Warning!

Violence, War, Magic & the Supernatural

The fictional worlds of Rifts® are violent, deadly and filled with aliens, war and supernatural monsters. Other-dimensional beings often referred to as "demons," torment, stalk and prey on humans. Alien life forms, monsters, vampires, ghosts, ancient gods and demigods, as well as magic, insanity, psychic powers and combat are all elements in this book. *All of it is fiction.*

Some parents may find the violence, magic and supernatural elements of the game inappropriate for young readers/players. We suggest parental discretion.

Please note that none of us at Palladium Books® condone or encourage the occult, the practice of magic, the use of drugs, or violence.

An epic sourcebook for the *Rifts*® series.

Compatible with the entire Palladium Books® Megaverse®

Dedication from Greg

To Jenn, my best friend, my wife, who despite her significant disdain for my hobby, did the best she could to support my work and offered her support and encouragement in any way!

To my three boys Caleb, Joshua and Noah who love to eat junk food and play with my coloured dice at our gaming nights.

To Harry, my hero and above all else my father! His words of encouragement, support and understanding even transcend the bonds of father and son.

To my gaming buddies who not only game with me on a regular basis, but were equally excited and enthusiastic about play testing and gaming with the Rifts® Lemuria material for the first time! Dennie Lutes (also my proofreader and concept check guy), Eric Lanctot (also my content check guy), Martin Scaiano, Chris Salter and Ryan McConanchie.

And last, but not least to Kevin, for creating a gaming system that has entertained me for nearly two decades, fighting with every last breath to keep Palladium Books alive and for offering a bunch of freelancers (myself included) the opportunity to make our own contribution to his work!

– Greg Diaczyk

Special Dedication

To G.A.M.E., Visioncon and Joe W. Ryan for their dedication to the role-playing game hobby and passion for Palladium Books and all things gaming. May they all prosper and game on.

– Kevin Siembieda

The cover, by *John Zeleznik*, depicts a Lemurian floating city nestled on the floor of an ocean or sea. A surface dwelling visitor to Lemuria rides a Mega-Ray, while a couple of Lemurian allies known as Merans scout the perimeter.

First Printing – April 2012

Palladium Online: **www.palladiumbooks.com** – also visit us at **facebook.com/PalladiumBooks**

Rifts® World Book 32: Lemuria™ is published by Palladium Books Inc., 39074 Webb Court, Westland, MI 48185-7606. Printed in the USA.

Palladium Books® Presents:

Rifts® World Book 32:

Lemuria

Conceived by: **Greg Diaczyk**

Written by: **Greg Diaczyk and Kevin Siembieda**

Additional Writing & Ideas: **Matthew Clements**

Editors: **Alex Marciniszyn**
Wayne Smith
Matthew Clements
Kevin Siembieda

Proofreader: **Julius Rosenstein**

Cover Painting: **John Zeleznik**

Interior Artists:
Amy L. Ashbaugh
Nicholas Bradshaw
Kent Burles
Allen Manning
Brian Manning
Michael Mumah
Charles "Chuck" Walton II

Additional Creatures & Armor Concepts: **Charles Walton II**

Maps: **Greg Diaczyk**

Art Direction: **Kevin Siembieda**
Typography and Layout: **Wayne Smith**

Based on the RPG rules, text, characters, settings, concepts and Megaverse® created by **Kevin Siembieda.**

Special Thanks to *Greg Diaczyk* for his inventiveness and breathing life into a project long shelved; to *John Zeleznik* for an elegant and evocative cover; to *Chuck Walton* for his inspiring Bio-Armor and monster designs; to *Kent, Mike, Nick, Brian, Allen* and *Amy* for kicking it up a notch, and to the intrepid Palladium crew, *Alex, Wayne, Kathy, Julius* and *Matthew*, each one a hero and a friend. And to the 359 *Megaverse Insiders* whose support helped make this book possible.

– Kevin Siembieda, 2012

Megaverse® Insiders

Inside Help

Nathaniel Baker, Joshua Bambrick, Anna Barrett, Ben Bingham, Vernon Atsumasa Brown, Alex Bunten, Phillip A Compher, Kimihiro Hamaura, Paul Herbert, Greg Hermann, A. Leonard Hogan, James Terrill Holt, Damian Kavanaugh, Christopher Kavanaugh, Rick Kelley, Lee Kleint, Joshua Krebs, Matt Krebs, Jennifer R. Levenson, Sophia A. Levenson, Jeffery S. Levenson, Robert M. Levenson, Frank Loose, Kat MacDougall, Jason Martin, Jeremy McKenna, Jonah Lucas Paslawski, Lily Fae Paslawski, Johathan Powell-Mark, Morgan Smith, Gregory Spivey, Lois l Terrill, James Terrill, Nicole Terrill, Laura Terrill, Tristan Terrill, Zander Terrill, Alexis Terrill, Ethan l Terrill, Alan Valentine, Jake Walkenhorst, Christopher Wilmer

In Memoriam

Fred J Allman, Jim "Angus" Blakley, Anne "Dementer" Brett, Lee "Navigator" Carroll, Rebecca Ann Cloer, Toumani Dembele, Gregory Fordham, Chris Joas, Richard Newman, Azariah Perez, Peter Porcaro Sr, Orville Rose, Paul Selice, Richard C Steele, Pearl Steele, Melvin Terrill, James Howard Thomas, Boyd Tracy, Tom Whittemore

A Real Character Tribute

Alejandro DeLaCruz, Amaranth Nox, Angelle Davis, Bambi "The Borg" Carruthers, Daimyo Shi, Daventhalas de Mont Hault, 'DeskTopTrooper' SeyfertSluw, Dollop the Dragon, Felix, Gabriel Corhst, Garner Varzerius Harmon, Jerick Rollie, Karl Logen, Kenjo Dekai, Kyan Redblade, Magnus, Max Eumaeus, Me is Michael, Orion Atlason, Paul Crocker, Pvt. 54SH4 "Sasha", Ray Blackheart, Roderick "Flashpoint" Green, Sakura Hayase, Sir Caldwell, Tempest Manslaughter, The Mysterious Tattooed One King Zarchron, Torq, Trip Stan Vic, Victor & the Dragon, Wemic Pandemic

Cyber-Insiders

Sabrina Akins, Thomas Andary, Carl Arterbury, Mark Assar, Nathaniel Baker, Ben Bonds, Jeff Bunde, Brent Burnett, Kevin Carpenter, Anthony Casab, Oswin Chang, David Chittim, Phillip A Compher, Mike Creelman, Michael Dawson, James Diefenderfer, Jason Domke, Michael Estrada, Jeffrey Farrar, Allan Fierro, Brandon Fong, Jon Foster, Scott Gibbons, Travis Guerrero, Harley Hacker, Alexander Heck, Paul Herbert, John Horton, Clifford Hoyt, Neil Johnson, Demetrius Karanikolas, Nolen Keith, David Lang, Scott Leapold, Joseph MacIsaac, Sara McLaughlan, David Moffatt, Rog Myrant, Aaron Nelson, Matthew Newton, Leigh O'Neil, Victor Peterson, James Plowman, Matt Powell, Jeffrey Reade, Tim Robertson, Michael Rose, Scott Rubin, Stephen Schneider, Troy Scoughton, Christopher Shields, Michael Smith, Adam Soliday, Christopher Spencer, Damien Titchener, Chad Trantham, H. E. Werkheiser, Jeffrey White, Jason Williamson, Jeff Woodman, Frank Wrege

Palladium Insiders

Dylon Amerasinghe, Michael Barakofsky, Rex Barkdoll, Bayton Befoe Jr, Richard Bray, Brent Burnett, Eric Campion, David Chittim, Allen R Cogar, Cory Crandall, Steven Daniel, Stuart J Davis, Matthew "Nekira" Daye, Carl Douglas, Brett Easterbrook, Melissa Eaton, Bryan Ellis, Todd Ferrullo, Trevor Fitch, Steve E Gibson, Todd Gilbert, Carl L Gilchist, Carl Gleba, Denny "Kegleneq" Ham, Kairam Hamdan, Brian Harrison, Brenda L Heck, Gregory Hermann, James Hicks Jr, Seth Johnson, John "Sinder" King, John Kretzer, James LaFlamme, Chadd Leath, James Lukow, David Manz, Wayne Maynard, Andy McElravy, Kevin McGoldrick, Casey Michels, Patrick E T Miller, Thomas Molen, Trevor Morehead, Rod Myrant, Warren Nelson, Charles Pickering, Allan "ZeroArmour" Randall, Ryan Rawlings, Bradley Reeser, Daniel Ritchie, Bill Schaffer, Ken Stewart, Josh Stoddard, Erin "Chakat Cait" Sullivan, Austin Suzuki, Seraphine Swalve, Thor Swenson, Daniel "Ogre" Thomas, Nick Warren, Steven Whittredge

Emerald Insiders

Kristopher Akers, Brandon K Aten, Graham Bailey, William J Bailey, Scott A Banzhaf, Jon Bruning, Jeff Costello, Jeremy Davis, John J Dorch, Brett Easterbrook, Gregory Hermann, Michael Holland, Dennis Hughes, Jeremy Johnston, Christopher Kavanaugh, David Klett, Jason Lamb, Matthew Lane, Heath Langemann, Chad Lasecki, Jonathan "Iscerus" Lum, Scott Norman 783, Evan Odensky, Boone Oshel, Kris Perlock-Campeau, Steve Robbins, Matthew Robertson, John Santa Barbara, Edward J Sauerland, Raymond D Spencer, Dave Waller, Paul Wehde, H E "Hew" Werkheiser, Stanley Woo, Kelly Zolnoski

Emerald-Plus Insiders

Peter Adams, Chris Beacock, Joshua Curry, Erich Eisenmenger, Michael Henre, Perry G Jones, Stephen B Keith, Shawn Kennedy, John J King, Magnar Laska, Jeff A Lee, Russell S Lenhares, Timothy Letts, Jorel J Levenson, Ryan Mahoney, Kris Main, Chris Miller, Cupcake Miser, Richard J Perez, James Eric Ritchie, Jeffrey Schuler, Sgt Scott Simpson, Larry Todd Stanley, Richard Steele, Michael Swain, Christopher M M Thomas, Charles Viaud, Christian Weidelman, Steven "Chief Executive GM" Yeung

Top Insiders

Jamey Adams, Eric Auger, Chris Axtell, Ryan Bacon, Brent Casavant, Anthony Castorino, Jonathon E Conroy, Robb F Dunn, Jessica Frost, Torrey Jones, John Kallil, Andrew Kelsoe, Chris Kluge, Andrew Kohler, Brandon Landry, Derrick "Omote" Landwehr, Rich and Becky Lints, Christina Liu, Kai Martin, Charles McComb, Jason Mendoza, Ramzie Othman, Donovan Pankratz, Ron Placentia, Ammon Redman, Albert Rosado, Michael Satran, Frederick R Seibel 5th, Geoffrey Setjo, Chris S Steinbrenner, Robert Steiner, Tracy Sykes, Brian Terrill, Jason Volinsky, J. Patrick Walker, Robert J Walsh, Thomas Walters, Jason Webster, Christopher Wilmer, Athena and Anthony Young

Ultimate Insiders

Christopher Arnwine, B.D.J.P (Alan Beck) Gaming, Matthias Belfast, Kerry Cook, Joshua Hill, Shawn Johnson, Jesse Mihalik-Howard, Jeff Monahan, Peter Porcaro Jr, Leonard Smith, David Snell, Todd Spencley, Shephard A Williams

Benefactors

Benjamin Barton, Derek Boudreaux, Lucas Buck, Charles Bucklew, David Dunham, Todd Flippo, Federico Franceschi, Ryan Fuerst, Travis Guerrero, Shawn Johnson, John Kelley, Scott Kendrick, John Klinkel, Arnaldo Lebebre, Michael Lord, Becky Northaven, Ronald Robinson, Douglas Rood, Anthony Santaferra, Jonathan Scolamiero, Leonard Smith, Ed Surrett, Kevin Valonis, Brad Whitcomb

Contents – Rifts® Lemuria

Quick Find

A Note from the Author:

Like many of the fans of **Rifts®** I have been an avid reader of every world book published, curious and excited to read about the next amazing place it will take me and my adventuring group. However, not every aspect of Rifts Earth gets covered as quickly as our imaginations can explore. Many such places are left unexplored or not revealed in official canon and are left up to G.M.s to create on their own (which isn't a bad thing). Then there are books that for some reason are envisioned but fizzled out due to lack of commitment from the writer who volunteered to work on it. **Rifts® Lemuria** was once such book. It was vividly hinted at in **Rifts® World Book 7: Underseas** and all of us gamers were tantalized and teased with the possibilities of seeing just what it was the Lemurians were all about. Some of us had our own preconceived ideas, but nonetheless, would accept the awe-inspiring thoughts that are often the end result of Kevin's brainchild (or his conglomerate of like-minded freelancers). Rifts® Lemuria was unfortunately scrapped due to the freelancer being unable to carry through with his original proposal and the book was shelved indefinitely.

Like all gamers who had been awaiting details on this part of the world, I was understandably crushed. So as the old adage goes, "if you want something done, do it yourself!"

So I started writing down ideas that I thought should have been in the book, and my thoughts coalesced into a rough outline of what I was thinking of sending to Palladium Books as a proposal. Only having one **Rifter®** article under my belt at the time, and the "recent" news that Palladium Books was no longer accepting unsolicited manuscripts from outsiders, my hopes dropped even further. I decided to keep up my work however, sending in a couple more Rifter® articles and managed to get them published. It was during this phase that I decided to do something with my ragtag set of notes, and I thought about submitting a small article to the Rifter® about the Lemurians in hopes of getting the approval to whip up a full-scale World Book. It was about this time that I noticed that a number of other Rifter® freelancers were getting some of their own books, so I took a giant leap of faith and sent in a letter to Kevin, letting him know my ideas and what I had outlined for a *Rifts®: Lemuria World Book.* To my amazement, Kevin was equally surprised and excited that a freelancer wanted to tackle the project and, after some banter back and forth, we hammered out a decent outline... the resurrection of Rifts® Lemuria was well on its way. The rest is essentially what you are about to read. I hope you enjoy the book and have as much fun reading it and using the material presented here as I had writing it.

– Greg Diaczyk, 2009

The Lemurians

Lemuria originally emerged during the same *prehistoric era* as *Atlantis* and *Nazca*, and like the other two civilizations, mysteriously disappeared into myth and legend, leaving a murky but lasting legacy. Lemuria rose as a world power far more advanced than the majority of her primitive neighbors. During the kingdom's original reign, it dominated much of the coastal regions in and around the Indian Ocean, and it is the place Lemurians still consider the cradle of their civilization.

For the most part, Lemurians have always been a people of a high moral fiber, tending to the needs of the individual as much as to the needs of the community. At the pinnacle of their early civilization they had mastered many different sciences, practiced advanced holistic medicine, harnessed the Earth and magic to power and operate their cities, tamed the wilderness and brought peace and prosperity even to their barbaric neighbors.

True Atlanteans and Lemurians shared a deep friendship, and with it, the secrets of *Stone Magic* and the creation of stone pyramids to channel and control the mystic energy of ley lines. In fact, there was some friendly debate between the two civilizations as to which first invented the ancient craft. While both claim to have originated Stone Magic and pyramid technology, neither knows for certain if their claim is accurate. Regardless of which civilization was the first to develop the magic and implement the use of pyramids, Stone Masters of both great civilizations learned to tap into, channel and manipulate what they called "Earth Energy" (P.P.E./magic). This involves the making of giant stone structures, pyramids and stone megaliths. Unlike the Atlanteans, who focused on reaching into the heavens and piercing the inter-dimensional barrier with pyramid technology, the Lemurians turned their efforts inwards. Instead of plain stone pyramids, Lemurians built thriving ziggurats teeming with gardens, hydroponics, waterfalls and water fountains. Such places were natural refuges for a host of wild and exotic birds, insects and animals. The harmonious and friendlier stone ziggurats offered Lemurian mages a different range of powers than the pyramids of Atlantis. Instead of inter-dimensional travel, Lemurian edifices had the power to rejuvenate and heal, aiding the Lemurians in their quest to understand the mechanics of life.

Though Lemurians are said to have originated as ordinary human beings, their mastery over Biomancy and understanding of biology enabled them to transform themselves into something more than human. Lemurians always loved exploration and nature. After having explored many parts of the surface world, they began to wonder what wonders existed below the waves. Oceans and seas dominated more than two-thirds of the planet, and Lemurians found themselves craving to be part of the bigger, unseen world underwater. To explore the oceans, Lemurian Biomancers genetically altered their people to survive above and below the waves. Their cities, powered by energies of the Earth (P.P.E./magic), were already designed to float on the waves and in the air, now they were made to float *underwater* as well. Lemurian cities, even ones as vast as the City of Mu, could travel over land or sea or under the waves with comfortable ease and good speed. Traveling and spending time underwater also kept the peaceful Lemurians safe from the rise of aggressive, human civilizations given to war and conquest. One of the Lemurians' greatest achievements was the construction of the enormous **City of Mu.** Mu was the total sum of Lemurian mystic knowledge and achievement of the time. From this magnificent city, Lemurians explored the world around them and collected samples of flora and fauna, above and below the waves. Wherever the great floating city traveled, they collected new specimens of life and added them to their already impressive areas of knowledge, medicine and science, all of which were carefully guarded secrets.

One such secret was the **Code of Life.** A blueprint found in all living creatures that dictated their form and function. (Modern surface dwelling humans call this "Code of Life" DNA.) Through several centuries of in-depth research, Lemurian Biomancers and scientists were able to change, copy and create new codes from pieces of other code, building *chimeras*, tweaking existing genetic designs and improving the quality of life for their people and others.

Global disaster came without warning. The Atlantean civilization vanished, continent and all, and most of the planet's magic energy vanished with it. The Lemurians called magic "Earth Energy" because P.P.E. or magic energies radiated from the very planet. These lines of Earth Energy had become the basis of Lemurian technology as well as a renewable source of clean energy. Suddenly, that energy all but vanished. Somehow, the global loss of magic coincided with the disappearance of Atlantis. Several Lemurian floating cities had received distress calls from Atlantis before communications went dead. Like any good friend, the Lemurians gathered their cities and went to investigate and rescue survivors. Details of Atlantis' fate were pieced together from the little physical and anecdotal evidence that could be found. Other bits of information were filled in by a tiny handful of Atlantean survivors gathered by the floating cities. Even without it, the Lemurians would have guessed what happened.

Their Atlantean friends had always been fascinated with dimensional travel to other realities. Something clearly went terribly wrong during one of their dimensional experiments, taking the entire continent of Atlantis with it. Nobody knew where Atlantis had vanished to, or whether it even existed anywhere, anymore. The number of survivors from a continent that had a population in the millions, were a terrifying few thousand.

The disappearance of Atlantis sent shock waves across the planet. With the continent gone – just gone – (accidentally sent to another dimension until the Splugorth brought her back after the Great Cataclysm), water levels and coastlines changed, people died, and the world was irrevocably altered. Lemurians felt the loss on a personal level, as their long time friends, allies and trading partners had vanished in the blink of an eye. The many small Atlantean coastal colonies located on other continents and islands were wiped out by the changing seas and Ley Line Storms that erupted when Atlantis disappeared.

And the catastrophe was not over.

The level of magic energy plunged to terrifying lows never before experienced. Ley lines that had once roared with energy like a mighty river were reduced to a mere trickle. Demons and monsters went on the warpath, and dimensional travelers like dragons and the sphinx found themselves stranded on Earth without enough magic energy to open a portal to leave.

Things were no better on the mainland. Without levels of magic strong enough to cast spells and work magic, overnight the old power base of Druids, priests and sorcerers found themselves nearly powerless and very, very vulnerable. Suddenly, those who had used magic to keep barbarians and warlike primitive people at bay were without means to defend themselves. Yes, magic still existed, but reduced to pathetic power levels. Civilizations that

had risen to power before the Sumerians and Egyptians crumbled and faded without ever being recorded in the pages of history. The worldwide loss of magic energy also had an impact on true of *creatures of magic* like dragons, as well as Deevils, demons and all manner of supernatural beings. Though the magic powers and spell casting abilities of such creatures had been reduced to almost nothing, these monsters still possessed brute strength and enough physical and/or psionic power to haunt, hunt and battle humankind for millennia. The last dragons did not perish until the middle ages, some 14,000 years after the disappearance of Atlantis and the obliteration of magic. Many mythic creatures lingered on Earth for thousands of years before being wiped out completely or forced to hide from the growing civilizations of humanity that would rise in the centuries that followed. Many ancient "myths" about dragons, vampires, demons and monsters are based upon real creatures that existed in considerable numbers until the Atlanteans made magic all but vanish. However, the truth and specific details about these beings became jumbled and forgotten as the growing numbers of humans wiped them out and science became the new magic. By the 20th Century, the truth about these creatures was indeed lost to myth, and few believed they had ever truly existed.

As magic continued to wane, the floating cities of Lemuria, whether above or below the waves, began to float slower and the infrastructure and machines that ran on Earth Energy began to grind to a halt. Lights, heat and fuel to run the machines had all been based on magic. Without it, everything began to shut down. Eventually, Lemuria's floating cities would have come crashing down, perhaps ending their glorious civilization then and there, had it not been for the massive reserves of Earth Energy contained within their stone ziggurats. Still, it was only a matter of time, counted in months, before their floating cities would have to settle on a final resting place and stop moving. Magic was dying and with it, the Lemurian way of life.

Perhaps because the floating cities of Lemuria, of which the City of Mu was the greatest, still contained dwindling magic energy within their mighty ziggurats, supernatural horrors began to besiege them in an attempt to get at that magic. Many of the supernatural and magic creatures hoped to steal enough P.P.E. to escape Earth and go home, or at least to another dimension with natural reserves of mystic energy. To evade the clamoring supernatural hordes, the Lemurians went *underwater*. There, concealed and much less accessible, Lemuria's greatest minds formed a plan. To stay on Earth meant forfeiting magic and the sciences of magic. Life below the waves without magic seemed a viable solution, but it would be a very different way of life and long-term survival was not assured. However, if they could find a portal to another Earth-like world with enough magic energy to sustain their machines, they could travel to it and continue to live as always.

It was a risky proposition, so the choice was made voluntarily. Mu and the majority of cities decided it was a chance worth taking. A few Lemurian cities opted to stay behind and resettle on land. A few would remain underwater. While those that stayed behind would survive for centuries, some contributing to new megalithic and stone pyramid societies of other human civilizations, each would eventually perish.

Those looking for a way out traveled to one of the most powerful underwater nexuses the Lemurians had uncovered in their past explorations. In the Pacific Ocean years earlier, mages had detected great magic and dimensional energy among a trio of massive and powerful ley lines in the *Marianas Trench*. Lemurian psychics also felt the presence of danger and supernatural evil, so they did not linger to explore much of it. Thus, it was an unknown quantity, but they had gleaned enough information to know there was an open portal to another dimension present. They also knew it led to an alien realm of water and magic much like their own beloved Earth. Acting quickly, the floating cities gathered with the hope of going through the Rift and making a new life.

Upon returning to the Marianas Trench, the mages of the floating cities found the portal floundering and fading. Lemurians quickly assessed the Rift and determined it could collapse at any time. It was a miracle it was still there at all. In fact, the mages determined it was only the efforts of an unknown outside force that was somehow enabling the shriveling ley lines to hold the portal open. It was now or never. There was no time to send probes or reconnaissance teams through the portal. They had to take a leap of faith and go. As the first two cities passed through the dimensional Rift, something attacked the third, destroying it in minutes. Feeling they had no other choice, the other floating cities made a mad dash to the open portal. Each time such a massive object with so many people on board passed through it, the Rift shuddered and threatened to close. Meanwhile, the force that destroyed the city went on to attack two others. It was madness. As the City of Mu went through the dimensional portal, after making certain a few smaller cities were able to slip through before it, the Rift collapsed.

Without sufficient energy left to reopen the massive Rift, the **Lord of the Deep** was trapped on Earth where it would languish as an angry shadow of its true self for thousands of years. Perhaps needless to say, this has earned the Lemurians the monster's eternal enmity. The Lemurians had no idea the Lord of the Deep existed, nor that the Rift was his means of escape. All they knew was that an evil force had destroyed at least two of their cities and clung to one other, preventing it from going through the Rift. The survivors could only imagine that those left behind were destroyed.

The good news for the Lemurians who made it through the Rift was that the new dimension was almost exactly like Earth. What the Lemurians could not have known was they had not gone to an alien world, but to a kind of pocket dimension created by the Lord of the Deep. An ocean-like space capsule the size of a small ocean that could maintain the evil Alien Intelligence as it traveled to other worlds in the Megaverse. For every thousand years that passed on Earth, one decade passed for the Lemurians, but that's still 150 years from then to the present day.

If not for the **Coming of the Rifts**, the Lemurians might have been trapped in the Lord of the Deep's private, dimensional ocean forever. When the Rifts came, and magic flooded back more powerfully than ever, the Lord of the Deep's dimensional portal to Earth reopened and the contents of the pocket dimension were disgorged into the Atlantic Ocean, including the floating cities. Half-asleep and disoriented by the sudden surge of renewed energy, the *Lord of the Deep* was too distracted to take immediate action against the returning Lemurian population, but the monster did close the underwater Rift. Confused and frightened themselves, the Lemurians fled into the larger ocean around them. It would take decades before they realized that they (and Atlantis) had been returned to Earth 15,000 years in the future, and that the planet Earth was, once again, in upheaval because of Earth Energy.

This was a much more hostile and alien Earth than the one known to their ancestors. The Lemurians spent most of their first 250 years back on Earth hiding, adapting and battling the forces of chaos and the wrath of the vengeful Lord of the Deep. Most of that time was spent underwater, where things seemed less tumultuous and safer than the surface world. Lemurians again found themselves exploring the oceans and seas of the world, learning about the new underwater realm and developing new magicks, defenses and armies to ward off frequent attacks by the Lord of the Deep, Naut'yll, Horune Pirates and other monstrous forces. It also took time to figure out and learn to live within the Earth's new ecosystem. During this period of survival and adaptation, Lemurians were kept on their toes and the loss of life was high. Still, they made new developments in Biomancy magic, weapons and armor, as well as the development of Symbiotes and methods to alter the genetic structure of their sea mounts. It has only been in the last 50 years that the Lemurians have felt they can hold their own against the monsters of the deep and keep their people safe. With that accomplished, they have once again begun to quietly explore the underwater and surface world in greater depth. Lemurians are, overall, thrilled to be "back home" even if Earth is a very, very different place. In the last decade, Lemurians have decided to take a much more active role in this bold, new Earth. They are hiding less and have begun to send out individuals and small squads to "walk among the new people of Earth" and make contact with sentient life forms below and above the waves. This is why, for many, rumors about an aquatic species of humanoids calling themselves Lemurians have only started to surface over the last few decades.

For the most part, life is good for the average Lemurian. They've even come to terms with having to deal with the wrath of a vengeful god like the *Lord of the Deep* and have become more militaristic to survive. The Lord of the Deep is the Lemurians' arch-enemy. The supernatural monstrosity hates them above all others and will not rest until every last Lemurian is slain. To that end, the fiend sends members of the Cult of the Deep, monsters, minions, sea serpents, demons, evildoers, dupes, and trouble their way whenever it can. For this reason, Lemurian floating cities *never* stay in one place for long. Instead, they are constantly on the move, spending equal time underwater, floating on the water's surface and floating in the air. They are so elusive that most surface dwellers aren't sure if the Lemurians are real or myth, and few know when, where or how to find them. More often than not, it is the Lemurians who decide when they make contact with people on the surface.

Lemurians are fond of helping others, and have a reputation for assisting floundering ships, rescuing people from storms and drowning, and saving people from pirates and sea serpents, especially from the clutches of the Lord of the Deep. Half the time, however, surface dwellers are unaware that Lemurians have intervened on their behalf. Until very recently, the Lemurians operated in secret, using magic from a distance to help those in trouble. Tales of "miracles" at sea, storms mysteriously stopping or changing direction, rough seas suddenly becoming calm, being pulled to the surface by an unknown force or animals, and encounters with "mermaids", helpful "aliens" or "Elemental beings" are more than likely to have been Lemurian rescuers. They don't identify themselves nor wait for a thank you, they just appear out of the blue and quietly vanish when people are safe.

Long ago, Lemurian society developed a great respect for life – all life – from plants and animals to sentient beings – as well as a keen sense of responsibility to other life forms and the environment. To the average Lemurian, all life is precious and all intelligent beings are responsible for the care and nurturing of Mother Earth. Lemurians take that sense of responsibility several steps farther than most people and see themselves as the caretakers and protectors of the planet Earth and the environment. That is why Lemurians try to live in harmony with the planet and everyone in it. There was a time when no Lemurian would raise a finger to hurt another creature. Not to harm a fellow human being, swat a fly or cut down a tree. Over time, the secrets of Biomancy enabled them to mold and manipulate plant and animal life on a genetic level, and even their own bodies. Ancient Lemurians were the first to use methods of conservation, hydroponics (and magic) to grow crops, and have always tried to replenish forests and replace whatever resources they take. It has only been their return to Rifts Earth and the constant onslaught from the *Lord of the Deep* that has turned Lemurians into warriors and a much more proactive force for good.

Other people with the knowledge and power of the Lemurians might have become embittered and vengeful, or aggressive and militant, conquering other civilizations or destroying their enemies. Not Lemurians. Though they have become skilled fighters and warrior mages, they revere the life and freedom of other people more than ever. They battle the *Lord of the Deep* only to escape his onslaughts with minimal loss of Lemurian life. They fight primarily in self-defense, and their first priority is always to avoid collateral damage to innocent people and the environment. Whenever they can flee without confrontation, they do so.

However, there is one big change in Lemurian philosophy: they are not hesitant or afraid to take the life of an evildoer to protect themselves, innocent people everywhere and the environment. While Lemurians do not go looking for trouble or conflict, they will not turn their backs on someone in need. Not when they are in a position to do something about it. They have also come to accept that the forces of supernatural evil are real and not going away. That there are supernatural creatures whose very reason for existence is to cause suffering, sorrow and death. That the Lord of the Deep is one such being, demons and Deevils another two. The verdict remains out on the Splugorth and their mortal minions.

There is one type of vile creature Lemurians have never balked at destroying: **the undead**. Lemurians (and Atlanteans) see the undead, living dead, walking dead and similar beings that defy death and prey upon the living, as the very antithesis of life. From their point of view, vampires and other types of undead are the equivalent of what *anti-matter* is to matter – *anti-life* – monsters who enslave, torment and destroy the living, and who thrive in darkness and shun life as the natural world knows it. To allow the undead to exist is to endanger all sentient life forms. As far as the Lemurians are concerned, these unnatural, anti-life monsters must be destroyed wherever they are found. Likewise, **Necromancy** is seen as a type of *anti-life magic*, which is why its practice is forbidden and repulsive to Lemurians dedicated to protecting the planet.

The dramatic changes to the Earth since the *Coming of the Rifts* have made the planet a nexus to infinite worlds across the Megaverse, introducing new life forms into the planet's ecosystem. The alien people (D-Bees), flora and fauna are all embraced by the Lemurians, who see life as constant change and motion. However, the Rifts have also unleashed the undead and wicked monsters of countless variety into the world. The undead, along with any vile supernatural being or creature of magic who threatens the innocent or the environment, are seen as the Enemies of Life. Enemies to be driven away, back through a Rift, or destroyed. That kind of thinking and commitment has led current day Lemurian people to think of themselves as *Protectors of the Earth.* A new and unfamiliar role they are trying to figure out.

Lemurians are becoming increasingly bold about visiting and exploring the surface world to get a better understanding of the many diverse people and cultures that now claim Earth as their home. Ever curious about new ideas, people, places and life forms, Lemurians have also begun to bring surface dwellers down into the watery depths of the oceans. Surface dwellers are given aquatic capabilities via the use of magic, Symbiotes, special herbs and sometimes, machines, all of which enable land dwellers to function underwater as if they were fish.

Even with greater contact among other civilizations of Rifts Earth, Lemurians remain an enigma, and to most people, the stuff of myth. Reports of underwater cities floating through the oceans or even in the sky are dismissed as hallucinations and fairy tales by most surface people. So far, Lemurians have kept their numbers and magic a secret, preferring to make tenuous forays into the surface world and picking when, where and with whom they make contact. Their main area of operations has been the waters of the Pacific Ocean, avoiding the Atlantic and the Minions of Splugorth, whom they fear.

Lemurians have adapted to the higher levels of magic across the face of the planet since the Great Cataclysm. They have made Lemurian magic, their bio-constructs and stone creations more powerful than they ever were in the past (i.e. S.D.C. to Mega-Damage). Even with this advantage, the Lemurians still find themselves faced with surviving in a chaotic and dangerous environment with enemies like the *Lord of the Deep* hounding their every move. They now find themselves grasping at any and all means to rout the monster and its evil servants, and are even entertaining the idea of seeking assistance from surface dwellers and the mysterious *Captain Nemo* and his *New Navy.* Clever enough to avoid the wrath of more than one dark god or powerful nation at a time, Lemurians are careful about open opposition to the Vampire Kingdoms, the Xiticix, the Splugorth of Atlantis, and the Yama Kings, but fear they may all represent grave danger to the future of Mother Earth and her people.

The Lemurian People

Long ago, the Lemurians were completely human. However, they have used Biomancy to genetically re-engineer themselves for a dual life above and under the sea. This means they have the ability to breathe air as well as gills to breathe underwater. Their "ascension" to their current state has been brought about by millennia of tweaking and fine-tuning their *Code of Life* (DNA). The current genetic structure of Lemurians has not changed in centuries, and most Lemurians agree that they have found the perfect level of physical development for their people. As one might expect, this means Lemurians are tall, physically fit, attractive people free of genetic illnesses and immune to most disease.

Though Lemurian ancestry probably goes back to the people of Southeast Asia, genetic modification has made Lemurians look quite different. Most surface dwelling people assume Lemurians look like a mermaid with the upper body of a human and the tail of a fish, but that is not the case. Lemurians have chosen to keep their human bodies. As a result, they are an attractive, graceful people with muscular bodies, slight builds, and delicate features. Lemurians have two arms and legs, their fingers are not webbed, they have human faces with a nose, lips, two almond-shaped eyes, a pair of small, pointed ears, and a thick mane of hair on their heads, usually grown long. Other than their eyebrows and the hair on their heads, Lemurians have no other body hair and cannot grow mustaches or beards. Gills for breathing underwater are located just behind back of the jaw near the ears. The skin color of Lemurians ranges from gold to a warm grayish brown with flecks of iridescent blue or green along the sides of the neck and shoulders and down the tops of the forearms. The color on the throat, underarms, inner leg and belly is 10-20% lighter than the rest of their body and has faint hints of blue, green or yellow. Lemurians have a wide range of hair color from light brown, blonde (almost golden), red, copper, violet and purple to shimmering silver and white hair with streaks or tints of light blue, light green, dark green or dark blue. Though they can move their mouths underwater to speak, they create noises and sonic impulses like dolphins and whales. *To actually vocalize words* they must be on the surface. Lemurians can also use Telepathy and Empathy to communicate.

Underwater, Lemurian warriors dress in any number of different types of Biomancy living armor. Otherwise, citizens and most people wear a wide range of different clothing. Casual wear for men may range from a pair of swimming trunks or trousers to shirt and pants. Women may wear the equivalent of a bikini to a light silk blouse and skirt. Others wear organic clothing that more resembles a second skin or a weave of seaweed. Lemurian women have a thing for wispy scarves, capes and cloaks that sometimes appear to be gossamer wings or the frilly-fins of a Lion Fish that flow as they swim. The material used in such clothing for both males and females often looks and feels like silk, but is actually spun from a variety of marine plants that creates a fabric that is lighter than silk, but several times stronger and more durable. Many Lemurian women wear sexy, exterior waist garments that resemble ornate corsets, some of which appear to be made of fine or large fish scales, others appearing to be made of leather covered in pearls or fish bone, or gems or seashells. Men tend to stay away from jewelry, but Lemurian women enjoy rings, necklaces, bracelets, anklets, earrings, hair combs and tiaras. Pearls are very popular, as is jewelry made of seashells, coral and, of course, gemstones. Bare feet, partial nudity and minimal clothing are commonplace and completely acceptable in Lemurian society, especially

when underwater or swimming. Lemurians are accustomed to the tactile feel of the water on their bodies and say it makes them feel at home. That having been said, boots are very common, especially among males, while females seem to prefer sandals or short boots that resemble pixie boots. Long hair is the fashion whether the Lemurian is a child, male, female or a soldier, and Lemurians do not lose their hair as they age. Of course, genetic manipulation and magic have made it so Lemurians look youthful even when they are ancient. An elder Lemurian in his hundreds seldom looks older than a human in his thirties, forties or early fifties.

On the surface, Lemurians tend to cover their bodies more, but when not wearing living body armor, still prefer airy, loose fitting clothing that resemble the togas and light silk gowns and blouses reminiscent of the ancient Egyptians, Greeks, Romans and Persians. On the surface, males and females may wear baggy pants that tuck into boots or end below the knee. Short and long cloaks, capes and hooded robes are also very popular. Some Lemurians choose to wear the clothing of other cultures, be it China or Chi-Town. Lemurian adventurers out in the world tend to wear clothing that is suitable for travel and exploration, and which fits in with the local culture. Adventurers and warriors may also wear one of the many different suits of living, environmental Biomancy body armor.

The Lemurian navy is an unconventional force of warriors that use a wide range of weapons, armor and equipment that combine high-technology, magic and living weapons and symbiotic constructs. Most soldiers are **Oceanic Guardsmen** which make up 40-50% of their armed forces. Psychics such as Zappers or Spouters make up elite combat troops in Special Forces, and represent 20% of their troops. Lemurians prefer hit and run and other guerilla tactics instead of full frontal assaults, which is more suitable to the powers of psychics, mages and Special Forces. Experienced Master Psychics, mages and hardened combat veterans make up the majority of leaders and ship commanders. The rest can be almost any adventurer and men-at-arms O.C.C. including **Lemurian Scouts** (many with Major Psionics), **Biomancer Gene-Mages** and support personnel.

Occupations that serve or call upon the supernatural such as *Witches, Shifters, Necromancers* and even *Priests* and *Warlocks* are frowned upon by most Lemurians who see these people as "tainted" by inhuman and otherworldly beings. Those who choose to select any of these O.C.C.s are looked upon with worry and distrust, even revulsion, and some, like Necromancers and Witches, may be cast out for their beliefs and pursuit of evil magic. To counter this negative image, *Lemurian Priests* try to associate with benign and aquatic deities such as Poseidon/Neptune. *Warlocks* find greater acceptance if they dedicate themselves to the elemental forces of Water (50%) or Air (20%), though any element may be selected.

Dark magicks go against the Lemurian culture and way of life. *Shifters, Temporal Wizards, Necromancers,* and any magic that enslaves, harms or kills the living as a matter of practice are very rare among Lemurians, who generally revere life and freedom. Only outcasts and evil individuals practice these dark types of magic in secret. A few Shifters and Temporal Wizards are known to practice within Lemurian society, but most avoid making a link to the Supernatural and focus on inter-dimensional magic and travel rather than commanding sinister, evil beings. However, after the Atlantean Catastrophe, dimensional travel and manipulation of the Rifts and dimensional energy are considered too unpredictable and dangerous, and best to be avoided like the plague. Moreover, its practice within city limits, where an "accident" or magic "gone wrong" could unleash demons and monsters or dimensional forces that could hurt or kill scores of innocent people, is forbidden. This is seldom a problem as less than 0.32% of Lemurian practitioners of magic pursue Temporal or dimensional magic. *Stone Magic, Biomancy, Warlock/Elemental, Ley Line Magic, Invocations, Wizardry* and other types of *spell casting* are the most common and popular of the mystic arts among Lemurians.

Lemurian Technology

Lemurian "technology" is magic, and most devices, vehicles and everyday utilities run on Earth Energy (P.P.E.) stored up in stone pyramids and ziggurats. Biomancy and Stone Magic are the two major magic arts used in creation and building, control and dispersal of energy, and are combined with other sciences from botany and farming to the manufacture of weapons, armor and clothing. Lemurian technology is a synthesis of magic, nature and technology, even when it comes to the making of cities, vehicles and everyday items, but in a very different way from Techno-Wizardry. Many Lemurian devices are alive or made of stone and other natural materials such as plant fiber. As a result, Lemurian technology is considered *alien technology* to most outsiders (-40% skill penalty to understand and use it, -50% to copy or repair it; half those penalties for Atlanteans and the Splugorth). This also means very few Lemurians learn to master conventional science as practiced by the Coalition States, Triax and other human nations, so O.C.C.s like Scientist, Operator and Technical Officer are uncommon among Lemurians. Biomancers are the scientists and Stone Masters the builders in their civilization.

Biomancy and Stone Magic are the cornerstones of Lemurian technology, but other magicks also play a role. Ancient Lemurians learned how to manipulate stone with Stone Magic to better harness and control Earth Energy (magic/P.P.E.), ley lines and nexus points, as well as to stabilize dimensional anomalies and quell Ley Line Storms and other ley line related concerns. Unlike other uses for magic, Lemurians direct Earth Energy to build, heal, nurture and understand and protect nature. This has led to an in-depth understanding of the genetic codes and structures of plants and animals that are the keys to life, and in the case of the Lemurians, the creation of living armor, weapons, and even vehicles and houses made of living coral, woven from living plants and creatures, or castaway fibers, resin and other natural materials. Thus, Lemurians have unlocked many secrets of genetics and use Biomancy to modify their environment, the living creatures around them and even their own bodies. They have learned to live in harmonious synergy with the natural world. So while one might classify the stone megaliths, pyramids and ziggurats as "technology," and the creation of fantastic, new animal life forms as "genetic engineering," the Lemurians see them simply as extensions of the Earth and life – even if they were designed and altered by Lemurian Biomancer Gene-Mages into their current configuration and functionality.

Lemurians rely heavily on their gene-tweaked psionic abilities to communicate with the animals and Symbiotes they create and tame, and use Biomancy Bio-Constructs to meet their daily needs (tools, equipment, weapons, armor, vehicles, food, medicine, clothing, companions, etc.). While a surface dwelling warrior might rely on a suit of power armor, an M.D. laser rifle, cybernetics and computers, a Lemurian warrior uses living Bio-Armor, Bio-Weapons, Biomancy altered animals and his own psionics and aptitude for magic. Plant and animal byproducts (fruits, plant fiber to make fabric and cords, resins, herbs, extracts, etc.) are also used in eco-safe Lemurian manufacturing. Even some of the stuff one might classify as "technological," like Lemurian aircraft, are actually an amalgamation of Biomancy and Stone Magic – a stone construct/structure that houses a living organism which functions with a Lemurian pilot to make it work.

Much of the Lemurians' "technology" melds Earth Energy (magic/P.P.E.) with *living* plants and animals that serve the purpose of a machine or piece of equipment. As their technology advanced via Biomancy, Lemurians (who still think of themselves as human) changed themselves, the living organisms they use and their environment to fit their needs. Magic and technology have been taken to the point that it is, in effect, *genetic engineering.* Biomancy and bio-manipulation improves the quality of life and creates living organisms and animals that help Lemurians safeguard their people, preserve nature, and protect the Earth. They are used to fight monsters, dark magic and evil supernatural forces that would enslave and harm people, and destroy the natural environment. Lemurians are so resolute about this that even ordinary citizens believe it is their destiny to destroy the evil supernatural horrors that run rampant across the planet. If the Coalition States didn't consider Lemurians to be "magic using D-Bees," Emperor Prosek would hang a medal on them and welcome Lemurians into the CS with open arms. Unfortunately, Lemurians, though human in origin, are much too alien and mysterious to be accepted by the Coalition. Furthermore, the culture clash between these two would be catastrophic (Lemurians are educated, tolerant and open to all people; the CS is notoriously intolerant and closed to all of the above).

Creatures the Lemurians call "Bio-Constructs" – living armor, living weapons, living vehicles – as well as symbiotic organisms and animals used for riding, labor and other purposes, pose no threat to the environment and are biodegradable resources. They draw upon renewable Earth Energy/ley lines, the P.P.E. of individuals, and I.S.P. (psionic energy and force of will). Lemurian Symbiotes and Bio-Constructs are altered on a biological and genetic level to serve the specific needs of Lemurian society. Since the relationship between man and organism is *symbiotic,* both accept, need and draw upon each other and there is no resistance between the symbiotic organism and its user. Both meld and benefit from the union and function as one. To that end, the control and proper use of living Symbiotes and Bio-Constructs usually requires a minimum of P.P.E. or inner strength (I.S.P.) and at least minor psionics, such as Empathy, Telepathy and/or *Empathic Connection with Animals* (an ability that is much like the Psi-Stalkers and Simvans' power to communicate and control animals) or the Biomancer power of *Communicate with Plants and Animals.* **Note:** The psionic power of Telemechanics does NOT work to control or operate any Lemurian living armor, weapon or machine.

For Lemurians, magic and psionics are not only part of every day life and abilities possessed by them all, but the very foundation of their ecosystem, technology and civilization. Without them, they would be lost.

Lemurian Caste System & Government

The Lemurian caste system bears some similarities to the Japanese and Hawaiian caste systems of ancient times.

Ali'i: At the top of the list are the Ali'i, Lemurian families that have achieved near mythic status for generations of humanitarian efforts and legendary contributions to Lemurian civilization. These families are highly educated, wise and live to serve the Lemurian people in positions of leadership and guidance. They can be considered "royalty," and only a member of this class is worthy of taking the position of King. The King is the ultimate leader within Lemurian society, with his Ali'i family members as his court, advisors and other members of the ruling body. However, unlike many societies, there is little corruption or abuse of power and position. The Ali'i truly live to serve and see their position as an honor and privilege.

The Ali'kili, or "King," is the head of government, chief representative of the citizenry and is said to be the "soul of the people." As such, he has only the best interests of the populace at heart. When the Ali'kili finds his task too daunting or boring, he may step down, appointing another member of the royal family in his place as the new King (or Ali'i aimoka/Queen). After several decades of leading the people, most will volunteer to step down and pass the mantle to another worthy member of the Ali'i while the former King/Queen goes off to pursue other humanitarian or educational efforts, or engage in personal pursuits. The current Ali'kili is Tangaroa, however, his older twin brother, Rongo, passed on the mantle of leadership to him because he felt that Tangaroa was better suited for the job. And it seems he was correct, as Tangaroa is proving to be a kind and capable leader, as well as a clever military strategist and tactician in the campaign against the Lord of the Deep and other enemies.

Kahuna: The Kahuna are what one could call the master or professional class. Each member of this caste is typically an educated specialist and well-trained individual who strives to master his profession and attain a degree of perfection. Biomancer Gene-Mages, Stone Masters, Ocean Wizards and most practitioners of magic, psychics, healers, engineers, architects, writers, artists, philosophers and academics are of this class.

Maka'ainana: This is the working class occupied by farmers, laborers, builders, salvage experts, Wilderness Scouts, Psi-Druids, entertainers, explorers, Vagabonds and the occasional Biomancer Gene-Mage whose focus is on tending to crops and the care of animals. Warriors/soldiers – seen as servants of the people and protectors of the Earth – also fall into this class, the intention being to keep warriors and heroes grounded and humble.

Kauwa: Outsiders/non-Lemurians. These are, as a general rule of thumb, visitors, friends and associates who do not seek citizenship nor necessarily share Lemurian values. However, because Lemurians value all people, surface-dwelling humans and D-Bees who wish to become citizens of Lemuria may achieve any position within Lemurian society, except for the office of Ali'kili (King).

Maui-Kau: Criminals, Outcasts, traitors and evildoers. Members of the Mauian Order fall into this category, as do Lemurians and outsiders who exhibit no respect for life and murder, enslave or torment others.

The Mauian Order

The enemy within

Lemurians were shocked and horrified by the sudden disappearance of Atlantis and the profound impact it had on the entire planet. In the aftermath of the disaster, most Lemurians felt a great sense of grief, fear and uncertainty. Their world had changed overnight. The disappearance of Atlantis caused a massive depletion of magical Earth Energy. What had been a small but steady stream of Earth Energy turned into a minuscule trickle. Atlantis' folly had transformed the world. Magic was virtually gone, and with it, the

Lemurians' way of life. Without sufficient magic, their machines would soon stop working and their floating cities would fall from the sky. Atlanteans had not only doomed themselves, but Lemuria as well. The catastrophe was beyond belief and emotions ran hot. Faced with a world without magic, the Lemurians would have to change and adapt to the world of ordinary men (most other people of that era were barbarians and savages) or flee to a different planet. One with sufficient magic energy to support their magic based technology and lifestyle. As already recounted, most Lemurians chose to leave Earth.

Despite the shock and raging emotions, the vast majority of Lemurians felt sorrow over the destruction/disappearance of their Atlantean friends. They wondered about their fate and prayed that a few had somehow survived. Most Lemurians did not hold ill-will toward the Atlanteans. Rather they felt a deep loss, sadness and sympathy. Lemurians treasure life and considered True Atlanteans to be their closest friends and allies – a mirror image of themselves. As a result, the vast majority of Lemurians understood that people make mistakes, and they forgave their friends for the disaster that now threatened their own existence. Magic is a tricky tool. Dimensional magic is the trickiest. If anything, the disaster that caused Atlantis to vanish, and all but erased magical energy from the planet, was *a lesson* to the Lemurians that taught them to be very careful with their own pursuits in the mystic arts. It served as a cautionary tale that would curb their own magical experimentation and make them careful to be sure their own actions did not have dire consequences for their entire civilization, other people or their beloved planet.

Not all Lemurians were so forgiving.

A small group calling themselves the **Mauian Order** blames the Atlanteans for all the woes that have befallen their civilization and damaged Mother Earth for thousands of years. These bitter misanthropes are determined to see *True Atlanteans* and their *Chiang-Ku dragon* mentors pay for their crimes against the planet and its inhabitants. Pay in blood.

The Mauian Order was founded under a charismatic leader by the name of **Maui-tikitiki** (pronounced: mow-wee-teek-key-teek-key), and they live for a simple agenda of revenge: destroy every last True Atlantean and Chiang-Ku as punishment for the unforgivable sins of their fathers. Some have even convinced themselves that as long as any Atlantean lives, there remains the danger that another mistake that damages the flow of magic or alters an entire world could take place. Though Lemurian society condemns such madness and embraces True Atlanteans as ancient allies, the Mauian Order will not listen to reason. To them, any Lemurian who chooses to stand in the way of their punishment of Atlanteans is a fool and shall pay a harsh price for their misplaced loyalty.

Though the Mauian Order is few in number – believed to be no greater than one thousand total – they are zealots dedicated to the destruction of all True Atlanteans and the Chiang-Ku. The cult's leader, Maui-tikitiki, is a man consumed with hatred and fueled by self-righteous indignation. He has a brilliant mind, but is hardened by hate and consumed by unreasoning paranoia, anger and an unrelenting need for revenge. Maui-tikitiki is so twisted by hate and imagined fears that he regards his fellow Lemurians as blind fools for not condemning Atlanteans as he and his followers have. According to Maui-tikitiki and the members of the Mauian Order, what the Atlanteans did, accident or not, is unforgivable and must be punished. The Mauians insist Atlanteans have not suffered enough for their hubris and crimes against the Earth itself. To them, Atlanteans are monsters who must be destroyed before they cause more harm to the Earth and, perhaps, the Megaverse. They insist Atlanteans have learned nothing from the destruction of Atlantis or the damage they did to the Earth 15,000 years ago. If anything, they are worse than ever, traversing the Megaverse and interfering in the lives of countless humanoid civilizations and provoking trouble with such powerful beings as the Splugorth. Someone has to put a stop to the insanity, and that someone is Maui-tikitiki and his followers.

The Mauian Order believes that the arrogant, dimension-trotting Atlanteans might one day shatter the very fabric of reality across the dimensions. They even blame them for the Minion War (as well as many other wars and troubles the Atlanteans had nothing to do with) and believe they must be stopped at all costs. As a result, members of the Mauian Order have become dimensional travelers themselves and consort with the enemies of True Atlanteans, including the Splugorth, Deevils, demons and other evil beings. If fellow Lemurians are injured by the Mauians' actions, they consider it unfortunate collateral damage.

While this may sound like utter madness to a rational person, Maui-tikitiki is adored by his followers, who revere him as a visionary and a living god. They accept everything he tells them as truth and obey his every command. All members of the Order are willing to lie, cheat, steal, murder and die for him and their campaign of genocide. To that end, the members of the Mauian Order are willing to trick and manipulate anyone to do their dirty work. They don't care if their actions may jeopardize their own people or allow evil to triumph, provided Atlanteans or Chiang-Ku dragons are made to suffer and die in the process.

The Mauian Order and their leader believe all dragons are a danger and a scourge upon the Megaverse. No dragon is ever to be trusted, and when the opportunity presents itself, it is best to destroy them. The Chiang-Ku – allies of True Atlanteans and the creators of Tattoo Magic – are regarded as the worst of the worst and top the list of dragons to be wiped from existence. In fact, some people believe the Mauian Order's efforts to destroy the fabled dragons have been so successful over the last 300 years, they have helped bring the species to the edge of extinction, at least on Rifts Earth.

Obsessed with hatred for the Atlanteans, Maui-tikitiki and some of his followers have mastered magicks that allow them to travel to other worlds and dimensions. Most Lemurians (99%) avoid dimensional travel and Temporal Magic, but Maui-tikitiki believes he must master such mystic arts to fight fire with fire and to track down and destroy True Atlanteans wherever they hide in the Megaverse. Thus, members of his inner circle include Shifters, Temporal Wizards, Ley Line Rifters, Necromancers, Demon Mages, Witches, Fire Warlocks, Soulmancers, Blood Mages and other practitioners of dark magicks forbidden by Lemurian society. They also recruit *Serpent Hunters* to become destroyers of the Chiang-Ku and other dragons deemed by the Mauian Order to be dangerous or untrustworthy. In fact, it was Maui-tikitiki, before he fell from grace within Lemurian society as a madman, who organized and trained the very first *Serpent Hunters.*

Since then, Maui-tikitiki has given up on Lemurian civilization, and he and his Mauian Order continue to track down and slay Chiang-Ku dragons and True Atlanteans at a relentless pace. A large part of the knowledge Maui-tikitiki and his men have collected across the Megaverse deals with uncovering the secrets of dragons, True Atlanteans and other "monsters," so that they might better hunt and destroy them.

In a bid to win over new recruits and allies, the Mauian Order accepts select outsiders into their secret society. They have even gone so far as to teach a few fledgling civilizations many of the Lemurian philosophies and teachings to make the world a better place. Of course, such potential acts of kindness are always twisted with the sordid tale of what the Atlanteans have done to the Earth, how they are responsible for the Great Cataclysm and the Coming of the Rifts, and why they should be feared, hated and destroyed. The most notable civilization to be heavily influenced by the Mauian Order is the *Jungle Elves of South America.* These beings have accepted the Mauian Order's teachings, believe the lies about Atlanteans and dragons, and have been so steadfast in the teachings of the Order that some consider Maui-tikitiki to be a sort of demigod.

The Mauian Order represents a danger not only to the beings they have targeted for eradication, but to Lemuria itself. First, the actions of the Order may reflect badly on the rest of Lemuria. After all, the Order proudly kills in the name of Lemuria and makes no bones about being Lemurians.

Second, the Mauian Order's campaign of hate is corrupting fledgling civilizations and people of Rifts Earth, like the Jungle Elves of South America and a number of tribal people in Polynesia, to fear, hate and murder True Atlanteans, dragons and other targets designated by the Mauian Order. There are Lemurian outcasts, terrorist groups and secret members of the Order scattered across Rifts Earth and the Megaverse who spread lies, corrupt naive individuals and entire cultures to engage in acts of murder and genocide. There are also members of the Mauian Order who travel the Megaverse in search of dark secrets, new magicks, and ancient artifacts, as well as Chiang-Ku dragons and True Atlanteans to murder in their sleep.

Third, the Order is a menace within Lemurian civilization. As a "secret society," no one knows how many members of the Mauian Order exist, who they are or where they operate. As with any secret society, the membership is exclusive, elite and very secret. Secret members of the Mauian Order use their positions within Lemurian society to influence and manipulate people, events, laws and attitudes to further the Order's own agenda. This includes painting the Chiang-Ku and True Lemurians in a bad light, locating them for extermination, interfering with diplomatic relations with them (along with their allies, and dragons in general), and creating general unrest in matters involving them. This means that a senator or social leader, war hero or businessperson or hard-working laborer could be a secret member of the Mauian Order quietly pushing their agenda or using his or her influence to cover up their activity, bankroll their operations and help the Order in any number of ways. Though it is believed their numbers are small, nobody knows for sure. Try as they might, the leaders of Lemurian society have not been able to completely root out the Mauian Order.

Each member of the Mauian Order has his or her given name and a *chosen name* within the Order. The chosen name almost always starts with 'Maui' in respect to their illustrious leader, *Maui-tikitiki.* So Klayn Valotiki may be Maui-valto or Maui-Valiant – something similar, or something completely dissimilar, to his true name. At this time, 95% of the members of the Mauian Order are Lemurians. The Mauian Order is essentially a full-blown terrorist cult, fully rooted within Lemurian society, with operatives working on the surface world and within Lemuria. Their continued efforts and covert operations have allowed the Mauian Order to keep in touch with the supernatural forces that hate True Altanteans, which include the Splugorth and their minions, Deevils and demons. They are known to associate with members of the Federation of Magic, the Jungle Elves of South America, the Blood Druids of France, Temporal Raiders, the Yama Kings and others of questionable character. Rumor has it that Maui-tikitiki's secret base of operations is on Splugorth-occupied Atlantis, is safeguarded by one of Lord Splynncryth's elite squads, and that Maui-tikitiki has the ear of the Lord of Atlantis himself. And that cannot possibly be a good thing for anyone.

Secret quest for the Blade Eternal

While on one of his many dimensional travels, Maui-tikitiki has come across information that may be a piece to the Current-Riders' enigmatic prophecy. He has heard stories about an ancient magic sword said to be in the possession of a powerful aquatic creature on an alien water world. The weapon is known as the **Blade Eternal** and is said to burn even in the depths of the sea, where it radiates a heat so intense that it boils the water around it. The weapon is also said to be indestructible (probably an ancient, Greater Rune Weapon), able to fire a beam of heat so hot that it can even burn demons and Deevils (does 1D6x10 M.D., double damage to Lords, evil gods and Alien Intelligences; 2,000 foot/610 m range), make its wielder impervious to both fire and cold, and enable that person to survive in *any* environment as long as the Blade Eternal remains in his possession (in hand or on his person). Moreover, legend claims the Blade Eternal can cut through anything. Only the **Sun Scabbard** can contain the Blade Eternal's fiery essence without radiating heat and fire. Some legends say the Blade Eternal was made from the heart of a sun, others claim it was forged by a powerful engine of creation in a distant galaxy. The Mauian Order believes the sword may indeed be the Eternal Flame Blade described in the infamous prophecies known to the Current-Riders, and the Order wants to get their hands on the magical item for Maui-tikitiki. They have information that points to a half dozen planets that might be the actual water world where the blade might be located, the planet Earth among them.

The Mauian Order is on the constant lookout for this fabled blade and rumors about it, as well as other legendary magic items. They are seriously thinking about hiring several groups of trustworthy mercenaries and adventurers to go looking for it. Their concern is that to hire outsiders is to share the existence of the lost relic with other people, and worry that if the lords of Hell learn about the weapon, they will try to find it for themselves. Thus, caution and secrecy are of the utmost importance.

Maui-Tikitiki, Leader of the Mauian Order

Maui-tikitiki is an aging Lemurian who, unlike most of his kind, has rough looks, scars and an aura of confidence and danger about him that many people find quite chilling. He has traveled the Megaverse in search of power, the secrets of magic and dark arts for two centuries. The acquisition of such power has made him a formidable mage – a Shifter – and won him an unusual amount of mystic energy (P.P.E.). However, this acquisition of power and forbidden knowledge has marred his Lemurian good looks, scarred his body, and some say, his very soul. He has shoulder-length, white hair braided with seaweed and seashells into dread locks. His beard is white with hints of blue, and his athletic body is "decorated" with a number of deep scars he wears like badges of honor. Each scar has a story. Many represent narrow escapes from death, while some are the marks of power won from dark and deadly sources.

Once, long ago, he was filled with high ideals and an insatiable lust for knowledge. His hatred and resentment of the Chiang-Ku dragons and True Atlanteans has warped his sense of right and wrong, but it has been his pursuit of forbidden magic that has turned him into a twisted monster. While his physical appearance has changed to the point where few would mistake him for a handsome Lemurian, it is his heart that has changed most of all. Not only is he a cold, calculating killer bent on the genocide of True Atlanteans and Chiang-Ku dragons, but he has decided that he knows what is best for Lemuria and should be the leader of his people. Worse, he has grown to see ordinary Lemurians as dull-witted weaklings – sheep – instead of tigers and sharks who should conquer and rule over the lesser people like "humans" and D-Bees. Maui-tikitiki believes Lemurians have risen above their human ancestry and are now superior beings with the knowledge and power to reclaim and rule the planet Earth. They just lack the will and proper leadership. Leadership he could provide if only they would stop being pacifists and listen to him. Thankfully, only a tiny number of Lemurians share his sense of superiority, and most of them are already members of his Mauian Order.

Those who knew Maui-tikitiki in his youth insist that it has been the corrupting influence of the demons and monsters he commands as a Shifter that has turned his heart black. Others say it is the dimensional travels he has taken that have not only cast a shadow over his soul but driven him quite mad. The truth is, both are certain to have contributed to the corruption of a brilliant mind, but Maui-tikitiki always had a dark side going back to his youth and stemming from his bitter, abusive father.

So it is, Maui-tikitiki is almost the opposite of his Lemurian brethren. He lacks compassion and empathy for the human condition and shares little appreciation for life. He is a sociopath consumed with the acquisition of power and a need to prove he is better, smarter and more fit to rule than any Lemurian. Though he has his own twisted code of honor, he is a monster with an agenda of misplaced retribution against True Atlanteans and Chiang-Ku dragons, both of whom he seeks to destroy. Though he and the Mauian Order take action to destroy all enemies of Lemuria (Atlanteans and Chiang-Ku first among them), the Dark Son of Lemuria seeks to undermine Lemurian civilization so he may one day step in as a hero and seize the position of King.

The long reach of Maui-Tikitiki. During his travels across the face of the Earth and through many dimensions, Maui-tikitiki has made many questionable and dangerous friends and associates. People and beings he can call upon for help and information when he really needs it. The least of them include fellow Biomancers, Ley Line Walkers, Ley Line Rifters, Mind Melters, Mystics, Stone Masters, Shifters, Temporal Raiders, Wizards, Wilderness Scouts and Jungle Elves. Among the more powerful and least human allies are various dragons, the Minions of Splugorth, the Splugorth themselves, and, some say, dark gods. If such rumors are true, one or more of the Yama Kings may be a friend and ally of Maui-tikitiki. It is also rumored that Maui-tikitiki has visited the fabled **Green World** (probably as a favor from his vile Splugorth allies), and knows secrets of Biomancy that are not known to Lemurians or Jungle Elves. Still other rumors warn that within the Lemurian elite there are some Biomancers who are more loyal to him than to Lemuria, and work, in secret, on his behalf. Some circles whisper that his campaign to slay the wise Chiang-Ku has much less to do with revenge than the acquisition of power via the dark arts and the blood sacrifice of the ancient dragons.

Maui-Tikitiki NPC Villain

Also Known As: Maui-Mu, the Lone Traveler, and the Dark Son of Lemuria.

Alignment: Once, long ago, he was Scrupulous, but his extreme views, prejudice and arrogance have turned him Aberrant evil.

Attributes: I.Q. 25, M.E. 29, M.A. 22, P.S. 22, P.P. 23, P.E. 24, P.B. 9 (was once 21), Spd 30.

Hit Points: 74

S.D.C.: 53

Size: Five feet, eight inches tall (1.7 m); 135 lbs (60.7 kg).

Age: 329; looks to be in his early 50s.

P.P.E.: 548

Level of Experience: 15th level Shifter O.C.C. and founder of the Mauian Order. Some say he also derives power and knowledge from one or more dark gods who serve as his benefactor(s) (or does he serve them as an agent of darkness?), but most believe this is merely a tall tale.

Natural Abilities: As per all Lemurians, plus supernatural level of P.P.E. and extensive knowledge of forbidden magic; most notably Shifter, Ley Line Magic and Temporal Magic.

Psionic Powers: As per all Lemurians: Empathic Connection with Animals, Empathy (4), Mind Block (4), Object Read (6), See the Invisible (4), Speed Reading (2) and Telepathy (4). Considered a Minor Psychic and has 79 I.S.P.

Magic Knowledge: As a 15th level Shifter, Maui-tikitiki is well versed in transdimensional and anti-supernatural magic. He possesses the following Shifter abilities: Dimensional Sense 98%, Dimensional Travel, Communication Rift, Dimensional Teleport Home (Rifts Earth), Sense Rifts and Familiar Link (Iki the Lemur). Despite the rumors to the contrary, he does not have a "link" to the supernatural, as he considers such things vile and a tainting of the pure and noble human spirit. However, he associates and makes deals with the Splugorth and other dark gods and powerful forces of supernatural evil.

Summoning and Minions: While Maui-tikitiki claims disdain for supernatural creatures and demons, and clearly treats them as the scum of the Earth, he makes an exception in associating with their Lords and the deities who rule over them. This means he has no qualms about summoning and using demons and supernatural beings to do his bidding and fight his enemies. He calls it "fighting fire with fire." The Shifter also surrounds himself with powerful animals, sea monsters, sea dragons and sea serpents, using them as his minions, protectors, mounts and pets (any in this book or **Rifts® Underseas™**).

Maui-tikitiki knows many spells, but those listed below are among his favorites and most often used: All Ley Line Magic spells, Animate and Control Dead ((20), Annihilate (600), Armor of Ithan (10), Aura of Power (4), Banishment (65), Befuddle (6),Blinding Flash (1), Breathe without Air (5), Calling (8), Call Lightning (15), Calm Storm (200), Carpet of Adhesion (10), Circle of Travel (600), Cloud of Smoke (2), Compulsion (20), Constrain Being (20), Control and Enslave Entity (80), D-Step (50), Desiccate the Supernatural (50), Dimensional Portal (1,000), Dimensional Teleport (800), Dispel Magic Barrier (20), Distant Voices (10), Domination (10), Energy Disruption (12), Energy Sphere (120), Expel Demons (35), Forcebonds (25), Influence the Beast (12), Invisibility: Simple (6), Ley Line

Transmission (30), Locate (30), Magic Pigeon (20), Magic Net (7), Magic Warrior (60), Metamorphosis: Animal (25), Metamorphosis: Insect (60), Meteor (75), Multiple Images (7), Mystic Alarm (5), Mystic Portal (60), Negate Magic (30), Phantom Mount (45), Plane Skip (65), Power Bolt (20), Protection Circle: Simple (45), Protection Circle: Superior (300), Repel Animals (7), Re-Open Gateway (180), Reality Flux (75), Reduce Self (20), Rift to Limbo (160), Rift Teleportation (200), Sanctum (390), See Aura (6), See the Invisible (4), Sense Evil (2), Sense Magic (4), Shadow Meld (10), Sheltering Force (20), Summon Ally (600), Summon and Control Animals (125), Summon and Control Canines (50), Summon Fog (140), Summon and Control Sea Serpents (350), Summon and Control Rain (200), Summon and Control Storms (300), Summon and Control Rodents (70), Summon Shadow Beasts (140), Sustain (12), Tame Beast (30), Teleport: Lesser (15), Teleport: Superior (600), Time Hole (210), Time Slip (20), Tongues (10), Trance (10), Turn Dead (6), Watchguard (10), and Wink-Out (20+).

Maui-tikitiki also knows the following Temporal Spells: Attune Object to Owner (30), Dimensional Pocket (20 or 140), Dimensional Envelope (60 or 380), Remote Viewing (45), See Dimensional Anomaly (30), Sense Dimensional Anomaly (30), T-Dep: Time Deprivation (20), Time Warp: Slow Motion (45+), Temporary Time Hole (100), and Time Warp: Fast Forward (75).

And not to stray too far from his aquatic lineage, Maui-tikitiki knows the following Ocean Magic spells: Armor of Neptune (20), Coral Armor (10 or 45), Metamorphosis: Fish (50), Metamorphosis: Crustacean (60 or 120), Metamorphosis: Shark (90 or 160), Mystic Sea Horse (15), Strength of the Whale (20), and Summon Sea Friend (40).

Combat Skill: Hand to Hand: Kapu Kuialua.

Attacks per Melee: Seven.

Bonuses: +6 on Perception Rolls, +5 on initiative, +9 to strike, +8 to parry and +9 dodge, +7 to roll with impact, +4 to pull punch, +3 to disarm, +11 damage, +1 to body flip/throw, +1 body block/tackle and a Critical Strike from behind on a Natural 17 to 20, +7 to save vs magic, +5 to save vs poisons, +9 to save vs psionics, +11 to save vs Horror Factor, 70% to Trust/Intimidate and 45% to Charm/Impress.

Skills of Note: Language & Literacy: Lemurian, Dragonese/Elven, English/American, Spanish and Chinese; Language: Cetacean, Demongogian, Faerie Speak and Oceanic; Astronomy, Basic and Advanced Mathematics, Computer Operation, Horsemanship: General and Exotic, Lore: Demons & Monsters, Lore: Dimensions, Lore: Magic, Lore: Cattle and Animals, Lore: Sea Creatures, Lore: D-Bees, Lore: Faeries and Creatures of Magic, Undersea and Sea Survival and Underwater Navigation, all at 98%.

Weapon Proficiencies: W.P. Blunt and W.P. Trident at 15th level, W.P. Sword and W.P. Knife at 6th level proficiency.

Weapons of Note: He has access to pretty much any weapon created by the Lemurians, but the ones of note are:

T-Club (also known as Te Kauae Maro Muri-ranga-whenua (Jawbone Club of Muri-ranga-whenua). This simple looking Bio-Weapon looks like a paddle with a very short handle and was created by Maui-tikitiki's ancestor Muri-ranga-whenua. She presented it to Maui-tikitiki on his first voyage, and it was her stories and insight into magic that sparked his curiosity about the Megaverse beyond Earth.

The club inflicts 3D6 M.D. as a melee weapon, but does double damage to *temporal creatures* and those using Temporal Magic, including Temporal Wizards, Temporal Warriors, and Temporal Raiders (as well as Prometheans, Phase Adepts and Phase Mystics). It also provides the wielder with a +1 to save vs any kind of Temporal Magic.

Guardian Staff. No one knows where Maui-tikitiki got this magical staff, but many are well aware of its power and abilities, especially when fighting against the supernatural. Those who dare speculate as to its origins point to its cold stone appearance and gem facets to indicate that it might be some kind of Rune Weapon. The staff is a long, octagonal cross-sectioned staff with strange patterns and carving down its length. The head of the staff is also octagonal in shape but is twice the diameter of the base of the staff. Each face on the staff's head holds a colored gem; red, orange, yellow, green, teal, blue, purple and violet. From each of the crystals emerges a glowing, colored energy ball which then circles the staff while Maui-tikitiki uses that particular feature or power. When it is not in use, the ball of light returns to the staff and turns off. Activating a gem or changing to a new gem uses one action, but otherwise each attack counts as one of his own. When used as a blunt weapon it does 4D6 M.D. to most foes, but 6D6 M.D. against supernatural opponents, including creatures of magic.

Red: Unleashes a crimson beam not unlike a laser that inflicts 4D6 M.D. and has a range of 4,000 feet (1,219 m).

Orange: Unleashes a stream of fire that does 5D6 M.D. and has a range of 300 feet (91 m). Does NOT work underwater.

Yellow: Launches a golden orb made of telekinetic energy that hits with the force of a cannonball, does 2D6 M.D. and has a range of 1,000 feet (305 m).

Green: Launches a green orb up to 200 feet (61 m) that causes plants/trees and living coral to grow and entangle anything or anyone within 12 feet (3.6 m) of it. Requires a 16 or greater to dodge out of the way of the growing tendrils and takes 1D4+3 melee rounds to pull or chop free of the entangling vegetation, or until the end of the magic's duration. If fired at a mortal humanoid or large mammal, the specific individual is bestowed with life energy and gets an extra 2D6+10 Hit Points (or is healed of equivalent H.P. or S.D.C. damage). Duration: 2D4+3 melee rounds.

Teal: This one launches an orb that soaks an individual with water and does 1D6x10 damage to vampires, 1D6x10 M.D. to Fire Elementals and other creatures vulnerable to water, or douses a 12 foot (3.6 m) diameter of fire.

Blue: Fires a beam of cold that does 2D6 M.D.; double damage to beings vulnerable to cold or ice.

Purple: Launches an orb of darkness that conceals the wielder and creates a Horror Factor of 12 up to 300 feet (91 m) away.

Violet: Fires a beam that cauterizes wounds, stops bleeding and purges poisons (immediately stops further damage). The beam restores 1D6 Hit Points, S.D.C. or M.D.C. per wound that is healed.

Armor of Note: Barnacle or via magic.

Lemurian Floating Cities

The City of Mu

A template for all Lemurian Floating Cities

Location: Mobile, always changing; seldom stays at the same locale for more than 2D4 days and may spend days, weeks and months at a time slowly floating from one place to another or just drifting.

Speed: Maximum Speed Underwater: 70 mph (112 km/60.8 knots); increase by 50% along ley lines.

Maximum Speed on the Surface of Water: 70 mph (112 km/60.8 knots); increase by 50% along ley lines.

Maximum Speed Flying: 320 mph (512 km); maximum altitude is 22,000 feet (6,705.6 m); increase by 50% along ley lines.

Favorite Resting Places: The heart of the Indian Ocean (30°00'S 87°13'E), the bottom of the world's oceans, seas, and large, deep lakes, as well as remote mountaintops and other remote places.

Estimated Population: 375,000

Racial Breakdown:

90% Lemurians.
5% Merans.
2% Ichthyleans.
2% Pneuma-Biforms, dolphins and whales.
1% Other, mostly Amphibs, humans and mutants.

The ancient city of Mu dates back to when Lemurians were still completely surface dwelling humans. The city was the product of their highly advanced civilization and drew upon the Lemurians' vast knowledge of Stone Magic and the use of ley lines and other magic in its construction. It would eventually become the template for all the cities that followed. Today, it remains the jewel of the Lemurian civilization and is the biggest of the floating cities. It can glide along ley lines without drawing on the P.P.E. reserve held inside its own stone pyramids and ziggurats, and can teleport the entire city from one ley line nexus to another anywhere in the world. While drifting along a ley line or loitering at a ley line nexus, the city's pyramids draw upon the ambient magic energy, funneling it into their ziggurats and pyramids to recharge and restore the city's energy reserves. This way, Mu can float and maintain operations for up to 1D4+2 weeks away from available Earth Energy along ley lines. These same stone edifices provide all the energy throughout the city, from streetlights to heating. As a monument to peace and exploration, Mu carries no obvious built-in armaments or fortifications. Mind you, it is not completely defenseless. The stone pyramids and ziggurats are Mega-Damage structures with walls several feet thick and contain vast reserves of P.P.E. with which to cast a dazzling array of magic defenses and offensive spells. The pyramids also harness the energy collected from ley lines and channel it throughout the city as the primary renewable energy. This means magic can be worked from all the stone ziggurats to erect magic defenses, calm or create Ley Line Storms, and work a wide range of magic to defend the city and protect the innocent. Remember, all Lemurian cities have a large population of practitioners of magic (20-30%) as well as a contingent of elite warriors who can leap into action to fend off an attack or rain down destruction upon invaders.

The City of Mu is the largest and most beautiful of them all. Like all Lemurian cities, there are streets lined with trees and the city is dotted with manicured parks, gardens and courtyards. Parks with trees, flowers and sculpted gardens, or urban farms are also found on the rooftops of almost every building in the city, and small, private gardens are seen crowning or dangling from most terraces, trellises and down the sides of some buildings. As a result, the city is teaming with birds, woodland creatures, butterflies, insects and plants of all kinds. However, as a center for the arts, education and magic, Mu is also filled with works of artistry, from paintings and mosaics to sculptures and architectural wonders. Every building seems to be adorned with engravings, sculptures, wall paintings, mosaics and all sorts of tasteful carvings and artistic touches that are pleasing to the eye. The architecture of the city is equally delightful, making the city seem welcoming and itself a giant, sprawling work of art. Mu, like most Lemurian cities, feels like it is part city and part nature preserve, or a city built within a forest without imposing its profile upon the beauty of the wildlands. All Lemurian floating cities travel the world studying other people and life forms, collecting specimens, learning about the mysteries of life, and developing new ways of living in harmony with the planet, and Mu is no different.

Lemurian floating cities each have a large **central or "Master" ziggurat** (pyramid) that functions as the central nervous system and main power hub for the city. Dozens of smaller ziggurats (terraced pyramids) that encircle the main one are found in straight lines away from the central ziggurat. As the city travels along a ley line or rests on a nexus, the city orients itself to maximize the collection of energy into the central ziggurat. That energy is then channeled to the smaller stone pyramids until all are filled to maximum capacity and stored. While perched over a ley line, the pyramids of the floating city maintain absolute control over that ley line. This grants the Lemurians the ability to sense dimensional anomalies, open and close Rifts, and prevent Rifts from opening while the city is at the nexus point, as well as the ability to control the weather, wind and sea currents around the city and along the ley line, calm rough seas and inclement weather, adjust water temperature and perform a wide range of magic boosted by the energy of the ley line or nexus. Even severely depleted energy reserves are brought to full power levels within 24 hours and can power a floating city for 1D4+1 months depending on the level of energy use. However, the leaders of floating cities seldom let power levels drop below 60% before taking measures to power up.

Most surface dwellers assume Lemurian cities are submerged and filled with water like a ceramic castle in a fish bowl. The truth is, all Lemurian cities are dry and filled with a renewable, temperature controlled, breathable atmosphere. The city is enveloped by a great, transparent *Bio-Skin* that is virtually invisible underwater. It covers the city like a giant, semi-visible membrane, giving the habitat something of a giant jellyfish appearance when the city rises up out of the sea and into the air. The membrane lets in sunlight, and removes oxygen from the water and circulates it into the city via Biomancy magic to purify existing air. The vast amount of vegetation in each city also helps to purge toxins and produce breathable air. The magical process that cleans and creates the breathable atmosphere also collects carbon dioxide, methane and other toxins from the city and releases them into the sea. Magic circulates the

air, and the entire process is powered by renewable Earth Energy (magic). Like so many things in Lemurian civilization, the membrane is a Mega-Damage structure (200 M.D.C. per 10 foot/3 m diameter) and a living organism that "heals" from damage inflicted to it (recovers 1D4x10 M.D.C. per hour, double on a ley line). Condensation can sometimes create a light fog on city streets, or a mist in the air. Once in a while, water even falls from the top of the membrane like a light spring shower.

A network of water-filled tubes, tunnels, channels, canals and pools run throughout the city to accommodate aquatic allies and Lemurian citizens who prefer water as a method of travel. These manmade waterways are also the way in and out of the city, with exits to the sea located at various locations. The actual "door to the sea" is a somewhat thicker membrane that works like an airlock. Biomancers and the Lemurian Warrior caste, Oceanic Guardsmen and Sea Sentinels (including their combat vehicles) can use these exits, but also have the ability to pass right through the living membrane that encloses the rest of the city.

Vehicles are uncommon in Mu and most Lemurian cities, as most people walk or swim everywhere. The city's mass transit system uses pressurized transport tubes filled with water that carry passengers much like a modern day subway. People can wait for a transit car, swim through these tubes or ride the current to their next destination. The tubes are made of transparent Bio-Skin which lets travelers see where they are and where they are going. When ready to leave, the individual can press through the tube membrane to exit without spilling more than a small amount of water. Ley Line Phasing and using the ziggurats to teleport from one location in the city to another are also common ways of getting around town, particularly by mages and city authorities, though using a ziggurat requires the aid of a Stone Master or Ley Line Walker. There are also roads and walking paths throughout the city and its many parks. Most parks appear to be natural forests and jungle habitats with clear paths and places to sit along the way. Such places are likely to harbor wild animals. Lemurians with their empathy with animals and nature have nothing to fear from the wild beasts of these habitats, but human and D-Bee visitors must exercise caution, and are recommended to stay on the paths and not stray into the thicket. Other parks are well manicured botanical gardens with areas for specific species of plants, trimmed hedges, flower gardens, courtyards with places to sit, fountains, statues, mosaics and other works of art. Art and decorations are found everywhere, indoors and out. The many gardens and courtyards are open to everyone and are used as places to sit, relax and meditate.

Rising up from the top of the central ziggurat is the communications center in the form of a tower, usually making the central ziggurat, located in the heart of the city, the tallest building. Meanwhile, laboratories and animal habitats designed to operate entirely underwater or to hold aquatic animals are located in the thick base of the floating city.

The city is fully capable of travel underwater or floating on the surface of the water at a maximum speed of 70 mph (112 km/60.8 knots), or rising off the ocean floor, breaking the surface of the water and floating into the air. Maximum altitude is 22,000 feet (6,705.6 m), with a maximum flying speed of 320 mph (512 km). Be it on water or in the air, however, the floating city usually moseys along at a much more relaxed pace of 20-40 mph (32 to 64 km). It can also hover in place, make a dead stop in water, or perform a vertical ascent or descent, making it a truly all-terrain, mobile habitat. **Note:** Travel speeds in the air, on the surface of water or underwater can be increased by as much as 50% when traveling along a ley line.

It is the versatile, all-environment capabilities of Lemurian cities that has kept them from falling to the Lord of the Deep and other supernatural enemies. It is also what has kept Lemurian cities concealed from land dwellers and rendered Lemuria the stuff of myth and legend for centuries. One story reports the city on the floor of the Indian Ocean, another floating through the waters of the South Pacific, the next claims it was drifting through the air above Africa or Australia, and the next reports the city resting on a mountaintop in Tibet. Since most people (99%) do not realize Lemurian cities are mobile with naval, submersible and flight capabilities, reports of such "airborne" and "underwater cities" are dismissed as hallucinations, myths and lies. The Lemurians are always on the move, spending time underwater, then on the surface of oceans or in the air, sometimes resting on the bottom of the sea or atop mountains or hovering over land, so that the Lord of the Deep and other supernatural enemies cannot find them. Being always on the move keeps their enemies guessing and confused as to their numbers, resources and whereabouts. It is a tactic that has worked for the last three hundred years.

Key City Design Elements

Mu was the first and foremost of the floating cities, and served as the *design template* for all that followed. Thus, unless noted otherwise, all Lemurian floating cities, regardless of size and population, have the following key locations and elements of city design. Only size, scope and population vary.

Outer Ring of Ziggurats

There are a total of 16 other ziggurats (pyramids) in two rings around the main ziggurat at a radius of 4-8 miles (6.4 to 12.8 km), depending on the size of the city. Each of the ziggurats is aligned on one of the eight cardinal directions (N, NE, E, SE, S, etc.). These peripheral ziggurats align with ley lines visited by the city, typically four along one axis while traveling along a ley line. At a ley line nexus the city is oriented so that the maximum potential number of ziggurats are in line with the intersecting ley lines to collect as much magic energy as possible in 24 hours or less. The way the network of ziggurats is set up allows all of them to tap into the pyramid powers which are normally associated with stone pyramids on a ley line or nexus. The network also channels and stores mystic energy in all the ziggurats for trips away from ley lines. All of the ziggurats on the outer ring (eight total) straddle the Bio-Skin barrier, acting as passageways/airlocks into the city. That means they function as defensive bunkers as well, housing a large number of troops in barracks style fortifications to respond to attacks, regulate and monitor the flow of traffic, especially by outsiders, and to deal with trouble outside the city and monitor the surrounding area. They are also set up to receive guests (not that the Lemurians get too many) with royal reception chambers to meet with ambassadors and allies; Lemurians don't let any non-Lemurians into the main, central ziggurat. Each outer ziggurat also has a small contingency of labs and research facilities, quarantine areas and holding cells.

"Hale Atua" – The Halls of Lemuria: In each of the outer ring ziggurats there is a reception area. Some are set up as trade centers where aquatic races who find or are invited to the ancient city of Mu can trade, share news and meet with Lemurians. Ambassadors can also be seen and invited to a more secure area within the ziggurat to meet with council members, or the King himself, in private.

"Hale Ua" – The Oceanic Guard Barracks: Each of the ziggurats is protected by a contingent of Oceanic Guardsmen. Many are housed in the same ziggurats they protect while others operate from one ziggurat but travel all over the city or outside to engage in military operations, protect outposts, and perform search and rescue missions. As a rule, 100 Oceanic Guardsmen are posted at an outer ziggurat, 40 (a platoon) at each inner ziggurat and over 200 at the central ziggurat. An additional 200 elite Oceanic Guardsmen (1D4+6 level) serve as the *Royal Guard*, staying with the King and his council wherever they go. The King always lives in the City of Mu. The other cities have regents who oversee and run city operations.

"Hale Mana" – Healing Centers: All of the outer ziggurats have healing centers where psychics, doctors, Biomancers and other mages can offer wounded troops, adventurers, visitors and citizens medical care. "Visitors" are always taken to an outer ziggurat to keep them away from the heart of the city. A host of pyramid powers, healing as well as Biomancers, Bio-Constructs and related magic, can be made available to guests at healing centers.

Inner Ring of Ziggurats

The inner ring of ziggurats are not as heavily guarded, relying on the protection of the outer ring, the Bio-Skin and defenders to keep the city safe and invaders out. A small contingent of Oceanic Guardsman, Spouters and Zappers watch over the inner ziggurats and their operations. This second tier of pyramids is where the bulk of Lemurian Biomancy and other magical and scientific research is conducted. Live specimens, medical experiments, genetic engineering and magical experiments and pursuits are conducted within the safety of the inner pyramids.

"Hale Ua" – The Oceanic Guardsmen Barracks: While essentially identical to the barracks on the outer ring of ziggurats, the guards here are often more relaxed and less experienced (level 1D4+2). While their duties are still strict and a high degree of professionalism is required, they get the chance to try out and work with many of the new Biomancer creations, including Bio-Armor, Bio-Weapons, Bio-Symbiotes, and new animals created as pets, riding animals and other applications.

"Hale Mana" – Research Centers: Each of the inner ring ziggurats houses a massive, multi-level research center. Many of these centers are interdisciplinary and one can find mages from a variety of walks of life – Biomancer Gene-Mages, Line Walkers, Ocean Wizards, Sea Druids, Whale Singers, etc. Each ziggurat usually focuses on one specific area or one specific problem, so that all related minds can work together, share notes and study issues as a diverse team to meet their research objectives. While the term "research" is used, the methods are less scientific and more metaphysical - as is the way of Lemurians.

Northern Ziggurats (NE and N): The northern ziggurats house mages and researchers studying and mapping the genetic structures of newly discovered M.D.C. animals. Live specimens of these "new" animals (both young and ancient, predatory and otherwise) are kept onsite at the facilities in special habitats.

Southern Ziggurats (SE, S and SW): More genetic and scientific research and studies take place at these locations. One project conducted at such facilities is the attempt to unravel the secrets behind a mysterious animal gene dubbed the *"Primordial Gene."* This gene is believed to be present in dinosaurs, dragons, some ancient species of reptiles, fish, and sea serpents, and a few giant-sized mammals. The elusive "Primordial Gene" is believed to be responsible for transforming these megalithic beings into M.D.C. creatures and providing them with Supernatural Strength. Some have theories that the Primordial Gene responds to the high ambient level of magical energy in magic rich environments like Rifts Earth. Here, the return of magic is believed to have triggered the gene and somehow channels and redirects Earth Energy (P.P.E.) to make a creature into an M.D.C. being. Put those same creatures in a low magic environment (which are most common throughout the Megaverse) and they revert to S.D.C. beings in a matter of minutes. Lemurians hope to someday isolate the gene sequence that does this to alter their own genetic structure and become M.D.C. beings. However, such a mystery is likely to take centuries or eons to unravel, if ever, and years more to figure out the means to transform humans.

Western Ziggurats (NW and W): The study and application of the mind, psionics, and dimensions in the understanding of life, human nature and the working of the human brain. Everything from scientific studies, philosophical debate and metaphysical studies are pursued at these facilities. The ultimate goal: to better understand the human animal, psychic phenomena, the Megaverse and humanity's place in it. Another is to learn how Lemurians can find greater harmony with the Megaverse and bring balance to their lives. Other areas of study include psychic research about the Astral Plane and other dimensions, dimensional travel using the mind, reaching out to the minds of other sentient beings, psychic imprinting, developing and expanding psychic abilities and using psionics to better communicate with and fight supernatural beings. This includes how and why some extra-dimensional energies can mutate and make super-monsters as well as dimensional phenomena like the Bermuda Triangle, Fade Towns, the Rifts and other anomalies. While the results and hypotheses portions of dimensional research take place at these ziggurats, any actual experiments and field testing are conducted outside and away from the city. It is interesting to note that the King of Lemuria and the Council of Elders are uneasy with this research and even mental exercises about the nature, function and use of dimensions and dimensional travel; they allow it as a necessary evil.

The Eastern Ziggurat (E): The research here is cataloging and understanding new and alien species that are foreign to Rifts Earth. While no dramatic biological experiments are performed here, there are laboratory experiments, and a small degree of medical research, as well as practical applications of the use of new species and their genetic material in curing alien-spawned diseases, combating the supernatural and discerning native Earth species from alien species and mutations.

Hale Papa'a – Learning Centers/Training and Knowledge Centers: While all the ziggurats contain at least one *Tree of Knowledge*, learning centers have several and function like a traditional university with students, young and old, who come to study and learn a wide range of subjects from a wide range of educators and scholars that include mages, psychics and Trees of Knowledge. The most popular subjects are Lemurian history, magic, psionics, communing with nature, farming, botany, biology, ocean sciences, medicine, meditation, philosophy, ethics and the arts. Students can seek the wisdom of elder Lemurians and engage in their own research and extrapolations. Those studying magic enter into an apprenticeship program.

The Master Ziggurat

Also known as the Royal Ziggurat

When on a ley line, ALL stone pyramids/ziggurats collect and store Earth Energy (P.P.E.), but it is the Master Ziggurat that channels and distributes that energy throughout the city, charging up the reservoirs of all ziggurats and redirecting energy wherever it is needed across the city. In some respects, the stone pyramids function like power plants, with the Master Ziggurat being the main plant and primary point of control and distribution. This provides the floating city with weeks of energy even when away from ley lines or nexus points. A *central control chamber* in the Master Ziggurat is where all energy distribution of the city takes place, with reserves for powering lights, heat and city systems, as well as automated energy management systems. From this location, the ebb and flow of energy of all other pyramids is managed, and in the case of an emergency, the Master Ziggurat can drain, direct, redirect, and even cut off the flow of energy to any pyramid or part of the city. Consequently, there are many failsafes and defenders in place, and only the most trusted mages and engineers handle Master Operations.

Heiau – Master Control Chamber: The mages in this room control every aspect of the city, from flight, speed of travel and defenses (i.e. ley line storms and other magicks) to the mundane, as well as monitor all sections of the city and areas just outside the city's protective membrane. A central platform big enough for up to a dozen practitioners of magic is used to channel and direct pyramid energy, (and/or the P.P.E. of the mages) to perform any of the normal powers and functions of a Stone Pyramid or to cast spells within the city and its exterior. The Master Control Chamber is heavily guarded and the pyramid itself prevents invaders from Teleporting, Rifting or using Ley Line Phasing to appear at or within any of the ziggurats. Those using magic or dimensional power to appear in the city or at a ziggurat find themselves magically *redirected* into a heavily guarded and sealed off location known as the **Central Reception Area**, away from the Master Ziggurat. Here, "visitors" are greeted by Oceanic Guardsmen, mages and psychics where they are questioned and if necessary, subdued. Violence and aggression is met in kind and any perceived threat or hostile forces are "neutralized" and "pacified." Translation, forced into submission and placed in confinement for additional questioning, or exterminated.

Hale Ali'i – Royal Annex: This is where the King and his council members meet to discuss matters of city policy, politics, education, defense, exploration, city services, transportation and the needs of the city and its citizens. The King and the Council of Elders often reside in the Master Ziggurat, each with their own spacious and luxurious quarters fit for a prince. No one save the King, his direct family and the council members and their immediate families have access to the Royal Annex within the Master ziggurat.

Hale Ua – The Royal Guard Barracks: A permanent contingent of 144 Oceanic Guardsmen (levels 1D6+5) who have earned the position of "Royal Guard" live on site inside the Master Ziggurat. They are on call 24 hours a day and are regarded as heroes and the best of the best. An additional 1D4x100 Oceanic Guardsmen (levels 1D4+2) can be called upon for additional support and have a response time of 1D4+1 minutes. Any excursions made by the King or any royal council member is escorted by at least a pair of the Royal Guard; at least 8 for the King and the immediate members of his family (function like the Presidential Secret Service).

Other Locations

The Archive of Omatu: A subterranean complex built into a circular ring directly around the Master Ziggurat contains the sum of Lemurian knowledge, including several ancient Trees of Knowledge, many heralding back to the days before the city was even built. These ancient trees bear the original memories and knowledge of many of the first Lemurians and the way things were before the Atlantean Catastrophe or the Coming of the Rifts. Besides the wealth of knowledge stored in the mystical trees, is a vast library of books, parchments, stone tablets, pre-Rifts artifacts and data files that have been recovered and restored. The keeper of these archives is an ancient Lemurian academic named *Puta Toa.* It is said that he knows everything there is about Lemurian civilization as well as a great depth of knowledge about Mother Earth.

Serpent Hunters' Citadel: A large, stone citadel in the center of the southwestern quadrant is home to the *Serpent Hunters* and their *Thrall Sea Serpents.* Their ideal location near the southern ziggurat enables them to help regulate the large variety of dinosaurs, sea serpents and riding animals in this quarter of the city. The citadel is part castle (the upper level) and part network of tunnels and caves. There is a huge underground complex of caves, labyrinths and dwelling places for sea serpents and other exotic riding animals. Of course, there are several transit tubes that link to the rest of the city and others that provide a quick, secret exit and entry in and out of the city for the Serpent Hunters and their monstrous riding animals.

The Garden: The most illustrious section of the city is a large, beautiful, terraced botanical garden filled with trees, flowers, fruit, vines, patches of vegetables gardens and exotic plants native to Earth and other worlds. Much to the surprise of many surface dwellers, the Garden is also home to a wide range of insects, birds and a host of exotic creatures. Many Lemurians work long and hard managing this wondrous site and their love for their work and devotion to nature is apparent at a moment's glance. Many artists, philosophers and mages come to *the Garden* to meditate and absorb the quiet splendor. Others come to play, rest or eat lunch or dinner. The Biomancer groundskeepers make their home right in the Garden, bending trees to form their homes and furniture – enclosing and decorating their sectioned off area with flowers and designs that bloom all year round to their own personal preference. The power of the stone pyramids is said to increase the average lifespan of those who sleep under and within them, and that feature also applies to the Garden. Many believe it is because the Garden's plants are interwoven and linked to the ziggurats of the city and help to bolster the reservoirs of magic energy held in each ziggurat, which then allows the plants to draw on that energy to create a *magical garden paradise* in the floating cities.

Private Habitats, Realms and Oases: Though the Garden is the largest and most impressive collection of flora in the city, almost all homes and places of business have their own flower gardens, vegetable gardens and plant-filled courtyards. In fact, trees, vines and gardens are found on the roofs, ledges, terraces and balconies of even the tallest buildings. In addition to private gardens there are dozens of city parks, gardens and courtyards filled with flora and fauna from around the world. These mini-ecosystems are like an oasis containing many different ecosystems, some isolated (such as the arctic chamber) while many others are open to everyone. The more exotic habitats are controlled by magic and Biomancer communication to keep specific species in one particular location. However, wildlife is found throughout all Lemurian cities. Since the Lemurian people can commune with nature and, in effect, talk to plants and animals, there is seldom a problem with what surface dwellers would consider "wild animals," though predators are kept to a minimum. While Lemurians take this closeness to nature in stride as the harmonious way to live, outsiders may be startled to have deer run by or leap over the park bench they are sitting on; probably a natural stone or tree, vine or plant woven into a seat. Even more startling is to see an ocelot, lion, wolf or something more exotic like a dinosaur or alien animal. Again, most animals stay in their fenceless habitat without bothering people, and do not attack unless threatened. However, such animals may be encountered almost anywhere in a Lemurian floating city.

City Defenses

Lemurian floating cities have come to rely upon moving and hiding above and below the waves to avoid conflicts and attacks. The ability to remain concealed and unnoticed is their first line of defense. To that end, the Lemurians have developed a number of powerful ley line spells/magicks that enable them to use the ley lines and nexus points to hide, shelter and defend their underwater cities. Everything from creating magical illusions and camouflage to ley line avatar defenders have been used to deter and confuse would-be invaders. When one of the cities does fall under attack – usually by undead and/or demonic forces, Nauty'll, Minions of Splugorth and the servants and pawns of the Lord of the Deep – they rely on magic, ley lines and their elite warriors to fight back. Enemies and assailants should not forget that the floating cities of Lemuria are populated by people with Minor to Master Psychic abilities, and at least one third are practitioners of magic. Mages, psychics and warriors often command sea monsters and sea dragons, and all floating cities are defended by a standing army with unique abilities and Biomancy weapons, armor, vehicles and monsters at their command. Furthermore, Lemurians are friends of cetaceans and other aquatic people and sea creatures who are quick to come to their aid and defense.

Lemurian floating cities, with all their pyramids and ziggurats, contain Earth Energy (magic) on a scale not known to most surface dwellers (with the possible exception of the Splugorth's Atlantis). This means the Lemurian cities have the powers of stone pyramids at their command, are capable of controlling and summoning Ley Line Storms, the weather, casting Ley Line Magic and other magicks, and when actually on a ley line, possess even greater power, range and resources. When on a ley line nexus, a Stone Master or Rifter can Rift the entire city to any location along the interconnecting ley lines or to another, known ley line nexus. (**Note:** Takes two melee rounds to prep and costs 1,500 P.P.E. from each of the 16 stone pyramids to jump the entire floating city from one location to another, half if it is to a location on the same ley line).

Each Lemurian stone pyramid/ziggurat can fire a directed bolt of magical energy much like a Ley Line Storm's lightning bolt. The blast is too slow to strike small, fast and maneuverable targets like power armor or a vehicle the size of a van, but it is quite effective against large warships, buildings, marching troops and other large, slow or stationary targets. **Note:** In most circumstances the blast does 1D4x100 M.D., but increases to 1D6x100 M.D. when on a ley line, and 2D4x100 M.D. when drawing upon the energy of a nexus point. Range is 4,000 feet (1,219 m), increase by 30% when on a ley line, and 50% greater at a nexus. Each ziggurat/pyramid can fire once every minute (4 melee rounds).

Garden Valley

According to rumor, not all Lemurian cities and outposts are mobile. One such exception is known as the Garden Valley, said to be nestled in an undersea mountain valley at a secret location someplace on the ocean floor.

In reality, the "Garden Valley" is several, sprawling, underwater farm settlements concealed in the valleys of a particular ocean mountain range. All manner of plants are grown at the Garden Valleys. Biomancy magic helps these fields of aquatic plants to flourish with rich, dense crops for food, but also for the making of fabric, clothing and other material (rope, netting, paper, etc.). These rich underwater farms, in turn, attract a large array of fish and other aquatic animals that are used for food, riding animals and other purposes.

Wildlife. A host of fish and sea creatures are attracted to the lush fields of the Garden Valleys, but others are kept and raised for food and as riding animals.

Exotic crops. In addition to plants native to Earth, there are crops that have come to Earth from alien worlds carried in from the Rifts, as well as genetically engineered plants created by the Biomancer Gene-Mages. A few are noted here, but also see the *Biomancy Gardens* in the comprehensive section on Biomancy.

Gardens of kelp and aquatic plants nurtured by ley line energy rather than sunlight are grown and used as the base for a variety of Lemurian foods as well as Bio-Construct rituals.

Bioluminescent Forests are vast underwater farms of aquatic plants that bear fruit that are glowing bulbs. Besides their obvious light producing properties, Lemurians use them for many magical rituals and healing.

The Lemurians' fabled Crystal Gardens are found at some of the Garden Valley locations, creating forests of gems, crystals and the mystical *Crystal Trees.*

Animal ranges are also scattered throughout the mountains and are considered part of the *Garden Valley complex.* Some animals are kept for research and study, others are raised for food and the big sea serpents and monsters are trained as riding animals. The latter are often ferocious looking beasts, though many behave like puppies in the hands of their Lemurian trainers and riders. The training of sea monsters means there is always a strong presence of *Serpent Hunters* and *Oceanic Guardsmen* picking out or training their combat steeds along with the *Biomancer Gene-Mages* who alter and raise them. Such animals and training centers are usually outdoors, but there are a number of massive training areas and habitats built inside the mountains and within ocean canyons.

Merans. An underwater village of Merans live near the Garden Valley complex. They have been trusted allies for centuries and share in all the secrets of the Garden Valley. In fact, the Merans work some of the Lemurian farms for a share of the crops and enjoy life among their Lemurian friends as complete equals. When danger appears, Merans are quick to lure interlopers away and come to the Garden Valley's defense.

Concealment of the Garden Valley. Though these farms are out in the open, they are nestled in remote, undersea mountain valleys and ravines where even aquatic people are not likely to stumble across them. In addition to the natural concealment of the ocean and mountains, Lemurian Ocean Wizards, Biomancers and Ley Line Walkers use magic to shroud and hide the Valley from those who might discover it.

A common tactic is to lure underwater explorers and outsiders who are getting too close to one of the Valley Gardens away from them. This can be done by Lemurians or Merans, via magic or illusion, or schools of fish, blooms of algae, strange lights or noises, the appearance of Lemurian vehicles, and even direct contact in which the outsiders are met by one or more Lemurians and taken to the surface or an underwater outpost, or even a floating city, that is *away from* the Garden Valley. If the interloper is a surface dweller, the natural inclination is to head for the surface under the guise that the landlubber feels more comfortable and safe there.

A lure can include having the intruders chase a mermaid, a group of Lemurians or Merans riding sea monsters, a Lemurian vessel, strange noises, magic phenomena, a school of exotic animals and so on. If a lure fails to draw the intruders away from a secret outpost or garden, one or more whales, sharks or sea serpents (an entire school of them if necessary) can be sent out to scare and chase the unsuspecting interlopers out of the area. If they don't depart, or put up too much of a fight, Lemurians and/or Merans will attack with the intention to disable the intruders' underwater capabilities and vessels to the point where they must flee, or be towed away to someplace safe and far away by the Lemurians. These tactics are, of course, reserved for innocent travelers, adventurers and explorers who happen to get dangerously close to stumbling across one of the Garden Valleys. *Enemies*, especially the undead minions and evil henchmen of the Lord of the Deep, are destroyed when a lure fails to work. However, if the Lemurians can remain hidden or if the outsider can be lured or chased away, even an enemy will be spared destruction.

Hidden within. There are thousands of miles of tunnels within the mountains of the Garden Valleys that lead to chambers, living areas, storage bays and animal habitats hidden inside and under the mountains. *Some tunnels* also lead to the valley farms of aquatic plants and crops. In the event of a mass attack by an enemy, people can be evacuated through the secret labyrinth under the sea floor and through the mountains. *Tunnel Hubs* are intersections and connection points where several interconnecting tunnels intersect. Depending on the tunnel, it may lead to one of the valley farms, animal training areas, storage or to the ocean deep. In mountain chambers that are kept dry and contain breathable air, the tunnels lead to an airlock-like structure controlled by an aquatic Symbiote that opens and closes huge rolling stone doors or organic membranes that allow people to pass from water to airlock to the dry chamber. Such chambers range from living quarters, storage facilities, labs and work areas, to massive air-filled chambers that serve as training areas, stadiums, animal habitats and even farms and parkland with vegetation you would expect to find on dry land, not under the sea.

Finding Lemuria

Many an adventurer has asked, "If Lemuria is real, how does one get there?"

The easy answer is, by accident or when someone from a Lemurian city wants to be discovered and makes contact.

There are some things to keep in mind when dealing with the question of finding Lemuria.

Lemuria is unlike any other nation or civilization on Earth. Though other people of the world don't realize it, Lemuria does not occupy any one continent or location anywhere on the planet. Lemuria is divided into several, massive floating cities that are constantly on the move. In that sense, Lemuria is *nowhere* and *everywhere*. This fits with their philosophy that all of Mother Earth is their home and the home of all sentient beings who embrace the Earth Mother. All of the floating cities are pieces of "Lemuria" and represent the Lemurians' culture and civilization. The city of Mu is where the King of Lemuria resides, but he and his family visit and stay at the other floating cities from time to time for days, weeks and sometimes, months at a time.

As a civilization composed of many floating cities that are always on the move and call no land (above the waves) home, it is nearly impossible to find, track or follow even one city for long, let alone locate and keep tabs on several of them. Even the Lemurian cities themselves are often separated by hundreds of miles of sea, land and air. Large enemy fleets and armies have an even harder time coming up on a Lemurian city, because they are detected by the floating cities while they are still many miles away. If a Lemurian floating city sees trouble coming, it can usually escape the incoming combat force by going deep underwater, high into the air, over land, up into the mountains, back down into the water, can use magic to cloak or defend themselves and ley lines and nexus points to teleport the entire city to a new, unknown location with less than a minute of preparation.

If, by some miracle, a Lemurian floating city is encountered by outsiders, peaceful visitors of any race and species are welcomed. Attackers are met in kind, and usually held at bay, chased off or destroyed. In the event that a massive invasion force is successful in attacking a Lemurian city, destroying it will take a lot of firepower. And if a floating city is destroyed, it is a tragedy limited to that one city. The rest of Lemuria remains hidden, safe and on the move.

So far, only the **Lord of the Deep** has been successful in destroying a few Lemurian floating cities. However, if they could keep eyes on one long enough and muster the proper force of Metztla and minion warriors, **the Splugorth of Atlantis** have the power and resources to destroy Lemurian floating cities as well. So far, however, the Splugorth and their minions have been satisfied with raiding, capturing and enslaving Lemurians and their exotic array of riding animals, rather than launch an all-out attack to destroy them or conquer and enslave the entire civilization.

To keep safe, Lemurians do not tell even their most trusted friends and allies exactly how many floating cities and outposts exist, nor the names of the cities. Those with some knowledge of Lemurians believe there to be at least one dozen and as many as two dozen cities as well as a handful of small outposts. There are rumors about the *Garden Valley,* but no one seems certain if it really exists, and no one knows that there are actually many Garden Valleys. As for the names of specific cities, the only one known to most outsiders is the **City of Mu**, however, even they do not realize Mu is the capital city of Lemuria. It is interesting to note that when outsiders are welcomed to a Lemurian floating city, they are told, "Welcome to Lemuria," regardless of the specific city's name. The true name of the city is seldom revealed, and most outsiders don't think to ask. They hear "Lemuria" and think that is where they are. Remember, most surface dwellers (99.9%) have no idea Lemuria even exists, and certainly don't know Lemurian cities are mobile, all-terrain environments capable of any type of travel.

Small raiding parties, groups of adventurers, pirates and lone ships have had the best luck at stumbling across a Lemurian floating city. However, finding that same city again – sometimes even after only a few hours – is near impossible unless the Lemurians *want* to be found. Seafarers and adventurers who make it publicly known through as many channels as possible that they desire to meet with Lemurians out at sea *may* get lucky and encounter a floating city, but only because the curious Lemurians sought them out and allowed their city to be seen. Even under such circumstances, it is likely that a Lemurian scouting party would make contact with the outsider, not the entire city. It would be only after a careful assessment of the people seeking them out that the Lemurian Scout *might* consider taking the outsiders to a city underwater. If this is the case, the outsiders will be blindfolded, and after some travel or via magic, simply appear at a Lemurian city resting someplace below the waves. When Lemurians allow an outsider to visit one of their cities, it is almost always done underwater with the city settled on an undersea mountain or the ocean floor to give visitors the idea that the city is a fixed location just like any surface city. They don't want people to know their cities are mobile and especially not that they can fly in the air. Even the Splugorth don't realize Lemurian cities can float and fly, but suspect they use magic to teleport to different locations on the floor of the ocean or may straddle two different dimensions to make themselves undetectable. As a rule, the vast majority of announcements by outsiders requesting to meet with Lemurians are simply *ignored.*

Surface dwellers are much more likely to meet a Lemurian or small group of Lemurian adventurers in their own lands. Few realize Lemurians are amphibious and can function as well as any human on dry land. As a result, they don't expect to meet a Lemurian in the Chi-Town 'Burbs, fighting vampires in the plains of Mexico or in the mountains of Tibet. The fact that Lemurians look reasonably human, especially when they want to pass for "Joe Adventurer," means most people don't realize they have even met one. As Lemurians begin to make their existence known, it is they who are going out into the surface world in Biomancy armor or riding the backs of exotic animals, and saying, "Hello, I'm a Lemurian, may I help you?" Even then, Lemurians seldom talk about their home or their history. They may cheerfully discuss life under the waves and how beautiful it is, but they do not talk about their cities moving from one place to another, nor that the entire city can pick up and float or fly anywhere. They leave the impression that their cities are located on the floor of the ocean and that Lemurians are an aquatic people. They don't often lie outright, but avoid providing details that could compromise Lemurian security, and dodge direct questions of that nature. This can be very easy because they simply let people make erroneous assumptions about cities and life under the sea without correcting them. If these Lemurian explorers see any value in taking a new surface friend to a floating city, they may arrange it, but as noted previously, all "visitors," even trusted ones, are blindfolded and taken to the city at an underwater location they cannot easily identify.

Lemurians are famous for coming to the rescue of people out at sea. This includes saving sinking ships, shipwrecked castaways and vessels under attack from monsters or villains like pirates, the Naut'Yll and the Minions of Splugorth. However, if they can avoid bringing seafarers and refugees to their city, they will. Even though the Lemurians are a bit paranoid (with good reason) and tend to have a bit of an isolationist leaning, they are very caring and helpful by nature and feel it is their duty as protectors of the Earth to help people in trouble, especially victims of the Lord of the Deep and those left to the mercy of the sea.

Lemurians can be encountered pretty much anywhere, but are most often found in the Pacific Ocean, Indian Ocean, South Atlantic and Mediterranean Sea as well as places and with people fighting the undead, demons, the Lord of the Deep, Naut'Yll and other dark forces. Lemurians frequent the northern Atlantic Ocean the least due to the strong presence of the Splugorth and their minions.

Easter Island

Lemurian Outpost: Rapa Nui

Location: 27°09'S, 109°27'W.
Size: 63.9 sq. miles (163.6 km^2) pre-Rifts, 75 sq. miles (192 km^2) on Rifts Earth.
Estimated Population: 52,000
Racial Breakdown:
54% Lemurians.
43% Tangata Manu (Lemurian Birdmen).
3% Other.

One of Lemuria's few fixed outposts is the island of Rapa Nui, more famously known as *Easter Island.* Easter Island was a Lemurian city-state 15,000 years ago when Atlantis vanished, taking Earth magic with it. The island was one of the places where some Lemurians remained behind to build a new life apart from magic. They did well for a while, but without magic, the island kingdom was eventually abandoned, and Lemurians were assimilated into the people of South America and except for myths and legends, forgotten.

Easter Island has always been one of those places of mystery. No one knows its true history, but many cultures have made an impact on the area. The standing stones and giant stone heads have intrigued explorers for centuries, without any of them ever understanding what they really represent or who built them – the Lemurians.

Easter Island is located on one of the most powerful ley line nexus points on the planet. Long ago, the ancient Lemurians sensed this was a special place and set out to make it one of three sanctuaries to guard against the supernatural. That included erecting several circles of standing stones similar to Stonehenge and 999 magical stone guardians called **Moai**. The magic used to create the circles of stone and the Moai involved magic known only to an elite sub-cult of Stone Masters. The magic used by the ancient Lemurians was so secret and so powerful that only a handful of elite mages in the royal family knew its secrets. It made the island itself completely free from the influence of the supernatural, and it would be only the first of many. Only they knew how to make the Moai and work such magic. When that news leaked out to dark forces, they conspired to destroy the Stone Masters with that special knowledge, and succeeded. No more Moai or Sanctuary Islands could be made.

The Moai's sole purpose was to wait for supernatural invaders and upon the proper orders, come to life to battle them. The methods to create these stone guardians were lost a few hundred years before the Lemurians left Earth, and no one knows how to make new Moai. However, Lemurian Stone Masters know how to activate and command the behemoths to battle supernatural evil. For now, the Moai remain a Lemurian secret weapon, with only one or two being activated from time to time.

Of the 999 Moai originally placed on the island, 887 Moai Stone Guardians have survived the ages. And unknown to any but the Lemurians, an additional 317 Moai are buried in the earth on the ocean floor around the island.

Today, a small contingent of Lemurian Stone Masters, Biomancers, Ocean Wizards, researchers and their families live on Easter Island and in the small underwater village of **Mataveri**, which was formed partially by adding onto the old lava tunnels be-

neath the island. They have spent a great deal of effort restocking and rebuilding Easter Island's ecosystem after the cataclysm. Now the island is a lush jungle paradise sculpted by the Biomancers, transforming the new plant life into living homes woven from trees and plants. Meanwhile, many of the Stone Masters and researchers try to rediscover the magical processes by which the fabled Moai Stone Guardians were made. Besides the village of Mataveri, the Lemurians have built three lookouts on the peaks of the three highest points of the island: *Terevaka, Tuutapy* and *Puhi*. Each lookout allows Lemurian Birdmen a good overview of the island and the surrounding oceans. Their avian Bio-Armor enables the Birdmen to travel quickly between lookouts or anywhere else on the island and at rocket speeds along ley lines.

The island's two ley line triangles not only provide ample energy to supercharge all the Moai, but also provide plenty of ambient Earth Energy (P.P.E.) for all kinds of mystic studies, experimentation and research. Thus, it is home to many mages. Intense volcanic activity during the Great Cataclysm has raised and enlarged the island, and covered the entire island and everything within a two hundred mile (320 km) radius with a coating of ash 100-200 feet (30.5-61 m) deep. However, the magical nature of the Moai caused them to rise to the surface of the ash, where they continue peering out at the waters around them. Magic also erected any Moai that had fallen, and any damage was restored by magic to make the giant stone sentinels look like new. In fact, it was this magic restoration that made accurate dating of the Moai in the past impossible and erroneous.

The volcanoes on the island raged for decades after the Coming of the Rifts, but have settled down over the last 200 years. Still, the two eastern volcanoes, *Rana Roratka* and *Puakatike* continue to emit streams of smoke and rumble whenever supernatural forces gather at the edges of the supernatural free zone. Both volcanoes are under the complete control of the Lemurian mages, as are the ley line triangles that are located at Easter Island. The ley lines also link the island to the mountains of Chile and Peru, South America.

Moai

Stone Guardians of Easter Island

The Moai appear as massive stone figures usually carved out of a single block of volcanic stone. They are sometimes mistaken to be only a massive stone head, especially from a distance, but they have bodies. There are a few reasons for this: 1. The disproportionate size of the massive head dwarfs the small, stout body. 2. The detail on the body is minimal. 3. The Moai often sink their bodies into the ground, leaving only the head showing from the shoulders up.

The average Moai (64%) is roughly 13 feet (4 m) tall and weighs 14 tons. Large Moai (34%) are 33 feet (10 m) tall, and the largest, of which there is only one on the island and another 21 buried on the ocean floor around the island, is 72 feet (21.9 m) and 150 tons. Moai are giant, stone guardians created to protect Lemurians and the Earth from supernatural monsters and the undead. When given the proper command, they come to life to battle supernatural enemies as automatons that follow the verbal or telepathic commands of a Lemurian commander or can be piloted like a giant robot. Before the Great Cataclysm, the Moai used special pedestals called *ahu* which siphoned the energy of the island's ley lines to power and recharge the stone sentinels as needed. When the Atlantean disaster caused magic to fade from the Earth, the Moai lacked sufficient power to function and became inert, giant statues. With the super-charging of Earth's ley lines since the Great Cataclysm, the Moai are recharged simply by being on Easter Island, and can recharge at a ley line or nexus anywhere in the world.

Now, fully charged, the Moai are a power to be reckoned with. Among their many abilities, the Lemurian Stone Guardians are robot-like automatons that obey the commands of Stone Masters. Even when simply standing guard, the Moai watch for the presence of the supernatural. Upon the detection of the supernatural the Moai start to "sing" a deep, bellowing moan, which reverberates and can be heard clearly throughout the entire island. When asked where the danger lies, the Moai can indicate what the danger is (i.e. the type of supernatural menace), approximately where it is located (within a 1,000 mile/1,600 km radius of the island), and the direction it is heading. When supernatural evil gathers in great numbers, like the Vampire Kingdoms and the Splugorth's Atlantis, the Moai can sense it up to 5,000 miles (8,000 km) away. If the evil being(s) should somehow manage to reach Easter Island, the Moai would rise up and engage it/them in combat. However, the ancient and forgotten Stone Magic of Rapa Nui is so powerful that no evil supernatural force, not even an Alien Intelligence like the *Splugorth* or dark god like the *Lord of the Deep,* has been able to come within 10 miles (16 km) of the edge of the island.

The Moai Stone Guardians can also be activated by Lemurian Stone Masters and members of the royal family and commanded like obedient robots. When activated, the giant head rises up from the earth and onto its feet. The humanoid body is about the same height as the head, and has two arms and hands, two legs and feet, and its trademark massive, narrow head that tapers at the top. The hands have three fingers and an opposable thumb, the feet, four toes. The body is small and never more than the same height of the massive head that rests on its shoulders. The end result is a tall stone head on a disproportionate, stubby body. Since magic is involved, the small body never seems to have any problem with carrying the oversized head. Though the body can engage in physical combat, it is the head that wields all the real power. The moment the Moai is activated, the eyes glow with bluish-white energy and streams of energy seem to rise from the head like steam. The glow from the eyes gets brighter and the plumes of streaming energy larger when the Moai is on a ley line and during peek astronomical periods when the energy levels of magic are higher.

Moai Guardian Statues

Also Known As: Moai, Guardian Statues, Lemurian Stone Guardians and Stone Guardians of Easter Island.

Class: Magical Stone Automaton.

Crew: Optional. A Stone Guardian can be given commands and sent on its way, led via verbal or telepathic commands, or piloted by someone inside it.

The commander or pilot can be a Stone Master of 6th level or greater experience and good alignment, or a member of the Lemurian royal family (regardless of level) or a trained Lemurian Moai pilot. In all cases, the pilot must be Lemurian, must be of Principled or Scrupulous alignment (nothing else is acceptable) and the person must know the secret activation and command word sequence. The activation and command sequence is known only to a small number of people, including the most trusted Stone Masters, key members of the royal family, and a few officers among the Birdmen, Sea Sentinels and Royal Guard.

As automata, one to seven Stone Guardians can be given a command and sent on their mission. However, without direct Lemurian input, the Moai function at a lower level with fewer attacks and lack human decision making capabilities and reasoning. Thus, it is best if the Moai is piloted or accompanied by a Lemurian who issues verbal or telepathic commands. In the alternative, 1-7 Stone Guardians can be led by a single Lemurian Stone Master (or other, as noted above) who functions as a squad leader, directing the megalithic stone juggernauts. **Note:** In all cases, the commander of one or more Moai must be a Lemurian and Principled or Scrupulous alignment. The Moai will not follow or obey anyone who does not have 100% Lemurian genes and a good alignment.

Pilot and Passengers: Lemurians and humanoids can climb inside through the mouth or back of the head (magically opens with the right command) to gain access to the passenger chamber in the head, but all passengers must be of good or at least selfish alignment. Characters of an evil alignment cannot even enter a Moai. The number of passengers varies with the size of the Moai:

Small Moai (13 feet/4 m; most numerous type): Pilot only (or one passenger who has no influence over the Moai can be carried passively inside).

Large Moai (33 feet/10 m; second most common): Pilot and two passengers.

Giant Moai (72 feet/22 m; rare): Pilot and five passengers.

Sealed Environmental Chamber for Pilot and Passengers: Pilot and passengers sit inside the head of the Moai. To enter and exit the head of the Moai, a magic phrase must be spoken (or sent via Telepathy) which enables the pilot and passenger to enter through the mouth or an opening that magically forms in the back of the head. Once everyone is inside or the pilot issues the command to seal the chamber, the openings turn into solid M.D.C. stone (takes 245 M.D.C. to blast into the pilot and passenger chamber though an open mouth or back of the head). Inside the chamber, there are seats made of vines, nothing else. There is no control panel as the Stone Guardian responds to the voice or telepathic commands of the pilot. However, all passengers are able to see through the Moai's eyes as if they had a view screen in front of them.

M.D.C. by Location:

Small Moai (13 feet/4 m):
- **Head – 400
- Arms (2) – 110 each
- Hands (2) – 50 each
- Legs (2) – 150 each
- *Main Body – 330

Large Moai (33 feet/10 m):
- **Head – 1,100
- Arms (2) – 220 each
- Hands (2) – 95 each
- Legs (2) – 300 each
- *Main Body – 900

Giant Moai (72 feet/22 m):
- **Head – 2,000
- Arms (2) – 330 each
- Hands (2) – 140 each
- Legs (2) – 560 each
- *Main Body – 1,700

* Depleting the M.D.C. of the main body to zero or less causes the Moai to shut down and fall flat on its face. Anyone inside is expelled and the Stone Guardian is reduced to an inanimate statue. If the head retains even one M.D.C. point, the Moai can be transported to a ley line, nexus or back to Easter Island, where it regenerates damage to the main body at a rate of 1D6x10 M.D.C. per hour and is immediately reactivated and available for combat with the restoration of the first 10 M.D.C. Of course, it is not recommended to send the unit back into action until at least half the M.D.C. has been restored. **Note:** Any lost appendages and damage to the other parts of the body can be restored to the Moai, with lost limbs seeming to grow out of thin air, but only after all the damage to the main body is restored does any damage to the head and then appendages get restored. Going into combat before all M.D.C. is restored means the Stone Guardian may be vulnerable to attacks, because even if fighting on a ley line, the Moai must be in "rest mode," not active, in order to regenerate lost M.D.C.

** Destroying the head causes the Moai to shatter into 1D6+1 pieces. Unless it was shattered on Easter Island or while on a ley line or nexus point, it is permanently destroyed; nothing but the remains of a statue. However, when destroyed on a ley line or nexus, and if the shattered remains are left on the line, the Moai begins to reform and regenerate after 48 hours. First, the shattered pieces reunite with the body and head, one at a time (one piece per hour). When the Moai is back together, it starts to regenerate 1D6x10 M.D.C. per hour to the main body and is immediately reactivated and available for combat with the restoration of the first 10 M.D.C. Any lost appendages regrow. If a Moai is destroyed away from a ley line, it can be restored only if the pieces of the head and as much of the body as possible are returned to Easter Island and the stone undergoes a special restorative ritual by Stone Masters. **Note:** Since the secrets of making the Moai Stone Guardians are lost to antiquity, if any are completely destroyed, they are gone forever. It is estimated that 10-14 Moai were taken to cities around the world and may be buried among the ruins of certain pre-Rifts historical museums.

Speed:

Running: 40 mph (64 km), double along a ley line; same speeds running along the bottom of the ocean.

Fly in the Air: 60 mph (96 km) in the air, double along a ley line. Maximum Altitude: 5 miles (8 km). The Moai can also hover in air and water.

Rocket Through Water: 50 mph (80 km/43 knots) underwater, double along a ley line. Maximum Depth: 6 miles (9.6 km). This applies both to the Moai and those who may be inside.

Statistical Data:

These unusual, statue-like golems have large heads and small bodies. Some Moai also have a round "hat" or "topknot." All Moai are infused with magic energy, but most of that is hidden deep within the Moai with the exception of the eyes.

Size (Varies): There are three sizes of Lemurian Stone Guardians:

Small (64%) Moai are 13 feet (4 m) tall, 7.5 feet (2.3 m) wide at the shoulders and 6.6 feet (2 m) in length from nose to the back of the head at the neck. Weighs 14 tons and can hold only the pilot, no passengers.

Large (34%) are 33 feet (10 m) tall, 16 feet (4.9 m) wide at the shoulders, 14 feet (4.3 m) in length from the nose to the back of the head at the base of the neck. Weighs 82 tons and can hold one pilot and two passengers.

Giant (2%, only 22 Moai) are 72 feet (21.9 m) tall, 34 feet (10.3 m) wide at the shoulders, and 26 feet (7.9 m) in length at the base of the head. Weighs 150 tons and can hold one pilot and five passengers.

Physical Strength: Small: Supernatural P.S. of 27. Large: Supernatural P.S. of 37. Giant: Supernatural P.S. of 47.

Cargo: None, Moai are combat machines and never used for labor except in the most extreme of emergencies.

Power Supply: Magic. A small Moai needs to recharge its magic batteries once a month at a ley line by standing motionless in "rest mode" for 8 hours.

A large Moai needs to recharge once every two weeks at a ley line by standing motionless in "rest mode" for 16 hours.

A giant Moai needs to recharge at least once every week at a ley line by standing motionless in "rest mode" for 24 hours.

Note: Reduce recharging time by half when at a ley line nexus or on a ley line triangle.

Penalties for Low Energy: In all cases, when unable to power up as needed, the Moai is sluggish and functions at half its usual levels – half speed, half damage, half P.S., half the number of attacks, half range weapons and senses, etc. The Moai can function at this low energy capacity for 1D4+1 days before it freezes up like a statue. If it freezes from lack of fuel/energy, the Moai remains an inanimate statue until it can be recharged. Most pilots power up as often as they can long before the *Moai* needs recharging.

Powers & Weapons of a Moai:

Damage Note: Remember, the Moai is designed to protect against and fight *supernatural evil.* Thus, in all cases, the Moai levels the greatest amount of damage against the supernatural forces of evil, not mortal men.

ALL ATTACKS inflict double damage against Necromancers, animated dead, vampires and all forms of the undead.

1. Breath Attack: The Moai can unleash a stream of steam from its mouth that does 4D6 M.D. against supernatural evil or 4D6 S.D.C. against mortal foes. Range: 100 feet (30.5 m).

2. Eye Beams: The Moai can fire energy blasts from the eyes.

Range: 3,000 feet (914 m).

S.D.C. Damage: 1D6 S.D.C. to 5D6 S.D.C./Hit Points; can be increased in increments of 1D6 up to 5D6 S.D.C. against mortal opponents and S.D.C. targets.

Mega-Damage (varies with size of the Moai): Mega-Damage is inflicted to supernatural evil and other M.D.C. opponents.

Small Moai (13 feet/4 m; most common): 4D6 M.D. against supernatural evil, 1D6x10 M.D. against greater supernatural evil and deities. Does 3D6 M.D. against all other M.D.C. opponents.

Large Moai (33 feet/10 m): 6D6 M.D. against supernatural evil, 2D6x10 M.D. against greater supernatural evil and deities. Does 4D6 M.D. against all other M.D.C. opponents.

Giant Moai (72 feet/21.9 m; rare): 1D6x10 M.D. against supernatural evil, 3D6x10 M.D. against greater supernatural evil and deities. Does 6D6 M.D. against all other M.D.C. opponents.

Rate of Fire: Four if an automaton or as per the number of attacks of the pilot. Each eye blast counts as one attack.

Payload: In all cases, the payload is effectively unlimited.

3. Hand to Hand Combat: As an unmanned robot and piloted by a Lemurian.

Hand to Hand Combat as Automaton: As an unmanned stone robot, the Moai have *four attacks per melee round* and inflict damage as per the weapons noted above or via hand to hand combat and Supernatural P.S.

Mega-Damage: Punches, kicks and head butts is per Supernatural Strength and does double damage to greater supernatural beings.

Combat Bonuses Against Supernatural Evil: +5 on Perception Rolls, +3 on initiative, +6 to strike, +4 to parry and +2 to dodge, +4 to pull punch, +2 to roll with impact, impervious to Horror Factor and is impervious to all forms of possession (the Moai itself cannot be possessed and controlled by outside forces, Entities or other supernatural beings, magic or psionics, but the pilot is a different story). **Note:** Reduce bonuses by half when fighting mortal opponents; round down.

Hand to Hand Combat by Moai Pilot: When the Lemurian Stone Guardian is piloted, the Moai moves as if it were an extension of the pilot's own body and responds with the speed of thought. All the pilot has to do is think it and the Moai fires its eye beams, throws a punch, dodges, jumps, flies, etc.

The number of attacks, bonuses and types of moves are the same as the pilot's plus the following bonuses: +2 attacks per melee round, +2 on Perception Rolls (double against supernatural evil), +2 on initiative, +2 to strike and parry, +3 to pull punch, +2 to roll with impact, +4 to save vs Horror Factor and +3 to save vs all forms of possession and mind control while inside and piloting the Moai.

4. **Ley Line Healing:** As described under the single asterisk (*) and double asterisk (**) in the **M.D.C. by Location** section above. Requires time to stand motionless and access to a ley line, nexus point energy, or being within a triangle of ley lines like the Bermuda Triangle or at Easter Island.
5. **Resistance to Magic:** The enchanted Stone Guardians are resistant to some magic attacks. Impervious to possession and magic fire, heat and lava attacks. Magic cold does half damage, but electricity/lightning and other magic energy attacks inflict full damage, as do physical attacks, missiles and high-tech weapons.
6. **Spell Casting Through the Moai via Voice of the Moai:** The mouth and voice/singing ability of the Moai enables the pilot and/or passengers who are practitioners of magic to cast spells through the Moai. When they speak, the Moai speaks.

   Most spoken spells and Whale Songs can be cast using the Moai as a conduit. This doubles the range of a spell and increases the damage of the spell (as cast by that individual) by 50%. Only one mage/person can speak/cast spells through the Moai at a time, so if more than one mage wants to cast spells through the Stone Guardian, they must take turns. **Note:** The following magic can NOT be used or cast by the Moai even if the passenger knows the spells: Temporal Magic, rituals, Animate and Control Dead, Create Zombie, Metamorphosis spells, disguise and concealment magic and illusions, nor Necromancy, Demon Magic, Soulmancy or any dark/evil magic. The Moai cannot make Techno-Wizard devices, magic items, wards, circles or other magical constructs, nor perform any task requiring a delicate touch or small fingers and hands.
7. **Senses:**

   Auditory Senses: Equal to that of a human.

   Olfactory Senses: About twice as keen as a human.

   Optics: Moai have full color, supernatural vision and can see a bird on the horizon at 6 miles (9.6 km), can see in absolute darkness (one mile/1.6 km), and see the invisible (including Astral Travelers and the fragmented essence of Alien Intelligences).

   Touch: Equal to that of a human; Supernatural P.S. as noted above.

   Voice of the Moai: Though a Moai seems almost alive, it is, in effect, a giant robot made of stone and powered with magic. One passenger can speak through the Moai. This is usually the pilot and is done to communicate and issue warnings. The Moai's voice is a deep baritone. As noted above, speaking through the Moai enables the pilot or passengers to cast spells using the Moai as a conduit that amplifies the power of the spell.
8. **Sense Ley Line Location (special):** Range is 30 miles (48 km). A Moai needs to recharge its P.P.E. batteries on a regular basis, so locating ley lines is a necessity.
9. **Sense the Supernatural (special):** The Moai can instantly sense the presence of supernatural evil. Upon their detection, the Moai starts to "sing" a deep, resonating moan, alerting their masters to the presence of the supernatural. Upon receiving an order from their master the Moai can then seek out and destroy the supernatural invader. Range: 100 miles (160 km), their "singing" can be heard throughout the island, but only about a mile (1.6 km) out to sea.

Lemurian Agriculture & Food

As masters of the powers of life, the Lemurians are some of the best farmers and planters on the planet. They cultivate whole fields of kelp, kale, sargassum, other seaweed and certain coral, letting them grow in the wild and periodically stopping in to check on their crops. And while Lemurian cities travel continually, they also maintain a continuous link to outposts, settlements and farms. Sites are chosen either for their rich nutrient currents or for being safe and out of sight. Fresh and dried seaweed, kelp, algae, kale and other ocean crops make up a huge percentage of the Lemurians' diet, especially because the vegetarian and vegan outlooks are so prevalent.

Certain products only grow above the waves, however. The Lemurians have developed gardens and greenhouses within their undersea cities, but space comes at a premium in such places and true farmland is still a necessity. To get around this, they establish small garden-islands to grow things like coconuts, bananas, yams, papayas, macadamia nuts, palm trees, pomelos, grapefruits, oranges, limes, lemons, soursops, kiwi, guava, dragonfruit, starfruit and mangoes. The first step is to locate an isolated island or raise one using magical means. Then, Biomancers and agricultural specialists come in and terraform the island, creating jungles and mangroves on barren volcanic outcroppings and coral reefs. From there, the necessary animals and insects are introduced, and finally, the desired crops are planted in organic terraces and patches, very different from the regimented rows found in the farms of surface dwellers. Most garden-islands will focus on three or four primary crops, possibly with small fields or stands of others.

Unlike most surface farmers, Lemurian agriculturalists do not live alongside their fields. Lemurian cities are always moving, and shifts of farmers, tenders and Biomancers go out on long patrols to bring in the harvest and check up on their efforts. Scouts are usually sent ashore first to make sure the coast is clear. Matters are

complicated greatly if surface dwellers are found, and the agriculture team must decide if they should abandon the island, gather their crops by night or under the cover of magic, or call in armed reinforcements to show the intruders who the real property owners are. Surface dwellers who do wash up on the beach will find an island to be a paradise covered in plentiful edible plants. Across the vast emptiness of the Pacific, however, many Lemurian garden-islands go undiscovered for years, if not decades.

Underwater crops are also grown under the waves, often hidden in mountain valleys and ravines. Most are crops of aquatic plants, but there are also crops of surface plants grown inside caves and enclosures using Biomancy to create an environment with air. The mythical location known as the Lemurian Paradise Garden or simply, "The Garden," is the most expansive of these undersea gardens.

Lemurian Food Vats

The Lemurian diet is similar in many ways to the traditional diet of Japan and Korea. Heavy in seafood, they make use of whatever resources can be found and have several traditional dishes that are made out of seaweed and other base ingredients that have been processed through simple means; drying, smoking, mashing, fermenting, salting. Dried sheets of kale, plankton cakes, algae spread, krill paste and many other concoctions are good examples. Natural sources are sometimes used to make these local delicacies, but many animal products come from the mystical Lemurian food vats.

The vats are magical nutrient baths that boost the growing properties of living things. A bubbling nutrient bath is prepared by a Biomancer or agriculturalist and balanced with just the right types of minerals and nutrient compounds. Introduce a single plankton, krill, egg or shrimp to the baths, invoke the proper enchantments, and the magical growth process will initiate a burst of supernatural development. Using this method, batches of shrimp, caviar, smelt, roe, plankton, algae, krill and sardines can be produced without taxing the local environment. Larger fish are "grown" in smaller tanks that have individual cells and compartments where pieces of fish flesh begin to form. Entire fish are not produced this way, merely cuts and filets, similar to sashimi. Many of the animal products consumed by the Lemurian people come from the food vats, along with a substantial percentage of their seaweed and plant dishes.

Hunting

The Lemurians are a people who have a close connection to life and can sense the pain and distress of all living things. They are also keenly aware of the natural cycle of life, and that death is an integral part of the process. Lemurians never hunt for sport or amusement, and have the utmost respect for animals that give their lives so that they may eat. They make every attempt to use as much of the animal as possible, and give away excess food to the hungry or offer it to helpful animals.

When Lemurians do decide to hunt, they are careful in their selection of prey. Going for a prized alpha male or female can be dangerous, and is detrimental to the overall health of the species. Fish and other animals that are too sickly and weak to eat are also a bad idea, and will be picked off by some predator eventually, anyway. The ideal target is older or otherwise different from the rest of the school, mature enough to have bred and passed on its genes, but not young enough that it will have many more breeding seasons.

While many Lemurians abhor the idea of killing an animal for any reason, those who live and work outside the cities often do not have the luxury of choice. Lemurian explorers, Scouts, Serpent Hunters, Sea Sentinels and Oceanic Guardsmen may all have to resort to fishing or hunting when out in the field. Like any Lemurian, they will be considerate and respectful in the act, and will seek to use as much of their kill as possible, and take care not to cause unnecessary pain and suffering of the animal. With their psychic Empathy toward animals, Lemurians can even soothe and calm the animal, ensuring its last few moments are not full of fear and confusion. To use their powers to call animals to them just to be killed is a violation, however. Prey must be hunted honorably, with no use of psychic manipulation and control.

Biomancer Gardens

The Lemurians tend to vast acreage of gardens they use to produce food, medicine, Symbiotes and a host of other products. Some are as small as a few square miles, while others are thousands of miles in size! Most are found on the ocean floor, some in shallower waters to take advantage of the sunlight, while others reside near ley lines and nexus points to siphon magic energy, or are hidden in underwater mountain valleys, and a few are even close to volcanic vents to take in the abundant thermal heat and mineral-rich waters. Below are a list of some of the more interesting gardens and products grown at them. Most aquatic races with the *Sea Holistic Medicine* skill will have a passing familiarity with most of these herbs. Game Masters should feel free to expand on these ideas and create their own Lemurian gardens and herbs. **Cost Note:** The price listed is what the item sells for in Lemuria. In the surface world and elsewhere, the same item is likely to be rare and sell for 5-20 times the listed price.

Carnivorous Blue Fruit Trees

The Carnivorous Blue Fruit Tree, more commonly known simply as **Blue Death**, was an early Lemurian Biomancy creation that was later deemed a mistake and abandoned. They are seldom created by Lemurians anymore, but a number of the organisms have gotten out into the ocean where they have multiplied and now exist in the wild. They are also created and grown by evil and rogue Biomancers, including some members of the Mauian Order.

This uncommon underwater plant and coral hybrid resembles a long field or cluster of coral protruding like giant tendrils or large tubes of grass from the coral bed. Each long, blue stem resembles a tentacle or length of thick plastic tubing. At the base of several such tentacles is a cluster of blue, round fruits about the size of a grapefruit. Each fruit has a faint glow of energy from within it. Magic energy that can be sensed by practioners of magic, creatures of magic, and the supernatural.

Blue Death was originally created with a number of different applications in mind. One was to harness the P.P.E. generated at death. That's the energy glowing within the fruit. It was thought the "fruit" could later be gathered and the energy within could be drawn upon by practitioners of magic to power Biomancy machines and fuel magic rituals and spell casting.

Two, the carnivorous plant could consume the remains of the dead, as well as organic waste, making it a natural way to dispose of organic matter, including rotten food, animal remains and the remains of the dead. Though not as effective when feeding on Lemurian table scraps or the deceased, the plant could survive on dead organic material. However, Blue Death prefers feeding on the living, be it fish, mammals, humanoids, demons or sea monsters.

Three, demon and monster slaying trap. The Blue Death's instinct to feed on the living, particularly beings that possess high levels of P.P.E., led to the ill-conceived idea of using the coral plant to lure demons and sea monsters into its tentacles and destroy them like a giant *Venus Flytrap*. The problem is, there is no way to get the Blue Death to discriminate between monsters and people. In short, it ensnares, kills and eats whoever falls into its clutches. Even Biomancers using their psionic and magical Empathy with plants and living creatures cannot stop the ever hungry creature from attacking innocent people and wildlife.

To feed, the Blue Death first ensnares its prey with its long tendrils. Then it strangles them or drags them into its giant maw concealed at the base of the plant. The P.P.E. released at the moment of death is channeled into the organism and stored in the blue fruit bulbs of the plant. The fruit from the Blue Death can be picked and eaten for nutrition or to access the 3D6+13 P.P.E. contained inside each fruit. The trick is getting to the fruit without being ensnared, slain and eaten. A difficult task since they lay in clusters at the base of the plant/coral and one must swim through the tendrils to get to them. Touch one of the tendrils, let alone one of the fruits, and the tendrils lash out to entangle and kill.

Creatures of magic, such as dragons and many sea serpents, as well as supernatural beings and mortals sensitive to magic energy, can sense the P.P.E. energy in the fruit. There is also a sort of magical aura that attracts mages and creatures of magic. In this regard, the carnivorous plant uses its fruit as *bait* to attract unsuspecting victims. In addition, the fruit has a powerful, sweet and alluring scent detectable to most aquatic animals and supernatural beings from miles away. In this way, a steady stream of small fish and aquatic animals are lured to their doom, their energy captured and stored in the blue P.P.E. bulbs. Though sea serpents, dragons and demons, make much more formidable prey, they too can be drawn to their doom, entangled by a dozen or more M.D.C. tentacles, drained of their life essence and/or bitten until they are slain and eventually consumed. When its prey draws near, the plant launches several tendrils to ensnare it and pull the unfortunate victim into a hidden maw concealed in the coral bed.

The dangerous and uncontrollable nature of the Carnivorous Blue Death plant has led to their use being discontinued by the Lemurians, but they still exist in the wild and are used in remote hideouts by the Mauian Order to prey upon trespassers and enemies. Though one might imagine a bed of bones and skulls around the carnivorous plant, it consumes all remains and no trace is left of its victims or anything fed to it.

Also Known As: Hungry Blue Fruit Trees (Poloi Uli Hua'ai Kumula'au) and Carnivorous Coral.

Alignment: Considered evil.

Attributes: Most attributes are irrelevant as it functions on instinct and reflexes, responding to motion and stimuli (touch, body heat, etc.), but it does have the equivalent of Supernatural P.S. 1D4+20 and a P.P. of 1D4+16.

M.D.C. by Location:

Tentacles (4D6+13) – 2D6+16 M.D.C. each

Main Body – 6D6x10

Size: The coral bed stretches over an area 100-200 square feet (9.3 to 18.6 square meters).

Tendrils look to be about 6 feet (1.8 m) long, but can stretch and reach 18 feet (5.5 m).

Weight: 2,000-3,000 lbs (900 to 1350 kg).

P.P.E.: 4D6x10 for the coral formation, but each fruit has 3D6+13 P.P.E. points. The more frequently the Blue Death eats, the more fruit it bears and the stronger the alluring scent and amount of P.P.E. present. A typical Blue Death Tree is likely to have 6D6+13 fruits. A very well-fed one may have twice as many.

Natural Abilities: Resistant to cold (half damage), unlimited depth tolerance, attractive and alluring scent of fruit six mile (9.6 km) radius, magic energy aura one mile (1.6 km), and tentacles negate magic by touch (see below for details).

The plant regenerates 2D6 M.D.C. per hour and regrows lost tentacles with full M.D.C. in 24 hours.

It senses and locates the presence of the living by motion, touch and heat. The Blue Death's heightened sense of touch enables it to sense the vibrations, noises and movement of its prey. When something comes within striking distance, 1D4+2 tentacles lunge out to entangle the prey. The tentacles constrict to hold tight and may strangle prey, but the tendrils ultimately pull the prey to its hidden, massive mouth. Actually, there are typically 1D4+1 mouths spread across the expanse of its body, each concealed under the sand, rocks or debris until they are needed to attack. More than 80% of the carnivorous tree's body is buried and concealed, so would-be attackers who think they have destroyed the creature usually succeed only in injuring it enough to escape destruction.

Attacks per Melee: Three by bite or entanglement, but 1D4+2 tendrils strike out to entangle in unison and each holds tight until severed or the victim manages to pull away; needs a combined Supernatural P.S. of 30 per every three tendrils. For every melee round the prey struggles and pulls, another 1D4+2 tentacle-like vines are sent out to hold and drag the prey to one of the mouths.

Damage: Special Attack: Magic Draining Tendrils. Practitioners and creatures of magic entangled by the monster's tendrils are prevented from casting spells or activating magical abilities, as the Blue Death absorbs the P.P.E. unleashed by spell casting. To successfully cast a spell, the victim must expend *double* the usual P.P.E. required, a fact most victims are painfully not aware of. Unable to cast a spell, most beings reliant on magic panic and squirm more, causing the Blue Death to tighten its grip or send out more tendrils to hold the thrashing prey. Furthermore, each tendril drains the victim of 1D4 P.P.E. per melee round until the victim breaks free or is slain.

M.D. Bite Attacks: Each bite does 4D6 M.D., but the magical nature of the Blue Death means that damage inflicted can not be Bio-Regenerated until the victim manages to break free of all the magic draining tentacles. Even if ensnared by only one tendril, Bio-Regeneration is not possible. Blue Death live to feed and will bite and gnaw on an entangled victim for as long as it takes to kill it. Unless the entangled prey is very large, such as a whale or sea serpent, only one mouth can bite at a time. Extremely large prey can be bitten by two or three of the maws.

Tendril Strikes: A tendril that lashes out as a whip to deliver a striking blow inflicts 2D6 M.D. Such an attack may be used to bat away others trying to pull or cut entangled prey loose. Or 1D4+2 tendrils may reach out to entangle them as well and pull them toward a different mouth.

Bonuses (in addition to possible attribute bonuses): +1 to strike and +4 to entangle with its tendrils, +2 for a tendril to dodge. The creature itself is impervious to Horror Factor, mind control and possession, and usually keeps fighting until all its tentacles are destroyed, the prey manages to escape (gets out of striking distance) or the Blue Death is destroyed (reduced to zero M.D.C.). **Note:** This aggressive plant/coral predator does not respond well to the Empathic nature of Lemurians and often ignores requests to release prey or spare a captive.

Blue Death Fruit: The fruit of the Blue Death tastes indescribably delicious and some people have reportedly paid as much as 8,000 credits for one. A single fruit provides the sustenance of a full meal as well as an energy boost. Those who consume Blue Death Fruit fatigue at half the usual rate and are +1 on initiative, +1 to strike, +2 to save vs vampire bite and undead mind control, and +1 to save vs disease and toxins for 1D6+1 hours after eating.

When plucked from the tree, the fruit keeps fresh for 1D6+11 *years!* The fruits have only 1D4 S.D.C. but seem impervious to bruising, incidental damage, cold and heat, thus they store and travel well even when jostled about and dropped.

Each fruit also serves as a reservoir of magic energy containing 3D6+13 P.P.E. Any practitioner of magic can draw upon the P.P.E. in the fruit as if it were a talisman or amulet. When the P.P.E. is used up, the fruit won't last long. If eaten after the P.P.E. is drained, the Blue Fruit has only a mild sweetness tinged with an unpleasant metallic taste. If left uneaten, it shrivels up and is inedible within 1D4 hours. Psi-Stalkers and other beings who can draw upon P.P.E. of the living, can also feed upon the P.P.E. in the Blue Death Fruit.

Cost: 1,000 credits each (much more outside of Lemuria).

Crystal Trees

Also known as Sunwater Trees

Another strange experiment conducted by the Lemurian Biomancers was an attempt to grow living crystals as an alternative source of mystic energy. Skilled Biomancers and Stone Masters developed a process that enabled them to create precious gems and stones from other natural materials. This allows them to make a supply of gems for the Stone Master to use without the need to mine natural sources of gemstones. The process, however, is extremely arduous, time consuming and requires several different sub-species of a special kind of deep sea bacteria and raw minerals from an active volcano vent to "grow" the crystals to a viable size. This attempt to use this technique to create a living crystal that could harness ambient magical energy came with limited success.

While the Lemurian Biomancers felt the experiment was a failure (i.e. it could not be used as a long-term P.P.E. battery) and abandoned it for other avenues, Stone Masters continued along the path and developed a pseudo-living crystal. Melding the deep sea bacteria into the growth of the crystal's structure, they were able to make the bacteria use the crystal as a latticework for its own growth. The bacteria were also developed to harness and use the crystal in the production of magical feats, not unlike some of the Stone Masters' own gem powers.

The final product of this development is a network of crystal branches, roots and other intertwined structures that resembles a large crystal tree, including vine and leaf-like structures on the end and the occasional "fruit" or crystal orb. These crystal trees radiate the full spectrum of color and produce a radiant rainbow effect when there is light to illuminate them. In the deep darkness of the ocean they are next to invisible, except for a faint magical glow seen only by spell casters and creatures of magic. At least until exposed to light, at which point a single tree can illuminate a 2,000 foot (610 m) radius as if it were daylight under the waves. Even a small light, such as a Globe of Daylight or a flashlight, is enough to create this effect. Include other Crystal Trees and one can light up the floor of the ocean for miles.

The living crystal continues to expand and "grow" on its own as a sort of crystal tree up to 20 feet (6.1 m) tall. But such growth is slow and Crystal Trees of that size are thousands of years old. As they grow, the bacteria generates and stores energy in the walls of the crystal, turning it into P.P.E. conduits and storage receptacles. Thus, each branch of the tree contains a small but usable supply of P.P.E., plus the Crystal Trees possess a handful of spells based on light and stone which the trees use for self-defense. These same spells can be tapped by any practitioner of magic who understands the powers and function of a Crystal Tree. As a result, the branches of the Crystal Tree can be used as magical wands and staves with the same light and magic abilities as the tree, and are particularly effective in fighting the undead and other supernatural creatures vulnerable to sunlight.

Also Known As: Sunwater Tree (La Wai Kumula'au) and Magic Power Tree (Mana Kumula'au).

Size: On average 7-12 feet (2.1 to 3.6 m) tall, with the oldest being 16-20 feet (4.9 to 6.1 m) tall.

Weight: 600 lbs (270 kg) per foot of height.

P.P.E.: Living Tree: Available P.P.E. for an entire tree varies with age and size. A small Crystal Tree sapling (under 5 feet/1.5 m tall) has 1D6x10 P.P.E. available to spend to protect itself.

A medium tree (5-10 feet/1.5 to 3 m) has 2D6x10 P.P.E.

A large/adult tree (11-15 feet/3.3 to 4.6 m) has 5D6x10 P.P.E.

An ancient Crystal Tree (16-20 feet/4.9 to 6.1 m) has 2D4x100 P.P.E. **Note:** All trees regenerate 5 P.P.E. points per hour regardless of size or age.

Staff-Sized Branch: 4D6+7 P.P.E., no P.P.E. regeneration.

Twig or Wand-Sized Branch: 2D6+5 P.P.E., no P.P.E. regeneration.

Leaf or Small Gem: 1D6+3 P.P.E., no P.P.E. regeneration.

Stone Orb/Fruit or Large Gem: 4D6+11 P.P.E., no P.P.E. regeneration.

Natural Abilities of the Living Crystal Tree: Bio-Regenerates 1D6 M.D.C. per hour, and is a natural P.P.E. battery which can be used by any who touch it.

Magic Abilities of the Living Crystal Tree:

Spell Magic: The tree possesses the following stone and light manipulation spells: Blinding Flash (1), Chromatic Protection (10), Cloak of Darkness (6), Globe of Daylight (2), Lantern Light (1), Life Blast (15), Shatter (5), and Throwing Stones (5). These spell are also available in Crystal Tree wands, staves and stones.

These powers make a forest of Crystal Trees an ideal barrier for the undead and provide the trees with self-defense capabilities against attacking anyone who tries to pluck its stones, leaves or branches unless they are Lemurians and select other recognized "friends," such as Merans. Most other intruders with an alignment of Anarchist or evil are likely to be attacked and chased away.

Uses of the Crystals as Magic Items: These living crystals possess a number of unique, magical properties. **Note:** Only characters of a good alignment can use the staves, wands and stones of the Crystal Tree, and even Unprincipled characters have trouble with them (reduce range by half and the P.P.E. cost of casting its spells is 30% greater). The magic of a Crystal Tree wand, staff or stone will not work in any capacity for Necromancers, Witches, demons or characters of an evil alignment.

1. P.P.E. reservoir. The P.P.E. contained in the crystal (as noted above) can be drawn upon by practitioners of magic as an extra reserve of P.P.E. energy when needed. Though the spent P.P.E. does not regenerate, the mage can *refill* it with his own P.P.E. up to whatever the crystal's original P.P.E. capacity was (see above as per type and size). Furthermore, the item can refill its P.P.E. reservoir when on a ley line or at a stone pyramid at a rate of 1D6+2 points per hour.

2. Spell casting. The mage wielding a gem, orb, wand or staff of a Crystal Tree can channel his own P.P.E. through it to cast any of the spells listed above possessed by the trees. This includes spells he does not normally know. All he has to do is channel the P.P.E. necessary to cast the spell and think of the desired effect. Of course, it helps if one knows the abilities of the Crystal Tree to begin with, but all Lemurian Biomancers and mages have this knowledge, as do some Lemurian academics and farmers. Anyone with knowledge of the Crystal Trees' light and related abilities and who has sufficient P.P.E. can cast the spells inherent to the Crystal Trees.

3. Use as a weapon. The leaves/gems, stones and branches of the magical trees can be used as magic items and weapons.

Crystal Tree Staves inflict 2D6 S.D.C. to mortal opponents, but do 4D6 damage to vampires, other undead and creatures vulnerable to light. They do 2D6 M.D. (or equivalent damage) to other types of evil supernatural beings. The weapon can also be used to cast the spells known to all Crystal Trees. Cost: 50,000-70,000 credits (x10 outside of Lemuria).

Crystal Tree Wands inflict 1D6 S.D.C. to mortal opponents when used as a weapon, but do 2D6 damage to vampires, other undead and creatures vulnerable to light. They do 1D6 M.D. (or equivalent damage) to other evil supernatural beings. The weapon can also be used to cast the spells known to all Crystal Trees. Cost: 25,000-30,000 credits (x10 outside of Lemuria).

Crystal Tree Gems or Leaves: These are small, often leaf or arrowhead-shaped gemstones. They range from the size of a shelled almond to about the size of a human's thumb and can be used as an arrowhead, small spearhead or small knife. Damage as a cutting/slashing weapon is 1D4 S.D.C. to mortal opponents, 2D4 damage to vampires and undead, and 1D4 M.D. to evil supernatural beings such as demons. The weapon can NOT be used to cast the spells known to all Crystal Trees. Range: As per usual.

When *stabbed into vampires and other undead,* whether fired as an arrow or impaled inside the monster at the end of a spear, the arrow or spear does 5D6 damage and prevents the monster from using metamorphosis until the shaft with the crystal is removed. Cost: 25,000-30,000 credits (x10 outside of Lemuria).

Crystal Tree Stones or Fruit: These are round or oval-shaped stones that vary from the size of a chicken egg to that of a tennis ball. They can be used as medallions or mounted into the heads of scepters, war clubs or staves made of wood or coral. Weapons that utilize Crystal Tree "Stones" in this fashion function the same as a staff described above (same damage, same spells).

However, Crystal Tree Stones can also be turned into Amulets and Talismans (as per the spells), but increase the usual bonuses by 50% for Amulets. As a Talisman that functions as a P.P.E. battery, the Crystal Tree Stone Talisman can hold 100 P.P.E., double the usual amount. As a Talisman that contains the ability to cast the same one spell three times, the Crystal Tree Stone Talisman can do the same, plus it can also cast three of the light spells possessed by the trees once (the three light spells are always the same three; pick from those listed under magic, above).

Dark Seed Kelp

This mysterious species of seaweed feeds on everything and anything: ambient sunlight, radiant energy from a ley line, heat and mineral currents from volcanic vents, even nuclear radiation. Rumors persist that it can also steal P.P.E. at the moment of death and absorb decomposing organic material left near its roots or in its vines.

The seaweed is black, dark blue or dark purple in color and produces fist-sized M.D.C. nodules or seed pods reminiscent of giant almonds. These nodules are dark purple or black in color with a faint glow of bioluminescence coming from along the seam of the seed. The nodules are the main apparatus for energy absorption and draw on whatever ambient energy is in the area to feed the plant. While the nodules themselves are not actually seeds, the plant is a tenacious survivor and a root or a nodule can grow into a full plant when given enough time and energy. Lemurians and other aquatic people harvest these seed pods for their M.D.C. and potent magical properties.

Also Known As: Black Seaweed ('Ele'ele Limu) or Black Coconut Seaweed ('Ele'ele Niu Limu).

Horror Factor: 6; the eerie purple bioluminescence often makes it appear evil or scary, despite not radiating such a presence.

Size: The plant is 6-20 feet (1.8 to 6.1 m) tall, but the roots may creep for several hundred yards/meters under the surface of the ocean floor. The seed pod is the size of a human's opened hand.

M.D.C.: Only the seed pod is a Mega-Damage structure with 2D4+15 M.D.C. per each pod.

Weight: 60-180 lbs (27 to 81 kg) for the exposed portion of the plant, but the entire underground root system may be several tons.

P.P.E.: Negligible for the vines and roots, but the nodules have 1D6 each, with your average stalk having 2D6 nodules.

Natural Abilities: The tenacious and hardy plant needs but a fraction of itself to survive and re-grow, though its growth rate is slow and highly dependent upon available energy.

Dark Seed Weapons: Used to make axes, war hammers and spears, such weapons inflict 1D6 M.D. Cost: 1,500-2,000 credits per weapon.

Dark Seed Amulet: A crude "magical amulet" can be made from the nodules that provides the wearer with a bonus of +1 to save vs magic and absorbs the first magic attack leveled at the wearer. This absorption of one incoming spell attack is good once every 48 hours. Cost: 10,000 credits.

Other Uses: The M.D.C. shell of the seed pod may also be used to make non-environmental scale armor, and a variety of items, from spoons and ladles to jewelry (necklaces, armbands, bracelets, mantles, etc.) and headdresses. Cost: Varies. Simple items may cost as little as 300 credits and jewelry depends on the size, quality and number of Dark Seeds used (and additional gems and craftwork), but ranges from 1,000 to 20,000 credits. Scale armor has 4D6+70 M.D.C. and sells for 45,000-60,000 credits.

Mana Limu Magic Algae

While the Lemurians have thousands of genetically engineered species of algae and bacteria they use in a variety of herbal remedies and magical rituals, their understanding of microorganisms and their importance to the environment only emphasizes their mastery of the ecosystem and "science" of Biomancy. One particular species stands out due to its general use and widespread application, not only by the Lemurians but by many aquatic races. When Lemurians refer to "Magic Algae" they mean *Mana Limu*. This algae is found growing in the upper stratum and on the surface of the ocean, but only in so-called "Triangles" like the Demon Sea (also known as the *Bermuda Triangle*) in the Atlantic Ocean and *Dragon Triangle* off the coast of Japan in the Pacific. It is green or blue-green in color and resembles green algae, except it is brighter and glows at night. Somehow, Mana Limu is packed with high amounts of P.P.E. and has magical properties. The Magic Algae can be consumed by most species of fish, marine creatures and people, and is harvested by many undersea communities. Eating it promotes health and vitality, and provides a proper balance of vitamins, minerals and nutrition for most people.

When the proper Biomancy rituals are performed, the following magic products can be created from Mana Limu. Most are very simple processes and common throughout Lemuria. The "cost" listed is the price within Lemurian civilization. On the surface, the same item may sell for 10-20 times more.

Cure-All Potion: Drinking a four ounce (118 ml) vial of a Manu Lima healing potion reduces the symptoms (and penalties) of most bacteria and virus based illnesses by half, including the common cold and hangover symptoms. The person also recovers in half the time. Drinking multiple amounts of the Cure-All does NOT increase the recovery time or reduction of symptoms. Cost: 50 credits per vile.

Food Supplement: Eating 8 ounces (236 ml) of Mana Limu, whether raw or as a paste, or 12 ounces (354 ml) of soup/broth provides the full nutritional value of a balanced meal and quells hunger. Cost: 10 credits per serving.

Healing Salve: Applied to cuts, abrasions and burns, the Mana Limu healing salve heals them in 1D4 days and leaves no permanent scar. Cost: 30 credits per 8 ounce (236 ml) jar. Unless the wound is large, one ounce is usually good for one application.

Miracle Growth Agar: This gelatinous paste can be created as a food-base for bacterial cultures and seed germination. Its enriched magical properties double the rate of growth of any plants that germinate in it and allow them to produce some of the most delicious fruits and vegetables, as well as a natural resistance to disease. Cost: 15 credits for a one pound (0.45 kg) container.

Oxygenating Potion: From the algae, a potion can be extracted that grants those who drink it the ability to hold their breath for an extraordinarily long time. Water-breathing species are able to walk on land without suffocating and surface dwellers can swim below the waves or breathe in a toxic environment. Duration: For humans and most D-Bees, the potion provides oxygen for 2D4+6 minutes; 2D6+15 minutes for amphibious beings and 2D6+6 for most fish/aquatic/water-breathers. Cost: 30 credits.

Note: P.P.E. Booster: Eating a regular diet of Mana Limu (at least one meal every day for a 1D4 years) increases the person's base P.P.E. by 10%. The bonus fades when the individual hasn't eaten any in a month. Those who have eaten Mana Limu most of their lives don't lose the P.P.E. boost until they've been deprived of it for 1D6+5 years.

Missile Anemones

This strange creature appears to be a transplant from an alien world. Lemurian Biomancer Gene-Mages insist it is not one of their creations and use it with caution. The Missile Anemone has a set of tentacles it can launch like rubbery projectiles at approaching predators or intruders such as humans (the Lemurians' communion with wildlife keeps them safe from attacks unless they threaten the anemone). When large predators like sharks, D-Bees, or sea monsters approach, the anemone launches one of its tentacles, which swim quickly towards the predator. Most predators are foolish enough to attempt to swallow and eat the approaching tentacle (double damage and no save for stun if the tendril is bitten or swallowed). The projectile unleashes an electrical jolt when it hits that often stuns the victim and serves as a warning to stay away from the anemone.

The Missile Anemone also has tentacles that cannot be shot out like a torpedo, but they possess the same stun capabilities. The stun attack is used to kill small fish and sea creatures, which the anemone feeds upon.

Also Known As: Fire Eel Seaweed (Ahi Puhi Limu).

Attributes: Not applicable for the plant itself, however the detached tentacles swim at a speed of 68 (46 mph or 74 km).

S.D.C.: 2D6x10

Size: Anemone can grow up to six feet (1.8 m) in diameter. Tentacles are 4-6 feet (1.2 to 1.8 m) long.

Weight: 100-300 lbs (45 to 135 kg).

P.P.E.: 2D6

Number of Missile Tentacles: 3D6+24 and an equal number of appendages that cannot be launched like a projectile.

Natural Abilities: Resistant to cold (half damage), sense motion, heightened sense of touch, heightened sense of hearing (equivalent of the cybernetic implants Amplified Hearing and Ultra Ear), Bio-Regeneration 3D6 S.D.C. per 12 hours of healing; Missile Tentacles Bio-Regenerate in 1D4+2 days.

Attacks per Melee: Two, however it usually fires a volley of 1D4 tentacles.

Damage: Missile Tentacles: The Anemone has 3D6+24 Missile Tentacles which it uses to kill fish and other small prey. Each tentacle travels at a speed of 68 (46 mph or 74 km), is +2 to strike and has 1D6 S.D.C.

Humanoids and large animals struck by the tentacle(s) must roll a 16 or higher to save vs this non-lethal attack. Mega-Damage creatures and those clad in M.D.C. body armor are +2 to save. Characters who fail to save take 1D4 S.D.C. damage and are stunned for 1D6+1 melee rounds. A stunned individual is -8 on all combat maneuvers (strike, parry, dodge, etc.), and reduce the number of attacks per melee, Speed and the performance of skills by half. The attack kills most small fish, shrimp and other small creatures.

A successful save means one point of S.D.C. damage from the jolt (per tentacle), the victim loses initiative, and is -1 on all combat maneuvers (strike, parry, dodge, etc.) for 1D4 melee rounds; otherwise the character is fine. Lemurians using Biomancy or their empathic connection with animals allows safe passage.

The anemone senses the size and number of approaching targets and launches an appropriate number of tentacles (1D4 per target). If the tentacle misses or the target dodges the Missile Tentacle turns around and continues to pursue the target, unless there is easier prey to hit. The Missile Tentacle has two attacks the first melee round it hits a target before becoming inert and sinking.

Sun Seaweed

Bioluminescent Seaweed

These forests of seaweed are made up of a kelp-like plant that bears tennis ball-sized nodules that glow with a warm yellow or orange bioluminescent light. Seeing a forest of this seaweed from afar is reminiscent to seeing a town covered in Christmas lights. Their soft, friendly glow is a beacon to undersea life, and such places are often a refuge from the cold, blackness of the abyss, especially if Lemurians are present. Sun Seaweed is always found in the deeper parts of the ocean where there is a complete absence of sunlight. The leaves and bulbs have minimal value as a food to humans and Lemurians, but are consumed by several species of fish and aquatic animals. The glowing liquid inside the orbs tastes quite bitter and may upset the stomach of humanoids who consume it (33% chance). It is interesting to note that two of the Sun Orbs, about the size of a tennis ball or small apple, contain enough liquid to cover the body of a full-sized man. Any object or person covered in the dense liquid (it is heavier than water and sinks when a bulb is punctured) glows for 1D4 hours. Lemurians sometimes use Sun Seaweed to mark a trail or location, send a signal, mark equipment and even write a message. Puncturing the orbs and letting the yellow glowing liquid slowly drizzle down into the depths is also used to mark an area, signal for help and to lure sea monsters who are attracted to the squiggles of light. **Note:** Covering one's body is useful in keeping track of people in a group or their equipment, but in dark waters, the glow attracts large predators and sea monsters, in effect, marking the person as "prey."

Each bulb of Sun Seaweed glows a different shade of yellow or orange and gives off the equivalent of a 60 watt lightbulb. A Sun Bulb on a living plant generates light for 2D6+20 days before it fades out. A Sun Orb plucked from the plant but kept in water continues to glow for 2D6+6 days. Taken out of water, the Sun Orb shrivels and its light fades within 1D4 days.

The Sun Orbs are actually the plant's seed casings and are meant to be carried away and discarded, allowing the plant to spread. Likewise, puncturing the bulb/orb/seed casing and leaking out the glowing fluid releases the hundreds of tiny seeds inside the liquid. Lemurians grow the plants not only as food, but for their light and medicinal properties. Some elite Lemurian warriors, most notably *Serpent Hunters* and *Oceanic Guardsmen*, use the bioluminescent fluid like war paint to mark themselves for battle and look more intimidating (+1 to Horror Factor).

Also Known As: Sun Seaweed (La Limu), Fire Seaweed (Ahi Lima) and Sunfire Seaweed (La Ahi Lima).

Size: 6-20 feet (1.8 to 6 m) tall/long.

Weight: 50-175 lbs (23 to 79 kg).

P.P.E.: Negligible.

Natural Abilities: Each of its nodules glows with the vibrancy of a 60 watt lightbulb in a variety of different shades of yellow and orange. A typical Sun Seaweed plant has 4D4x10 glowing seed pods/light nodules.

Sun Orb/Bulb: Used for light or paint. Cost: An individual, glowing orb costs one credit. Common at all Lemurian cities, outposts and gardens.

Sun Orb Poison Antidote: The orbs have limited healing properties and serve as the antidote to many different poisons, including stingray stings and snake bites. The orb is broken open and the bitter, glowing liquid drank or rubbed into the poisoned wound. One orb is sufficient to stop the effects of most poisons and even restores 1D6 Hit Points/S.D.C. of damage (or one M.D.C.) caused by the poison. It takes 1D4 melee rounds for the Sun Orb's neutralization to take effect.

Sungrass Seaweed

This long, straight, grass-like seaweed is green with yellow, vertical stripes and grows in shallow waters where ample sunlight is present. It is a natural antibiotic and antibacterial agent good for clearing out infected cuts, wrapping wounds and fighting colds and bacterial infection. It is common enough that most undersea inhabitants have access to it.

Also Known As: La Mau'u Limu (Sungrass Seaweed) and Sunweed.

Size: 1-4 feet (0.3 to 1.2 m) tall/long.

Weight: 2 lbs (0.9 kg) per root clustering.

P.P.E.: Negligible.

Natural Abilities: Antibacterial.

Consumed: Eating or chewing on the Sungrass Seaweed imparts its healing properties and provides a +2 to save vs disease or toxins for the next 1D6+2 hours and heals 1D6 Hit Points damage caused by poison, bacterial diseases and simple toxins, including food poisoning and dysentery. Cost: A single leaf good for 4-8 doses costs one credit.

Woven Wrap Bandages: Used as strips or woven into sheets, Sungrass Seaweed can be used to wrap and bind wounds as if they were bandages. The natural antibacterial agents in the seaweed prevent further infection and stimulate healing, doubling the natural rate of healing on the wound wrapped with Sungrass. Cost: Woven bandages sell for 2-5 credits per three inch (7.6 cm) wide and three foot (0.9 m) long strip.

Tangleweed

This seaweed is a long, tall and stringy grass that is more like a vine that floats upward in the water. From a distance, the dark green and grey Tangleweed looks like an eerie undersea savanna of extraordinarily tall grass. The real danger is not the sea serpents and large predators that like to sleep and hide in the weed's embrace, but from the vines themselves. Tangleweed grabs and holds anything from about the size of a child or sea turtle to that of a man or dolphin. It doesn't bother smaller fish and creatures, nor very large creatures (orca and larger) that are powerful enough to break free or tear the weeds out by their roots, but those in between are fair game.

Tangleweed entwines itself around man-sized prey, holding it in place until it dies from suffocation or starvation. As the body decays, the plant feeds on the corpse, absorbing the nutrients through its skin. Boats and other vehicles going through a field of Tangleweed are likely (01-75% chance) to get their propellers entangled and frozen, and engines and intake valves choked and clogged with it. This knocks out the engine and propulsion system until the weed can be removed; a process that can take hours, especially at sea.

Also Known As: Kapu Limu (Forbidden Seaweed), Grappleweed and Tangled Forests.

Attributes of Note: I.Q. 2 and P.S. 20 (Supernatural).

Hit Points: An individual plant has 2D6 Hit Points, but each vine is tough and has 1D6+4 S.D.C. When entangled in one vine, let alone 1D6+6 (which is typical), a P.S. of 18 or higher is needed to break free. When entangled by four or more vines, a P.S. of 50 or Supernatural P.S. of 18 is needed to break free. Double the P.S. requirement if the arms are pinned or entangled and the victim lacks leverage. In many cases, someone who is not entangled must spend time cutting each vine one at a time. However, swimming into a crop of Tangleweed puts every character who enters it at risk of becoming entangled as well.

Size (individual plant): 6-12 inches (15-30 cm) in diameter, while the individual vines are 15-20 feet (4.6 to 6.1 m) long. A typical "patch" or field of Tangleweed is 3D6x100 plants and covers a square mile (2.6 square km). A forest of Tangleweed can stretch 2D4 square miles.

Weight (of the plant): 100-175 lbs (45 to 79 kg).

P.P.E.: 1D6

Natural Abilities: None per se. This is a plant, but its stem and leaf system is such that medium-sized creatures and boats get entangled in the viney mesh. Even M.D. robots and power armor sometimes get stuck in the vines despite their M.D. strength.

Tangleweed Nets: Harvested Tangleweed enhanced via Biomancy can turn a hand-woven net using the vines into a net with 11 M.D.C. per 10 square feet (0.9 sq m). Cost: 500 credits (much more on the surface).

Tangleweed Rope: Biomancy manipulation and careful tying of several lengths of Tangleweed can create Mega-Damage cord/rope about half the thickness of a grapevine that requires 6 M.D. to cut. A P.S. of 50, or Robotic P.S. of 35 or Supernatural P.S. of 20 is needed to break it. Can hold/pull 10 tons without fear of snapping. Cost: 200 credits per 20 foot (6.1 m) length (much more on the surface).

Tree of Knowledge

The Tree of Knowledge looks like an ancient oak tree with a thick trunk and roots, its branches spread out wide instead of high. Each branch has oval shaped bulbs that resemble giant, polished stones instead of conventional leaves. Each bulb is blue-green, light blue or purple-blue in color and radiates a cool, refreshing light that soothes and calms all in its presence. Small vines, each covered with blueberry-sized bulbs, also extend from the larger branches like hair or tentacles and float freely in the current or wind. A Tree of Knowledge can grow on the surface or underwater, but is always found on a ley line or at a nexus point. Ley lines enable the trees to communicate and share their knowledge with other Trees of Knowledge. Like the *Trees of Wisdom* and the *Jungle Elves' Memory Trees*, a Tree of Knowledge can turn into an acorn-like seed (looks like a smaller version of the blue stone it has in place of leaves) to preserve itself and its knowledge. The seed can then be carried away and planted when the danger has passed. In the event that the tree falls under attack or is about to be harmed or destroyed, it can collect its essence into the seed and launch it up to one mile (1.6 km) in any desired direction to escape and preserve itself. The tree's body remains as a decoy and begins to decay, losing 1D4x10 Hit Points/M.D.C. per minute until it crumbles into sawdust.

A Tree of Knowledge feeds on mystical energy and needs to be planted along a ley line in order to sprout from a seed and grow. In its seed form, the tree enters a hibernation state that can last for eons. However, in this state the tree is not connected to the network of other sentient trees and only retains the old knowledge of the collective; nothing new is learned since becoming a seed.

All Lemurian Floating Cities have several Trees of Knowledge, as the trees contain the collective history of the Lemurians and they teach young Lemurians about nature, history, Biomancy and understanding themselves as a people and their place in the world.

Also Known As: Kahuna Kunela'au (Wizard Tree).

Attributes: Most physical attributes are meaningless, I.Q. 2D6+12, M.A. 2D6+12, M.E. 1D6+20, and P.E. 1D6+18.

M.D.C. by Location:

Vines (2D4x10 of them) – 2D6 each
Main Branches (2D4x10 of them) – 2D4x10 M.D.C. each
Small Branches (1D4x100 of them) – 2D6 M.D.C. each
Seed (1, to contain life essence & knowledge) – 1D4x1,000
Main Body/Trunk – 3D6x100 M.D.C.

Height: 20-50 feet (6.1 to 15.2 m) tall.

Weight: 8-25 tons.

P.P.E.: 2D6x100+200 P.P.E., but can also draw from the ley line or nexus it is planted on.

Natural Abilities: Sense environment around it without needing vision (unaffected by invisibility or darkness), with a range of 1,200 feet (366 m) regarding humans and animals, but 20 miles (32 km) when involving forest fires, floods, storms, droughts, plagues, earthquakes, ley line eruptions, ley line ebbs and flow, Rifts opening and similar natural occurrences. The tree Bio-Regenerates 1D6x10 M.D.C. every minute, is immune to normal fire, heat and cold, and even Mega-Damage and magic heat and cold inflict half damage; impervious to ocean depths. The tree communicates and transmits images and knowledge directly into other minds and absorbs thoughts and memories from other people via a form of Telepathy. This works as a sort of a mental exchange of information. A Mind Block can stop either transmission, and intense fear, hate or a strong desire to close off one's mind/thoughts also severs and blocks communication. Also see Psionics.

Equivalent Skills: Most Trees of Knowledge have an equivalent of a 98% skill in most skills *common* to its region, to within 300 miles (483 km). This includes Anthropology, Art, Astronomy, Biology, Biomancy, Boat Building, Botany/Plants, Camouflage, Carpentry, Dowsing, Farming/Growing, Firefighting, Fishing, History, Holistic Medicine, Languages, Lores, Mathematics, Navigation, Philosophy, Preserving Food, Wilderness Survival and general knowledge similar to the people around them. They are also quite versed in the principles of magic, how it works and ley lines. A few have even had a chance to study and understand some aspects of technology and the laws of men.

Bonuses (in addition to possible attribute bonuses): +2 to save vs magic and psionic attacks, +8 to save vs Horror Factor and possession, impervious to mind control and illusions.

Magic: Most trees are versed in at least one form of magic. The most ancient Trees of Knowledge know two disciplines of magic. Choose one (or two if ancient) from the following or roll for random determination:

01-25% Biomancy
26-50% Ley Line Walker/Wizard Magic/Spell Invocations
51-75% Ocean Magic
76-90% Stone Magic
91-00% Whale Songs

Psionics: All Sensitive psionic abilities plus Empathic Transmission, Mind Bolt and Hydrokinesis <u>or</u> Radiate Horror Factor for defense. I.S.P.: 1D4x100, double for ancient trees. Trees of Knowledge communicate with humanoids and other creatures using Empathy and Telepathy at no I.S.P. cost (range: 1,200 feet/366 m).

Wizard Wrap Kelp

This turquoise species of kelp grows in the deep ocean along and within a few miles of ley lines, at nexus points and within ley line triangles, where it feeds off of ambient mystic and dimensional energy, granting it a number of unique properties. It is favored by Ocean Wizards and other practitioners of magic who like to rest in the comforting folds of the kelp. It is also a favorite resting place for sea dragons and creatures of magic such as dragons and Faerie Folk which often make their homes in such pleasant environments near a ley line. A limited market exists for magic hammocks, sleeping bags and bedding made from the Wizard Wrap Kelp which aid in the recovery of P.P.E.

Also Known As: Wizard Seaweed (Kahuna Limu).

Size (of an individual plant): 4-12 feet (1.2 to 3.6 m) tall.

Weight (of the plant): 100-300 lbs (45 to 135 kg).

P.P.E.: 1D6

Natural Abilities: Resistant to cold (half damage) and actually keeps the waters around it still, preventing heat loss and retaining much of the thermal energy in the cold abyss, like a warm blanket.

Ley Line Rejuvenation: Those who enjoy the warm embrace of the plants are granted a recuperative ability identical to the Ley Line Walker's ability of *Ley Line Restoration* and can use it to recover from injuries while at the ley line. If they also possess *Ley Line Restoration*, they may use either as a second use of this power to further heal and restore themselves.

Recuperative Aura: Resting amongst or even wrapping yourself in the kelp doubles the natural rate of recovery for P.P.E., I.S.P. Hit Points and S.D.C.

Wizard Wrap Sleepware: Harvested kelp can be made into surprisingly comfortable blankets, quilts, bedrolls, sleeping bags and hammocks that calm the nerves and help the person achieve a deep, restful sleep. While asleep, the mage recovers an extra +1 P.P.E. per hour (+1D4 when also sleeping inside a triangular tent also made of Wizard Wrap Kelp). The perfect cure for insomnia. <u>Cost</u>: 500-700 credits each for Wizard Wrap blankets to sleeping bags, 3,000 credits for a Wizard Wrap Tent.

Wizard Wrap Headgear: Hats, helmets, turbans and headdresses made of Wizard Wrap are said to promote mental calm, focus and imagination. Some Lemurian academics and mages swear by them and insist they provide much greater benefits than the +1% to skill performance they actually grant. Others claim any additional benefits are a placebo effect. <u>Cost</u>: Varies with the style and other accessories to the hat, helm or headdress; 500-3,000 credits.

Wizard Wrap Canteen: Keeps water fresh and pleasantly cool for as long as six months. <u>Cost</u>: 300 credits.

Wizard Wrap Bandages: Promote increased healing (10% faster) and reduce scarring (33%). <u>Cost</u>: 100 credits for a four foot (1.2 m) bandage wrap.

Aquatic Races

By Greg Diazcyk and Kevin Siembieda

Ichthylean R.C.C.

Ichthyleans (Ick-thih-lee-ans) are odd-looking creatures that appear to be half man and half fish; not in the pleasing appearance of the Merans but more like the *Creature from the Black Lagoon*! Ichthyleans are covered from head to toe with fish scales and possess large, clawed, webbed feet and hands. They have webbed spines that run down their backs and a membrane under their arms. Though these fish-men may look eerie they have a heart of gold, are peaceful people and only wish to live a simple life. It is theorized that they were an experiment by the Lemurians as a possibility for their new aquatic form during their descent into the oceans.

The Ichthyleans have been misunderstood and hunted as a race for centuries. Their frightful appearance and unusual method of communication have made it all the more difficult for them to trade and associate with other people. Misunderstood, especially by surface dwellers, Ichthyleans are often seen as monsters and attacked on sight. Feared and hated anyway, some have resorted to raiding ships at sea as well as villages along waterways, stealing food, supplies, weapons and gear they desire. However, even Ichthylean raiders don't kill if they can avoid it nor cause malicious damage, and otherwise keep to themselves, hidden. Most avoid surface dwellers and associate only with other aquatic races. Tribes and villages are usually found underwater in oceans and seas worldwide, but there are some tribes found in deep freshwater lakes and remote places, including the heart of wilderness swamps and jungle waterways.

Most Ichthyleans are kind, gentle people among their own kind and with allies. As a rule, they wish to live a quiet, peaceful existence. However, Ichthys are quick to fight back when attacked or taken advantage of, and are capable warriors. A provoked Ichthylean or one backed into a corner, protecting loved ones or defending his or her young, fights like a hungry shark. Most survive as hunters and gatherers, though some also farm and raise livestock. All tend to hunt only enough to satisfy their needs, and use as much of the slain animal as they can.

Also Known As: Ichthys, Lee-anns and Water Lions.

Alignment: Any, but most are Principled (15%), Scrupulous (30%), Unprincipled (20%), or Anarchist (15%).

Attributes: I.Q. 3D6, M.E. 2D6+5, M.A. 1D6+6, P.S. 2D6+18 (Robot), P.P. 2D6+6, P.E. 2D6+6, P.B. 1D6+3, Spd 2D6+10 running, triple Spd when swimming in water and swimming fatigues Ichthys at 10% the usual rate. P.S. is the equivalent to Robot P.S.

Size: 6 feet + 2D6 inches (1.8 to 2.1 m).

Weight: 200-350 lbs (90 to 157 kg); all muscle and blubber.

M.D.C.: P.E. attribute number x2 to start, +1D6 per level of experience. Skills that provide an S.D.C. bonus only add 1D6 M.D.C. to this character. Armor or magic may be used to provide additional M.D.C. protection. (On S.D.C. worlds Ichthyleans have Hit Points equal to their P.E. attribute number +1D8 per level of experience, 2D4x10 S.D.C. and a Natural A.R. of 15.)

Horror Factor: 13 to humans and most D-Bees.

P.P.E.: 5D6

Disposition: Ichthyleans are cautious and suspicious of outsiders and seldom let their guard down around them. Among their own, they are open, friendly, playful and caring. They really only open up their feelings to trusted friends and loved ones and are pragmatic about life. Though peaceful, they are quick to action and willing to fight and kill without hesitation to protect their species and defend hearth and home. Most dislike and distrust surface dwellers, and are wary of any outsider or stranger.

Life Span: 1D6x10+60 years.

Gender: Ichthylean males and females look very similar, except females have brighter colors. Males are a rich green with light to deep blue accents and colored fins, while females are a light green with yellow webbing and fins, and the long fin crest that runs from their head, down their spine is twice the size as the males and is orange or red. Females bear 2D4 eggs, which are watched in a nest for four months. Young reach physical maturity at age 10.

Natural Abilities: Swimming 98%, Nightvision 1,000 feet (305 m), keen normal and underwater vision, depth tolerance of 2 miles (3.2 km) and resistant to cold (half damage).

Amphibious: Survive on Land and Water: The Ichthyleans use gills to extract oxygen from the water. However, unlike most fish, their gills are inside gill sacks within their chest, like lungs. The gill sacks store and funnel water past the gills and out their backs (water goes in through their mouth). When out of the water, the back exhaust section seals up, allowing the Ichthylean to carry oxygenated water with him. Through churning and "gargling" the water every 10 minutes to re-oxygenate it, the Icthylean can survive indefinitely out of the water. On dry land, they use their "gargling" effect to also make noises, grunt and to speak.

Chemoreceptors/Advanced Sense of Taste: Ichthyleans have a superior sense of smell/taste while in water and can taste/sense blood and chemicals in the water up to two miles (3.2 km) away. In fact, part of their communication with their own kind involves chemicals by quickly depositing molecules in the water that disperse and speak to their species. Such scents communicate love, joy, anger, fear, concern, caring, welcome, and short messages like join me/us and share, all is well, awarning to back off/stand down, a warning to be alert, a warning to hide, a warning of immediate danger, a warning to flee, a call to come, a call for help, and a call to attack.

Communication: All Ichthyleans communicate using chemical exchanges, gurgling, clicks, sounds, and the occasional words and short phrases as well as Empathy and Telepathy. Their chemical/gurgling language is referred to as Ichthylean and thus far, can only be spoken by Icthyleans and Milu, though humans and other races can try to mimic the sound by gurgling water in their mouth to duplicate the Ichthyleans' dialect. Ichthyleans can learn to understand and even speak other languages, however their vocal cords and gurgling noises often make it difficult for them to reproduce certain sounds or be understood by others. All spoken languages are at -15% and they sound like someone trying to talk with their mouth full of water or while gargling water.

Track by Smell/Taste Underwater (only): Ichthyleans can identify blood and most chemicals common to ocean waters and track it to its source at 50% +3% per level of experience (+12% if it's an Ichthylean scent).

Vulnerabilities & Penalties: Cannot breathe air directly; see gill sacks above for their limitations and restrictions. -1 to save vs poison and drugs. Tend to be passionate and hot-tempered, which can get them in trouble.

R.C.C. Skills: The Ichthyleans are a simple wilderness people who enjoy a tribal way of life. They rely on their cunning, physical strengths, natural abilities, psionic powers, and some magic to survive on Rifts Earth.

Male Ichthylean R.C.C. (97%): Advanced Fishing (+20%), Barter (+12%), Carpentry (+10%), Climbing (+10%), Fishing (+20%), Gardening (+12%), Hand to Hand: Expert, Horsemanship: Aquatic Animals (+10%), Horsemanship: Sea Monsters (+15%), Hunting, Language (Native): Ichthylean/Milu at 90%, Language: Lemurian (+10%, but no bonus to speak it), Lore: Sea Creatures (+20%), Physical Labor, Prowl (+10% on land and underwater), Skin and Prepare Animal Hides (+10%), Tailing (+10%), Track & Hunt Sea Animals (35%/25% +5%), Underwater Navigation (+20%), Undersea & Sea Survival (+25%), Wilderness Survival (+15%), W.P. Knife, W.P. Trident, W.P. Ancient (one of choice), and W.P. Modern (two of choice).

Female Ichthylean R.C.C. (94%): Animal Husbandry (+15%), Appraise Goods (+10%), Camouflage (+20%), Cook (Prepare Food; +20%), Hand to Hand: Basic, Horsemanship: Aquatic Animals (+10%), Identify Plants and Fruits (aquatic and land; +20%), Language (Native): Ichthylean/Milu at 92%, Language: Lemurian (+15%, but no bonus to speak it), Marine Biology (+20%), Preserve Food (+15%), Sea Holistic Medicine (+20%), Sewing, Undersea Farming (+25%), Underwater Navigation (+10%), Undersea & Sea Survival (+15%), W.P. Blunt, W.P. Knife, W.P. Modern (one of choice).

O.C.C. Note: 3% of males and 6% of female Ichthyleans become mages, mostly Ocean Wizards and Sea Druids, but sometimes Biomancer Gene-Mages or other practitioners of magic.

Experience Level: 1D6+1 or as set by the Game Master for NPCs. Player characters should start at first level. Use the *Oceanic Guardsman* experience table.

Attacks per Melee: As per Hand to Hand Combat skill and R.C.C. bonuses.

Mega-Damage: As per Robot equivalent P.S. or by weapon, +3 M.D. from claw attacks and an Ichthy bite does 1D6 M.D. (a nip does 2D6 S.D.C.).

R.C.C. Bonuses: Males: +1 attack at levels 1, 5 and 10 (this is in addition to those gained from Hand to Hand Combat skill), +1 on Perception Rolls (+2 for rolls pertaining to taste/smell in water), +1 on initiative, +2 to automatic dodge underwater only, +1 to disarm and pull punch, and +1 to save vs Horror Factor at levels 1, 3, 5, 7, 9 and 11.

Females: +3 on Perception Rolls (+5 for rolls pertaining to taste/smell in water and caring for young), +4 to automatic dodge underwater only, +1 to save vs psionics and magic, and +5% to save vs coma/death.

Magic: Rare, by O.C.C. only.

Psionics: All Ichthyleans have the following psychic abilities: Empathy (4), Telepathy (4), Telepathy Aquatic Sentient Beings (Special: Can be used indefinitely without any I.S.P. cost to communicate with other members of their own race, Milu, Amphibs, Junk Crabs, Naut'Yll, the Lord of the Deep, Cetaceans, Lemurians, many of the Splugorth Minions and other intelligent, aquatic beings.), +1D4+1 additional psi-abilities selected from *one* of these categories: Healing, Physical or Sensitive. Considered Major Psychics. I.S.P. Base: M.E. attribute number x2 +1D6 per level of experience.

Habitat: Ichthyleans travel the waters of the world, but prefer the Pacific Ocean and other warm waters. Some have even made it into the waterways of the Americas, Africa, India and Southeast Asia. They tend to avoid the mid-Atlantic where they are stalked by Splugorth Slavers and Metztla. They may be encountered as a lone hunter, in pairs or a small family group or hunters up to 1D6+2. A typical tribe/village has 2D6x10 members, 5D6x10 for a large one.

Allies: They are heavily influenced by the Lemurians and consider them as brothers, which means they share their views and philosophies, emulate their way with nature, and often live near or with Lemurians. Even those who are not friends or fans of Lemurians consider them to be a friend of their people and the sea. They are also friends with cetaceans (dophlins and whales), but most other people are seen as invaders, rivals or enemies. Merans, Milu, Junk Crabs, Ocean Wizards, Sea Druids, Amphibs and the New Navy, on the other hand, are judged on an individual basis, and generally considered with uneasy indifference. The humans of Tritonia are especially suspect and viewed with disdain and distrust.

Enemies: The Splugorth and their minions, Horune Pirates, Naut'Yll, demons, undead, and the Lord of the Deep and his minions are among the most hated and feared of enemies. Surface dwellers are also regarded as wicked and cruel monsters who hate and kill anyone they don't understand. While their Lemurian allies insist not all surface dwellers are evil, most (75%) Ichthyleans are not convinced.

Cybernetics: None.

Money: Salvage and trade goods worth 1D4x1,000 credits.

Junk Crab R.C.C.

Junk Crabs are among the strangest new life forms on Rifts Earth. Imagine a Hermit Crab the size of a man. Carried on its back is a giant shell 10-15 feet (3 to 4.6 m) tall, but the "shell" is made of junk the creature has gathered and cobbled together. If the word "cobbled" suggests intelligence, you are correct, as Junk Crabs, also known as "Crab People" and "Salvage Crabs," have human-like intelligence. So now imagine this man-sized crab-creature waves you down and offers "free repairs" for your boat, body armor or equipment. Do you accept the offer?

Junk Crabs are sentient D-Bees from another dimension. They have an average human intelligence, a gift for mechanics, salvage, and recycling, and enjoy tinkering and building weird conglomerations of, well, everything. They make surreal sculptures, underwater bridges and towers to nowhere, and love to gather junk and salvage for later use. They are fascinated by all types of technology though they seem to have difficulty with high-technology and their sense of design and artistic aesthetics is, umm, junk. That being said, Crab People are skilled at making hull repairs to vessels and armor, and building, repairing and maintaining rafts, small boats, and simple machinery. They are happy to try their hand at repairing just about anything, if only to have a chance to figure out how it works, learn about a new piece of technology and to get some M.D.C. scrap metal, weapons, E-Clips, or other "desirable junk" *in trade* for their services.

After one's initial shock at meeting a giant, talking crab-thing, Junk Crabs can be quite amusing, affable and helpful. They look more animal than human, with four legs and two arms covered in a natural shell-like exoskeleton, a long flexible neck, and a pair of large, round eyes mounted on flexible stalks that can turn 360 degrees; so can the neck. The mouth is more like a tiny beak with a pair of small tendrils and a pair of large ones that droop down above the mouth, giving Crab People the appearance of having a mustache. (The "mustache" is smaller on females.) A pair of long feelers rise up from the top of the head, providing more tactile and sensory capabilities. The hands are comparatively small and armored like the rest of the appendages, but have only two, long fingers and an opposable thumb. The part of the Junk Crab that earns them their name is their custom-made shell pieced together from M.D.C. materials, scrap metal, machine parts, old tires, anchors and anything else the Junk Crab finds suitable or decorative. Of course, to the Junk Crab, pipes, chain, old license plates, tin cans and pieces of glass may be "decorative." While predominantly used for protection and carrying all of their personal effects, including tools, the shell is filled with concealed weapon systems to protect themselves.

Crab People may look like walking junk piles, but they are a lot smarter than their appearance and behavior suggests. They think differently from humans and what humans consider a "civilized culture," but are clever and resourceful. Junk Crabs also lack sophistication and social skills, as well as the capacity for spoken language. Their natural language is clicks, barks and hums similar to the Milu (effectively the same), so when they speak human languages they tend to speak in phrases and short, simple sentences. This contributes to the misconception that Junk Crabs are dull-witted.

Many Crab People are shy and tentative, especially when they meet strangers. Like young children, they get much more friendly and boisterous after they feel more comfortable with the strangers. They also get excited about technology, junk, scrap and the chance to fix or build something. Junk Crabs have an eye made for technology and seem to be able to fix just about anything they can get their little claws on, except for really high-tech stuff and Techno-Wizard items. They also seem to understand machines better than they do people. As a result, they tend to blurt out what they are thinking, and say things that may seem outspoken, rude and ill-mannered because they have no concept of culture, decorum, law, politics or etiquette. However, they do possess a strong sense of what is right and wrong, and try to be friendly and do what's right. Thus, they behave more like rambunctious children than stuffy adults.

Though initially shy, they welcome strangers, if for no other reason than to learn about their machines. Visitors from the surface world and other places means people with more technology. Some Junk Crabs have even set up underwater or floating barges with radio or sonar beacons broadcasting the phrase, "I Fix" or "Free Repairs" to attract people willing to trade technology, scrap and junk with them. And that's an important point, although Junk Crabs advertise "free repairs" they usually want something in exchange. That trade item may be junk, scrap or something perceived as having little or no value, but it's still a trade for services rendered. That having been said, most Junk Crabs will take an I.O.U. or promise to "bring something back the next time I'm in the area." Furthermore, many are truly willing to do free repairs for people in trouble, heroes and Lemurians, though most people feel obligated to bring them some kind of trinket or scrap to repay the favor. It's important to note that a Junk Crab may consider a worthless chunk of debris or broken gun as a fair trade for a great deal of work.

Special R.C.C. Abilities of the Junk Crab D-Bee:

1. Amphibious Beings: Junk Crabs can breathe water and air, and can survive on dry land for as long as four days without submerging themselves in water (one third that time in desert environments). However, they prefer to come in and out of the water frequently, and feel at home under the waves in oceans and seas, not on dry land. If kept out of water for more than four days, Junk

Crabs quickly become weak (reduce all physical attributes, attacks/actions per melee round and M.D.C. by half for every additional 12 hours out of water) and will die in 1D4 days from dehydration.

2. Intuitive Mechanical Aptitude: One might think of Junk Crabs as mechanics or machine savants with instinctive abilities to build and repair. See Natural Abilities, Magic, Psionics and R.C.C. Skills.

3. Create Armored Defensive Shell or "Junk Shell:" These handcrafted armored shells have 5D6x10+35 M.D.C. to start, and are more than just a protective home, they provide additional M.D.C. protection and give the Junk Crabs greater confidence. Maybe it's the security offered by the armor or the plethora of weapon systems contained within it, but without their shell, Crab People are shy, skittish and tend to avoid contact with outsiders.

The main shell is made from M.D.C. scrap metal and junk, while the outer covering is adorned with decorations made of anything the Junk Crab considers to be attractive, artistic or interesting. Junk Crabs call this housing their "Armored Techno-Shell." It is designed to allow the Junk Crab to retract completely inside the shell and seal it shut with a sliding door or simply a large sheet of M.D.C. plating. When tucked completely inside his shell, the Junk Crab looks like nothing more than a debris pile. In a ship graveyard, shipwreck or battlefield, the Junk Crab is indistinguishable from the rest of the wreckage until it moves. Looking around while inside is easy, because he can extend one or both of the feelers or eye stalks without being noticeable.

The Armored Techno-Shell conceals a number of automated weapon systems to defend and protect the Junk Crab, as well as clubs, swords, and handheld guns the D-Bee can pull out from concealed locations as needed. The shell may be bulky, but it is easy and comfortable enough for the Junk Crab to carry around with his Robot equivalent strength and body built for an outer shell; many add air ballasts and buoyancy mechanisms to make it easier to swim and move quickly underwater, and some even install turbo jets to rocket along at 30-40 mph (48-64 km or 26 to 34 knots an hour).

Creating an Armored Techno-Shell(a.k.a. "Junk-Shell"): Players and Game Masters are encouraged to design their own wacky Junk-Shells using the array of common features listed below. Pick 1D4+1 weapons (any) and 1D4+4 other features at level one. Add one new feature (weapon or other) for every new level of experience (starting at level 2). The character may elect not to spend all of his selections or save up a new selection upon reaching a new level of experience to add items or additional armor at a later time, or to get a feature that counts as two or three selections. Unless it states otherwise, these features can be selected several times.

Common Design Features of Junk Crab Shells:

Concealed Cargo Container: One large container the size of a steamer trunk (4x3x3 feet/1.2 x 0.9 x 0.9 m), or three small ones the size of a tackle box; all can be locked and sealed watertight.

Concealed Handheld Gun/Energy Assault Weapon: This is a handheld energy pistol or rifle that the Junk Crab has found, waterproofed and modified for use underwater and on dry land. May include Biomancy and Techno-Wizard weapons and wands, scepters and staves that fire energy bolts or have other long-range capabilities, but the Junk Crab cannot make any modifications to magic items. Primary Purpose: Combat and Defense. Range on Dry Land: As per what's normal for that weapon. Range Underwater: One third. Mega-Damage on Dry Land: Standard as per that weapon. Mega-Damage Underwater: Half. Rate of Fire: Each blast counts as one melee attack. Payload: Standard as per that weapon. **Rail Gun Note:** Rail guns and most projectile weapons have much reduced value underwater, are bulky and require a large, heavy ammo-drum, so they are seldom used by Junk Crabs. Range on Dry Land: As per what's normal for that weapon. Range Underwater: One third. Mega-Damage on Dry Land: Standard as per that weapon. Mega-Damage underwater: Half. Rate of Fire: Each burst counts as one melee attack. Payload: Standard as per that weapon.

Concealed Melee Weapon: This is a handheld, close-combat weapon that has a concealed housing where it is hidden and stowed until needed. If one looks closely, you might be able to see the weapon's handle sticking out of the Junk Shell, but that's all. It may be an M.D. or S.D.C. weapon of any variety, but most Junk Crabs prefer clubs/bludgeons, war clubs, hammers, Neural Maces, axes, knives and swords. They love Vibro-Blades, Techno-Wizard blades, and magic weapons.

Concealed Extendable & Retractable Laser Weapon: This is a light weapon that may look like a gun/rifle that slides or pops-up out of a housing in the shell. The weapon can turn 180 degrees and has a 45 degree up and down arc of fire. Primary Purpose: Defense. Range: 1,000 feet (305 m) underwater, 2,000 feet (610 m) on dry land or shooting from the surface of water into the air. Mega-Damage: 2D6 M.D. Rate of Fire: Each blast counts as one melee attack. Payload: 120 shots hooked up to a series of E-Clips or a small generator. If the latter, it recharges at a rate of 30 blasts per hour.

Concealed Extendable & Retractable Ion Weapon: This is a light weapon that may look like a gun/rifle that slides or pops-up out of a housing in the shell. The weapon can turn 180 degrees and has a 45 degree up and down arc of fire. Primary Purpose: Defense. Range: 500 feet (152 m) underwater, 1,000 feet (305 m) on dry land or shooting from the surface of water up into the air. Mega-Damage: 4D6 M.D. Rate of Fire: Each blast counts as one melee attack. Payload: 60 shots hooked up to a series of E-Clips or a small generator. If the latter, it recharges at a rate of 15 blasts per hour.

Concealed Extendable & Retractable Power Tools: Any "bionic" power tool such as a drill, jackhammer, saw, laser torch, etc. can be mounted on a retractable and extendible arm or as a handheld tool. Range: Handheld or 10 feet (3 m) if on an extendable arm. Damage: As per the tool.

E-Clip Charger: The Junk Crab has an E-Clip charger and portable generator (with a 1D4 year life) built into his shell. A better power supply, like a nuclear one with a 15 year life, is a separate purchase. **Note:** Counts as two feature selections.

Electrified Shell: The Junk Crab can activate electrified nodules on the outside of the shell to deter predators and attackers. The D-Bee must retract completely inside his shell before activating. Range: Touch. Damage: The field does 3D6 M.D. every time someone tries to touch the shell and 1D4 M.D. per melee round to anybody who even comes within four feet (1.2 m) of his electrified shell. Note that fish and most other aquatic animals will sense and feel the tingle of electricity at 100 yards/meters away and know to avoid getting too close to the shell. Payload: 12 periods of electrification. Duration of the Electric Field: 1D4+1 minutes per use. **Note:** This feature can only be selected *once*.

Extra M.D.C. Armor for the Shell: Add 2D4x10+20 M.D.C. every time this feature is selected and increase shell size and weight 10%. Cannot be selected more than five times.

Fixed Position Laser Weapon: This is a light laser that looks like a pipe or barrel of a rifle sticking out from the Junk Shell. It is locked in a fixed position which means it can only shoot in the direction it is pointing. To change its position, the Junk Crab must tilt, turn and reposition his entire body. For most humanoids, a fixed weapon is mounted in the front of their combat vehicle or armor, however, since Crab People can extend and turn their long necks and eye stalks 360 degrees to see up, down, under, around, and behind themselves, a fixed weapon can be mounted in the front, back, sides, top and underbelly of their shell (each location counts as one selection). Primary Purpose: Defense. Range: 1,000 feet (305 m) underwater, 2,000 feet (610 m) on dry land or shooting from the surface of water up into the air. Mega-Damage: 2D6 M.D. Rate of Fire: Each blast counts as one melee attack. Payload: 120 shots hooked up to a series of E-Clips or a small generator. If the latter, it recharges at a rate of 30 blasts per hour.

Fixed Position Ion Weapon: Same as the Laser, above, except for combat stats. Primary Purpose: Defense. Range: 500 feet (152 m) underwater, 1,000 feet (610 m) on dry land or shooting from the surface of water up into the air. Mega-Damage: 3D6 M.D. Rate of Fire: Each blast counts as one melee attack. Payload: 80 shots hooked up to a series of E-Clips or a small generator. If the latter, it recharges at a rate of 20 blasts per hour.

Hover and Flight Capabilities: Enables the Junk Crab to hover and fly thorough the air. Requires some sort of E-Clip, battery or generator to provide the power. Speed: Hover, VTOL capabilities, 60 mph (96 km) maximum. Maximum Height: 3,000 feet (914 m). Bonus: +1 to dodge when flying. Power Supply: One standard E-Clip provides 48 hours of flight before it needs to be recharged. A long E-Clip provides 60 hours of use. A nuclear battery provides unlimited flight. **Note:** This feature counts as two selections.

Mini-Missile or Torpedo Launcher: This is a small, two shot launcher that can be built almost anywhere on the shell. Range: One mile (1.6 km). Mega-Damage: As per the type of torpedo or mini-missile. Rate of Fire: One or both torpedoes or mini-missiles at a time; counts as one melee attack. Payload: Two, with others carried on its back or belly or in a concealed storage container.

Nuclear Power Supply: The same type as used in power armor. Concealed and fixed energy weapon systems built into the shell are linked to the power supply and have an unlimited payload. Average life is 15 years. **Note:** This counts as three selections and can only be selected once.

Radio, Long-Range and Directional: Range: 700 miles (1,120 km) under water, 500 miles (800 km) on dry land or on the water's surface; multiple communication frequencies.

Seating for Passengers: Two or three seats on the outside of the shell to accommodate passengers who want to ride on the D-Bee's back. Each seat comes with a seatbelt and shoulder harness.

Sensor Pod: This item, usually sticking out from the top or the sides, is a sensor pod. The Junk Crab either can control it through his Telemechanics or has a remote control system and display console he can pull out of a housing in the chest or underbelly of his shell and control by hand. The sensor pod typically has a combat and targeting computer linked to all integrated weapon systems built into the shell and sonar and radar systems like the types used in aquatic power armor, plus a radiation detector, compass, gyroscope, depth gauge, and temperature gauge. Bonuses: +1 to strike with weapons built into the shell and +2 to dodge. **Note:** Multiple sensor pods only serve as backup systems, they do not provide additional bonuses.

Underwater Hover Jet System: Enables the Junk Crab to move slowly through water and hold his position against the current without having to swim. Requires some sort of E-Clip, battery or generator to provide the power. Speed: 12 mph (19.2 km or 10.4 knots) maximum. Power Supply: One standard E-Clip provides 120 hours of propulsion before it needs to be recharged. A long C-Clip provides 164 hours of use. A nuclear battery provides unlimited use. Can only be added once.

Underwater Turbo-Jet System: Enables the Junk Crab to rocket through water like a torpedo or across the surface like a speedboat. Requires some sort of E-Clip, battery or generator to provide the power. Speed: 50 mph (80 km or 43 knots) maximum. Power Supply: One standard E-Clip provides 50 hours of propulsion before it needs to be recharged. A long E-Clip provides 66 hours of use. A nuclear battery provides unlimited use. **Note:** This feature counts as two selections and can only be added once.

Junk Crab Stats

Also Known As: Crab People, Mechanic Crabs and Salvage Crabs.

Alignment: Any, but most are Anarchist (50%), Unprincipled (30%) and Scrupulous (10%).

Attributes: I.Q. 1D6+9, M.E. 1D6+8, M.A. 2D6+11, P.S. 2D6+20 (Robot), P.P. 1D6+11, P.E. 2D6+7, P.B. 2D4+1, Spd 2D6+15 (double Spd when outside their shell). Robot equivalent P.S., -5 to M.A. and -3 to M.E. and P.B. when seen outside of their junk shell.

M.D.C. by Location:

Head & Neck – 40 (triple if the character wears a helmet and armored protection along the neck).

Hands (2) – 30 each

Arms (2) – 55 each

Legs (4) – 115 each

Main Body (without shell) – P.E. attribute number x2 +1D6 per level of experience.

*Shell Housing – 4D6x10+35 to start.

* Think of the armored shell as a portable house or fortified bunker carried on the back of the Junk Crab. This "shell" is not a physical part of the Crab Person's body, but a construct the D-Bee builds and wears. Thus, he can completely exit the shell when necessary or desired, but that is a rarity. Any M.D.C. damage can be repaired by the character provided he can find the right materials to weld and add to it. Such repairs take 1D4 hours. The M.D.C. of the shell can be replaced, but never exceeded except for the *Extra M.D.C. Armor for the Shell* "feature" described previously.

Horror Factor: Not applicable; in fact,they often look comical.

Size: 5-6 feet (1.5 to 1.8 m) tall from their toes to the top of their heads, but they can stretch their necks an additional 5 feet (1.5 m) and the feelers on the top of their heads are three feet (0.9 m) long. Furthermore, the armored shells can tower up to 8 feet (2.4 m) tall and 6 feet (1.8 m) in width and length.

Weight: The Junk Crab himself is rather small and slight when he steps out of his large, bulky shell; 100-150 lbs (45 to 67.5 kg), the shell varies but is typically 1,000-2,500 pounds (450 to 1,125 kg).

Average Life Span: 60-90 years.

P.P.E.: 1D6x10 + P.E. attribute number, +1D6+1 P.P.E. per level of experience. Considered to be a strange sort of D-Bee Mystic (see Magic and Psionics).

Disposition: All Crab People are socially awkward. They tend to be shy until a piece of technology or something to build or repair catches their eye, then they behave like a curious, precocious child with a million questions ("What is that?" "What's it do?" "How much does it weigh?" "How fast can it go? "What's the range?" "Can I try it?" "Why not?" "Please?" "Can I take it apart?" "Why not?" "I'll fix your engine if you let me take it apart." "I'll put it back together the right way, I promise." "Wait! What's that over there!?"). They also get bored easily, and when bored, they wander off or take something apart or fix something and putter around. They don't know or care about money or valuables, have no interest in or understanding of politics, and would rather be exploring, meeting people, building, fixing stuff and acquiring "cool" tech, scrap and junk than waiting around.

Natural Abilities: Swimming 88%, Climbing 76%/56%, P.S. is the equivalent to Robot Strength, Nightvision 400 feet (122 m), resistant to cold (half damage, even magic cold does half damage), tolerate depths up to 5 miles (8 km). Outside their shells they are fast and agile swimmers, but are vulnerable to attack which makes them shy, skittish and prone to avoiding contact with others. In their shell, most are confident and cheerful.

Chemoreceptors (special): A highly advanced sense of taste/smell that lets the Junk Crab detect salinity and toxicity of the water, and they are especially keen at picking up the scent of metal, oil, and other technological byproducts they can track to their source at 68% +2% per level of experience (-20% to track other scents).

Feelers (special): Their prehensile feelers can be used like hands to feel and figure out shapes and what an object might be. They are also sensitive to light, water temperature, water currents and their direction, scents (see Chemoreceptors) and motion. All this means the penatlies for being blind/functioning in total darkness are only -3 for Junk Crabs.

Limited Bio-Regeneration (special): Can regrow lost feelers (and mustache tendrils) in 1D4+1 days; regrows an eye and/or eye stalk in 1D4+1 weeks; a hand in 1D4+2 weeks and a leg in 1D6+4 weeks. Otherwise, heals twice as fast as humans.

Prehensile Neck and Eye Stalks (special): The neck is two feet (0.6 m) long to begin with and can stretch an additional 5 feet (1.5 m) when necessary. It is also extremely flexible and can bend to look around, over, under and behind its shell; the head can turn 360 degrees.

Likewise, the eye stalks can stretch 2 feet (0.6 m) and can also turn 360 degrees to see in all directions. The D-Bee has such control that he can stretch and/or turn just one eye stalk to look in one direction, while the other looks in a different direction. This makes the Junk Crab difficult to surprise or attack from behind; see Bonuses.

Also see *Magic* and *Psionics*.

R.C.C. Skills: All Junk Crabs know the following skills: Barter (+6%), Basic Electronics (+15%), Basic Mechanics (+20%), Boat Building (+20%), Carpentry (+10%), Field Armorer & Munitions Expert (+15%), General Repair and Maintenance (+20%), Jury-Rig (+20%), Mathematics: Basic (+30%), Optic Systems (+10%), Pick Locks (+10%), Pilot: Water Scooters (+12%), Water Skiing and Surfing (+20%), Radio: Basic (+20%), Recognize Weapon Quality (+15%), Recycle (+25%), Salvage (20%), Sensory Equipment or T.V./Video (+10%), Undersea Salvage (+25%), Weapon Systems (+10%), and Wilderness Survival (+20%), plus W.P. Blunt, W.P. Sword, W.P. Energy Rifle, and two W.P.s of choice (any).

Additional Skills: Junk Crabs are natural builders and mechanics, so one additional skill is chosen from the skill categories of Electrical, Mechanical and Technical Skills (in the latter case, provided they involve building, excavation, making things or working with machines and materials) at levels 2, 5, 7, 10 and 13. Each of these skills gets a +10% skill bonus.

Experience Level: 1D4+3 or as set by the Game Master for NPCs. Player characters should start at first level. Use the *Birdman* experience table.

Vulnerabilities: They can survive without their armored shells, but are even worse off socially without them and lose the confidence to do any kind of mechanical work, with the exception of rebuilding a new shell.

Attacks per Melee: Three, six if technology is being used.

Damage: A punch from a closed claw does 2D6 S.D.C., a clawed pinch does 3D6 S.D.C.

Bonuses (in addition to possible attribute bonuses): +4 on Perception Rolls (+6 to detect a surprise attack or attack from behind, and to find salvage or when working with scrap and machines), +2 on initiative, +1 to strike, parry, and dodge, +1 to disarm, +3 to pull punch, +4 to roll with impact, and +2 to save vs disease. When outside their armored shell (a rarity), Crab People are +3 to dodge and have the Prowl skill at 64%.

Magic: Similar to a human Mystic, the Junk Crab's intuitive understanding of technology enables him to cast the following spells: Frequency Jamming (15), Mend the Broken (10+), Mystic Fulcrum (5), and Negate Mechanics (20). Pick one additional spell from levels one ot two Spell Invocations when the character reaches levels 3, 6, 9 and 12. Base P.P.E.: 1D6x10 + P.E. attribute number, +1D6+1 P.P.E. per level of experience.

Psionics: An intuitive understanding of technology augmented by the psionic abilities of Object Read (6), Telemechanics (10) and Telemechanic: Mental Operation (12). All enable them to build, repair and operate most machines, devices and make simple structures as well as incorporate them into their armored shells. Base I.S.P.: M.E. attribute number x3 +1D6+3 per level of experience. Additional Psionics: Select one new psychic ability from the *Physical category* at levels 1, 5, 8, 11 and 15.

Habitat: Junk Crabs may be encountered as lone individuals, pairs and small groups of 3D4 in all the oceans of the world, however, nobody knows where they actually live or whether there are large communities of them. Lemurians have found the occasional village of 1D6x10, but like many tribal people (and the Lemurians themselves), Junk Crabs appear to be nomadic and always on the move.

Allies: Anyone willing to trade junk, salvage or share technology. Junk Crabs are always quick to offer their services to repair the exteriors of ships, robots, armor and simple or small machines in exchange for M.D.C. scrap metal, salvage, E-Clips, and bits and pieces of technology, oftentimes even if it is broken. Many are also thrilled to take what humans and others might consider "junk." In other cases, the friendly and tech curious D-Bees will do simple repairs if given the opportunity to simply explore the interior of a submarine, visit the engine room or examine an exotic artifact or alien device. If a person is in trouble and in need of repairs, but has nothing to trade, a Junk Crab may make the repair anyway, telling the person to pay him the next time they meet, or to bring some salvage to his shop in the future. However, a Junk Crab can usually find something he'll take in trade even if it's a Vibro-Knife or spent E-Clip in need of recharging.

Enemies: Junk Crabs do not like pirates, demons, the undead, and the supernatural, and some rumors suggest Metztla hunt and eat them.

Value: As slaves they are generally useless, giving up and dying as if they could not survive in captivity. However, given a free hand and a chance to "be their own boss" or an "equal partner," Crab People can be a good ally and become quite the entrepreneur. Many Junk Crabs establish an amphibious repair shop, trading and repairing technological goods near an island, the mainland, Dead Pools or ship graveyards. They don't understand the concept of money (or credits) and will fix just about anything to see how it works or for what they (the Junk Crab) consider a "fair trade." Which, by the way, most surface dwellers consider a deal in their favor.

Lemurian R.C.C.

All Lemurians are well educated, literate (in Lemurian, if nothing else), versed in mathematics and ethics, open-minded, and never stop seeking knowledge or the attainment of harmony with the natural world.

Lemurians of Rifts Earth see themselves as the "human" protectors and healers of the planet Earth. Most have a high regard for life, are ecologically minded, love nature and wildlife, and care about the well-being of the ocean and all life on Earth. They live in harmony with the environment and value all life forms. They see destructive and wicked supernatural beings such as demons, dark gods and evil Alien Intelligences as their natural enemies and the enemies of mortal beings. Chief among these vile horrors are the *undead* of the Milu and minions of the *Lord of the Deep*, but the Minions of Splugorth are also a serious problem. The Lemurians of Rifts Earth see themselves as the safeguards of nature and life in the natural world and have begun to oppose the forces of darkness to defend the innocent and obliterate the undead and supernatural evil from the planet. They see magic as part of the *natural world* and have no enmity toward creatures of magic unless they behave as a force of destruction and evil.

Genetically altered via Biomancy to what Lemurians consider the peak of perfection, grace and beauty, most are tall, thin, muscular and attractive people. They look relatively human even though they are amphibious.

Special R.C.C. Abilities Common to All Lemurians:

1. Life Sense: All Lemurians can sense the presence of the living through their connection with nature. If given a few moments (takes one melee round/15 seconds), the Lemurian can focus his concentration to pinpoint a specific *type* of animal or plant within his sensing range. Of course, if the animal is hiding, he may feel that it is near, but remain unable to locate it. The presence of the *undead* and *evil supernatural beings* is like a bullhorn broadcasting the monsters' presence and general proximity. Thus, a Lemurian can feel when a vampire, zombie, other type of undead, or supernatural evil, is nearby and avoid it (or attack it). This ability is even more acute in Biomancer Gene-Mages and a few other Lemurian O.C.C.s.

Range: 25 foot (7.6 m) radius plus 5 feet (1.5 m) per level of experience. Base Skill: 20% +5% per level of experience to locate/track/find a specific type of animal or plant, +5% when in an underwater environment. Adds a +5% bonus to the Tracking, Hunting and Identify Plants and Fruit skills when this ability is in play.

2. Empathy with Animals – equates to being "Animal Brothers:" This ability is similar to those of the Psi-Stalker and Simvan. All Lemurians have an automatic affinity with animals of all kinds. Domesticated animals always take an immediate liking to them and will try their best to please them, which automatically gives Lemurians the ability to ride any horse (wild or tame) or any other non-predatory, terrestrial or aquatic animal at a +10% bonus. The same applies to skills that involve working with any domestic animals.

Wild animals, with the exception of monsters, felines, sharks and mutant or alien predators, react to a Lemurian as if he were a fellow wild creature and allow him to walk among them without fear or moving away to avoid him. This ability enables Lemurians to operate in the wild without causing animals to react to their presence: birds do not fly away, fish do not swim off, animals do not run, crickets do not stop chirping, and therefore, do not indicate the Lemurian's approach or presence. Even watchdogs do not sound a bark of alarm at their presence unless the Lemurian takes a hostile action or invades the animal's territory, and *Psi-Stalkers, Dog Boys, mutant bears, Merans, Ichthyleans* and *Amphibs* usually get along with Lemurians.

This affinity with animals means Lemurians see wildlife as their "brothers" – just as the animals see them as a fellow or "brother" animal. This sense of brotherhood means animals, even predators, take no immediate hostile action toward the Lemurian, provided the person behaves in a nonthreatening manner. That changes the moment the Lemurian takes any action to capture, attack, kill, or threaten the animal. In the case of pack animals, the dominant animals (usually the males, but in some cases, females) become defensive and hostile if the Lemurian adopts a dominant or threatening posture, let alone any outright aggressive or challenging behavior. Aggression by a Lemurian, even the threat of it, causes wild animals to flee or fight depending on their nature and the situation. Bulls will attack to protect the herd, and all animals fight to protect their young and mates.

The Empathy with Animals only goes so far, and *animal predators* like sharks, sea serpents, sea dragons, felines, intelligent mutant animals and "monsters" are not welcoming nor accepting of Lemurians. Indeed, Lemurians are seen as fellow hunters, threats and rivals. As such, the creature is likely to target them first in battle, and will not respond to the character in a positive manner regardless of how nice or submissive the Lemurian may behave. **Note:** Xiticix, other insectoids and all types of undead sense Lemurians as *natural enemies.*

The Empathy with Animals means Lemurians *feel* the fear and anguish of animals when they are in distress, scared, ill or injured whether the characters open themselves to such psychic vibes or not. This contributes to their high regard for all living creatures and why Lemurians do not raise livestock for slaughter and consumption. With the exception of *Lemurian Scouts* and a few other O.C.C.s, Lemurians seldom hunt animals for any reason and tend to avoid eating meat, especially the meat of higher animals such as birds and mammals. It is one thing to eat fish, shrimp, lobsters and other simple life forms, but mammals, even those surface people consider to be livestock and cattle, are never raised for food by Lemurians. Most Lemurians also refuse to eat the highly intelligent octopus and squid, and some don't even eat fish if they can avoid it. At least 40% of Lemurians are dedicated vegetarians while 50% include fish, crustaceans and other simple animals as part of their diet along with fruit and vegetables, but seldom mammals. Only 10% – mainly *Lemurian adventurers* who explore and travel the surface world – will consider hunting and eating fowl, cattle, livestock, dinosaurs and wild animals to survive in the wilderness and/or to fit in with surface dwellers. *Lemurian Scouts* who hunt do so out of necessity and make a point to use as much of the slain animal as they possibly can. Many offer up a prayer of gratitude and thanks for their "brother" animal's sacrifice so they may live.

3. Pets and Familiars: The bond Lemurians share with nature and animals is such that most Lemurians have pets. The term "pet" is used very loosely because the animals are more like *friends, helpers* and *companions* than a caged beast or even a house pet. Any animals at a Lemurian's home are likely to have free reign of the house and yard and be treated like members of the family. A favorite animal companion is the traditional *Lemur* and the Biomancy tweaked *Aquatic Lemur* (both described below). Two-thirds of all households have at least one Lemur and many have one for each member of the family. Lemurs can be seen running along side or riding on the shoulders of many a Lemurian mage and citizen alike. Mages love lemurs as Familiars, however most animals, from lemur, dog or cat to monkey, lion, tiger or small dinosaur, may serve as a pet or Familiar.

Lemurian adventurers are likely to be accompanied by a lemur or other animal companion/buddy as well as have a riding animal of some kind. Riding animals can range from the conventional to the monstrous. If given the choice, most Lemurians prefer to ride an animal or walk rather than ride inside of a vehicle. Boats and vehicles that float in or on the surface of water or in the air are the exception, but even then an animal would be preferred.

4. Ultrasonic Communication (special): Besides being able to hear into the ultrasonic sound range, Lemurians can also create high-frequency noises to communicate just like the cybernetic Inaudible Frequency Transmission implant to communicate underwater with whales, dolphins and other Lemurians. This also lets them use the full range of *Whale Singer Spellsongs* for those who study that form of magic (uncommon). Range of Communication:

2,000 feet (610 m) underwater, 400 feet (122 m) on the surface/ in the air.

5. Ley Line Powers (special): Due to their connection to the Earth and their natural aptitude for magic, all Lemurians heal twice as fast as a normal human when on a Ley Line or at stone pyramids. They also recover spent P.P.E. at twice the usual rate and swim 25% faster when along ley lines.

6 R.C.C. Bonuses: +1 on Perception Rolls in general, +2 on Perception Rolls involving plants and nature, plus bonuses gained from high attributes, O.C.C.s and certain skills.

Also see Natural Abilities.

Lemurian Stats

Alignment: Most Lemurians are of a good alignment, Principled (30%) and Scrupulous (38%); some are Unprincipled (10%), Anarchist (7%), Aberrant (5%) and other (10%).

Attributes: I.Q. 2D6+8, M.E. 2D6+8, M.A. 2D6+9, P.S. 2D6+10, P.P. 2D6+8, P.E. 2D6+10, P.B. 2D6+12, Spd 2D6+14 running, double Spd when swimming in water and Lemurians fatigue at half the usual rate; all Lemurians are genetically engineered to be prime specimens.

Hit Points: P.E. attribute number x2 to start, +1D6 per level of experience.

S.D.C.: 3D6 to start, plus those from O.C.C. and some skills.

M.D.C.: By armor or magic only.

Height: 5 feet +3D8 inches (1.6 to 2.1 m).

Weight: 100 lbs to 220 lbs (45 to 99 kg) depending on height, but all muscle. The re-engineered genetic structure of Lemurians makes it difficult for them to become obese, nor do they lose their hair or show signs of aging until quite old.

P.P.E.: 5D6 + P.E. attribute number is the base P.P.E. of the ordinary Lemurian. This base P.P.E. does not increase with experience. Only the P.P.E. of practitioners of magic grows with experience.

The high amount of permanent P.P.E. is due to Lemurian genetic improvements, pre-disposition for channeling magic and their close relationship with nature. The Lemurians' high base level of P.P.E., among those who do *not* take up a magic O.C.C., helps them to bond with Biomancy creations, use Bio-Constructs, and though many Lemurians have had little exposure to Techno-Wizard items (those who have are leery of them and feel the magic is too close to *machine technology* to be acceptable for general use), can intuitively use TW items. **Note:** Lemurians who possess *Master Psionics* have less P.P.E.: 1D6 P.P.E. + P.E. attribute number for their base.

Horror Factor: None. Lemurians look very similar to humans.

Age: Due to their advances in magic, holistic medicine and their re-engineered genetic structure, the average life span of a Lemurian is 300 years, with reports of some reaching 400. Most retain a youthful appearance – look to be in their twenties or thirties – well into their second hundred years, so a Lemurian who looks to be in his forties or fifties is ancient (300 or 400 years old).

Lemurian females may give birth as young as 21 years old and as late in life as 110. Pregnancy is nine months and newborn Lemurians have the ability to breathe air or water as soon as they are born. It is commonplace to give birth *underwater* as it is believed to be much more natural and comfortable for the infant. Lemurian infants, however, cannot swim. Just as human children must learn to walk, Lemurian children must learn to do both. That having been said, most Lemurian children are swimming by seven months and walking by 16 months.

Lemurian children start exhibiting their Empathic Connection with Animals as early as age three, though most do not use it on a frequent basis until age five or six. Other psionic abilities begin to manifest at the onset of puberty, ages 12-13. Master Psychics may start to manifest psionic powers as early as age ten.

Disposition: Lemurian culture is dedicated to peace, learning and compassion. They believe in living in harmony with nature, love the outdoors and enjoy all forms of artistic expression. Even their fighting force is made up of compassionate warrior poets. A curious people by nature, they love to explore and learn about everything. Most Lemurians have a curiosity that knows no bounds and they find almost everything interesting to some degree. Most are intrigued by all things having to do with nature, flora, fauna, science, medicine, history, philosophy, arts and entertainment. While magic is a major part of Lemurian life and the foundation of their technology, the average Lemurian takes it for granted as a "science" rather than mystical; an estimated 20% of Lemurians practice magic.

The optimistic Lemurians tend to be naive and trusting of other people, and they try to accept everyone. Experience on Rifts Earth has taught the open and friendly Lemurians to try to be more wary of new people and unknown magicks, but that is difficult for these beings. Once someone has earned their trust and friendship, most Lemurians are loyal and protective of them to a fault. Their empathic natures also make Lemurians courteous and kind. It is rare to encounter a Lemurian who is demeaning, arrogant or impatient. Their high regard for all life and philosophical points of view prevents them from seeing themselves as better than the next human or D-Bee, just different.

Experience: Non-player characters may range from levels 1-8 (2D4) or as the Game Master desires. *Player characters* should start at *first level* and advance in experience as per their chosen O.C.C.

Natural Abilities Common to ALL Lemurians: High amount of base P.P.E., perfect color and underwater vision, Nightvision 100 feet (30.5 m), keen sense of hearing, resistant to cold (half damage), heals twice as fast as normal humans, and can breathe underwater (gills are located just behind back of jaw near the ears). Though they can move their mouth to speak underwater, they cannot speak words, but can create noises much like a dolphin and speak in tones, clicks and songs much like dolphins and whales.

Depth tolerance of one mile (1.6 km). To go deeper requires environmental body armor, Bio-Skin, Bio-Armor, magic or vehicle. **Note:** While all Lemurians can swim, they must learn the skill just as human children must learn to walk. Of course, they take to it like a duck to water, and most learn to swim before they can walk.

Also see *Psionics* (below) and *Special Lemurian R.C.C. Abilities* (above).

Skills Known by All Lemurians:

Language: Lemurian and Oceania at 96%.
Literacy: Lemurian at 85% +1% per level of experience.
Mathematics: Basic 82% +1% per level of experience.
Swimming at 78% +2% per level of experience.

Common O.C.C.s: As with any civilization, there is a great diversity of occupations and a Lemurian can be any O.C.C. HOWEVER, a Lemurian player character is likely to be one of the *Adventurers & Scholars, Lemurian Men-At-Arms, a Biomancer Gene-Mage* (or other Practitioner of Magic) or a *Psychic O.C.C.* described in this book.

Attacks per Melee: As per hand to hand combat from O.C.C. The average citizen (65%) has *no* combat training. Player characters are the exception and combat skills are as per O.C.C.

Magic: Lemurians have a high affinity and natural aptitude for the use of magic. At least 20% of the Lemurian population are practitioners of magic.

Psionics: Modification to Lemurian DNA insure that all Lemurians have at least *Minor Psionics,* including the following abilities: Empathy (4), Mind Block (4), Telepathy (4), and two Physical or Sensitive psionic abilities of choice. **Note:** The Lemurian Men-at-Arms and some other Lemurian O.C.C.s provide a specific set of psionic abilities different from those listed here; use only those listed for that O.C.C., do not add them to those listed here.

I.S.P. Base for Lemurian Minor Psychics: Equal to the character's M.E. attribute number +1D6 I.S.P. per level of experience.

I.S.P. Base for Lemurian Major Psychics: Equal to the character's M.E. attribute number +8, +2D4 I.S.P. per level of experience.

I.S.P. Base for Lemurian Master Psychics: As per psychic O.C.C. If the character is a *Master Psychic*, a specific Psychic Character Class such as the Mystic or Mind Mage should be selected.

Table for Random Determination of Psychic Abilities:

01-60% Lemurian Minor Psychic. Powers as noted above.

61-90% Lemurian Major Psychic. Empathy (4), Mind Block (4), Telepathy (4), and a total of four additional psionic abilities of choice selected from Healing, Physical and/or Sensitive Categories (7 total), or the abilities specifically named above, plus two of choice from one of the following categories: Healing, Physical or Sensitive, or one Super Psionic Power.

91-00% Lemurian Master Psychic. Roll on, or pick one from, the table below or select any desired Psychic O.C.C. **Note:** If the player does not want to play a Master Psychic, then give the character Major Psionics and pick a non-psychic O.C.C.; ignore the rest that follows.

Players who want to play a Master Psychic for their Lemurian character can select any Psychic O.C.C. from this book, *Rifts® Ultimate Edition* or *Rifts® World Book 12: Psyscape*. Or roll on the table below for random determination:

01-10% Mind Melter (see Rifts® Ultimate Edition)
11-30% Spouter (in this book)
31-50% Shrieker (in this book)
51-60% Psi-Druid (see Psyscape)
61-70% Psi-Healer (see Psyscape)
71-80% Psi-Ghost (see Psyscape)
81-90% Zapper (see Psyscape)
91-00% Burster (see Rifts® Ultimate Edition)

Note: As a special option, the Lemurian character with Major Psionics may trade three of these psionic abilities for ONE of the following Super-Psionic powers: Bio-Manipulation (10), Bio-Regeneration (20), Electrokinesis (varies), Empathic Transmission (6), Hydrokinesis (varies), Psychic Body Field (30), or Psionic Invisibility (10).

Magic: As per O.C.C.

Bionics & Cybernetics: None, ever.

Money: As per occupation (or O.C.C.).

Lemurian Ring-Tailed Lemur

A Common Pet and Familiar

Lemurians have an deep fondness for lemurs. Just as surface dwellers keep cats and dogs as pets, many Lemurians have a lemur. There are several varieties of lemurs, but the *Ring-Tailed Lemur* is the most preferred. Attractive, clever and curious animals to begin with, Lemurian Biomancers have tweaked the animal to make it more domesticated, loyal and smart – as smart as a chimpanzee. The subtle re-design has worked so well that lemurs are the favored Familiar of Lemurian Biomancers and other mages.

In the wild, Ring-Tailed Lemurs associate in groups, called "troops," of 20-40 individuals. The females and young form the core while the males move from group to group. The females are dominant over the males and both genders have scent glands,

which they use to mark their territories. These lemurs are active throughout the day, with most of their time being spent on the ground. They feed on fruit, leaves, bark, grass and resins/sap. Females produce one young after a gestation period of about five months.

Alignment: Considered Anarchist in the wild, but domesticated lemurs are, generally, the equivalent of Scrupulous (20%), Unprincipled (45%) or Anarchist (30%), but can be any.

Attributes of Note: I.Q. 1D6+6 high animal intelligence, M.E. 1D6+5, M.A. 1D6+14, P.S. 1D6+2, P.P. 1D6+14, P.E. 2D6+7, P.B. 2D6+11, Spd 2D6+12 on the ground and climbing, double running and swinging through trees, and swimming is half running speed.

Size: Body is 18 inches (0.4 m) long, plus a long, bushy tail that adds another 22 inches (0.56 m).

Weight: 3-7 lbs (1.3 to 3.1 kg).

Hit Points: 1D6+7. **S.D.C.:** 1D6+9.

A.R.: Not applicable.

P.P.E.: 2D6+4

Disposition: Inquisitive, playful and loyal.

Average Life Span: 7-10 years in the wild, but Familiars and domesticated lemurs live 2D6+15 years.

Natural Abilities: Acrobatics 90%, Climbing 95%, Nightvision 200 feet (61 m), swim 55%, can leap 8 feet (2.4 m) high and 12 feet (3.6 m) across, heightened sense of smell (can track by scent 45%, detect or find plants by smell 65%), exceptional sense of hearing, good daytime vision, and sensitive to the supernatural and magic much like canines, cats and other animals.

Attacks per Melee: Three.

Damage: Bite does 1D4 S.D.C.

Bonuses: +3 on Perception Rolls, +2 on initiative, +1 to strike, +4 to dodge, and +4 to roll with impact/fall.

Value: As a pet, 100-200 credits, as food or fur/tail, 30 credits.

Habitat: Forests, jungles and Lemurian cities.

Range: Used to be found only in and around Madagascar and the African Coast, but can now be found throughout parts of Africa and India, and, of course, all Lemurian cities and outposts.

Allies: As an animal, none per se, but are favored by Lemurians and some humans as pets and Familiars.

Enemies: Are hunted by many large predators, dislike the supernatural and are wary of people.

Lemurian Aquatic Lemur

A Common Pet and Familiar

The Aquatic Lemur is the product of Biomancy genetic engineering. The little fellow resembles the Ring-Tailed Lemur but with somewhat different markings. The most obvious differences are the animal's webbed feet and hands, short fin on its back, gills behind the jaw, and a long tail that looks more like the smooth body of an eel than the fluffy tail of a land lemur. Like its Lemurian pet owners, the Aquatic Lemur can breathe on land and in water, and is equally comfortable in both environments. Even with a fin on the top of its head and back, and a hairless tail, Aquatic Lemurs are clever, cute and playful.

Also Known As: Water Lemur, Ocean Lemur and Sea Monkey.

Alignment: All Aquatic Lemurs are domesticated and live among Lemurians whom they regard as the leaders of their pack. Generally, the creature is the equivalent of Scrupulous (30%), Unprincipled (50%) or Anarchist (15%), but can be any.

Attributes of Note: I.Q. 1D6+7 high animal intelligence, M.E. 1D6+5, M.A. 2D6+12, P.S. 1D6+2, P.P. 1D6+14, P.E. 2D6+8, P.B. 2D6+12, Spd 2D6+10 on the ground and climbing, 50% faster running and swinging through trees, and double Spd when swimming.

Size: Body 18 inches (0.4 m) long, plus a long, hairless tail that resembles an eel and adds another 22 inches (0.56 m).

Weight: 4-8 lbs (1.8 to 3.6 kg).

Hit Points: 1D6+7. **S.D.C.:** 1D6+10.

A.R.: Not applicable.

P.P.E.: 2D6+7

Disposition: Inquisitive, playful and loyal.

Average Life Span: 4-7 years in the wild, but Familiars and domesticated lemurs live 2D6+14 years.

Natural Abilities: Acrobatics 80%, Climbing 75%, Nightvision 300 feet (91.4 m) and can see in murky water, swim 97%, can leap 5 feet (1.5 m) high and 8 feet (2.4 m) across, can dive 100 feet (30.5 m), heightened sense of smell (can track by scent 40%, detect or find plants by smell 60%), exceptional sense of hearing, good daytime vision, resistant to cold (half damage), and can survive depths of up to 8 miles (12.8 km). Aquatic Lemurs are also sensitive to the supernatural and magic much like canines, cats and other animals.

Attacks per Melee: Three.

Damage: Bite does 1D4 S.D.C.

Bonuses: +2 on Perception Rolls when on dry land, +4 to Perception Rolls underwater, +3 on initiative, +2 to strike, +4 to dodge and +2 to roll with impact/fall.

Value: As a pet, 100-200 credits among Lemurians, to the outside world 500-1,000 credits as an exotic pet or oddity.

Habitat: Lives among the Lemurians as pets and Familiars; not found in the wild.

Allies: Lemurians, upon whom they are dependent.

Enemies: The enemies of Lemurians.

Meran R.C.C.

Outsiders do not know whether the Merans are a successful experiment on humans (or Lemurians?) or a friendly, aquatic D-Bee race that has won the confidence and favor of Lemuria. Whatever the truth, the two races don't share that information with outsiders. What is known is that Merans (*mermaids* and *mermen* to the outside world) have been spotted on Earth and other worlds for millennia, coexist with nature and are protectors of the sea. Merans are a race of aquatic humanoids with the upper body of a humanoid and the lower body of a fish, including a tail. Male Merans are typically blue, green, gray, or a combination of those colors with yellow, red or black markings. Female Merans are a myriad of different bright colors such as white, yellow, orange, and light green with dark red, purple or blue markings. For brief intervals of time, both genders of Merans can transform into bipedal form as a sort of "fish person," or can, for a shorter period of time, assume a completely Lemurian or human appearance. This transformation into full human form, with legs, provides Merans the ability to walk on land and, if so desired, among humans without being noticed. Their only limitation is dependence on seawater; without it a Meran will dehydrate, become ill and eventually die.

Earth Merans have thrived as a largely unknown aquatic species, appearing in human records only as myths and stories about "mermaids." They have kept their existence and society a secret for millennia by living in the depths of the oceans, mostly unseen by the people of the surface world. Whether they are D-Bees who arrived on Earth or evolved as a sentient aquatic species, or might even be a forgotten sect of Lemurians who "evolved" themselves further into a truly aquatic species, is unknown. What is known is that they have been around since the rise of the Greek and Egyptian empires dating back at least 8,000 years.

The current monarch of the Merans is *Queen Jennara*, who inherited the throne upon her father's death 50 years ago. Though the Meran population has never been large, their numbers have been severely reduced since the Coming of the Rifts and appearance of the Lord of the Deep. Those who reject the evil god are hunted down and destroyed, and the noble and fiercely independent Merans have suffered at his tentacles. Queen Jennara rules what is left of the small Meran kingdom with compassion and competence. Their realm stretches across what was once known as *French Polynesia* in the South Pacific. With the advent of the Rifts and the rising sea levels, the tropical islands that once populated the area have been submerged, creating a vast undersea paradise of new reefs, underwater mountains and a plethora of fish and other sea life that the Merans have come to cherish.

Meran civilization, though ancient, is not what surface dwellers would consider to be "advanced." Most Merans inhabit small to medium-sized villages (1D4x1,000 is a common population range) and live simple lives. The average Meran village is a collection of stone dwellings underwater. The villagers go to the surface to fish, hunt and gather fruits and vegetables, or to interact with landlubbers. While they appreciate some technology, most of what they use has been salvaged from shipwrecks or acquired through trade with the Lemurians and other aquatic people. They survive by hunting, gathering and undersea farming. It is important to note that unlike Lemurians, who are making contact with the surface world as well as fellow aquatic people, Merans are reclusive and do not trust outsiders, even other aquatic people. Their friendship with Lemurians since the Great Cataclysm is unusual for them. The Merans' high moral standards combined with their love for nature and harmonious existence have made them immediate and easy allies of Lemurians. The two civilizations get along famously, and often refer to each other as "brother" and "sister."

Meran females give birth to one live young underwater and newborns can immediately breathe water and swim. However, though the young have the ability to also breathe air and transform themselves to walk on land or look completely human, most need to be shown this ability and it seldom manifests before age three or four. Merans speak underwater with dolphin-like high-frequency calls, but can speak in air atmospheres without difficulty, and are able to understand and speak any language after being exposed to them for only 1D4 days.

Meran Stats

Optional Player Character or NPC

Also Known As: Mermaids, Mermen and Merfolk.

Alignment: Any, but tend to be Principled (30%), Scrupulous (30%), Unprincipled 10%) and Anarchist (10%).

Attributes: I.Q. 3D6, M.E. 3D6, M.A. 3D6+3, P.S. 3D6+8, P.P. 3D6+2, P.E. 2D6+6, P.B. 1D6+7 (+6 additional in human or Lemurian form), Spd 3D6+32 swimming, reduce by half on dry land/running.

Size: 6 feet (1.8 m) +1D4+3 feet (1.2 to 2.1 m) additional for their tail as Merans. 6 feet +1D6 inches (1.85 to 1.98 m) in Lemurian/human form.

Weight: 200-270 lbs (90 to 121.5 kg), all muscle and they look tall and lean in human guise.

M.D.C.: Since the Coming of the Rifts Merans have been transformed into M.D.C. beings. M.D.C. is P.E. attribute number x4 +2D6 per level of experience. Additional M.D.C. can be added by wearing M.D.C. armor or the use of magic, however, Merans prefer *not* to wear armor, not even Lemurian Bio-Armor. (In S.D.C. environments, Hit Points are P.E. attribute number x2 +1D8 per level of experience, and 1D4x10 S.D.C. plus those from certain skills and O.C.C.)

Horror Factor: None.

P.P.E.: 5D6+25

Disposition: Merans are creatures of the sea who prefer to live in the ocean depths rather than interact with surface dwellers. A curious race by nature, they love to explore and learn about the people around them. However, curiosity has killed many a Meran, so most do so by watching from a safe distance or in human disguise, avoiding direct contact with humans and D-Bees; Lemurians are the exception to the rule. Otherwise, they tend to be brave, noble, and heroic people who are reclusive and voyeuristic beings that keep to themselves or hang with Lemurians.

Average Life Span: 1D6x10+100 years.

Natural Abilities: Swimming 98%, Nightvision 1,000 feet (305 m), keen normal and underwater vision, extraordinary sense of hearing, depth tolerance of 5 miles (8 km), breathe underwater or in air, resistant to cold (half damage), and recover lost M.D.C. at a rate of 1D6 per 12 hours, double at ley lines and at stone pyramids.

Echolocation System: Merans can also hear and discern the reflections or echoes they make using clicks and sounds, like a dolphin, to sense objects around them. While not as precise as a whale or dolphin's echolocation sense, it does help them navigate underwater and detect unseen objects in darkness (reduces penalties for being blind or fighting invisible foes by half, instead of the usual -10). **Base Skill:** 30% +3% per level of experience. **Range:** 500 feet (152 m).

Metamorphosis: Humanoid: Merans may have evolved from humans/Lemurians, which could explain why they are born with the ability to shape change into bipedal imitations of them to travel on land. Merans have two humanoid forms. The "fish-man" retains his natural, fish-like appearance and scales, but turns his tail into humanoid legs. In this form a Meran can stay on land and out of water for 24 hours per level of experience and maintains all his attributes, M.D.C. and natural ablities.

By focusing just a little harder, Merans can take on the appearance of a Lemurian, True Atlantean or human. However, in this "human" guise, reduce M.D.C. and P.S., P.P. and P.E. attributes by 40%, depth tolerance is reduced to one mile (1.6 km), and the human form can only be maintained for two hours per level of experience.

When a Meran is forced to stay on dry land beyond his humanoid limit, the character returns to his normal, fish form, with tail, cannot change back into a human for 48 hours after he has been revitalized by water (assuming he survives), and suffers penalties from dehydration: Reduce the M.D.C., attributes and abilities of his previous humanoid form by half, attacks per melee round and all combat bonuses are also reduced by half, and crawling speed on land in fish-man form is 1D4+3. Reduce M.D.C. by half for each additional 24 hours denied submersion in water. Being placed in a tank of water restores the Meran by 25%, but the individual must be released back into the sea to recover completely (full abilities within 1D6 hours and recovers lost M.D.C. as usual, but cannot transform into a humanoid for 48 hours).

Ultrasonic Communication: Besides being able to hear into the ultrasonic sound range, Merans can also create high-frequency noises to communicate just like the cybernetic Inaudible Frequency Transmission implant. They use this ability to communicate underwater with whales, dolphins, Lemurians and other Merans.

R.C.C. Skills: Swimming 98%, Fishing 88%, Underwater Navigation 85% and Undersea Survival 70%.

Available O.C.C.s: 60% of Merans are Wilderness Scouts of one variety or another, 15% an Adventurer O.C.C. or Vagabond, 11% Oceanic Guardsmen (or the equivalent), and 10% are practitioners of magic (Ocean Wizard, Sea Druids, Sea Inquisitors and Whale Singers being the most common, though there a few Biomancer Gene-Mages). Only 4% of the Merans select a technology based O.C.C. like the Salvage Expert, Operator, Scientist, Body Doc, etc., or join up with Tritonia or other outsiders, and are typically viewed with suspicion in Meran society.

Experience Level: 1D6 or as set by the Game Master for NPCs. Player characters should start at first level. Experience table as per O.C.C.

Attacks per Melee: As per Hand to Hand Combat skill.

Damage: As per combat skill, weapon or magic.

Bonuses: +2 on sound based Perception Rolls, +1 on initiative, +2 to parry and dodge, +3 to automatic dodge underwater only, +2 to disarm and pull punch, +1 to save vs magic and psionics.

Vulnerabilities: Merans need seawater to keep their skin hydrated and their bodies functioning properly; without it they die.

Psionics: None.

Magic: By O.C.C. only; uncommon.

Standard Equipment: As per O.C.C.

Money: As per O.C.C.

Cybernetics and Bionics: None to start. Though Merans are not afraid of bionic enhancement, any bionic system installed on the tail or legs will be rejected during shape-changing.

Habitat: Merans are found throughout the oceans of the world, though they tend to avoid the Mid-Atlantic due to the presence of the Minions of Splugorth, particularly Conservators, Slavers and Metztla. These days, they are found mainly in the Pacific and Indian Oceans and among Lemurians. The main Meran colony is in and around the group of sunken islands once known as French Polynesia, though only a handful of those islands pierce the surface today. Their kingdom is an aquatic paradise just below the waves. As curious and adventurous people, over the centuries, thousands of Merans have traveled to other ocean worlds, many making new homes in those dimensions.

Alliances and Allies: The Merans consider Lemurians to be their brothers and sisters, and both people would lay down their own lives to save the other. As a result, one seldom encounters a group of one without the other being present. Whales, dolphins and Sea Druids are generally considered friends and allies, while Ichthyleans are regarded as friendly rivals. Amphibs, Junk Crabs, the New Navy and other outsiders are viewed with suspicion and caution, but not enmity.

Enemies: For Merans, the invading Naut'Yll are seen as the most dangerous and hated of enemies, as the two have clashed many times, and Merans fear the threat they represent is underestimated by Lemurians and most other people. The Minions of Splugorth, the Lord of the Deep and his minions, Davey Jones, the Milu undead, demons and anyone who threatens Merans, Lemuria or the oceans, round out the list of enemies. Merans are suspicious of human Tritonians, dislike and distrust them, and believe Amphibs are their dupes and second-class citizens. As close allies of Lemuria, the enemies of Lemuria are the enemies of most Merans. Meanwhile, surface dwellers, in general, are viewed as unpredictable and potentially dangerous people judged on an individual basis.

New & Notable Skills

Aquatic Skills

Advanced Fishing (30% +5%)
Horsemanship: Aquatic Animals (40%/20% +4%)
Horsemanship: Sea Monsters (30%/20% +4%)
Horsemanship: Serpent Hunter (70%/50% +3%)
Language: Cetacean (30% +4%)
Language: Ichthylean/Milu (Ick-thih-lee-an/Me-loo)(15% +2%)
Language: Lemurian (50% +5%)
Language: Oceanic (50% +5%)
Lore: Sea Creatures (25% +5%)
Marine Biology (35%/25% +5%)
Ocean Geographic Surveying (15% +5%)
Sea Holistic Medicine (20% +5%)
Swimming & Fatigue Note
Track & Hunt Sea Animals (35%/25% +5%)
Undersea Farming (35% +5%)
Underwater Navigation (30% +4%)
Undersea Salvage (30% +5%)
Undersea & Sea Survival (25% +5%)

Physical Skill

Hand to Hand: Demon Combat (Kapu Kuialua) (Ka-poo Koo-ee-ah-loo-lah)

Piloting Skills

Advanced Deep Sea Diving
Pilot Related: Navigation
Submersibles (40% +4%)
Symbiotic Conduit Vehicles Combat (60%+2%)
Warships & Patrol Boats (40% +4%)
Water Scooters (50% +4%)
Water Skiing and Surfing (40% +4%)

Weapon Proficiencies

W.P. Net
W.P. Harpoon & Spear Gun
W.P. Torpedo
W.P. Trident

Note: The following skill descriptions are either new or reprinted from **Rifts® Underseas™** for your convenience.

Aquatic Skills

Advanced Fishing (Also a Technical Skill): The normal Fishing skill has to do with the recreational sport of fishing with a hook, pole and line. *Advanced Fishing* is the knowledge of commercial fishing techniques, including the use of nets, cages (for lobsters and crabs), trolling, explosives, harpoon guns and other methods and techniques used in commercial fishing of mass catches from the ocean. It also includes a knowledge of baiting, as well as cleaning, preparing, storing and preserving catches for transport to market. **Base Skill:** 30% +5% per level of experience. **Note:** -15% when dealing with alien creatures and mutants.

NEW: Horsemanship: Aquatic Animals: This skill is fundamentally the same as *Horsemanship: General* except the riding animals are not horses, but aquatic animals such as giant manta rays, giant stingrays, sea turtles and other large aquatic beasts of Earthly, otherworldly and Biomancy origin. **Note:** This skill also applies to riding cetaceans (dolphins and whales), except these mammals are intelligent and can only be ridden when the cetacean agrees to let a humanoid ride on its back. **Base Skill:** 40%/20% +4% per level of experience (+20% on a cetacean that is willing to let one or more people ride on its back).

NEW: Horsemanship: Sea Monsters: This skill is fundamentally the same as *Horsemanship: Exotic Animals* except the riding animals are not horses, but large to massive aquatic monsters and sea serpents of Earthly, otherworldly and Biomancy origin. **Note:** This skill also applies to riding sea dragons, other types of dragons and sentient monsters that willingly agree to let humanoids ride on their backs. **Base Skill:** 30%/20% +4% per level of experience (+20% if the monster is intelligent and is willing to let one or more people ride on its back).

NEW: Horsemanship: Serpent Hunter: This skill is fundamentally the same as *Horsemanship: Cyber-Knight* except it applies to any large aquatic animal, sea monster or sea serpent. **Base Skill:** 70%/50% +3% per level of experience (+10% if the monster is intelligent or a serpent, and is willing to let the Serpent Hunter ride on its back).

NEW: Language: Cetacean. This is the language used by dolphins, whales and pneuma-biforms through their ultrasonic communication. It can be learned and spoken by any race with the ability to hear and communicate into the *ultrasonic range*, including Lemurians, Merans and cyborgs with the Ultra Ear and Inaudible Frequency Transmission implants. Each species of whale, dolphin and porpoise has a distinct "dialect" as does each family group, but for game simplicity it is assumed to be one common language spoken by all cetaceans. Understanding or speaking this language is impossible without the ability to hear into the ultrasonic range or create ultrasonic tones/sounds. Some legends speak of pre-Rifts scientists creating a device that enabled them to learn the Cetacean language and communicate with dolphins and whales, but any such device is presumed to have been lost in the Great Cataclysm. **Base Skill:** 86% +1% per level of experience for characters with whom this is a "native" language (this includes *Lemurians* and *Merans*). Characters learning it as an additional language have a base of 30% +4% per level of experience. Provides a +5% bonus to learn Ichthylean/Milu.

NEW: Language: Ichthylean (includes Milu). All Ichthyleans communicate underwater using Telepathy, chemical exchanges, clicks, chirps, thumps and body language; out of water they also use gurgling noises. Their chemical/gurgling language is referred to as Ichthylean and thus far, can only be spoken by Ichthyleans, though humans and other races have tried to understand and mimic the sounds to communicate with them. **Base Skill:** 88% +1% per level of experience for Ichthyleans. All others attempting to learn it as an additional language have a base of 15% +2% per level of experience. As a result, Ichthyleans communicate with humans and most sentient life forms via Empathy and Telepathy.

NEW: Language: Lemurian. This is an ancient form of Polynesian (which later expanded into the seven main Polynesian cultures of Aotearoa, Hawai'i, Rapa Nui, Marquesas, Samoa, Tahiti and Tonga) with a few root words that have been carried over into Chinese, Indian/Hindi and some African tribal dialects. **Base Skill:** 88% +1% per level of experience for Lemurian native speakers; -20% to speak other dialects and forms of Polynesian. Non-Lemurians may take this skill as an additional language and start at a Base Skill of 50% +5% per level of experience.

NEW: Language: Oceanic. This is a blending of several Southeast Asian and Pacific Rim languages (much like Euro) that share a common root. In essence it is a blend of Thai, Malaysian, Indonesian, Vietnamese, Chinese and Polynesian. **Base Skill:** 88% +1% per level of experience for native speakers; those learning it as an additional language have a base of 50% +5% per level of experience. Those who speak Lemurian enjoy a +10% bonus when they take this language skill as well.

NEW: Lore: Sea Creatures. General knowledge and practical information about the sea and sea life from seaweed, reefs, crustaceans, fish, aquatic mammals and other animals, to stories, myths and legends about sea monsters, sea serpents, Lemurians, Merans, Milu, the Lord of the Deep and his minions, as well as the New Navy. Includes tips about watching your step in certain areas of the beach and lagoons, being careful of poisonous or sharp/stinging fish, mollusks and other sea life, as well as first aid treatments such as urinating on jellyfish stings to relieve the pain and symptoms, to what to do when one encounters a shark, how to stay alive and what to do during a shark feeding frenzy. **Base Skill:** 25% +5% per level of experience.

Marine Biology (Also a Science Skill): This skill is a general knowledge of the ecology of oceans and seas, with an emphasis on undersea habitats, environments, and the types of fish and sea animals living in such places. This skill also gives the character the knowledge of where to look for particular types of sea creatures (e.g. in coral reefs, under rocks, inside caves, warm water, cold water), the types of food sea animals eat/prey upon, migration patterns of fish and sea mammals, and a knowledge of tides, water composition, and ocean plant-life.

The Marine Biology skill also gives the character specific medical and scientific knowledge about the behavior, habits, evolution, physiology, cells, anatomy, and genetics of fish, marine mammals and other types of sea life. This knowledge enables the character to perform surgery, remove glands and sacs of poison or chemicals, prepare antidotes to poisons (from sea creatures only) and the care, keeping, and medical treatment of marine animals, including dolphins and whales. **Basic Skill:** 35%/25% +5% per level of experience. The first number is the character's general knowledge. The second number is specific medical and scientific applications, including making antidotes to poison, capturing animals without killing them (+10% to hunt/kill), surgery (sea animals only; -60% on humanoids), and the care, keeping and medical treatment of marine animals. **Note:** -30% when dealing with alien and mutant life forms. **Requirements:** Biology, Advanced Mathematics and Chemistry.

Ocean Geographic Surveying (Also a Science Skill): The methods and ability to identify natural geographic formations (mountains, trenches, coral reefs, etc.), identify wreckage and underwater cities, identify Earth minerals, damage caused by earthquake and earthquake zones, determining depth, accurate map making, accurate map reading and geographic photograph identification and evaluation, as well as a basic knowledge of geology and oceanography. **Base Skill:** 15% +5% per level of experience (+15% to read maps).

Sea Holistic Medicine (Also a Medical Skill): Training in the recognition, preparation, and application of natural medicines derived from aquatic plants/seaweed and animals, including ink, blood, poisons and other secretions and chemicals. This skill also includes the knowledge of where to find the necessary plants or animals, how to extract the necessary components and some knowledge of legends as they pertain to the healing properties of the sea and sea animals. Otherwise, the skill is fundamentally the same as the standard Holistic Medicine skill. **Note:** The standard skill does NOT include medicines derived from the oceans and seas, likewise, the sea holistic knowledge does NOT include most of the land herbs and plants (only a handful of the very most common and basic items). **Base Skill:** 20% +5% per level of experience. A failed roll means the treatment or concoction did not work.

Swimming & Fatigue Note: For humans and similar surface dwelling D-Bees, the act of swimming on the surface has the same fatigue rate as running and medium to heavy exertion, especially at great speed or very long periods of time. Swimming underwater with S.C.U.B.A. equipment or other underwater equipment is considered to be light activity, unless extremely active, involved in combat or fast swimming (in which case it is considered strenuous or heavy activity).

For most aquatic life forms, including Amphibs, Naut'Yll, Lemurians, aquatic D-Bees and mutants, sharks, dolphins, whales, and sea mammals, underwater activities such as fast swimming, diving, playing and underwater acrobatics are considered light activities and can be conducted for hours without fatigue. Pulling a heavy load and combat are both considered medium to heavy activity.

Remember that the buoyancy of water *reduces the weight of most items by 30%* when used/carried underwater. This means the fatigue rate for carrying a heavy load is reduced by 30% or 30% more can be carried at the normal fatigue rate. Characters can also lift 30% heavier weights.

Track & Hunt Sea Animals (Also a Wilderness Skill): General knowledge of the oceans and seas, with an emphasis on undersea habitats and environments, and the types of fish and animals that live in such places. The character knows where to look for particular types of fish and sea creatures (i.e. in coral reefs, under rocks, inside caves, in warm water, cold water, etc.), the types of food the sea animals eat/prey upon, migration patterns of fish and sea mammals, and notable types of seaweed and their uses (edible, poisonous, etc.). **Basic Skill:** 35%/25% +5% per level of experience. The first number is the general knowledge, and the second is the character's ability to locate and capture small and large undersea creatures (crustaceans, fish, eels, sea mammals, etc.). **Note:** -20% when dealing with mutants and alien creatures.

Undersea Farming (Also a Science Skill): The knowledge of cultivating undersea plants, algae, and/or breeding aquatic animals/fish for harvesting and production. Undersea Farming includes, but is not limited to, growing crops (either through hydroponics or on the ocean floor), lobster farms, oyster beds, and fish hatcheries. **Base Skill:** 35% +5% per level of experience.

Underwater Navigation (Also a Wilderness Skill): This skill is the deep sea version of Land Navigation. The character can identify his whereabouts, direction, traveling speed, and stay on course by means of observation. This method includes mentally marking and recognizing underwater landmarks (mountain ranges, reefs, sunken wreckage, cities, animal habitats, etc.), as well as noting the direction of currents, tides, determining the time of day, recognizing sounds, surface landmarks, the positions of the stars and sun, and other navigational tricks. The character should roll once for every ten miles (16 km) traveled in order to stay on track. A failed roll means he is drifting off course by 1D6x100 yards/meters. Consecutive failed rolls means the individual does not realize that he's off course and continues in the wrong direction. His course can only be corrected when he makes a successful roll. **Base Skill:** 30% +4% per level of experience. Penalty: -25% when in deep ocean waters away from the bottom of the sea where there are no discernable underwater landmarks, only water.

Undersea Salvage (Also a Technical Skill): The character knows how to locate and identify objects (ships, armor, gold, etc.), recognize salvageable components and materials (valuable parts, electronic equipment, E-Clips, weapons, coins, magic items, precious metals and gems, etc.), retrieve (with minimal damage and effort), evaluate (estimate approximate resale value based on the item's condition), clean/restore (restoration gets top salvage price), and sell salvaged underwater artifacts, equipment, parts, and scrap metal. The skill also offers methods of exploiting and capitalizing on some of the simple resources under the seas, including rudimentary mining, excavation, and gathering coral, rocks, seaweed, sponges, clams, oysters, and starfish. The character is also familiar with underwater cutting tools, cranes, pulleys, and tow lines, and can strip/cut apart and retrieve wreckage and machinery for use as scrap metal. Those with Mechanical Engineering can salvage working parts, make repairs on slightly damaged items, and even raise small sunken ships, subs, and 'bots! **Base Skill:** 30% +5% per level of experience; add a bonus of +5% if a mechanical engineer.

Undersea & Sea Survival: Methods and information for surviving in an underwater environment or lost at sea (on the water's surface). Includes a basic knowledge of what sea animals and fish are edible and easiest to find and catch, how to make simple fishing hooks and lines, dangerous predators and D-Bees to avoid, how to protect oneself from the sun, water and food rationing, and fundamental survival techniques. **Base Skill:** 25% +5% per level of experience. **Note:** At the G.M.'s option, this can be included as part of a character's basic *Wilderness Survival skill* rather than as a separate skill. This is especially likely of Navy men, Sailors, Pirates, Sea Druids, Ocean Wizards, Lemurians and aquatic D-Bees.

Hand to Hand: Demon Combat

NEW! Hand to Hand: Kapu Kuialua: Also known as Pa Kuialua or Lua or Lemurian Demon Combat, this martial art form was created by the *Mauian Order* and roughly translates as "Forbidden way to fight," but its secrets leaked outside of the order and the martial art has been adopted by Lemurian *Ocean Guardsmen* and *Serpent Hunters*. Though it may, in theory, be learned by anyone, few ordinary Lemurians, let alone outsiders, learn Kapu Kuialua. First, it is one of the Lemurians' less shared secrets. Second, the practitioner must have a reserve of P.P.E. he can call upon in order to inflict Mega-Damage to the supernatural. Third, the mastery of the demon slaying martial art requires intense mental focus, many physical demands, and years of practice and training. Though practitioners of magic have more than enough P.P.E. most lack the physicality, stamina and time necessary to master magic *and* this demanding martial art. Thus, Biomancers never learn Kapu Kuialua, and rarely do other mages, such as Ocean Wizards, learn this martial art. When a practitioner of magic does learn Kapu Kuialua, his personal P.P.E. number, O.C.C. bonuses and starting number of spells are *reduced by half* compared to other mages of the same O.C.C. Likewise, the usual Kapu Kuialua bonuses listed below are also reduced by half when learned by a mage.

Kapu Kuialua was developed by the Mauian Order using their knowledge of the supernatural and, some say, dark and forbidden arts from other worlds. It is a form of physical martial arts that draws upon magic energy and the fighter's chi (inner spirit) to inflict physical damage against supernatural creatures impervious or resistant to ordinary weapons and attacks. Furthermore, the focus and training hardens the fighter, physically and mentally, against supernatural attacks. As a result, Kapu Kuialua fighters are able to inflict M.D. to flesh and blood supernatural beings and creatures of magic with their bare hands, but not to man-made M.D.C. structures (i.e. body armor, robots, vehicles, walls, etc.). This is due, in large part, to *the focus* of the combat training, which is to slay the supernatural and dangerous creatures of magic like dragons.

To engage in Kapu Kuialua Mega-Damage combat, the trained warrior needs one full melee round (15 seconds) to focus and prepare himself for battle. Then, he draws upon his chi and expends 13 points of P.P.E. For the next minute or several minutes, the human warrior is able to fight, parry and inflict M.D. to his inhuman adversary via punches, kicks and other martial arts maneuvers. Though not a magic spell, this martial art requires its user to draw upon his P.P.E. base or ambient P.P.E. such as the energy of a ley line or stone pyramid. P.P.E. must be spent to make M.D. attacks via Kapu Kuialua. Without sufficient P.P.E., the fighter's combat bonuses remain, but he only inflicts S.D.C. damage. Furthermore, even when Kapu Kuialua combat is in force, only Hit Point/S.D.C. damage is inflicted against mortal (Hit Points/S.D.C.) opponents. Mega-Damage attacks are only possible when leveled against M.D.C. supernatural enemies and creatures of magic; no damage to man-made M.D.C. armor or D-Bees, though the Kapu Kuialua fighter can parry attacks from Mega-Damage opponents with his bare hands.

Range: Empowers self only.

Mega-Damage: The character's usual S.D.C. punch and kick damage does Mega-Damage (M.D.) when it is directed against supernatural and magical creatures. Each S.D.C. point becomes M.D., including P.S. and skill bonuses to damage. For example, if the character's normal punch or kick does 1D6+7 S.D.C. damage (the "bonus" coming from skill and/or P.S. attribute bonuses), it now does 1D6+7 M.D. to the supernatural and creatures of magic. If the warrior is a D-Bee who already does M.D. damage (a rarity), then increase his normal M.D. by 50%. (In an S.D.C. setting, a fighter trained in Kapu Kuialua does double damage to supernatural beings and creatures of magic, and a Critical Strike goes direct to the monster's Hit Points.)

The martial artist can also parry the M.D. punches, kicks, claw strikes and other attacks of man-sized Mega-Damage opponents (beings under 10 feet/3 m tall), but he may need some type of M.D.C. armor or magic to survive any attacks that get past his defenses. **Note:** The bonuses and M.D. of Kapu Kuialua combat do not apply to handheld weapons such as clubs, knives, swords, etc. Damage is either inflicted by the bare hand martial art or by the M.D. of the weapon, not both.

Duration: One minute per level of experience; double at a ley line, stone pyramid or Lemurian ziggurat, quadruple at a nexus point.

P.P.E. Cost: 13 points must be expended to engage in Kapu Kuialua Mega-Damage combat with supernatural opponents.

Limitations: Developed by Lemurians and seldom taught to outsiders. Only a character dedicated to martial combat and possessing at least 16 P.P.E. points can learn Kapu Kuialua. Even among Lemurians, the practitioners of the martial art are limited to *Oceanic Guardsmen* (60%), *Serpent Hunters* (36%), select members of the *Mauian Order* (2%) and *others* (2%).

Level 1: The following techniques and maneuvers are known at first level. Body flip/throw, body block/tackle, holds, roll with impact, pull punch, disarm, punch (1D4 damage), knee and elbow strikes (1D6 damage), kick attack (2D4 damage), plus the usual strike, parry and dodge. **Note:** Whenever an attack or saving throw indicates the word "demon," this includes all types of supernatural beings, including demons and Deevils.

Starts with four attacks/actions per melee round, +1 to roll with impact and +2 to pull punch.

Damage Against the Supernatural: As described above, normal punch and kick damage inflicts M.D. to supernatural beings and creatures of magic when the necessary focus and 13 P.P.E. are spent. Duration: One minute/four melee rounds per level of experience.

Hardened Against the Supernatural: +1 on Perception Rolls and +1 to save vs Horror Factor.

Level 2: +1 on initiative and +1 to strike.

Damage Against the Supernatural: Snap kick (1D6 damage) and knife hand (2D4 damage).

Hardened Against the Supernatural: +2 to save vs Seduction.

Level 3: +1 to disarm, +1 to entangle and +1 to save vs Horror Factor.

Damage Against the Supernatural: Snap kick (1D6 damage) and knife hand (2D4 damage).

Hardened Against the Supernatural: +2 to save vs demonic possession (does not apply to psionic attacks).

Level 4: One additional attack per melee and +1 to parry.

Damage Against the Supernatural: Karate kick (2D6 damage).

Hardened Against the Supernatural: +3 to save vs insanity and magic-based illness.

Level 5: +1 to strike and disarm, and +1 to save vs Horror Factor.

Damage Against the Supernatural: +2 to punch and kick damage, and +1D6+1 points to the character's base P.P.E.

Hardened Against the Supernatural: +2 to save vs demonic mind control and +5% to save vs coma and death.

Level 6: +1 to dodge, and Critical Strike on a Natural 18-20.

Damage Against the Supernatural: Palm strike (2D6 damage), and Critical Strike from attacks made from behind.

Hardened Against the Supernatural: +2 to save vs attacks directed at the soul.

Level 7: Paired weapons, +1 to strike and +1 to save vs Horror Factor.

Damage Against the Supernatural: Stone fist strike (3D6 damage).

Hardened Against the Supernatural: Stone hands enables the warrior to grapple, hold or parry beings and weapons made of or covered in fire or energy.

Level 8: One additional attack per melee and +1 to disarm.

Damage Against the Supernatural: Palm strike (2D4+2 damage).

Hardened Against the Supernatural: Impervious to demon fire, heat blasts and lava attacks, as well as dragon fire breath attacks. **Note:** Magic fire from spells and magic weapons, as well as man-made weapons, still do full damage.

Level 9: +1 on initiative, +1 to strike, and +1 to save vs Horror Factor.

Damage Against the Supernatural: +3 to punch and kick damage, +2D6+2 to the character's base P.P.E.

Hardened Against the Supernatural: +3 to save vs curses (including magical curses), +2 to save vs dark magic, including Demon Magic, Necromancy, Soulmancy, and magic that changes alignments, corrupts, compels or dominates/controls.

Level 10: +1 to Perception Rolls and +2 to pull punch.

Damage Against the Supernatural: Stun Kick, a special move and type of kick that is either directed at the head or spine. The kick does 3D6 damage and if the roll to strike was a Natural 15 or greater, the supernatural opponent is momentarily stunned/impaired/slow to react: reduce the monster's bonuses and remaining number of attacks for that one melee round by half. Recovers by the next melee round.

Hardened Against the Supernatural: +2 to save vs all forms of possession (including psionic) and insanity.

Level 11: +1 to strike and entangle, and +1 to save vs Horror Factor.

Damage Against the Supernatural: Lightning Kick – two rapid-fire kicks, each doing 2D6 damage (4D6 total), but counts as one melee attack. On a roll of a Natural 19 or 20 the victim is also stunned and loses 1D4s attack that melee round.

Hardened Against the Supernatural: Impervious to demonic petrification.

Level 12: +2 to body flip/throw and +1 to pull punch.

Damage Against the Supernatural: Double damage to the undead, including vampires, zombies and the animated dead (skeletons, etc.).

Hardened Against the Supernatural: Breathe Without Air (same as the third level Spell Invocation) and impervious to vampire mind control and Trance magic and psionic attacks.

Level 13: Death Blow! See core rule book for details. Triple damage on a Natural Twenty and the creature's body cannot Bio-Regenerate the damage inflicted by the Death Blow for 1D4 hours. +1 to save vs Horror Factor.

Damage Against the Supernatural: Double damage to Lesser Demons.

Hardened Against the Supernatural: +3 to save vs illusion magic and Seduction, and impervious to demonic cold attacks.

Level 14: +1 attack per melee round and +1 to strike.

Damage Against the Supernatural: Double damage to Greater Demons.

Hardened Against the Supernatural: The warrior using Kapu Kuialua can erect a light, magical force field, reminiscent to Armor of Ithan, that has 1D4+3 M.D.C. per level of experience. Duration is five minutes or until all M.D.C. is gone. P.P.E. cost to erect this magic force field is 6 points.

Level 15: Critical Strike on a Natural 17-20, +1 initiative, and +1 to save vs Horror Factor.

Damage Against the Supernatural: Triple damage to the undead, including vampires, zombies and the animated dead (skeletons, etc.), and can hit and inflict normal punch and kick damage (no damage bonuses) to ghosts/Entities, Astral Beings and other ethereal and energy beings.

Hardened Against the Supernatural: Impervious to possession and +15% to save vs coma/death.

Piloting Skills

Advanced Deep Sea Diving: Skill in the methods, techniques and equipment used in deep sea diving and exploration. Includes the use of most types of diving suits, diving pods (attached to tethers/life lines) and light to medium *power armor*! It does not include combat models.

Pilot Related: Navigation Note: Navigating marine vessels is an aspect of the standard Navigation skill. The basic skill described in the **Rifts®** core rule book enables the character to pilot ships, war ships and other water vessels that ride on the surface of the water by charting the stars and landmarks and using instruments. Likewise, the character can navigate *submersibles* using instruments and other data, but does so with a -10% penalty.

Submersibles: The knowledge and skill of piloting all types of submersibles, including underwater sleds, mini-subs and most types of submarines, including military submersibles. For Lemurians, this skill offers +20% to pilot Cloud Wind, Cloud Shell and Scuttler units underwater and is necessary to pilot Wave Shadow submarines. **Base Skill:** 40% +4% per level of experience. **Note:** -20% when using alien or unusual submarines. Does not include power armor or deep sea diving suits.

Symbiotic Conduit Vehicle Combat: Lemurian combat vehicles are powered and controlled via a link to an organism known as the Symbiotic Conduit. In theory, most anyone can pilot these vehicles as they virtually fly themselves, but Lemurian warriors with this skill get the following bonuses. **Base Skill:** 60% +2% per level of experience (plus any O.C.C. bonus). **Combat Bonuses for Trained Lemurian Pilots:** +1 on initiative, +2 to strike using the vehicle's weapon systems, +2 to dodge, half the usual penalty for evasive maneuvers, stunt flying and crash landings, and +1 attack per melee round at levels 2, 4, 8 and 12. **Note:** All bonuses are in addition to the pilot's own hand to hand combat training and attribute bonuses. They do *not* apply to the pilot's physical abilities outside the vehicle.

Pilot : Warships & Patrol Boats: Special training in the use of military warships, combat hydrofoils, patrol boats and amphibious beachcraft/transports. Includes a basic idea of how to use sonar and targeting equipment, depth charges, torpedoes, and other common weapon systems, as well as evasive maneuvers and piloting. **Base Skill:** 40% +4% per level of experience. **Note:** Characters with the Boat: Motor or Boat: Ships skill can also pilot these vessels, but at a -12% penalty.

Pilot Water Scooters: The knowledge and skill of piloting all types of one- and two-man water sleds (underwater) and jet skis (surface sleds). **Base Skill:** 50% +4% per level of experience.

Pilot: Water Skiing & Surfing: All water skiing techniques, methods and use of most types of recreational forms of "riding the waves," including skis, ski jet boots, water boards, surfboards and sail boards. **Base Skill:** 40% +4% per level of experience.

Weapon Proficiencies

W.P. Net: Usually thought of as a gladiator or slaver's skill, the net is used by many aquatic people and fishermen. As a weapon, it is used to parry, trip and snare/entangle. To trip an opponent the net is slung in such a way that it hooks the foot, ankle or leg, followed by a quick, strong tug that knocks the opponent off his feet or stumbling to keep his balance (loses initiative and one melee attack). When used like a whip, a net does 1D4 S.D.C. damage. **Bonuses:** +1 to strike at levels 2, 5, 8, 11 and 15. +1 to entangle at levels 2, 5, 8, 11 and 15. +1 to parry at levels 2, 4, 6, 9 and 12. Bonuses are in addition to those gained form other skills such as Hand to Hand Combat.

There are two other types of attacks possible with a net:

1. Snaring an opponent's weapon: The weapon becomes entangled and is pulled out of the opponent's hand. A natural, unmodified (no bonus) roll of 18, 19 or 20 will disarm an opponent in this way, unless he can roll an equally unmodified high parry (no bonuses).

2. Snare/entangle an opponent by throwing or looping the net over him. The intended victim must dodge or be netted. Only characters with a *spear, pole-arm or staff* can parry a thrown net attack. If caught in the net, the victim is -8 to strike, -10 to parry and dodge, and running is impossible. If netted underwater, the trapped individual is unable to swim and immediately begins to sink at a rate of 6 yards (6 meters) per melee round (15 seconds). It takes 1D4+1 melee rounds to cut free of a net provided the trapped individual has a cutting tool or weapon and that his adversary doesn't press his attack to slay or further bind and incapacitate the netted character.

If the character dodges or the net thrower misses, it is the net wielder who may suddenly find himself weaponless. Even if the net has a drawstring attached to it, the thrower needs one melee action/attack to pull it back to him or to grab a different weapon. The throwing of a net to capture an opponent requires the use of *two hands* (no bonuses to strike or entangle when thrown with one hand). However, if the net is being used to parry, entangle or whip an opponent, it can be used with one hand, while the other wields a sword or other weapon; parry the same as usual. Using the net as a whipping weapon does 1D4 Hit Point/S.D.C. damage. **Underwater Note:** Cannot be "thrown" underwater more than 10 feet (3 m) unless the net is being tossed down to a lower depth, but the attacker is -2 to strike targets at a further distance.

W.P. Harpoon & Spear Gun (Rifle-Size): Proficiency with the harpoon gun. The weapon can be used either with a plain pointed end (2D6 S.D.C. damage) or with an explosive head (4D6 M.D.). **Bonuses:** +1 to strike at levels 2, 4, 7, 10 and 15. **Range:** 700 feet (213.3 m) in the air, half that range underwater.

W.P. Torpedo: Maintenance and a keen understanding of a torpedo's speed, range, trajectory, and most effective use. **Bonuses:** +1 to strike at levels 2, 6 and 12. +1 to strike with a depth charge at level four.

W.P. Trident: The practiced use of the trident as a weapon. The Trident is a spear-like weapon with three sharp points similar to a "pitchfork." It is especially useful underwater because it can jab, stab and slice, as well as being an exceptional weapon for disarming and pinning opponents.

"Catch" or "Pin" an opponent's arm, hand, foot or weapon between the prongs: +1 at levels two, five, ten and fifteen. If a limb is caught or pinned, the trident user can twist and swing the trident with a quick movement that forces the "pinned" opponent to follow the movement and be "flipped" off his feet or upside down underwater. The victim of a body flip is thrown to the ground/down/over and loses initiative and one melee action/attack. An underwater victim is flipped upside down or out of the way and loses initiative and one melee action/attack. A trident can also be used to pin an opponent by snagging the hand or ankle between the prongs or through an article of clothing and stabbing the business end of the weapon into a coral reef, a sunken boat, floor, wall, etc. to hold his opponent in place. The pinned appendage is stuck until the trident is pulled out. If the attacker lets go of the trident the pinned victim needs 1D4+1 melee rounds to pry the trident loose due to lack of leverage. Of course, the attacker has a distinct advantage if he abandons the stuck trident and presses his attack with another weapon or even his bare hands.

Typical damage is 3D6 S.D.C. or 3D6 M.D. depending on what it is made of or whether it is a magic weapon. It can be thrown 50 feet (15.2 m) in the air or 30 feet (9 m) underwater. **Bonuses:** +1 to strike and parry at levels 1, 3, 7, 11 and 15.

Underwater Combat (Optional)

By Matthew Clements

Fighting underwater is far different from fighting on land. Visibility is dramatically reduced, speed and accuracy are both affected and the reality of fighting in a three-dimensional space is difficult for surface dwellers to get used to. A different fighting style must be adopted, and those with no experience in underwater combat will see themselves at a significant disadvantage.

Restricted Vision: The biggest differences underwater are in vision and propulsion. Humans and most humanoid D-Bees are simply not equipped with the fins, flaps and webbing necessary for moving through water. Our eyes are also designed to see in air, and even with goggles or masks, the maximum visibility in most water, especially deep water, is 100 feet (30.5 m) or less.

Underwater Combat Penalties for Surface People: Non-aquatic races like humans suffer penalties of -2 on initiative and Perception Rolls and -2 to strike, dodge or parry when fighting in close combat underwater. Accuracy with ranged weapons is unchanged. Amphibious races like Lemurians, Splugorth Slavers, the Naut Y'll and Amphibs are unaffected, and fight equally well on land or underwater.

Fatigue: In addition to the listed penalties, humans and other land dwellers also fatigue at twice their normal rate in water.

Cold Waters: In cold water less than 50 degrees Fahrenheit (F) or 10 degrees Celius (C) with no wetsuit or armor, humans and humanoid D-Bees will be unconscious in 4D4x10 minutes, and likely to be dead 2D6x10 minutes after losing consciousness.

In water near or below freezing (32 degrees F/zero C), unconsciousness or exhaustion generally sets in within 3D6+15 minutes, and death follows within 1D4x10+25 minutes of exposure. Penalties: Double combat penalties, above, for humanoids in cold water less than 50 degrees F (10 C), and triple penalties in freezing water less than 32 degrees F (0 C). Of course, none of this is applicable to those in power armor, Bio-Armor or protected via any number of magic spells, including Swim as a Fish and Armor of Ithan. Even full environmental body armor can keep its wearer warm (and breathing)for five hours; indefinitely if an external source of oxygen is available.

Underwater Weaponry

Combat beneath the waves requires different weapons and fighting techniques.

Thrown weapons are almost useless underwater. However, throwing a *spear, trident* or similar weapon works to a limited degree. The attack is -2 to strike, and the spear will slow down until it is no longer a threat after traveling *one third* its normal surface throwing distance, but such attacks are possible.

Firearms. Modern bullets may be able to fire underwater, but guns are designed for air in between their moving parts, not water. Bullets are also not suitably hydrodynamic, and will slow dramatically once they leave the barrel, making them non-lethal beyond 15 feet (4.6 m). Hollow-point rounds break into pieces becoming ineffective after only five feet (1.5 m). Traditional firearms are not very common on Rifts Earth.

Rail guns are operational underwater, as they rely on electrical current running between rails to push their projectiles, not chemical explosions. However, reduce rail gun range by *half.*

Different types of **energy weapons** all perform at various levels underwater. **Normal lasers** work, albeit at *half range*. **Blue-green lasers** are specifically made for aquatic use; full damage and range. **Ion weapons** work as well underwater as in air, and are popular amongst pirates, salvagers and divers. **Plasma** and **particle beams** both boil their way through the water in front of them, throwing up clouds of bubbles and superheated liquid that can make it difficult for the shooter to see. It also reduces their range and damage by 70%.

Weapons that Work Underwater

- Punches, kicks and most close combat attacks.
- Knives, hatchets and short swords.
- Vibro-Blades.
- Spears, harpoons and tridents.
- Spear guns and harpoon guns.
- Ion weapons.
- Blue-green lasers.
- Magic spells that are not fire based.

Weapons with Reduced Effect Underwater

- Laser weapons: 50% normal range, full damage.
- Rail guns: 50% normal range, full damage.
- Particle beam and plasma weapons: 30% normal range and damage, and each blast obscures the shooter's vision (-3 to strike on all shots fired for 1D4 melee rounds after the first shot).
- Crossbows: 40% normal range, full damage.
- Electrical weapons: 30% normal range and inflicts 20% of normal damage as an *area effect to everything* (including the shooter!) within 25 feet (7.6 m). Includes magic electricity.
- Conventional firearms: Full damage at point-blank range (under 5 feet/1.5 m); half damage from 6-15 feet (1.8 to 4.6 m); no damage past 15 feet (4.6 m).
- Hand grenades and most explosives will explode and do full damage to their full radius. HOWEVER, they cannot be thrown underwater. Dropping a grenade downward is -4 to strike, and sinks slowly so the person dropping it will get caught in the spherical blast radius unless quickly swims in the opposite direction. This is why shaped charges used underwater, placed exactly where wanted, and detonated remotely or on a timer.

Weapons That Do Not Work Underwater

- Flying kicks, leap kicks and body throws (still deprives target of initiative/melee attacks, but inflicts no damage).
- Most blunt weapons like bats, clubs, war hammers and staves.
- Thrown weapons, including darts, shuriken and throwing knives.
- Bows and arrows, including compound bows.
- Flamethrowers and fireballs.
- Slings, slingshots and whips.
- Magic fire and magical flight capabilities.

Lemurian O.C.C.s of Note

By Greg Diaczyk and Kevin Siembieda

There are a wide range of occupations and character classes in Lemuria, from academics and experimenters, to a variety of practitioners of magic, but the O.C.C.s presented in this section are the most likely to go forth into the world, go on adventures, join adventurer groups, fight evil and make excellent player characters.

Lemurian Practitioner of Magic

Biomancer Gene-Mage

Lemurian Men-At-Arms

Birdman Warrior
Oceanic Guardsman
Sea Sentinel
Serpent Hunter

Lemurian Adventurer

Lemurian Scout

Lemurian Psychic

Spouter

Lemurian Practitioner of Magic O.C.C.

Biomancer Gene-Mage

By Greg Diaczyk and Kevin Siembieda

Inspired by the source material found in **Rifts® World Book 6: South America**, created by C.J. Carella and Kevin Siembieda.

The Biomancer Gene-Mage practices a more developed and advanced version of the Biomancy known to the Jungle Elves of South America. Lemurian Gene-Mages have learned to use Biomancy to create living weapons, tools, armor, and riding animals to meet most of their and Lemurian society's needs without using machines or killing living beings. Since Lemurian Biomancers inhabit both the terrestrial and underwater environments, they have tailored many Biomancy spells for life both undersea and on dry land.

Biomancy is one of the most powerful systems of magic ever devised, but it is also one of the rarest and is virtually unknown throughout most of the Megaverse. The main reason for this is the

fact that the users of Biomancy must have a very close relationship to nature and an incredibly high regard for life – all life. So while in theory, Gene-Mage Biomancy can be learned by anybody, few are able to embrace the natural world enough to do so. For Lemurian Biomancers, it means becoming vegetarians, giving up city ways and big city comforts, forsaking the use of machines, electronics and technology, and becoming absorbed with the preservation of nature, wildlife and living in harmony with the environment. Things most people are not willing to do. This mindset is much more difficult to achieve than one might suspect, and it greatly limits who can and cannot wield Gene-Mage Biomancy. This is why beings like the Splugorth have given up trying to learn the mystic art and mock and trash-talk its practitioners.

Many Lemurian Gene-Mages are so committed to the natural world that they will not enter a city or civilized area unless absolutely necessary. For many Biomancer Gene-Mages this includes Lemurian cities, which are often more like botanical gardens than what most surface dwellers would consider to be cities. Likewise, self-contained underwater habitats and submersibles with hydroponics or botanical gardens are entered with a bit of reluctance. This disdain for all things mechanical, technological and cities is due to the fact that such things often harm, if not destroy, large expanses of nature, pollute the air and water, play havoc with wildlife and ecosystems, and create an ugly, unnatural, artificial environment. For many Lemurians, not just Biomancer Gene-Mages, technology is viewed with distrust, disgust and as an unholy alliance with "dead" things. From their perspective, reliance on machines and technology is to become cut off from the natural world and become partially dead oneself. By Lemurian standards, the *Coalition States* with their megalithic fortress cities, squalid 'Burbs, massive war machines, Dead Boy armor, and Skelebots are the poster child for how not to live.

The only known dimensions where Biomancy exists are the Green World from which the Jungle Elves migrated, and now, Rifts Earth, which has been influenced by the Lemurians and Jungle Elves.

Biomancy is life. Biomancy is based on life, healing and living. As a result, Biomancy is the direct magical and philosophical opposite of *Necromancy* and practitioners of these two schools are deadly enemies. *Biomancy* should not be confused with *Splugorth Bio-Wizardry*, which also affects living beings, but is intrusive, enslaving and damaging to both the recipient of the magic and the organisms used in it. To most Biomancers, Splugorth Bio-Wizardry is a mockery of life that creates abominations via a synthesis of dark magic, enslavement, and monstrous symbiotes and parasites used for foul purposes. Biomancer Gene-Mages also abhor the creation of Rune Weapons, and never use them. After all, Rune items are powered by the life force of innocent victims forever enslaved within the weapon.

Three Schools of Biomancy

There are three basic "schools" of Biomancers. They are known as *the Acceptors, the Patient Ones* and *the Defenders*. The O.C.C. abilities and skills are fundamentally the same for each. It is the view of the world and the Biomancer's relationship within it that defines the three different philosophies.

The Acceptors, like their name indicates, tolerate the crimes committed by sentient beings against nature as part of the process of evolution. They only object to the most extreme acts of inhumanity, pollution and deforestation; many *Merans* and a few Lemurians and Biomancer Gene-Mages are Acceptors. The Acceptors can be found in or near cities and are not above traveling in vehicles, living in artificial houses or using technological items. However, they avoid cybernetics, Techno-Wizardry, Bio-Wizardry and Rune Weapons and exhibit an obvious respect for life and nature. These characters are often vegetarians and will not hunt or kill any animal or plant except in self-defense.

The Patient Ones do not accept crimes against nature. They prefer to live away from such people and the stench of their cities in remote all-natural communities. They take no action against the misguided destroyers and polluters, except to try to repair the damage they have inflicted and to defend the land or sea they have claimed as their domain. Patient Ones are close to nature and use technology and Techno-Wizard items only as a temporary, last resort. They absolutely abhor Bio-Wizardry, Rune Weapons and other forms of magic that enslave or damage any life form. Most *Lemurians, Ichthyleans* and *Biomancer Gene-Mages* are Patient Ones. Many are vegetarians and abstain from eating, hunting or harming animals, even fish and insects.

Patient Ones get along best with characters who have a high regard for all life. They find the use of robots, cybernetics, bionics and artificial augmentation distasteful and treat such characters coolly or with open disdain or revulsion.

The Defenders are the most militant and extreme of the Biomancers. Not only do they reject technology, machines and the "ways of death" used by most civilized sentient species, but they also take an active role in stopping damage to nature by others. They reject all technology as evil and unnatural and only use it under the most extreme circumstances, and sometimes not even then. Many have gone so far as to declare war on city people of all levels of technology, destroying polluting factories, sabotaging mining and lumber operations, and sometimes killing those responsible. Most will not hesitate to punish or slay anyone who dares to damage forests or slay animals or kill their fellow beings in their presence. The most brutal and extreme punishments are reserved for those who kill or destroy deliberately for pleasure or profit without regard for people, fauna or the land. An estimated 7% of Lemurians and Biomancer Gene-Mages are Defenders, and 30% of the members of the *Mauian Order*. Defenders are always vegetarians and abstain from eating, hunting or harming animals, fish, insects and even plants. They inflict brutal retribution upon those who exhibit no respect for nature or life.

Biomancer Defenders try to avoid associating with meat-eaters, supernatural beings, scientists, cyborgs, Robot Pilots, Techno-Wizards, Operators and other tech-based individuals, and find City Rats, Headhunters, Cyborgs, robots, Crazies, Juicers, and others who use cybernetics, bionics, robotics or artificial augmentation to be absolutely repugnant. Many even frown upon the *Acceptor Biomancers* who are regarded as too tolerant, and *Patient Ones* for being weak (but acceptable). The most hated of all are the undead, the Milu, Necromancers, demons and Deevils (both of whom thrive on hate, enslavement, torment, war and the destruction of life), the Splugorth, their minions, Bio-Wizards and the makers of Rune Weapons/items. Defender Biomancers get along best with other Biomancer Defenders, Serpent Hunters, Patient Ones, Faerie Folk, wilderness people and characters dedicated to defending life and preserving and nurturing nature.

The Lemurian Philosophy of Life. Many Lemurian civilians in other walks of life fall into one of the three philosophical outlooks described above. They tend to see sea creatures, plants and animals as their "brothers" worthy of the same respect, honor and right to live as any human being. The Lemurians and their Biomancer Gene-Mages understand that living creatures must eat and use plants and other animals to survive. They recognize that the way of the predator is part of the circle of life, and an aspect of nature. Thus, while they may be disappointed and unsupportive of hunters and cattlemen, and their practice of slaying and eating animals and wearing their skins, *most Lemurians* do not consider such people to be monsters or criminals. The same is true of the *Serpent Hunters* and their sea serpents, who the Biomancer Gene-Mages feed with fish and try to minimize their impact on other species. However, sentient beings who kill only for sport, pleasure or for one small part of the animal (fins, oils, skin, tusks, feet, teeth, etc.) and discard the rest or take only trophies are seen as monsters and despoilers of nature.

The Lemurians' high regard for life makes them patient and tolerant of other life forms and their unpleasant ways, but they don't like it. When they can, they try to teach people to live in harmony with nature, and hope their own good example will inspire others to live better. The only beings Lemurians have learned to destroy without mercy are vampires and other undead, demons and evil supernatural beings. They have learned the hard way that such wicked beings are born filled with hate and driven by vile instincts to torture, harm and destroy all that is good, beautiful and natural. Lemurians have taken an "attack first and ask question later" approach when dealing with such loathsome creatures. Their link to nature helps them sift out evil supernatural despoilers from the native Earth and alien life forms that now call Earth home.

Lemurians, especially Biomancer Gene-Mages, try to never become destroyers themselves. Slavery of any kind is despised and Biomancer Gene-Mages, Oceanic Guardsmen, Sea Sentinels, Spouters, Scouts and Serpent Hunters are quick to rescue and free the enslaved, and slay any enslavers who try to stop them. This judgment includes cruel Shifters, Bio-Wizards, masters of Rune Magic, and the Lord of the Deep and his minions. They have little respect or appreciation for robots, artificial intelligences and automated machines. (Should they ever find out about A.R.C.H.I.E. Three, they'll freak out and want to hunt it down and destroy it.)

Plant P.P.E. and Biomancer Gene-Mages

Plants, like all living creatures, gather and store ambient P.P.E. as a natural part of life. Unlike animals, humans and D-Bees, the amount of P.P.E. held within a plant is comparatively tiny, but nonetheless, it still exists. Most practitioners of magic consider the amount negligible and subconsciously ignore what little P.P.E. is available, preferring to draw their energy from ley lines, nexus points, human volunteers or blood sacrifices. Another reason why plant P.P.E. is often ignored is the difficulty in extracting it. Most plants are unwilling to give up their P.P.E. freely (as well as have a natural immunity to P.P.E. loss due to the intrinsic properties of the plant's cells), and cutting them down won't kill them quickly so their P.P.E. remains intact and lingers for a long time (many species of plants can be plucked and replanted or at least continue to live if placed in water). Only completely destroying a plant, typically by fire, kills it quickly and releases the doubled amount of its P.P.E., which still is miniscule. However, the Biomancer Gene-Mage's connection with plants enables him to get past the plant's natural resistance and encourage it to share its available P.P.E. with the Gene-Mage. They can draw P.P.E. from one acre of land at a time.

Most grasses, flowers, ferns, small shrubs, patches of algae, seaweed and other small plants can typically offer *1D4 P.P.E.*

from one acre (43,560 square feet/4,047 square meters) a day; add 2 P.P.E. if the plants are bearing some kind of fruit.

Coral is not a plant, but P.P.E. can be drawn from it in a similar way as plants. In this case, the Gene-Mage coaxes coral into sharing up to *3D6 P.P.E. from one acre* (43,560 square feet/4047 square meters) a day. The Great Barrier Reef off the coast of Australia is an exception as it is not true coral, but a mysterious being, much like the Millennium Trees. Its stats, magical artifacts and communities of creatures that live in and around it will be detailed in a future sourcebook.

Medium to large shrubs, small trees and columns of seaweed can provide *1D6 P.P.E. from one acre* (43,560 square feet/4047 square meters) per day; add another 1D6 P.P.E. if the plants are bearing some kind of fruit.

Fully grown trees provide *3D6 P.P.E. from one acre* (43,560 square feet/4,047 square meters) per day; add another 1D6 P.P.E. if the plants are bearing some kind of fruit.

Large (over 100 feet/30.5 tall), ancient (over 200 years) trees and giant trees (like the Redwoods of British Columbia, Canada) and similarly long-lived or gigantic plants may provide as much as 2D4+1 P.P.E. per *each tree*; add 1D4 P.P.E. per 1,000 years of age.

The Gene-Mage can draw upon 1D4+1 large or ancient trees at a time when channeling the trees' P.P.E. In the case of smaller plants and coral, the Biomancer Gene-Mage can tap into *one acre* at a time. As always, once the P.P.E. has been channeled from those plants and spent by the Biomancer Gene-Mage, it is no longer available until 24 hours have passed. Add one additional acre of P.P.E. at levels 4, 8 and 12.

Note: Only the Biomancer Gene-Mage can tap into and draw upon the negligible amounts of P.P.E. in plant life. Also note that Lemurian stone pyramids and ziggurats are almost always covered in fruit bearing plants and trees, providing additional P.P.E. for Gene-Mages to tap into, as well as for the aesthetics, fruit, nuts and vegetables.

O.C.C. Abilities and Bonuses of the Biomancer Gene-Mage:

1. Life Sense: Like all Lemurians, the Biomancer Gene-Mage can sense the presence of the living through his connection with nature. However, the Gene-Mage's sensitivity is twenty times greater than the average Lemurians. If given a moment (counts as one melee action), the Gene-Mage can focus his concentration to pinpoint a specific *type* of animal or plant within his sensing range. Of course, if the animal is hiding, he may feel that it is near, but remain unable to locate it. The Biomancer Gene-Mage can also tell if a living creature or plant is dying and why (old age, injury, sickness, etc.), and roughly how long it has left to live.

The presence of the *undead* and *evil supernatural beings* is like a bullhorn broadcasting the creatures' presence, proximity and general location. Also see #2, Sense Death and the Unnatural.

Range: 500 foot (152 m) radius plus 50 feet (15.2 m) per level of experience. Base Skill: 35% +5% per level of experience to locate/track/find a specific type of animal or plant (+5% when in an underwater environment), and adds a +10% bonus to Tracking, Hunting and Identify Plants and Fruit skills.

2. Sense Death and the Unnatural: The Biomancer Gene-Mage's awareness of all "living" things around him in the "natural" world makes him keenly sensitive to supernatural evil, the undead and death in general. The mage can also sense major disturbances and destruction in nature, be it caused by people or natural phenomena. Thus, the Biomancer Gene-Mage can sense a dead forest, deforestation, strip mining, poisoned or polluted water, radiation zone, and similar areas of blight and destruction. Anything that interferes with the natural order of life is felt by the Biomancer Gene Mage. They radiate their alignment and foul intentions, which the Biomancer Gene-Mage senses like a sickening nausea.

This ability is automatic, meaning the character does not have to concentrate nor expend P.P.E. or I.S.P. to feel death or unnatural forces at work. (Remember, Lemurians consider magic to be a force of nature.) The sensation is very general, especially at first, alerting the Biomancer Gene-Mage to the presence of death, destruction or supernatural evil, and a general direction, but without any other information. The closer the Gene-Mage gets to the source of the disturbance in nature, the stronger the sensation gets, but he still lacks specific data. All that might change is a sense that the destruction or death is minor, serious, major or horrific. In the case of the supernatural, the Biomancer Gene-Mage may be able to sense that the creature is a lesser, greater or deific level of evil and power, or that there are few, many or very many present. The mage can also tell if the supernatural evil is near or far, approaches, waits or is leaving the area. Range: 500 feet (152 m) plus 100 feet (30.5 m) per level of experience. Quadruple the range to sense the presence of extraordinarily powerful evil creatures such as the Lord of the Deep or the Reachers of the Deep. This also applies to any other Alien Intelligences or god-like beings of malevolent nature, like the Splugorth.

3. Psionic Empathy with Animals: Same as all Lemurians.

4. Communicate with Plants and Animals: The Biomancer Gene-Mage (and a few other Lemurian O.C.C.s) can make contact with nearby terrestrial and aquatic animals and plants. This form of communication does not occur in words, but in a manner similar to Empathy. The Biomancer gets *flashes* of past or ongoing events involving the animal or plant, but the flashes of insight and images are limited to the creature's senses and perception. For example, a tree notices when a man climbs it. It feels his weight and touch, just as it will feel heat if someone shoots an energy weapon near its trunk or branches, or sets fire to it, but the tree is not able to "see" the individual or identify his features. This means the tree can only relate what it knows to the Gene-Mage and a face is not part of that information. HOWEVER, plants hear and respond to sound, so it may know a name, or some other identifying sound. Or know that one hand was hard and not made of flesh, and may be able to offer the approximate weight, size and shape, as well as smell.

The communication also allows the mage to calm down enraged animals, but only if he can project a sense of peacefulness towards the creature. Chance of Success: The communication is automatic, and the attempt to calm the animal has a base chance of 40% plus 5% per level of experience (does not work against supernatural monsters). Range: 120 feet (36.6 m).

In the case of the Lemurian Biomancer Gene-Mage, he can make contact with terrestrial and aquatic plant and animal life, from sea mammals and fish to mollusks, crustaceans, coral, plankton, algae and similar sea life. Plankton, krill and beds of algae and seaweed can fill several square miles and such colonies may be able to provide information as to the directional bearing of a boat or swimmer, or whether the target or traveler is still within its body or colony. The same applies to coral reefs. For example, a coral reef notices if a boat goes screaming by overhead and feels the waves and engine vibrations. If the boat is still traveling along the length of the reef, it can give the Gene-Mage a good idea of its location and the direction the boat is traveling. Likewise, the coral reef knows if people or items were dropped from the boat and are resting on the reef or where they may be swimming within the reef's frame of reference. However, the coral reef is unable to see what kind of boat it is or how many people are aboard, what it is carrying, etc.

Animals are a different story as they see things, and so visual information should be available to the Gene-Mage. However, the images come in "flashes" and the impressions are from the animal's point of view. The ability to communicate with animals also enables the Biomancer Gene-Mage to calm down enraged or frightened creatures, but only if the mage can project a sense of peacefulness toward it. This may be impossible if the animal is reacting to having already been attacked or if it is injured (reduce Chance of Success by half). Creatures that take an aggressive or defensive posture or are consumed by pain are nearly impossible to communicate with, and the only information one can get from them is pain, hostility and a desire to strike out and kill in retaliation. Animals locked into a hunting bloodlust or feeding frenzy, like sharks, can only be calmed down if the source of blood and death that has made them frenzied is removed or sealed up, but the chance of success is only one-quarter the normal rate.

Chance of Success: Communication with plants and animals is automatic. The attempt to calm an animal has a base chance of 35% +5% per level of experience (+10% for Biomancer Gene-Mages communicating with sea creatures). Half if the animal is alien to Earth, a quarter if the animal is in the throes of a blood frenzy or is injured and in pain. This ability does not work on supernatural monsters, creatures of magic or intelligent beings, such as humans and other sentient beings.

Range: 60 feet (18.3 m) plus 10 feet (3 m) per level of experience, increase by 50% for Lemurian Biomancer Gene-Mages when underwater (unchanged on dry land). This ability combined with the Lemurian's natural psionic ability of *Empathic Connection with Animals* provides the Lemurian Biomancer Gene-Mage a bonus of +15% to any skill that relates to, or interacts with, animals such as Horsemanship and Animal Husbandry.

5. Healing Touch: The Biomancer Gene-Mage can manipulate the tissues of living things, repairing damage from wounds, burns, bruising, poisons, etc., with but a touch and a focused desire to heal. The touch restores 1D6 S.D.C./Hit Points or 1D4 M.D.C. points per level of experience to any one plant, animal or person. The Biomancer Gene-Mage can also use this healing power on himself. This ability requires no expenditure of P.P.E. or I.S.P. but can only be performed *three times per 24 hours* at first level experience, then four times a day at 5th level, five times a day at 10th level, and six times a day at 15th level.

6. Gifts of Nature: All Biomancers can convert living organic matter into edible food! By concentrating and expending 8 P.P.E., the Biomancer can convert any part of a living plant into a fruit-like organ (the "Gift") with enough nutritional value to keep a person fed for one day. This applies to plants above and below the waves. As a result, Biomancer Gene-Mages can turn seaweed and algae into a delicious, edible fruit.

The magic only works on trees, bushes or larger plants, or in the case of seaweed and algae, a patch that is at least 10 feet (3 m) in diameter. The transformation can only be done on one plant a set number of times. As a rule of thumb, a bush will only provide one Gift, a man-sized plant 1D4 Gifts, a medium-sized tree 1D4+2, and so on, with the largest trees able to provide 1D6x10 Gifts. In the case of seaweed and algae, a dense, 10 foot in diameter patch produces one Gift of fruit. Trying to exceed a plant's limit (the Biomancer senses exactly how many times he can ask for a Gift) inflicts 2D6 S.D.C. damage to the tree/plant and generates a psychic backlash that does 1D4x10 S.D.C. to the mage (or M.D. to a Mega-Damage being or Biomancer clad in Bio-Armor). **Note:** This power cannot be used on Millennium Trees or any sentient plant life. When tried on a Millennium Tree, the attempt results in temporary injury to the Tree and a Mega-Damage explosion to anybody near the tree (see **Rifts® World Book 3: England** for details about the energy releases of the Millennium Tree).

7. Gift of Peace: The Biomancer's unique link to the ecosystem gives him an aura that protects him from most animals and even some monsters. Animals from mosquitos to elephants never attack the Biomancer, except in self-defense. Undersea this includes fish, jellyfish and sharks – even sharks under the effects of a blood frenzy. Most of the time, the animals get out of his way or swim around him. Creatures affected by a blood lust/frenzy, like sharks, carry on with their normal frenzied behavior, but do not attack the Biomancer, even if he is the source of the blood. Even predatory animals and some alien monsters with animal intelligence, like mutant sharks and dinosaur-like creatures, will not attack the Biomancer Gene-Mage unless the animal is cornered, injured or attacked first, or is extremely hungry and desperate, or the Gene-Mage is unable to defend himself. Intelligent creatures, supernatural monsters, demons, creatures of magic and people are unaffected by the Gift of Peace.

8. Create Bio-Constructs: Biomancers can create weapons, armor and equipment by magically altering living matter. The process is somewhat similar to Eco-Wizardry and Bio-Wizardry, but it affects living animals and plants without hurting them. The magic essentially creates a symbiotic union between the animal(s) and the Biomancer and allows him to form a *Bio-Construct* he can wear or use. The more advanced creations of the *Biomancer Gene-Mage* often take a higher degree of scientific knowledge and understanding of living organisms (biology and genetics) to facilitate the creation of complex weapons, armors and symbiotic unions. The most elaborate creations like Bio-Armor and genetically-engineered war steeds are brought to life by powerful, high-ranking Gene-Mages with the help of assistants and special facilities. The rituals necessary for their development are carefully guarded secrets reserved for masters of the art, and not available to standard player characters. See **Standard Equipment** at the end of the stat block for the range of Symbiotic Bio-Constructs, Bio-Weapons and Bio-Skins to start.

9. Bonuses: +4 on Perception Rolls involving Biomancy, symbiotic organisms and genetic manipulation (half involving other magicks and nature), +1 to save vs magic at levels 4, 7, 10, 12 and 15, +2 to save vs Horror Factor, +20% to save vs coma/death, +3 to save vs Bio-Manipulation magic (including Agony, Blind, Mute, Life Drain, Sickness, Curses, Metamorphosis and Transmutation), and +1 to save vs disease. The Gene-Mage also gains a +1 to Spell Strength (the number others must save against when you cast a spell) at levels 3, 6, 9 and 12.

10. P.P.E.: 3D6x10 plus P.E. attribute number to start, +3D6 P.P.E. per each additional level of experience. The Biomancer Gene-Mage can also draw P.P.E. from ley lines, nexus points, and other people the same as the Ley Line Walker and other mages, as well as plants (see Plant P.P.E., above).

11. Initial Spell Knowledge: The Biomancer Gene-Mage's understanding of magic comes from his link with nature and develops much like a Mystic. As the mage grows in experience he is able to hone and master his magical abilities, and develop Biomancy talents that go beyond spell casting and simple manipulations of plants and animals. At the highest levels, (NPC) Biomancer Gene-Mages can manipulate their subjects on a molecular level, adjusting D.N.A. or what they call the "Code of Life," from modifying and improving existing creatures to creating living armor and monstrous life forms – as reflected in some of the new, higher level Biomancy spells, Bio-Armor and Riding Beasts.

Selecting Magic Spells: At first level, the Biomancer Gene-Mage selects a total of *six Biomancy spells* from levels 1-4, plus three Ocean Magic spells. Biomancer Gene-Mages learn at least a handful of Ocean Magic spells.

At level two the Biomancer Gene-Mage gains four new spells selected from levels 1-5 Biomancy or Ocean Magic spells.

At level three the Biomancer Gene-Mage gains a total of four new Biomancy spells from levels 1-6 and two Ocean Magic or common Invocation spells.

At level four and every level after that, the character gains two new Biomancy spells that can be selected from any level up to four levels higher than his own current level of experience.

Biomancer Gene-Mage O.C.C.

Also Known As Pauu Goltar, Lemurian Biomancer, Lemurian Gene-Mage and just Gene-Mage or Biomancer.

Alignment Restrictions: Any, but Principled (30%), Scrupulous (35%) and Unprincipled (12%) are most common.

Attribute Requirements: A minimum I.Q. and M.A. of 14 or higher are required, a robust P.E. (13 or higher) is suggested, but not required.

Race Restrictions: Gene-Mage Biomancy has been developed by Lemurians so it is known only to Lemurians and the handful of people with whom they associate. The Biomancer Gene-Mage is nearly exclusive to Lemurians (94%) and nobody is better at it than they. However, a few other beings have been taught the secrets. They include Merans (5%) and a handful of rare others (1%), including a few humans. **Note:** Lemurians only share the secrets of Gene-Mage Biomancy with individuals they believe have the potential to do great good with the magic and share their philosophy of life.

Skills Known by All Lemurians:

Language: Lemurian and Oceanic at 96% +0.5% per level of experience.
Literacy: Lemurian at 86% +1% per level of experience.
Mathematics: Basic at 82 +2% per level of experience.
Swimming at 76% +2% per level of experience.

O.C.C. Skills:

Biology (+20%)
Botany (+30%)
Chemistry (+10%)
Language: Other: Two of choice (+10%).
Literacy: One of choice (+20%).
Lore: Animals/Cattle (+25%)
Lore: Demons and Monsters (+15%)
Lore: Sea Creatures (+20%)
Lore: Vampires (60% +3% per level of experience)
Marine Biology (+30%)
Mathematics: Basic (+20%)
Mathematics: Advanced (+15%)
Sea Holistic Medicine (+25%)
Undersea and Sea Survival (+10%)
W.P.: Two of choice (any).
Hand to Hand: Basic, which may be upgraded to Expert at the cost of two O.C.C. Related Skills, Martial Arts at the cost of three and *Hand to Hand: Kapu Kuialua* at the cost of four O.C.C. Related Skills.

O.C.C. Related Skills: Select four skills at level one. Plus select one additional skill at levels 4, 8, 10 and 14. All new skills start at level one proficiency.

Aquatic: Any (+5%).
Communication: Any, but the following skills in that category get a +10% bonus: Barter, Creative Writing, Language, Literacy, Performance, Public Speaking and Sing only.
Cowboy: None.
Domestic: Any (+5%).
Electrical: Basic only.
Espionage: Detect Ambush, Detect Concealment, Intelligence and Tracking only.
Horsemanship: General or Exotic Animals only (+10%).
Mechanical: Basic only.
Medical: Any (+15%), except Cybernetic Medicine.
Military: None.
Physical: Any, except Boxing and Acrobatics.
Pilot: Boat: Paddle, Boat: Sail, Jet Pack (Squid Pack), Water Skiing & Surfing all get a +10% skill bonus. Other Pilot skills, except military ones, can be taken but with a penalty of -10%.
Pilot Related: Any.
Rogue: Gambling, Imitate Voices and Sounds, Palming, Seduction and Tailing only.
Science: Any (+10%), except Artificial Intelligence.
Technical: Any (+10%), except Computer Operation, Programming, Cybernetics: Basic and Jury-Rig.
W.P.: Any, except Heavy Weapons.
Wilderness: Any (+10%).

Secondary Skills: The character also gets to select three Secondary Skills from the Secondary Skills list in **Rifts® Ultimate Edition**, page 300, plus one additional Secondary Skill at levels 3, 5, 9 and 13. These are additional areas of knowledge that do not get any bonuses, other than any possible bonus from having a high I.Q. All Secondary Skills start at the base skill level.

Standard Equipment: Special and/or additional weapons and gear may be assigned for special situations and missions. See the *Bio-Construct section* elsewhere in this book for the full range of Bio-Armors, Bio-Weapons, symbiotes and gear.

Bio-Constructs: Bio-Armor: ANY; select two; one is kept in stasis/suspended animation until needed. Also has access to all types of Bio-Skins.

Bio-Constructs: Symbiotes: ANY. Starts with a Living Saddle, Morphic Riding Bio-Barding, Sea Doctor and 1D4+1 other Symbiotic Bio-Constructs of choice, which may include other non-lethal types of weapons.

Bio-Constructs: Bio-Weapons: ANY. Starts with one Bio-Construct melee weapon and one long-range weapon of choice (any).

Lemurian War Steed: ANY; starts with 1D4 War Steeds, but can only use one at a time and is extremely unlikely to lend them out to others, especially outsiders. Plus one animal companion, usually an Aquatic Lemur.

Miscellaneous: A knife, 1D4 ceremonial robes, a set of dress clothing and casual clothes, a set of traveling clothes, a cloak, backpack, duffle bag or satchel, bedroll, utility belt, canteen or water skin, box of wooden matches, mess kit, small flashlight, pocket mirror, sunglasses, goggles, compass, an air filter and gas mask, language translator, distancing binoculars, laser distancer, magnifying glass, 20 feet (6.1 m) of rope/cord, 1D4+1 small specimen jars, 2D6+6 plastic specimen bags, sketchbook, pocket notebook, 2D4 pencils, a small sack, a medium sack, a large sack, and various common personal items. Fanatically anti-tech Gene-Mages will forsake things like binoculars and gas masks, replacing them with symbiotes or magical equivalents.

Cybernetics: None. Lemurians have no interest in bionics, not even Bio-Systems.

Money: Monthly salary of 3,200 credits or trade goods; starts off with 2D6x1,000 credits in savings. Most Biomancers have a family estate and live there in one of the floating cities, or Lemurian Gardens, but many also establish several homes and getaways in remote parts of the world above and below the waves. Those working with the Lemurian military can also use barracks for extended stays or special assignments that require long periods of time of being on duty. The typical barracks has room for two Biomancers, one lavatory and a sitting room.

Lemurian Men-At-Arms O.C.C.s

Only the following Men-At-Arms O.C.C.s are available to Lemurian characters. There are no mercenaries, cyborgs, Juicers, robot pilots or other tech-based soldiers among Lemurians.

Birdman Warrior

The "Tangata Manu" (Birdmen) of Easter Island

This ancient order of warriors dates back to before the Atlantean disaster. Much like the newer warrior caste, the Tangata Manu were not aggressive soldiers in search of conquest, but rather the protectors of Lemuria. They were chosen from a cult of Lemurians who admired birds and had a unique identification with birds and birds of prey. For a time, the Tangata Manu worshiped nature and birds, and it is said that it was Stone Masters among this clan who invented the Maoi Stone Guardians. Later, they invented a bird inspired suit of flying Bio-Armor.

Only the bravest of the Tangata Manu clan would apply to become Birdman Warriors. In these ancient times, once every year, as part of their initiation into the order of Lemurian Birdmen defenders, new initiates climbed down a steep cliff on Rapa Nui (Easter Island) and swam out into shark-infested waters to a small island just off the coast named *Motu Nui* to bring back a bird's egg from the fabled Sooty Tern. The lucky initiate who succeeded, without having to be rescued and pulled from the water, would raise the hatchling as his own and upon completion of his combat training and the maturing of the hatchling into an adult Sooty Tern, would bond with the bird in the same manner as some practitioners of magic bond with a Familiar. Ready for combat, the high Biomancer of the clan would bestow upon the new Birdman a suit of Bio-Armor specifically designed for him. Upon receiving his Avian Bio-Armor, the young protector of the realm would join the ranks of the Birdman Warriors. To hone the warrior's sense of humility and connection and respect for others, he would be thrust

into a position of leadership over a small local village. For one year, it would be his responsibility alone to protect and help the people of the village in all matters. The following year, he would be relieved of his responsibility by the next initiate and join a position within the Birdman hierarchy of peace-loving defenders. It was the responsibility of the Birdmen to help keep the peace, resolve disputes without violence and defend Lemuria and her people against supernatural threats, creatures of magic, monsters and any who might seek to enslave, hurt or destroy them.

The Birdmen served as the lone protectors of Lemuria for nearly one thousand years. It was the Birdmen who began the tradition of warrior poets and philosophers as defenders of civilization. It has only been since returning to Rifts Earth that the Oceanic Guardsmen, Sea Sentinels and Serpent Hunters have been formed as additional fighting forces in a world swarming with supernatural invaders and demonic enemies hungry for Lemurian blood.

Birdmen are considered elite warriors from a long line of heroes entrusted with the protection of Lemuria. They might be considered the Lemurian air force since the Birdmen are more at home in the sky than under the waves. The main force of Lemurian Birdmen are based at Easter Island, where the first of their kind took wing so many millennia ago. The most trusted and heroic of them are among the few allowed to command the Moai Stone Guardians and often fight the most dangerous supernatural threats in tandem with the Moai.

Birdman Special O.C.C. Abilities & Bonuses:

1. Special R.C.C. Abilities Common to Lemurians: See the Lemurian racial description for full details.

Life Sense: Same as all Lemurians. Range: 25 foot (7.6 m) radius plus 5 feet (1.5 m) per level of experience. Base Skill: 20% +5% per level of experience to locate/track/find a specific type of animal or plant, +5% when in an underwater environment.

Empathy with Animals: Same as all Lemurians. An automatic affinity with animals of all kinds, except monsters, predators and sentient creatures.

Ley Line Powers: Same as all Lemurians; heals and recovers P.P.E. twice as fast as a normal human when on a ley line or at stone pyramids. Swim 25% faster when along ley lines.

Natural Abilities: Same as all Lemurians.

Pets and Familiars: Same as all Lemurians. Birdmen occasionally keep pets and Familiars or make use of flying riding animals, usually taking in birds and other airborne creatures.

Ultrasonic Communication: Same as all Lemurians. Hears and creates high frequency noises to communicate. Range of Communication: 2,000 feet (610 m) underwater, 400 feet (122 m) on the surface/in the air.

2. Communicate with and Control Moai (exclusive to Birdmen): The Birdmen all have a natural link to the Moai and can intuitively feel when one reacts to the presence of supernatural evil. This connection enables the Birdmen to instantly know where the supernatural threat is located as well as give them a good idea of the nature of the threat and the level of danger (low, medium, high). It also tells the Birdmen when a Moai is under attack, how many enemies it faces and its exact location. When fighting together with a Moai, the link between the Birdmen and the Stone Guardian provides the following additional bonuses to the avian warriors: +1 on Perception Rolls, +1 on initiative and +2 to automatic dodge (the act of dodging does not use up a melee attack/action).

A select handful of trusted and combat proven Birdmen possess the secret words to activate and pilot Moai. This is a rare and high honor among Lemurian warriors. It is a privilege bestowed to more Birdmen than any of the other fighting classes of Lemuria. (See Moai in the *section on Easter Island* for details about these massive stone automatons.)

3. Ride the Moai: Though designed for flight, aerial combat, aerial reconnaissance and search and rescue operations, Lemurian Birdmen can also "fly" underwater with a maximum depth tolerance of two miles (3.2 km). However, when Birdmen perch themselves on the top or sides of the head of a Moai and hang tight, they are covered in a thin crust of hardened lava that makes them a temporary part of the Moai. When this happens, the Birdmen warriors can function as observers carried to great depths (as deep as 6 miles/9.6 km) on the back of the Moai. They must remain connected to the Moai and can take no action of their own nor disengage from the Stone Guardian until they are at a survivable depth of two miles (3.2 km) or less. To disengage from the Moai at greater depth is to be crushed by the incredible pressure of the deep ocean.

4. Psionics: Standard as per all Lemurians.

5. Birdman O.C.C. Bonuses: +6D6 S.D.C., +1 on Perception Rolls, +2 to automatic dodge (the act of dodging does not count as a melee attack), +1 to save vs Horror Factor at levels 2, 4, 8, 12 and 15, +1 to save vs magic at levels 3, 8 and 12, and +2 to save vs possession.

6. Manutara Companion: The Birdman is linked to a "manutara" – a Sooty Tern bird Familiar. Once the "manutara" (bird Familiar) has reached full maturity, the animal is bound to the warrior and functions as his companion and Familiar.

Sooty Tern Stats: This marine bird nests on rocky or coral islands, laying 1-3 eggs. It feeds on small fish, which it plucks from the surface or shallow waters. Its wings and deeply forked tail are long, having a white underside with dark gray upper parts and a black bill and legs. Babies are scaly gray all over.

Size: 13 to 14.2 inches (33 to 36 cm) in length, with a 32.3 to 37 inch (82 to 94 cm) wingspan.

Attributes of Note: Speed: 8 on dry land, 12 in the water, 55 flying (35 mph/56 km).

Hit Points: 1D8+2. **S.D.C.:** 2D6+2.

A.R.: Not applicable.

P.P.E.: 2D4+1

Natural Abilities: Fly, Swim 90%, depth tolerance 10 feet (3 m), keen hawk-like vision and exceptional endurance – have been known to fly or glide out at sea for 3-10 years at a time! +2 to save vs toxins and magic, and resistant to cold (half damage).

Attacks per Melee: Two.

Damage: Bite or peck does 1D4 S.D.C., claws do 1D4 S.D.C.

Bonuses for the Bird: +2 to Perception Rolls, +1 on initiative, +2 to strike and +5 to dodge.

Note: A seagull or most any aquatic bird can be substituted, but tradition among the Birdmen is to bond with the Sooty Tern.

Birdman Warrior O.C.C. Stats

Also Known As: Lemurian Birdmen, Birdmen of Easter Island and Rapa Nui's Warriors.

Alignment: Usually Principled or Scrupulous.

Attribute Requirements: M.E. P.P. and P.E. of 12 or higher.

Racial Requirements: So far, all Birdmen are Lemurians from the Tangatu Manu clan.

Skills Known by All Lemurians:

Language: Lemurian and Oceanic at 98%.

Literacy: Lemurian at 85% +2% per level of experience.

Mathematics: Basic at 82 +1% per level of experience.

Swimming at 86% +1% per level of experience.

O.C.C. Skills:

Acrobatics or Boxing (pick one).
Climbing (+5%)
Intelligence (+10%)
Land Navigation (+15%)
Language: Oceanic (+20%)
Lore: Faeries and Creatures of Magic (+20%)
Lore: Demons and Monsters (+20%)
Navigation (+20%)
Prowl (+10%)
Tracking (+15%)
Wilderness Survival (+15%)
W.P. Ancient: One of choice (Sword is common).
W.P. Energy Pistol or Energy Rifle.
W.P.: Two of choice, any (Ancient or Modern).
Hand to Hand: Martial Arts. Can be changed to Hand to Hand: Kapu Kuialua at the cost of two O.C.C. Related Skills.

O.C.C. Related Skills: Select five skills at level one, plus one additional skill at levels 3, 5, 7, 9, 11 and 13. All new skills start at level one proficiency.

Aquatic: Any (+5%).
Communication: Any; Barter, Creative Writing, Language, Literacy and Public Speaking are at +5%.
Cowboy: None.
Domestic: Any (+5%).
Electrical: None.
Espionage: Any (+5%).
Horsemanship: General or Exotic only.
Mechanical: None.
Medical: Animal Husbandry, Brewing, First Aid or Holistic Medicine (+5%).
Military: Camouflage, Find Contraband, Military Etiquette, Naval History, Naval Tactics and Recognize Weapon Quality only (+10%).
Physical: Any.
Pilot: Any, excluding military, power armor and robots. Pilot: Boat (any type) and Jet Pack are at +10%.
Pilot Related: Any (+5%).
Rogue: Tailing (+15%) only.
Science: Astronomy & Navigation and Mathematics: Advanced only (+10%).
Technical: Any (+5%), except Computer Operation, Computer Programming, Cybernetics: Basic and Jury-Rig.
W.P.: Any.
Wilderness: Any (+10%).

Secondary Skills: The character also gets to select two Secondary Skills from the Secondary Skills list in **Rifts® Ultimate Edition**, page 300, plus one additional Secondary Skill at levels 3, 6, 9 and 12. These are additional areas of knowledge that do not get any bonuses, other than any possible bonus from having a high I.Q. All Secondary Skills start at the base skill level.

Standard Equipment: Avian Bio-Armor (described in the Bio-Armor section), one weapon for every W.P. (+3 extra clips where applicable; may include Biomancy Weapons), 1D4+1 symbiotes of choice, two Bio-Construct Weapons, survival knife, canteen, bedroll, backpack, a few sets of clothes and some personal items. They also have access to all Bio-Skins and may be assigned additional weapons, gear or symbiotes for special missions. Birdmen may also be assigned as aerial troops on any but the smallest Lemurian stone vehicle and submarines.

Cybernetics: None. Lemurians have no interest in bionics, not even Bio-Systems.

Money: Monthly salary of 2,000 credits or trade goods, double for squadron leaders; starts off with one month's pay. Even low ranking warriors often have a spacious apartment or small family home in one of the floating cities or at Easter Island. There are also barracks for extended stays or special assignments that require long periods of time of being on duty. The typical barracks has room for three Birdmen, one lavatory, a sitting room, study and small kitchen.

Oceanic Guardsman

The Oceanic Guardsmen may be thought of as warrior-poets or philosopher soldiers. These noble warriors are the first line of Lemuria's defense. All have had tremendous experience fighting the minions, monsters and undead of the Lord of the Deep, Milu and other supernatural forces of evil, as well as pirates and other threats.

The Oceanic Guardsmen fill the roles of infantry shock troops, sentries, power armor pilots (clad in heavy Bio-Armor), police and protectors of the people. Though some might think of them as "grunts," they are well trained and skilled combatants with a broad range of skills and experience. Many Lemurians, though not the Guardsmen themselves, insist they are the bravest of the brave, for it is the Oceanic Guardsmen who rush out, first in line, to meet *all* enemies and face all dangers. Lemurian society is so polite and considerate of each other that there is little crime and even fewer acts of violence, so there is little need for police as we think of them. Instead, Oceanic Guardsmen are very much "servants and protectors," first to Lemurians and their allies (including animals), and second, to all sentient beings. Oceanic Guardsmen are also first responders in times of disaster. Thus, all Guardsmen are happy to help, comfort and assist any person in trouble and are quick to protect them from every sort of danger. Being Rifts Earth, there seems to be no end to the number of threats from the outside world, even underwater. Some common threats include monsters from the Rifts, the undead of the Milu, the minions of the Lord of the Deep, the Naut'Yll invaders, Minions of Splugorth, slavers, pirates, raiders, sea monsters and a host of others.

Though skilled and deadly warriors, Oceanic Guardsmen are compassionate and merciful, without being fools or foolish. They show mercy where mercy is deserved, and battle the forces of evil with ruthless resolve. Their humanity, nobility and valor have earned the best of these warriors the position of *Royal Guardsmen*, the highest honor in Lemurian society for men-at-arms, and they are revered by the people above all other Lemurian fighting forces. Oceanic Guardsmen also have special forces teams, reconnaissance specialists and civil and military investigators, making them one of the most versatile military forces around.

Special O.C.C. Abilities and Bonuses of the Oceanic Guardsmen:

1. Special R.C.C. Abilities Common to Lemurians: See the Lemurian racial description for full details.

Life Sense: Same as all Lemurians. Range: 25 foot (7.6 m) radius plus 5 feet (1.5 m) per level of experience. Base Skill: 20% +5% per level of experience to locate/track/find a specific type of animal or plant, +5% when in an underwater environment.

Empathy with Animals: Same as all Lemurians. An automatic affinity with animals of all kinds, except monsters, predators and sentient creatures.

Ley Line Powers: Same as all Lemurians; heals and recovers P.P.E. twice as fast as a normal human when on a ley line or at stone pyramids. Swim 25% faster when along ley lines.

Natural Abilities: Same as all Lemurians.

Pets and Familiars: Same as all Lemurians. Lemurian Guardsmen are likely to be accompanied by an Aquatic Lemur and have a designated Lemurian War Steed (player's choice).

Ultrasonic Communication: Same as all Lemurians. Hears and creates high frequency noises to communicate. Range of Communication: 2,000 feet (610 m) underwater, 400 feet (122 m) on the surface/in the air.

2. Trained in Combat and Rescue. The Guardsmen's training includes combat and weapons, but also rescue and helping others in all situations. Their O.C.C. Skills reflect this wide range of training.

3. Psionics (Guardsman): Death Trance (2), Empathy (4), Intuitive Combat (10), Mind Block (4), See the Invisible (4), Stop Bleeding (4), Suppress Fear (4), and Telepathy (4). I.S.P.: 1D6x10 plus M.E. attribute number to start, +2D4 I.S.P. per level of experience. Considered a Major Psychic. No other psionics are available to this character.

4. O.C.C. Bonuses (Oceanic Guardsman): +2 to P.S., +1 to P.P., +3D6 to S.D.C., +2 on Perception Rolls in general and involving plants and nature, +1 attack per melee round, +2 to pull punch, +1 to save vs Horror Factor at levels 2, 4, 6, 8, 10, 12 and 14, +1 to save vs possession and mind control, plus any bonuses gained from high attributes and certain skills.

Oceanic Guardsman O.C.C. Stats

Also Known As: Maku Toa and Lemurian Guardsman.

Alignment: Any, but most are Principled (40%), Scrupulous (35%), Unprincipled (15%) or Aberrant (3%; honorable).

Attribute Requirements: Minimum P.S. 14 and P.E. of 11 or higher, other high physical attributes and I.Q. are also suggested, but not required.

Race Restrictions: Lemurians (85%), Merans (8%), Ichthyleans (6%) and assorted other species (1%) have become Oceanic Guardsmen.

Skills Known by All Lemurians:

Language: Lemurian and Oceanic at 96%.
Literacy: Lemurian at 85% +1% per level of experience.
Mathematics: Basic at 82 +1% per level of experience.
Swimming at 80% +2% per level of experience.

O.C.C. Skills:

Boxing
Climbing (+10%)
Detect Ambush (+12%)
Detect Concealment (+10%)
Excavation (+10%)
Firefighting (+15%)
Land Navigation (+5%)
Language and Literacy: Lemurian (Native) at 98%.
Language: Two of choice (+12%).

Law (+15%)
Literacy: Lemurian at 96%.
Literacy: One of choice (+20%).
Mathematics: Basic (+20%)
Military Etiquette (+10%)
Paramedic (+10%)
Tailing (+10%)
Undercover Ops (+10%)
Undersea and Sea Survival (+10%)
Underwater Navigation (+8%)
W.P. Energy Rifle
W.P. Spear or Sword (pick one).
W.P. Ancient: Two of choice.
W.P. Modern: Two of choice.
Hand to Hand: Expert, which may be upgraded to Hand to Hand: Martial Arts at the cost of one O.C.C. Related Skill or Hand to Hand: Kapu Kuialua at the cost of two O.C.C. Related Skills.

O.C.C. Related Skills: Select five skills at level one, plus select one additional skill at level 3, 5, 7, 9, 11 and 13. All new skills start at level one proficiency.
Aquatic: Any (+10%).
Communication: Barter, Creative Writing, Language, Literacy, Performance, Public Speaking and Sing only (+5%).
Cowboy: None.
Domestic: Any (+5%).
Electrical: None.
Espionage: Any (+10%).
Horsemanship: General or Exotic only.
Mechanical: None.
Medical: Animal Husbandry, Brewing, First Aid, or (Sea) Holistic Medicine (+5%).
Military: Camouflage, Military Etiquette, Military Fortifications, Naval History, Naval Tactics, Recognize Weapon Quality and Trap/Mine Detection only (+10%).
Physical: Any.
Pilot: Bicycling, Boat (sail or paddle type only), Jet Pack (Lemurian Squid Packs), Jet Aircraft (Lemurian only), Submersibles (Lemurian only), Water Skiing & Surfing only (+5%).
Pilot Related: Any (+5%).
Rogue: Any (+5%), except Computer Hacking, Roadwise, Safe-Cracking and Streetwise.
Science: Astronomy & Navigation and Mathematics: Advanced only (+5%).
Technical: Any (+5%), except Computer Operation, Programming, Cybernetics: Basic and Jury-Rig.
W.P.: Any.
Wilderness: Any (+5%).

Secondary Skills: The character also gets to select three Secondary Skills from the Secondary Skills list in **Rifts® Ultimate Edition**, page 300, plus one additional Secondary Skill at levels 3, 5, 9 and 13. These are additional areas of knowledge that do not get any bonuses, other than any possible bonus from having a high I.Q. All Secondary Skills start at the base skill level.

Standard Equipment: Special and/or additional weapons and gear may be assigned for special situations and missions.

Bio-Constructs: Bio-Armor: Select one of the following Bio-Armors: *Chitin, Coral, Dolphin, Kelp, Wood* or *Shark*; a growing number (currently 17%) select *Shark Bio-Armor* which is exclusive to Guardsmen. The type of Bio-Armor often reflects the Guardsman's personality and assignment; Chitin, Coral and Crustacean Bio-Armor is typical for defensive positions, guard duty or front-line combat, while Kelp Bio-Armor is used for stealth, reconnaissance and scouting, Dolphin for patrols and quick response, and Shark Bio-Armor for special operations and all types of combat, and so on. Also has access to all types of Bio-Skins.

Bio-Constructs: Symbiotes: Living Saddle, Morphic Riding Bio-Barding and any three Symbiotic Bio-Constructs of choice, which may include one other non-lethal type of weapon.

Bio-Constructs: Bio-Weapons: Stonecaster Pistol is the standard sidearm, plus one Bio-Construct melee weapon and long-range weapon of choice (any). Spears, staves and pole arms are especially popular among Royal Guardsmen.

Lemurian War Steed: All Guardsmen have a specific war steed assigned to them, but may be given access to others depending on their assignment.

Miscellaneous: Organically grown and woven clothes (uniforms, dress/formal wear, and combat clothes; most are conducive to underwater use), backpack, utility belt, water skin, rope and other common personal items.

Cybernetics: None. Lemurians have no interest in bionics, not even Bio-Systems.

Money: Monthly salary of 2,100 credits or trade goods, double for Royal Guardsmen and top officers; starts off with one month's pay. Even low ranking Oceanic Guardsmen often have a family estate and live there in one of the floating cities. There are also barracks for extended stays or special assignments that require long periods of time of being on duty. The typical barracks has room for four Guardsmen, one lavatory, a sitting room, study and small kitchen.

Sea Sentinel

Sea Sentinels are the Lemurians' equivalent to naval fighter pilots. These are the men and women who pilot Stone Flyers – stone combat vessels that fly through the air like jets and cruise through water like submarines. Sea Sentinels are also known as the "Rann-gii" (Ran gee) named after the man who founded this defense force and designed the first water-to-air flyers. It was his crazy idea of using ley line energy and stone magic to create the flying submersibles, and it was he who designed and built the very first Stone Flyers. The idea was to make small, fast fighters able to outmaneuver the *Reachers from the Deep* and even withstand a few direct hits from them. Their addition to the Lemurian defense force has been vital in countering attacks from the Lord of the Deep, the Milu undead, other supernatural terrors and high-tech invaders from the surface. Commander Rann-gii led this bold, new defense force until his untimely death at the tentacles of the Lord of the Deep. The loss of Commander Rann-gii, however, has only seemed to strengthen the Sea Sentinels' determination to protect Lemuria and all people from the wrath of dark gods and supernatural horrors everywhere.

Sea Sentinels are committed to the protection of Lemuria, the protection of all innocent people, and the preservation of nature. However, not unlike the flying aces of World War I, Sea Sentinels share an unbreakable camaraderie among their fellow flyers, and have developed a sense of elitism among their forces. Many see themselves as swashbuckling heroes to whom the rules do not always apply. Their quest for speed, excitement and the opportunity to tangle with evil supernatural forces threatening Rifts Earth has

led many Sentinels to engage in daring and dangerous operations. Sea Sentinels are becoming known for taking ridiculous risks to rescue the innocent, exhibiting no fear against impossible odds, and engaging in high-speed chases, death-defying maneuvers and heart-stopping dogfights above and below the waves. When questioned or reprimanded for their feats of daring-do and crazy antics, a Sea Sentinel is likely to smile and retort with a wink, "Apologies, Sir, but there was no risk. We make our own luck." As arrogant as such a statement may sound, most Sea Sentinels have an uncanny aptitude for flying and diving at shattering speeds, and are able to fly circles around most of their aerial and aquatic adversaries. It is almost as if they were born to glide through water and the air.

Though the amphibious stone vehicles of Lemuria are the Sea Sentinels' favorite vessels, they find all submersibles, aircraft and flying power armor fascinating, and like to try their hands at piloting the vehicles of other people. Through the use of Telemechanics and Object Read, Sea Sentinels are able to fly almost any kind of aircraft, but at a penalty of -15% to their usual piloting skill and -1 attack/action per melee round. This interest in non-Lemurian technology has led some Sea Sentinels to fall from grace in the eyes of their Biomancer brethren who fear that flying tech-aircraft and submersibles may lead the Sentinels astray and cause them to lose their connection with nature and Earth Energy (magic).

Special O.C.C. Abilities and Bonuses of the Sea Sentinel:

1. Special R.C.C. Abilities Common to Lemurians: See the Lemurian racial description for full details.

Life Sense: Same as all Lemurians. Range: 25 foot (7.6 m) radius plus 5 feet (1.5 m) per level of experience. Base Skill: 20% +5% per level of experience to locate/track/find a specific type of animal or plant, +5% when in an underwater environment.

Empathy with Animals: Same as all Lemurians. An automatic affinity with animals of all kinds, except monsters, predators, and sentient creatures.

Ley Line Powers: Same as all Lemurians; heals and recovers P.P.E. twice as fast as a normal human when on a ley line or at stone pyramids. Swim 25% faster when along ley lines.

Natural Abilities: Same as all Lemurians.

Pets and Familiars: Same as all Lemurians. Sea Sentinels may be accompanied by an Aquatic Lemur or other pet and some may even have a personal riding animal (player's choice).

Ultrasonic Communication: Same as all Lemurians. Hears and creates high frequency noises to communicate. Range of Communication: 2,000 feet (610 m) underwater, 400 feet (122 m) on the surface/in the air.

2. Born to Soar! Can Pilot Any Aircraft or Submersible: When piloting any Lemurian stone vehicle, submersible or Stone Flyer, the Sea Sentinel does so at a base skill of 80% +2% per level of experience, and gets a bonus of +1 attack/action per melee round, +2 on initiative, +2 to automatic dodge, and reduced penalties for evasive and trick maneuvers. Furthermore, the usual penalties for aerial acrobatics, dog fighting, evasive action, and trick maneuvers are *half* to begin with and -1% per level of the pilot's experience (the latter is subtracted from the penalty, lessening its severity).

Sea Sentinels are natural born pilots and their focus on fast flying and amphibious vehicle combat enables the characters to pilot any human, D-Bee and even alien aircraft, submersibles, amphibious vehicles, and suits of power armor that have air and/or underwater capabilities. However, when flying technology based machines not made of stone or powered by magic, the Rann-gii flyers suffer the following penalties: -15% to piloting skills, all the standard penalties for trick maneuvers apply, and they are -1 attack per melee round.

3. Machine Awareness: Much like the Zen Combat Abilities of the Cyber-Knights, Sea Sentinels are keenly aware of machines, sensors and targeting devices functioning around them.

This awareness enables them to react to the combat vehicle and all mechanical devices and tech-weapons used by one specific opponent, including targeting systems, radar and tracking systems, Vibro-Blades, Neural Maces, handheld guns, weapons and targeting systems built into environmental body armor, power armor, cyborg, robot or robot vehicles, combat vehicles and other combat/targeting war machines. Basically, any combat machine with moving parts or that uses electricity and/or a computer chip (which is virtually an advanced peoples' entire armory) is *felt* by the Sea Sentinel when it targets or tracks him.

This awareness lets the Sea Sentinel know the very instant a targeting computer or radar locks on, the moment he falls into the cross-hairs of a gun, when a trigger is about to be squeezed, when an energy cell charges to fire, a cybernetic muscle tenses or a turret begins to aim at him. More than that, the Sea Sentinel can actually feel the weapons and war machines as they come online or are drawn to be used against him. It is like he can see them as clearly as if the weapon were being pointed in his face.

Bonuses & Abilities Against Weapons and Technology:

- Negates any bonuses his *attacker* might have from the weapon/machine/targeting device he is operating.
- The Sea Sentinel knows what his opponent is doing the same instant his opponent does it, enabling the warrior to react a split second faster: +1 on Perception Rolls involving machines and technology, +1 on initiative and +1 to automatic dodge against attacks from "manned" guns, weapon systems and machines (bionics, power armor, vehicular weapon systems, etc.), double against "automated" attackers such as artificial intelligences, computers and unmanned robots like Skelebots and automated defense systems.
- At first level of experience, the Sea Sentinel can only focus and be aware of *one opponent* and all the weapons and weapon systems of that *one*, primary opponent. The number of opponents he can "sense" and react to increases by +1 at levels 4, 8 and 12.

Note: A Sea Sentinel can also sense when a robot or automated optic system is targeting, watching, videotaping or following him. He may not be able to locate the surveillance device if it is well hidden or concealed, but he'll know it is present and watching.

4. Ley Line Powers: Though the Sea Sentinels have no spell casting abilities, their constant exposure to magic energy, ley lines and unique relationship with the symbiotes inside all Lemurian stone vehicles have given them a few unique magic abilities in relation to their duties as fighter pilots.

Increase the speed of any Lemurian stone aircraft, submersible or amphibious vehicle by 50% without strain or damage to the vehicle when traveling along a ley line. Can only increase the speed of man-made tech vehicles by 10%.

Increase range of weapons built into Lemurian vehicles by 5% per level of the Sea Sentinel's experience. Not applicable to man-made tech vehicles.

Increase damage of weapons by 1D6 when on a ley line (or as stated under specific weapon systems).

Erect a magical force field with 2D6+10 M.D.C. per level of experience around the vessel once per every six hours, but possible only when traveling along a ley line. Duration: Ten minutes per level of experience or until the field is reduced to zero M.D.C.

Miracle crash landing. The vehicle takes the entire force and all the damage in a crash landing, enabling the pilot (and any passengers) to walk away unscathed when the landing takes place on or within two miles (3.2 km) of a ley line.

5. O.C.C. Psionics and Intuitive Machine Operations: Sea Sentinels possess Telemechanics and other psionic abilities which enable them to understand and use the machines and technology of other people. All Sea Sentinels develop the following psychic abilities, including an understanding of machines that is uncharacteristic to most Lemurians: Empathy (4), Machine Ghost (12), Meditation (0), Mind Block (4), Object Read (6), Sense Time (2), Telemechanics (10), Telemechanic Mental Operation (12), and Telepathy (4). I.S.P.: 2D4x10 plus M.E. attribute number to start, +2D4 I.S.P. per level of experience. Considered a Major Psychic. No other psionics are available to this character.

6. O.C.C. Bonuses: +1 to M.E. and P.P. attributes, +2D6 S.D.C., +2 to roll with impact, +1 vs Horror Factor at levels 2, 5, 7, 9, 11, 13 and 15, and loves speed and excitement.

7. Penalties: Most Sea Sentinels develop a psychological need for speed and excitement. They thrive on action and are bored, fidgety and irritable when not on patrol, racing, adventuring, engaged in rescue operations, combat, sports or other competitive or exciting activity.

Sea Sentinel O.C.C. Stats

Also Known As: Rann-gii Flyers, Rann-gii and just Sentinels.

Alignment: Any, though most are Principled (20%), Scrupulous (40%), Unprincipled (20%) or Anarchist (10%).

Attribute Requirements: A minimum I.Q. and P.P. of 12 or higher is required, a high M.E. is suggested, but not a necessity.

Race Restrictions: Exclusive to the Lemurians, no other race is permitted.

Skills Known by All Lemurians:

Language: Lemurian and Oceanic at 96%.
Literacy: Lemurian at 85% +1% per level of experience.
Mathematics: Basic at 86 +1% per level of experience.
Swimming at 76% +2% per level of experience.

O.C.C. Skills:

Astronomy & Navigation (+20%)
Land Navigation (+10%)
Language: Two of choice (+10%)
Literacy: One of choice (+15%)
Literacy: Techno-Can (+10%)
Mathematics: Advanced (+20%)
Navigation (+30%)
Pilot (special): Can pilot *any* aircraft, submersible or amphibius vehicle (the latter can be water-to-air, water-to-ground, or all-environment); see Special Abilities, above.
Sensory Equipment (+15%)
Underwater Navigation (+20%)
Weapon Systems (+10%)
Wilderness Survival (+10%)

W.P.: One of choice (any; typically a melee weapon or pistol).
Hand to Hand: Basic, which may be changed to Expert at the cost of one O.C.C. Related Skill, or Martial Arts at the cost of two O.C.C. Related Skills.

O.C.C. Related Skills: Select five skills at level one, plus select one additional skill at level 2, 5, 8, 11 and 14. All new skills start at level one proficiency.
Aquatic: Any (+5%).
Communication: Any (+5%).
Cowboy: None.
Domestic: Any.
Electrical: None.
Espionage: None.
Horsemanship: General or Exotic only.
Mechanical: None.
Medical: First Aid (+5%) only.
Military: Camouflage, Military Etiquette, Military Fortifications, Naval History, Naval Tactics, Recognize Weapon Quality and Trap/Mine Detection only (+10%).
Physical: Any.
Pilot: Bicycling, Boat (sail or paddle type only), Jet Pack (Lemurian Squid Packs), Jet Aircraft (Lemurian only), Submersibles (Lemurian only), Water Skiing & Surfing only (+5%).
Pilot Related: Any (+5%).
Rogue: Gambling and Tailing only.
Science: None.
Technical: Any (+5%), except Computer Operation, Programming, Cybernetics: Basic, and Jury-Rig.
W.P.: Any.
Wilderness: Any.

Secondary Skills: The character also gets to select two Secondary Skills from the Secondary Skills list in **Rifts® Ultimate Edition**, page 300, plus one additional Secondary Skill at levels 3, 5, 9 and 13. These are additional areas of knowledge that do not get any bonuses, other than any possible bonus from having a high I.Q. All Secondary Skills start at the base skill level.

Standard Equipment: Special and/or additional vehicles, weapons, and gear may be assigned for special situations and missions.

Combat Vehicles: All Sea Sentinels are assigned a *Sea Dart Interceptor* (depicted in the illustration), but can be assigned *different* vehicles depending on the pilot's mission and available vessels. The pilots' dependence and connection to their amphibious stone vehicles means they don't need much else in the way of other weapons.

Bio-Constructs: Bio-Armor: Select one of the following light Bio-Armors: Barnacle, Dolphin, Kelp or Wavestrider. Also has access to all Bio-Skins.

Bio-Constructs: Symbiotes: A Sea Doctor and one of choice.

Bio-Constructs: Bio-Weapons: One melee weapon and one short-range weapon of choice (any), but tend to select small, compact weapons that can fit in the cockpit of most vehicles.

Miscellaneous: Organically grown and woven clothes (uniforms, dress/formal wear, and combat clothes; most are conducive to underwater use), backpack, utility belt, water skin, rope and other common personal items.

Cybernetics: None. Lemurians have no interest in bionics, not even Bio-Systems.

Money: Monthly salary of 2,300 credits or trade goods, double for squadron leaders; starts off with one month's pay. Even low ranking Sea Sentinels often have a spacious apartment or family home in one of the floating cities. There are also barracks for extended stays or special assignments that require long periods of time of being on duty. The typical barracks has room for three Sea Sentinels, one lavatory, a sitting room, study and small kitchen.

Serpent Hunter

Lemurian Serpent Hunters have captured the imaginations of most surface dwellers and the outside world. They are the warriors who specialize in the fighting, capturing and taming of sea serpents, dragons and sea monsters. Moreover, Serpent Hunters always have one or more sea serpents or other exotic, Biomancy enhanced riding animals of their own, and are said to be able to tame and ride *any* sea serpent or monster.

Serpent Hunters are comparable to what surface dwellers think of as paladins, both in spirit and fighting ability, but instead of a grand warhorse to carry them into battle, they ride upon the backs of giant sea serpents and other monsters. It is the Serpent Hunter who captures sea serpents in the wild, tames and trains them, or when necessary, slays them. Biomancer Gene-Mages have mutated several creatures to create an interesting array of Lemurian War Steeds that most outsiders would consider "monsters." Indeed, War Steeds are living weapons, and in the hands of the Oceanic Guardsmen, and especially *Serpent Hunters*, they are combat partners that can be dismounted to attack the enemy on their own, or watch their warrior partner's back, or to carry civilians out of harm's way. Spurred on by new challenges of magical genetic engineering, Biomancer Gene-Mages have created stranger and stranger creatures for Serpent Hunters to ride. While a large range of War Steeds are available to Serpent Hunters, each warrior has two that are specifically his and no one else's.

Serpent Hunters have perfected their natural psychic abilities and know so much about handling monstrs, that the creatures are almost a living extension of the warrior. The symbiotic relationship between man and monster is so strong, the two can even separate yet still fight in tandem. The mental and physical training to achieve such unity and discipline is unparalleled in Lemurian society. When a Serpent Hunter dies, his two riding animals are tagged to insure no other Lemurian ever rides them and are set free in the wild or let loose at a Lemurian Garden to graze, but also serve among the Garden's protectors. If an animal is slain, the Serpent Hunter mourns for weeks before selecting and taming a new one.

Serpent Hunters are renowned for their fighting acumen and legendary bravery. Young, brash and strong-willed Lemurians dream of becoming Serpent Hunters, but only the most worthy earn a position among these heroes – protectors of the oceans and defenders of the traditions, honor and people of Lemuria.

Serpent Hunters are selected for their aptitude in combat and general physical fitness, but also for their mental stability, sense of honor, duty and ability to work as a member of a team. Serpent Hunters inspire trust and respect, and most warriors are willing to follow one even into the most harrowing combat situations. Though not every Serpent Hunter is a natural leader, it is the Hunters' job to rally the troops and lead the charge into battle. It is interesting to note that the training and mettle of the Serpent Hunters is such that few are arrogant or boastful glory hounds. Rather, the typical Serpent Hunter is humble and down to earth. They care about people and have a high regard for life, be it the life of surface dwellers, Lemurians, or noble sea creatures. This makes

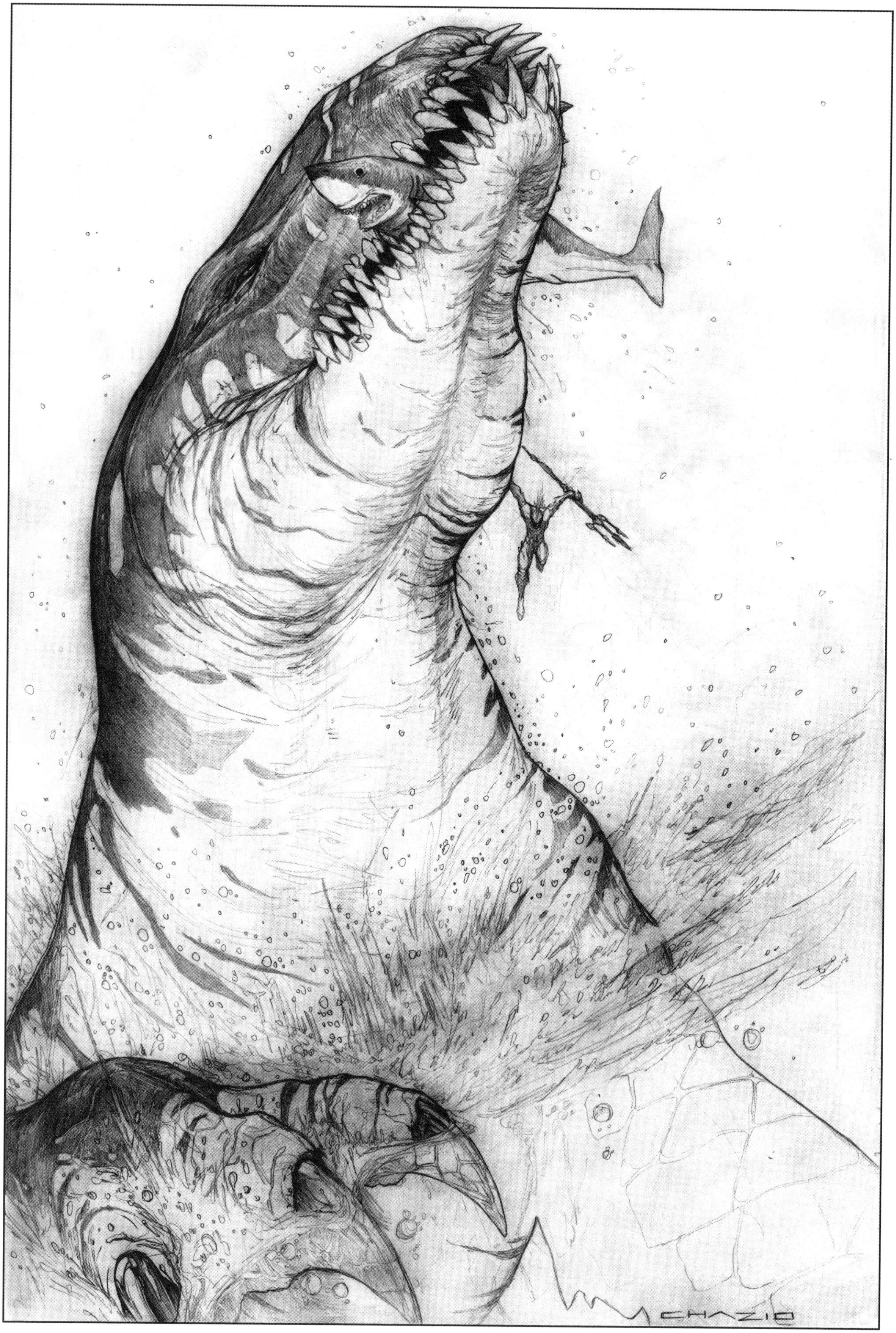

them gentle, kind and compassionate when dealing with civilians in need. However, you'd never know it on the battlefield, where Serpent Hunters fight with merciless tenacity and have no qualms about destroying enemies and monsters. They are especially ruthless when facing the minions of the Lord of the Deep, the Milu and the undead, their three most hated of enemies.

Special O.C.C. Abilities of the Serpent Hunter:

1. Special R.C.C. Abilities Common to Lemurians: See the Lemurian racial description for full details.

Life Sense: Same as all Lemurians. Range: 25 foot (7.6 m) radius plus 5 feet (1.5 m) per level of experience. Base Skill: 20% +5% per level of experience to locate/track/find a specific type of animal or plant, +5% when in an underwater environment.

Empathy with Animals: Limited; replaced with *Empathy with Serpents and Monsters*, see #2, below, for details.

Ley Line Powers: Same as all Lemurians; heals and recovers P.P.E. twice as fast as a normal human when on a ley line or at stone pyramids. Swim 25% faster when along ley lines.

Natural Abilities: Same as all Lemurians.

Pets and Familiars: Same as all Lemurians. Lemurian Guardsmen are likely to be accompanied by an Aquatic Lemur and have a designated Lemurian War Steed (player's choice).

Ultrasonic Communication: Same as all Lemurians. Hears and creates high frequency noises to communicate. Range of Communication: 2,000 feet (610 m) underwater, 400 feet (122 m) on the surface/in the air.

2. Empathy with Serpents & Monsters: The Serpent Hunter's *Empathy with Animals* is replaced by a more specific Empathy with Serpents & Monsters. As a hunter, the usual Lemurian's aura of peace, harmony and animal brotherhood does not apply nor work. However, the Hunter's intense study, familiarity and experience in dealing with serpents, sea serpents, sea monsters, snakes, large reptiles, predators and other monsters provides them with great insight into the personality, behavior and handling of these magnificent beasts. (**Note:** Dinosaurs fall into the "monster" category.) Furthermore, Serpent Hunters have the ability to *approach* predators and monsters without them feeling threatened or immediately attacking. If the Serpent Hunter makes a successful empathic connection (roll under skill percentage), the serpent or monster is wary and watchful of him, but does not attack. If the hero moves slowly and makes no threatening gestures, the monster will allow him to draw it away from prey, let him touch/pet it, handle it, examine it, clean a wound, groom it, extract venom, enter the creature's lair, share its food and sit with it or stay in its presence/proximity, without fear of attack or violence. This all establishes a tenuous sense of trust, rapport and acceptance by the creature. **Base Skill:** 80% +1% per level of experience, +8% when the animal/monster is an actual serpent. A failed skill roll means the creature growls a clear warning to back off. Failure to do so causes it to attack.

Dominance and Control: Once a rapport is established, as noted above (takes 1D4 melee rounds of grooming and petting), the Serpent Hunter can use the Empathy with Serpents & Monsters to establish *dominance*. **Base Skill:** 70% +1% per level of experience, +10% when the animal/monster is an actual serpent of some kind, and +15% when the animal is already a tamed War Steed or domesticated animal. -20% when dealing with sentient monsters with even low human equivalent I.Q., and not applicable to true dragons and greater supernatural beings. A failed dominance roll means the creature growls a clear warning to back off. Failure to do so causes it to attack.

Successful dominance means the creature accepts the Serpent Hunter as his equal or superior – but not its master. This enables the Serpent Hunter to play and wrestle with the beast (and its young!), care for its young, handle it roughly, hunt alongside it, have it accompany him as an ally/brother, and ride on its back. The Serpent Hunter can even ask or encourage the serpent/monster to attack and fight with him against humanoids and other monsters/prey; an offer most predators are apt to accept. However, the animal cannot be forced to fight or made to do anything it does not want to do. In life and death situations or against a foe or force that the animal is ordinarily afraid of, the animal can decline to fight or even serve as a steed or companion, and leave. However, the monster may hang back and watch what unfolds from a hiding place or safe distance, joining the battle when it senses an advantage or easy kill. Or not. 50/50 chance.

Penalty Handling Other Animals: Ironically, Serpent Hunters do not have the Lemurian's usual Empathy with Animals and suffer a -20% penalty to riding and other skills that involve all other types of animals, even domesticated ones, from cattle to bunny rabbits.

3. Horsemanship: Serpent Hunter (Ride Sea Monsters & Sea Serpents): Like any knight of the realm, the warrior needs a war horse, but in this case, that steed is a sea monster or sea serpent. Training includes riding and fighting with a saddle and bareback, as well as the skills necessary to dismount and continue to fight together but separately in a coordinated combat. The warrior also knows how to maneuver across the entire length of his sea monster, swinging from spines and fins, avoiding tentacles and natural weapons of the animal, riding from the side or tail, hiding under a fin, upside down or even inside the creature's mouth! **Base Skill:** 70%/50% +3% per level of experience (+10% when the War Steed is one of the Hunter's two personal War Steeds, and +10% if the monster is intelligent and willing to let the Serpent Hunter ride on its back or is an actual serpent of some kind).

4. Sense Sea Serpents, Sea Monsters and Aquatic Monsters: Centuries of spending time hunting sea serpents, dragons and aquatic monsters has given the Serpent Hunter a knack for locating his quarry and sensing when such creatures are near (within one mile/1.6 km) or the beast is stalking him. Of course, finding such creatures and capturing or slaying them are two different things. **Base Skill:** 50% +4% per level of experience, -20% on dry land.

5. Dragon, Sea Serpent and Sea Monster Slaying: Years of training to hunt and slay sea monsters has given the Serpent Hunters knowledge of weak points and the best strategies and tactics to kill monsters.

Special Bonuses:

+1 attack per melee when battling serpents, dragons and monsters.

+2 to automatic dodge when battling serpents, dragons and monsters; the act of dodging does not use up a melee attack.

Double damage from behind.

Critical Strike (double damage) on a Natural (unmodified roll of) 19 or 20 at level one.

Critical Strike (double damage) on a Natural (unmodified roll of) 18-20 at level Four.

Critical Strike Death Blow (triple damage) on a Natural (unmodified roll of) 18-20 at level eight.

6. Spell Knowledge (Limited): While magic is not their true focus, Serpent Hunters understand how magic works and are taught a handful of magic spells to help them hunt, capture and fight sea serpents, dragons and monsters.

Serpent Hunter Spell Knowledge: Breathe without Air (5), Globe of Daylight (2), Impervious to Fire (5), Lightblade (20), Magic Net (7), Magic Shield (6), Armor of Ithan (10), Sense Evil (2), Sense Magic (4), Tongues (12), and Chameleon (6). **Note:** The Serpent Hunter is limited to this initial spell range and may not learn new spells. **P.P.E.:** P.E. attribute number x2 to start, plus 2D6 per level of experience.

7. Psionics (Serpent Hunter): Death Trance (2), Empathy (4), Impervious to Poison (4), Levitation (varies), Mind Block (4), Resist Fatigue (4), See the Invisible (4), Telekinetic Leap (8), and Telepathy (4). I.S.P.: 1D6x10 plus M.E. attribute number to start, +2D4 I.S.P. per level of experience. Considered a Major Psychic. No other psionics are available to this character.

8. O.C.C. Bonuses: +1D4 to M.E., P.S. and P.E., +4D6 S.D.C., +2 on Perception Rolls dealing with snakes, serpents, sea serpents, dragons and monsters, +1 attack while riding a War Steed or sea serpent, +1 to strike, parry and dodge while riding a sea serpent or War Steed, +2 roll with impact, +3 to save vs Horror Factor (+6 vs H.F. when fighting serpents, sea serpents, dragons and aquatic monsters).

Serpent Hunter O.C.C. Stats

Also Known As: Serpent Riders and Serpent Bringers.

Alignment Restrictions: Any, but most are Principled and Scrupulous.

Race Restrictions: Lemurians (95%), Ichthyleans (2%), Merans (1%), humans and others (2%) can learn the Way of the Serpent Hunter.

Attribute Requirements: A minimum M.E., P.S. and P.P. of 15, a high P.E., I.Q. and other attributes are recommended, but not required.

Skills Known by All Lemurians:
Language: Lemurian and Oceanic at 96%.
Literacy: Lemurian at 85% +1% per level of experience.
Mathematics: Basic at 82 +1% per level of experience.
Swimming at 90% +1% per level of experience.

O.C.C. Skills:
Horsemanship: Aquatic Animals (+10%) or Exotic Animals
Horsemanship: Sea Monsters (+25%)
Language and Literacy: Lemurian at 98%.
Language: One of choice (+10%).
Literacy: One of choice (+10%).
Lore: Demons and Monsters (+5%; +25% when dealing with serpents and sea monsters).
Lore: Faeries and Creatures of Magic (+5%, +15% when dealing with dragons)
Track and Hunt Sea Animals (+20%)
Undersea and Sea Survival (+20%)
Underwater Navigation (+15%)
W.P. Energy Rifle
W.P. Spear or Pole Arm (pick one).
W.P. Trident
W.P.: Three of choice (any).
Hand to Hand: Martial Arts or Hand to Hand: Kapu Kuialua at the cost of one O.C.C. Related Skill.

O.C.C. Related Skills: Select four skills at level one. Plus select one additional skill at levels 3, 6, 9, 12 and 15. All new skills start at level one proficiency.
Aquatic Skills: Any (+5%).
Communication: Barter, Creative Writing, Language, Literacy, Performance, Public Speaking and Sing only (+5%).
Cowboy: Any (+5%).
Domestic: Any (+5%).
Electrical: None.
Espionage: Any (+5%).
Horsemanship: None, other than O.C.C. Skills.
Mechanical: None.
Medical: Animal Husbandry or First Aid only (+10%).
Military: Camouflage, Military Etiquette and Recognize Weapon Quality only (+5%).
Physical: Any (+10% where applicable).
Pilot: Boat (sail or paddle type only), Jet Pack (Squid Packs), Water Skiing & Surfing only (+10%).
Pilot Related: None.
Rogue: Imitate Voices & Sounds, Prowl and Tailing only (+10%).
Science: Anthropology, Archeology, Astronomy & Navigation, Mathematics: Advanced, Ocean Geographic Surveying and Undersea Farming only (+5%).
Technical: Any (+5%), except Computer Operation, Programming, Cybernetics: Basic, and Jury-Rig.
W.P.: Any.
Wilderness: Any (+5%).

Secondary Skills: The character also gets to select four Secondary Skills from the Secondary Skills list in **Rifts® Ultimate Edition**, page 300, plus one additional Secondary Skill at levels 3, 5, 9 and 13. These are additional areas of knowledge that do not get any bonuses, other than any possible bonus from having a high I.Q. All Secondary Skills start at the base skill level.

Standard Equipment: Special and/or additional vehicles, weapons, and gear may be assigned for special situations and missions.

Lemurian War Steed: The Serpent Hunter is assigned a *Thrall Serpent* or *Serpent Seahorse*, and one other "serpent" as his two, personal War Steeds. However, the warriors can usually get access to any *Lemurian War Steed* depending on availability and the mission; sometimes serpents don't make the best steeds on land operations.

Bio-Constructs: Bio-Armor: Leviathan Bio-Armor is standard issue, but a few of these warriors prefer other Bio-Armors (any); also has access to all Bio-Skins.

Bio-Constructs: Symbiotes: 1D4 Talisman Shells and one other type of Bio-Construct of choice.

Bio-Constructs: Bio-Weapons: A Serpent Blade and Serpent Trident, and two other Lemurian Bio-Weapons of choice (any).

Miscellaneous: Organically grown and woven clothes (uniforms, dress/formal wear, and combat clothes; most are conducive to underwater use), backpack, utility belt, water skin, rope and other common personal items.

Cybernetics: None. Lemurians have no interest in bionics, not even Bio-Systems.

Money: Monthly salary of 2,300 credits or trade goods, double for squadron leaders; starts off with one month's pay. Even low ranking Serpent Hunters often have a has a spacious apartment or family home in one of the floating cities. There are also barracks for extended stays or special assignments that require long periods of time of being on duty. The typical barracks has room for three Serpent Hunters, one lavatory, a sitting room, study and small kitchen.

Lemurian Adventurer O.C.C.

Lemurian Scout

By Kevin Siembieda & Matthew Clements

As the Lemurians make their presence known to the world at large, they have a growing need for information about the rest of the planet, especially the surface world. Whether the job is to investigate neighboring aquatic species or make daring runs up to the surface, it is Lemurian Scouts who function as their eyes and ears. While they are proficient in the depths of the ocean, Lemurian Scouts spend a lot of time on the surface, where they interact with surface dwellers. They have learned to mask their true identity and assume the role of a D-Bee or alien visitor amongst most outsiders. When they do not wish to be seen at all, however, Lemurian Scouts disappear beneath the surface of the waves or vanish into rivers and lakes.

A large portion of Lemurian World Trekkers pursue their love of nature and knowledge by traveling the oceans and surface of the world in search of adventure and experiences. Along the way, they help those in need, battle monsters, slay the undead, and save lives one ecological incident at a time. They rely on Bio-Weapons and Bio-Armor for protection and survive on the bounty of nature. Some use symbiotes as well and/or collect the occasional tool, weapon or useful salvaged artifact from the surface world. But the World Trekker's most valuable commodities are his intelligence and resourcefulness. Most of these Lemurian Scouts are hardy, rough-and-tumble types (much like their surface dwelling counterparts), who have learned to adapt quickly to changing circumstances and environments. They live by the seat of their pants, are open to D-Bees and new cultures and ideas, and find everything about nature and travel exciting. Lemurian Scouts always have a high regard for life, living to the fullest and marveling at nature. Though predominantly individuals and loose bands of explorers and travelers, the Lemurian Scouts have formed an unofficial brotherhood and have created a network of information exchanges. Haumia-tiketike leads this group and reports their findings to the King of Lemuria directly.

Special O.C.C. Abilities and Bonuses of Scouts

1. Special R.C.C. Abilities Common to Lemurians: See the Lemurian racial description for full details.

Life Sense: Same as all Lemurians. Range: 25 foot (7.6 m) radius plus 5 feet (1.5 m) per level of experience. Base Skill: 20% +5% per level of experience to locate/track/find a specific type of animal or plant, +5% when in an underwater environment.

Empathy with Animals: Same as all Lemurians. An automatic affinity with animals of all kinds, except monsters, predators, and sentient creatures.

Ley Line Powers: Same as all Lemurians; heals and recovers P.P.E. twice as fast as a normal human when on a ley line or at stone pyramids. Swim 25% faster when along ley lines.

Natural Abilities: Same as all Lemurians.

Pets and Familiars: A Lemurian Scout is likely to be accompanied by one small and one medium to large animal companion. A lemur or Aquatic Lemur and a land animal such as a dog, fox, wolf or predatory feline (puma, lynx, lion, etc.) are likely choices. Also has a Lemurian War Steed capable of both land and water travel (player's choice).

Ultrasonic Communication: Same as all Lemurians. Hears and creates high frequency noises to communicate. Range of Communication: 2,000 feet (610 m) underwater, 400 feet (122 m) on the surface/in the air.

2. Trail Blazing: The ability to cut and mark trails through the wilderness for others to follow. Lemurians use normal trail markings, enchanted signals and psychic traces to designate trails. **Base Skill:** 45% +5% per level of experience. A failed skill roll means the trail cannot be followed by others as intended.

3. Cross-Country Pacing: Scouts are known for pacing themselves for cross-country travel. This not only includes pacing their physical exertion and speed, but also pacing their food and water intake, enabling them to cover great distances on foot, mounted or by propulsion pack for a maximum speed that can be maintained for days. This skill, combined with Undersea or Land Navigation, also enables the Lemurian Wilderness Scout to accurately predict how long a trip will take (for him alone or with others in tow - the latter always taking at least twice as long) within 2D6x10 minutes, 6D6 hours if unfamiliar with the area.

This makes the Scout an excellent messenger between parties, able to cut across country avoiding sea lanes and other well trafficked areas, in favor of little known canals, crevasses, waterways and shortcuts, often ensuring secrecy and safety for travel. These guys come and go without anyone knowing how, when or where they've been. Once a Scout travels out of sight, he seems to simply vanish into the wilderness. **Note:** A Scout never reveals his most secret and favorite routes to clients or strangers accompanying him unless it is an absolute emergency.

On foot, this skill enables the character to move at full running speed cross-country for a time equal to his P.E.x5 in minutes without overexerting himself. In the water, the character can swim at full speed for a time equal to his P.E.x6. Taking a more relaxed pace of 50% his maximum speed can be maintained, with proper breaks, food and water, for days on end. **Base Skill:** 35% +5% per level of experience.

4. Cartography: The specialized art of mapmaking, Cartography is one of the most important skills that a Scout learns. Characters with this skill can produce highly accurate maps with a wide variety of tools, including pen and paper, computer plotting and even advanced holographic displays. (Computer mapping requires a character to have the Computer Operation skill.)

The Cartography skill also includes the rudiments of mathematics. A character with the Cartography skill has the equivalent of the Basic Math skill at a fixed base of 50%, plus any applicable bonus for an exceptional I.Q. attribute, or provides a bonus of +5% to Math: Basic if it is also selected as an O.C.C. Related Skill. (This mostly just applies to non-Lemurians, as all Lemurians already have a strong foundation in Basic Mathematics. **Base Skill:** 40% +5% per level of experience. A successful roll means the map is not only accurate and easy to use, but elegant and aesthetically pleasing. A failed roll indicates that some details are wrong, other details have been left out, and the scale and specified locations are off by 1D10 miles.

5. O.C.C. Bonuses (Scout): +2D6+6 to physical S.D.C., +1 to P.S. and +2 to P.E. attributes, +2 on Perception Rolls involving

C. WALTON

nature, hunting and tracking, +1 on initiative, +1 to pull punch, +2 to roll with impact, +3 to save vs poison and disease, +10% to save vs Coma & Death, and +1 to save vs Horror Factor at levels 2, 4, 7, 9 and 13.

Lemurian Scout O.C.C. Stats

Also Known As: World Trekkers, Out-Reachers and Lemurian Wanderer.

Alignment: Any, as per Lemurians, so typically good.

Attribute Requirements: I.Q. 8 and P.E. 12 or higher, a high P.S. and M.E. are helpful but not mandatory.

Racial Requirements: None.

Skills Known by All Lemurians:

Language: Lemurian and Oceanic at 96%.
Literacy: Lemurian at 85% +1% per level of experience.
Mathematics: Basic at 82 +1% per level of experience.
Swimming at 76% +2% per level of experience.

O.C.C. Skills:

Language: Other: Two of choice (+15%).
Climbing (+10%)
Cooking (+15%)
Fishing (+25%)
Horsemanship: General (+5%) or Pilot Paddle-Type Boats.
Horsemanship: Sea Monsters (+10%)
Identify Fruits and Plants (+20%)
Land Navigation (+10%)
Lore: Sea Creatures (+15%)
Undersea Survival (+15%)
Underwater Navigation (+20%)
Pilot: Water Scooters (+10%) or Submersibles (+10%).
Wilderness Survival (+15%)
W.P. Ancient: One of choice.
W.P. Modern: One of choice.

O.C.C. Related Skills: Select three skills of choice from the available categories listed below, +1 at levels 2, 5, 8, 11 and 14. All new skills start at level one proficiency.

Aquatic: Any (+10%).
Communications: Barter, Language (any; +10%), Literacy (any), Performance, and Public Speaking only.
Cowboy: Any.
Domestic: Any (+10%).
Electrical: None.
Espionage: None, except as a part of a Speciality Skill Package.
Horsemanship: Exotic Animals (+5%) only.
Mechanical: Basic Mechanics only.
Medical: First Aid (+10%) or Holistic Medicine (+20%), but the latter counts as two skill selections.
Military: Camouflage (+10%) only.
Physical: Any, except Acrobatics (+5% when applicable).
Pilot: Any, except robots, power armor, military or large, noisy vehicles.
Pilot Related: Any, except military vehicles and giant robots.
Rogue: Gambling, Imitate Voices & Sounds, and Tailing only (+5%).
Science: Any. Also see Speciality Skill Packages.
Technical: Any (+10% bonus applies only to Art, Breed Dogs, Lore (any), Rope Works, Recycling, Salvage and Whittling & Sculpting).
W.P.: Any.
Wilderness: Any (+15%).

Area of Specialty Skill Package (Pick One): Lemurian Scouts tend to be more educated, interested in science, and are more specialized than the Wilderness Scout known to the surface world. As a result, the Scout specializes in a particular type of scouting and investigation. These include exploration, naturalistic/botanical studies, salvage/treasure hunting, zoological/animal studies, and rescue/tracking. PICK ONE of the following skill sets:

Explorer Specialty Skill Package: This is the all-purpose explorer who enjoys traveling and exploring new places, and discovering and meeting new people, places and wildlife. This character is most at home and alive in the wilderness.

Anthropology (+20%)
Barter (+10%) or Archaeology (+15%).
Carpentry (+20%) or Escape Artist (+10%).
Excavation (+10%) or Spelunking (+10%).
Prowl (+10%) or Boat Building (+20%).
Track & Hunt Sea Animals (+15%) or Track & Trap Animals (+20%); pick one.
Tracking (people; +10%)
Hand to Hand: Expert, but can be changed to Martial Arts (or Assassin if evil) for the cost of two O.C.C. Related Skills.

Naturalist Specialty Skill Package: This is an individual whose focus is on the study of flora and fauna, with an emphasis on plant life, herbs, medicinal uses of plants, and exotic and previously unknown plants and wildlife.

Animal Husbandry (+15%)
Botany (+20%)
Brewing (+20%)
Brewing: Medicinal (+15%)
Dowsing (+20%)
Chemistry (+10%) or Biology (+10%).
Holistic Medicine (+20%) or Entomological Medicine (+20%).
Preserve Food (+20%) or Undersea Farming (+10%).
Hand to Hand: Basic, but can be changed to Expert for the cost of one O.C.C. Related Skill.

Ranger Specialty Skill Package: A Ranger Scout often engages in search and rescue operations and assists military forces, governments and industry to explore, gather information on a particular region or people, establish trails and supply lines, observe indigenous people and map the wilderness.

Detect Ambush (+20%)
Camouflage (+15%)
Intelligence (+16%)
Ocean Geographic Surveying (+10%)
Undersea Salvage (+10%)
Tracking (people; +20%)
W.P.: Any, two of choice.
Hand to Hand: Expert, but can be changed to Martial Arts for the cost of one O.C.C. Related Skill, or one of the above.

Treasure Hunter Specialty Skill Package: This Scout is a treasure hunter who specializes in finding and collecting salvage and valuables from sunken ships, crashed cargo vehicles, and ancient ruins. They love uncovering hidden treasure, ancient relics and artifacts, and salvage for fun and profit. This character may also establish trade with other people, outposts and civilizations, with an eye for exotic herbs, spices, animals and goods.

Archaeology (+10%)
Appraise Goods (+20%)
Barter (+10%)
Excavation (+15%)
Gemology (+15%)
Ocean Geographic Surveying (+10%)
Salvage (+20%)
Undersea Salvage (+10%)
Hand to Hand: Basic, but can be changed to Expert for the cost of one O.C.C. Related Skill.

Zoologist Specialty Skill Package: This is an individual whose focus is on the study of flora and fauna, with an emphasis on animals, particularly exotic and previously unknown animals, mutants, aliens and wildlife.
Biology (+20%)
Marine Biology (+20%)
Skin & Prepare Animal Hides (+10%)
Track & Hunt Sea Animals (+20%)
Track & Trap Animals (+20%)
Veterinary Science (+15%)
Zoology (+20%)
Xenology (+10%) or Medical Doctor (+5%).
Hand to Hand: Basic, but can be changed to Expert for the cost of one O.C.C. Related Skill.

Secondary Skills: These skills are replaced by the Area of Specialty Skill Package, above.

Standard Equipment: Special and/or additional weapons and gear may be provided for special assignments and missions.

Bio-Constructs: Bio-Armor: Select one of the following Bio-Armors: Barnacle, Dolphin, Wood or Wave Strider. Also has access to all types of Bio-Skins. In the alternative, the Scout may wear "human" body armor.

Bio-Constructs: Symbiotes: Living Saddle and any 1D4+1 Symbiotic Bio-Constructs of choice that are not weapons.

Bio-Constructs: Bio-Weapons: Waterjet Gun, Bio-Weapon Wood Staff or Walking Stick or other wood weapon.

Lemurian War Steed: One animal suitable for land and water travel. In the alternative, may have a horse or similar conventional surface animal and a pack horse or mule. Plus two animal companions as noted above.

Miscellaneous: One "surface dweller" sidearm, one knife or sword, a set of traveling clothes, a poncho or cloak, wide brim hat, baseball cap, backpack, duffle bag or satchel, bedroll, utility belt, canteen or water skin, box of wooden matches, cigarette lighter, mess kit, fishing kit and collapsible pole, small flashlight, pocket mirror, sunglasses, goggles, compass, an air filter and gas mask, language translator, distance binoculars, laser distancer, magnifying glass, 20 feet (6.1 m) of rope/cord, 1D4+1 small specimen jars, 2D6+6 plastic specimen bags, digital camera, sketchbook, pocket notebook, 2D4 pencils, a small sack, a medium sack, and various common personal items.

Cybernetics: None. Lemurians have no interest in bionics, not even Bio-Systems.

Money: 1D6x1,000 in Universal Credits, gems and/or trade goods for travel. Savings: 2D6x1,000 credits worth of artifacts, works of art and items from other cultures; all probably tucked safely away at home. If working for the Lemurian government or military, the Scout gets a monthly salary of 1,500 credits or trade goods. Otherwise, lives off the land, sleeps under the stars, picks fruits and berries and hunts for food.

Lemurian Psychic O.C.C.

Spouter

Spouters are Master Psychics with influence over water. In fact their control is so impressive that 50% of them are employed by the Lemurian military defense force, where they are known as **Spouter Guardsmen**, though they do not share the same degree of respect or accolades as Oceanic Guardsmen. About 25% work as Lemurian scouts and explorers, and the rest in various roles from farmers to builders to healers and teachers. Spouters who spend a lot of time on dry land in the surface world find their hydrokinesis powers make them well suited as vampire hunters. Against undead Milu, water powers mean little, but against the vampires and undead of the surface world, Spouters are vampire slaying dreadnaughts. Of course, they must be careful in picking their battles and making sure there is plenty of water for them to draw upon. A Spouter out on the prairies or in a desert is out of his element. The majority of the Spouter's powers require the presence of large amounts of water, which some people might see as a vulnerability, but which Spouters see as a challenge.

Like most Master Psychics, the Spouter has less education and fewer skills than others. This is due to having spent much of his time learning and mastering his Hydro-Psionic powers, and exploring the underwater environment in ways that even aquatic life can't. This also means Spouters rely on their psionic powers and wits more than book learning. This makes them even more connected to the aquatic environment than other Lemurians. The typical Spouter loves everything about water, both while deep in its embrace and on dry land. To them, water is the elixir of life. Whether it's cruising a beach, surfing and riding the waves with or without a surfboard, or fighting sea monsters in the deep or the undead on the surface, Spouters use and enjoy water. And though they claim to enjoy the peace and quiet of nature as much as any Lemurian, Spouters relish excitement and thrive in dangerous environments. They think quickly on their feet, adapt well to new and frightening situations, and love to use their powers. That includes having fun with them and going out and "playing" much like an impetuous teenager. To most Spouters, everything is an adventure or challenge, and they love both, which is why so many become warriors, scouts and explorers.

Special O.C.C. Abilities of the Spouter:

1. Special R.C.C. Abilities Common to Lemurians: See the Lemurian racial description for full details.

Life Sense: Same as all Lemurians. Range: 25 foot (7.6 m) radius plus 5 feet (1.5 m) per level of experience. Base Skill: 20% +5% per level of experience to locate/track/find a specific type of animal or plant, +5% when in an underwater environment.

Empathy with Animals: Same as all Lemurians. An automatic affinity with animals of all kinds, except monsters, predators, and sentient creatures.

Ley Line Powers: Same as all Lemurians; heals and recovers P.P.E. twice as fast as a normal human when on a ley line or at stone pyramids. Swim 25% faster when along ley lines.

Natural Abilities: Same as all Lemurians.

Pets and Familiars: A Spouter is likely to be accompanied by one small animal companion, typically an Aquatic Lemur, but can be anything. Also has a Lemurian War Steed capable of both land and water travel (player's choice).

Ultrasonic Communication: Same as all Lemurians. Hears and creates high frequency noises to communicate. Range of Communication: 2,000 feet (610 m) underwater, 400 feet (122 m) on the surface/in the air.

2. Traditional Psionic Abilities: Starts with Empathy (4), Hydrokinesis (varies), Impervious to Cold (2), Meditation (0), Mind Block (4), Resist Thirst (6), Sense Time (2), and Telepathy (4). **I.S.P. Base:** 2D6x10 +M.E. attribute number and 1D6+4 I.S.P. for each additional level of experience.

3. Water Based Psionic Powers (new): Spouters are Master Psychics with dramatic Hydrokinetic abilities, influence over water and related psychic abilities via the medium of water. A Spouter cannot create water but can use existing sources of water. This requires water to be available to him within the range of the particular Hydro-Psionic ability being used.

Hydro-Psionic Abilities to Start: Hold Breath (2), Hydro-Propulsion (7), Sense Water (2), and 1D4+1 of choice, and one Hydro-Super-Psionic ability at level one.

Additional Hydro-Psionics: Select one Hydro-Psionic ability for each new level of experience. Also select one Hydro-Super-Psionic power at levels 3, 5, 8, 10 and 13.

Alphabetical Listing of Hydro-Psionics:

Hold Breath (2)
Hydro-Ice Skate (3)
Hydroplane Skating (5)
Hydro-Propulsion (7)
Psychic Purification: Liquid (7)
Resist Dehydration (4)
Sense Water (2)
Water Breakout (2)
Water Levitation (8)
Water Telekinesis (varies)
Water Telekinesis Attack (M.D.) (10 or 20)
Water Telekinesis Bolt (S.D.C.) (6)
Water Telekinesis Punch (7 or 21)
Water Telekinesis Rain (5)
Water Walk Telekinesis (6)

Alphabetical Listing of Hydro-Super-Psionics:

Hydro-Magnet (10)
Hydration (15)
Water Breathing (8)
Water Pressure Endurance (12)
Water Shield (30)
Wave Attack (10 or 20)

4. The Influence of Ley Line Energy: The duration and range of the Spouter's water abilities and other psychic powers are increased by 50% whenever near (within one mile/1.6 km) or on a ley line. The duration, range and damage of his powers are *doubled* when at a ley line *nexus*.

5. Other Bonuses: +2D6 S.D.C., +3 to Perception Rolls involving water and psionics, +1 to parry and dodge while in the water or using water, +1 to save vs magic illusions and possession, and +1 to save vs Horror Factor at levels 1, 3, 6, 9, 12 and 15.

Spouter Psychic O.C.C. Stats

Also Known As: Hydro-Warriors and Water Psychics.

Alignment Restrictions: None, but tends to lean strongly toward good (Principled or Scrupulous) or selfish (Unprincipled or Anarchist).

Attribute Requirements: None, though a high M.E. or a high P.E. as well as an I.Q. of 8 or higher is suggested, but not required.

Race Restrictions: Most common among Lemurians (64%), Merans (11%), Ichthyleans (11%), Humans (8%), Elves (3%) and a host of other aquatic and non-aquatic D-Bees (3%). Essentially, any psionic capable race, though most that do develop it have a connection to water, the sea or oceans.

Skills Known by All Lemurians:

Language: Lemurian and Oceanic at 96%.
Literacy: Lemurian at 85% +1% per level of experience.
Mathematics: Basic at 82 +1% per level of experience.
Swimming at 90% +1% per level of experience.

O.C.C. Skills:

Brewing (+10%)
Fishing (+10%)
Language: One of choice (+5%).
Pilot: Water Scooters (+15%)
Pilot: Water Skiing & Surfing (+20%)
Undersea & Sea Survival (+15%)
Underwater Navigation (+10%)
W.P. Trident or Spear (pick one).
W.P.: Two of choice (any).
Hand to Hand: Basic, which can be changed to Expert for the cost of one O.C.C. Related Skill, Martial Arts (or Assassin if an evil alignment) for the cost of two, or Kapu Kuialua at the cost of three O.C.C. Related Skills.

O.C.C. Related Skills: Select five other skills. Select an additional skill at level 4, 8 and 12. All new skills start at level one proficiency.

Aquatic: Any (+10%).
Communication: Any (+10%).
Cowboy: None.
Domestic: Any (+10%).
Electrical: Basic Electronics only.
Espionage: Wilderness Survival only.
Horsemanship: General or Exotic only.
Mechanical: Basic, Automotive and Submersible Vehicle Mechanics only.
Medical: First Aid, Brewing and (Sea) Holistic Medicine only (+5%).
Military: None.
Physical: Any.
Pilot: Any, except Robots, Power Armor and Military Vehicles.
Pilot Related: Any (+5%).
Rogue: Any.
Science: Astronomy and Math only (+5%).
Technical: Any.
W.P.: Any, except Heavy Weapons.
Wilderness: Any (+5%).

Secondary Skills: The character also gets to select four Secondary Skills from the Secondary Skills list in **Rifts® Ultimate Edition**, page 300, plus one additional Secondary Skill at levels 3, 5, 9 and 13. These are additional areas of knowledge that do not get any bonuses, other than any possible bonus from having a high I.Q. All Secondary Skills start at the base skill level.

Standard Equipment: Special and/or additional vehicles, weapons, and gear may be assigned for special situations and missions, especially for Spouters in the military.

Bio-Constructs: Bio-Armor: Select one of the following Bio-Armors: Dolphin, Kelp, Wood or Wave Strider. Also has access to all types of Bio-Skins. In the alternative, the Spouter may wear "human" body armor.

Bio-Constructs: Symbiotes: Living Saddle and any 1D4 Symbiotic Bio-Constructs of choice that are not weapons.

Bio-Constructs: Bio-Weapons: Two of choice.

Lemurian War Steed: One animal suitable for land and water travel. In the alternative, may have a steed that is predominantly or entirely a sea creature.

Miscellaneous: One weapon for each W.P., a survival knife, surface dweller gun as a sidearm (probably an ion weapon), a set of traveling clothes, a poncho or cloak, wide brim hat, baseball cap, backpack, duffle bag or satchel, bedroll, utility belt, canteen or water skin, box of wooden matches, cigarette lighter, mess kit, fishing kit and collapsible pole, small flashlight, pocket mirror, sunglasses, goggles, an air filter and gas mask, language translator, distance binoculars, laser distancer, silver cross, walkie-talkie, compass, magnifying glass, 20 feet (6.1 m) of rope/cord, 1D4+1 small specimen jars, 2D6+6 plastic specimen bags, digital camera, sketchbook, pocket notebook, 2D4 pencils, a small sack, a medium sack, and various common personal items.

Cybernetics: None. Lemurians have no interest in bionics, not even Bio-Systems.

Money: Monthly salary of 2,000 credits or trade goods, double for high ranking officers in the military. Otherwise, 2D4x1,000 in credits, gems and/or trade goods in savings. Those with regular jobs earn 2D4x100+900 credits as monthly salary or may be a vagabond or adventurer type of person, making money from odd jobs and exploration. Most Spouters don't mind living in the wild in the ocean depths, or exploring and living under the stars on dry land.

New Water-Based Psionics

Hydro-Psionics exclusive to the Spouter

By Kevin Siembieda,
inspired by Greg Diaczyk and Alex Marciniszyn

Hold Breath

Range: Self.
Duration: Ten minutes +1 minute per level of experience.
I.S.P.: 2

This is a form of Bio-Manipulation in which the psychic is able to breathe in a maximum amount of air into his lungs and reduce his body's consumption of oxygen to hold his breath for a long period of time. Ideal for short dives into lakes, rivers and seas.

Hydro-Ice Skate

Range: Self.
Duration: Five minutes per level of experience.
Limitations: Ice must already exist, and the character can only follow the path of the ice covered surface.
I.S.P.: 3

The Spouter can walk, slide and skate across any ice covered surface in shoes, boots or bare feet, at triple his running speed and without fear of breaking through even the thinnest of ice.

Hydroplane Skating

Range: Self.
Duration: Three minutes per level of experience; double when raining.
Limitations: Water must be available.
I.S.P.: 5

The Spouter simultaneously causes a thin film of water, drawn from an existing water source (rain, morning dew, swimming pool, sewer drain pipes, toilet, sink, pond, lake or other body of water up to 1,000 feet/305 m away), to create a path of water that is always just in front of him, and which he can slide across as if he were skating on a sidewalk of ice. Hydroplane Skating speed is twice the character's running speed.

The water path must be a relatively level surface, but can flow up hills and inclines up to a 45 degree angle, and up and over parked vehicles and debris piles that have a low starting point no higher than two feet (0.6 m); cannot skate straight up the sides of fences and walls or the sides of buildings, nor upside down.

Hydro-Propulsion

Range: Self.
Duration: Five minutes per level of experience.
Limitations: A body of water large enough and deep enough to swim in must be available.
I.S.P.: 7

The psychic can travel on and under water at a good speed.

Underwater Torpedo. Increases the forward speed of water in a horizontal path to carry the Spouter forward at considerable speed. Underwater the Spouter is rocketed through water like a human torpedo.

Ride Waves. On the surface of water, it's as if the pyschic is riding an invisible surfboard or a wave.

In both cases, the psychic can change direction with a thought, but it is always sharp turns; cannot go sideways. To travel in a circle requires greater concentration, speed is half, and it uses up all but one attack/action in a melee round. Each change of direction counts as one melee attack/action. Speed is 5 mph (8 km) per level of experience whether riding on the surface of water or underwater.

Psychic Purification: Liquid

Range: Touchs
Duration: Permanent results in one melee round.
Limitations: Half a gallon (1.9 liters) per level of experience.
I.S.P.: 7

The Pyschic must place his hands on a container of water or other drinkable liquid (milk, broth, juice, wine, etc.) and channel his psychic energy to cleanse and purify the liquid for human consumption. It takes one full melee round (15 seconds) and kills all dangerous bacteria, parasites and germs. For twice the I.S.P., the psychic can turn salt water into drinkable, desalinated water.

Resist Dehydration

Range: Self.
Duration: 2 hours when on the move; six when sitting still and meditating.
I.S.P.: 4

A mind over matter discipline which slows the dehydration process by half when the psychic continues to exert himself. This requires moving at a slow, measured pace – half Spd, and in combat is -2 on initiative and -2 attacks per melee round. However, if sitting still and meditating, even in the blazing hot sun, the body's metabolic rate is slowed and dehydration is slowed to a crawl, 10% its usual amount, though the psychic feels very thirsty and will suffer from sunburn unless he is covered (even sunburn is reduced by half).

Sense Water

Range: Self up to a distance of a 1,000 foot (305 m) radius +100 feet (30.5 m) per level of experience.
Duration: 2 minutes per level of experience.
I.S.P.: 2

The psychic can sense the presence and general location of sources of water, whether they are natural bodies of water (pond, swamp, lake, river, sea, ocean, underground spring, etc.) or a man-made storage or means of water conveyance (swimming pool, filled bathtub, toilet, water tank, fountain, drain, sewer, reservoir, etc.) within a 1,000 foot (305 m) radius +100 feet (30.5 m) per level of experience. He can also sense if the water is clean, pure and drinkable, impure but drinkable, foul and unsafe to drink, fresh or sea water, and whether it is has dangerous parasites or disease.

Water Breakout

Range: 15 feet (4.6 m) per level of experience; line of sight required.
Duration: Instant result.
Limitations: The liquid filled container must be available.
I.S.P.: 2
Saving Throw: To avoid being sprayed, dodge at -2.

The Spouter can cause sealed containers of water and other thin liquids (broth, soda, coffee, tea, juice, milk, alcohol, cleaning solutions, and similar) to disgorge their contents in a spraying burst. Think a shaken can of carbonated soda pop. Likewise, he can cause a faucet to release a burst of water as if someone had turned it on full blast for one second. The spray hits everyone within a four foot (1.2 m) diameter. **Note:** Does not affect petroleum products (oil, gasoline, etc.), or thick solutions like mud, stew, paint or paste. Has no effect on open containers, glasses, bowls, etc., the container must be closed, capped or covered with a lid to "breakout."

This ability may be used to startle, distract, confuse and frighten the people, especially the unsuspecting. It may also be used to create enough water for the Spouter to use one of his other abilities, or to momentarily impair an opponent. A bursting container is going to draw the attention of everyone in the immediate area and cause them to look in that direction. Those in a 10 foot (3 m) radius are -2 on Perception Rolls, -2 on initiative and pause to see what's going on or move out of the way. Double these penalties to anyone splashed by the liquid, and they also loses one melee attack/action. In addition, depending on circumstances, splash victims may be further distracted and preoccupied if they feel the need or desire to clean themselves up, or dry off, or to change their clothes.

If the liquid was hot, caustic or burns when splashed in the eyes (as most soaps and cleansers, alcohol, and chemicals will do), those victims caught in the spray or hit directly in the face get no Perception Rolls, lose initiative, lose two melee attacks and fight blind (-10 on all combat rolls) until the substance is washed from the eyes. In the case of hot water, the penalties last 1D6+1 melee rounds before the eyes recover enough to see.

Water Levitation

Range: Affects the Spouter or another person weighing up to 200 pounds (90 kg), raising him/it up on a pillar of water to a height of 10 feet (3 m) per level of experience. Goes straight up only, but water can be drawn from an existing water source (rain, swimming pool, sewer pipes, water drain, toilet, sink, pond, lake or other body of water) up to 100 feet (30.5 m) away per level of experience.
Duration: 3 minutes per level of the psychic.
Limitations: Water must be available.
I.S.P.: 8

The Spouter rides a pillar of water that can be made to rise up and out of a body of water. In the alternative, the water can flow from a body of water, up to 100 feet (30.5 m) per level of experience, over land and then made to levitate upward with the Spouter or another person.

Water Telekinesis

Range: Throw/Hurl Water: 60 feet (18.3 m) away; double underwater. Flow Water: 100 feet (30.5 m) per level of experience; double underwater.
Duration: Two minutes per level of experience.
Limitations: Can only move water and watery liquids, and a water source must be available. *Flowing water* moves at a pace of 50 feet (15.2 m) per melee round, unless it is already flowing from a source at a faster pace. *A Water Blast/Pulse* is telekinetically hurled water and an instant attack the same as any thrown object.
I.S.P.: 12 to *flow* an unlimited amount of water (in two minutes), provided there is a source for it; when the water runs out, no more can be flowed across surfaces.

Throwing water varies. 3 I.S.P. for a *small amount* of water (half gallon/four pints/1.9 liters); 5 I.S.P. for a *medium amount* (up to one gallon/3.8 liters); or 5 I.S.P. for a *large amount* (5 gallons/19 liters per level of experience).
Saving Throw: Dodge with a penalty of -2.

Telekinesis is the ability to move objects without any means other than directed psychic energy. In the case of the Spouter and Water Telekinesis, that force uses water as the medium for the psionic power.

Water Telekinesis can make water flow backward, up the side of a building and walls, across the floor or ceiling, up steep vertical inclines, and in specific patterns, shapes and even write words using water and thin, watery liquids. It can also stop the flow of water at a specific point or area specified and maintained by the psychic, causing the water to flow around, or back up into (and possibly fill up) an area. The psychic can also stop water from flowing out of a faucet, into a hose or container, or direct the water coming out directly into a container or at a specific target. Water Telekinesis can also draw water out of a faucet or hose when the tap is turned off (though at a slow pace), or any open container.

In order to move water, it or its source (sink, drain, bowl, etc.) must be clearly visible and within the psychic's range. As usual, the psychic must concentrate on what he's doing, so each telekinetic feat counts as one of his melee attacks. The total number of attacks is equal to the character's number of physical attacks per melee.

Throwing Water/Water Pulse: Water Telekinesis can hurl pulses or bursts of water from a bowl, bucket, toilet, sink, puddle, pool, drain, and other sources of water, making it seem to leap from its place and fly through the air to hit a person or target with the intent of getting it wet/soaked (does 3D6 damage to vampires).

Water Blast: Water Telekinesis can blast a burst of water with such force as to inflict one S.D.C. point of damage from a small amount, 1D4 from a medium amount, and 2D4 S.D.C. from a large amount of water. In this latter case, anything five gallons or more, regardless of how much more, does a total of 2D4 S.D.C. (The large amount does 5D6 to vampires, all lesser amounts do double normal damage.)

Water Telekinesis Attack (M.D.)

Range: 30 feet (9.1 m) +10 feet (3 m) per level of experience. Double range underwater.
Duration: Instant.
I.S.P.: 10 for S.D.C. damage, 20 for Mega-Damage.
Saving Throw: Dodge or parry; -2 underwater.

The psychic summons up a whirling vortex of water from a nearby body of water to slam into an opponent with the force of a sledgehammer. Damage: 1D6x10 S.D.C. when 10 I.S.P. are spent, 2D6+2 M.D. when 20 I.S.P. are spent. 2D6x10 or 4D6x10 Hit Points to vampires or double damage to other creatures vulnerable to water.

Water Telekinesis Bolt (S.D.C.)

Range: 10 feet (3 m) per level of experience. Double range underwater.
Duration: Instant.
I.S.P.: 6
Saving Throw: Dodge or parry, -2 underwater.

The psychic summons up a small, whirling vortex of water from a nearby body of water and fires it at an opponent with enough force to inflict 3D6 S.D.C.; double damage to vampires and other creatures vulnerable to water.

Water Telekinesis Punch

Range: Touch or one foot (0.3 m) per level of experience.
Duration: One melee round; each punch counts as one melee attack.
I.S.P.: 7 underwater. 21 on dry land, but water must be nearby.
Saving Throw: Dodge or parry, -2 underwater.

The psychic summons up a small, whirling vortex of water around his fist from a nearby body of water to slam into an opponent with enough force to inflict 2D6 S.D.C./Hit Point damage plus P.S. damage bonus (if any); double damage to vampires and other creatures vulnerable to water.

Water Telekinesis Rain

Range: 10 foot (3 m) diameter per level of experience around the psychic or up to 30 feet (9.1 m) away from him per level of experience.

Duration: One melee round per level of experience.
Limitations: Must have sufficient water available.
I.S.P.: 5

The ability is used to send water droplets up in the air and release them to drop down to water or shower an area. Ideal for making an area wet, watering crops, dowsing small fires, and showering. Equivalent to a light rain (inflicts 1D4 Hit Points per melee round to exposed vampires.)

Water Walk Telekinesis

Range: Self.
Duration: Five minutes per level of experience.
Limitations: Must have sufficient water available.
I.S.P.: 6

By increasing the surface tension of the water, the psychic can walk on its surface or ride the waves as if on an invisible raft. Speed is the character's normal walking/running speed or the speed of the waves, allowing him to ride the wave like a raft. This means he can only go as fast as the waves and is carried in the direction of the tide/waves, and not any faster. Walking against the tide and into the waves, or sideways/cross-grain to the waves is done at one quarter his normal walking speed.

Hydro-Super-Psionics

Hydro-Magnet

Range: Self.
Duration: Three minutes per level of experience.
Limitations: Water must be available.
I.S.P.: 10

The wielder can cause water in a 50 foot (15.2 m) radius, per level of experience to flow to him and keep coming, up to 100 gallons/378 liters (think two full bathtubs of water) per level of experience, per melee round. The water starts to cover and soak a 20 foot (6.1 m) diameter around him. If in a room or vehicle that is not water/airtight, it starts to fill up. If in a boat or a room on a boat, it starts to fill up, and depending on its size, could be in jeopardy of sinking. This is usually done to create panic and confusion, chase people away, or dowse a fire, but depending on the circumstances, can sometimes be used to drown people and certainly to chase vampires away.

Hydration

Range: Self, or one other by touch.
Duration: Instant results.
Limitations: Water must be available.
I.S.P.: 15

A mind over matter and bio-feedback discipline that restores the dehydrated psychic or another by touch, to a healthy level of hydration within a matter of 1D6+1 minutes. All penalties and impairments from dehydration are removed and 2D6+11 Hit Points (or 2D4 M.D.C.) are restored at the end of this healing period. The victim of dehydration must be placed in a bath of water or covered in soaking wet blankets for re-hydration to work. If being performed on someone other than the psychic, the Spouter must place his hands on the subject to be healed, meditate the entire period and channel his own psychic energy into the dehydrated being to stimulate that person or animal's own psychic energy.

Water Breathing

Range: Self.
Duration: 10 minutes per level of experience.
I.S.P.: 8

The name says it all, the Spouter is able to draw oxygen from the water he is in, feels completely at ease in any water environment, and is able to endure depths 25% greater than normal.

Water Pressure Endurance

Range: Self.
Duration: 10 minutes per level of experience.
I.S.P.: 12

The Spouter can survive double his normal depth tolerance without any protective gear. Living Bio-Armor or symbiotes worn by/attached to the psychic are also affected, enabling them (and the Spouter inside) to survive depths 30% greater than their normal capacity.

Water Shield

Range: Self or up to a distance of 40 feet (12.2 m) per level of experience within line of sight.
Duration: 10 minutes per level of experience on the surface of water, on dry land, or underwater.
M.D.C. of the Shield: 25 M.D.C. per level of experience when created on the surface of water or on dry land, but it takes half damage from heat, fire and plasma attacks. 35 M.D.C. per level of experience when created underwater.
Limitations: There must be sufficient water (10,000 gallons/37,850 liters, minimum) within 100 feet (30.5 m) of the Spouter in order to create a Water Shield.
Saving Throw: -5 to dodge.
I.S.P.: 30

This is, in effect, a version of Telekinetic Force Field channeling and using water. See the *Rifts® Ultimate Edition RPG* for the complete description.

When cast on the surface of water, the Water Shield remains on the surface of water. When created underwater, the shield hangs in the water at the same level/depth, but floats on the tide.

On the surface or underwater, the Water Shield absorbs incoming attacks just like a force field, however, heat, fire and plasma attacks do half damage to it and vampires take 3D6 damage, themselves, if they touch the Water Shield.

Wave Attack

Range: 50 feet (15.2 m) per level of experience.
Duration: Instant.
Limitations: Water must be available and counts as two attacks.
Saving Throw: -3 to dodge.
I.S.P.: 10 for S.D.C. damage, 20 for M.D.

The Spouter causes a wave to rises up (six feet/1.8 m tall per level of experience) and slam into the intended target in a slapping motion. The wave can be made small or as wide as 12 feet (3.6 m).

Knockdown Wave Attack (S.D.C.): Victim loses 1D4 melee attacks and initiative, loses Perception, and is carried 2D4 yards/meters away). Damage is 4D6 S.D.C., but even Mega-Damage beings and robots weighing less than two tons are knocked off their feet and carried off for a few yards.

Damaging Wave Attack (M.D.): Victim loses 1D4+1 melee attacks and initiative, loses Perception, is carried 3D6 yards/meters away and suffers 5D6 M.D. Even Mega-Damage beings, robots and vehicles weighing less than four tons are knocked off their feet and carried off for a few yards.

Note: If the Spouter should desire to do so, he can ride the Wave Attack. He is not harmed when the wave strikes, but he is right there to continue to run past the target being struck by the wave or to press the attack while the victim is down. He is vulnerable for 3-4 seconds as the wave rises and slams forward, but to be hit, the attacker must announce a "Called Shot" and the shooter is -3 to strike. Riding a Wave Attack is not possible if it is slamming into a wall or cliff (the Spouter would take double damage).

Experience Tables

Birdman & Junk Crab

1 0,000–2,100
2 2,101–4,200
3 4,201–8,400
4 8,401–17,250
5 17,251–25,500
6 25,501–35,900
7 35,901–51,000
8 51,001–71,000
9 71,001–96,000
10 96,001–131,700
11 131,701–181,900
12 181,901–232,200
13 232,201–282,400
14 282,401–342,500
15 342,501–403,000

Gene-Mage & Milu

1 0,000–2,450
2 2,451–4,900
3 4,901–9,800
4 9,801–19,600
5 19,601–29,000
6 29,001–39,000
7 39,001–55,000
8 55,001–75,000
9 75,001–102,000
10 102,001–142,000
11 142,001–195,000
12 195,001–240,000
13 240,001–295,000
14 295,001–360,000
15 360,001–420,000

Oceanic Guardsman & Ichthyleans

1 0,000–2,130
2 2,131–4,260
3 4,261–8,520
4 8,521–17,040
5 17,041–25,040
6 25,041–35,040
7 35,041–50,040
8 50,041–70,040
9 70,041–95,040
10 95,041–130,040
11 130,041–180,040
12 180,041–230,040
13 230,041–280,040
14 280,041–330,040
15 330,041–380,040

Sea Sentinel & Lemurian Scout

1 0,000–2,100
2 2,101–4,200
3 4,201–8,400
4 8,401–17,200
5 17,201–25,400
6 25,401–35,800
7 35,801–51,000
8 51,001–71,200
9 71,201–96,400
10 96,401–131,600
11 131,601–181,800
12 181,801–232,000
13 232,001–282,200
14 282,201–342,400
15 342,401–402,600

Serpent Hunter

1 0,000–2,140
2 2,141–4,280
3 4,281–8,560
4 8,561–17,520
5 17,521–25,520
6 25,521–35,520
7 35,521–50,520
8 50,521–75,000
9 75,001–101,100
10 101,101–136,200
11 136,201–186,300
12 186,301–246,400
13 246,401–306,500
14 306,501–366,600
15 366,601–416,700

Spouter

1 0,000–2,050
2 2,051–4,100
3 4,101–8,250
4 8,251–16,500
5 16,501–24,600
6 24,601–34,700
7 34,701–49,800
8 49,801–69,900
9 69,901–95,000
10 95,001–130,100
11 130,101–180,200
12 180,201–230,300
13 230,301–280,400
14 280,401–340,500
15 340,501–400,600

Lemurian Biomancy

By Greg Diaczyk, Kevin Siembieda and Matthew Clements

Lemurians believe they are the most sophisticated and advanced practitioners of Biomancy on Rifts Earth, and perhaps throughout the Megaverse. There can be no doubt that they know more Biomancy spells than even the Jungle Elves of South America.

Lemurian Biomancy Spells Alphabetical Listing

A note on new Biomancy Spells. If the Game Master so desires, any of the new Biomancy spells can be made available to the Biomancers living in South America (see **Rifts® World Book 6: South America**), however the ocean/water based Biomancy spells available to Lemurian Biomancers are only available to them and not the Jungle Elves/Biomancers of South America nor Ocean Mages. The same is true of the spells concerning Bio-Armor.

Level One

Algae Bloom (New)

Range: 50 foot (15.2 m) bloom radius per level of experience, double along a ley line, quadruple size at a ley line nexus. The spell is cast on the magic user's location, and the caster himself will be affected unless the mage swims away from the area.
Duration: It takes 1D4 melee rounds for the algae to bloom. The multiplied amount of algae is permanent, and dissipates into the ocean or other body of water over time.
Saving Throw: None.
P.P.E.: Four

Algae must already be present in order to create a "bloom." The algae bloom can be used to block sunlight and "muddy" the water, impairing vision much like an *underwater fog* or cloud of smoke. Anyone caught inside an algae bloom is blinded (-10 to strike, parry, dodge and other combat moves) until they can manage to swim out of the area of effect. Algae is not dense enough to impair movement or swimming, though it may (01-25% chance) clog air hoses, vents and small light motors. An algae bloom may also be created to feed aquatic animals.

Bio-Scan (New)

Range: Touch or up to 5 feet (1.5 m) away for a full scan, 20 feet (6.1 m) for monitoring vitals.
Duration: Two melee rounds per level of experience; a complete scan takes 1D6 melee rounds. However, the Gene-Mage Biomancer can engage in continuous monitoring of *one* specific patient for 30 minutes per level of experience.
Saving Throw: None for animals. Standard for sentient beings, but only if the subject does *not* want his vitals to be read. Does not work on supernatural beings or creatures of magic. Automatic success for willing subjects. The use of a *Mind Block* or *Alter Aura* adds a bonus of +3 to save vs Bio-Scan. A successful save means the spell caster is unable to get a reading of that person and cannot read any of his vitals. Beings who are unconscious or out of their head with fever, pain, etc., do not get a saving throw and the spell is an automatic success. Beings who are asleep are -2 to save vs magic.
P.P.E.: Four

The spell enables the Biomancer to conduct in-depth diagnostics of sentient or animal patients. The spell also establishes a mystic link with one specific subject so the mage can continue to monitor his vital signs. The spell cannot look into the mind or read the thoughts or emotions of the patient, nor can it be used to identify mental illness unless it has a physical root cause (e.g. chemical imbalance in the body, brain tumor, etc.). Doing a magical Bio-Scan reveals the following about a patient/subject:

- Vital bio-stats such as heart rate, blood pressure, respiration, body temperature and similar. The spell caster recognizes when the subject is at rest and relaxed, or in pain, having a heart attack, anxiety attack, seizure or suffering other types of physical distress.
- Indicates tissue and muscle damage, broken bones, hairline fractures, sprained and pulled muscles, damage to organs, organ failure, internal bleeding, and other types of physical trauma.
- Detects/locates bullets, fragments and other foreign objects in the subject's body.

- Indicates the presence of foreign chemicals in the body, including poison, toxins, recreational drugs, alcohol, and chemical imbalance in the body which may indicate a more serious or chronic disease (diabetes, cancer, etc.).
- The presence of disease, infection, parasites, symbiotes, and other invading organisms in the patient's body. Does not reveal the presence of supernatural, magical or mental possession.
- Detects/locates cybernetics and bionic implants, including Bio-Systems. Though the enchantment cannot diagnose or help the Biomancer repair "machine parts," it can indicate if the surrounding connective tissue and nerve endings have been injured/damaged due to trauma to the body or from the implant.
- Identifies the source of physical pain and nerve damage.
- Unique to the Gene-Mage Biomancer only: Able to review and examine sections of the Code of Life (DNA) and be alerted to the presence of genetic anomalies, defects and disease.

Note: The Bio-Scan spell provides a wealth of information to the Biomancer, but that information is useless unless the individual understands biology and medicine. The Bio-Scan does not magically find and diagnose disease and physical trauma, but provides the Biomancer with enough information that he can make an accurate diagnosis and take appropriate action to remedy the problem. Using this spell provides +30% to diagnose the problem and +20% to treat disease and injury. Bio-Scan can not be used as a lie detector or to treat plants.

Bio-Scan: Plants (New)

Range: Touch or up to 5 feet (1.5 m) away for a scan, 30 feet (9.1 m) for monitoring vitals.
Duration: Two melee rounds per level of experience; a complete scan takes 1D6 melee rounds. However, the Gene-Mage Biomancer can engage in continuous monitoring of *one* specific patient for 30 minutes per level of experience.
Saving Throw: None for ordinary plants. Standard for sentient plant-beings, but only if the subject does *not* want his vitals to be read. Automatic success for willing subjects. The use of a *Mind Block* or *Alter Aura* adds a bonus of +3 to save vs Bio-Scan. A successful save means the spell caster is unable to get a reading of that person and cannot read any of his vitals. Beings who are unconscious or out of their head with fever, pain, etc., do not get a saving throw and the spell is an automatic success. Beings who are asleep are -2 to save vs magic. Does not work on supernatural beings or creatures of magic, such as a Millennium Tree, Memory Tree, or similar plant life forms.
P.P.E.: Three

This spell enables the Biomancer to conduct in-depth diagnostics of his plant patients. The spell also establishes a mystic link with one specific plant or patient, enabling the mage to continue to monitor that one specific plant's vital signs. The spell cannot look into the mind or read the thoughts or emotions of the patient/plant, nor can it be used to identify mental illness unless it has a physical root cause (i.e. chemical imbalance in the body, brain tumor, etc.). Doing a magical Bio-Scan reveals the following about a plant-patient/subject:

- Monitors vital bio-stats such as hydration, CO2 consumption, photosynthesis, pollen, and access to light, water and proper nutrients.
- Indicates the presence of disease, infection, toxins, rot, mold, blight, parasites, insect infestation, animal habitation/nests, symbiotes, and other invading organisms in the plant's body. Does not reveal the presence of supernatural, magical or mental possession.
- Indicates physical trauma such as broken limbs, dead leaves and branches, damaged tissue, burnt areas, dehydration, cell wall damage, root damage, and the effects of herbicidal poisons and other chemicals dangerous to plants.
- Identifies the source of damage, dead parts, distress and cell damage.
- The Biomancer is able to review and examine sections of the Code of Life (DNA), be alerted to the presence of genetic anomalies, defects and disease.
- Provides all the same information as the Bio-Scan spell when used on sentient vegetative and plant beings.

Bio-Scan: Plants only provides information to the Biomancer. The spell itself does not have healing properties, and actual treatment requires an applicable skill such as Botany or Gardening. Using this spell provides +30% to diagnose the problem and +20% to treat disease and injury. Bio-Scan can not be used as a lie detector or to treat animals.

Commune with Nature

Range: One mile (1.6 km) radius per level of experience.
Duration: Instant.
Saving Throw: None.
P.P.E.: Two

The Biomancer meditates and receives a general feeling for the surrounding ecosystem. On land, the spell informs the character if the ecosystem is unbalanced or damaged and why, such as a drought, flooding, storm/tornado/hurricane, extensive pollution, deforestation, fire, war, etc. Likewise, the spell indicates any ley lines within sensing range.

Aquatic: Underwater, the spell reveals changes in water temperature, salinity, toxicity, currents and other characteristics. The character understands the ecosystem and its threats, from pollution to over-fishing, de-oxygenation, volcanic activity, invasive alien species or reef die-offs. The spell also reveals if there is Earth Energy/ley lines within sensing range.

Heal Plants

Range: One tree or 10 foot (3 m) area per level of experience.
Duration: Permanent.
Saving Throw: None.
P.P.E.: Five, Ten or Twenty P.P.E. depending on the size of the plant, with the most applicable to trees.

If a plant has a broken or damaged stem, branch, or trunk, this spell heals the break or damage to normal and increases the usual S.D.C. by 10%. The effects are immediate and the magic is used to repair and heal repair damage to plants and trees.

Ink Cloud (New)

Range: Self.
Duration: 1D4 melee rounds +1 per level of experience (half in strong currents).
Saving Throw: None.
P.P.E.: Three
Note: Also available as an *Ocean Magic spell* for the same P.P.E. cost.

The spell caster projects a cloud of dark, blinding ink around himself, just like the defense mechanism of the octopus. The Ink Cloud covers a 50x50x50 foot (15x15x15 m) area (double area of effect at levels 5, 10, and 15). Those inside the Ink Cloud are blind (-10 to strike, parry, dodge, disarm or entangle, etc.) and lose their sense of direction.

Insect Signals (New)

Range: Self.
Duration: 10 minutes per level of experience.
Saving Throw: None.
P.P.E.: Three

The spell caster is able to understand the sounds, scents and actions of any insects he can see or hear. For example, he will be able to tell if an insect is agitated, frightened or hostile (which means it is likely to attack if bothered or touched), or whether it is content/happy (as happy as an insect can be, of course), hungry, hunting or foraging for food, mating, calling others to its location, leaving a trail for others of its kind to follow, or is sounding a warning, and so on. If a warning, frightened or hostile, the mage is able to tell if the warning has to do with a threat specific to the insects or a danger to the wider area and environment.

Shape Plants

Range: Touch.
Duration: Permanent.
Saving Throw: None.
P.P.E.: Four

The Biomancer can reshape a tree limb or small plant at will. He can alter its position and even bend, twist and reform the trunk and branches of a small tree, bush or plant without fear of harming it. Large trees and intricate designs, such as sculpting a normal tree into a humanoid or animal shape, requires multiple castings of the spell with each creating one minor effect. Sculpting a large tree or kelp frond takes 1D4+8 castings. This power only works on living or freshly cut trees and plants.

Weather Sense

Range: One mile (1.6 km) radius per level of experience.
Duration: 24 hours.
Saving Throw: None.
P.P.E.: One

The spell caster knows what the weather will be for the next 24 hours. The spell provides a reliable weather report: cloud cover, wind direction and speed, temperature highs and lows, humidity, weather fronts moving into the area, the likelihood of precipitation or foul weather, and approximately (within 5D6 minutes) when it will arrive and how long it will last. **Note:** The spell cannot forecast weather changes caused by magic or ley line disturbances during that period, but if the weather does not turn out as reported, the mage will know an outside force is responsible.

Whale Speak (New)

Range: One mile (1.6 km) per level of experience.
Duration: 15 minutes per level of experience.
Saving Throw: None.
P.P.E.: Four
Note: Also available as an *Ocean Magic spell* for the same P.P.E. cost.

Whale Speak grants the spell caster the ability to communicate with cetaceans, including whales, dolphins and orcas. The spell is not telepathic communication, and the caster must call out to the cetacean he is speaking with using high-frequency clicks and whistles for dolphins and orcas and low-frequency whale songs for most large whales. Other cetaceans and those with the Cetacean language skill will be able to understand and overhear the speaker if he or she is not careful.

Level Two

Amphibious (New)

Range: Self or one individual or animal per spell casting.
Duration: 20 minutes per level of experience, triple duration along a ley line.
Saving Throw: None.
P.P.E.: Six
Note: Also available as an *Ocean Magic spell* for the same P.P.E.

The spell gives fish and other sea creatures that cannot ordinarily function out of water the ability to temporarily breathe air and walk, slither or crawl on land (Speed: 1D6+6; double for octopus and other creatures with tentacles or legs).

When cast upon a land animal or humanoid, fingers and toes become webbed, being in water feels natural, and the individual can breathe and swim underwater for the duration of the spell. Max depth is one mile (1.6 km) and swimming Spd is the same as the running Spd attribute number. Being amphibious means the enchanted person or animal can function both on land and in the water with equal ease for the duration of the magic.

Animate Plants: Minor

Range: 60 feet (18.3 m) per level of experience.
Duration: One melee round (15 seconds) per level of experience.
Saving Throw: None.
P.P.E.: Four

The Biomancer can cause one plant as large as an average tree to move. The plant remains rooted to the spot, but can be made to move its limbs/branches or stems, bend over, seem to bob and dance, and so on. Animated trees make a lot of noise when they flail their limbs, rustling leaves and rattling branches. The mage can also make a tree or branch bend and rise back to its original position to assist him in climbing, hold a package, or to provide camouflage. The animated plant/tree can not attack, entangle or hinder people, but its movement and sound can distract, frighten or appear threatening to people not expecting the plant to move or, with proper forewarning, entertain and delight observers. Horror Factor: Seeing a large tree suddenly move its branches or bend as if to bow calls for a save vs Horror Factor 10. Perception Rolls: The animated movement of a plant, bush or tree is distracting if not outright threatening, reducing the Perception Rolls of all people watching the plant by half.

Animal Weaponry: Simple

Range: Self.
Duration: One minute per level of experience.
Saving Throw: None.
P.P.E.: Six

The spell caster alters his own body to make his fingers transform into animal-like claws or bird-like talons, or his teeth into fangs. Damage: Claws inflict a bonus of 3D6 S.D.C. damage in addition to normal punch damage and any applicable P.S. damage bonus. Sharp, pointed teeth or fangs inflict 2D6 damage and can be used to chew through rope, plastic and similar S.D.C. materials.

Bait Ball (New)

Range: 100 feet (30.5 m) per level of experience, line of sight, double along a ley line.
Duration: Takes 1D4 melee rounds for the bait ball to form and lasts for two minutes (8 melee rounds) per level of experience.
Saving Throw: None.
P.P.E.: Six
Note: Also available as an *Ocean Magic spell* for the same P.P.E. cost.

This spell makes a school of fish or plankton cluster into a tight ball instead of swimming in a loose school to evade potential predators. This is done to attract, feed or distract an animal predator, but may also be used to catch vast numbers of fish by causing them to ball and then netting them or moving them into a pen/cage. As a balled school of fish, there is only the one type of fish, not an array of different species typical of traditional net fishing. The number of fish in the ball is 1D6x10 (1D4x1,000 if plankton), but works only on small fish (less than two feet/0.6 m long) and plankton, not crustaceans, large fish, aquatic mammals or sentient beings. Chance of success using Bait Ball: 84% when predators have been seen and known to be in the area. 62% in an area known to be inhabited by or visited by the type of predator one is looking to attract (shark, sea serpent, etc.). 33% when the area is unknown to the mage. Note that a predator other than the one desired is likely (55% chance) to be attracted instead or as well as the target animal.

Bioluminescence (New)

Range: 30 feet (9.1 m) per level of experience.
Duration: 5 minutes per level of experience.
Saving Throw: Standard.
P.P.E.: Seven
Note: Also available as an *Ocean Magic spell* for the same P.P.E. cost.

The spell caster's body lights up with a highly noticeable glow. Bioluminescence is used by creatures that live in the darkest depths of the ocean to communicate, attract prey and make their presence known. Mages may use it for the same purposes, as well as to mark targets. When the spell is cast upon an opponent or target such as the front or end of a submersible, the glow becomes a giant sign calling out for people to take notice. The intense glow also washes out the facial features of the person or animal it is cast upon, making clear identification of the individual impossible unless seen within 15 feet (4.6 m). The light is bright enough to read a book or see details on a sunken ship, illuminating everything within 20 feet (6.1 m) of a person aglow with Bioluminescence. Unobstructed, the glow can be seen underwater for at least 650 feet (198 m).

Bio-Electric Touch (New)

Range: Touch only.
Duration: Instant.
Damage: 3D6 S.D.C. or 1D6 M.D. per touch.
Saving Throw: None.
P.P.E: Four for the S.D.C. attack, Ten P.P.E. for the M.D. touch.
Note: Also available as an *Ocean Magic spell* for the same P.P.E. cost.

Bio-Electric Touch is an electrical attack that inflicts 3D6 S.D.C. damage or 1D6 M.D., as desired by the spell caster and when sufficient P.P.E. is spent.

Underwater, the main target of the "touch" takes full damage, but everything within a 5 foot (1.5 m) radius of the electrical discharge takes 1D4 S.D.C. damage or 1 M.D. in the case of the Mega-Damage Bio-Electrical Touch. The touch can also be used as a defibrillator, restarting the heart when it has stopped. (01-25% chance of success when used by someone who doesn't know what he's doing, 65% when performed by a doctor, Biomancer or someone directed by a character knowledgeable in biology or medicine.) The touch can also recharge S.D.C. batteries, providing them an additional 1D6+4 minutes of life, or "jump" starting a weak car battery.

Filter Feeder (New)

Range: Self or others by touch.
Duration: 15 minutes per level of experience.
Saving Throw: None.
P.P.E.: Ten
Note: Also available as an *Ocean Magic spell* for the same P.P.E. cost.

The Filter Feeder spell enables the enchanted individual to feed upon, and gain nourishment from plankton, like certain whales and fish, by swimming around and magically absorbing the plankton in the water. It only takes 1D6+8 minutes for the average human or human-sized D-Bee to eat their fill. For larger creatures, feeding requires 1D6+8 minutes per 100 lbs (45 kg) of their overall mass.

Harvest (New)

Range: Touch.
Duration: 2D4 melees to perform, but the result is permanent.
Saving Throw: None.
P.P.E. Cost: Five for small plants, Eight P.P.E. for medium-sized plants, Fifteen for trees and plankton blooms.

The spell is able to coax a plant to give up a portion of its body as a "harvest gift." The gift can be bearing 1D4 pieces of fruit, nuts or vegetables in a matter of seconds even when out of season, or a small balloon-like pouch, about the size of a man's fist, containing 1D4+5 ounces of seeds, syrup, sap, root, leaves, petals, blossoms, pollen, or plant extract such as poison or chemicals that are something the plant normally can produce. Such "harvest gifts" are often used in medicine, cooking and magic, and are "harvested" without harming the plant.

For 30 P.P.E. the spell can compel insects and simple animals, like snakes, that have poison, chemicals, teeth or quills that the creature can secrete, fire or remove without injury to itself, to give up 1D4 of them (or 1D4 doses of chemicals) and put them in the hand or a container without attacking or hurting the spell caster.

This spell can also turn non-edible plants, grass, seaweed, leaves, stalks, flowers, berries and roots, as well as plankton and mashed insects, into a thick, nutritious soup or paste (like poi or porridge) that is surprisingly good tasting and packed with protein, vitamins and fiber. One spell makes enough food for one human-sized person per level of experience for the cost of 8 P.P.E. or two people per level at the cost of 15 P.P.E. May be used in conjunction with the various "Bloom" spells.

Insect Chemical Trail (New)

Range: Self only.
Duration: 10 minutes per level of experience. Scent lingers for 28 hours +2 hours per level of experience. Reduce the duration of the scent by half during or after rain; reduce by 90% in snow that is deeper than three inches (7.6 cm) or in a downpour.
Saving Throw: None.
P.P.E.: Five

Many insects can secrete chemicals to mark their territory, leave a trail or warn of danger. This spell enables the spell caster to mark such an invisible chemical trail on everything he touches – the path he walks upon, every leaf he brushes against, every tree he touches with his hands, and so on. The scent is left behind whether touched by the mage's bare skin, armor or clothing. Only other Biomancers using the *Chemical Trail* spell, *Insect Signals* and/or *Commune with Nature* can detect the unique insect scent and recognize what it is, what it means and follow the trail. (**Base Skill:** 90%, reduce by half in a downpour or snow deeper than a couple inches). **Note:** Insects and Insectoids like the Xiticix can also follow the chemical trail. Canines and other beings with superior sense of smell can NOT detect the Insect Chemical Trail. The scent is used by Biomancers to mark an invisible trail they can follow back later, or for other Biomancers to follow after.

Insect Leap

Range: Self.
Duration: Instant; one leap.
Saving Throw: None.
P.P.E.: Five

This spell enables the character to make an enormous grasshopper-like leap. This can be either a broad lengthwise leap or a high jump upward. A broad jump for distance carries the character 50 feet (15.2 m) plus 10 feet (3.0 m) per level of experience from a standing still position. High jumps, leaping up rather than for distance, are 10 feet (3 m) plus 6 feet (1.8 m) per level of experience. An Insect Leap counts as one melee attack/action.

Plankton Bloom (New)

Range: 90 foot (27.4 m) radius per level of experience, double along a ley line, quadruple the size at a ley line nexus.
Duration: Takes 1D6 melee rounds for the plankton to bloom and grow in volume. The multiplied amount of plankton is permanent.
Saving Throw: None.
P.P.E.: Eight
Note: Also available as an *Ocean Magic spell* for twice the P.P.E.

Plankton Bloom causes an explosion of plankton – the tiny, floating creatures found in the waters of the ocean and that make up the bottom of the ocean food chain. Unlike the dense cloud of algae created by the Algae Bloom spell, plankton are more dispersed.

Plankton must already be present in order to create a "bloom" and can be used to block sunlight and "muddy" the water, impairing vision much like a light *underwater fog*. Anyone caught inside a Plankton bloom has their vision obscured (-5 to strike, parry, dodge and other combat moves) until they can manage to swim out of the area of effect. Plankton is not dense enough to impair movement or swimming, though it may (01-30% chance) clog air hoses, vents and small, light motors. In their mystically-enhanced blooming frenzy, plankton swim and wriggle into every crack and crevice of technological items. Any piece of technology, vehicles, weapons and underwater tech with water intakes has a 30% chance of failing. Only taking apart the item, cleaning and reassembling it restores it to its working state. In the case of vehicles, running the engine at a high speed for 2D4+1 melee rounds should clear them without needing a overhaul.

The Plankton Bloom spell is also used to feed aquatic animals, has a 01-33% chance of attracting certain types of whales, rays and other plankton eaters, and can be used in conjunction with the Harvest spell to create food edible for humans.

Plant Virtual Sight

Range: 100 feet (30.5 m) per level of experience.
Duration: One melee round (15 seconds).
Saving Throw: None.
P.P.E.: Six

The spell caster can "see" from the vantage point of any plant, be it a blade of grass low to the ground or the tallest treetop. For instance, a character needing to see past a jungle's heavy canopy could use this spell to magically move his eyesight to the top of a tree. This spell can also be used on seaweed in the water to see underwater or on plants floating on the surface to see what rests on the surface of water. The spell caster has to specify the angle and the direction he intends to look and cannot change direction once the virtual sight is established.

Weave Plants

Range: Touch.
Duration: Permanent.
Saving Throw: None.
P.P.E.: Fifteen

The spell enables the mage to take portions of a plant (never the whole plant, but small pieces like leaves, vines, fibers, strips of bark, and so on) and magically reform them into a plant fiber that is lightweight, resilient and waterproof to create a fabric suitable for making cloth and clothing. The resulting material is like a cross between plastic and cotton. Color is manipulated by the selection of the base materials. Fabric made of bark, branches and roots are shades of brown; leaves and vines are shades of green; grains make yellow and orange colored fabric, while flower petals and fruits make the color of the petals or the skin of the fruit.

As the Biomancer weaves the plant fiber, he or she can shape it into clothes, sheets, strips, belts, bags, ropes or any article that can be made out of fabric or weaving. However, the Sewing skill is necessary to make a functional set of clothes (any style). Characters without the Sewing skill can only make simple cloaks, robes, blankets, sheets of material, sacks, rope and other simplistic articles. Each casting creates three square feet (0.3 square meters) of material per level of experience. Seaweed works perfectly well to make clothing, rope, nets, rigging, and sails. **Note:** Coral is a collection of a variety of different animals and cannot be transformed via this spell.

S.D.C. armor can be made by using bark or roots and layering and interlacing several layers of the material. Such armor has 1D6+45 S.D.C. and an A.R. of 13. **Note**: The Ironwood spell can be used to turn S.D.C. bark or wood armor into M.D.C. armor (1D6+45 M.D.C.).

Mend M.D.C. armor. This spell can be used to mend M.D.C. wood or plant armor, including Lemurian Bio-Armor, Millennium

Tree bark and leaf armor, and other M.D.C. wood or plant-based armor, restoring *five M.D.C.* every time the spell is cast.

Level Three

Accelerate Plant Growth

Range: Touch.
Duration: Permanent.
Saving Throw: None.
P.P.E.: Five for a small plant, Ten for a small tree and Twenty for a large tree.

The Biomancer can speed up the normal growth of a plant. Full-grown plants sprout a full year's worth of output in a melee round (including fruit production) and a sapling will grow up into a full-sized adult plant. Adult trees grow another 4D6% of their current size. A seed needs two castings, one after the planting to create a sapling and another spell to make the plant reach full size.

Animal Weaponry: Poison (New)

Range: Self.
Duration: One melee round per level of experience.
Saving Throw: None.
P.P.E.: Ten

The spell is an add-on effect to the Animal Weaponry: Simple and Major spells. This requires the *Animal Weaponry: Simple* or *Major* spell to be cast first. When this spell is cast next, the Biomancer's claw and bite attacks also release a poison that has one of the following effects. While casting the spell, the Biomancer must decide which type of poison his Animal Weapons will release: paralyzing, lethal or feverish. The ability to poison with bites and claw strikes lasts for one melee round per level of experience.

Paralyzing Toxin: A successful strike that cuts an opponent inflicts a poison that paralyzes the appendage (hand, arm, leg, wing, tentacle, etc.) that is cut or bitten, causing it to immediately go numb for 1D4 melee rounds. In the case of a hand or arm, the victim cannot use the numb limb to fight, use a weapon or even hold or carry an object. Skill performance requiring that limb is -40%. When a leg is paralyzed, reduce speed by 50%, kick attacks are impossible and the performance of skills requiring that limb is reduced by half. The victim must roll to save vs non-lethal poison (16 or higher) each time he is cut or bitten. (**Note**: Bite and claw damage as per the Animal Weaponry spell.) A failed save means paralysis. A successful save means the limb feels cold and tingles, but retains enough feeling for continued function but at -1 on all combat rolls (strike, parry, etc.) and -5% on skill performance. Each additional paralyzing strike to the same limb adds 1D4 melee rounds of paralysis to the duration unless the character manages to save (no extension of duration nor additional penalties). Roll to save for each successful poisoning attack.

Paralyzing attacks made to the head, neck and torso affect the main body by making the victim sluggish with accumulating penalties for each successful paralyzing claw or bite attack. In this case, a successful roll vs poison means no damage or penalties.

However, each failed roll to save vs non-lethal poison (15 or lower) inflicts the following penalties: reduce Spd by 5%, -1 penalty on initiative and dodge, and -5% to skill performance with accumulating effects per each attack. When Spd is reduce by 60% the victim also sees his attacks per melee and all other bonuses reduced by half.

Fever Poison: The victim of this attack must make a save vs non-lethal poison (16 or higher). A failed roll means the victim suddenly suffers the effects of high fever for 1D4+1 melee rounds. The victim finds it difficult to concentrate and focus, vision is blurry and he is -25% on the performance of all skills, reduce Spd by 30%, -1 melee attack, -2 on all combat moves, -4 on Perception Rolls and has no initiative. Penalties and fever last for 1D4 melee rounds. A successful save means no penalties whatsoever.

Lethal Poison (Hit Points): A successful strike that cuts an opponent inflicts poison and requires the victim to make a save vs lethal poison (14 or higher). A failed roll means the victim suffers 2D6 damage direct to Hit Points from each poisonous strike that is successful. A successful save vs poison means the character only suffers 1D4 damage to his S.D.C.; when S.D.C. is gone, damage is applied to Hit Points.

Lethal Poison (Mega-Damage): For twice the P.P.E. cost, the lethal poison can affect Mega-Damage beings and inflicts 2D6 M.D. A successful claw strike or bite inflicts poison and requires the victim to make a save vs lethal poison (14 or higher). A failed roll to save means the victim suffers full damage. A successful save means only 1D4 M.D. is inflicted. Non-M.D. targets take Hit Point damage rather than M.D.

Note: Damage from poison is in addition to the usual claw or bite attack. Damage from the actual claw strike or bite can be reduced by the attacker if he rolls to pull punch, in which case a successful pulled punch inflicts one point or one die of damage rather than the full amount. The poison still has full effect.

Chitin

Range: Self or other by touch.
Duration: 10 minutes per level of experience.
Saving Throw: None.
P.P.E.: Fifteen

The character's skin is magically covered in a hard, insect-like exoskeleton that is a dark, vaguely organic substance that looks like melted wax with short spikes at the joints and shoulders. This mystical chitin protects the spell caster, or one person by touch, with 40 M.D.C. +5 M.D.C. per level of experience. Chitin body armor is the equivalent of living, light body armor that has little impact on the ability to swim or climb (-5% Prowl and movement penalties). No other armor can be worn over Chitin, but it can be concealed under a cape, cloak, poncho or robe. The Chitin-clad individual can be easily mistaken for a monster or D-Bee. The spikes on the chitin inflict an extra 1D6 S.D.C. in hand to hand combat – 1D6 M.D. if this spell is combined with the spell *Animal Weaponry: Major.*

Coral Growth (New)

Range: 50 foot (15.2 m) radius of growth per level of experience.
Duration: Permanent.
Saving Throw: None.
P.P.E.: Eight

Live coral or the living organisms that create coral must already be present in order to "grow" coral. The spell stimulates and speeds up the growth of coral by 100 times their natural growth rate to repair damage to coral reefs, enlarge or spread such reefs or to create new ones.

Electrolocation (New)

Range: Self, with a sensing range of 100 feet (30.5 m) per level of experience.
Duration: Two minutes per level of experience.
Saving Throw: Standard.
P.P.E.: Ten
Note: Also available as an *Ocean Magic spell* for the same P.P.E. cost.

Many fish use electrical receptors to locate prey buried in the sand or hidden in muddy waters. All living things produce a small electrical field, and keying in on that allows the spell caster to find people and animals in complete darkness, silt-laden rivers, intense blizzards, magical illusions and other visual impediments. The spell caster sees visual traces of bioelectricity indictating the presence and location of life forms and electrical energy, including wiring and conduits. Can judge the actual position to within five feet (1.5 m) even in total darkness and reduces the penalties for being blind by half. The spell also enables the enchanted individual to sense strong lines of electromagnetic energy and magnetic north.

Fish Skin (New)

Range: Touch.
Duration: Permanent.
Saving Throw: Not applicable.
P.P.E.: Ten or Thirty-Five

This spell is similar to the Weave Plant invocation, only the Biomancer accelerates the growth cycle of one or two large fish or a school of 1D4x10 small fish to shed a layer of skin and scales, which are then magically molded together to form a fabric that is like the skin of a fish. The "Fish Skin" is lightweight, flexible, waterproof and reminiscent of a rubber diving suit or heavy spandex. Color depends on the fish used to acquire the fish skin and can range from white, silver/gray and black to yellow, orange, red, violet and blue. This magic can be used on monsters and sea serpents with fish-like skin to similar effect.

As the Biomancer creates the Fish Skin, he can shape it around himself or another person to create a skintight, second skin similar to a diving suit. This second skin is used to stay warm at colder depths underwater and as a simple armor without movement penalties.

S.D.C. Armor: For the cost of 10 P.P.E. the Fish Skin has an A.R. of 14 and 30 S.D.C. +5 per level of experience.

M.D.C. Armor: For the cost of 35 P.P.E. the Fish Skin has 10 M.D.C. +5 M.D.C. per level of experience.

Unlike many spells that provide a temporary suit of armor, Fish Skin is permanent and remains a functioning suit of armor until the armor is destroyed (loses all its S.D.C. or M.D.C.).

Insect Climb (New)

Range: Self or another person by touch.
Duration: Two melee rounds (30 seconds) per level of experience.
Saving Throw: None.
P.P.E.: Eight

The spell enables the recipient of this magic to climb any but the most smooth or icy of surfaces like a bug, including walls and ceilings. **Base Skill:** 98%, -30% when climbing faster than 75% of the character's full running speed, -60% when trying to climb on glass, ice or similar slick or smooth surfaces. The spell lasts for a brief time, so it is often used to get to a particular ledge or perch before the spell wears off.

Life Link (New)

Range: Self or other by touch. Once the link has been established, the affected individual can travel up to 3,000 miles (4,800 km) away and remain in contact with the animal or area to which he is linked. The spell caster can end the connection at any time. A link to an area picks up the general feelings and sensations of everything within a 100 foot (30.5 m) radius or may be limited to one specific animal or plant.
Duration: Five minutes per level of experience.
Saving Throw: Standard for animals and people.
P.P.E.: Eight to link to a specific animal or plant, Fifteen for an area link. Double the P.P.E. cost and triple the duration when the mage links *himself* to an individual, animal or area to monitor and protect it.

This unusual spell can be used in a few different ways. In all cases, the mage can break the link at will.

1. To monitor. The mage may link himself to a specific animal, person, plant/tree or 100 foot (30.5 m) area of nature to monitor it. He cannot read its mind nor see through its eyes, but does feel the animal, plant or area's general emotions and will instantly know when it feels relaxed, content, fearful, hostility or pain and suffering. Any of these emotions indicate the general state of the animal, person or environment, and a sudden change may indicate play, rest or the appearance of someone special, an enemy, imminent danger, and being attacked/hurt or killed. **Note:** Remember, the emotions of plants and wild animals will be different from people. For example, a flower, bush or tree is not likely to fear the appearance of a monster (or an army of monsters) unless it is uprooting, setting fire to, or destroying vegetation. **Penalties:** While linked in this manner, the mage or other recipient is distracted and suffers the following penalties: -4 on Perception Rolls, -2 on initiative, reduce all combat bonuses by half, and -20% to skill performance.

2. Relaxation and meditation. In the alternative, a Biomancer may link himself or another to a healthy, beautiful area of nature or a vibrant animal so he may experience the splendor, majesty and joy of nature. Same disorientation and penalties apply as in #1 above, but gets the benefits of being in a relaxed state similar to meditation and Lemurians and Biomancers are +10% to commune with nature.

3. To teach a lesson. The Life Link spell may also be used as a teaching tool to make despoilers of nature understand the consequences of their actions. In this case, the spell links a person other than the spell caster to a particular animal or plant, or to a specific wilderness area. Whenever that plant or animal is hurt (or a 100 foot/30.5 m radius of a specific wilderness area) the linked individual feels every emotion and every ounce of pain or discomfort to which he is bound. The recipient of the link is not physically injured or harmed, even if the creature he is linked to is hurt or dies. However, feeling the emotions and pain of the suffering animal/environment is a powerful experience. It often brings about an awakening and awareness as to the consequences of one's actions. **Penalties:** While linked to the suffering animal or carnage to an area, the linked individual is flooded with sensations that make fighting and skill performance difficult: reduce the number of attacks and combat bonuses by half, he has no initiative or Perception Rolls, and skills suffer a penalty of -50%.

Optional: At the G.M.'s discretion, have the target of the link make a save vs Insanity (15 or higher). A failed roll means roll for one of the following results:

01-05% Hateful. Good or evil, the experience does nothing to change the individual's ways, except now he has a lasting hatred of all Biomancers. He'll never trust them or their cursed magic and looks for ways to make them suffer as payback for what was done to him by this spell; +2 to save against this spell in the future.

06-10% Callous. Good or evil, the individual likes the suffering or carnage he's unleashed and does not change his ways in the least. In fact, he *may* even become more callous, cruel or destructive. Repeat exposure to this spell is a pleasant experience that reinforces his callous attitude.

11-30% No lasting effect. Good or evil, the individual feels remorse for a while (1D6 days), but falls back to his old ways. Roll on this table again if subjected to this spell in the future.

31-50% Changed. Good or evil, the individual's eyes are opened and he tries to be more aware and considerate of the environment in the future. He is less careless and callous, and much more humane and concerned about the welfare of animals and the environment. Repeat exposure to this spell reinforces the "Changed" attitude, nothing more.

51-70% Self-Enlightenment. Good or evil, the individual's eyes are opened and he tries to be much more aware about the humane treatment of animals and responsibility to the environment. He, himself, is never cruel to animals nor careless or destructive to the environment. Repeat exposure to this spell reinforces the "Self-Enlightened" attitude, nothing more.

71-90% Crusader. Good or evil, the individual's eyes are opened and he becomes a crusader for the humane treatment of animals, appreciates nature and fights for the preservation of the environment. He is now prone to lecturing others on the matter, condemning foolish and dangerous behavior that could cause damage to the environment or the inhumane treatment of animals, and may even threaten and punish (beat up, humiliate, sabotage, etc.) offenders who ignore his words. Repeat exposure to this spell reinforces the "Crusader" attitude and may make him even more proactive and/or violent toward those who do not share his view.

91-00% Obsessed. The individual sees the world through new eyes and no longer wishes to pursue his careless, callous or deliberate ways of destruction. He is now obsessed with trying to right his past wrongs. He is part Crusader (see above) and quite zealous in his views. The character is likely to give up the hunting and eating of animals (or seldom eats the meat of any animal), and is likely to threaten, beat up and even kill offenders who ignore his words. Repeat exposure to this spell reinforces the "Obsessed" attitude and may make him even more proactive and/or violent toward those who do not share his outlook. Bonuses: +5% to all skills involving the care, breeding and riding of animals, and +5% to the Botany, Gardening, I.D. Plants & Fruits and Recycling skills.

Nutrient Bath (New)

Range: 12 feet (3.6 m) per level of experience.
Duration: Roughly 2 minutes (8 melee rounds).
Saving Throw: None.
P.P.E.: Eight
Note: Also available as an *Ocean Magic spell* for twice the P.P.E.

Nutrient Bath creates a bubble of water around the mage or a specific target that is infused with nutrients and vitamins. The enchanted water scours the target's skin and infuses into his or her body, scrubbing away dirt, mud, algae, seaweed, skin parasites and skin disease and healing burns, minor cuts, scrapes and abrasions. The spell straightens wrinkles, evens skin tone and removes acne and blemishes, providing +1 to P.B. for up to a month after its application (can only be done once per month). The spell can also be used to clean and care for riding animals like sea monsters, purify sick or rotten fish/squid for consumption and to clean plants of rot and disease.

Repel Sharks (New)

Range: 10 foot (3 m) radius per level of experience around the spell caster.
Duration: Five minutes per level of experience.
Saving Throw: Standard.
P.P.E.: Ten
Note: Also available as an *Ocean Magic spell* for the same P.P.E. cost.

Sharks and rays hunt using the ability to sense electrical activity in the water produced by living prey and muscle movement. This also makes them extremely sensitive to overloads of electricity, especially since water is an excellent conductive medium. This spell creates a low level electrical field around the caster. Any shark, ray or other S.D.C. creature able to sense electricity is likely to stay outside the range of the electrical field. Those that come within the spell's radius suffer 1D4 S.D.C. damage and must save vs Horror Factor 17. A failed H.F. roll shocks and compels the creatures to leave the area, swimming 1D6x1000 yards/meters away. It has the same effect on spell casters using the *Senses of the Shark* spell and those who have taken on *the form* of a shark or ray. No effect on M.D.C. sea monsters, sea serpents, demons, supernatural creatures or beings not sensitive to electricity.

Seaweed Net (New)

Range: Net appears in the spell caster's hands and can be thrown 20 feet (6.1 m) with surprising accuracy (magically assisted).
Duration: One melee round per level of experience (half when removed from water or cast on dry land).
Saving Throw: Dodge vs the attacker's toss of the net; high roll wins.
Note: Counts as two melee attacks/actions; one to make the net and one to throw it.
P.P.E.: Nine

The spell creates a net out of available seaweed that can then be thrown to snare as many as four human-sized victims or large fish/animals within an 8 foot (2.4 m) radius. Normal weapons can cut the seaweed netting, but the damage is instantly repaired and the netting magically restored. Only damage greater than 18 M.D.C. inflicted at one time can destroy the netting, causing it to fall apart. A Dispel Magic Barriers spell also causes the net to fall apart, freeing its captives. Those caught in the net are temporarily immobilized (down to one physical attack without benefit of bonuses and applicable only when someone comes close enough to be struck by the netted victim) until the net is destroyed, the captured are released or the duration of the spell elapses. The spell caster can cancel the net at any time.

Seaweed netting may also be strung up to create a light, temporary barrier or pen. **Note:** If there is no seaweed within a 100 foot (30.5 m) radius of the spell caster, the netting cannot be created.

Shrink Plant

Range: Touch.
Duration: One minute per level of experience or permanent.
Saving Throw: Standard; supernatural plants get a +6 to save.
P.P.E.: Ten temporary or Two-Hundred for permanent shrinking.

This spell shrinks any one plant by as much as 90%, reducing a 30 foot (9.1 m) tree to a mere 3 feet (0.9 m). The spell caster can determine the degree of shrinkage in gradations of 10% to a maximum of 90%. Once shrunk, the spell cannot be used on that plant again to make it any smaller. Expending 200 P.P.E. points makes the reduction in size permanent.

Tracking Barnacle (New)

Range: Self by touch or up to 30 feet (9.1 m) away; line of sight required.
Duration: One hour per level of experience.
Saving Throw: None.
P.P.E.: Fourteen

The Biomancer summons a mystic barnacle with a special link to him. The barnacle can be attached by hand to a vessel, object or large creature, or cast from a distance up to 30 feet (9.1 m) away. In either case, the barnacle attaches itself securely to the target and assumes the color of the object/vessel to which it is attached. As per the magic, the spell caster can sense the general direction, distance and location of the barnacle, no matter the distance between them. **Note:** Works best underwater and stops working after 15 minutes when taken out of water.

Weaponize Sea Anemone (New)

Range: Self or other by touch.
Limitations: The Biomancer can transplant and weaponize two anemones per level of experience.
Duration: 30 minutes per level of experience.
Saving Throw: None.
P.P.E.: Twelve

The Biomancer takes an anemone, a little creature with poisonous tentacles that lives attached to rocks and coral, and gently coaxes it off its perch. The anemone can then be magically transplanted to another underwater object and location. This can include a door, doorknob, chest/container, weapon or other object, and even to Mega-Damage or S.D.C. armor or the flesh of the Biomancer.

Once attached, the sea anemone lives and functions as it would at a coral reef, stinging fish and people with its poisonous tentacles when they come too close or touch the anemone. Any bare skin that comes in contact with the anemone suffers 1D4 S.D.C. damage. In combat, that means sparring and grappling with an anemone covered opponent causes pain and damage from 1D4 anemones every time the opponent tries to grab, hold, parry, punch or touch a part of the body that has anemones on it. Even accidentally brushing up against the anemone while engaged in combat inflicts 1D4 S.D.C./ Hit Point damage per touch. **Note:** Each anemone has 1D6+1 Hit Points, but can only be killed when the attacker specifically intends to do so and strikes with the purpose of killing the anemone, not the person, armor or object to which it is attached. An anemone is typically the size of a tangerine or small apple and its tentacles are much too tiny, short and weak to grab an opponent or a weapon.

Level Four

Animal Weaponry: Major

Range: Self.
Duration: One minute per level of experience.
Damage: Mega-Damage as described below.
Saving Throw: None.
P.P.E.: Twenty

The Biomancer alters his own body by making his fingers magically elongate into bony animal-like claws and/or his teeth into large fangs. The character can even make a pair of horns or antlers grow out of his head. The Major spell makes these growths Mega-Damage weapons.

Claws inflict 2D6 M.D. in hand to hand combat and are +1 to strike and parry. Horns or antlers do 2D6 M.D. and are +1 strike with head butt and ram attacks. Fangs inflict 1D6 M.D. per bite and can be used to chew through S.D.C. material and light M.D.C. cord, chains and very thin metal (i.e. has less than 12 M.D.C.).

Forest Camouflage

Range: Self.
Duration: Two minutes (8 melees) per level of experience.
Saving Throw: None.
P.P.E.: Fifteen

The Biomancer can blend into any plant-covered or seaweed-filled landscape, becoming totally invisible! Unlike the Chameleon spell, the mage can move around without cancelling the cloaking capabilities of the spell. Not even the See Invisible spell or creatures with that ability are able to see the Forest Camouflaged character as long as he stays among the trees or scrub (bushes, tall grass and/or weeds, and other tall vegetation). Nor can he be detected by any technological imagers, motion detectors or heat sensors. While the spell is in effect, the character has an effective Prowl skill of 60% (or +20% to an existing Prowl skill, whichever is greater), and as long as he stays still and among tall vegetation, he cannot be located.

The Biomancer's location/hiding place is revealed only when he calls attention to himself by making noise, talking/shouting, waving, stepping out of tall vegetation or attacking. Once revealed, the spell is broken.

Similarly, this spell can be cast upon a parked vehicle with it's engine and other noise making devices turned off, crates, bundles, tents, gear, etc., to make them camouflaged. Someone would literally have to bump into or trip over the item to find it.

Remember, the spell only works in places where trees and tall vegetation are present and numerous: forests, jungles, city parks, gardens and fields with tall grass, weeds, flowers or scrub. In the case of fields with tall vegetation, the Biomancer must crouch low for the spell to work; standing above the vegetation reveals him. The spell does not work at beaches, deserts, rocky landscapes, lawns or fields where the grass and brush is shorter than four feet (1.2 m) nor areas devoid of plant life.

Insect Silent Walking (New)

Range: Self only.
Duration: Five minutes per level of experience.
Saving Throw: None.
P.P.E.: Ten

The enchantment enables the Biomancer to walk silently, even across squeaky floorboards, dry leaves, gravel, and through underbrush without making a sound, provided he doesn't move faster than half his maximum running speed/Spd attribute. Moving faster negates the magic and generates the normal amount of noise.

Insect Silent Walking provides the equivalent of the Prowl skill at 70%. If the mage already has the Prowl skill it functions at 94% and leaves a minimal trail to be followed (-25% penalty to the Tracking skill of those trying to follow character's trail).

Re-Hydrate (New)

Range: Touch or 20 feet (6.1 m) per level of experience; line of sight required.
Duration: Permanent.
Saving Throw: None.
P.P.E.: Ten

Re-Hydrate completely restores water levels within one large plant or one human-sized living creature or 1D6+2 small animals (lemur or squirrel size or smaller). For humans and similar D-Bees, going two or three days without fresh water is life-threatening. Re-Hydrate not only stakes the thirst and provides them with a full normal allotment of water, but it also heals the ravages of dehydration, from a cracked and parched tongue and mouth to dangerously dried-out brain and body tissue.

Plants are much more resilient and many can go for long stretches without water. Even though the plant may look withered and nearly dead, as long as the plant is still alive, Re-Hydrate will bring it back to its full glory, no matter how dried out and dessicated it appears. The spell can be used on one large tree, two medium trees, 1D4+2 saplings, or a 10 foot (3 m) radius of plants, flowers, crops, bushes and shrubs, or double that size of grass.

Safe Fire (New)

Range: Touch or up to 10 feet (3 m) away; line of sight required.
Duration: 30 minutes per level of experience.
Saving Throw: None.
P.P.E.: Seven

The spell creates a magic campfire suitable for cooking and keeping a small area warm. The fire does not spark or flare, even in a high wind, and when it goes out, it is instantly cold and dead; there is no hot ash or embers that could accidentally start a forest fire.

Scent Cloak (New)

Range: Self or others by touch.
Duration: 15 minutes per level of experience.
Saving Throw: None.
P.P.E.: Eleven

Water carries scents and traces of blood, oil and chemicals for many miles, and most marine predators are adept at tracking by smell. Scent Cloak completely masks the smell of those enchanted by this magic, making them impossible to track by scent on land or in the water, and indistinguishable from the normal chemistry of the water or air. As long as the spell is active, those cloaked by the spell produce no scent whatsoever and can only be tracked by sight or other means.

Seaweed Floating Platform (New)

Range: 6 foot (1.8 m) radius per level of experience.
Duration: 12 hours per level of experience.
Saving Throw: None.
P.P.E.: Ten
Note: Also available as an *Ocean Magic spell* for twice the P.P.E.

The spell causes seaweed within a mile (1.6 km) radius to come together to create a soft, spongy platform strong enough for a person or several people to stand upon, walk across or ride upon like a semi-submerged life raft on the surface of the water. Although those on the seaweed platform will get wet, and receive no protection from the elements, the soggy seaweed raft prevents its passengers from sinking and drowning. The platform cannot be summoned out of nowhere, so there must be seaweed present in the area for the spell to work. To keep the platform from eventually falling apart, the spell may have to be recast, and the spell caster responsible can cancel the magic at any time.

Strengthen Plant

Range: One tree or 10 foot (3 m) area per level of experience.
Duration: One minute per level of experience or permanent.
Saving Throw: None
P.P.E.: Temporary effects: Blades of grass, a shrub or bush 20 P.P.E., a small tree 30, an adult tree 40 or a giant redwood type tree 60 P.P.E. 400 P.P.E. will permanently transform a living plant of any size into a Mega-Damage structure.

This spell transforms normal trees and plants into M.D.C. structures! A blade of grass has one M.D.C. point (and is like stepping on a nail, pointed end up), small shrubs and bushes acquire 4D6 M.D.C., larger bushes and small trees have 1D6x10 M.D.C., good sized trees have 4D6x10 M.D.C. and trees towering 200 feet (61 m) or higher have 1D6x100+100 M.D.C.!

Some biomancers use rituals and ley line energy to permanently transform whole forests into living Mega-Damage structures. This is especially effective in foiling logging operations and turning seaweed and kelp into deadly obstacles for ships. In addition to their new Mega-Damage strength, transformed plants are immune to disease, insects and to normal fires. M.D. and magic/psychic fire inflict normal damage.

Once a Mega-Damage plant or tree is cut down/killed, however, it reverts back to normal S.D.C. wood and fiber, so people trying to exploit the capabilities of the strengthened plants by killing them get nothing for their troubles.

Weaponize Eel (New)

Range: Self or others by touch.
Duration: 15 minutes per level of experience.
Saving Throw: None.
P.P.E.: Sixteen

Similar to the Weaponize Sea Anemone spell, the Biomancer is able to attach and use eels. The eel can be a Moray or other large, aggressive, S.D.C. type of eel. The Biomancer convinces the animal to join with him or her, affixing the animal to his armor or own skin, often along the forearm and shoulders. The eel(s) remains docile until the mage enters combat, at which point the eel(s) snaps at opponents independently (has two attacks per melee round) and bites anyone who comes within range or tries to grapple with or strike the Biomancer.

Moray Eel: The animal has 3D6 Hit Points/S.D.C., its bite does 1D6 S.D.C. damage, and it is +1 to strike and dodge.

Electric Eel: The animal has 3D6 Hit Points/S.D.C., its bite does 1D4 S.D.C. damage and the electric shock does 2D4 S.D.C. damage and has a 01-50% chance of stunning fish and animals smaller than a foot (0.3 m) in length.

Unleash Eels: At any time, the mage can unleash one or more of the eels attached to him, point at an adversary and have the eel(s) attack him. The eels fight for one melee round per level of the Biomancer or until they are slain, whichever comes first.

Level Five

Amplified Scent (New)

Range: 50 feet (15.2 m) per level of experience.
Duration: 10 minutes per level of experience.
Saving Throw: Standard.
P.P.E.: Twenty-One

The spell caster enchants a person, animal or object to amplify its natural scent. Whether on land or submerged, any animal or individual attempting to track the enchanted individual/target by scent receives a +35% bonus. The enhanced scent is highly noticeable, even for those with a poor sense of smell, and the scent is just as strong in water as it is in the air. Those in the presence of the enchanted creature or object will find the scent so strong as to be unappealing and probably want to stay away and downwind of him/it.

Animal Phantom

Range: 10 feet (3.0 m) per level of experience.
Duration: One minute per level of experience.
Saving Throw: Standard.
P.P.E.: Twenty

This spell, also known as Animal Ghost, can be used along a game trail, a drinking spot, or any place frequented by animals. The spell creates a seemingly real image of any one animal that is known to the area. The phantom animal appears real, especially from a distance, and it behaves as one might expect the normal animal to do. A duck would swim, fly, waddle and quack, a rabbit hop and eat greens, a deer would run and leap, a bear forage for food and stand up threateningly and roar when startled before dropping to all fours and running off, and so on. Many Biomancers use this spell to trick and lure hunters into an ambush or away from the real game animals.

Animate Plants: Major (New)

Area of Effect: 40 feet (12 m) plus 5 feet (1.5 m) per level of experience.
Duration: One minute per level of experience.
Saving Throw: None.
P.P.E.: Twenty

This spell enables the Biomancer to mentally manipulate all the plant life within a 40+ foot area in front, behind or around him. Thus, he can cause vines, weeds, seaweed, shrubs or trees to tangle and ensnare animals or people or bend and reposition to cover and camouflage an object/vehicle or to create cover for him or others to hide. The mage can also make the larger plants attack using their branches or bodies/trunks to hit, swat or grab and hold an opponent, and vines to strike like a whip. Although the limbs of trees can be made to move like hands and arms, they are still restricted by the fact that they are hard wood, lack true fingers and human dexterity and are rooted to one spot. However, while incapable of articulated movement, trees hit with great force and mass and can block, grab and hold opponents and even vehicles in their arms/branches, as well as trip and entangle with their roots.

Attacks per Melee: Those of the spell caster +2 (+1 more at levels 5, 10 and 15). Each attack by a tree or area of vegetation counts as one of the Biomancer's own as he turns, points and waves his arms and hands like a conductor directing an orchestra, except he's directing the action of the plants and tree attacks. This spell requires the full concentration of the Biomancer, preventing him from casting any other spells as long as he is orchestrating the attacks of plants.

Damage: Damage can be M.D. due to the mass of the tree branch used to strike. Tree branches are much larger and heavier than one might expect when looking at them from the ground up. Add the force of momentum, weight and Supernatural equivalent strength of trees, and it strikes with significant force. Of course, the tree also takes damage, but it is incidental (5% of what it inflicts) and probably appears as a shower of leaves and broken twigs and small branches. Not applicable for seaweed; see Entanglement.

- Whip attacks from a vine inflict 2D6 S.D.C. damage.
- Underbrush, bushes and saplings (trees 12 feet/3.6 m and smaller) inflict 2D4 S.D.C. damage strike.
- Medium-size adult trees (15-30 feet/4.6 to 9.1 m) inflict 5D6 S.D.C., 1D6x10 S.D.C. or 1D4 M.D. depending on the amount of damage desired by the mage controlling the tree.
- Large adult trees (35-90 feet/10.6-27.4 m) inflict 6D6 S.D.C., 2D4x10 S.D.C. or 2D4 M.D. depending on the amount of damage desired by the mage.
- Massive, giant trees taller than 100 feet (30.5 m) or with a trunk thicker than 10 feet (3 m) in diameter – rare – inflict 2D4x10 S.D.C., 3D4 M.D. or 4D4 M.D. depending on the amount of damage desired by the mage.

Note: The heaviest damage is done by the largest, thickest branches or the trunk of the tree which can be made to bend down in a pummeling hammer strike or baseball bat-like sideswipe.

Entanglement:

- Short weeds, grass, flowers and soft plants grab and entangle the feet and legs to impair movement, reducing speed by 15% (20% for seaweed)
- Tall weeds and/or tall grass, light vines and seaweed impair movement and reduce speed by 30% (40% for seaweed).
- Many and/or thick vines reduce speed by 40% and there is a 01-40% chance of becoming completely tied up or tied down to one location when one remains in one spot for more than two melee rounds. To break free of the vines in two melee actions requires a combined P.S. of 40 or Robotic or Supernatural P.S. of at least 18, otherwise it takes 1D4+2 melee actions to cut free of the entangling vines (60% for seaweed).
- Dense scrub and sapling trees reduce speed by 45% (65% for a dense mass of seaweed).
- Small to average-sized trees impair movement, reducing speed by 60% (70% for seaweed).
- Large trees (or a clump of seaweed) impair movement, reducing speed by 85%. Trees can be made to lean and bend to block a

path with a dense weave of branches to make places difficult to nearly impossible to pass through without going around, climbing through or chopping or blasting through the mass of branches (takes two melee rounds to blast through 20 feet/6.1 m using M.D. weapons or tools). Characters who try to climb through the weave of branches may suddenly find themselves 20-50 feet (6.1 to 15.2 m) above ground if the controlling Biomancer has the tree rear back up with its branches reaching up into the air. Being thrown or shaken out of a tree does 3D6 S.D.C. fall damage with a 01-75% chance of losing initiative and two melee attacks from the fall.

Birth Giver (New)

Range: Self only.
Duration: As long as the birth takes.
Saving Throw: None.
P.P.E.: Twenty

This enchantment enables the spell caster to assist in the birth of any living animal, from a hamster or horse to a human or D-Bee. The enchantment lasts until the young is born and enables the Biomancer to handle most birth related medical procedures and emergencies (breached birth, etc.). Though the mage can handle most complications in birth like a seasoned professional, the magic imparts no lasting medical knowledge or skill. The Birth Giver spell empowers the Biomancer to help females (and certain unisex aliens) through childbirth, but the magic also has a soothing effect on the mother, keeping her calm, reducing pain and, as a rule, preventing serious complications. As a result, the birthing process takes half as long as usual and there are seldom complications for the mother or child during or after birth.

Insect Brother (New)

Range: Self or one or two others by touch.
Duration: Ten minutes per level of experience.
Saving Throw: None.
P.P.E.: Eleven

The spell creates an aura and pheromones that make insects and arachnids see the enchanted individual as one of their own kind. As such, the individual is ignored by insects and arachnids, and is able walk among them, even through a cloud of angry bees, hornets, etc., without fear of getting attacked. All insects see the individual as one of their own and will not bite or attack, not even mosquitos. This also means the enchanted individual can handle poisonous insects and arachnids without fear. However, if the insect is startled or believes it is about to be attacked by its Insect Brother, it will fight back and bite or sting him. This spell does not make a character immune to insect poison and he will suffer the full effects. **Note:** This spell can be used to mask the "scent" of humans and D-Bees to make them undetectable to *Xiticix* and other insect beings. However, Xiticix and intelligent insectoids immediately know they are being fooled the instant they make *visual contact* with humanoid intruder(s).

Metamorphosis: Plant

Range: Self only.
Duration: 5 minutes per level of experience.
Saving Throw: None.
P.P.E.: Thirty

The Biomancer can transform himself into a plant. The size can range from a shrub to a tree. While in this state, the Biomancer cannot move, attack or use magic (except to end the spell), but remains in control of all his senses other than speech. Turning into a shrub or tree temporarily gives the character 60 additional S.D.C. for normal plants or 200 S.D.C. for a large tree or kelp frond.

Revitalize Plant Life (New)

Range: Touch or up to a casting distance of 50 feet (15.2 m) per level of experience; line of sight required.
Area of Effect: 25 foot (7.6 m) radius per level of experience.
Duration: The effects take 1D6 melee rounds to become apparent, but are permanent once the spell has been cast.
Saving Throw: None.
P.P.E.: Fifteen

Channeling his or her magic power into the local environment, the Biomancer restores all the plant life within the area of effect to their normal level of vitality and health. Plants within the area appear healthy and hydrated. Damage which may have been caused by drought, heat, flooding, bad weather, frost, toxic spills/exposure to chemicals and trampling are all undone. The spell does not actually replace or regrow grass, trees or seaweed, but restores those still present to a healthy state.

Seaweed Bloom (New)

Range: 60 foot (18.2 m) bloom radius per level of experience, double along a ley line, quadruple size at a ley line nexus. The spell is cast at the magic user's location, and he will also be affected unless he swims away from the area.
Duration: It takes 1D4 melee rounds for the seaweed to bloom. The multiplied amount of vegetation is permanent, and dissipates into the ocean or body of water over time.
Saving Throw: None.
P.P.E.: Twenty

Seaweed, whether it is kelp, sargassum or other type of plant, must already be present in order to create a "bloom." The seaweed bloom is used to block sunlight, impair vision and create an underwater barrier. The thick tangle of seaweed clogs the engines and entangles and binds the propellers of most vessels going faster than two miles per hour (3.2 km/1.7 knots). Any motorized sea vessel trying to pass through the bank of seaweed at faster speeds will grind to a halt until the seaweed can be removed from the engine or prop (2D6 minutes).

Power armor units, swimmers and animals can travel through the thick seaweed at a speed of 6 mph (9.6 km/5.2 knots) with minimal difficulty, but even they find it difficult to navigate or see through the thick tangle of seaweed. Visibility is 1D6+10 feet (11-16 feet/3.3 to 4.9 m) and those trying to Prowl or hide in the seaweed enjoy a +15% bonus. However, even at this ponderous speed they are -5 to Perception Rolls, -3 to initiative, -4 to strike using ranged weapons, -35% to Underwater Navigation and lose their sense of direction. Double the penalties when moving faster than 6 mph (9.6 km/5.2 knots) with a maximum swimming speed that is half when swimming through the floating mass of seaweed (reduce speed by 50%) and the character also loses two melee attacks/actions as he literally fights his way through the mass of weeds.

Seaweed Lift (New)

Area of Effect: Creates a four foot (1.2 m) diameter platform per level of experience. The spell caster can control the size of the platform.
Range: Self, with the range of movement for the platform being 10 feet (3 m) per level of experience.
Duration: One minute per level of experience, double at a ley line or within a ley line triangle like the Demon Sea/Bermuda Triangle.
Limitations: Can lift/move a maximum of two tons per level of experience.
Saving Throw: None.
P.P.E.: Fourteen
Note: Also available as an *Ocean Magic spell* for twice the P.P.E.

The spell causes seaweed within a mile (1.6 km) radius to come together to create a soft, spongy platform strong enough for one or more people or cargo to rest upon. While this may sound similar to the Seaweed Floating Platform, the difference is, the Seaweed Lift is able to rise up from the water like an elevator and carry the spell caster and passengers, or cargo, up into to the air (or through the water) 10 feet (3 m) per level of the mage's experience. The Seaweed Lift can also be made to move side to side, forward and backward as long as the movement is within the spell's range of movement. The platform does not fly, but is rather lifted up and out of the water by a long, woven length of seaweed with a relatively flat surface platform at the top. The platform can be made to go up and down as fast as it can be offloaded and reloaded for the duration of the spell. Of course, the speed at which it moves is slow, equal to a Spd attribute of 9.

The platform cannot be summoned out of nowhere, there must be enough seaweed present in the area for the spell to work and to reach whatever height and distance the spell caster requires. To keep the platform from eventually falling apart, the spell must be recast before the duration of the previous one ends. The spell caster can cancel the magic at any time. **Note:** Only the spell caster can make the Seaweed Lift move, so he must either be on the platform or within 20 feet (6.1 m) of its base in the water to control it.

Level Six

Barnacle Armor (New)

Range: Self or one person by touch.
Duration: Permanent.
Saving Throw: None.
P.P.E.: Twenty-Four or Eighty-Five

The Biomancer summons forth a magical confluence of barnacles that the mage shapes around himself, or another person, to create a surprisingly mobile, outer covering that serves as body armor. Moments after the armor has formed, the barnacles turn rock-hard, but remain lightweight. This hard, second skin is used to stay warm at colder depths underwater and as a tough, simple armor with slight movement penalties (-10% to skills such as Acrobatics, Climbing, Gymnastics, Prowl, Swimming and Tailing).

S.D.C. Barnacle Armor: For the cost of 24 P.P.E. the Barnacle Armor has an A.R. of 18 and 48 S.D.C. +10 per level of experience.

M.D.C. Barnacle Armor: For the cost of 85 P.P.E. the armor has 24 M.D.C. +8 M.D.C. per level of experience.

Unlike many spells that provide a temporary suit of armor, Barnacle Armor is a permanent Biomancy creation and remains a functioning suit of armor until the armor is destroyed (loses all its S.D.C. or M.D.C.). It can be taken off in pieces like man-made armor.

Barnacle Armor Repair: After a Biomancer creates a suit of Barnacle Armor for himself, the mage can repair his armor with 40 S.D.C. or 16 M.D.C. per 24 P.P.E. spent on repairs (never more than the starting amount for the armor). Repairs can only be made as long as the suit of armor has at least 25% of its S.D.C. or M.D.C. remaining.

Barnacle Projectile Attack: After a Biomancer creates a suit of Barnacle Armor for himself, he can spend 4 P.P.E. to fire a single volley of 1D4+4 hardhitting barnacles that inflict 5D6 S.D.C. damage or 12 P.P.E. to inflict 2D6 M.D. per blast. Each blast costs 4 or 12 P.P.E. depending on the level of damage unleashed. Range: 20 feet (6.1 m) per level of experience underwater, 40 feet (12.2 m) per level of experience out of water. Rate of Fire: Each blast/spell casting counts as one melee attack/action.

Bio-Blast

Range: 100 feet (30.5 m) per level of experience.
Duration: Instant.
Saving Throw: None, except dodge, but the victim must know the attack is coming and must roll an 18 or higher to dodge.
P.P.E.: Fifteen

The Biomancer fires a bolt of life energy at a target, disrupting living beings and destroying inanimate objects. The blast does 2D6 S.D.C./Hit Point damage and causes neural disruption to living creatures. Victims lose initiative and their number of melee attacks and combat bonuses are reduced by half for one melee round. Against inanimate objects, such as weapons, robots, vehicles, machines, rock and buildings, the blast inflicts 1D6 M.D. per level of the Biomancer; double damage against vampires, other undead and supernatural monsters. The Bio-Blast can be fired from the fingertips or eyes of the spell caster.

Coral Whispering (New)

Range: Self. The link is limited to a 300 foot (91.4 m) diameter per level of the spell caster.
Duration: Five minutes per level of experience.
Saving Throw: None.
P.P.E.: Thirty

The underwater equivalent of Tree Whispering, the Coral Whispering spell allows the Biomancer to commune with a local coral reef, or even just sparse outgrowths of coral. There are both shallow, tropical reefs and deep-water coral that can grow in colder temperatures and less light. The Biomancer can pose simple and basic questions to the reef or simply sense its general condition and outlook, using it as a source of information and direction. The coral may be able to tell the Biomancer who has passed by recently or what the seabed is like around and below it. See the Tree Whispering spell also in this level of Biomancy spells for more details.

Immune System Push (New)

Range: Self or others by touch.
Duration: Permanent.
Saving Throw: None.
P.P.E.: Eighteen for short duration illnesses like the flu or measles, Eighty to cure chronic and life-threatening diseases.

Immune System Push is an extremely powerful healing spell that restores the immune system to its natural working order. Many debilitating diseases work by suppressing the immune system. This spell strengthens it, allowing the body to fight off disease and disorders by itself. Properly used, the spell can cure AIDS, lupus, cancer and all types of immune system deficiencies. Using it on someone who has a cold, flu or other common disease reduces the length/duration of the illness and its symptoms and penalties by half.

Degree of Healing for Serious, Chronic Illnesses: Roll percentile dice to determine the level of healing of chronic or life-threatening disease. **Note:** This spell can only be performed on the same person once in his lifetime.

01-33%: Progress of the disease has slowed to a crawl, reduce severity of symptoms and penalties by half for 4D6+8 years. Life is also extended by at least that amount. At the end of that period, the disease returns in full force.

34-66%: Progress of the disease has stopped and it has gone into remission for 6D6+15 years. During that time the individual appears to be completely cured. At the end of that period, the disease returns in full force.

67-00%: Gone. Completely cured and health is restored to full in 1D4 weeks.

Nutrient Feed (New)

Range: Touch or an area.
Area of Effect: 30 foot (9.1 m) radius per level of experience.
Duration: The spell takes about 1D4 melee rounds to complete its work with permanent results.
Saving Throw: None.
P.P.E.: Fifteen

Nutrient Feed channels bio-energy and magically-summoned nutrients into the plants of a given area to provide them with a full day's worth of nutrients, food and water in under a minute. Nutrient Feed can be used to feed and boost the health and growth of a single plant by touch or all the vegetation, coral or kelp of a particular area. In the alternative, the Biomancer can select one particular type/species of plant and only "feed" them with the magic, skipping, for example, weeds or unwanted plants. Edible plants and those with medicinal properties or which bear fruit, vegetables or nuts will have a 50% greater yield when fed via this spell every day for one month. The spell also attracts helpful insects and repels harmful ones.

Seaweed Path (New)

Range: The spell can be cast up to 50 feet (15.2 m) away per level of experience, double along a ley line or within a ley line triangle.
Area of Effect: A length up to 120 feet (36.6 m) long and 15 feet (4.6 m) wide per level of experience, double along a ley line or within a ley line triangle. Also double the length and width when 48 P.P.E. are spent. The spell caster determines the direction of the path.
Duration: Two minutes per level of experience.
Saving Throw: None.
P.P.E.: Twenty-Four or Forty-Eight
Note: Also available as an *Ocean Magic spell* for the same P.P.E.

The spell creates a clear path through seaweed to allow quick passage through it. Underwater, this passage is a tunnel up to 15 feet (4.6 m) in diameter. On the surface of water, the area clear of seaweed is 15 feet (4.6 m) deep for the entire length of the path. The higher number of P.P.E., which doubles the size of the path, is usually reserved for the passage of ships and submarines. Visibilty beyond the clear path is zero, and the environment and penalties described under the Seaweed Bloom spell apply should an individual venture beyond the path.

Tree Teleport

Range: 200 feet (61 m) per level of experience.
Duration: Instant.
Saving Throw: None.
P.P.E.: Twenty

The Biomancer can temporarily transform himself and up to 150 lbs (68 kg) of equipment into bio-energy and "jump" to a nearby tree. The tree acts as a lightning rod for the bio-energy and enables the Biomancer to disappear from one location and reform himself at another; line of sight or knowledge of the area is required. The effect is just like a Teleport spell, enabling the character to pop in, out and around an area without leaving tracks or to surprise or escape an enemy. The spell needs a tree to "ground" itself and to give the spell caster a fixed target location; he appears right next to the target tree.

If a foolish character attempts the spell when there are no trees in range, he cannot re-materialize! Instead, the character will temporarily turn into energy and drift randomly for 1D6 minutes, after which time he finally reappears next to a tree 1D4x10 miles (1D4x16 km) from his jump point (or the next closest tree if none are within that range).

Tree Whispering (New)

Range: Self. The link is limited to a 300 foot (91.4 m) diameter per level of the spell caster.
Duration: Five minutes per level of experience.
Restriction: Trees only, not other plants.
Saving Throw: None.
P.P.E.: Thirty

When this spell is cast, the Biomancer can hear the trees as voices whispering in his ear. The spell caster may listen to what the trees have to say in general, or ask specific questions of them. Trees always see a Biomancer as their friend and are happy to comply. The communication is nothing like a true conversation, but rather sensations, words, phrases, and simple sentences repeated until the mage responds, asks a new question or cancels the spell. Only the Biomancer who casts the Tree Whispering spell hears their communication rather like Empathy and Telepathy combined. This means the Biomancer may see flashes of images and/or sensations as well as words. Ask if a missing girl passed this way and the mage may hear, "Yes, yes," accompanied by the sounds of her little feet running across the ground, and/or the image of a girl looking frightened or laughing and running through the woods. If she has not come this way, the words, "No, no" may be accompanied by the sound of the wind and an image of deer running by or pheasant flying off into the sky. If looking for something, someone, or someplace in particular, the whispers may say, "this way, this way, not far," accompanied by a flash image of sunlight through the trees to indicate time or direction. Trees sense time differently than people and the use of numbers is minimal, thus time is often represented as "since sunrise," "since sunset," "since the full moon," and so on, or "since yesterday" may be about the best one can get for a moment of time. Numbers are one, two, a few, many, a great many, an army or "there were so many their numbers made the ground tremble."

The trees can help the Biomancer find and locate surface and underground water, specific plants and herbs, fruit and edible plants, and even minerals such as silver, gold, coal, etc. They can also reveal things about themselves and their environment, such as what lies directly beneath their roots, the quality of the soil around them, if water is nearby, if edible plants, fruits or nuts are nearby, and what animals live within their branches, trunk or under their roots. They can also reveal if a tree is sick or healthy, troubled with rot, fungus or carpenter ants, and so on.

The more pointed and simple the question, the better. A vague question such as, "Who has come this way recently?" means nothing to a tree as many animals have come and gone. Furthermore, what is recent to a tree that can live for centuries? A month, a year, a decade? And 'who' is 'who' to a tree? A rabbit, a deer or hawk may have as much, or more significance than a person. Unless the individual frequents the area, asking something like "have you seen Coalition Troops?", or a particular person by name is likely to draw a blank. However, ask if men clad in black metal and adorned in white skulls have passed by since morning, and the trees can answer that question. Ask if a red dragon or fellow Biomancer or child with brown hair has passed by since yesterday, and the trees can answer that too.

Level Seven

Animate Plants: Superior (New)

Range: Affected area is 40 feet (12.2 m) per level of experience.
Duration: One minute per level of experience.
Saving Throw: None.
P.P.E.: Twenty-Five

This spell might be thought of as possess and animate plants. The Biomancer takes direct control of one large tree or a mass of seaweed and animates it like a puppet. He can manipulate its shape to create a vaguely humanoid body with a face, 2-4 arms, a pair of legs (though they may be very short or it may walk using the roots like the tentacles of an octopus). Unlike previous Animate Plant spells, the Biomancer can uproot the tree (or seaweed) and make it walk like a giant Tree Golem. The magic even lets the spell caster project his voice through the tree to give it a voice (his own voice or something that sounds different and monstrous). Controlling the tree takes all of the Biomancer's focus and attacks per melee, but the tree is now an extension of himself made to mimic his movements. However the Biomancer moves, the animated tree emulates as best it can.

S.D.C. of the Large Tree: 3D6+12x100 (or the equivalent of one M.D.C. per 100 S.D.C.).

Speed Factor: Five +1 point per level of the spell caster.

Damage: Same as Large Trees described under *Animate Plants: Major*.

Bonuses: Resistant to cold and pain (half damage), impervious to possession and mind control (the tree is already possessed), and +2 attacks per melee and +2 to strike in addition to the number of attacks and bonuses of the spell caster.

Restore Bio-Armor (New)

Range: Touch or 15 feet (4.6 m); line of sight required.
Duration: Instant.
Saving Throw: None.
P.P.E.: Forty

Biomancer Gene-Mages are the creators of Bio-Armor, a type of living power armor. This spell was developed to maintain and repair that armor. Restore Bio-Armor can do any one of the following per spell casting:

1. Instantly restore 1D6x10 M.D.C.
2. Instantly repair or regrow any one sensor or weapon system such as an antenna, fin, retractable blade, etc. The item is immediately functional but possesses one third its usual M.D.C.
3. Instantly recharge one weapon system with a full payload.

See the section on *Bio-Armor* for more details.

Seaweed Bridge (New)

Range: The spell can be cast up to 300 feet (91.5 m) away per level of experience.
Area of Effect: Up to 300 feet (91.4 m) long and 10 feet (3 m) wide per level of experience.
Duration: Five minutes per level of experience.
Saving Throw: None.
P.P.E.: Forty (240 P.P.E. to make the bridge last one hour per level of experience).

This spell creates a sturdy seaweed structure that is long and held in place against waves, current and wind. The Seaweed Bridge is not suitable for use as a life raft, and must be anchored firmly to something on at least one end. The bridge formed by the spell can be placed underwater, made to float on the surface of the water, or attached to dry land and suspended in the air (in the latter case, reduce the extended hour duration by half). While it won't keep your feet dry and has the bounce of a rope bridge, it is strong enough to support vehicles and robots that weigh 30 tons. The spell can be cancelled by the caster at any moment, but there is a 1D4 melee round delay with clear indications that the bridge is unraveling.

Suspended Animation: Bio-Armor (New)

Range: Touch or 15 feet (4.6 m); line of sight required.
Duration: Hours to months; up to 30 days per level of experience.
Saving Throw: None.
P.P.E.: Forty

Bio-Armor are a type of living power armor. They are also symbiotic organisms that must be worn at least 1D6+6 hours every week or the suit's link with its host breaks and the suit dies a few hours later. This can be avoided by wearing the suit often, but sometimes that's not possible. To avoid the connection being broken and the armor dying, a Biomancer Gene-Mage can place the suit in a state of suspended animation for days to months. This keeps the armor alive for a much longer time until its owner can reclaim possession of it. Suspended Animation: Bio-Armor may also be used to store one type of Bio-Armor while another is being deployed by the same warrior. See the section on *Bio-Armor* for more details.

Tree Phasing (New)

Range: A specific direction desired by the spell caster.
Area of Effect: A 100 foot (30.5 m) length per level of experience in whatever direction the Biomancer is looking. Width of the path is 15 feet (4.6 m) per level of experience.
Duration: Five minutes per level of experience.
Saving Throw: None. Spell does not work on sentient plants.
P.P.E.: Twenty-Two

Tree Phasing enables the Biomancer and his allies to pass through forests, jungles, living reefs, masses of seaweed and other collections of plant growth as if they were not there. The spell renders the area's trees and vegetation intangible and semi-transparent. This allows people and vehicles to pass right through them. However, the Biomancer must remain behind and stay in physical contact/touch with a tree at the start of the area being phased out. This is done by touching a tree (or large plant) with his hand or body (leaning on a tree works just as well). This limits the area of trees and plant life that can be phased out from a distance (see Area of Effect above). As long as the Biomancer remains in contact with a tree at the start of the path to be made intangible, the vegetation along that path becomes and stays intangible (for a maximum of five minutes per level of the spell caster). This however, means the Biomancer and the tree he is touching remain solid the entire time. The moment the mage breaks contact, the trees and vegetation become solid again.

Once travelers reach the end of the intangible tree line and wait in a clearing, the Biomancer can let go of the tree and he, himself, is able to move again. However, the Tree Phasing spell remains active, provided the mage keeps his focus and does NOT cast any other magic or perform any skill (walking/moving does not count as a skill). This means the spell caster (and only the spell caster) can walk through trees and brush as if they were still intangible. By placing his hand on another tree when he catches up with the rest of the group and concentrating, he can make another swath of trees and vegetation intangible so the vehicles and people can pass through another stretch of forest. Rendering the Biomancer unconscious or dragging him away from the tree contact point cancels the spell, which may leave the mage's companions severely entangled in undergrowth.

In the alternative, the Biomancer can move through trees and underbrush as if he were a ghost (even though it is the trees and vegetation that are momentarily phased out as he passes by) for the duration of the magic. Running through a forest while *Tree Phasing* enables the mage to move at full speed as if running across a well manicured lawn with no vegetation to entangle or block his way. However, he must still be careful to avoid stones, boulders, animals, people, vehicles and debris, as they are not intangible and he'll crash right into them. Similarly, the Biomancer can turn a single tree intangible with a touch, so that he may step through it as if it were not there at all. This can be used to move quickly through a forest or to walk through a tree in order to hide behind it when it becomes solid again.

Trees and plants under the spell's effects are semi-transparent and obviously intangible. When contact is broken, cancelled or the duration period runs out, the plants become solid again, requiring people and vehicles to go around trees or crash into them. People and vehicles cannot be trapped inside an intangible tree that becomes solid. However, a vehicle or group may find themselves stranded in the middle of a thick, unnavigable forest or seaweed cluster.

Tree Warrior

Range: Immediate area.
Duration: 30 minutes per level of experience.
Saving Throw: None.
Limitations: The Biomancer who created the Tree Warrior can only cast one other spell per melee round as long as the Tree Warrior is created, and only one Tree Warrior can be created at a time.
P.P.E.: Thirty

This spell enables the Biomancer to animate a tree and imbue it with Supernatural Strength and Endurance. The tree then pulls itself up by the roots and follows the Biomancer to fight his enemies. At the end of the spell, the tree will root itself in the nearest convenient spot (if possible, its original position) and return to normal. The tree can serve as a bodyguard, spy, or scout. Tree Warriors are ideal for ambushes because they can remain immobile like an ordinary tree until an unsuspecting victim/target comes within reach. Biomancers who carelessly cause the death of a tree with this spell have a 10% chance of losing their Biomancy powers until they can somehow redeem themselves! This 10% chance is cumulative, so repeated Tree Warrior deaths will most definitely result in the loss of Biomancy powers.

Tree Warrior

- M.D.C.: 200
- 8-15 feet (2.4 to 4.6 m) tall, I.Q. 7, P.S. 25, P.P. 17, Spd 16, +3 to strike, +4 to parry and dodge, Bio-Regeneration of 2D6 M.D.C. per melee round and M.D. fire and plasma do half damage.
- Can shoot bio-energy bolts inflicting 3D6 M.D., double against vampires and the undead. Range: 100 feet (30.5 m).
- Four physical attacks or bio-bolts per melee. Punch inflicts 2D6 M.D., power punch does 4D6 M.D. (counts as two attacks).
- The Tree Warrior obeys only the person who summoned it. Even then it tends to follow instructions on a literal basis, so it is best to keep them simple.

Undo Undead

Range: Touch or 30 feet (9.1 m) per level of experience.
Duration: Instant.
Saving Throw: 14 or higher.
P.P.E.: Twenty-Five

The Biomancer causes an undead creature to be surrounded by bio-energy that reacts to its necromantic energies like matter does to anti-matter! If a vampire, zombie, animated skeleton, corpse or other undead or animated dead fails its saving throw (14 or higher), the abomination begins to smolder and take damage. The spell inflicts 1D6x10 M.D. or Hit Point damage +2 points per level of the Biomancer's experience. A successful save means the undead suffers only 1D6 points of damage and recognizes the dangerous life magic wielded by its opponent. The latter makes Biomancers one of the undead's primary targets to incapacitate or destroy.

Level Eight

Coral Menace (New)

Range: Immediate area.
Duration: 20 minutes per level of experience.
Limitations: The Biomancer who created the Coral Menace can only cast one other spell per melee round as long as the Coral Menace is created, and only one Coral Menace can be created at a time.

Saving Throw: None.
P.P.E.: Sixty

This spell enables the Biomancer to animate a section of coral and imbue it with Supernatural Strength and Endurance, turning it into a living, rock-like monster. A section of coral roughly twice the size of a normal human pulls itself away from the coral reef and follows the Biomancer, fighting by his side, protecting him or attacking designated enemies. At the end of the spell, the section of coral will bind itself to the nearest convenient spot (if possible, its original position) and return to normal. The Coral Menace can serve as a bodyguard, spy, or scout. Coral Menaces are ideal for ambushes underwater because they can remain immobile like an ordinary section of coral, melding into an existing reef or lying dormant on the ocean floor as a coral patch until an unsuspecting victim comes within reach. Biomancers who carelessly cause the death of the Coral Menace with this spell have a 15% chance of losing their Biomancy powers until they can somehow redeem themselves! This 15% chance is cumulative, so repeated Coral Menace deaths will most definitely result in the loss of their Biomancy powers.

Coral Menace
- M.D.C.: 300
- 10-15 feet (3 to 4.6 m) tall, I.Q. 7, P.S. 40, P.P. 17, Spd 12 walking. The Menace is heavy and has a difficult time swimming, preferring to walk along the ocean floor or on dry land; swimming speed is 6. +3 to strike and parry, +1 to dodge, Bio-Regenerates 2D6 M.D.C. per melee round.
- Can shoot bio-energy bolts inflicting 3D6 M.D., double against the undead; range 100 feet (30.5 m).
- Four physical attacks or bio-bolts per melee round and punches and kicks inflict 4D6 M.D., power punch does 1D4x10 M.D. (counts as two attacks).
- The Coral Menace obeys only the person who summoned it. Even then it tends to follow instructions on a literal basis, so it is best to keep them simple.

Remove Parasites (New)

Range: Touch.
Duration: Results are permanent; takes 1D6+1 minutes to remove parasites.
Saving Throw: None.
P.P.E.: Fifty

This spell enables the Biomancer to identify, locate and remove parasites without injury to the infested host body. However, any damage the parasite(s) may have done prior to removal remains. Likewise, any benefit or powers the parasite may have provided is removed along with it. Neither the parasite or the victim are harmed in this procedure. Parasites inside the body are forced out by the magic spell, but the Biomancer must observe the entire process, coaxing them out with strange noises and magical gestures. Cancelling or interrupting the spell early will cause the parasite to dig back into the host body and replant itself. Does not work on symbiotes.

Suspended Animation

Range: Self only.
Duration: Days or years, up to five years per level of experience.
Saving Throw: None.
P.P.E.: Eighty

The Biomancer can place himself in a total state of suspended animation, slowing all bodily functions to a crawl, but remaining alive and nourished for the entire duration, even it if is decades. While in suspended animation, the mage appears to be dead, except his body doesn't deteriorate. The Biomancer ages one year for every five that he sleeps. While in the suspended state, the Biomancer cannot cast spells or think, only dream. His physical body is not protected in any way by the spell so he should find a safe, dry, warm place with some form of protection or guardian, as he is vulnerable to attack while asleep. The character can be roused only by a Tree of Wisdom, Memory Tree, Tree of Knowledge or via telepathic or empathic communication, but awakes only if he can be convinced to end his magical sleep. Otherwise, he sleeps for the time period he had in mind (days, months, years) when he went into a state of suspended animation. Awakes with all his senses, abilities and P.P.E.

Touch of Life

Range: Touch.
Duration: Permanent.
Saving Throw: None.
P.P.E.: Humans and other sentient beings as well as giant animals (20-80 feet/6.1-24.4 m long): Sixty. Very large animals (12-20 feet/3.6 to 6.1 m): Forty. Large animals (African lion to elephant size): Thirty. Animals of moderate size (fox to wolf size). Twenty. Small animals (raccoon to mouse size): Fifteen. Tiny animals (shrimp to flea size): Ten.
Permanent P.P.E. Loss: Each time the Touch of Life is used successfully, the Biomancer permanently loses half the P.P.E. required to bring the being back to life. Once spent to bring the dead back to life, the P.P.E. is forever gone.

The Biomancer can revive someone who has died within the last 24 hours by infusing him with bio-energy. The corpse can be no more than one day old (less is better). The chance of success is 01-70% plus 1% per level of experience. If successful, the corpse is restored to 1D6 Hit Points above zero and the damage or injury that killed him is magically repaired. The individual will be weak and sick until the rest of his Hit Points are restored. The Touch of Life does not restore missing limbs, heal burns or disease, nor does it cure insanity or remove curses.

Lasting effects of having died. Victims of death are likely to be traumatized and suffer lasting penalties of having died and returned to life. Roll on each of the following percentile tables.

Insanity:

01-10% Lucked out. None.

11-20% Phobia: Death (afraid to die and tries to avoid it, takes fewer risks, etc.).

21-40% Phobia: Of whatever it was that caused the character's demise.

41-45% Phobia: Dead bodies, corpses and skeletons, animated or not. Does not include vampires and other undead as they tend to look and behave quite alive, though monstrous.

46-50% Phobia: Ghosts and Entities.

51-80% Random Phobia. Roll on the table found in the Rifts® core rule book.

81-90% Obsessed with revenge or bringing the person/creature responsible for his demise to justice (or to kill him in return). May apply to the *type* of creature if the thing that slew him was a demon or monster.

91-00% Random Obsession. Roll on the table found in the Rifts® core rule book.

Permanent Penalties: These are in addition to any obvious loss of limb or disability that may have resulted in the character's demise.

01-20% Reduce P.B. by 10%.

21-40% Reduce Spd by 10%.

41-60% Reduce all combat bonuses by one point.

61-80% Reduce Hit Points (or M.D.C. if a Mega-Damage creature) by 10%.

81-00% -2 to save vs vampire mind control and possession.

Level Nine

Bio-Energy Weapon (New)

Range: Self, i.e. a weapon held and used by the spell caster.
Duration: One melee round per level of experience.
Saving Throw: None.
P.P.E.: Sixty

The Biomancer can summon forth a deadly M.D. weapon by temporarily infusing any weapon made of organic material including wood, coral or bone with Bio-Energy. The common Bio-Energy Weapons are staves, spears, war clubs and bludgeons, but can also include blade weapons made of wood or wood and animal teeth, or wood and coral. The Bio-Energy Weapon can be used to fight and kill, or to heal.

Heal: The energy-filled blade can be gently placed on a wound to negate poison, expel foreign objects (bullets, shrapnel, etc.) and then seal and heal the wound with minimal scarring. The healing effect restores 2D6 Hit Points/S.D.C. or 1D6 M.D.C. per touch; can make one touch per melee round. Touching the bio-energy blade to an unconscious or comatose individual has a 01-70% chance of awakening him or her instantly and provides that person with a +20% bonus to save vs Coma/Death.

Harm: The energy imbued into the enchanted weapons makes it a Mega-Damage weapon that inflicts 1D6 M.D. per level the Biomancer's experience. Against supernatural evil, the weapon does an additional +10 M.D. and against the undead, the Bio-Energy Weapon inflicts double damage! A safeguard in the spell requires the Biomancer to willingly want to harm somcone for it to inflict Mega-Damage, otherwise it does only 1D6 S.D.C. Similarly, when facing an S.D.C. opponent, the weapon automatically switches power levels, changing from M.D. to 1D6 S.D.C. per level of the spell caster's experience. Against inanimate inorganic objects like metal or plastic body armor, robots, vehicles and cyborgs, as well as force fields, the Bio-Energy Weapon inflicts *half* the usual damage. **Note:** Living armor, Lemurian Bio-Armor, and any armor that is alive or made from organic material (wood, coral, plants, barnacles, etc.) takes full damage.

Creature of the Forest (New)

Range: Self.
Duration: 10 minutes per level of experience.
Saving Throw: None.
P.P.E.: Seventy

This is a hybrid type of metamorphosis that transforms the Biomancer into a small, forest-dwelling humanoid one third his normal size which more resembles a lemur or monkey than a man. As a Creature of the Forest, the Biomancer is covered in fur, has a fluffy tail equal to half his body length, is able to climb, run and swing through tree branches at full running speed as if it were as easy and natural as walking, can leap 10 feet (3 m) high and 15 feet (4.6 m) across (increase by 50% with a running start), is unafraid of heights, Nightvision 300 feet (91.4 m), has the equivalent skills of Acrobatics, Climbing, Rappelling and Tailing, each at 82% +1% per level of experience, Prowl at 58% +1% per level of experience, +10 to running speed, +2 on Perception Rolls from tree branches or an elevated position (rooftop, rafters), +1 on initiative, +4 to automatic dodge (the act of dodging does not use up a melee attack), +5 to roll with impact/fall and has a 01-50% chance of landing on his feet and taking no damage from a fall or leap as great as 100 feet/30.5 m), and feels at home in the forest and trees. Retains all human memories and skills, and can use any psionic abilities the Biomancer may possess. Other arboreal animals, such as squirrels, raccoons, lemurs, monkeys and apes, accept the Creature of the Forest as one of their own and are not afraid of him.

Limitations of the Form: Cannot speak full sentences nor cast spells in this form, but can say single words ("run," "go," "stop," "help," etc.) or short phases ("come quick," "this way," "vampires coming," "follow me," etc.), and is too small to use weapons, guns or tools, but can press buttons, flick switches, and work a keyboard.

Heal the Earth

Range: By touch or up to 1,000 feet (305 m) away; line of sight.
Area of Effect: 100 foot (30.5 m) radius per level of experience.
Duration: Permanent.
Saving Throw: None.
P.P.E.: Two Hundred

This spell "heals" the earth, as in the very ground itself, purging it of poison, chemicals, pollution, radioactivity, and any other damaging substances, and revitalizes the soil so that it is capable of supporting life again. An area thus treated becomes perfectly suited for the development of life as determined by the region's ecosystem. If cast on farmland, yields for the area affected will increase by 10% per level of the spell caster's experience.

Reconfigure Bio-Armor (New)

Range: Touch.
Duration: A ritual that takes 15 minutes.
Saving Throw: None.
P.P.E.: One Hundred

When an owner of Bio-Armor dies, so does the armor. Likewise, the fragile symbiotic organism is connected to its owner. When that connection is broken from lack of use, the Bio-Armor dies. From time to time, Lemurian warriors and explorers either want to switch from one type of Bio-Armor to another, or retire and no longer have a need for their symbiotic partner. Rather than let it waste away and die, a Biomancer Gene-Mage can reconfigure the armor, severing the old link and connecting and configuring it to the exact specifications (and DNA) of the new owner. This is done more often than one might believe, and reconfigured Bio-Armor always works as good as new.

This magic can also be used to re-establish a broken link between a negligent existing owner and his disconnected (and soon to die) Bio-Armor. See the section on *Bio-Armor* for more details about it.

Level Ten

Bio-Field (New)

Range: Self.
Duration: One minute per level of experience.
Saving Throw: None.
P.P.E.: One Hundred

The spell causes the Biomancer to radiate with life-giving energy. As he walks, plants and flowers appear in full bloom around his feet, as if by magic. They return to normal a few moments later after he has moved on. While in place, the Bio-Field turns the spell caster's Hit Points into M.D.C. (in S.D.C. environments, triple the character's H.P.) and he Bio-Regenerates 6D6 M.D.C./Hit Points/S.D.C. once per melee round, including the M.D.C. of any living Bio-Armor or symbiotes he may have on him, as well as his riding animal or animal companion, provided he is riding it or it is at his side. As long as the Bio-Field is in place, the character is also +50% to save vs Coma/Death, impervious to diseases and poison, and +5 to save vs possession.

Creature of the Sea (New)

Range: Self.
Duration: 10 minutes per level of experience.
Saving Throw: None.
P.P.E.: One Hundred

This is a hybrid type of metamorphosis that transforms the Biomancer into a whale-like humanoid three times his normal size with a whale- or dolphin-like tail. As a Creature of the Sea, he can breathe water (but not air until he changes back to human form), P.S. becomes Supernatural, add 2D6+20 to swimming speed, depth tolerance is 8 miles (12.8 km), Hit Points and S.D.C. are combined to become M.D.C. (regenerates 2D6 M.D.C. every melee round), he has a large maw with sharp teeth that inflict 3D6 M.D. from a bite attack, punches and tail swipes do damage as per Supernatural P.S., has Nightvision 1,000 feet (305 m), and being in water feels completely natural. Other sea mammals and fish accept the Creature of the Sea as a fellow aquatic animal.

Limitations of the Form: Cannot speak full sentences nor cast spells in this form, but can say single words ("run," "go," "stop," "help," etc.) or short phases ("come quick," "this way," "follow me," etc.), and is too large to use most human weapons, guns or tools, and the webbed fingers are too large and clumsy to press buttons, flick switches, or work machines. Most important, the character cannot survive on dry land for more than 1D4 melee rounds without switching back to his true humanoid body.

Reverse Undead (New)

Range: Touch.
Duration: Instant.
Saving Throw: 18+, Standard.
P.P.E.: One Hundred

This powerful spell breaks the influence a vampire has over a living victim via the Killing Bite or undead mind control, and restores the vampire's victim to normal and full health. No longer under the vampire's control, the process to turn said person into an undead must be started all over again.

Furthermore, a recently created vampire that has yet to feed on the blood of another living humanoid has a 01-75% chance of being changed back to the living via this healing magic. If successful, roll on the same two tables as found under the *Touch of Life* spell for permanent side effects, but the character is no longer a vampire. If unsuccessful, the magic fails and the vampire remains one of the living dead.

This spell can also undo/negate Necromancy magic and turns animated dead or animated body parts back into inanimate, bones and parts.

Level Eleven

Nutrient Push: Soil (New)

Range: 500 foot (152 m) radius per level of experience.
Duration: Permanent.
Saving Throw: None.
P.P.E.: One Hundred Eighty

The Biomancer plants his or her hands in the earth or sea floor and pumps nutrients and Bio-Energy into it to stimulate the growth of any plants in it. Any crop seeds or young plants in the soil sprout and grow to the point of being ready for harvest in 1D6 minutes. Tree seeds turn into saplings. Saplings become small trees. Mature trees, coral reefs and kelp fronds grow an additional 25% and are at the peak of health. In addition, the soil remains rich and fertile for one year per experience level of the spell caster. Plants that grow in "pushed" soil grow a full 50% larger and yield 50% greater crops for 2D6 years, creating a super-farm or an oasis of life.

Remove Symbiotes (New)

Range: Self only.
Duration: Permanent results, takes one hour to remove a symbiote.
Saving Throw: -2 if the removal is wanted, because the symbiotic organism resists the magic. +5 to save if the removal is unwanted by the sentient being to which the symbiote is attached. Unwanted procedures are often painful as well.
P.P.E.: One Hundred Fifty

This spell enables the Biomancer to identify, locate and remove symbiotic organisms, including those used in Bio-Wizardry by the Splugorth. Injury to the host body is minimal. However, any damage done to it by the symbiote prior to its removal remains. Moreover, removal of a symbiote will almost certainly leave scars and any benefits, bonuses and powers the monster may have provided are removed along with it. In most cases, neither the symbiote nor its host suffers in this procedure, but sometimes removal of a symbiotic organism kills it and/or does permanent damage to the host. Parasites inside the body are forced out by the magic spell, but the Biomancer must observe the entire process, and parasites will quickly retreat back into their host if the spell is left incomplete.

Level Twelve

Forest Walk (New)

Area of Effect: 40 foot (12.2 m) radius per level of experience.
Duration: The plants can walk for 10 minutes per level of experience.
Saving Throw: None, unless the plants are magical or sentient creatures, in which case they may make a standard saving throw of 12 or greater vs magic. Millennium Trees and other such powerful plant beings are immune to this spell and move only if they choose to do so.
P.P.E.: One Hundred Ninety-Five

This spell "awakens" all the plants in a particular area and enables them to pull themselves up out of the ground, by their roots, and march to a new location of the Biomancer's choosing. This includes every type of plant from the tallest trees to tiniest blades of grass. Lemurian Biomancers use this spell to uproot areas of plant life to transplant them to a safer, better or different location, and to safeguard them when they need access to the rocks and minerals underneath. This spell can also be used to plant farmland and orchards, to landscape gardens and parks, clear land for roads and development, re-plant land areas decimated by fire or other disasters, and to change the environment to confuse travelers or to hide secret camps, bases and underground entrances and similar uses. Sometimes, an animated forest is used to frighten and intimate as it can seem like a marching army. However, the plants animated by this spell cannot attack in any way and are still S.D.C. structures easily destroyed by fire and Mega-Damage weapons. For an extra 20 P.P.E., the Biomancer can separate the plants by type and command each type/species to move to specific locations.

Mimic Animal or Plant (New)

Range: Self.
Duration: 15 minutes per level of experience.
Saving Throw: Standard if the person does not wish to be transformed.
P.P.E.: Five Hundred

The Biomancer metamorphs into a specific or generic form of almost any animal or plant. The Biomancer must place one hand on the creature or plant he wishes to mimic and then cast this spell. He can either transform into an exact physical duplicate of the original creature or a more general version of the creature's species. In the case of the general mimicry, the character transforms into a member of that species with all the corresponding racial abilities, powers and attributes.

A specific mimic transformation turns the spell caster into an exact duplicate, right down to every birthmark, fingerprint and genetic marker. The only thing that does not change is the mind of the character. He retains all of his own memories, personality, skills and mental attributes, but has all the physical attributes and abilities of the species he is mimicking. This spell works on all living creatures that use DNA as their blueprint for life.

Reconstruction (New)

Range: Self or other by touch. Can be performed on sentient beings, animals and plants.
Duration: Permanent.
Saving Throw: None, unless the person does not want to be healed, or have something removed/restored, in which case they are +7 to save.
P.P.E.: Six Hundred Seventy-Five

This Biomancy spell takes and restores everything natural about the person or animal subjected to the magic. Reconstruction is based on the information in the subject's Code of Life (DNA). Tattoos (both mystical and mundane), parasites, symbiotes, M.O.M. (Crazies) implants, missing limbs, cybernetics, bionics (even full conversions), Bio-Wizard augmentations, Juicer augmentation, chemicals and chemical damage, etc., are all removed and the body, organs, appendages, and tissue restored to their natural state. Full conversion cyborgs will have their bionics expelled and a whole new body regenerated.

A skilled Biomancer Gene-Mage can use this spell to remove one, several or all such "unnatural" implants/symbiotes/parasites and restore the subject's body to its natural state of being. Those who have abused their bodies, like Juicers, can have their systems restored to normal without the temptation of addiction or other dependencies. Crazies and those affected by brain altering chemistry can have their minds mostly restored (keeps only half of any insanities), but they also lose the powers, bonuses and psionics the M.O.M. implants provided, returning them to a state of normal that may not be desired.

The spell also heals (without scarring) any damage done in combat, burns, poisons or chemical exposure and completely restores the recipient to full health (Hit Points and S.D.C. or M.D.C.), and good as new, physical condition.

Note: This spell does not eliminate emotions, memories, insanity or curses. Nor can it alter genetic defects or mutations (good or bad), or change the genetic code, only restore the body to what it was.

Invocations available to Biomancers

Biomancer Gene-Mages also have knowledge of select Wizard/ Ley Line Walker Invocations that fit their orientation and connection to nature. The available spells are listed below. The P.P.E. cost and spell effects remain unchanged.

Ocean Magic as an alternative. As Lemurians, Biomancer Gene-Mages may elect to study and select Ocean Wizard spells *instead* of selecting some of the spell invocations listed below, but not both. The P.P.E. cost and spell effects of Ocean Magic remain unchanged. **Note:** Ocean Magic is not available to the Biomancers of South America.

See the Biomancer Gene-Mage O.C.C. for details about the number and types of spells he can know.

Level One

Death Trance (1)
Globe of Daylight (2)
Lantern Light (1)
See Aura (6)
Sense Evil (2)
Sense Magic (4)

Level Two

Aura of Power (4)
Chameleon (6)
Cleanse (6)
Climb (3)
Concealment (6)
Detect Concealment (6)
Turn Dead (6)

Level Three

Armor of Ithan (10)
Breathe without Air (5)
Create Wood (10-20)
Energy Bolt (5)
Impervious to Fire (5)
Invisibility: Simple (6)
Life Source (2+ Special)
Light Healing (6)
Orb of Cold (6)
Wave of Frost (6)

Level Four

Carpet of Adhesion (10)
Cure Minor Disorders (10)
Electric Arc (8)
Energy Field (10)
Fireblast (8)
Fist of Fury (10 or 50)
Magic Net (7)
Repel Animals (7)
Shadow Meld (10)
Swim as a Fish (6)

Level Five

Armor Bizarre (15)
Energy Disruption (12)
Escape (8)
Heal Wounds (10)
Influence the Beast (12)
Lifeblast (15)
Sleep (10)
Superhuman Endurance (12)
Sustain (12)

Level Six

Cure Illness (15)
Fire Blossom (20)
Fortify Against Disease (15)
Impervious to Energy (20)
Magic Pigeon (20)
Reduce Self (20)
Sheltering Force (20)

Level Seven

Dispel Magic Barrier (20)
Fly as the Eagle (25)
Heal Self (20)
Invisibility: Superior (20)
Invulnerability (25)
Lightblade (20)
Metamorphosis: Animal (25)
Purification (20)

Level Eight

Commune with Spirits (25)
Eyes of the Wolf (25)
Exorcism (30)
Forcebonds (25)
Greater Healing (30)
Lifeward (40)
Magical-Adrenal Rush (45)
Metamorphosis: Human (40)
Negate Magic (30)

Level Nine

Metamorphosis: Insect (60)
Purge Self (70)
Summon and Control Canine (50)
Tame Beast (60)
Water to Wine (40)

Level Ten

Metamorphosis: Superior (100)
Purge Other (100)
Restore Limb (80)
Summon and Control Rodents (70)
Super-Healing (70)

Level Eleven

Remove Curse (140)
Summon and Control Animals (125)

Level Twelve

Ironwood (50+)
Metamorphosis: Mist (250)

Level Thirteen

Restore Life (275)
Sanctum (390)

Level Fourteen

Restoration (750)
Resurrection (650)
Summon and Control Sea Serpents (350)

New Ocean Magic Spells

New Ocean Magic Spells

Buoyancy Blast

Range: By touch or can be cast 20 feet (6.1 m) away per level of experience.
Duration: Five minutes per level of experience on inanimate objects, two minutes per level on the living.
Limitations: Can only be placed on one person, animal or object per casting. Weight is limited to 200 lbs (90 kg) +50 lbs (22.5 kg) per level of experience. This limitation means the spell is ineffective when used on heavy objects, boats, ships, subs, and most Bio-Armor or power armor clad opponents.
Saving Throw: None for inanimate objects, standard for surface dwellers, +2 to save for aquatic/amphibious people, +3 to save for fish, crustaceans, cetaceans, and other aquatic animals.
P.P.E.: Nine
Level: Third

The spell imparts the properties of buoyancy upon an object or person. This can be used to rescue someone who has fallen overboard or to save cargo that would otherwise sink. Handheld melee weapons and guns being used underwater and affected by the Buoyancy Blast spell are -2 to strike as the weapon bobs and tugs upward, and will float up and away if the holder loosens his grip. Cast upon sunken treasure and salvage that has already been dug out of the silt/ground, or is only resting on the sea floor, and it rises toward the surface without the necessity of ropes and pulleys or carrying it by hand. Of course, anything made buoyant is vulnerable to currents and waves.

If cast on a person underwater, unless he saves vs magic, the individual immediately begins to slowly float up toward the surface. He can resist this pull by swimming hard against it. However, such intense resistance uses up half the character's melee attacks/actions and inflicts the following penalties: -4 on Perception Rolls, no initiative, -2 to strike, parry, dodge and all other combat rolls, -20% on skill performance and it takes twice as long to perform the skill, and reduce Spd by half unless it is up. If able to hold on to something to keep's one place, the effect and penalties of buoyancy are reduced by half, but the enchanted person must hang onto whatever it is that's preventing him from floating to the surface.

If cast upon a fast moving target (40 mph/64 km or faster) like a torpedo, harpoon or spear, the mage must roll to strike, and needs a 16 or higher to hit. If he hits, the torpedo/projectile/moving target continues to move forward (if it is a propelled object) but will veer upward and off course 1D4x10 degrees. If he misses, the spell is spent, the P.P.E. is used and the projectile remains on target.

Capture Moisture

Range: Self.
Duration: One minute per level of experience, with permanent results.
Saving Throw: None.
P.P.E.: Three
Level: First

This spell enables the mage to capture moisture from dew, fallen rain that forms droplets on leaves, even fog and humidity hanging in the air. The spell caster can then collect it into a container or direct it to coalesce and water a particular plant, tree, or area of plants/crops (5 foot/1.5 m diameter per level of experience). Up to one gallon (3.7 liters) of water per level of experience, per minute, can be gathered in this manner, double within 15 minutes after a rain shower or within 30 minutes after a thunderstorm. All water gathered this way is suitable for drinking or watering crops.

Current Curtain

Range: 20 foot (6.1 m) diameter sphere of influence per level of experience, and can be cast up to 100 feet (30.5 m) away per level of experience.

Duration: One minute per level of experience.
Saving Throw: None. Must fight the current to break free or be pulled out, otherwise the victim is trapped within for the duration of the spell or until the spell caster cancels its effect.
P.P.E.: Forty-five
Level: Ninth

This powerful spell has a few possible effects. One is to create a sphere of influence that is not affected by the current and waves of the waters around him, creating a zone of calm water.

Another is to create an area of violently turbulent water and powerful, swirling currents. Any animals, people and small boats or mini-subs that enter the sphere are swept up into it and caught in an undercurrent that requires a Robot P.S. of 40 or a Supernatural P.S. of 26 to be able to swim out of the tide, and even that takes 1D4 melee rounds. While held and buffeted by the powerful forces of the Current Curtain, victims are -1D4 attacks per melee round, long-range attacks are -5 to strike (including any torpedoes or projectiles fired from within the Curtain), all other combat bonuses are reduced by half, -30% to skill performance, and any handheld items/weapons will be swept away unless held tight. Once a victim has swum free or is pulled out, he'll have to swim around the Current Curtain or get stuck again.

Torpedoes and projectiles that hit the Current Curtain are slowed down by 30% and knocked 1D4x10% off course, unless they are smart bombs that can course correct after they exit the Curtain. Ships, submarines, and sea monsters that pass through the magic sphere experience shaking and turbulence, sonar and communications systems go down while in the Current Curtain and speed is reduced by 2D6%, but that's all.

Depth Tolerance

Range: Self or one other by touch.
Duration: 30 minutes per level of experience.
Saving Throw: Standard.
P.P.E.: Six
Level: Second

A simplified version of the Impervious to Ocean Depths spell, Depth Tolerance does not allow those under its effects to travel to the bottom of trenches and abyssal plains, but does provide shallower depth capacity; 50% greater than what is typical for that species (for example, 600 feet/183 m is the normal range for humans) or to a depth of one mile (1.6 km/5,280 feet/1,609 m), whichever is greater. (For humans, that would be one mile/1.6 km.) The spell can only be cast on one individual at a time, and if it wears off while at great depths, the person is in serious trouble.

Draw Water

Range: 100 feet (30.5 m) per level of experience.
Duration: One minute per level of experience.
Saving Throw: None for the water; -2 to dodge for those targeted for a soaking.
P.P.E.: Fifteen
Level: Fifth

The spell caster can draw water up and around him to be used for a number of different applications. The first is to grab and channel that water to soak a target, to put out a fire aboard a ship or wash away garbage or debris. Drawing water and using it against vampires does 6D6 damage per melee attack (counts as two attacks/actions; one to draw the water, another to direct it at the target).

Another application is to draw up the water and suspend it around the mage, who can then use it to conceal his features (only his shape can be seen), or to wash items or clothing, take a shower, or to create a circular wall around himself to keep biting insects or small animals away, or fire at bay. Any vampire punching through it takes 3D6 damage, (no damage if using a melee weapon.) The simplest use, of course, is to draw water up, like a fountain, from a well or recessed water source to get a drink or fill containers with water.

Light up the Deep

Range: Lights up a 50 foot (15.2 m) diameter per level of experience and can be cast up to 200 feet (61 m) away per level of experience.
Cannot be cast on land; underwater only.
Duration: One minute per level of experience.
Saving Throw: Standard.
P.P.E.: Fifteen
Level: Fifth

The spell caster summons a magical approximation of the sun's light. A brilliant sphere of yellow-white light appears, its rays saturating the area. All living things accustomed to the dark of the deep ocean will flee the area (roll vs Horror Factor 15), and those that stay are blinded for the duration of the spell. While the light will not damage aquatic undead, it will drive them back to outside the spell's radius. Those beings who can see in light need 1D4 melee rounds for their eyes to adjust, during which time they lose one melee attack and are -5 on Perception Rolls and all combat rolls. Lighting up a light area underwater has no special effect. This spell can be used to help search the ocean depths, read, signal for help, and other practical applications.

Manipulate Thermoclines

Range: Affects a one mile (1.6 km) radius per level of experience.
Duration: 5 minutes per level of experience.
Saving Throw: None.
P.P.E.: Twenty-Four
Level: Sixth

Thermoclines are layered temperature boundaries found in large bodies of water. Passing through a thermocline creates a noticeable temperature difference, and the various layers of water have an effect on sonar and scent currents. Moving a thermocline layer above or below a target will confine their sonar and scent-tracking abilities to that layer, essentially blinding them to scents and sensor readings from the other side of the thermocline. A thermocline is not a physical wall, however, and anyone or anything with swimming capabilities can pass right through it. Thermoclines are always horizontal in nature and parallel to the water's surface, and cannot be cast as vertical walls or boundaries that wrap around an object.

Water Shield

Range: Self or another person or object by touch or 10 feet (3 m) away; line of sight required.
Duration: One minute per level of experience to remain dry. Instant drying.
Saving Throw: None.
P.P.E.: Twenty
Level: Seventh

If cast prior to going into water or being exposed to water, the recipient is protected from water by an invisible magic aura. When cast on vampires, other creatures, or objects (paper, electronics, etc.) which can be hurt or damaged by water, they are completely protected by this spell. Those beings or objects protected by a Water Shield can walk through rivers, swim in the water and dive underwater without injury or ill effect (provided they can get over the possible psychological fear/aspect of their condition).

In the alternative, the Water Shield spell can be used to instantly *dry off* a person or object. Great for drying waterlogged clothes, books, and items, but any damage done by the water remains. For example, food will be ruined, there is only a 01-45% chance electronics will work, paper is permanently wrinkled and warped, the pages of a book are likewise warped and will not close/is bloated to three times the thickness of the original book. 01-90% chance that a dried out gun will work with new ammunition. **Note:** Has no effect on water beings and does not dry out or dessicate fish, fruit, etc., it simply dries the surface/skin and any apparel worn by a person.

Biomancy Bio-Armor

By Matthew Clements, inspired by the ideas of Greg Diaczyk, Kevin Siembieda and the art of Chuck Walton. Additional text by Kevin Siembieda.

Avian Bio-Armor
Barnacle Bio-Armor
Chitin Bio-Armor
Coral (Heavy) Bio-Armor
Crustacean (Heavy) Bio-Armor
Dolphin Bio Armor
Kelp Bio-Armor
Leviathan (Heavy) Bio-Armor
Shark Bio-Armor
Wood Bio-Armor
(Wave Strider Body Armor – for civilian use)

Features Common to All Bio-Armor:

The Bio-Armor Symbiote: Each suit of Bio-Armor is a living construct that has a symbiotic relationship with its owner. This means it <u>needs</u> the host to survive. The suit can be removed (come off completely), but needs to be worn at least 1D6+6 hours every week or the suit's link with its host will break and the suit dies 1D6 hours after the break. As a result, most warriors wear the suit 50% to 90% of the time, only in its concealed mode, covering 25-50% of their body. Because the armor is alive, form fitting and, in effect, a second skin, it is quite comfortable to wear, and most warriors come to forget they are even wearing it.

After the symbiotic link is broken and the armor dies, a Biomancer can create a completely new suit of the same type or a different type. Under the right circumstances, the Biomancer Gene-Mage can recreate the original suit of Bio-Armor, provided he was able to get a DNA sample from it before it perished. Likewise, a Biomancer Gene-Mage can reconnect a broken link between the Bio-Armor and its owner before the suit dies by performing a slight variation of the original creation ritual. However, if the suit has been neglected in the past and was close to dying because its owner does not wear it often enough for a second or third time, the armor is less compliant and when the link is reestablished, the Bio-Armor has 10% less M.D.C. and all of its other stats and attributes (Spd, P.S., etc.) are also 10% less than before. **Note**: Biomancer Gene-Mages are able to sense exactly how long a disconnected suit has to live.

All Terrain Functionality: Bio-Armor can survive and function in all terrestrial environments and does not suffer damage out of the water for long periods of time. Whether the wearer has gills or lungs, the Bio-Armor can breathe (intake air) on the surface and underwater for itself as well as provide breathable air to its wearer. Bio-Armor also screens and filters out toxins, gases and pollution, typically providing +3 to save vs air and waterborne toxins/gas and disease when the armor is sealed and +2 even when the helmet is removed. Most also have an emergency one hour air supply. Bio-Armor also enables the wearer to speak clearly in air and water environments, keeps him warm and comfortable in cold conditions, cool in hot conditions, indicates approximate depth underwater and warns when they are reaching the limit of its depth tolerance. Bio-Armor is operated via the mental commands and muscle movements of the wearer.

Custom Fitting: The creation process typically takes 10-30 minutes and requires the presence of a Biomancer Gene-Mage, the recipient of the Bio-Armor (can be the Biomancer himself, another Biomancer or someone else) and the creatures enlisted to aid the Biomancer Gene-Tech in the creation of the suit. Each suit of Bio-Armor is custom made, linked to its specific owner and cannot be worn by anyone else. If the owner has natural shape-shifting powers like the Merans, or is magically transformed, the suit conforms its owner's new body shape and size as necessary. When the owner dies, so does the armor within 1D6 hours.

Concealment: All suits of Bio-Armor can retract to reveal the face, head, hands, etc. of the wearer as necessary or desired. The armor can even retract and compact itself enough to be easily concealed under clothing; it must cover a minimum of 25% of the body, typically retracting to the chest and back or lower body.

Feeding Bio-Armor: Bio-Armor feeds on natural ambient P.P.E. from the environment and the dead skin that is constantly being shed by its host as well as trace elements and organisms encountered while filtering water and air. Psychics are able to detect the aura of a particular Bio-Armor and it registers on infrared as a living thing.

Organic Healing: Bio-Armor is alive and heals at a rate of 2D6 M.D.C. per hour, double at a ley line, triple at a nexus or Stone Pyramid; its M.D.C. can also be restored via psionic healing and magic.

P.P.E. of Bio-Armor: Each suit, though alive, has a low amount of P.P.E. (2D6+2) that is not available to its wearer, with the exception of the Barnacle Bio-Armor.

Suiting Up: To don a Bio-Armor suit takes about 15 seconds (about one melee round). Activation of a retracted suit is nearly instantaneous, taking only a single melee action to completely seal the suit.

Utility Clasps: All suits of Bio-Armor can extend little tendrils, hooks or arms depending on the creature the armor is based upon. For example, Kelp Bio-Armor has vine-like tendrils of seaweed to hook and hold accessories, while the Crustacean Bio-Armor has appendages that resemble little crab claws or legs to strap things to the suit. These "Utility Clasps" are used to hold weapons on the side or back, pouches and bags to the waist, upper leg and chest, and so on. Even a full-sized trident or heavy weapon can be carried and kept neatly out of the way, clasped to the back of the Bio-Armor suit.

Destroying Bio-Armor: Depleting the M.D.C. of the *main body* shuts the Bio-Armor down, causing it to retreat into concealed mode and go dormant. A depleted and dormant Bio-Armor no longer provides its wearer with any M.D.C. protection, bonuses, combat or travel capabilities, Supernatural P.S., or any other armor features and abilities. In fact, the wearer suffers the following penalties due to the dead weight of the armor and loss of the familiar contact with his symbiotic partner: -1 attack per melee round, -1 to all combat bonuses and maneuvers, and reduce running and swimming speed by 20%.

Armor Recovery: HOWEVER, unless the living Bio-Armor has been reduced to 100 points below zero, it remains alive and will recover from its dormant state as soon as it recovers a minimum of 10 M.D.C. Remember, Bio-Armor heals as at a rate of 2D6 M.D.C. per hour, double at a ley line, triple at a nexus or Stone Pyramid. **Note:** While in the non-responsive dormant state, the Bio-Armor provides no protection to the wearer even though it is still attached to him. For an attacker to inflict additional damage to the Bio-Armor at its concealed location, an attacker must deliberately target it and make a "Called Shot" with a -4 to strike penalty unless at point-blank range. If M.D.C. is reduced to more than 100 points below zero, the Bio-Armor is completely "killed" and destroyed. There is no recovery.

Exclusive to the Military: The Warrior's Legacy. With a few exceptions, most Lemurian Bio-Armor is designed specifically for the warrior castes within Lemurian society, and is not available to the average Lemurian citizen or most other O.C.C.s other than the Biomancer and Scout. Some are exclusive to specific Military O.C.C.s only, and no one else. Even Biomancer Gene-Mages respect this and never select these "exclusive" armors. Each O.C.C. indicates which armors are available to it.

Avian Bio-Armor

Exclusive to Birdmen Warriors

By Kevin Siembieda and Greg Diaczyk

The magical creation process enchants a flock of Sooty Terns (other aquatic flying birds can be substituted) into weaving a cover of feathers around the Birdman. The Biomancy ritual takes 20 minutes and must be in an open area along the ocean waters, be it a beach, the shoreline or at the top of a cliff. A flock of sea birds (Sooty Terns are the traditional animal used to make *Lemurian Avian Armor*) descend upon the Birdman Warrior, completely covering him under their fluttering wings. The recipient of the armor must remain as still as possible while immersed in the flock of birds. The enchantment weaves their feathers, essence and energy into a thick blanket of feathers with stringy wisps extending from the back between the shoulders. As the birds fly away, unharmed, the blanket of feathers transforms into a dense mesh that seems to take shape and mold into plates of armor over the chest, shoulders and lower legs. A tough, flexible M.D.C. fabric forms over the rest of the body and extremities. Soon a helmet takes shape over the defender's head and a pair of wings and tail form on the back.

When the ritual is completed, the Lemurian Birdman is clad in a suit of magical Avian Bio-Armor, complete with a beaked helmet, hands and feet with bird-like talons, and a pair of wings. The wings fold to be more compact when on the ground. The way they fold gives them a deceptive butterfly-like appearance, but when they unfurl to fly, they very much take the shape of bird wings. The wings can lower, raise and adjust to catch and ride wind currents, but they do not beat up and down like real birds. Avian Bio-Armor is exclusive to the Lemurian Birdmen Warriors. While one might imagine it takes some time to master this unique armor, the affinity the Tangata Manu clan has with birds (all Birdmen Warriors come from this clan) enables them to take wing like they were born to it. Most master the use of the armor within a matter of 2D6 hours of flying time and 1D6 hours underwater.

Avian Bio-Armor is sealed, environmental armor with a magical, independent air supply to protect against pollution and toxins in the air or water. The armor can "breathe" new air as needed, filtering most gases and dangerous substances. Even when temporarily unsealed, the warrior inside the armor gets a +2 to save vs toxic gases, airborne poisons and diseases. The wearer controls his pair of wings with mental commands and muscle movement. Wings remain folded and compact until they are needed. In the air, the wings fold out like those of a bird or airplane and change position and configuration as needed to ride air currents. Underwater, the wings take on a low profile V-shape to minimize resistance and cut through the water at good speeds. The wings operate by mental command and the suit responds to the pilot as if it were a second skin – which in many respects, it is.

Until the last 70 years when the heavier Bio-Armors were first designed, Avian Bio-Armor was used in all combat missions. Now, with a wider variety of armor and specialization, the Birdmen engage primarily in scouting operations, reconnaissance and intelligence gathering, search and rescue, surprise attacks, stealth attacks, sabotage, espionage and Special Forces operations.

Lemurian Avian Bio-Armor

Exclusive to the Lemurian Tangata Manu Clan and select heroes.

Model Type: Avian Bio-Armor.
Class: Light Aerial Combat Armor – the Biomancy Gene-Mage equivalent of medium, environmental power armor.
Crew: One.
M.D.C. by Location:

* Head – 110
Arms (2) – 67 each
* Clawed Hands (2) – 37 each
Legs (2) – 122 each
* Clawed Feet (2) – 70 each
* Wings (2) – 117 each
** Main Body – 257

* A single asterisk indicates a small or difficult target to hit that can only be struck when the attacker makes a Called Shot, and even then the attacker is -4 to strike. Destroying the head/helmet eliminates all forms of optical and sensory enhancement, leaving the pilot to rely on his own human senses without any of the bonuses granted to him by the Bio-Armor.

** Depleting the M.D.C. of the *main body* shuts the Bio-Armor down and Supernatural P.S., all bonuses, combat and special capabilities provided by the armor to its wearer are gone. See Features Common to All Bio-Armor above for full details.

Speed:

Running: 35 mph (56 km) maximum. The act of running *does* tire out its wearer, but at half of the usual fatigue rate.

Leaping: 10 feet (3 m) high or lengthwise from a stationary position, 30 feet (9.1 m) high or across with a running start without actually attaining flight.

Flying: Can take flight from a standing still position, running start or leap from a height. Avian Bio-Armor can hover stationary in mid-air or fly up to a maximum speed of 100 mph (160 km), triple along a ley line or within a ley line triangle, but cruising speed is considered to be 50 mph (80 km). A power dive in the air doubles the Birdman's current speed and is always a sharp, downward angled dive. Maximum altitude of the suit is 20,000 feet (6,096 m), but it is typically used at low altitudes and is so agile and mobile it can fly at treetop level, through a forest (at half speed), through streets and around buildings, and even down hallways and narrow passages. This means it can also hug the ground and slip under enemy radar. **Note:** As a magical and living construct, Avian Bio-Armor is *silent* (except for the rush of the wind) even when flying at top speed. Unless an enemy looks up he is not likely to notice the Birdman.

Underwater Capabilities: The Avian Bio-Armor can swim/rocket through water at a maximum speed of 30 mph (48 km or 26 knots), triple along a ley line, and can swim and walk along the bottom of shallow seas at half the running speed. Can make an underwater dive of 300 feet (91.4 m) underwater from the air or the surface of the water. Maximum depth is two miles (3.2 km).

Mobility: Good; -5% to Prowl or use other Physical skills due to the bulk of the suit's wings.

Statistical Data:

P.P.E. Cost to Create: 570 P.P.E.

Height: 7-8 feet (2.1 to 2.4 m) with wings folded as small as possible.

Width: 2.6 to 3 feet (0.8 to 0.9 m) at the shoulder.

Length: 4.5 feet (1.4 m) with wings folded to be upright and compact.

Wingspan: 14 feet (4.3 m) with wings fully extended.

Weight: 200 pounds (90 kg).

Physical Strength: Supernatural P.S. of 20.

Cargo: None, though belts, bags and other carrying cases can be strapped to or carried by the Birdman.

Power System: Magic. The living armor feeds on and is powered by the P.P.E. of its wearer or available ambient P.P.E. As long as it has at least 15 P.P.E. per day, it can function at full capacity.

Continuous flight can be maintained for two hours per each of the Birdman's P.E. attribute points. After that he must rest or suffer exhaustion.

Cost: Exclusive to Lemurians and never sold on the open market, nor are the secrets of its creation ever shared with outsiders, no matter how trusted they may be. Easily worth 6-10 million credits.

Weapon Systems:

1. **Clawed Gauntlets (2):** The gauntlets of the armor end in short claws for slashing and raking attacks. As armored, clawed gauntlets, the Birdman can parry melee weapons with his hands without injury to himself or the gauntlets. They are also useful for scaling the walls of buildings and cliff facings, and hanging onto Moai and the sides of water vessels. **Note:** The Bio-Armor Gauntlets are damaged only when an attack specifically targets them; requires a Called Shot and the attacker is -4 to strike.

Primary Purpose: Close Combat.

Secondary Purpose: Climbing.

Range: Hand to hand/arm's reach.

Mega-Damage: 2D6 M.D. (factors in the Supernatural P.S. of 20), double damage from a Power Strike but counts at two melee attacks.

2. **Clawed Feet/Boots (2):** The boots of the armor end in clawed toes for slashing and raking attacks and inflict more damage from flying rake attacks and kicks. They are also useful for scaling the walls of buildings and cliff facings, and hanging onto Moai and the sides of water vessels. **Note:** The Bio-Armor boots are damaged only when an attack specifically targets them; requires a Called Shot and the attacker is -4 to strike.

Primary Purpose: Close Combat.

Secondary Purpose: Climbing.

Range: Hand to hand/arm's reach.

Mega-Damage: 3D6 M.D. (factors in the Supernatural P.S. of 20) from a typical kick, 4D6 M.D. from a flying rake or flying kick.

3. **Side Arms (2; Optional):** One or two pistols or Biomancy Power Rods can be strapped to the waist and secured to each leg for additional firepower. Likewise, a utility belt with pouches and gear can be hooked around the waist or chest.

   Birdmen may also use any type of Lemurian or outsiders' rifle or long-range power rod as a third handheld, ranged weapon. Of course, staves, tridents, spears, swords and other melee weapons may be used in addition to or in place of a blaster or gun.

4. **Hand to Hand Combat:** Rather than use a weapon, the pilot can engage in Mega-Damage hand to hand combat. The number of attacks and bonuses are as per the skills and attributes of the armor's wearer, plus the following bonuses provided by the armor.

   Avian Bio-Armor Combat Bonuses:

   +1 additional attack per melee at levels 2, 5, 10 and 15.

   +2 to Perception Rolls from the air only.

   +2 to strike and parry, +3 to *automatic dodge* (the act of dodging does not use up an attack/action), +2 to disarm, +1 to pull punch, +2 to roll with impact, and +2 to save vs toxic gases, airborne poisons and diseases.

+10% to Climbing, Land Navigation and Prowl skills when the armor is worn.

5. Sensor Systems & Special Features of Note: These are in addition to features common to all Lemurian Bio-Armor.

Bio-Regeneration of the Armor: The Bio-Armor suit is alive and regenerates 2D6 M.D.C. per hour, double at a ley line, triple at a nexus or Stone Pyramid.

Magic Healing of the Wearer Inside the Armor: One Hit Point or S.D.C. point per hour, double at a Stone Pyramid or at a ley line or nexus.

Optics: Perfect color vision and telescopic vision 5,000 feet (1,524 m), Nightvision 2,000 feet (610 m), see the invisible 300 feet (91.4 m), polarization filters to eliminate glare above and below the waves.

Resistant to Cold: Suffers one-third damage.

Sense Altitude, Depth and Wind: The armor enables the Birdman to sense the altitude/height he is flying, depth level underwater and limitations of the armor with exact precision. It also enables him to calculate wind direction, strength and speed, updrafts, waves, tide and undercurrents and compensaten for them to maximize speed of travel.

Barnacle Bio-Armor

This is an unusual form of Bio-Armor that uses barnacles to create the armor and then invites them to climb aboard for a free ride. In return, the wearer can harness and channel the P.P.E. held and collected by each barnacle! This feature makes Barnacle Armor particularly popular among Biomancers, other spell casters and troops armed with magic weapons they can recharge using the suit's P.P.E. The armor resembles a netting-like mesh of the barnacles' connective strands and bony shell sections linking key parts of the body armor together (like joints). One can still see the wearer's skin through the mesh, but the magical properties of the suit protect the wearer completely. The rest of the suit is encrusted with 3D4x10 barnacles. The barnacles' filtering properties also provide a +6 to save vs toxic gases, poisons and impurities found in the water or air, so Barnacle Armor is sometimes used as a kind of hazmat suit and appreciated for its P.P.E. reserve (1 P.P.E. per barnacle). **Note**: If the host/armor dies, the surviving barnacles will resume their normal life cycle, settling into the environment.

Lemurian Barnacle Bio-Armor

Model Type: Barnacle Bio-Armor.

Class: Amphibious Combat Armor – the Biomancy Gene-Mage equivalent of light, environmental power armor.

Crew: One.

M.D.C. by Location:

* Head – 90

Arms (2) – 50 each

Legs (2) – 85 each

** Main Body – 147

* A single asterisk indicates a small or difficult target to hit that can only be struck when the attacker makes a Called Shot, and even then the attacker is -4 to strike. Destroying the head/helmet eliminates all forms of optical and sensory enhancement, leaving the pilot to rely on his own human senses without any of the bonuses granted to him by the Bio-Armor.

** Depleting the M.D.C. of the *main body* shuts the Bio-Armor down and Supernatural P.S., all bonuses, combat and special capabilities provided by the armor to its wearer are gone. See Features Common to All Bio-Armor above for full details.

Speed:

Running: 35 mph (56 km) maximum. The act of running *does* tire out its wearer, but at half of the usual fatigue rate.

Leaping: 10 feet (3 m) high or lengthwise from a stationary position, 16 feet (4.8 m) high or across with a running start.

Flying: None.

Underwater Capabilities: The Barnacle Bio-Armor can swim or rocket through water at a maximum speed of 30 mph (48 km or 26 knots), triple along a ley line, and can swim and walk along the bottom of shallow seas at half the running speed. Maximum depth is three miles (4.8 km).

Mobility: Excellent; no movement penalties.

Statistical Data:

P.P.E. Cost to Create: 750 P.P.E.

Height: 7-8 feet (2.1 to 2.4 m).

Width: 2.6 to 3 feet (0.8 to 0.9 m) at the shoulder.

Length: 3.5 feet (1 m).

Weight: 130 pounds (59 kg).

Physical Strength: Supernatural P.S. of 20.

Cargo: None, though belts, bags and other carrying cases can be strapped to or carried by the wearer.

Power System: Magic. The living armor feeds on and is powered by the P.P.E. of its wearer or available ambient P.P.E. As long as it has at least 20 P.P.E. per day, it can function at full capacity.

Cost: Exclusive to Lemurians and never sold on the open market nor are the secrets of its creation ever shared with outsiders, no matter how trusted they may be. Easily worth 3-4 million credits.

Weapon Systems:

1. Barnacle Grenade: A single barnacle charged with Bio-Energy can be discharged from the surface of the suit, detonating in an explosion of clamshell fragments that distracts opponents and gives the wearer an opportunity to regroup or make a run for it.

Primary Purpose: Anti-Sea Monster/Anti-Submarine.

Secondary Purpose: Defense.

Mega-Damage: 4D6 M.D. to everything within a 4 foot (1.2 m) blast radius.

Range: 350 feet (106.7 m).

Rate of Fire: Each launched barnacle counts as one melee attack/action.

Payload: 6 barnacles. The suit recharges at a rate of one explosive barnacle per hour.

2. Barnacle Fists (2): The armor's gauntlets feature knuckles with protruding barnacle edges. They are extremely sharp and hard, able to inflict M.D.

Primary Purpose: Close Combat.

Secondary Purpose: Defense.

Range: Hand to hand/arm's reach.

Mega-Damage: 2D6 M.D. (factors in the Supernatural P.S. of 20), double damage from Power Strike but counts as two melee attacks.

3. Side Arms (2; Optional): Any type of side arm or melee weapon may be used; same as the Avian Bio-Armor.

4. Hand to Hand Combat: Rather than use a weapon the pilot can engage in Mega-Damage hand to hand combat. The number of attacks and bonuses are as per the skills and attributes of the armor's wearer, plus the following bonuses provided by the armor.

Barnacle Bio-Armor Combat Bonuses:

+1 additional attack per melee at levels 3, 7 and 11.

+2 to Perception Rolls underwater only.

+1 to strike and parry, +1 to disarm and +1 to pull punch, +2 to roll with impact, and +6 to save vs toxic gases, airborne poisons and diseases.

+10% to Climbing, Underwater Navigation and Undersea Salvage skills when the armor is worn.

5. **Sensor Systems & Special Features of Note:** All the same common features, except for the following.
Bio-Regeneration: 3D6 M.D.C. per hour.
P.P.E. Battery/Reservoir: The 3D4x10+220 barnacles provide a total of 1D4x10+50 P.P.E. at full power. The wearer of Barnacle Bio-Armor can draw upon the P.P.E. reserve of the suit to use in casting magic. The barnacles, en masse, recover P.P.E. at a rate of 5D6 per hour, so there should be 5-30 P.P.E. available most of the time, even when drawing on the suit on a frequent basis. **Note:** A barnacle is roughly an inch and a half (4 cm) in diameter, but they do not cover every inch of the armor.

Chitin Bio-Armor

The creation process for Chitin Bio-Armor enchants a group of insects into weaving a chitinous substance around the recipient of the Bio-Armor. The actual ritual takes about 20 minutes and can take place wherever insects are plentiful, though forests, jungles and marshlands seem to be preferred by most Biomancer Gene-Mages. A swarm of insects arrive and surround the subject of the spell, completely covering him under a solid, living mass of bugs. The insects are temporarily enchanted and able to secrete a gooey substance over the subject from head to toe. The recipient of the armor must remain as still as possible while immersed in the crawling insects and goo. The G.M. might require characters that aren't Biomancers, Lemurians, psychic sensitives or Jungle Elves to make a save vs a Horror Factor of 10. Failure means the character thrashes around and/or flees and the spell is ruined, no Bio-Armor is created, and the P.P.E. is lost.

When the ritual is successfully completed, the cloud of insects withdraws to reveal the warrior clad in a suit of insect plate armor, complete with a helmet and transparent eye goggles. Its perfect fit provides excellent mobility (no Prowl or other skill penalties) as well as two sets of unobtrusive wings that fit flush against the body. The Chitin Bio-Armor might not have the same speed or aerodynamics of the Avian Bio-Armor, but its four wings allow it to hover and fly at moderate speed, and it features impressive jumping and combat capabilities. The suit also has a pair of antennae which are sensitive enough to detect radar and sonar emissions.

Lemurian Chitin Bio-Armor

Model Type: Chitin Bio-Armor.
Class: Amphibious Combat Armor – the Biomancy Gene-Mage equivalent of medium environmental power armor.
Crew: One.
M.D.C. by Location:

* Antennae (2) – 10 each
* Head – 100
* Hands (2) – 57 each
Arms (2) – 95 each
Legs (2) – 157 each
* Insect Wings (4) – 35 each
** Main Body – 268

* A single asterisk indicates a small or difficult target to hit that can only be struck when the attacker makes a Called Shot, and even then the attacker is -4 to strike. Destroying the head/helmet eliminates all forms of optical and sensory enhancement, leaving the pilot to rely on his own human senses without any of the bonuses granted to him by the Bio-Armor. Destroying one pair of wings makes hovering and flight impossible.

** Depleting the M.D.C. of the *main body* shuts the Bio-Armor down and Supernatural P.S., all bonuses, weapons and special capabilities provided by the armor to its wearer are gone. See Features Common to All Bio-Armor above for full details.

Speed:
Running: 35 mph (56 km) maximum. The act of running *does* tire out its wearer, but at one quarter the usual fatigue rate.

Leaping: 20 feet (6 m) high or 40 feet (12.2 m) lengthwise from a stationary position, double with a running start without actually attaining flight.

Flying: Can take flight from a standing still position, running start or leap from a height. Chitin Bio-Armor can hover stationary in mid-air or fly up to a maximum speed of 50 mph (80 km), triple along a ley line or within a ley line triangle.

A power dive in the air doubles the wearer's current speed and is always a sharp, downward angled dive. Maximum altitude of the suit is 10,000 feet (3,048 m), but it is typically used at low altitudes and is so agile and mobile it can fly at treetop level, through a forest, through streets and around buildings, and even down hallways and narrow passages at full speed. This means it can also hug the ground and slip under enemy radar. **Note:** As a magical and living construct, Chitin Bio-Armor is extremely quiet, even when flying at full speed. The wings do make a distinctive buzzing sound, but the noise is much less than aircraft, hover vehicles, or jet packs. The suit must be within 500 feet (152 m) for the noise it produces to be audible. Silent underwater.

Underwater Capabilities: The Chitin Bio-Armor can swim/rocket through water at a maximum speed of 30 mph (48 km or 26 knots), triple along a ley line, and can swim and walk along the bottom of shallow seas at half the running speed. Maximum depth is three miles (4.8 km).

Mobility: Excellent; no movement penalties.

Statistical Data:

P.P.E. Cost to Create: 900 P.P.E.

Height: 7-8 feet (2.1 to 2.4 m) with wings folded as small as possible.

Width: 2.6 to 3 feet (0.8 to 0.9 m) at the shoulder.

Length: 3 feet (0.9 m) with wings folded flush against the suit.

Wingspan: 7 feet (2.1 m) with wings fully extended.

Weight: 180 pounds (81 kg).

Physical Strength: Supernatural P.S. of 25.

Cargo: None per se, though belts, bags and other carrying cases can be strapped to or carried by the wearer.

Power System: Magic. The living armor feeds on and is powered by the P.P.E. of its wearer and available ambient P.P.E. As long as it has at least 20 P.P.E. per day, it can function at full capacity.

Continuous flight can be maintained for two hours per each of the wearer's P.E. attribute points (half that underwater). After that he must rest or suffer exhaustion.

Cost: Exclusive to Lemurians and never sold on the open market nor are the secrets of its creation ever shared with outsiders, no matter how trusted they may be. Easily worth 5-8 million credits.

Weapon Systems:

1. Shoulder Beams (2): A "collar"-like ridge along the armor contains a pair of energy beam emitters. Their reach is limited, but they provide the wearer with long-range weapons while keeping his/her hands free for fighting hand to hand.

Primary Purpose: Anti-Personnel.

Secondary Purpose: Defense.

Range: 1,600 feet (488 m).

Mega-Damage: 2D6 M.D. per single blast, 4D6 M.D. for a dual blast.

Rate of Fire: Each blast or dual blast counts as one melee action.

Payload: Effectively unlimited as long as the suit is charged with P.P.E.

2. Serrated Forearm Blades (2): Each of the Bio-Armor's arms features dual, retractable blades similar to the arms of a praying mantis. They pull back when not in use and spring forward when the wearer engages in close combat.

Primary Purpose: Close Combat.

Secondary Purpose: Defense.

Range: Hand to hand/arm's reach.

Mega-Damage: 4D6 M.D. (factors in the Supernatural P.S. of 25), double damage from Power Strike but counts at two melee attacks.

3. Insect Mandibles: The mouth of the Chitin Bio-Armor features insectoid pincers that can be used to bite and snap in melee combat.

Primary Purpose: Close Combat.

Secondary Purpose: Defense.

Range: Hand to hand/arm's reach.

Mega-Damage: 2D4 M.D.

4. Side Arms (2; Optional): Any type of side arm or melee weapon may be used; same as the Avian Bio-Armor.

5. Hand to Hand Combat: Rather than use a weapon the pilot can engage in Mega-Damage hand to hand combat. The number of attacks and bonuses are as per the skills and attributes of the armor's wearer, plus the following bonuses provided by the armor.

Mega-Damage: As per Supernatural P.S. of 25. Restrained Punch: 4D6 S.D.C. Punch or Head Butt: 2D6 M.D. Power Punch: 4D6 M.D., but counts as two melee attacks. Kick: 3D6 M.D. Leap Kick or Power Kick: 5D6 M.D. Stomp: 1D6 M.D. Body Block/Ram: 2D6 M.D. plus has a 01-50% chance of knocking down opponents up to 14 feet (4.3 m) tall. Victims of knockdown lose initiative for the rest of the melee round and one melee attacks.

Chitin Bio-Armor Combat Bonuses:

+1 additional attack per melee at levels 2, 5, 10 and 15.

+2 to Perception Rolls on land only.

+2 to strike and parry, +1 to *automatic dodge* (the act of dodging does not use up an attack/action) at levels 1, 3, 5, 7, 9 and 11, +2 to disarm, +3 to pull punch, +2 to roll with impact, and +2 to save vs toxic gases, airborne poisons and diseases.

+15% to Climbing and Rappelling, +10% to Land Navigation and Tailing, and +5% to Prowl when the armor is worn.

6. Sensor Systems & Special Features of Note: All the same common features, plus those of the Avian Bio-Armor, plus the following.

Antennae: The Chitin Armor's antennae can detect radar signals at a range of up to 10 miles (16 km) and sonar signals from as far as 20 miles (32 km) away. The antennae tell the wearer the direction and distance of the signals, as well as whether a sonar pulse is biological or mechanical in origin, but they are incapable of determining what exactly is emitting the radar/sonar.

Coral Bio-Armor

This suit of Bio-Armor is created with the aid of the tiny organisms called polyps found in coral. The Biomancer Gene-Mage must perform this ritual near a living coral reef and the suit's recipient must be physically present. While the Biomancer chants the ritual (this takes approximately ten minutes), the recipient of the armor swims near the reef. As the spell progresses, the reef reaches up and engulfs him in a semi-liquid substance made of living polyps. When the ritual is over, the person is totally encased in coral. For 1D4 minutes he is blind and oblivious to the world. Some find

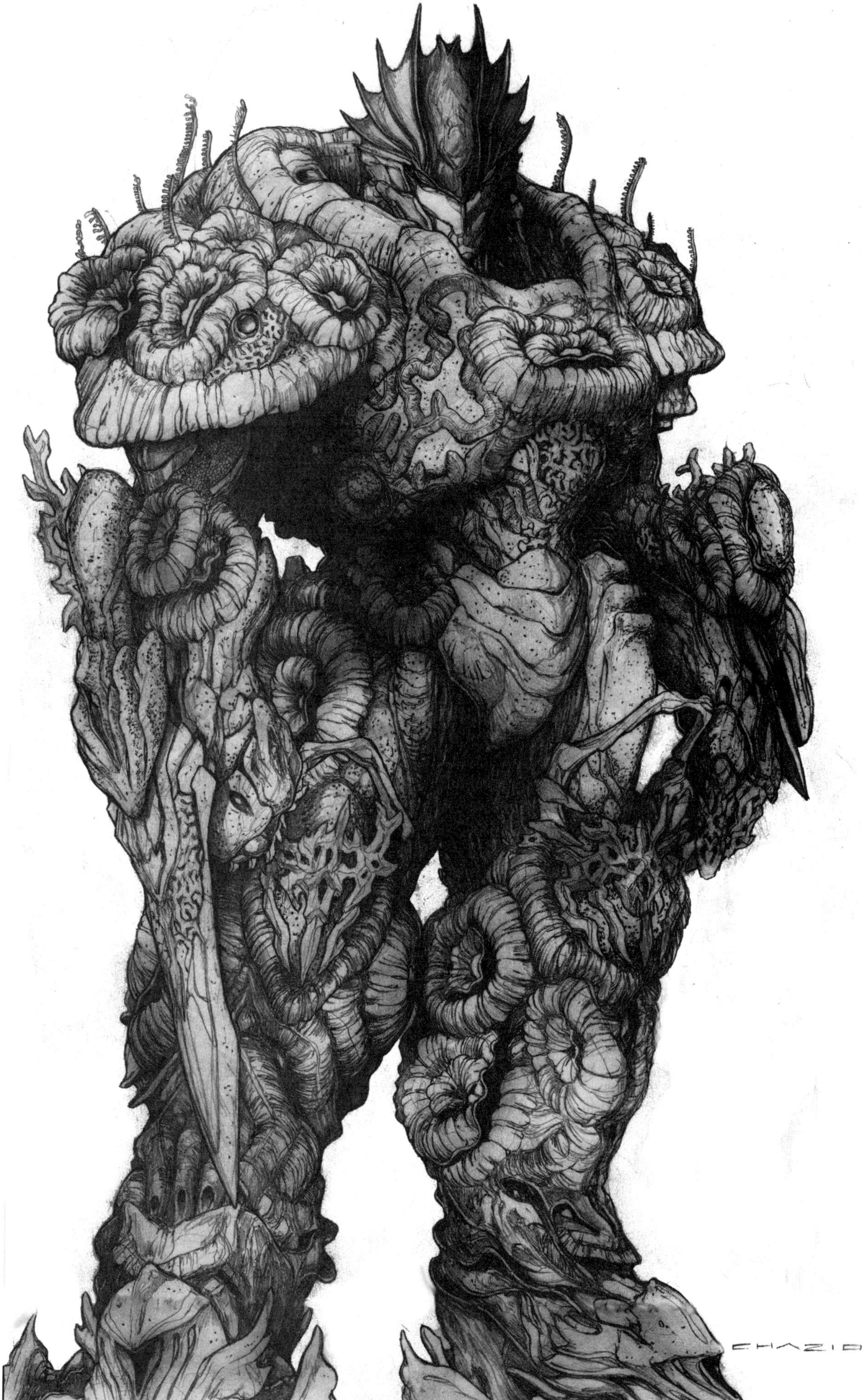

the experience disquieting and those with claustrophobia cannot endure the ritual. Most recipients take the opportunity to engage in deep meditation and enjoy bonding with the coral reef. After the 1D4 minute period is over, the reef resumes its natural appearance. Meanwhile, the coral encasing the person continues to transform into form-fitting, rock-like, Mega-Damage armor. The specific design of the armor varies with the Biomancer Gene-Mage and the emotions and temperament of the recipient, but it is always an organic shape with living organisms, colors and shapes that one would expect to find at a coral reef.

Lemurian Coral Bio-Armor

Model Type: Coral Bio-Armor.

Class: Amphibious Combat Armor – the Biomancy Gene-Mage equivalent of heavy, environmental power armor.

Crew: One.

M.D.C. by Location:

* Head – 120
* Hands (2) – 90 each
Arms (2) – 180 each
* Arm Sword – Blades (2) – 60 each
Legs (2) – 220 each
** Main Body – 357

* A single asterisk indicates a small or difficult target to hit that can only be struck when the attacker makes a Called Shot, and even then the attacker is -4 to strike. Destroying the head/helmet eliminates all forms of optical and sensory enhancement, leaving the pilot to rely on his own human senses without any of the bonuses granted to him by the Bio-Armor.

** Depleting the M.D.C. of the *main body* shuts the Bio-Armor down and Supernatural P.S., all bonuses, weapons and special capabilities provided by the armor to its wearer are gone. See Features Common to All Bio-Armor for full details.

Speed:

Running: 30 mph (48 km) maximum. The act of running *does* tire out its wearer, but at one third of the usual fatigue rate.

Leaping: 5 feet (1.5 m) high or lengthwise from a stationary position, 10 feet (3 m) high or across with a running start.

Flying: None.

Underwater Capabilities: The Coral Bio-Armor can swim/rocket through water at a maximum speed of 30 mph (48 km or 26 knots), triple along a ley line, and can swim and walk along the bottom of shallow seas at half the running speed. Maximum depth is four miles (6.4 km).

Mobility: Fair; -10% to Prowl or use other Physical skills.

Statistical Data:

P.P.E. Cost to Create: 700 P.P.E.

Height: 8.5-10.5 feet (2.6 to 3.2 m).

Width: 2.6 to 3 feet (0.8 to 0.9 m) at the shoulder.

Length: 3.5 feet (1 m).

Weight: 600 pounds (270 kg).

Physical Strength: Supernatural P.S. of 30.

Cargo: None, though belts, bags and other carrying cases can be strapped to or carried by the wearer.

Power System: Magic. The living armor feeds on and is powered by the P.P.E. of its wearer and available ambient P.P.E. As long as it has at least 25 P.P.E. per day, it can function at full capacity.

Cost: Exclusive to Lemurians and never sold on the open market nor are the secrets of its creation ever shared with outsiders, no matter how trusted they may be. Easily worth 12-15 million credits.

Weapon Systems:

1. **Coral Burst:** At the user's will, the Bio-Armor can fire a blast of dozens of tiny, razor sharp coral fragments from its hands and arms; point and shoot.
Primary Purpose: Anti-Personnel.
Secondary Purpose: Defense.
Range: 1,000 feet (305 m) underwater, double in an atmosphere.
Mega-Damage: 6D6 M.D. per blast from one arm, 1D6x10+6 from a simultaneous dual blast at the same target from both.
Rate of Fire: Each single or dual blast counts as one melee attack.
Payload: 60 blasts per arm, per hour.

2. **Retractable Arm Blades (2):** The arms of the Coral Bio-Armor sport a pair of extendible and retractable swords. They are used against sea monsters and humanoid opponents alike, and can retract fully into protective mountings when not in use.
Primary Purpose: Close Combat.
Secondary Purpose: Defense.
Range: Hand to hand/arm's reach.
Mega-Damage: 5D6 M.D. (factors in the Supernatural P.S. of 30), double damage from Power Strike but counts at two melee attacks.

3. **Side Arms (2; Optional):** Any type of side arm or melee weapon may be used; same as the Avian Bio-Armor.

4. **Hand to Hand Combat:** Rather than use a weapon the pilot can engage in Mega-Damage hand to hand combat. The number of attacks and bonuses are as per the skills and attributes of the armor's wearer, plus the following bonuses provided by the armor.
Mega-Damage: As per Supernatural P.S. of 30. Restrained Punch: 5D6 S.D.C. Punch or Head Butt: 3D6 M.D. Power Punch: 6D6 M.D., but counts as two melee attacks. Kick: 3D6+2 M.D. Stomp: 1D6 M.D. Body Block/Ram: 3D6+2 M.D. plus has a 01-60% likelihood of knocking down opponents up to 15 feet (4.6 m) tall. Victims of knockdown lose initiative for the rest of the melee round and one melee attack.
Coral Bio-Armor Combat Bonuses:
+1 additional attack per melee at levels 2, 5, 10 and 15.
+2 to Perception Rolls underwater only.
+1 to strike with Coral Burst at levels 2, 4, 6, 8, 10 and 12.
+1 to strike, +2 to parry and disarm, +3 to pull punch, +2 to roll with impact, and +2 to save vs toxic gases, airborne poisons and diseases.
+10% to Prowl and Camouflage skills in coral reef environments only.

5. **Sensor Systems & Special Features of Note:** All the same common features, except for the following.
Bio-Regeneration: 3D6 M.D.C. per hour, double at a coral reef.
Razor Coral: Coral reefs are known for their sharp edges that cut careless divers and undersea fishermen. The Coral Bio-Armor can temporarily ripple with razor-edged protrusions, making it extremely difficult to fight against the suit in close combat. When activated, anyone who strikes with their hands, feet, tail or body against the wearer takes 50% of the attack's damage themselves. Attackers who use a close combat weapon (sword, club, etc.) do not take damage, but see the damage they inflict reduced by 20%. Razor Coral lasts for one minute (four melee rounds), and can only be used twice per hour.

CHAZIO

Crustacean Bio-Armor

The mighty Crustacean Bio-Armor is the Lemurians' walking tank and an absolute monster in close combat. The creation process enchants a group of crustaceans (crabs, lobsters and other shellfish) into weaving a bone-like substance around the subject. The actual ritual takes 20 minutes, and must be performed at open sea or on an ocean beach. A swarm of crustaceans arrives and surrounds the subject of the spell, completely covering him under a solid, living mass of critters. The crustaceans are temporarily enchanted and able to secrete a gooey substance over the character. The recipient of the armor must remain as still as possible while immersed in the crawling crustaceans. The G.M. might require characters that aren't Biomancers, Jungle Elves, Lemurians or psychic sensitives to make a save vs a Horror Factor of 10. Failure means the character thrashes around or flees and the spell is ruined, the armor is not made, and the P.P.E. is lost. When the ritual is completed successfully, the cloud of crustaceans withdraws to reveal the character clad in a suit of bony plate armor, complete with a helmet and massive crab claw. Crustacean Bio-Armor has superior air and water filtering capabilities as well as heavy armor and impressive depth resistance. All of which make Crustacean Bio-Armor units perfect for attacks on the Lord of the Deep and other trench-dwellers.

Lemurian Crustacean Bio-Armor

Model Type: Crustacean Bio-Armor.

Class: Heavy Amphibious Combat Armor – the Biomancy Gene-Mage equivalent of heavy, environmental power armor.

Crew: One.

M.D.C. by Location:

* Head – 150
* Hand (1; usually right) – 130
Pincer Claw (1, usually left) – 350
Arms (2) – 220 each
Legs (2) – 310 each
** Main Body – 457

* A single asterisk indicates a small or difficult target to hit that can only be struck when the attacker makes a Called Shot, and even then the attacker is -4 to strike. Destroying the head/helmet eliminates all forms of optical and sensory enhancement, leaving the pilot to rely on his own human senses without any of the bonuses granted to him by the Bio-Armor.

** Depleting the M.D.C. of the *main body* shuts the Bio-Armor down and Supernatural P.S., all bonuses, weapons and special capabilities provided by the armor to its wearer are gone. See Features Common to All Bio-Armor for full details.

Speed:

Running: 30 mph (48 km) maximum. The act of running *does* tire out its wearer, but at one quarter of the usual fatigue rate.

Leaping: Cannot jump from a stationary position, 8 feet (2.4 m) high or across with a running start.

Flying: None.

Underwater Capabilities: The Crustacean Bio-Armor can swim/rocket through water at a maximum speed of 35 mph (56 km or 30 knots), triple along a ley line, and can swim and walk along the bottom of shallow seas at half the running speed. Maximum depth is seven miles (11 km).

Mobility: Poor, -15% to Acrobatics, Gymnastics, Prowl and similar skills requiring agility and movement, but not Climbing or Swimming.

Statistical Data:

P.P.E. Cost to Create: 1,000 P.P.E.

Height: 9-12 feet (2.7 to 3.6 m).

Width: 4.5 to 6 feet (1.4 to 1.8 m) at the shoulder.

Length: 4.5 feet (1.4 m).

Weight: 1,400-2,000 pounds (630 to 900 kg).

Physical Strength: Supernatural P.S. of 40.

Cargo: None, though belts, bags and other carrying cases can be strapped to or carried by the wearer.

Power System: Magic. The living armor feeds on and is powered by the P.P.E. of its wearer and available ambient P.P.E. As long as it has at least 30 P.P.E. per day, it can function at full capacity.

Cost: Exclusive to Lemurians and never sold on the open market nor are the secrets of its creation ever shared with outsiders, no matter how trusted they may be. Easily worth 18-25 million credits.

Weapon Systems:

1. Sonic Wave: The Crustacean Armor's hammerhead has the ability to emit piercing sonic energy directed into a broad wave and used as a ranged weapon. Larger targets take greater damage, while the wave's size means it can be fired at groups of infantry or small targets as well.

Primary Purpose: Anti-Personnel.

Secondary Purpose: Anti-Sea Monster/Anti-Submarine.

Range: 600 feet (183 m) on the surface, 1,200 feet (366 m) underwater.

Mega-Damage: Large targets (12 feet/3.6 m tall/long or larger) take 1D6x10 M.D. from absorbing the entire sonic wave. Smaller, man-sized targets take 3D6 M.D., but that damage is done to everything/everyone within 15 feet (4.6 m) of the point where the wave hits.

Rate of Fire: Each wave counts as one melee attack/action.

Payload: Effectively unlimited as long as the suit is charged with P.P.E.

2. Chest Beam (1): Mounted on the left side of the chest is a beam emitter that fires an energy beam. The damage is limited, but provides the wearer with a long-range weapon while keeping his/her hands free for fighting hand to hand.

Primary Purpose: Anti-Personnel.

Range: 1,600 feet (488 m); half underwater.

Secondary Purpose: Defense.

Mega-Damage: 2D6 M.D. per single blast.

Rate of Fire: Each blast counts as one melee action.

Payload: Effectively unlimited as long as the suit is charged with P.P.E.

3. Giant Crab Claw: The Crustacean's most noticeable weapon is its giant, distinctive crab claw. A massively powerful device, the claw can rip through tank armor and the hulls of ships with ease. Crustacean units are often used for boarding parties where they can create their own entrances and exits. For fighting onshore or deep below the waves, the Crustacean is as intimidating as any monster it is likely to come up against.

Primary Purpose: Close Combat.

Secondary Purpose: Assault.

Range: Hand to hand/arm's reach.

Mega-Damage: 6D6+10 M.D. (factors in the Supernatural P.S. of 40), 1D6x10 M.D. for a Power Strike, but counts at two melee attacks.

4. Side Arms (2; Optional): Any type of side arm or melee weapon may be used; same as the Avian Bio-Armor.

5. **Hand to Hand Combat:** Rather than use a weapon the pilot can engage in Mega-Damage hand to hand combat. The number of attacks and bonuses are as per the skills and attributes of the armor's wearer, plus the following bonuses provided by the armor.

Mega-Damage: As per Supernatural P.S. of 40. Restrained Punch: 6D6 S.D.C. Punch or Head Butt: 5D6 M.D. Power Punch: 1D6x10 M.D., but counts as two melee attacks. Crab Claw: 1D4x10+10 M.D. Stomp: 3D6 M.D. Body Block/Ram: 6D6 M.D. plus has a 01-78% likelihood of knocking down opponents up to 20 feet (6.1 m) tall. Victims of knockdown lose initiative for the rest of the melee round and one melee attack.

Crustacean Bio-Armor Combat Bonuses:

+1 additional attack per melee at levels 2, 4, 8, 12 and 15.

+3 to Perception Rolls underwater, +2 on land.

+2 to strike, +3 to parry, +1 to dodge (underwater only), +2 to disarm, +2 to pull punch, +3 to roll with impact, and +6 to save vs toxic gases, airborne poisons and diseases.

+10% to the Underwater Navigation and Land Navigation skills when the armor is worn.

6. **Sensor Systems & Special Features of Note:** All the same common features, except for the following.

Bio-Regeneration: 1D6x10 M.D.C. per hour.

Emergency Flotation: Due to the armor's significant weight and frequent use as a diving suit for combat at great depth, an emergency flotation feature is built in. When activated, the armor rockets upward towards the surface, moving much faster than its bulk would seem to allow. Granted, the only optional direction is straight up, but the Crustacean's heavy armor protects the user from any adverse effects of rapid pressure change. Opponents who the Bio-Armor is grappling and hanging onto may not have the same resistance, and ascending a few thousand feet in a matter of seconds could leave them victim to "the Bends" – disoriented, injured or even dead!

Hammerhead: Users clad in the Crustacean Bio-Armor are bulky and slow to react. To help make up for this, a "hammerhead" section on top of the armor has a pair of secondary eyes that allow the wearer to see in an almost 300 degree arc and perform head butts. Except for a small blind spot directly behind the armor, there is virtually no way to sneak up on the Crustacean Bio-Armor.

Dolphin Bio-Armor

Used almost exclusively by Lemurian Scouts and Sea Sentinels, this unusual looking suit of Bio-Armor possesses a full tail and fins. The ritual summons a pod of dolphins, which the Biomancer Gene-Mage then negotiates with, and enlists their aid in creating the suit for the recipient of the armor. If successful, the dolphins then agree to participate in the ritual, giving of themselves freely. The end result is a Bio-Armor suit with a mermaid-like dolphin tail and great speed, power and maneuverability in the water. The tail can be temporarily removed, allowing the Bio-Armor warrior to use his or her own legs. While separated, the tail section swims around like any other sea creature until it is called, recovered or given instructions. **Note:** Though physically separated, the tail section remains linked to its owner and can wait for an indefinite period of time to be reunited without suffering any ill effect. It is interesting to note that the "tail" can look like the traditional dolphin or whale style of tail, or that of a shark or other type of fish.

Lemurian Dolphin Bio-Armor

Model Type: Dolphin Bio-Armor.

Class: Undersea Combat Armor – the Biomancy Gene-Mage equivalent of light environmental power armor.

Crew: One.

M.D.C. by Location:

* Head – 90

Arms (2) – 90 each

Legs (2) – 120 each

Dolphin Tail Section – 221

** Main Body – 195

* A single asterisk indicates a small or difficult target to hit that can only be struck when the attacker makes a Called Shot, and even then the attacker is -4 to strike. Destroying the head/helmet eliminates all forms of optical and sensory enhancement, leaving the pilot to rely on his own human senses without any of the bonuses granted to him by the Bio-Armor.

** Depleting the M.D.C. of the *main body* shuts the Bio-Armor down and Supernatural P.S., all bonuses, weapons and special capabilities provided by the armor to its wearer are gone. See Features Common to All Bio-Armor for full details.

Speed:

Running: 40 mph (64 km) maximum. The act of running *does* tire out its wearer, but at half of the usual fatigue rate.

Leaping: 10 feet (3 m) high or lengthwise from a stationary position, 20 feet (6.1 m) high or across with a running start.

Flying: None.
Underwater Capabilities: Dolphin Bio-Armor can swim/rocket through water at a maximum speed of 50 mph (80 km or 43 knots), triple along a ley line, leap out of water 20 feet (6.1 m) high and across, and can swim or walk along the bottom of shallow seas at full running speed. Maximum depth is four miles (6.4 km). Without the dolphin tail attached, swimming speed is reduced by half.
Mobility: Excellent; no movement penalties.
Statistical Data:
P.P.E. Cost to Create: 800 P.P.E.
Height: 7-8 feet (2.1 to 2.4 m).
Width: 2.6 to 3 feet (0.8 to 0.9 m) at the shoulder.
Length: 2.5 feet (0.76 m) in bipedal mode without the tail, 16 feet (4.8 m) including the full length of the tail which is usually about 12 feet (3.6 m) long all by itself.
Weight: 100 pounds (45 kg), +250 (113 kg) with tail attached.
Physical Strength: Supernatural P.S. of 20.
Cargo: None, though belts, bags and other carrying cases can be strapped to or carried by the wearer.
Power System: Magic. The living armor feeds on and is powered by the P.P.E. of its wearer and available ambient P.P.E. As long as it has at least 15 P.P.E. per day, it can function at full capacity.
Cost: Exclusive to Lemurians and never sold on the open market nor are the secrets of its creation ever shared with outsiders, no matter how trusted they may be. Easily worth 6-10 million credits.

Weapon Systems:

1. Energy Bolt: Dolphin Bio-Armor can generate an energy blast from the hands; point and shoot.
Primary Purpose: Anti-Sea Monster/Anti-Submarine.
Secondary Purpose: Defense.
Range: 1,600 feet (488 m), half underwater.
Mega-Damage: 2D6 M.D. per blast; only single shots are possible.
Rate of Fire: Each blast counts as one melee attack.
Payload: Effectively unlimited as long as the suit is charged with P.P.E.

2. Tail Slap: The muscular tail can deliver powerful tail slaps when used in combat.
Primary Purpose: Close Combat.
Secondary Purpose: Defense.
Range: Hand to hand/tail's reach which is about 12 feet (3.6 m).
Mega-Damage: 3D6 M.D. (factor's in the Supernatural P.S. of 20). Counts as two melee attacks.

3. Side Arms (2; Optional): Any type of side arm or melee weapon may be used by the armor clad warrior; same as the Avian Bio-Armor.

4. Hand to Hand Combat: Rather than use a weapon the pilot can engage in Mega-Damage hand to hand combat. The number of attacks and bonuses are as per the skills and attributes of the armor's wearer, plus the following bonuses provided by the armor.
Mega-Damage: As per Supernatural P.S. Restrained Punch: 1D6 M.D. Power Punch: 2D6 M.D., but counts as two attacks.
Tail Slap: 3D6 M.D.
Dolphin Bio-Armor Combat Bonuses:
+1 additional attack per melee at levels 2, 6, 10 and 15.
+2 to Perception Rolls underwater only.
+1 to strike, +2 to parry, +1 to *automatic dodge* (the act of dodging does not use up an attack/action) at levels 1, 3, 5, 7, 10 and 13, +1 to disarm, +2 to pull punch, +1 to roll with impact, and +2 to save vs toxic gases, airborne poisons and diseases.
+15% to Underwater Navigation, Track & Hunt Sea Animals and Prowl skills when the armor is worn. No bonuses on land.

5. Sensor Systems & Special Features of Note: All the same common features, except for the following.
Bio-Regeneration: 2D6+2 M.D.C. per hour.
Dolphin Tail: Part of the Bio-Armor is a large, detachable dolphin tail. The tail provides additional speed and maneuverability in the water, but makes the suit unusable on land. To make up for this, the tail section is removable and when detached, behaves like an independent creature. It can be summoned and commanded to serve as a messenger or a distraction, or simply to wait/hide until the suit's wearer returns to it or calls it. The wearer of Dolphin Bio-Armor can send out a telepathic call, with the location to meet at up to 3,000 miles (4,800 km) away.

Kelp Bio-Armor

A large amount of kelp or other seaweed must be present to initiate the ritual. While the Biomancer Gene-Mage chants (this creation ritual takes 15 minutes), the recipient of the armor stands within the forest of kelp. As the spell progresses, the kelp begins to entangle and cover the recipient, completely engulfing him. When the ritual is over, the person is totally encased in seaweed. For 1D4 minutes he is blind and oblivious to the world. Some find the experience disquieting and those with claustrophobia cannot endure the ritual. After the 1D4 minute period is over, seaweed that is not part of the suit floats away, while the seaweed covering the individual continues to transform into form fitting, leathery looking, Mega-Damage Kelp Bio-Armor. The specific design of the armor is up to the Biomancer Gene-Mage and the temperament and influence of the recipient, although it always has a humanoid shape and organic appearance with many frills and ribbons of seaweed.

Kelp armor is used by Scouts, Serpent Hunters and ambush teams as its seaweed layers provide excellent undersea camouflage and even help hide the user from sonar. The kelp fronds that make up the suit also assist in climbing, entangling opponents in combat and can be used as a whip or rope as needed.

Lemurian Kelp Bio-Armor

Model Type: Kelp Bio-Armor.
Class: Undersea Combat and Reconnaissance Armor – the Biomancy Gene-Mage equivalent of medium environmental power armor.
Crew: One.
M.D.C. by Location:
* Head – 100
Arms (2) – 97 each
Legs (2) – 130 each
** Main Body – 247

* A single asterisk indicates a small or difficult target to hit that can only be struck when the attacker makes a Called Shot, and even then the attacker is -4 to strike. Destroying the head/helmet eliminates all forms of optical and sensory enhancement, leaving the pilot to rely on his own human senses without any of the bonuses granted to him by the Bio-Armor.

** Depleting the M.D.C. of the *main body* shuts the Bio-Armor down and Supernatural P.S., all bonuses, weapons and special capabilities provided to the wearer by the armor are gone. See Features Common to All Bio-Armor for full details.

CHAZID

Speed:

Running: 40 mph (64 km) maximum. The act of running *does* tire out its wearer, but at one third of the usual fatigue rate.

Leaping: 10 feet (3 m) high or lengthwise from a stationary position, 20 feet (6 m) high or across with a running start.

Flying: None.

Underwater Capabilities: The Kelp Bio-Armor can swim/rocket through water at a maximum speed of 40 mph (64 km), triple along a ley line, and can swim and walk along the bottom of shallow seas at half the running speed. Maximum depth is three miles (4.8 km).

Mobility: Excellent; no movement penalties.

Statistical Data:

P.P.E. Cost to Create: 650 P.P.E.

Height: 7-8 feet (2.1 to 2.4 m).

Width: 2.6 to 3 feet (0.8 to 0.9 m) at the shoulder.

Length: 2.2 feet (0.67 m).

Weight: 150 pounds (68 kg).

Physical Strength: Supernatural P.S. of 22.

Cargo: None, though belts, bags and other carrying cases can be strapped to or carried by the wearer.

Power System: Magic. The living armor feeds on and is powered by the P.P.E. of its wearer and available ambient P.P.E. As long as it has at least 20 P.P.E. a day, it can function at full capacity.

Cost: Exclusive to Lemurians and never sold on the open market nor are the secrets of its creation ever shared with outsiders, no matter how trusted they may be. Easily worth 6-10 million credits.

Weapon Systems:

1. **Kelp Whip:** A line of enchanted kelp extends from one of the wearer's hands to be used as a whip for combat purposes, but is even more useful as a climb-cord and nonlethal weapon. The whip has a mind of its own and can do tricks that no dumb piece of rope is capable of. The whip grabs and holds onto objects with minimal effort on the part of the user, an almost impossible trick that requires just the right skills and circumstances to perform with a normal whip. It can be used like a grappling hook or lasso to snare handholds when climbing and even pull the warrior up like a towline. The user of the armor doesn't need to actually climb much at all if he doesn't wish to; the whip can retract itself automatically and pull him along with it. The whip is fully prehensile, able to grab, hold and release objects at the whim of the wearer. It can also be used to disarm opponents, trip those who try to run, or tie a prisoner's arms and legs.

   The whip is permanently attached to the suit, however, and cannot be released like a bola or separated for use as a length of rope. The Kelp Whip is instantly responsive and releases itself upon command.

   Primary Purpose: Close Combat.

   Secondary Purpose: Defense/Climbing.

   Range: 15 feet (4.6 m) as a whip, 50 feet (15 m) as a rope/lasso/towline.

   Damage: 3D6 S.D.C damage or 2D6 M.D. when charged with Bio-Energy (double damage against undead opponents).

   Note: It takes 30 M.D. to cut the whip. If cut, the missing piece grows back at a rate of one foot (0.3 m) per hour until fully restored.

2. **Kelp Blades:** The sheets of overlapping kelp that make up the armor are studded with smaller, blade-like fronds. The Bio-Armor warrior can remove one at any time and use it as a throwing knife or melee weapon. Each blade is charged with Bio-Energy to inflict superior damage against undead targets. Most of the blades are concealed and look like just another piece of the armor until removed, and captors seldom find all of them when taking a Kelp Bio-Armored warrior prisoner.

   Primary Purpose: Anti-Undead.

   Secondary Purpose: Anti-Personnel.

   Range: 80 feet (24.4 m).

   Mega-Damage: 1D4 M.D. against most M.D.C. opponents, but 4D4 M.D. to undead.

   Rate of Fire: Each blade thrown counts as one melee attack/action.

   Payload: 8 blades. Discarded and lost blades regrow at a rate of one per hour.

3. **Side Arms (2; Optional):** Any type of side arm or melee weapon may be used; same as the Avian Bio-Armor.

4. **Hand to Hand Combat:** Rather than use a weapon the pilot can engage in Mega-Damage hand to hand combat. The number of attacks and bonuses are as per the skills and attributes of the armor's wearer, plus the following bonuses provided by the armor.

   Mega-Damage: As per Supernatural P.S. of 22. Restrained Punch: 3D6 S.D.C. Punch or Head Butt: 1D6 M.D. Power Punch: 2D6 M.D., but counts as two melee attacks. Kick: 2D4 M.D.

   Kelp Bio-Armor Combat Bonuses:

   +1 additional attack per melee at levels 2, 5, 10 and 15.

   +1 to Perception Rolls underwater only.

   +1 to strike, +2 to parry, +3 to disarm, +3 to entangle, +1 to pull punch, +1 to roll with impact, and +2 to save vs toxic gases, airborne poisons and diseases.

   +15% to Climbing and Rappelling, +10% to Land and Underwater Navigation and Prowl skills when the armor is worn.

5. **Sensor Systems & Special Features of Note:** All the same common features, except for the following.

   Bio-Regeneration: 2D6 M.D.C. per hour, double when nestled in a kelp patch or coral reef.

   Sonar Masking: The soft, rippling fronds of Kelp Bio-Armor help minimize and break up the user's sonar profile. Anyone or anything attempting to detect the suit on sonar is -15% to *Sensory Equipment*.

   Camouflage: The suit's leafy exterior provides the equivalent of the *Camouflage* skill at 45% for open areas, 65% for seaweed beds and 85% for kelp forests.

Leviathan Bio-Armor

Exclusive to Serpent Hunters

This rare and exclusive suit of Bio-Armor is only available to Serpent Hunters, as it is as much a symbol of their status and office as it is a link to their *Thrall Sea Serpents*. The armor is created like any other suit of Bio-Armor, but the Biomancer Gene-Mage performs the ritual with the Serpent Hunter and his Thrall Sea Serpent. The ritual grants the serpent the ability to give up elements of itself to form the suit of armor. The glowing biomass then descends upon the Serpent Hunter, engulfing him and forming into the iconic suit of armor.

Whether it is due to the Lemurians' genetic manipulation of the sea serpent or the sea serpent's distant relationship to dragons, the Serpent Bio-Armor is formed with a natural resistance to magic. The suit can only absorb a limited number of spells/psychic attacks before the nullification effect is overloaded, but it does give

the Serpent Hunter a huge advantage in combat against dragons, sea serpents, supernatural enemies, sorcerers and psychics. (See #6 below for details.)

Lemurian Leviathan Bio-Armor

Model Type: Leviathan Bio-Armor, a.k.a Serpent Bio-Armor.
Class: Amphibious Heavy Combat Armor – the Biomancy Gene-Mage equivalent of heavy environmental power armor.
Crew: One.
M.D.C. by Location:

* Head – 140
* Hands/Gauntlets (2) – 95 each
Arms (2) – 170 each
* Shoulder Light/Laser (1) – 35
Shoulder Cannon (1) – 140
Legs (2) – 230 each
** Main Body – 327

* A single asterisk indicates a small or difficult target to hit that can only be struck when the attacker makes a Called Shot, and even then the attacker is -4 to strike. Destroying the head/helmet eliminates all forms of optical and sensory enhancement, leaving the pilot to rely on his own human senses without any of the bonuses granted to him by the Bio-Armor.

** Depleting the M.D.C. of the *main body* shuts the Bio-Armor down and Supernatural P.S., all bonuses, weapons and special capabilities provided by the armor to its wearer are gone. See Features Common to All Bio-Armor for full details.

Speed:
Running: 30 mph (48 km) maximum. The act of running *does* tire out its wearer, but at one tenth of the usual fatigue rate.
Leaping: 8 feet (2.4 m) high or lengthwise from a stationary position, 16 feet (4.9 m) high or across with a running start.
Flying: None.
Underwater Capabilities: The Leviathan Bio-Armor can swim/rocket through water at a maximum speed of 30 mph (48 km or 26 knots), triple along a ley line, and can swim and walk along the bottom of shallow seas at half the running speed. Maximum depth is six miles (9.6 km).
Mobility: Fair; -10% to Acrobatics, Climbing, Prowl, and other skills requiring agility and freedom of movement.
Statistical Data:
P.P.E. Cost to Create: 2,000 P.P.E.
Height: 8.5-12 feet (2.6 to 3.6 m).
Width: 4 to 6 feet (1.2 to 1.8 m) at the shoulder.
Length: 4.5 feet (1.4 m).
Weight: 700 pounds (315 kg).
Physical Strength: Supernatural P.S. of 30.
Cargo: None, though belts, bags and other carrying cases can be strapped to or carried by the wearer.
Power System: Magic. The living armor feeds on and is powered by the P.P.E. of its wearer and available ambient P.P.E. As long as it has at least 25 P.P.E. per day, it can function at full capacity.
Cost: Exclusive to Lemurians and never sold on the open market nor are the secrets of its creation ever shared with outsiders, no matter how trusted they may be. Easily worth 10-14 million credits.

Weapon Systems:

1. **Light Stonecaster Cannon:** Mounted on the Serpent Hunter's off-hand is a large, high-powered version of the Lemurian Stonecaster infantry weapon. Its versatility takes care of most of the Leviathan's combat needs, making a secondary ranged weapon unnecessary.

Primary Purpose: Anti-Armor.
Secondary Purpose: Anti-Sea Monster.
Range: 4,000 feet (1,219 m), half underwater.
Mega-Damage: Sedimentary Rock: 3D6 M.D. to a 15 foot (4.6 m) area. Igneous Molten Rock: 4D6 M.D. on impact and 2D6 M.D. additional for the next two melee rounds. Metamorphic Stone (armor piercing): 6D6 M.D.
Rate of Fire: Each shot counts as one melee attack.
Payload: 60 blasts regardless of type. The weapon can be recharged/reloaded by placing it on a ley line, nexus or stone pyramid (regenerates one blast a minute), or by having any mage pump 60 P.P.E. into the cannon. Otherwise, it regenerates projectiles at a rate of one per hour when no source of magic energy is available.

2. **Shoulder Searchlight and Laser (1):** Mounted on the left shoulder is a mechanism with dual purposes. It can be used as a searchlight or as a laser weapon; both have the same range.

Primary Purpose: Search and Illumination.
Secondary Purpose: Combat and Self-Defense.
Range: 1,200 feet (366 m).
Mega-Damage: None as searchlight, 3D6 M.D. as a laser weapon.
Rate of Fire: Single shot; each counts as one melee attack.
Payload: Effectively unlimited.

3. **Clawed Gauntlets (2):** Each of the Leviathan armor's hands is tipped in sharp claws for fighting face-to-face.

Primary Purpose: Close Combat.
Secondary Purpose: Defense.
Range: Hand to hand/arm's reach.
Mega-Damage: 4D6+4 M.D. (factors in the Supernatural P.S. of 30), double damage from Power Strike, but counts at two melee attacks.

4. **Side Arms (2; Optional):** Any type of side arm or melee weapon may be used by the armor clad warrior; same as the Avian Bio-Armor.

5. **Hand to Hand Combat:** Rather than use a weapon the pilot can engage in Mega-Damage hand to hand combat. The number of attacks and bonuses are as per the skills and attributes of the armor's wearer, plus the following bonuses provided by the armor, below.

Mega-Damage: As per Supernatural P.S. of 30. Restrained Punch: 5D6 S.D.C. Punch or Head Butt: 3D6 M.D. Power Punch: 6D6 M.D., but counts as two melee attacks. Kick: 3D6+2 M.D. Stomp: 1D6 M.D. Body Block/Ram: 3D6+2 M.D. plus has a 01-60% likelihood of knocking down opponents up to 15 feet (4.6 m) tall. Victims of knockdown lose initiative for the rest of the melee round and one melee attack.

Leviathan Bio-Armor Combat Bonuses:

+1 additional attack per melee at levels 2, 5, 7, 9, 11 and 15.

+2 to Perception Rolls underwater only.

+2 on initiative, +3 to strike and parry, +1 to dodge, +2 to disarm, +4 to pull punch, +3 to roll with impact, and +3 to save vs toxic gases, airborne poisons and diseases.

Impervious to dragon fire breath and resistant to other types of dragon breath weapons (frost, acid, etc.), which do half damage.

+10% to Land Navigation and Underwater Navigation skills when the armor is worn.

Also see Spell Nullification, below.

6. Sensor Systems & Special Features of Note: Same as the Avian Bio-Armor with the following additions.

Bio-Regeneration: 4D6 M.D.C. per hour, triple at ley lines, stone pyramids and nexus points.

Magic Resistance: Magic and psionic energy attacks, from fire, lightning and Techno-Wizard weapons to Rune Weapons, inflict half damage. +5 to save vs illusions, +3 to save vs possession and mind control. But physical attacks, punches, Telekinetic and other "kinesis" attacks and cold do full damage.

Limited Spell Nullification: The Leviathan Bio-Armor can be set to stop up to three magic spells and/or psionic attacks per 24 hour period, +1 per each additional level of experience. When this automatic defense is switched "on," the suit protects the Serpent Hunter by canceling or dispelling the incoming magic or psionic attack before it has a chance to affect him. The wearer of the armor can pick and choose when he wants to put that magic defense in place, e.g., when he's going up against a dragon, Greater Demon, evil practitioner of magic, and so on. The Nullification effect recharges at a rate of one every three hours, twice as far at a ley line or within a stone pyramid or ley line triangle (e.g. the Bermuda Triangle).

Shark Bio-Armor

Exclusive to Oceanic Guardsmen

The creation process for this armor takes 30 minutes, must be performed in ocean waters (deep or shallow) and summons a swarm of bloodthirsty sharks. The animals surround the recipient of the magic, who must cut himself, releasing his blood into the water. This sends the sharks into an immediate feeding frenzy, but they don't attack the intended recipient of the armor nor the Biomancer(s) conducting the ritual. Instead, they nip each other, releasing more blood into the water, creating an ever wilder frenzy and bathing the intended recipient of the Bio-Armor in their blood. The blood magically engulfs the individual, covering his body as the sharks churn up the water around him until the warrior cannot be seen through the frothing water, red haze of blood and mass of frantic, thrashing sharks. When the ritual is over, the sharks depart to reveal a warrior clad in a suit of blood red Bio-Armor.

Shark Bio-Armor (depicted under the Oceanic Guardsman O.C.C. and another under the Biomancer Gene-Mage O.C.C.) seldom resembles the appearance of an actual shark. The closest one gets to "shark" imagery is the plating of the armor which often resembles the shape of shark's teeth. Otherwise, Shark Bio-Armor varies considerably from warrior to warrior, but most are adorned with ribbing, shark tooth styling, fins, spikes, spines, frills and leafy ribbons. Helmets are often monstrous looking combinations of shark, crustacean and fish, though a "Hammerhead" helmet is very popular, all of which are intended to intimidate the enemy. And the armor is always crimson to blood red.

Shark Bio-Armor is potentially dangerous for both the warrior wearing it and those around him. The creation process draws upon the killer instincts and blood frenzy of sharks, instilling those who wear it with the shark's hunger for blood and its cold ferocity. Even the most stable and strong-minded warriors find the aggression and bloodlust projected by this Bio-Armor difficult to control and capable of clouding one's judgement. Sometimes, the warrior becomes consumed by a berserker-like rage that drives him to fight as a relentless killing machine. In the worst cases, he has trouble recognizing his own allies during the heat of battle.

Many Lemurians have tried to tame the suit, but few outside the Oceanic Guardsmen have proven themselves up to the task. As a result, only elite members of the *Oceanic Guardsmen* are allowed to use Shark Bio-Armor. Among the most notorious is a Special Forces platoon known as the "Mano Toa" – or **Shark Champions** – renowned for their fierce courage in combat without succumbing to bloodlust or mindless slaughter. Despite the control exhibited by the Shark Champions and other warriors within the Oceanic Guardsmen, Shark Bio-Armor is not generally allowed even among the other protectors of Lemuria. Those within the Guardsmen who don Shark Bio-Armor are, as a rule, proven veterans who serve as special operatives assigned to handle search and destroy missions, prisoner rescues, and operations involving sabotage, surgical strikes and black ops. They often face what others might consider impossible odds and ops where there are usually few innocent people to get hurt from possible collateral damage or unchecked slaughter.

Lemurian Shark Bio-Armor

Model Type: Shark Bio-Armor.

Class: Undersea Combat Armor – the Biomancy Gene-Mage equivalent of medium environmental power armor.

Crew: One.

M.D.C. by Location:

* Head – 135
* Hands (2) – 55 each
Arms (2) – 120 each
Legs (2) – 160 each
** Main Body – 255

* A single asterisk indicates a small or difficult target to hit that can only be struck when the attacker makes a Called Shot, and even then the attacker is -4 to strike. Destroying the head/helmet eliminates all forms of optical and sensory enhancement, leaving the pilot to rely on his own human senses without any of the bonuses granted to him by the Bio-Armor.

** Depleting the M.D.C. of the *main body* shuts the Bio-Armor down and Supernatural P.S., all bonuses, weapons and special capabilities provided by the armor to its wearer are gone. See Features Common to All Bio-Armor for full details.

Speed:

Running: 50 mph (80 km) maximum. The act of running *does* tire out its wearer, but at one third of the usual fatigue rate.

Leaping: 10 feet (3 m) high or lengthwise from a stationary position, 20 feet (6 m) high or across with a running start.

Flying: None.

Underwater Capabilities: The Shark Bio-Armor can swim/rocket through water at a maximum speed of 45 mph (72 km), triple along a ley line, and can swim and walk along the bottom of shallow seas at half the running speed. Maximum depth is five miles (8 km).
Mobility: Good; -5% to Prowl and perform other Physical skills.

Statistical Data:

P.P.E. Cost to Create: 1,200 P.P.E.
Height: 7-8 feet (2.1 to 2.4 m).
Width: 2.6 to 3 feet (0.8 to 0.9 m) at the shoulder.
Length: 2.5 feet (0.76 m).
Weight: 220 pounds (99 kg).
Physical Strength: Supernatural P.S. of 25.
Cargo: None, though belts, bags and other carrying cases can be strapped onto the armor or carried by the wearer.
Power System: Magic. The living armor feeds on and is powered by the P.P.E. of its wearer and available ambient P.P.E. As long as it has at least 20 P.P.E. per day, it can function at full capacity.
Cost: Exclusive to Lemurians and never sold on the open market nor are the secrets of its creation ever shared with outsiders, no matter how trusted they may be. Easily worth 7-11 million credits.

Weapon Systems:

1. **Electric Arc:** The Shark Bio-Armor uses a shark's natural electroreceptors to collect, store and emit bursts of electricity. Emanating from the suit's head/helm, using the weapon does not require hands and leaves the wearer unencumbered in close combat.

Primary Purpose: Anti-Personnel.
Secondary Purpose: Assault.
Range: 1,500 feet (457 m) in air, 500 feet (152 m) underwater.
Mega-Damage: 3D6+3 M.D.
Rate of Fire: Each blast counts as one melee attack.
Payload: Effectively unlimited as long as the suit is charged with P.P.E.

2. **Shark Bite:** While it may appear to be an ordinary helmet made of a smooth piece of armor, or a regular mouth, it can open to reveal a large shark's maw lined with multiple rows of teeth; with new teeth rotating forward to replace those that are broken in combat.

Primary Purpose: Close Combat.
Secondary Purpose: Defense.
Range: Hand to hand/bite.
Mega-Damage: 3D6+2 M.D. (Takes into consideration the Supernatural P.S.)
Note: Each bite counts as one melee attack.

3. **Shark Tooth Blades/Spikes.** Along the forearm and/or gauntlets are 2-4 shark tooth-shaped blades or spikes used to slash opponents and parry weapon attacks.

Primary Purpose: Close Combat.
Secondary Purpose: Defense.
Range: Hand to hand.
Mega-Damage: 3D6 M.D. (Takes into consideration the Supernatural P.S.)
Note: Each bite counts as one melee attack.

4. **Side Arms (2; Optional):** Any type of side arm or melee weapon may be used; same as the Avian Bio-Armor. However, warriors clad in this armor have an affinity for weapons made of shark teeth and the teeth of dragons, sea serpents and monsters, as well as magic weapons, spears, pole arms and swords.

5. **Hand to Hand Combat:** Rather than use a weapon the pilot can engage in Mega-Damage hand to hand combat. The number of attacks and bonuses are as per the skills and attributes of the armor's wearer, plus the following bonuses provided by the armor, below.

Mega-Damage: As per Supernatural P.S. of 25. Restrained Punch: 4D6 S.D.C. Punch or Head Butt: 2D6 M.D. Power Punch: 4D6 M.D., but counts as two melee attacks. Kick: 3D6 M.D. Leap Kick or Power Kick: 4D6 M.D., but counts as two melee attacks. Stomp: 1D4 M.D.
Shark Bio-Armor Combat Bonuses:

+1 additional attack per melee at levels 2, 5, 9, 12 and 15.

+2 to Perception Rolls underwater only.

+1 on initiative, +2 to strike, +1 to parry, +3 to *automatic dodge* (the act of dodging does not use up an attack/action), +1 to disarm at levels 2, 5, 8, 11 and 15, +2 to pull punch, +2 to roll with impact, +2 to save vs toxic gases, airborne poisons and diseases, and +1 to save vs Horror Factor at levels 1, 3, 5, 6, 8, 10, 12 and 14.

+10% to Underwater Navigation and Prowl skills when the armor is worn.

Combat Frenzy/Bloodlust (special): Whenever the wearer of Shark Bio-Armor faces impossible odds, is outnumbered by more than 3 to 1, or when he or an ally is in imminent mortal danger, the character enjoys the following bonuses and penalties.

Duration of Frenzy: Until the odds even out, the enemy surrenders or retreats, the mission is accomplished without having to kill everyone, or all who oppose him are dead or unable to fight. Or until the frenzied individual is rendered unconscious or subdued and restrained.

Frenzy Bonuses:

A temporary 1D6x10 M.D.C. boost to the Shark Bio-Armor.

+1 attack per melee round.

+2 on initiative.

+2 to strike.

+3 M.D. to damage with handheld weapons, punches and kicks.

Critical Strike (double damage) on a roll of 17 or higher.

Double damage from behind.

Triple damage on a Natural 20.

+10% to save vs Coma/Death.

Frenzy Penalties:

-9 on Perception Rolls.

No bonuses at all to dodge, disarm, pull punch or roll with impact; straight die roll only. Obsessed with fighting and destroying all who oppose him.

Does not think about using other skills (consumed with combat) and is -20% if he does.

Those caught up in a Blood Frenzy will fight any enemy they encounter.

Roll percentile dice to determine if the frenzied warrior recognizes his friends, allies or innocent people. **01-60%** means yes, and he is able to stop himself from hurting them. **61-00%** means no, and he continues to fight, attacking with the intent of killing or taking down his "next enemy" as quickly and cleanly as possible. Thankfully, the frenzied warrior fights only until this opponent is rendered unconscious/unable to fight (a good time to play dead), surrenders, or runs away. After which, the still frenzied warrior turns to his next adversary. **Note:** Before the frenzied warrior delivers the "killing blow," roll again to see if he recognizes his ally or innocent person and stops short of killing him, or not. By the way, in a frenzy, the Shark Warrior has no time or interest in taking captives, so he expects anyone who surrenders to drop their weapons and leave the field of combat. To do otherwise means combat renews or continues.

Once the frenzy has run its course, the warrior is weakened and tired from the ordeal and should rest for 15 minutes. If the warrior is required to keep fighting or moving, he does so at -2 attacks per melee round, -50% to Spd, -3 on Perception Rolls, -2 to initiative, strike, parry, dodge, disarm, and entangle, and -10% in skill performance.

6. **Sensor Systems & Special Features of Note:** All the same common features, except for the following.
Bio-Regeneration: 2D6 M.D.C. per hour.
Detect Blood: The Shark Bio-Armor can detect even a few drops of blood in the water from up to 10 miles (16 km) away. On land, the armor can smell blood from a distance of one mile (1.6 km) and can track the blood scent to its source at a base skill of 50% +2% per level of experience.
Hammerhead (optional): Shark Bio-Armor that has a hammerhead configuration for the helmet has an extra pair of eyes at each end that provide a 300 degree field of view, making it extremely difficult to sneak up on. Whether or not the Blood Frenzy is active, the wearer of Hammerhead Shark armor is +1 on Perception Rolls and +1 to parry and dodge, and an extra 20 M.D.C. to the helmet.

Wood Bio-Armor

To create this Bio-Armor, one very large tree, two large trees or five medium-sized ones must be present for the ritual. Thus, as a rule, this creation ritual takes place in forests or jungles. While the Biomancer Gene-Mage chants the 15 minute ritual, the recipient stands with his back leaning against one of the tree(s) with his eyes closed the entire time. As the spell progresses, the tree(s) reaches out with its limbs stretching toward to the recipient of the armor. Meanwhile, sheets of bark seem to peel or flake off and cover the individual's entire body, from head to toe. When the ritual is over, the person is totally encased in bark. For 1D4 minutes he must remain still and is blind, deaf and dumb – oblivious to the world as the transformation finishes. People who are claustrophobic find the experience horrifying and cannot endure the ritual.

When the transformation is complete, the bark falls away to reveal Wood Bio-Armor that looks as if it was sculpted from driftwood. From a distance it resembles high-tech power armor with some aquatic flourishes. As with all Bio-Armor, the exact look of each suit reflects the personality and individual nature of the wearer, thus no two armors are exactly alike. The type of wood also varies depending on the trees used in the creation process.

Lemurian Wood Bio-Armor

Model Type: Wood Bio-Armor.
Class: Amphibious Combat Armor – the Biomancy Gene-Mage equivalent of medium environmental power armor.
Crew: One.
M.D.C. by Location:
* Head – 95
* Hands (2) – 55 each
Arms (2) – 95 each
Legs (2) – 145 each
** Main Body – 277

* A single asterisk indicates a small or difficult target to hit that can only be struck when the attacker makes a Called Shot, and even then the attacker is -4 to strike. Destroying the head/helmet eliminates all forms of optical and sensory enhancement, leaving the pilot to rely on his own human senses without any of the bonuses granted to him by the Bio-Armor.

** Depleting the M.D.C. of the *main body* shuts the Bio-Armor down and Supernatural P.S., all bonuses, weapons and special capabilities provided by the armor to its wearer are gone. See Features Common to All Bio-Armor for full details.

Speed:
Running: 40 mph (64 km) maximum. The act of running *does* tire out its wearer, but at half of the usual fatigue rate.
Leaping: 10 feet (3 m) high or lengthwise from a stationary position, 20 feet (6 m) high or across with a running without actually attaining flight.
Flying: None.
Underwater Capabilities: The Wood Bio-Armor can swim/rocket underwater at a maximum speed of 30 mph (48 km or 26 knots), 45 mph (72 km/39 knots) on the surface of water, triple along a ley line, and can swim and walk along the bottom of shallow seas at half the running speed. Maximum depth is 4 miles (6.4 km).
Mobility: Good; -5% to Prowl and perform other Physical skills.
Statistical Data:
P.P.E. Cost to Create: 650 P.P.E.

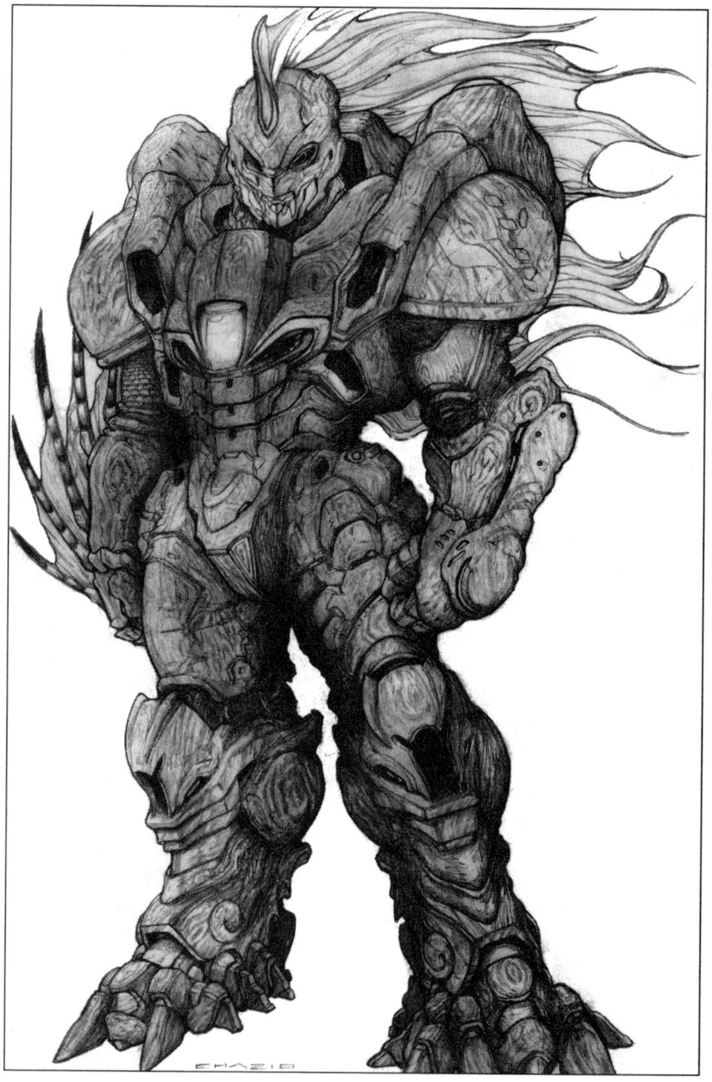

Height: 7-8 feet (2.1 to 2.4 m).
Width: 2.6 to 3 feet (0.8 to 0.9 m) at the shoulder.
Length: 2.5 feet (0.76 m).
Weight: 240 pounds (108 kg).
Physical Strength: Supernatural P.S. of 22.
Cargo: None, though belts, bags and other carrying cases can be strapped to or carried by the wearer.
Power System: Magic. The living armor feeds on and is powered by the P.P.E. of its wearer and available ambient P.P.E. As long as it has at least 20 P.P.E. per day, it can function at full capacity.
Cost: Exclusive to Lemurians and never sold on the open market nor are the secrets of its creation ever shared with outsiders, no matter how trusted they may be. Easily worth 5-8 million credits.

Weapon Systems:

1. Razorshell Launcher: A special projectile weapon is grown onto one of the Wood Bio-Armor's arms. Capable of firing sharp, flat shells, the weapon's razorshell ammo can cut through ropes and sails and makes bleeding, incisive wounds that attract sharks and other predators to the target.
Primary Purpose: Anti-Personnel.
Secondary Purpose: Assault.
Range: 2,000 feet (609 m), half underwater.
Mega-Damage: 2D6 M.D. per single shot.
Rate of Fire: Each shell counts as one melee attack.
Payload: 120 shells. The entire payload can be recharged in one hour when on a ley line or at a stone pyramid. Recharges shells at a rate of 1D4x10 per hour when no source of magic energy is available.

2. Arm Spines: The armor's other arm mounts a series of sharp spines used to slash at sea monsters as they rush past and to parry enemy attacks.
Primary Purpose: Close Combat.
Secondary Purpose: Defense.
Range: Hand to hand/arm's reach.
Mega-Damage: 4D6 M.D. (factors in the Supernatural P.S. of 22), double damage from Power Strike but counts as two melee attacks.

3. Side Arms (2; Optional): Any type of side arm or melee weapon may be used by the armor clad warrior; same as the Avian Bio-Armor.

4. Hand to Hand Combat: Rather than use a weapon the pilot can engage in Mega-Damage hand to hand combat. The number of attacks and bonuses are as per the skills and attributes of the armor's wearer, plus the following bonuses provided by the armor, below.

Mega-Damage: As per Supernatural P.S. of 22, but all do *double damage* (Hit Point equivalent) to vampires, the undead and other beings vulnerable to wood. Restrained Punch: 4D6 S.D.C. Punch or Head Butt: 2D6 M.D. Power Punch: 4D6 M.D., but counts as two melee attacks. Kick: 3D6 M.D. Leap Kick or Power Kick: 4D6 M.D., but counts as two melee attacks. Stomp: 1D4 M.D.

Wood Bio-Armor Combat Bonuses:

+1 additional attack per melee at levels 2, 5, 10 and 15.

+2 to Perception Rolls on land only.

+1 to strike, +3 to parry, +2 to disarm, +2 to pull punch, +3 to roll with impact, and +2 to save vs toxic gases, airborne poisons and diseases.

+10% to Climbing and Land Navigation skills when the armor is worn. +15% to Prowl and provides the Camouflage skill at 85% in wooded environments only.

5. Sensor Systems & Special Features of Note: All the same common features, except for the following.

Bio-Regeneration: 3D6 M.D.C. per hour.

Chlorophyll and Solar Energy Boost: On land in open, sunlit areas (grasslands, fields, desert, etc.) or in shallow water (less than 100 feet/30.5 m deep), the Bio-Armor can absorb the sun's energy to boost its power. Increases the suit's Supernatural P.S. to 25 and running speed to 75 mph (120 km), and also allows Wood Armor to Bio-Regenerate 1D6 M.D. per minute. **Note:** These bonuses fade within 1D6 minutes in shade and darkness.

Thorns: At will, the wearer can exude thorns from the fists, shoulders, elbows, knees and feet of the suit. The spiky protrusions add +1D6 M.D. to all close combat attacks.

Wave Strider Body Armor

Light Commercial Lemurian Armor

The Wave Strider is the primary survival suit used by Lemurian scouts, explorers, sailors, academics and citizens working outside the cities as well as visitors from the surface. While not technically a true Bio-Armor, it is made of organic parts using Biomancy processes. The end result is a suit that is not symbiotic in the same manner as full-fledged Bio-Armor, but has some of the same properties.

Wave Strider suits provide protection from damage, cold and pressure, slowly regenerates if given time (2D6 M.D.C. every 24 hours), and provide a boost to the user's swimming capabilities. Most Lemurians use Wave Striders for exploration and travel more than combat, though the suit's advanced aquatic capabilities are a benefit to both.

Class: Wave Strider Light, Commercial, Amphibious Body Armor.

Size: Adds 3 inches (7.6 cm) to the user's height; 9 inches (23 cm) counting the head crest, which can be retracted or folded to lie close to the back of the skull.

Weight: 19 lbs (8.5 kg).

Mobility: Excellent; no movement penalties.

M.D.C. by Location:

* Head/Helmet – 55
* Hands (2) – 18
Arms – 35 each
Legs – 45 each
Main Body – 87

* A single asterisk indicates a small or difficult target to hit. They can only be hit when the attacker makes a Called Shot, and even then the shooter is -3 to strike.

Special Features:

Breathe Underwater: The Wave Strider suit enables humans and other air-breathers to breathe underwater for an indefinite period of time.

Depth Gauge and Compass: A depth gauge and compass are built into the suit to assist in navigation. They are installed in the helmet and can be seen by the wearer at all times.

Depth Tolerance: 2.5 miles (4 km).

Enhanced Swimming: +10% to Swimming skill while wearing the suit.

Flotation System: Normally the armor is kept neutrally buoyant to allow for underwater swimming, but the user can increase the

CHAZ10

buoyancy and use the suit like a life preserver to float on the surface of water.

Resistant to Cold: Suffers one-third damage.

Wave Striding: The boots of the Wave Strider armor are enchanted to enhance the surface tension of the water when willed to do so. When activated, they allow the wearer to magically walk or run on top of a body of water. Waves greater than three feet (0.9 m) slow the wearer down 20%, waves up to 9 feet (2.7 m) reduce speed by half, waves 10-20 feet (3 to 6.1 m) by 75%, and larger, more violent waves make walking on the surface of water impossible (float only).

Webbed Fingers and Membrane: Assist in swimming; see Enhanced Swimming, above.

Cost: Exclusive to Lemurians and never sold on the open market nor are the secrets of its creation ever shared with outsiders, no matter how trusted they may be. However, as they are widely distributed amongst the Lemurian population and do not have to be linked to each individual user, Wave Strider suits are much easier for non-Lemurians to acquire from pirates and Splugorth traders than Bio-Armor or other weapons. 120,000-185,000 credits on the black market operating along ocean routes and at Atlantis; rare.

Lemurian Bio-Weapons

Features to Melee Bio-Weapons

Collapsible Construction: Bio-Weapons are, for the most part, rigid in their design, but a select few, typically the long, cumbersome or awkward weaponry, like pole-arms, staves, spears, etc., can retract or fold to one-third their normal length (just the pole section), to a typical overall length of about 2 feet/0.6 m for ease of carrying while swimming, to store during travel or while using another weapon.

Cost/Market Value of Bio-Weapons: Exclusive to Lemurians and never sold on the open market by Lemurians, nor are the secrets of their creation ever shared with outsiders, no matter how trusted they may be. However, Lemurian Bio-Weapons and gear may be lost and sometimes they are given to friends and allies from the surface world as a reward or in trade for a service or heroic deed (this may include Wave Strider armor and, once in a great while, even Bio-Armor). Bio-Weapons are considered to be magic weapons and are easily worth 50,000-200,000 credits depending on the weapon, amount of damage and special abilities.

Harm the Supernatural: Bio-Weapons are also charged with *Bio-Energy*, allowing them to harm creatures only vulnerable to special types of attacks like vampires and werebeasts. The weapons can inflict increased damage to the undead and the supernatural, even those only susceptible to specific substances like silver, wood or bone.

Proximity to Ley Lines and Nexuses: Close proximity to ley lines or nexus points does NOT, as a rule, increase the potency of direct weapon damage or the weapon's natural M.D.C. However, the energy aura of enchanted *Wood Bio-Weapons*, energy aura and energy blasts of *Coral Bio-Weapons* and the electrical blasts of the *Serpent Trident-Spear* are doubled on ley lines and tripled at a nexus, as are the payload/number of shots and damage.

Special Features: Bio-Weapons do not need to be linked to a host and can function on their own. However, to fire energy blasts or use special features in a Bio-Weapon (other than hacking, slashing of pummeling with the weapon itself) requires the use of Telepathy, Empathic Connection with Animals or the Biomancer's natural ability of Communicating with Plants and Animals. Many Bio-Weapons can hold large amounts of P.P.E., but this energy is not accessible to mages or those in possession of the Bio-Weapon for anything other than using the available P.P.E. to power the abilities of the weapon itself (a safeguard put in place by the Biomancer).

Super-Tough: Bio-Weapons are extremely strong and durable. Their overall armor capacity varies greatly due to inconsistencies in the construction/growth process, but any individual Bio-Weapon will have 1D6x10+20 M.D.C. if the weapon itself is targeted, and is capable of regenerating 1D6 M.D.C. per minute.

Barracuda Bio-Blades

These vicious bladed weapons might seem like silver Vibro-Blades with serrated teeth and fin designs on them. They are favored by Lemurian and Meran Wilderness Sea Scouts (and depicted on the cover of this book) for both combat and all-purpose functionality in the wild. Barracuda Blades also have alternate uses (as indicated below), but unlike the Bone of Shell Blades, do not receive any throwing enhancement. Creation Cost: 300-440 P.P.E.

Barracuda Dagger/Knife: Damage: 2D4 M.D. Alternate Use: Often used as a survival weapon, a filtration duct is built into the handle, and the knife can be used to filter salt from water, rendering it fresh and drinkable. Bonuses: Its serrated edge is also useful as a sawing tool and provides a +2% bonus to Wilderness and Undersea and Sea Survival skills.

Barracuda Spear: Damage: 2D6 M.D. Alternate Use: A special hook on the blade, its serrated teeth on the opposing side and its unique grip makes it an idea tool for spearfishing and/or dealing with large prey, cutting ropes from a distance and butchering large fish and animals. Bonuses: +2% bonus to the Fishing skill.

Barracuda Sword: Damage: 2D6+2 M.D. (large), 2D4 M.D. (short). Alternate Use: As depicted on the cover of this book, the sword has a serrated edge along the top, a pry bar-like tool attached to the hilt and a can opener edge on the pommel, making this a versatile tool for gaining access to sunken ships, locked cabinets and even oysters and clams. Bonus: +2% to the Undersea Salvage skill.

Barracuda Trident: Damage: 3D6 M.D. Alternate Use: Teeth, indents, ridges and holes in the trident make it an ideal tool for underwater surveying when the trident is held upright with the bottom end of the trident stuck into the sand. Bonus: +2% to Ocean Geographic Surveying.

Bone & Shell Bio-Weapons

All these weapons are made in the same fashion, using vertebrates (creatures with backbones) or crustaceans (lobsters, crabs and other shell fish) to create the Bio-Weapons. They typically resemble a jagged sharp edge or rough-cut blade weapon reminiscent of the edge of a crab claw or clamshell. **Magic Ability:** Bone and Shell Bio-Weapons are enchanted to *return when thrown* – specific throwing range is indicated for each. Creation Cost: 500-650 P.P.E.

Bone or Shell Club/War Club: Range: 100 feet (30.5 m), Mega-Damage: 2D4 M.D.

Bone or Shell Dagger/Knife: Range: 200 feet (6.1 m), Mega-Damage: 1D6 M.D.

Bone or Shell Spear: Range: 500 feet (152 m), Mega-Damage: 2D6 M.D.

Bone or Shell Sword: Range: 150 feet (45 m), Mega-Damage: 2D6+2 M.D. (large), 2D4 M.D. (short).

Bone or Shell Trident: Range: 400 feet (122 m), Mega-Damage: 3D6 M.D.

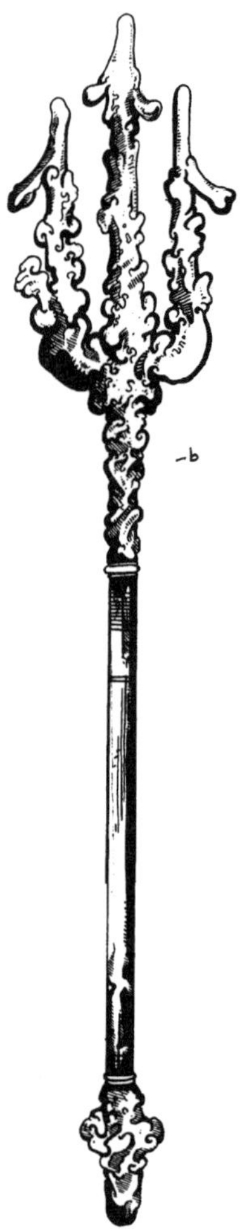

Coral Bio-Weapons

Coral Bio-Weapons are formed in a similar fashion as Coral Bio-Armor, and retain some mystical properties due to coral's natural abilities to collect and retain P.P.E. **Magic Ability:** The Coral Bio-Weapon can fire Bio-Energy blasts five times before the weapon needs to recharge. This can be done by waiting two hours, placing the weapon on a ley line or nexus, or by having a mage infuse the weapon with 21 P.P.E. points. When the weapon is charged, it can be used by anybody. **Note:** W.P. Energy Rifle (spears and tridents) or W.P. Energy Pistol (sword, dagger, knife and war club) can be used to provide bonuses to strike for ranged Bio-Energy blasts from Coral Bio-Weapons. Costs 550-700 P.P.E. to make such a weapon.

Coral Dagger or Knife: Range: 200 feet (61 m) above water, 240 feet (73 m) underwater. Mega-Damage: 1D4 M.D. in melee combat, or fire a blast of Bio-Energy that does 1D6 M.D.

Coral Spear: Range: 2,000 feet (610 m) above water, 2,400 feet (731.5 m) underwater. Mega-Damage: 1D6+2 M.D. in melee combat, or fire a blast of Bio-Energy that does 2D6 M.D.

Coral Sword: Range: 1,000 feet (305 m) above water, 1,200 feet (366 m) underwater. Mega-Damage: Short sword 2D4 M.D. in melee combat, or fire a blast of Bio-Energy that does 3D4 M.D.

Large sword 2D6 M.D. in melee combat, or fire a blast of Bio-Energy that does 3D6 M.D.

Coral Trident: Range: 2,000 feet (610 m) above water, 2400 feet (731 m) underwater. Mega-Damage: 3D6 M.D. in melee combat, or fire a blast of Bio-Energy that does 4D6 M.D.

Coral War Club: Range: 1,000 feet (305 m) above water, 1,200 feet (366 m) underwater. Mega-Damage: 2D6 M.D. in melee combat, or fire a blast of Bio-Energy that does 3D6 M.D.

Shark Tooth "Serpent Slayer" Bio-Weapons

These serrated weapons are swords and war clubs with saw teeth. Each features one or two rows of shark teeth that inflict Mega-Damage in clubbing, chopping and slashing attacks. They can also be used to saw wood and cut down trees. **Magic Ability:** Double damage to sea monsters, sea serpents, aquatic and reptilian demons, the Splugorth's Metztla and dragons! Throwing range as per usual for normal melee weapons of that type. It takes 300-600 P.P.E. to make one.

Battle-Axe (Large): Mega-Damage: 3D6 M.D.

Dagger or Hand Axe: Mega-Damage: 1D6 M.D.

Short Sword: Mega-Damage: 1D6+1 M.D.

Large Sword: Mega-Damage: 2D6+2 M.D.

Spear: Mega-Damage: 2D4 M.D.

Trident: Damage: 3D6+3 M.D.

War Club: Mega-Damage: 3D4+2 M.D.

Wood "Undead Slayer" Bio-Weapons

Wood Bio-Weapons are made using a single, living tree. Once the ritual begins, the weapon is drawn from the tree like a sword being drawn from its scabbard (in this case, the tree). **Magic Ability:** These weapons inflict S.D.C. damage until the owner wills it (through the use of a mental command using Telepathy, Empathic Connection with Animals or Communicate with Plants and Animals) to be imbued with a Bio-Energy field. When charged with Bio-Energy, the wooden weapon inflicts M.D. to Mega-Damage opponents. Each time the power is activated, the energy aura lasts five minutes (20 melee rounds). Activating a Wood Bio-Weapon takes one melee action of concentration. The weapon's energy aura can be activated up to four times per 24 hours, after that its P.P.E. base must be replenished. This can be done either by placing the weapon at a ley line, stone pyramid or ley line nexus for one hour, or by having a mage infuse the weapon with 30 P.P.E. When the weapon is charged, it can be used by anybody. **Note:** Wooden weapons inflict double damage to vampires and other beings vulnerable to wood even without an active energy aura. Costs 280-460 P.P.E. to make such a weapon.

Cane or Walking Stick: 1D6 S.D.C. or 1D6 M.D. with the aura activated.

Dagger or Stake: 1D6 S.D.C. or 1D6 M.D. with the aura activated.

Javelin: 2D4 S.D.C. or 2D4 M.D. with the aura activated.

Spear: The spear is a single piece of wood, with a pointed end (like a sharpened pencil) or "flat-spearhead" (arrow-like) tip. 2D6 S.D.C. or 2D6 M.D. with the aura activated.

Staff: 2D6 S.D.C. or 2D6 M.D. with the aura activated.

Short Sword: Available only as a short sword that does 1D6+2 S.D.C. or 1D6+2 M.D. with the aura activated.

Throwing Stick: Range: 80 feet (24.4 m), 2D4 S.D.C. or 2D4 M.D. with the aura activated.

War Club: 2D6 S.D.C. or 2D6 M.D. with the aura activated.

Serpent Bio-Weapons

These wicked looking Bio-Weapons are created using the Thrall Sea Serpents of the Serpent Hunters. The glowing biomass extracted from the creature descends in front of the Biomancer who shapes it into one of the following. These weapons are exclusive to Serpent Hunters and given to the occasional Oceanic Guardsman, Birdman and hero of Lemuria (including the rare outsider and surface dweller) for outstanding and heroic service to Lemuria or humanity.

Serpent Blade (750 P.P.E. to create): This magnificent Bio-Weapon is probably the Serpent Hunters' second favorite weapon. It is an elegant blade with a wickedly serrated inside curve. The weapon itself looks like it could have been pried from the back of some magnificent sea serpent or dragon and radiates a power all its own. As a normal weapon, it inflicts 2D6 M.D., but upon activating the blade the Bio-Energy inside it heats up. The blade itself starts glowing red hot like heated metal, leaving a trail of rippling water/air wherever it goes/swings. The "heat" is contained to the blade and very little of it leaks out into the surrounding air or water. Upon impact, however, it unleashes heat damage in addition to the cut of its blade.
Range: Hand to hand combat or heat blast: 100 feet (30.5 m).
Mega-Damage: 2D6 M.D. normal blade strike; 4D6 M.D. when hot with Bio-Energy. Heat Blast does 3D6 M.D. per shot. **Note:** Double damage to creatures vulnerable to fire or Bio-Energy, like the undead.
Payload: Each time the power is activated, the energy aura lasts five minutes (20 melee rounds). Activating the Bio-Energy of a Serpent Blade takes one melee action of concentration. The weapon's energy aura can be activated up to four times per 24 hours, after that its P.P.E. base must be replenished. This can be done either by placing the weapon at a ley line, ley line nexus or stone pyramid for two hours, or by having a mage infuse the weapon with 45 P.P.E. When the weapon is charged, it can be used by anybody.

Serpent Trident (950 P.P.E. to create): This unusual weapon is essentially a lance or long spear with a tri-prong arrangement of blades, the central blade slightly longer than the others. This weapon is typically used by the Serpent Hunters as their main weapon. Like most Bio-Weapon pole arms and spears, it can be retracted to

be made smaller and less cumbersome, however it can reduce itself to one-fifth its normal length (reducing to 2 feet/0.6 m.
Range: 500 feet (152 m) thrown. 2,000 feet (610 m) per electric bolt.
Mega-Damage: In its maximum shortened form it can be used as a melee weapon much like a *short sword* and inflicts 3D6 M.D.

Trident extended to full length: 5D6 M.D. (more from charge attacks on a riding animal/sea serpent steed; see the Serpent Riding ability/Horsemanship: Serpent Hunters for more details). **Note:** Does 1D6x10 M.D. to dragons, sea serpents, giant snakes and reptilian demons and monsters.

Electrical Bolt: 4D6 M.D. per blast.
Rate of Fire: Each blast counts as one melee attack.
Payload: 20 Electric Bolts can be fired before needing to be recharged. Recharging can be done either by placing the weapon at a ley line, ley line nexus or stone pyramid for three hours, or by having a mage infuse the weapon with 70 P.P.E. When the weapon is charged, it can be used by anybody.

Other Bio-Weapons

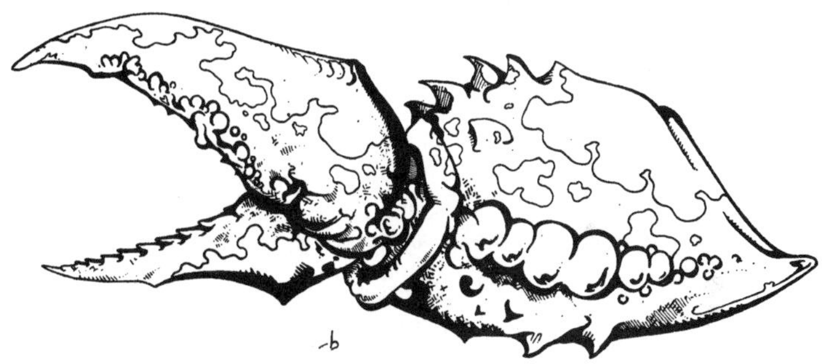

Crab Claw Gauntlet

This complex living weapon is worn like a glove. Two pincers protrude from the hand harness like a giant crab or lobster claw. On mental command the pincers snap open and shut like scissors, but are sharp on both sides of the pincer blades and can be used to stab, cut or slash an opponent. Each pincer has its own M.D.C., but is only damaged when an attacker targets the pincer itself. As a living creature, the gauntlet Bio-Regenerates damage at a rate of 2D6 M.D.C. per hour. Destroying one of the pincer blades reduces the damage by half and the claw cannot be used like scissors. Lemurians use the Crab Gauntlets in combat, to board enemy ships and cut through hulls, hatches, and take down rigging, etc., but they can also be used for penetrating other fortifications, excavation, cutting through wreckage (to rescue people pinned or trapped inside), salvage operations, construction and chopping up scrap.
Weight: A single gauntlet is 40 lbs (18 kg) and they are typically used by designated warriors and specialists.
Range: Close combat.
Mega-Damage: Stab or slash attacks do 3D6 M.D., scissor cuts inflict 5D6 M.D. but count as two melee attacks, and blunt strikes do 2D4 M.D.

Bonuses: +2 to parry and disarm. Crab Claw Gauntlets are good at parrying attacks and can even be used to parry bullets and energy blasts, but are -6 to do so.
M.D.C. of each Crab Gauntlet: 3D6+50 M.D.C., but they are damaged only when an attack specifically targets them for destruction.
Creation Cost: 450 P.P.E.

Serpent Entangler Net

This weapon looks like a net with bolas at the end. It is used to capture or contain unruly sea serpents, dragon hatchlings and other targets designated for capture instead of termination. Throwing Range: 200 feet (61 m), magically working equally as well above and below the surface. Damage: None. Bonuses: +2 to entangle. Creation Cost: 400 P.P.E.

The Serpent Entangler Net has a total of 3D4x10 M.D.C. (this applies only if an attacker targets the weapon itself). Attempting to cut through it to free oneself or a comrade is harder than it looks. To create a hole big enough to escape or untangle requires 3D6+10 M.D. (roll for *each* person or creature entangled). However, the net regenerates 2D6 M.D.C. per melee round. Failure to keep the net damaged enough to escape means the victim is re-trapped in the net! The net also returns after being thrown and missing its mark, to be re-thrown.

Tentacle Sword

The Tentacle Sword is a specialized anti-swordsman weapon. With so many different enchanted close combat weapons, the art of sword-fighting and fencing in Lemuria has grown quite sophisticated. The Tentacle Sword is designed as a sword-breaker for the many bouts of melee combat a Lemurian soldier is likely to face. It has a central blade that is used like a normal sword to thrust and parry, but also features two secondary tentacles that grasp and entangle an enemy's weapon. There is also a small tentacle at the base of the handle that wraps around the user's hand and prevents enemies from disarming him/her (attackers are -3 to disarm). Weight: 4.5 lbs (2 kg). Damage: 2D6+1 M.D. Bonuses: +3 to disarm, +4 to entangle, -3 to be disarmed by an opponent. Creation Cost: 150 P.P.E.

Lemurian Ranged Weapons

Lemurians and Guns. Remember, Lemurians leapfrogged through time inside the Dimensional Pocket of the Lord of the Deep. When they left Earth 15,000 years earlier, modern weapons such as pistols and rifles were not even imagined. A peace-loving people, they did not develop weapons during the 150 years locked inside the Dimensional Pocket. When they returned during the Great Cataclysm, though advanced in many ways and magically adept, their concept of war and combat was very much entrenched in the ways of ancient combat with swords and magic, not guns and missiles. It has only been in the last 60 years or so that Lemurians have begun to compensate for advanced weapons technology and create long-range assault weapons. Despite a growing variety of ranged weapons, Lemurians refuse to use land mines, naval mines, heavy explosives/missiles, or weapons of mass destruction.

Lemurian Weapons on the Black Market. The Lemurians are less militarized than many surface-dwelling societies, and as a result, weapons are normally only found in the hands of the military. The average Lemurian citizen may have a Barracuda Blade, Wood Bio-Staff, or other defensive weapon tucked away somewhere, especially for venturing out into the hostile oceans and wilderness of Rifts Earth, but most "guns," Bio-Armor and all symbiote vehicles are carefully monitored and exclusive to the military.

Outsiders with Lemurian weapons must have procured them in one of very few ways. Lemurians sometimes gift champions and heroes with their precious arms and armor, a just reward for those who stand with them against the many dangers of Rifts Earth. Other weapons may be salvaged from lost Lemurian vessels or taken off the dead after a great battle. Occasionally, stockpiles of weapons are lost in raids and pirate attacks. Horune Pirates, in particular, have learned to keep an eye out for high quality Lemurian weapons, and Lemurian symbiotes and Bio-Devices fetch an excellent price at the Dimensional Market of Splynn and on other worlds.

Bio-Energy Bow

This bow is grown from a living tree or coral and shaped with magic. Unlike a normal bow, this weapon has no visible string, yet it is curved in the shape of a strung bow. The bow is armed by a mental command (activated through Telepathy, Empathic Connection with Animals or Communicate with Plants and Animals) and the gesture of drawing back an imaginary string. The moment the imaginary string is released, an "arrow" or "bolt" of Bio-Energy is unleashed.
Weight: 4 lbs (1.8 kg).
Range: 1,200 feet (366 m), half underwater.
Mega-Damage: 3D6 M.D., double damage against vampires, the undead, Metztla and Alien Intelligences.
Payload: 40 energy bolts before needing a recharge by either placing it at a ley line, nexus or stone pyramid for two hours, or by having any wizard spend 35 P.P.E.
Cost on the Open Market: 35,000-70,000 credits.
Creation Cost: 200 P.P.E.

Clamshell Pistol

By Matthew Clements

A small, compact, defensive weapon, the Clamshell Pistol is a magically-engineered handgun that fires stinging pearl pellets. Typically issued as a backup weapon, the Clamshell Pistol's grip folds in when not in use to make the gun even smaller and less obtrusive. Controversy surrounds the weapon for its use in several notable assassinations, but it is too handy of a weapon for Sea Sentinels, submarine crewmen and scouts to be put out of service.
Weight: 0.75 lbs (0.34 kg).
Range: 500 feet (152 m); half underwater.
Mega-Damage: 2D4 M.D.
Rate of Fire: Each shot counts as one melee attack.
Payload: 15 shots. The weapon can be recharged by being placed on a ley line, nexus or stone pyramid for one hour, or having any wizard expend 20 P.P.E.
Cost on the Open Market: 7,000-15,000 credits.
Creation Cost: 100 P.P.E.

Ink Gun

By Matthew Clements

A combination underwater flare gun and smoke screen launcher, the Ink Gun shoots a magically charged ball of ink at high speed. When it reaches a certain desired distance, the ink ball explodes, filling the water with thick, opaque ink. Black or blue ink provides a dark, underwater smoke screen, while bright colors can be used to paint a target, signal for help or draw attention to a specific area. Ink Guns are issued frequently to Sea Sentinels and Lemurian Scouts.
Weight: 2 lbs (0.9 kg).
Range: 2,000 feet (610 m).
Damage: None. The Ink Gun creates a cloud of ink roughly 40 feet (12.2 m) in diameter.
Rate of Fire: Each blast counts as one melee attack/action.
Payload: 12 ink charges. Can be recharged by being placed on a ley line, nexus or stone pyramid for two hours, or by having any practitioner of magic expend 20 P.P.E. The weapon can also use spare ink packs when magical recharging is not an option.
Cost on the Open Market: 5,000-7,000 credits.
Creation Cost: 80 P.P.E.

Lava Projector

By Matthew Clements

An unusual weapon that uses a form of Stone Magic, the Lava Projector is a long staff or rod that emits blasts of molten rock. The weapon can be set to shower an area with magma, or to shoot more accurate streams. The lava temperature can even be cooled and the liquid stone used as a sealant or filler to plug gaps in ships' hulls or undersea fortifications.
Weight: 6 lbs (2.7 kg).
Range: 50 feet (15 m) for area-effect mode, 600 feet (183 m) for stream mode; half range underwater.
Mega-Damage: 2D6 M.D. to everything within a 10 foot (3 m) radius on area-effect mode, 4D6 M.D. to a specific target on stream mode.
Rate of Fire: Each blast/use counts as one melee attack. Using the weapon to seal a crack counts as one use.
Payload: 12 blasts/uses. The weapon can be recharged by being placed on a ley line, nexus or stone pyramid, or by having any practitioner of magic put 35 P.P.E. into the weapon.
Cost on the Open Market: 35,000-60,000 credits.
Creation Cost: 190 P.P.E.

Nematocyst Paralyzer

The Biomancer enlists the aid of a school of jellyfish to create a spear gun-like weapon which looks to be made out of semi-clear plastic or glass. This strange looking mini-staff or scepter/rod is reminiscent of a spear gun or pointed club. As a blunt weapon it functions very similar to a neural mace or taser, releasing nematocysts (exploding spines) that deliver a magical paralyzing toxin. Pointed and aimed like a shotgun or taser, it can fire off small arrow or mini-javelin-like projectiles of magical nematocyst stingers into the victim, paralyzing them from a short distance. The Lemurians use this Bio-Weapon to capture and incapacitate their subjects for questioning, or to handle difficult or dangerous creatures they do not wish to kill.
Weight: 2 lbs (0.9 kg).

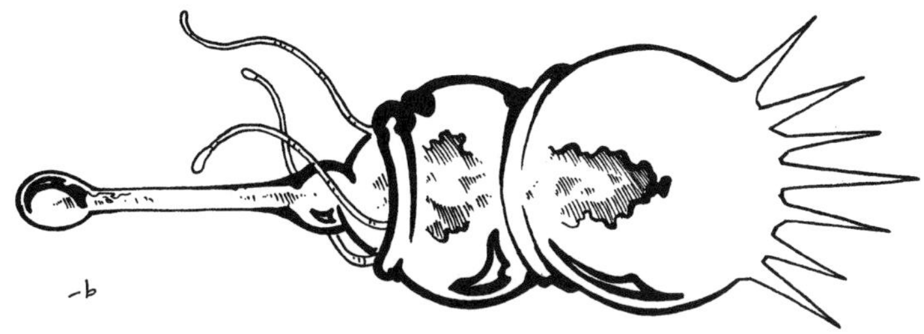

Range: 100 feet (30.5 m).
Damage: The blast/strike inflicts 1D4 S.D.C. to mortal S.D.C. creatures and one M.D. to Mega-Damage creatures. The victim must make a successful save vs non-lethal poison (16 or higher) or succumb to the stun effects of the weapon: Victims lose initiative and reduce the number of attacks per melee to two, -8 on Perception Rolls, -8 to strike and all other combat bonuses, the performance of all skills is -50%, and reduce Spd by 75% for 1D4+2 melee rounds. All penalties and duration of the stun effect are half for Mega-Damage creatures.
Rate of Fire: The weapon regenerates/re-grows a new projectile quickly enough for the user to fire one shot for every melee attack/action he has. **Note:** The weapon will not work through body armor, on robots or against bionics.
Payload: Six shots. The weapon can be recharged by being placed on a ley line, nexus or stone pyramid for two hours, or having a practitioner of magic put 40 P.P.E. into it.
Cost on the Open Market: 30,000-60,000 credits.
Creation Cost: 145 P.P.E.
Note: W.P. Harpoon & Spear Gun is needed to offer any kind of proficiency with this Bio-Weapon.

Sea Urchin Spike Launcher/Spear Gun

The Biomancer uses a group of sea urchins to create a spear gun like weapon that looks like a black mini-staff, rod or scepter with a texture/feel reminiscent of a crustacean's exoskeleton or chitin. The top edge has a couple of spines which, when used as a club, allows the weapon to inflict 2D6 M.D. As a spear gun it launches 6-inch (0.15 m) long spikes. The weapon grows/regenerates spikes so quickly that they can be used to fire short bursts from the spear gun (half the normal bonuses to strike) or used as single shots for more accuracy.
Weight: 3.5 lbs (1.6 kg).
Range: 800 feet (244 m), 500 feet (152 m) underwater.
Mega-Damage: Each spike does 1D6 M.D., or 3D6 M.D. for a burst of four.
Rate of Fire: Each shot or burst counts as one melee attack/action.
Payload: 30 P.P.E. will provide 12 shots.
Cost on the Open Market: 20,000-40,000 credits.
Creation Cost: 200 P.P.E.
Note: W.P. Harpoon & Spear Gun is needed to offer any kind of proficiency with this Bio-Weapon.

Sonic Blast Staff

By Matthew Clements

An area-effect weapon, the Sonic Blast Staff emits a shrieking pulse of sonic energy. Anything within range of the staff is affected, friend or foe, so careful use is advised. The user is protected from the sonic pulse, but any unshielded allies will suffer full damage. Sonic Blast Staves are typically issued to units of Bio-Armored troopers or practitioners of magic that can protect themselves from sound attacks.

Weight: 5.5 lbs (2.5 kg).

Range: 50 foot (15 m) diameter of effect.

Damage: Everything within 50 feet (15 m) of the staff takes 3D6 S.D.C. damage. Sea creatures and those without protection from sound waves (including Mega-Damage beings) suffer -4 on initiative, -2 to parry and dodge and -1 to strike for the next three melee rounds. Penalties are not cumulative.

Rate of Fire: Each use counts as one melee attack/action.

Payload: 8 uses. The staff can be recharged by being placed on a ley line or nexus or by having any mage expend 20 P.P.E.

Cost on the Open Market: 15,000-25,000 credits.

Creation Cost: 100 P.P.E.

Stonecaster Pistol

By Matthew Clements

The primary combat sidearm of Oceanic Guardsmen and Serpent Hunters, the Stonecaster Pistol uses the most basic properties of Stone Magic to generate several different types of ammunition. Sedimentary rounds fragment on impact and damage a small area. Igneous rounds stick to the target and burn like lava. Metamorphic ammo is hard, dense and has armor-piercing capabilities. No matter the situation or the target, the Stonecaster has the right magic projectile for the job. **Note:** Available as a pistol and as a rod or scepter.

Weight: 2.2 lbs (1 kg).

Range: 1,000 feet (305 m).

Mega-Damage: Sedimentary: 1D6 M.D. to a 10 foot (3 m) diameter. Igneous: 2D4 M.D. on impact and 1D4 M.D. for the next two melee rounds as the lava continues to burn. Metamorphic: 4D4 M.D.

Rate of Fire: Each shot counts as one melee attack/action.

Payload: 12 rounds. The weapon can be recharged by placing it on a ley line, nexus, or stone pyramid for two hours, or by having any mage expend 25 P.P.E. "Clips" of blank stone projectiles are sometimes issued to non-magic soldiers, and can be loaded into the weapon and then enchanted into whatever ammo type is desired.

Cost on the Open Market: 45,000-90,000 credits.

Creation Cost: 150 P.P.E.

Stonecaster Rifle

By Matthew Clements

As the name suggests, the Stonecaster Rifle is a larger weapon with long-range capabilities. All Stonecaster weapons are highly prized. In Lemuria they are only issued to the military caste.

Weight: 7.2 lbs (3.24 kg).

Range: 2,000 feet (610 m), half underwater.

Mega-Damage: Sedimentary: 2D6 M.D. to a 12 foot (3.6 m) diameter. Igneous: 3D6 M.D. on impact and 1D6 M.D. for each of the next two melee rounds. Metamorphic: 5D6 M.D.

Rate of Fire: Each shot counts as one melee attack/action.

Payload: 20 rounds. The weapon can be recharged by placing it on a ley line, nexus or stone pyramid for four hours by having any mage expend 60 P.P.E. Clips of neutral stone projectiles are also issued, and can be loaded into the weapon and then enchanted into whatever ammo type is desired.

Cost on the Open Market: 80,000-150,000 credits.

Creation Cost: 300 P.P.E.

Waterjet Gun

By Matthew Clements

The Waterjet Gun is a specialized weapon manufactured as a rod or staff, but sometimes also in a submachine-gun style configuration. It sprays an extremely concentrated "beam" of water, enough to inflict S.D.C. damage to normal targets and to pulverize vampires.

Weight: 4.5 lbs (2 kg).

Range: 800 feet (244 m).

Damage: 2D6 S.D.C. underwater, 4D6 S.D.C. on land. Vampires take 6D6+6 damage to Hit Points.

Rate of Fire: Each blast counts as one melee attack/action.

Payload: Effectively unlimited underwater, 20 blasts on land. The weapon can be recharged at any water source; the gun automatically "drinks" water when immersed and will recharge in 10 minutes. It can also absorb moisture in the air, recharging 1D4 water blasts per hour; +2 in jungles, forests and humid conditions, half in desert conditions.

Cost on the Open Market: 30,000-60,000 credits.

Creation Cost: 194 P.P.E.

Bio-Construct Symbiotes

Though technically all Bio-Constructs are symbiotes, these particular living items/symbiotic creatures are designated as weapons or armor and have more civilian applications.

Morphic Riding Bio-Constructs a.k.a. "Living Saddles"

While many Lemurians are quite adept at riding animals bareback, the rider often needs an extra pair of hands or something to hold weapons, secure cargo or even to carry extra passengers. This ingenious Bio-Construct allows for that. All Living Saddles are created using a Biomancy ritual known only to high level Biomancer Gene-Mages. When the saddle is not needed for riding, it shrinks and reconfigures to be a small, organic "patch" on the animal's back. If so desired, it can even be removed completely. As with Bio-Armor, however, a living saddle needs to spend time on a host animal at least 2D6+8 hours a week to survive. When a Living Saddle is placed on the animal to be ridden, large tendrils extend to secure the saddle to the animal's back. The saddle is comfortable for both the rider and the riding animal, and offers a number of advantages to both.

First, the saddle can extend itself, creating additional saddles on the back of a large creature to accommodate as many passengers as the animal can comfortably carry; typically one additional passenger for horse-sized creatures, but a dragon or sea serpent could easily accommodate 4-8 passengers depending upon its size.

Second, the saddle's tendrils not only attaches the saddle in a comfortable and secure manner, but its tendrils can be used to lash cargo to the back of the mount, allowing the animal to carry its maximum capacity without discomfort. It even redistributes the load and adjusts the cargo when the creature's back gets sore or stressed; empathetically sensing the feelings of the riding animal.

Third, a Living Saddle conforms in shape and size to the animal on which it is placed.

Weight: Roughly 90 lbs (40.5 kg).

Mega-Damage Capacity: The saddle itself has 1D4x10+40 M.D.C.

Cost on the Open Market: 15,000-30,000 credits (a third of that in Lemuria).

Creation Cost: 175 P.P.E.

Morphic Riding Bio-Barding

Bio-Barding is part Living Saddle and part living Bio-Armor that covers and protects the belly, neck and head of the riding animal. During the magical creation, thc Biomancer Gene-Mage doesn't stop with the creation of just a Living Saddle, but creates a sort of Bio-Skin, or second skin with heavy-looking organic plates or scales to provide even more protection for the animal's underbelly, neck and head. As the Bio-Barding is damaged, it flakes off like a turtle shedding the plates of its shell or a snake shedding its skin. However, it will regrow quickly. In the case of Bio-Barding, the extra armor is created from the animal itself and remains a permanent part of it. The "built-in" saddle appears as needed and can only accommodate one rider and one passenger (two passengers for large animals) and minimal gear on the back of the creature(about half the amount usual for the animal).

Weight: Increase the animal's weight by 20% and reduce its usual Spd and leaping ability by 10%.

M.D.C. by Location: Increase the M.D.C. of the animal by 50% over most of its body. Double the creature's M.D.C. for its underbelly, neck and head, as it has larger, thicker scales or flexible plating at these locations. Any natural protection or resistance of the creature (impervious to fire, resistance to cold, etc.) also extends to the Bio-Barding itself. **Note:** Bio-Barding regenerates at a rate of 2D6 M.D.C. per hour, double along a ley line or stone pyramid, triple at a nexus point.

Cost on the Open Market: Bio-Barding adds 150,000-300,000 credits to the cost of the animal.

Creation Cost: 820 P.P.E.

Bio-Skins

While similar to Bio-Armor, Bio-Skins are much more simplistic symbiotic organisms available to the Lemurian workforce and civilians. In their natural state, Bio-Skins appear to be some type of strange seaweed with one end anchored to the ocean floor and the other swaying with the current. Anyone wanting to use the Bio-Skin simply comes up to it and invites it to join them via Telepathy or Empathic Connection with Animals. An accepting Bio-Skin releases itself from the ground and wraps around the person.

There are a number of different types of Bio-Skin, each offering its own unique level of protection and abilities, but all function on an instinctive level and maintain their abilities as long as they are worn. Bio-Skin draws power from ambient P.P.E. and filter feeds on small animals and creatures like bacteria, algae and plankton.

In all cases, Bio-Skin feels so natural that most wearers forget they have it on.

Cost of Bio-Skin in Lemuria, where they are common, to Lemurians is 5% of the Open Market price listed. As with most Biomancy products and symbiotes, they are seldom sold or traded to surface dwellers or people not among Lemuria's most trusted of allies. However, they are sometimes traded or given as gifts and rewards to outsiders who have proven themselves to be good and well-intentioned, heroic and merciful, or have done a great service for Lemuria.

Bio-Skin Gill Suit: This suit is typically reserved for surface dwellers as it enables the wearer to breathe underwater as if he had gills without time limit, protects from cold, keeps the wearer dry and comforatable and enables him to survive depths up to two miles (3.2 km). The Bio-Skin Gill Suit is a medium green in color. M.D.C.: 2D6+22 main body and regenerates lost M.D.C. at a rate of 1D4 points per hour. Cost on the Open Market: 25,000-40,000 credits, though most non-Lemurian purchasers don't know how to care for Bio-Skin and it dies in 2D4+1 days. Creation Cost: 82 P.P.E.

Bio-Skin Dive Suit: This suit of Bio-Skin is used for deep sea excursions, exploration and salvage by Lemurians and their allies. Like the Gill Suit, it enables the wearer to breathe underwater as if he had gills, protects from cold, and enables the wearer to survive depths up to three miles (4.8 km). The skin is a Carribean blue color. M.D.C.: 2D6+33 main body and regenerates lost M.D.C. at a rate of 1D6 points per hour. Cost on the Open Market: 35,000-60,000 credits, though most non-Lemurian purchasers don't know how to care for Bio-Skin and it dies in 2D4+1 days. Creation Cost: 98 P.P.E.

Bio-Skin Protective Suit: This suit of Bio-Skin is obviously thicker and has what looks like a mass the size of an oxygen tank on the back. It is a dark green or green-gray color, and used for deep sea excursion, exploration, salvage and labor by Lemurians and their allies. Like the Gill Suit, it enables the wearer to breathe underwater as if he had gills, and protects from extreme cold (as low as -70 degrees Fahrenheit below zero/-56.6 Celius), heat (as high as 300 degrees Fahrenheit/148.8 C) and from lethal levels of radiation for up to two hours (the Bio-Skin starts to change color from dark to light orange as it reaches the limits of its protection to radiation). It also filters and protects against dangerous chemicals and toxins in the water (the wearer is +5 to save vs poison and disease) and has a depth tolerance of up to three miles (4.8 km). M.D.C.: 3D6+44 main body and regenerates lost M.D.C. at a rate of 2D4 points per hour. Cost on the Open Market: 45,000-80,000 credits, though most non-Lemurian purchasers don't know how to care for Bio-Skin and it dies in 2D4+1 days. Creation Cost: 118 P.P.E.

Bio-Skin Terrain Suit: This suit of Bio-Skin is used by Lemuria's aquatic allies (and sometimes by nervous Lemurians) for travel on the surface world, enabling the wearer to breathe air as if he had lungs, protects from heat/sun, keeping the wearer cool and hydrated for up to seven days (half in deserts or conditions of exposure), and helps to filter airborne and waterborne toxins (the wearer is +1 to save vs poisons, toxins and smoke). In the water, the suit enables the wearer to survive depths up to two miles (3.2 km). It is light brown or a green and brown camouflage pattern. M.D.C.: 2D6+22 main body and regenerates lost M.D.C. at a rate of 1D4 points per hour. Cost on the Open Market: 25,000-40,000 credits, though most purchasers don't know how to care for Bio-Skin and it dies in 2D4+1 days. Creation Cost: 90 P.P.E.

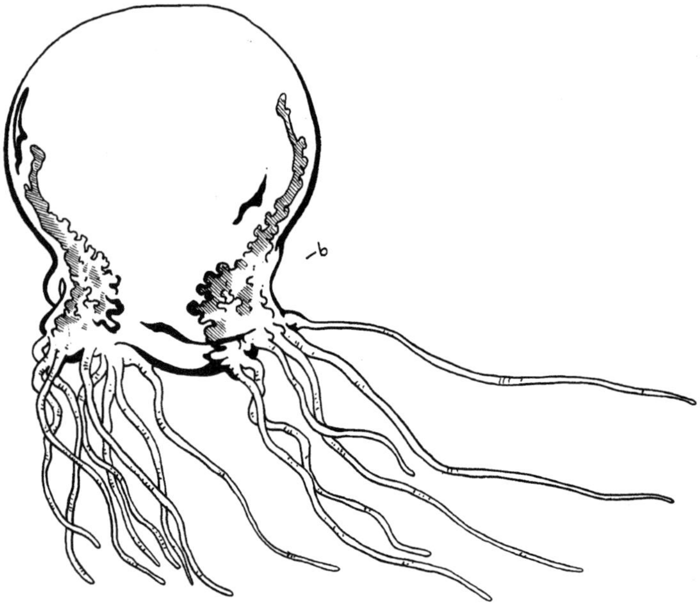

Breathers

These unusual jellyfish were created by Lemurian Biomancer Gene-Mages to enable surface dwellers to breathe underwater. They can also be used by Lemurians to filter out dangerous chemicals in the water (+4 to save vs poison and disease). They are frequently used by surface-dwelling Sea Druids and Ocean Wizards, as well as other seafaring people (and some pirates) who have figured out what Breathers can do and where to find them. (Usually at and near coral reefs, Lemurian Gardens, and Lemurian cities and outposts, but can also be found in the wild, in small numbers, at any location inhabited by other types of jellyfish.

Breather symbiotes are essentially a basketball-sized jellyfish with the usual array of tentacles. Their upper "shell" is clear and transparent and humanoids who want to wear it as a "breather" simply slide their head into this helmet-like part of the symbiote's body. Those unfamiliar with opening their eyes underwater see as if they were wearing a helmet, and water is kept out of their face. When placed over the head, the Breather's tentacles automatically wrap around the base of the neck to create a tight seal, then it pumps in fresh oxygen from its gills, filling the chamber with breathable oxygen. The Breathers feed/thrive on the carbon dioxide released by their host, as well as ambient P.P.E. and tiny water organisms. Lemurians sometimes wear a Breather when the water (or air) is too toxic to be filtered by other means, because the symbiote provides the wearer with clean and purified air. **Note:** Breathers themselves can breathe both air and water, but dehydrate and die when kept out of water within 2D4x10+60 minutes.

When not attached to a host, Breathers float to the surface and use their collected carbon dioxide and seawater to create food (sugar) through an odd form of photosynthesis. This form grabs all available light (including the green spectrum) using the clear "shell" to focus the light like a lens into their mitochondria (energy manufacturing center).

Attributes of Note: Has a low animal intelligence, a P.S. of 6 and a swimming speed of 6.

Hit Points: 1D6. **S.D.C.:** 2D4.

P.P.E.: 1D4

Natural Abilities: Swim 60% (kind of bobs around like a jellyfish), resistant to cold (half damage), impervious to poisons, toxins and other chemicals, including the stings of jellyfish, chemoreceptors enable the creature to taste/find hosts (50%), and it also filters toxins from the air and water.

Depth Tolerance: Three miles (4.8 km) for the Breather itself, but most surface dwellers cannot survive the pressure at more than 500 feet (152.4 m) without the additional protection of Bio-Skin, Bio-Armor or a high-tech diving suit/power armor.

Habitat: Typically in and around Lemurian cities and outposts, coral reefs and wherever other jellyfish are found, particularly in and around the Pacific Rim and Indian Ocean.

Allies: None per se, but will function with any air breathing species that exhales carbon dioxide.

Enemies: None per se, most creatures leave them alone as they often hide in and amongst other species of stinging jellyfish.

Value: To Sea Druids, Ocean Wizards, seafarers and those looking for a non-technological means of survival underwater, 1,500-5,000 credits.

Fin Pack

This unusual creature and the Squid Pack (described elsewhere in this section) are symbiotic organisms designed by Biomancy Gene-Mages to assist Lemurians in underwater travel, work and exploration. This creature is essentially a genetically engineered underwater *jet pack*, based on the abilities of a manta ray or stingray, or even a flying fish due to its odd "fin" or "wing" placement. Its shell also seems to indicate a possible melding of genetic material from a predatory snail such as the Episcopal Miter. Its compact design, however, requires it to rely more on magic for propulsion than the Squid Pack.

A large suction cup or snail's foot is used to secure the symbiote to the host's back. The Fin Pack – think a small pair of manta ray wings – positions itself over the central nervous system, allowing it to sense the host's muscle signals and reactions to swim for him in the same fashion as the ray. To engage the Fin Pack, the user must reach out to the symbiote with his mind, willing it to swim. Though the Fin Pack breathes water it can survive out of water for 1D6 hours, provided it remains linked to a host.

Attributes of Note: Has a low animal intelligence, a P.S. of 12 and a base swimming speed of 44 (30 mph or 48 kmph or 26 knots) using a pair of semi-retractable, ray-like wing-fins. Using its underwater wings and magic propulsion it can carry a humanoid weighing as much as 400 pounds (180 kg) for 1D6+8 hours before getting tired (reduce swim speed by half when it tires). A tired Fin Pack needs only an hour of rest to continue at full speed for another 1D4+2 hours, before requiring four hours of rest to get back to full level; half that time when resting at a ley line, nexus or stone pyramid.

M.D.C.: 3D6+12 M.D.C.

P.P.E.: 6D6+6

Natural Abilities: The Fin Pack is protected by a tough M.D.C. hide that feels like smooth rubber. The Fin Pack has a mouth full of sharp teeth to feed on small fish, crusteans and plants, but they are not suitable for combat. A bite does 1D6 S.D.C. damage and the symbiote cannot be sent to attack an opponent.

Habitat: In the wild, most Fin Packs live in and around Lemurian Gardens, outposts and cities, as well as coral reefs, shallow seas and locations where one would encounter manta rays.

Allies: None per se, as it is an animal. However, they readily accept and obey Lemurians and some friendly psychic races, Psi-Druids and Sea Druids with the manta ray or stingray totem.

Enemies: Predatory animals and monsters that prey upon large fish. The Splugorth also covet them as an ingredient for certain types of Bio-Wizardry.
Value: To anyone who can use them as an underwater jet pack, 15,000-30,000 credits. Lemurians who raise them sell them to other Lemurians for 2,000-3,000 credits.

Octo-Arm

This symbiotic organism resembles an octopus that attaches itself to the wearer's arm to provide a number of unique abilities and enhancements. The Octo-Arm creature has a small, bulbous head about the size of an apple or orange with eight long arms, each 3-4 feet (0.9 to 1.2 m) long. To join and use the Octo-Arm, a Lemurian simply uses his Communicate with Plants and Animals ability or Empathy and the Octo-Arm then wraps itself around the extended arm arm.

Special Abilities provided to the user/wearer:

1. Bonuses and Extra Attacks: The wearer of the Octo-Arm can use four of the tentacles as an extension of his own arm. It provides him with two bonus attacks per melee round, +4 to entangle, +1 to parry and disarm, and +10% to Climbing/Rappelling.

2. Limited Supernatural P.S. of the Tentacles. The Octo-Arm has a Supernatural P.S. of 20 and does 3D6 S.D.C. on a restrained punch/strike, 1D6 M.D. on a full strength strike (cannot do a Power Punch), and can wield melee weapons and simple tools and devices.

3. Chameleon. The Octo-Arm and its humanoid wearer can change their color and patterns to blend in with the environment to camouflage themselves. This provides a bonus of +15% to the skills Camouflage, Prowl and Tailing.

4. Enhanced Healing for the Wearer. The user of an Octo-Arm heals at a rate of 1D6 S.D.C./Hit Points per hour when wearing the symbiote, and is +1 to save vs poison, toxins and disease, and +5% to save vs coma and death.

Attributes of Note: Has an animal intelligence, a P.S. of 20 (Supernatural) and a basic swimming speed of 14.
M.D.C.: 3D6+18 for the main body of the Octo-Arm symbiote itself. Each tentacle has 1D6+6 M.D.C. The Octo-Arm Bio-Regenerates at a rate of 1D4 M.D.C. an hour and can completely regrow a lost tentacle in 24 hours.
P.P.E.: 4D6+6
Natural Abilities: The Octo-Arm looks and functions much like an octopus, eats small fish and crustaceans, as well as plankton, and lives a quiet, leisurely existence. In the wild and detached from a humanoid user, the Octo-Arm can also cast the *Chameleon (6) spell* on itself at the equivalent of a 4th level practitioner of magic. Each spell casting costs it 6 P.P.E.
Habitat: Most Octo-Arms live in and around Lemurian Gardens, outposts, and cities, as well as wherever octopus and squid are found.
Allies: Usually only Lemurians, though some friendly psychic races, Psi-Druids and Sea Druids with the squid or octopus totem may also be able to use them should they win their favor.
Enemies: They are often mistaken as octopus or squid and are preyed upon by the natural predators of those animals – who often get a nasty surprise – as well as sea monsters. Their M.D.C. bodies make conventional hunting and cooking by humanoids difficult.
Value: To anyone who can use them as an augmentation symbiote; 40,000 to 70,000 credits or more on the open market.

Sea Doctor

This unusual little creature looks like a lump of red or violet sea cucumber with nine small tentacles and a mouth at one end, but moves and functions more like a leech. The Sea Doctor feeds on parasites, bacteria, dead tissue, pus, jellyfish stings (nematocyst), and other infections commonly found in wounds and sea injuries. The Lemurians created this little fellow to accompany their people on long journeys and to provide assistance. When not in use the little fellow often curls up into a ball (about the size of a grapefruit) and hibernates until it is needed. They can survive out of the water in the hibernated state for 2D6+4 days, but will eventually need to be returned to salt water. The Sea Doctor is typically activated through the Empathic Connection with Animals ability, however placing a Sea Doctor that is in hibernation near an open wound or infected tissue causes it to awaken within 1D4+1 melee rounds as the smell of "dinner" reaches its senses.
Attributes of Note: Low Animal I.Q. that runs on instinct, has a swimming speed of 5.
Hit Points: 1D6
S.D.C.: 2D6
P.P.E.: 2D6+11

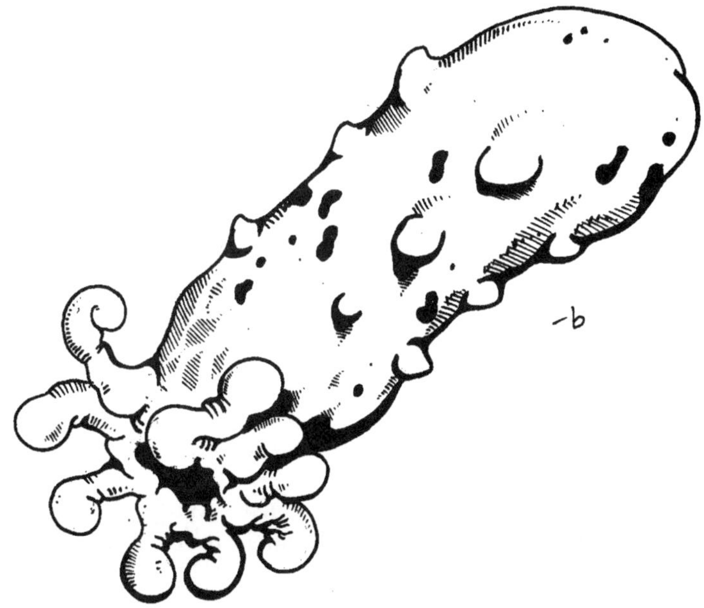

Natural Abilities: Swim 70%, depth tolerance of 8 miles (12.8 km), resistant to cold (half damage), breathes water but can survive in air for up to seven days, impervious to disease, poisons, toxins and other related chemical attacks (including the stings of jellyfish), chemoreceptors enable it to taste/find a wound. Goes into a hibernation state (curls up into a ball) that keeps it from needing to breathe/use its gills.

Innate Healing Abilities:

Chemoreceptor Diffuser: When attending to healing underwater, the Sea Doctor excretes an enzyme that breaks down and masks the odor of blood and flesh in the surrounding water, hiding itself and its patient from sensitive predators, like sharks, and has an 80% chance of not being detected or found if administered within one minute of the injury, otherwise the percentage drops 5% for every melee round after the first minute.

Fight Coma & Death: When the Sea Doctor is attached to a subject, it instills a boost to fight and survive coma and death; +15% bonus, double on a ley line or at a nexus or stone pyramid.

Ley Line Rejuvenation: If the Sea Doctor is on a ley line or at a nexus or stone pyramid, it can channel magic energy from it into the host while it is attached. The effect is to minimize scarring, heal wounds and restore vitality and health to the entire body as long as the symbiote remains attached. 1D6 Hit Points/S.D.C. (or one M.D.C. point) is restored for every hour until the wound is completely healed or healed enough to move on. The Sea Doctor recovers from injury it may have sustained itself at a rate of 1D4 Hit Points or S.D.C. per 20 minutes at a ley line, nexus and pyramid.

Regenerative Saliva: The saliva of the Sea Doctor is injected into and covered over open or infected wounds to kill infection and increase the natural rate of healing. Within 1D4 melees, the saliva breaks down and transforms into a powerful healing agent that restores 1D4 Hit Points instantly. It then increases the rate of healing in and around the wound, doubling the subject's natural rate of healing. This can be performed only once per *each* wound, healing another 1D4 Hit Points (or S.D.C.) per wound, but the increased rate of healing remains the same and lasts 1D4 days.

Removes Bacteria, Poisons and Toxins: After attaching itself to an injured or ill subject (humanoid or animal), the Sea Doctor drains him/it of any toxins, poisons, nematocyst and infection in the body, stopping any further deterioration/damage, and reducing any penalties, symptoms and their duration by 50%. The Sea Doctor feeds on the infection, dead or festering tissue, pus, a little on blood and other particles, which serve as food for it.

Psionics: In dire circumstances or when trying to heal a creature with a vast amount of Hit Points, S.D.C. or M.D.C., the Sea Doctor can tap into a hidden reserve of psionic abilities to further heal its host. For the most part, no one except for learned Lemurians know of these abilities; even the Lemurians' common allies who are given such a gift rarely find out about it. The Sea Doctor is almost constantly using its abilities *Mask Psionics and I.S.P.* and *Alter Aura* to conceal its true nature. In its hibernating state, its mind almost completely shuts down and is undetectable (for either psionics, intelligence or any other readings). Lemurians activate these abilities by placing a special request with their ability to Communicate with Plants and Animals/Empathic Connection with Animals, however normal Telepathy can also be used (simply asking for more help is sufficient).

The Sea Doctor has the following abilities: Mask Psionics and I.S.P., Alter Aura (on constantly), Healing Touch (6), Increased Healing (10), Deaden Pain (4), Induce Sleep (4), Psychic Surgery (14), Psychic Purification (8), and Psychic Diagnosis (4).

I.S.P. Base: 1D4x10+28

Habitat: Typically found in and around Lemurian Gardens, cities and outposts as well as at coral reefs. Many are found in Lemurian first aid kits and medic's bags.

Allies: None per se, though they like and favor Lemurians, Merans, Ichthyleans who all use the Sea Doctor, as do the occasional Ocean Wizard, Sea Druid, Whale Singer, and Holistic Doctors.

Enemies: None per se, animal. Seem to have a genetic disposition of avoidance of helping evil creatures such as the Splugorth, their minions and the undead. Otherwise, it has no qualms about helping any creature.

Value: To travelers, doctors and healers, the medical applications this little thing offers are amazing and can fetch 1D6x100,000 credits.

Sea Eye

Due to its appearance, some have equated this quaint little symbiote to a Zembahk, however, the symbiote is an animal, not a sentient being. Sea Eyes have a long, thick, cylindrical body with a large, round eye for a head and a flat, flipper-like foot for a tail. They are typically green, brown or gold with green flecks in color, with a large blue eye. When bonded with a humanoid host, the flipper mounts on the shoulder just like a shoulder pad and the worm curls up like a cobra, or a spring, on its flipper-tail/shoulder pad and the head and eye looks around like a second pair of eyes.

Also Known As: the Shoulder Worm and Eel Eye.

Attributes of Note: High animal intelligence and strong instincts on par with a monkey or lemur and is very curious and observant, always looking around and keeps an eye on everything that its host is not focusing on. When it is not attached to a host it has a swimming speed of 12, a crawling speed of 6, and is a filter-feeder.

M.D.C.: 1D6+4

P.P.E.: 3D6

Natural Abilities: Amphibious but prefers life in the sea and seldom leaves it on its own; breathes water and air, swim 98%, resistance to cold (half damage), nightvision 1,000 feet (305 m), keen hawk-like vision (can read a sign one mile/1.6 km away), see into the infrared and ultraviolet spectrums of light, sees the invisible and depth tolerance of 6 miles (9.6 km).

Bond with Host: While bonded with a sentient host, he sees everything the worm does and can even designate targets or where to point the wide beam of light to illuminate an area (see below). Bonuses: +2 to strike.

Enhanced Perception: Provides the humanoid it is attached to with the following bonuses: +2 on Perception Rolls, +1 on initiative, +1 to dodge, the humanoid cannot be surprised by attacks from behind or above, and is especially good at detecting danger and provides a +10% bonus on the skills Detect Ambush, Detect Concealment, Trap/Mine Detection, Track and Trap Animals, and Land and Underwater Navigation. Eye Energy Beam: Can also create light, either as a wide beam (like a flashlight) from its large eye or focused into a deadly laser-like beam of white energy. As a weapon, the eye beam does 1D6 or 4D6 S.D.C. and has a range of 100 feet (30.5 m) underwater or 200 feet (61 m) in the air, and is +1 to strike on its own.

Psionics: Unlimited Telepathy and Empathy with its human host/partner at no I.S.P. cost, but communications are images, emotions and sensations of danger, warning, happiness, etc. **Note:** The Sea

Eye also experiences the same thoughts, images, excitement and emotion as the humanoid it is linked with and enjoys the rush they supply. In this regard, the Sea Eye is an adrenaline junkie, who enjoys the wide range of emotions its human host provides, as well as the adventure and new sights and experiences.

Base I.S.P.: 2D6+11

Actions per Melee: Two; the Sea Eye has its eye beam as a means of attack or defense or it can dodge and hide.

Bonuses of the Sea Eye: +2 on Perception Rolls, +2 on initiative, +4 to automatic dodge, +2 to roll with impact, resistant to cold,

Habitat: Prefers interesting places filled with life and activity, including coral reefs, shallow seas, the Demon Sea/Bermuda Triangle, as well as coastal ports and Lemurian Gardens, cities, and outposts.

Allies: Tend to like beings of good alignments and kind dispositions, including Lemurians, Merans, Ichthyleans, Junk Crabs, Ocean Wizards, Sea Druids, and Whale Singers, but may assocaite with other beings.

Enemies: Seem to have a genetic disposition to avoid evil, angry and violent beings. Otherwise, it has no qualms about helping or bonding to any other creature.

Value: Have been known to sell for as much as 1D6x100,000 credits.

Squid Lock

The Squid Lock is another tentacled creature that uses its tentacles to bind and hold living creatures. Technically a parasitic organism, it then feeds on the life energy and P.P.E. of the creature locked in its embrace, consuming one point of S.D.C. and P.P.E. each per hour. This tiny amount seldom harms its captive, and after the Squid Lock has consumed 10 S.D.C./P.P.E. it has its fill and does not feed for another 1D6+6 hours. Lemurians and other aquatic beings use the Squid Lock to secure prisoners. It scrambles and interferes with magic and psionics, making it difficult to focus and cast spells or use psionics – requires a roll of 18 or higher for a prisoner to cast one spell or psionic ability, and can only try once every 2D6+8 minutes.

To be set free, the Squid Lock must be physically removed, which requires 1D4+1 sets of hands and a combined Supernatural P.S. of 45 or Robot P.S. of 75, or the creature must be destroyed (it will fight back) or it can be asked to let go nicely via Lemurian or equivalent Empathic Connection with Animals or Telepathy. However, Squid Locks are surprisingly smart and know who cares for them and feeds them regularly, answering to that person or persons (e.g. jail-keeper) above all others. All attempts to mind control a Squid Lock are made at -6. Furthermore, trying to pry and pull the animal off a prisoner hurts the captive and does 4D6 M.D. damage per tentacle that is pried away due to its hold and suction cup tentacles.

The Squid Lock can be placed on the body of a prisoner to bind the hands and arms, the legs, or both. Can also hold and bind tentacles and multiple limbs as the symbiote has eight tentacles of its own. Oddly enough, some Squid Locks look like squids, others like octopus, but all have a light gray or white body with dark blotches.

Attributes of Note: Has a medium animal intelligence, a P.S. of 30 (Supernatural) but its eight arms and suction cups makes it much more difficult to release its grip than its P.S. would suggest. Swimming speed is 22 (15 mph/24 km or 13 knots).

M.D.C.: 3D6+20

P.P.E.: 3D6+6

Natural Abilities: Drains P.P.E. and S.D.C. at a rate of one point per hour, but also disrupts focus and concentration, disrupting the abilty to cast magic or use psionics. Skill performance is also -30%.

The Squid Lock also Bio-Regenerates 1D4 M.D.C. of its own per minute and the stubborn creature will not release its prisoner or prey until near death – it reaches 1-4 M.D.C. points, at which point it lets go and swims away to hide until it regenerates. Tentacles regrow to full size in 1D4+1 days.

Attacks per Melee: As per the number of free tentacles; that's eight when not locked onto a prisoner or prey.

Bonuses: +1 on initiative, +3 to strike and parry, +2 to dodge, +6 to entangle, +4 to pin and hold, and does 3D6 M.D. from punches and whip attacks with tentacles. Whenever it is attacked while locked on to a prisoner, the Squid Lock is almost always able to fight back with at least two, often 3-4 of its tentacles.

Habitat: Wherever squid and octopus are found, as well as at Lemurian Gardens, cities and outposts.
Allies: Usually only Lemurians, though some friendly psychic races, coastal Psi-Stalkers, Sea Druids and Psi-Druids may also be able to use them.
Enemies: None, per se. Most predators don't like being entangled and preyed upon so they avoid them whenever possible.
Value: 5,000 to 30,000 credits depending on who is using the symbiote and for what purpose; only 10% that price in Lemuria among its military protectors and law enforcers.

Squid Pack

This unusual symbiotic animal was created by Lemurian Biomancer Gene-Mages for speed and underwater travel. While many Lemurians prefer to play and hitch rides from dolphins and whales, or ride a sea animal, the Squid Pack lets those looking for speed and simplicity to travel even faster and for longer periods of time. The Squid Pack is essentially a living underwater jet pack built upon the abilities of squids. The symbiote takes in and outputs great volumes of water to propel itself and its wearer/owner at top underwater speeds. The Squid Pack has four tentacles that it uses to hold onto and carry its rider/owner. It also uses its tentacles when there is no rider, to crawl along the bottom of the ocean at slower speeds and to catch prey; it eats small fish and crustaceans.

The Squid Pack lands on the host's back and wraps its four tentacles around him in a similar way that one might strap into a jet pack. Its position over the central nervous system of the host also allows it to sense the rider's reaction/intentions when trying to swim and assist where it is needed. To engage or activate the

Squid Pack, the user must reach out to the creature with his mind (Empathic Connection with Animals always works, Telepathy and Empathy also work), but one needs to charm and soothe the Squid Pack as one might a horse (use bonuses from M.A.) for maximum control and cooperation. Though the Squid Pack breathes water it can survive out of water for 1D6 hours, provided it remains linked to a host.

Attributes of Note: Has a medium animal intelligence, P.S. 20, P.P. 20, P.E. 20, and a normal swimming speed of 22 (15 mph/24 km or 13 knots).

Speed Bursts: Using its water propulsion system, the Squid Pack can rocket up to 66 (45 mph/72 km or 39 knots) underwater carrying a human-sized passenger; half that speed in Bio-Armor. However, unless the passenger is tough (i.e. has high S.D.C. or is M.D.C.), a more comfortable speed of travel is 20 mph (32 km or 17 knots). Maximum speed can be maintained for 1D4x10+60 minutes.

The Squid Pack can also "jump" out of the water (on its own or with its host), reaching heights of 20 feet (6.1 m) with a host and 30 feet (9.1 m) by itself. However, the act is a one shot deal, and the host must climb or jump back into the water for the Squid Pack to work again.

M.D.C. of the Squid Pack: 4D6+40

P.P.E.: 3D6+9

Natural Abilities (of the animal): The Squid Pack can alter its own coloration to appear as a normal leather backpack or to match the host's skin color, armor or preferred camouflage styling (a mottled color). Nightvision 1,000 feet (305 m), resistant to cold, and the animal has a depth tolerance of 7 miles (11.2 km).

Habitat: Wherever other squid are found, as well as in and around Lemurian outposts, gardens and cities.

Allies: Usually only Lemurians, though some friendly psychic races, Psi-Druids and Sea Druids with the squid or octopus totem are also able to use them should they win the animal's favor.

Enemies: Sea monsters and other predators that feed on large squid and M.D.C. animals as well as hunted by intelligent D-Bees and humans for food; the meat of the Squid Pack is delicious.

Value: Outside of Lemuria, 10,000 to 30,000 credits depending on who is using the symbiote and for what purpose; only 10% that price in Lemuria. As food, 10-20 credits a pound, the latter in Atlantis where the meat is considered a delicacy.

Talisman Shell

These small creatures are reminiscent of clams, snails and mussel shells. They collect and feed on ambient P.P.E. and have been infused with a biological form of the Talisman spell by Biomancer Gene-Mages. Each Talisman Shell is imbued upon creation with the ability to create one simple spell effect. Magical armor, enhanced attributes, stealth, protection and healing are most common, and only spells as high as level seven are possible. Furthermore, only spell invocations and Ocean Magic (not Biomancy or other types of spells) can be stored inside a Talisman Shell. The spell can be activated three times before it is without power. The magic can be restored by leaving the shell on a ley line for 48 hours or at a nexus for 24 hours, or by a mage pumping 200 P.P.E. back into the shell. Otherwise, the living being inside the shell collects enough ambient P.P.E. to cast one spell after 1D6+18 days.

To activate the spell, a simple Telepathic request or request with Empathic Connection with Animals is needed.

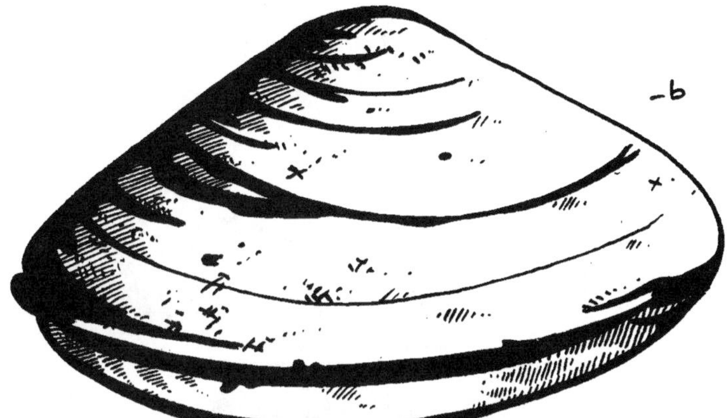

The spell-like ability held by the Talisman Shell functions at fifth level spell potency.

The magical energy stored in the little creatures also transforms them into minor M.D.C. beings with an M.D.C. of 1D4+4. Destroy the M.D.C. and the animal is killed and the Talisman Shell shattered.

Lemurian Transportation

Bubble Pack

The Bubble Pack is a conventional undersea propulsion system that is used by Wilderness Sea Scouts, Lemurian citizens, visiting surface-dwellers, and anyone else who wants a speed boost underwater. Surprisingly, the latter includes Merans seeking greater speed and/or light weapon capabilities. It is "conventional," however, only in the sense that it does not rely on magic. The advanced magneto-hydrodynamic propulsion drive that powers the pack and creates its signature "bubble trail" is an extremely sophisticated system with no moving parts to jam or clog (+10% to resist magic blooms and entanglement in thick seaweed). The Bubble Pack also comes with a mounted ion gun that can be aimed with the user's own vision thanks to a pair of special goggles with a built-in targeting device.

The over-the-shoulder placement of the ion blaster and hands-free operation of the Bubble Pack is ideal for underwater environments where the user has to keep his or her hands free for melee combat, swimming, carrying items and salvage efforts. Bubble Packs are small and compact, and the ion gun can rotate 360 degrees, tilt up and down 45 degrees and fold along the side of the Bubble Pack to minimize its size and drag when not needed. When not in use, the entire unit can be worn like a backpack or in the case of Merans, on the tail. The pack even features running lights that can be turned on or off to make the user more visible in the ocean depths. **Note:** A Bubble Pack worn by a Meran is pictured in use on the cover.

Weight: 14 lbs (6.3 kg).

M.D.C.: 28

Speed: 70 mph (112 km or 60 knots) maximum.

Bonuses: +1 to dodge at speeds above 35 mph (56 km).

Power System: P.P.E. reserve. Holds enough energy to power the pack for two weeks before needing to be recharged with 50 P.P.E.

Ion Blaster: Damage: 2D6+3 M.D. Range: 500 feet (152 m) underwater, 800 feet (244 m) on dry land/in the air. Payload: 50 blasts before needing to be recharged with 100 P.P.E. Recharges in 45 minutes on a ley line, 15 minutes on a nexus, or P.P.E. can be pumped into the device by a mage or anyone with sufficient P.P.E. and the desire to put his own energy reserve into the Bubble Pack.

Cost: 10,000 credits in Lemuria, 10x or more elsewhere.

Serpent Saddle

Not all Lemurians and undersea dwellers are good with animals or magic. Some are perfectly normal people with no control over mystical forces. For these types, there are conventional saddles used to direct sea serpents and other riding animals, as well as to add a little firepower.

Serpent Saddles come with seats for the rider and one passenger. They have built-in cargo compartments that allow the rider to carry personal possessions and salvage, and sport a pair of light ion cannons that turn their riding animal, be it a giant fish or a sea serpent, into a living attack submarine. The saddle was designed with giant rays, sea serpents and sharks in mind, but is adjustable and can fit almost any sea creature that is at least 18 feet (5.5 m) long.

Weight: 314 lbs (141 kg).

M.D.C.: 115

Cargo: 2x2x4 cubic foot (0.6 x 0.6 x 1.2 cubic meter) cargo locker behind the seats.

Power System: P.P.E. Reserve. Holds enough energy to power the two ion cannons for 30 blasts each before needing to be recharged with 160 P.P.E. Recharges in two hours on a ley line, 45 minutes on a nexus, or P.P.E. can be pumped into the device by a mage or anyone with sufficient P.P.E. and the desire to put his own energy reserve into the Serpent Saddle.

Light Ion Cannons (2): The saddle mounts two forward-facing, light ion cannons that the rider can aim and fire from his pilot's seat. The cannons face forward but can be adjusted in a 45 degree up and down arc of fire.

Primary Purpose: Anti-Submarine/Anti-Sea Monster.

Secondary Purpose: Defense.

Range: 1,500 feet (457 m) in all environments.

Mega-Damage: 3D6 M.D. for a single blast, 6D6 M.D. for a dual, simultaneous blast at the same target.

Rate of Fire: Each single blast or dual blast counts as one melee attack/action of the pilot.

Payload: 30 blasts per each cannon; costs 160 P.P.E. to bring both up to a full payload.

Cost: 18,000 credits in Lemuria, 10x or more elsewhere.

Lemurian Symbiotic Combat Vehicles

Features Common to Lemurian Symbiote Vehicles

All Are Made of Stone: All Lemurian combat vessels are made of stone, via Stone Magic and the help of the Symbiote Conduit. The symbiote also serves as the magic power source and onboard computer.

Symbiote Conduits: Living P.P.E. batteries called Symbiote Conduits are the power source for Lemurian combat vehicles. These symbiotes interact with the pilot/crew/passengers using psychic communication and also employ psychic powers as the vehicle's sensors. This includes the ability to "read" its pilot and tell whether he is in physical or mental distress and able to fly or not. This also means the vessel tends to support the decisions and feelings of its "partner" rather than outside commands, and never overrides him.

The Symbiote Conduit is a living component of the combat vehicle and might be thought of as a living computer and co-pilot. As such, it helps pilot the vehicle and imparts a basic piloting ability even if the person at the helm has no piloting skill whatsoever. Likewise, if the pilot is knocked unconscious or the symbiote needs to take over for some reason, it can operate the vehicle by itself at the following level of proficiency: Three attacks per melee round, no combat bonuses, and has the equivalent piloting skill at 60%. (Those without training in piloting Lemurian combat vehicles do so with the same 60% base ability.) The symbiote can also return to the Lemurian camp, base or city it departed from, patrol a preplanned route or wait until it is called to action.

The symbiote recognizes its pilot and designated passengers, friendly Lemurians and their allies, and locks anyone else out of the vehicle to prevent theft or sabotage. The symbiote does not respond to commands from anyone who has managed to force their way into the cockpit, unless the symbiote can be dominated via mind control or possession.

The living Symbiote Conduit can survive indefinitely in or out of the water (breathes both air and water), but is a permanent part of the vehicle. It can fill the crew compartment with filtered air, recycle and purify air or bring filtered, clean water into the pilot compartment depending on what its pilot and passengers prefer to breathe. In the event that the craft is taken into a hostile environment (such as outer space, polluted waters, etc.), the symbiote's magic can sustain itself and a breathable atmosphere for the pilot and passenger for an indefinite amount of time (the pilot and passenger would die of starvation and dehydration before running out of air). The outer shell of the symbiote is the stone of the vehicle itself. The magical force field provides additional protection for the symbiote and those inside, including radiation and the ravages of space and ocean depths.

Heal Outer Hull and Self: Any damage sustained by the stone vessel can be "healed" by the symbiote inside the vessel via its limited knowledge of Stone Magic. To do so, the symbiote must *stop* the vessel and hover or float stationary, or land or go to rest on the sea floor, extend one of its tendrils and remold the damaged stone shell. Such repairs restore 2D6 or 3D6 M.D.C. per melee round depending on the type of vessel. The symbiote itself regenerates at a rate of 2D6 or 3D6 M.D.C. per 24 hours (depending on vessel type), though magical healing can also be used to the same effect as on any living being.

Force Fields: Most Lemurian combat vehicles are equipped with a magic force field to offer additional protection. If the force field should be reduced to zero M.D.C. it can only be recharged along a ley line, nexus point or stone pyramid. Force fields require three hours at a ley line to recharge or an hour and a half at a nexus or stone pyramid. A depleted force field remains out of commission until it is fully recharged. In the alternative, a mage or being with sufficient P.P.E. can channel his own energy into the force field, restoring it at the cost of two P.P.E. per one Mega-Damage point.

The Lemurian Pilot of Combat Vehicles: Any Lemurian with the Symbiote Conduit Combat Vehicle skill, but most of the time, that's a *Sea Sentinel*.

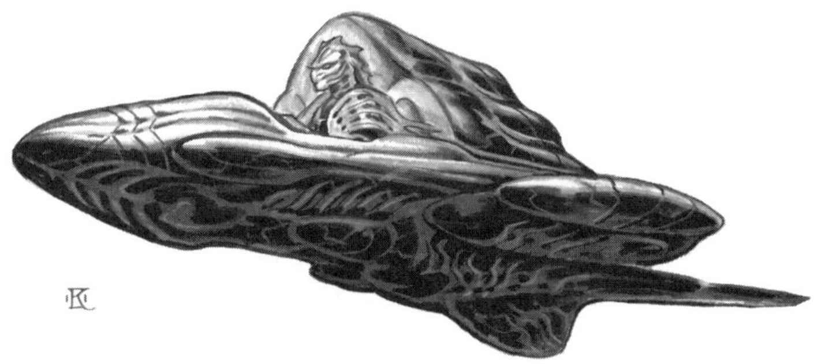

Sea Dart Interceptor

Submarine-Aircraft Fighter-Interceptor

The design of the Sea Dart Interceptor is a uniquely Lemurian amalgamation of stone magic and Biomancy. The hull of the ship is crafted by stone magic that uses a special variation of lodestone polished to a near perfect smoothness. The interior housing is a Biomancy symbiote that is essentially a living component of the ship. It is an all-purpose water and air vehicle that functions as a light attack sub and aerial interceptor, used in search and rescue operations, scouting and exploration, escort and defense. It is designed specifically for Lemuria's *Sea Sentinels,* who love high speed and maneuverability. Like all Lemurian craft, the Sea Dart Interceptor can fly in the air, hover, ride the surface of water and rocket through deep water. They are fast and maneuverable underwater and in the air, able to make tight and sharp turns most surface aircraft cannot perform. Furthermore, their small size and low profile makes them difficult to identify as fighters; they tend to read as missiles. Deployed in small "wings" of 3-6 the Lemurians call "tridents," Sea Dart Interceptors are especially effective in air to ship and underwater combat, where they are able to tear apart larger, slower vessels and sea monsters with high-speed hit and run attacks.

Sea Dart Interceptors are powered by basic symbiotes, using psionic powers as sensors and relying on Stone Magic to self-repair the craft. They are simpler versions of the larger, more sophisticated stone vehicles like the *Cloud Shell* and *Cloud Wind.*

All floating cities have many wings of Sea Dart Interceptors and they are also carried by the large Lemurian submarines to perform advance scouting, reconnaissance, pursuit and defense of the larger vessel.

Class: Flying Submersible Fighter-Interceptor.

Crew: One. There is no room for a passenger.

M.D.C. by Location:

Jet Thrusters (2, back) – 100 each

Force Field – 80

* Pilot Compartment/Symbiote – 6D6+30

** Main Body – 227

* The symbiote is inside the vehicle and cannot be targeted until the M.D.C. of the main body and the force field are both destroyed. The only exception is if the vessel opens up to pick up or release the pilot, at which point it can be struck with a "Called Shot." Destroying the symbiote renders the vehicle inoperable and a new symbiote must be implanted to make it work again.

** Depleting the M.D.C. of the main body shuts the vehicle down completely, making it useless. Those in the air plummet to earth, those underwater sink to the bottom of the sea/ocean. If the rear thrusters are destroyed, reduce speed by 60%, but the vehicle can still fly and propel itself through water.

Speed:

Land: None.

Flying: Mach 3 (2,310 mph/3,696 km) is maximum speed. The built-in TK Projectors allow the air-sub to hover and take off and land vertically.

Surface Speed: The Sea Dart can fly within 3 feet (0.9 m) of the ground or water surface at speeds up to Mach 1 (770 mph/1.232 km).

Water Surface: 120 mph (192 km) on the water's surface.

Underwater: 100 mph (160 km) maximum.

Maximum Depth Tolerance: 5 miles (8 km).

Statistical Data:

Height: 6 feet (1.8 m).

Width: 6.5 feet (2 m).

Length: 11 feet (3.3 m).

Weight: 2 tons.

Cargo: Minimal; room for a pistol, rifle and a basic survival kit.

Power System: Sea Dart Symbiotic Conduit: 100 year life span. Must spend at least three hours charging on a ley line (or one hour on a nexus or stone pyramid) every seven days or the ship is unable to use its weapons, recharge torpedoes, and is limited to a speed of 300 mph (480 km) in the air, 40 mph (64 km) on the water's surface and 30 mph (48 km) underwater.

Cost: 3 million credits to raise the symbiote and prepare the lodestone.

Weapon Systems:

1. Ionic Charge Imbalancer: Based on the weapons used by the larger Cloud Shell and Cloud Wind, the ionic charge imbalancer uses the Sea Dart Interceptor's magneto-hydrodynamic drive to channel ion pulses at targets. The imbalancer can be fired 360 degrees in any direction with no need to reorient the interceptor itself.

Primary Purpose: Assault.

Secondary Purpose: Anti-Aircraft.

Range: 1,500 feet (457 m) in all environments; double the range when on or within one mile (1.6 km) of a ley line or nexus point.

Mega-Damage: 5D6 M.D. per blast.

Rate of Fire: Each blast counts as one melee attack/action.

Payload: Effectively unlimited as long as the vessel is charged.

2. Symbiotic Living Torpedoes: Fish-like creatures that live and hibernate inside the vehicle and function as "living torpedoes." They are linked to the ship and the Sea Sentinel pilot, and follow his orders to the letter. They launch from the bottom of the vessel, activate a magical Bio-Energy Field and rocket through the water to strike enemy vessels with damaging force and magic energy. The Bio-Energy Field generated by these "Living Torpedoes" protects the fish from harm, and enables them to swim back to Sea Dart that fired them. However, as a last resort, the Living Torpedoes can commit suicide by detonating their reserve of Bio-Energy and doing more damage. The Living Torpedoes are capable of attacking only targets in and under water, but each can be given a specific target to attack or a Sea Sentinel can communicate and redirect the torpedoes (give them a new target) as he desires.

Bonuses and Stats for Living Torpedoes:

- Top speed of 120 mph (192 km/104 knots).
- The fish/torpedo has 25 M.D.C. Destroying its M.D.C. kills it and stops the attack, but it is a small, fast target able to dodge incoming attacks; +5 to automatic dodge any attacks leveled against it.
- Chase designated target. Being alive, this Biomancy "smart" torpedo can be assigned to target/attack a specific target among several and to "chase" it down for up to 4 miles (6.4 km); +3 to strike. (8 miles/12.8 km to return to their sub.)
- Each Living Torpedo has two attacks before needing to return to its Sea Dart to regenerate Bio-Energy for another attack (takes one minute/4 melee rounds to recharge).
- Damage (below) can be regulated to inflict a few different amounts.
- Unless told to commit suicide and detonate, Living Torpedoes automatically return to their designated vessel. This enables the Lemurians to reuse the same torpedoes many, many times. However, an enemy can use them to follow the torpedoes back to the location of the ship. Yet, these are living beings and they will take action to Prowl (50%) and lose anyone trying to tail them. Do not register on sonar/radar systems; must be tailed visually.

Primary Purpose: Anti-Ship.

Secondary Purpose: Anti-Submarine/Anti-Sea Monster.

Range: Living Torpedoes can travel roughly 4,000 feet (1,219 m) per melee round. Half this speed to return to the ship to recharge and attack again.

Mega-Damage: 2D6 M.D. for a warning shot, 4D6 M.D. for a full strength attack, and 1D4x10+2 M.D. for power attacks but it counts as both of the Living Torpedo's attacks.

In the event that a Living Torpedo is asked to commit suicide (01-90% likelihood the torpedo complies), the ensuing explosion of magic energy does 2D4x10 M.D. to the target, and the torpedo is destroyed. **Note:** Most Lemurian pilots ask their torpedoes to sacrifice themselves only when the situation demands it. Torpedoes do double damage to the undead due to the Bio-Energy.

Rate of Fire: Launching a Living Torpedo counts as one of the pilot's melee attacks/actions. After that, the creature, itself, has two attacks of its own. When those two attacks are finished, the Living Torpedo returns to its designated attack vessel. Once back on board, spent torpedoes are recharged with Bio-Energy (takes one

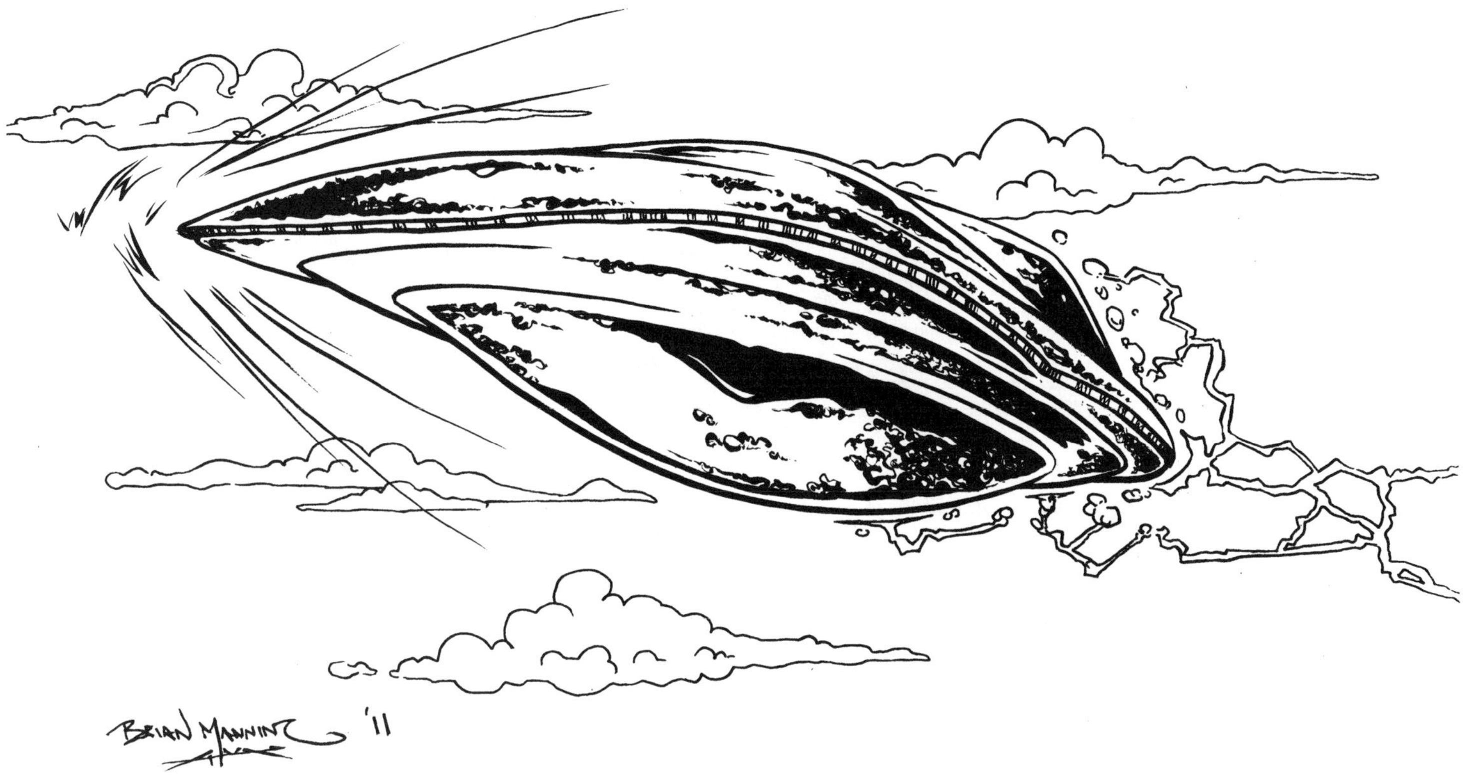

minute/four melee rounds) before being ready to attack again. This means the same Living Torpedoes can be used again and again, for years. If the vessel is not readily available, the "fish" will swim around and wait for 1D4+2 days to be retrieved, before swimming away to live an ordinary life.

Payload: Two, re-useable, Living Torpedoes.

3. **Sea Dart Symbiote and Repairs:** Any damage sustained by the interceptor can be "healed" by the symbiote inside the vessel via its limited knowledge of Stone Magic. To do so, the symbiote must *stop* the vessel (hover stationary or land), extend one of its tendrils and remold the damaged stone shell. It can repair 2D6 M.D.C. per melee round. The symbiote itself heals 2D6 M.D.C. per 24 hours, though magical healing can also be used.
4. **Sensor System Note:** The Sea Dart Interceptor does not use normal sensory devices. Instead, the symbiote relies on psychic powers for sensory input and has the following psychic abilities used as sensors: Empathy (4), Presence Sense (4), See the Invisible (4), Sense Dimensional Anomaly (4), Sense Time (2), Sixth Sense (2) and Telepathy (4).

Base I.S.P.: 1D6x10+33.

Range: 1,000 feet (305 m); double along ley lines.

Cloud Shell

Submarine-Aircraft Fighter

This sleek, almond-shaped craft is the pinnacle of Lemurian ingenuity. The small, one-man flying submersible is the final version of over a century of research and development into high speed and extreme maneuverability. In flight and underwater, it is virtually silent, and the technology proven in this series of craft was carried over into the Sea Dart, Cloud Wind Fighter-Bomber-Transport and the Wind Seer Drone.

The design of the Cloud Shell is a Lemurian amalgamation of Stone Magic and Biomancy. It is similar in design to a clam or oyster, with the top "lid" opening like a clam shell along one side to let the pilot and passengers enter. The hull of the ship is crafted by Stone Magic that uses a special variation of lodestone. The interior housing is a Biomancy created Symbiote Conduit that is essentially a living component of the ship. The symbiote can function on its own, performing basic tasks or following orders given to it by the pilot.

As a combat vehicle it can cut through water or air like a rocket with its sleek "arrowhead" shape and smooth, wingless exterior reducing air and drag resistance. It can also stop on a dime, hover, make VTOL (Vertical Take-Offs and Landings), and dive into water at full speed. After the Sea Dart Interceptor, this is the second favorite combat vehicle of the Sea Sentinels.

Model Type: Ao Pua "Cloud Shell."

Class: Flying Submersible Fighter-Interceptor.

Crew: One. There is room for three human-sized passengers behind the pilot or two in Bio-Armor, but the area is tight and will be uncomfortable for long trips.

M.D.C. by Location:

Stonecaster/Nose of the Vessel – 180

* Pilot Compartment/Symbiote – 6D6+50

Force Field – 120

** Main Body – 300

* The symbiote is inside the vehicle and cannot be targeted until the M.D.C. of the main body and the force field are both destroyed. The only exception is if the vessel opens up to pick up a passenger or to pick up or release the pilot, at which point it can be struck with a "Called Shot." Destroying the symbiote renders the vehicle inoperable and a new symbiote must be implanted to make it work again.

** Depleting the M.D.C. of the main body shuts the vehicle down completely, making it useless. Those in the air fall to the ground, those underwater sink to the bottom.

Speed:

Land: Not possible.

Flying: Mach 2 (1,540 mph/2,464 km). TK Projectors allow the air-sub to hover and take off or land vertically.

Water Surface: The Cloud Shell can fly within 3 feet (0.9 m) of the ground or water surface at up to 500 mph (800 km).

Underwater: 100 mph (160 km or 86 knots) maximum.

Maximum Depth Tolerance: 5 miles (8 km).

Statistical Data:

Height: 8 feet (2.4 m).

Width: 10 feet (3 m).

Length: 32 feet (9.8 m).

Weight: 12 tons.

Cargo: Without a passenger there is approximately a 4x6x6 foot (1.2 x 1.8 x 1.8 meter) space behind the pilot's seat for cargo.

Power System: Cloud Shell Symbiotic Conduit: 100 year life span. Must spend at least three hours charging on a ley line (or one hour and a half on a nexus or stone pyramid) every seven days. Otherwise, the ship is unable to use its weapons or recharge torpedoes, and is limited to a speed of 300 mph (480 km) in the air, 40 mph (64 km) on the water's surface and 30 mph (48 km) underwater.

Cost: 7 million credits to raise the symbiote and prepare the lodestone. However, such a vessel would be priceless to interests like the Federation of Magic, Psyscape or Lazlo.

Weapon Systems:

1. **Stonecaster Gun (Nose Weapon):** The Cloud Shell's primary long-range weapon uses Stone Magic to generate and fire heavy rock chips and stone fragments. Set in a fixed forward firing position, the Stonecaster nose gun works well in both aerial dogfights and underwater skirmishes.

Primary Purpose: Anti-Submarine/Anti-Sea Monster.

Secondary Purpose: Anti-Ship.

Range: 4,000 feet (1,219 m), half underwater.

Mega-Damage: Sedimentary: 4D6 M.D. to everything within an 8 foot (2.4 m) blast radius. Igneous: 5D6 M.D. on impact and 2D6 M.D. for the next 1D4 melee rounds. Metamorphic: 1D4x10+4 M.D.

Rate of Fire: Each shot counts as one melee attack.

Payload: 60 rounds. The weapon magically regenerates ammunition at a rate of two rounds per hour. Double the payload (and rate of regeneration) when inside the borders of a ley line triangle such as the Demon Sea (Bermuda Triangle), and quadruple payload on a ley line, at a nexus or at a Lemurian stone pyramid.

2. **Ionic Charge Imbalancer:** The Cloud Shell propels itself by magnetically pushing/pulling ionized fluids or gases past it as well as controlling direction by alternating which side of the craft produces the ionized molecules and which direction the magnets pull. This ionizing effect can be bumped up in power to shoot an ionized stream – essentially a lightning bolt – 360 degrees in any direction around the craft with no need to reorient the vessel itself.

Primary Purpose: Assault.

Secondary Purpose: Anti-Aircraft.

Range: 1,500 feet (457 m) in all environments; double the range when on or within one mile of a ley line or nexus point.

Mega-Damage: 1D4x10 M.D. per blast.

Rate of Fire: Each blast counts as one melee attack/action.

Payload: Effectively unlimited as long as the vessel is charged.

3. **Symbiotic Living Torpedoes:** Same as the *Sea Dart Interceptor*, except as follows.

Rate of Fire: One at a time or in volleys of two or four. Launching one or a volley of Living Torpedoes counts as one of the pilot's melee attacks.

Payload: Six re-useable, Living Torpedoes.

4. **Cloud Shell Symbiote and Repairs:** Any damage sustained by the vessel can be "healed" by the symbiote inside the vessel via its limited knowledge of Stone Magic. To do so, the symbiote must *stop* the vessel (hover or float stationary, on land or the sea floor), extend one of its tendrils and remold the damaged stone shell. It can repair 2D6 M.D.C. per melee round. The symbiote itself heals 3D6 M.D.C. per 24 hours, though magical healing can also be used.

5. **Sensor System Note:** Same as the Sea Dart Interceptor, which relies on psychic powers for sensory input, and has the following abilities: Empathy (4), Presence Sense (4), See the Invisible (4), Sense Dimensional Anomaly (4), Sense Time (2), Sixth Sense (2) and Telepathy (4).

Base I.S.P.: 2D4x10+28

Range: 1,000 feet (305 m); double along ley lines.

Cloud Wind

Flying Submersible Transport

The Cloud Wind is a troop and cargo transport combat vehicle, designed with the same magic and symbiotic technology as the Sea Dart and Cloud Shell. It resembles a giant, mechanical, tail-less manta ray made of stone. It functions using the magnetohydrodynamic propulsion system but can position and balance the magnetic field, creating openings to allow small vehicles and troops to enter or exit the craft while the propulsion system is engaged. This makes the Cloud Wind an ideal troop transport (can disembark when landed or dive out into the air or water while the vessel is moving), Bio-Armor carrier, bomber and cargo hauler. Along with similar weapon systems to the Cloud Shell, it can open up parts of its ionic flow to allow probes, missiles and torpedoes to be launched.

One popular tactic is to turn off the propulsion system and lie on the ocean bottom in silt, using the ship as a portable command post, observation point or forward base of operations. In this capacity, it also makes for a good field hospital or base for scientific research and study. Cloud Winds can also get into and out of areas that large vessels like Wave Shadow submarines would find impassable, including large inland bodies of water.

Model Type: Ao Maani "Cloud Wind."

Class: Flying Submersible Transport.

Crew: Six; captain, communication officer (typically a Mind Melter or other telepath), tactical officer or spell caster, pilot, co-pilot and an advisor (Biomancer, Sea Inquisitor, second Mind Melter, Scout, etc.), but can be operated by a crew of as few as three. **Note:** At least half the members of a full crew, if not all,

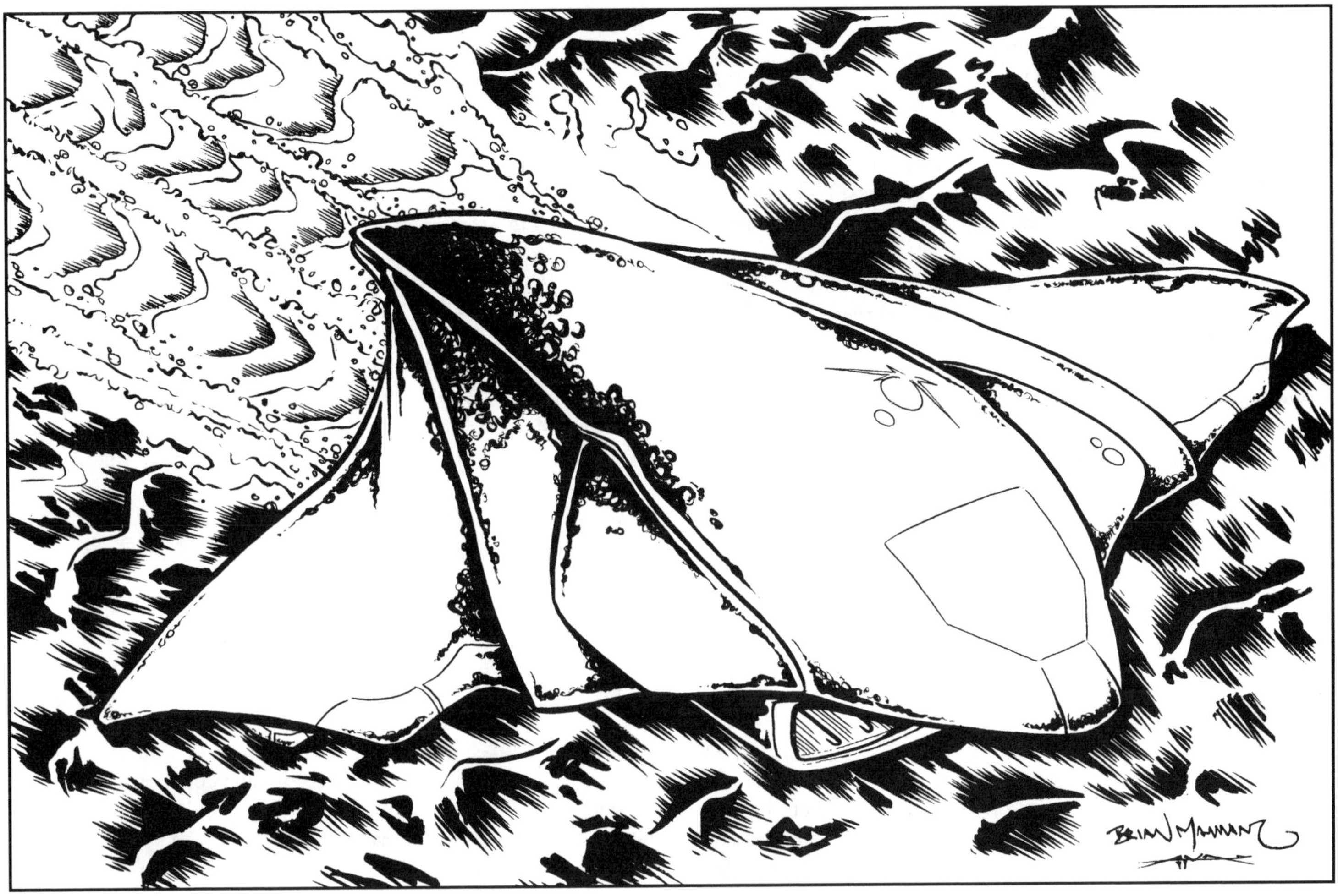

will be clad in Bio-Armor of one type or another which offers additional combat capabilities.

M.D.C. by Location:

Front Launch Bay Door – 300

Rear Cargo Door – 225

Wings (2; contains torpedoes and missiles) – 250 each

* Symbiote – 1D6x10+40

Force Field – 200

** Main Body – 920

* The symbiote is inside the vehicle and cannot be targeted until the M.D.C. of the main body and the force field are both destroyed. The only exception is if the vessel opens up to pick up a passenger or to pick up or release the pilot, at which point it can be struck with a "Called Shot." Destroying the symbiote renders the vehicle inoperable and a new symbiote must be implanted to make it work again.

** Depleting the M.D.C. of the main body shuts the vehicle down completely, making it useless. Those in the air fall to the ground, those underwater sink to the bottom.

Speed:

Land: Not possible.

Flying: Mach 2 (1,540 mph/2,464 km). TK Projectors allow the air-sub to hover and take off or land vertically.

Water Surface: The Cloud Wind can fly within 15 feet (4.6 m) off the ground or water surface at up to 500 mph (800 km).

Underwater: 80 mph (128 km or 69 knots) maximum.

Maximum Depth Tolerance: 5 miles (8 km).

Statistical Data:

Height: 30 feet (9.1 m).

Width: 160 feet (48 m).

Length: 120 feet (36 m).

Weight: 50 tons.

Cargo: Besides basic living quarters for the crew (6 rooms), there are bunk-bed style dormitories for up to 12 passengers in the cargo hold. There is also a small mess hall (seats five at a time), medical station and armory. There is also a cargo bay which can be used to house either a Serpent Hunter and sea serpent, 4 Wind Seer drones, 2 Scuttler tanks or 2 Sea Dart Interceptors, additional cargo or an extra 24 passengers or troops (18 if clad in heavy Bio-Armor).

Power System: Cloud Wind Symbiotic Conduit: 100 year life span. Must spend at least 24 hours charging on a ley line (12 hours on a nexus or stone pyramid) every seven days. Otherwise, the ship is unable to use its weapons or recharge torpedoes, and is limited to a speed of 100 mph (160 km) in the air, 30 mph (48 km) on the water's surface and underwater.

Cost: 30 million credits to raise the symbiote and prepare the lodestone.

Weapon Systems:

1. **Ionic Charge Imbalancer:** The Cloud Wind has a larger and more powerful propulsion system than the Cloud Shell, and can use it to make stronger ionic charges for use as a weapon. Essentially fires lightning bolts 360 degrees in any direction around the craft with no need to reorient the vessel itself.

Primary Purpose: Assault.
Secondary Purpose: Anti-Aircraft.
Range: 1,500 feet (457 m) in all environments; double the range when on or within one mile (1.6 km) of a ley line or nexus point.
Mega-Damage: 1D6x10 M.D. per blast.
Rate of Fire: Each blast counts as one melee attack.
Payload: Effectively unlimited as long as the vessel is charged.

2. Symbiotic Living Torpedoes: Same as the *Sea Dart Interceptor*, except as follows.

Rate of Fire: One at a time or in volleys of two or four. Launching one or a volley of Living Torpedoes counts as one of the pilot's melee attacks.
Payload: 12 re-useable, Living Torpedoes.

3. Mini-Missile Launchers (2): Concealed in each wing is a conventional, human-tech mini-missile launcher for water surface to air, air to land and air to air strikes.

Primary Purpose: Anti-Aircraft/Flyers.
Secondary Purpose: Anti-Missile and Defense.
Range: One mile (1.6 km).
Mega-Damage: Varies with missile type, but most pilots favor plasma missiles which inflict 1D6x10 M.D. to a 15 foot (4.6 m) radius.
Rate of Fire: One at a time or in volleys of 2, 4, 6 or 8.
Payload: 36 total mini-missiles, 16 in each wing.

4. Seaweed Chaff: Transports are larger targets than fighters and carry larger crews and numbers of troops inside. In order to provide them with a better defense against torpedoes and troops, the vessel can release a cloud of seaweed that fills a 60 foot (18.3 m) spherical diameter. This cloud of seaweed can then be increased in size by the Biomancer onboard casting the *Seaweed Bloom* spell. Even without the increased "bloom," any swimmer coming in contact with the cloud suffers the same penalties as the Seaweed Bloom spell (impaired speed and vision, etc.) and motorized vessels are likely to have their propellers entangled and stalled. Furthermore, there is 01-70% chance that any mini-, short-, medium- or long-range torpedo will detonate or lose its target lock when traveling through the mass of weeds. If one torpedo in a volley detonates, there is a 01-90% likelihood ALL the others in the volley explode prematurely as well. (If not, then only 1D4x10% of the torpedoes explode and the rest keep going.) Of course, Seaweed Chaff only works underwater or on the water's surface. Payload: 8 seaweed bundles.

5. Troops: The troops carried by the Cloud Wind can be released, even as the vehicle is moving (at a reasonable disembarkment speed), to join a fight or launch an attack.

6. Cloud Wind Symbiote and Repairs: Any damage sustained by the vessel can be "healed" by the symbiote inside the vessel via its limited knowledge of Stone Magic. To do so, the symbiote must *stop* the vessel (hover or float stationary, on land or the sea floor), extend one of its tendrils and remold the damaged stone shell. It can repair 3D6 M.D.C. per melee round. The Symbiote itself heals 3D6 M.D.C. per 24 hours, though magical healing can also be used.

7. Sensor System Note: Same as the Sea Dart Interceptor, which relies on psychic powers for sensory input, and has the following abilities: Empathy (4), Presence Sense (4), See the Invisible (4), Sense Dimensional Anomaly (4), Sense Time (2), Sixth Sense (2) and Telepathy (4) – plus Read Dimensional Portal (6).

Base I.S.P.: 2D4x10+40
Range: 1,000 feet (305 m); double along ley lines.

Wave Shadow Submarine

The Wave Shadow is Lemuria's most common class of submarine, a full-size underwater submarine that can deploy Serpent Riders, small vehicles and units of armored soldiers. Wave Shadows are the command centers for military operations, silent undersea platforms that bring heavy weapons to bear and can be used against the largest enemy ships and sea monsters.

Wave Shadows are built like other Lemurian subs, using a specially-grown Symbiote Conduit to power and help construct the shell of enchanted stone. Unlike other vessels, however, the Wave Shadow is powered by several Symbiote Conduits that work together and function redundantly in case one or more are destroyed. With such a big ship, the shell construction process takes almost a year, even with three symbiotes working in tandem.

These submarines lurk below the surface, running short and long-duration patrols around Lemurian cities, gardens and oceans around the world. Air-subs and smaller craft stage themselves out of the Wave Shadows and use them as mobile field bases. A single Wave Shadow carries enough troops and vehicles to launch raids and punitive expeditions all by itself; several of the ships working together constitutes a fleet of considerable power.

The Wave Shadow sub looks like a giant Cloud Shell air-sub with a large, low profile cannon mounted in the front, forward section of the ship, and two smaller cannons behind it.

Class: All-Purpose Combat Submarine – deep sea patrols, long-range reconnaissance, rescue, troop transport, cargo transport, defense and assault.

Crew: 12; captain, second officer, communications officer, sensor operator, 2 engineers, 4 gunners and two specialists (Biomancer, Sea Inquisitor, Mind Melter, Scout, etc.).

Combat Vehicle Standard Complement: 4 Cloud Shell air-subs, 8-10 Sea Dart Interceptors, 6 Scuttler Tanks, 2 Cloud Wind transports and 6 Wind Seer drones. May be reduced by half to two thirds when delivering cargo or on a mission to rescue a large number of people in need.

Troops, Standard Compliment: Two platoons of infantry (80 warriors in light to medium Bio-Armor), one heavy combat squad (10 warriors in heavy Bio-Armor), one reconnaissance squad (a mix of Scouts, Biomancers and other mages and/or psychics) and 1-4 Serpent Hunters and their sea serpent riding animals. The Serpent Hunters may be replaced by a platoon of medical personnel and a platoon of volunteers for humanitarian rescue missions.

M.D.C. by Location:

Main Cannon (1) – 180
Stonecasters (2) – 135 each
* Pilot Compartment/Symbiotes (3) – 6D6+60
Force Field (Main Body) – 200
** Main Body: Forward Section – 470
** Main Body: Mid-Section – 440
** Main Body: Rear Section – 460

* A Symbiote Conduit is inside each of the main sections of the submarine. They cannot be targeted until the M.D.C. of the main body for that section and the force field are both de-

stroyed. At which point it can be struck with a "Called Shot." Destroying the symbiote renders that section of the vehicle inoperable and a new symbiote must be implanted to make it work again.

** Depleting the M.D.C. of the main body of the *forward section* knocks out the three stonecasters and torpedo launchers.

Depleting the M.D.C. of the *mid-section* knocks out the ion weapon and dumps 2D4x10% of the troops and cargo carried by the sub into the sea. Also reduce speed by 30%.

Depleting the M.D.C. of the *rear section* reduces speed by 50%.

Depleting ALL M.D.C. of each section completely destroys the submarine, sending it sinking to the bottom.

Speed:

Land: Not possible.

Flying: Not possible.

Water Surface: 40 mph (64 km).

Underwater: 60 mph (96 km) maximum.

Maximum Depth Tolerance: 5 miles (8 km).

Statistical Data:

Height: 42 feet (12.8 m).

Width: 100 feet (30.5 m).

Length: 340 feet (103 m).

Weight: 2,200 tons.

Cargo: Has room for up to 500 tons of cargo, sea serpents and secondary vehicles.

Power System: Cloud Wind Symbiotic Conduit: 100 year life span. Must spend at least 48 hours charging on a ley line (24 hours on a nexus or stone pyramid) every ten days. Otherwise, the ship is unable to use its weapons, recharge torpedoes, and is limited to a speed of 30 mph (48 km) on the water's surface and underwater. The Wave Shadow has three symbiotes within it that work as a team. All three must be destroyed to shut down the sub.

Cost: 70-80 million credits to raise the symbiotes and prepare the lodestone.

Weapon Systems:

1. Main Gun Stonecaster Cannon (1): An oversized version of the Stonecaster Cannon fires enchanted mini-boulders that deal significant damage to enemy sea monsters, submarines and surface ships. It is mounted on a turret that can rotate 360 degrees and has a 90 degree up and down arc of fire.

Primary Purpose: Anti-Ship.

Secondary Purpose: Anti-Submarine/Anti-Sea Monster.

Range: 4,000 feet (1,219 m), half underwater.

Mega-Damage: Sedimentary: 6D6 M.D. to everything within a 20 foot (6.1 m) blast radius. Igneous: 1D6x10 M.D. on impact and 3D6 M.D. additional for the next 1D4 melee rounds. Metamorphic: 2D6x10 M.D.

Rate of Fire: Each shot counts as one melee attack/action of the dedicated gunner operating it (typically 4-5 attacks per melee round).

Payload: 100 shells. The weapon magically regenerates ammunition at a rate of two rounds per hour. Double the payload (and rate of regeneration) when inside the borders of a ley line triangle such as the *Demon Sea* (Bermuda Triangle), and triple the payload on a ley line, at a nexus or at a Lemurian stone pyramid.

2. Standard Stonecaster Cannons (2): The Wave Shadow's secondary guns are smaller stonecasters. The cannons can create different types of rock, useful against a wide array of targets. Each cannon has a dedicated gunner, can rotate 360 degrees and has a 45 degree up and down arc of fire.

Primary Purpose: Anti-Submarine/Anti-Sea Monster.

Secondary Purpose: Anti-Ship.

Range: 4,000 feet (1,219 m), half underwater.

Mega-Damage: Sedimentary: 5D6 M.D. to everything within an 8 foot (2.4 m) blast radius. Igneous: 1D4x10 M.D. on impact and 2D6 M.D. additional for the next 1D4 melee rounds. Metamorphic: 2D4x10 M.D.

Rate of Fire: Each shot counts as one melee attack/action.

Payload: 100 rounds each. The weapons magically regenerate ammunition at a rate of two rounds per hour. Double the payload (and rate of regeneration) when inside the borders of a ley line triangle such as the *Demon Sea* (Bermuda Triangle), and triple the payload on a ley line, at a nexus or at a Lemurian stone pyramid.

3. Symbiotic Living Torpedoes: Same as the *Sea Dart Interceptor*, except as follows. Fired by the captain or second officer.

Rate of Fire: One at a time or in volleys of two or four. Launching one or a volley of Living Torpedoes counts as one of the pilot's melee attacks.

Payload: 16 total; eight re-useable, Living Torpedoes in the launcher on each side of the sub.

4. Underwater Proximity Ionic Charge Imbalancer: The Wave Shadow can redirect its huge magneto-hydrodynamic drive to unleash torrents of ion energy upon nearby opponents. Small subs that try to latch onto the Wave Shadow and anyone trying to board her are in real trouble from this close-range defensive weapon system.

Primary Purpose: Defense.

Secondary Purpose: Anti-Submarine/Anti-Sea Monster.

Range: 100 feet (30.5 m). Double on a ley line.

Mega-Damage: 5D6 M.D. per discharge.

Rate of Fire: Each blast/discharge counts as one melee attack of its dedicated gunner.

Payload: Effectively unlimited as long as the vessel is charged.

5. Seaweed Chaff: Same enchanted seaweed chaff system as the Cloud Wind.

Payload: 8 seaweed bundles.

6. Troops: The troops carried by the sub can be released, even as the vehicle is moving (at a reasonable disembarkment speed), to join a fight or launch an attack.

7. Shadow Wave Symbiotes and Repairs: Any damage sustained by the vessel can be "healed" by section via the symbiote located in that specific section of the ship. To do so, the symbiote must *slow* the vessel to no more than 10 mph (16 km) or float stationary or settle on the sea floor, extend one of its tendrils and remold the damaged stone shell. It can repair 3D6 M.D.C. per melee round. The symbiote itself heals 3D6 M.D.C. per 24 hours, though magical healing can also be used.

8. Sensor System Note: Same as the Sea Dart Interceptor, which relies on psychic powers for sensory input, and has the following abilities: Empathy (4), Presence Sense (4), See the Invisible (4), Sense Dimensional Anomaly (4), Sense Time (2), Sixth Sense (2) and Telepathy (4) – plus Read Dimensional Portal (6).

Base I.S.P.: 2D4x10+40

Range: 1,000 feet (305 m); double along ley lines.

Scuttler Submersible Tank

Amphibious Assault Armored Vehicle

Used for defending cities, supporting raids and launching amphibious assaults against shorelines, Scuttlers are compact submarines used more like tanks than the traditional sub. Their heavy armor and slow speed means they must be carried aboard Cloud Wind aircraft or Wave Shadow submarines and deployed directly into battle. This necessity insures that when Scuttlers are seen the Lemurians are on the offensive or a city is close by.

For propulsion, Scuttlers do not use the complex and expensive magneto-hydrodynamic drives of other Lemurian craft. Instead, they have a "propulsion skirt" that rings the vehicle, providing forward momentum in the same way a cuttlefish swims, by rippling and pushing water behind the tank.

Scuttlers are amphibious, and can crawl right up out of the sea to mount attacks inland. Out of the water, their propulsion skirt creates a cushion of air below the vehicle and it operates just like a hover tank.

Class: Submersible Amphibious Armored Vehicle.

Crew: One, with room for one gunner and two passengers/troops.

M.D.C. by Location:

* Stone Cannon – 135
** Pilot Compartment/Symbiote – 6D6+50
Force Field – 120
*** Main Body – 320

* A single asterisk indicates a small and difficult target to strike, requiring the attacker to make a "Called Shot", but even then the attacker is -3 to strike.

** The symbiote is inside the vehicle and cannot be targeted until the M.D.C. of the main body and the force field are both destroyed. The only exception is if the vessel opens up to pick up a passenger or to pick up or release the pilot, at which point it can be struck with a "Called Shot." Destroying the symbiote renders the vehicle inoperable and a new symbiote must be implanted to make it work again.

*** Depleting the M.D.C. of the main body shuts the vehicle down completely, making it useless. Those on land grind to a dead stop, those underwater sink to the bottom.

Speed:

Land: 60 mph (96 km).

Flying: Not possible.

Water Surface: 60 mph (96 km).

Underwater: 35 mph (56 km).

Maximum Depth Tolerance: 4 miles (6.4 km).

Statistical Data:

Height: 8 feet (2.4 m).

Width: 10 feet (3 m).

Length: 22 feet (6.7 m).

Weight: 8 tons.

Physical Strength: TK projector is equal to a Robotic P.S. 40.

Cargo: Minimal. Enough room for a rifle, pistol and basic survival gear.

Power System: Scuttler Symbiotic Conduit: 100 year life span. Must spend at least two hours charging on a ley line (or one hour on a nexus or stone pyramid) every seven days or the tank will be unable to use its weapons and is limited to a speed of 20 mph (32 km) on land or underwater.

Cost: 4 million credits to raise the symbiote and prepare the lodestone.

Weapon Systems:

1. Stonecaster Cannon: The Scuttler's main gun is a cannon that uses Stone Magic as a weapon. The cannon can create different types of rock, useful against a wide array of targets. Sedimentary rounds break up on impact and throw stone chips and flying sand into the air. Igneous rounds are pellets of lava that melt when they hit and cause continuing damage. Metamorphic ammo is extremely hard and dense and functions as armor-piercing rounds. The cannon has a dedicated gunner, can rotate 360 degrees and has a 45 degree up and down arc of fire.

Primary Purpose: Anti-Submarine/Anti-Sea Monster.

Secondary Purpose: Anti-Ship.

Range: 4,000 feet (1,219 m), half underwater.

Mega-Damage: Sedimentary: 5D6 M.D. to everything within an 8 foot (2.4 m) blast radius. Igneous: 1D4x10 M.D. on impact and 2D6 M.D. additional for the next 1D4 melee rounds. Metamorphic: 2D4x10 M.D.

Rate of Fire: Each shot counts as one melee attack/action.

Payload: 100 rounds. The weapon magically regenerates ammunition at a rate of two rounds per hour. Double the payload (and rate of regeneration) when inside the borders of a ley line triangle such as the *Demon Sea* (Bermuda Triangle), and triple the payload on a ley line, at a nexus or at a Lemurian stone pyramid.

2. TK Defense: The Scuttler is equipped with an experimental Telekinetic Defense system to fight in close combat against monsters and combat robots, punching, blocking and parrying attacks just like a pair of invisible hands. **Note:** Cannot be erected as a sustained invisible wall or shield.

Primary Purpose: Inertial Dampening System.

Secondary Purpose: Telekinetic Close Combat against giant opponents 10 feet (3 m) tall or larger; cannot be used against man-sized targets.

Range: 50 feet (15.2 m) in all environments.

Mega-Damage: 1D6 M.D. per punch, a Power TK-punch does 2D6 M.D. but counts as two melee attacks, and a restrained TK-punch does 3D6 S.D.C.

Rate of Fire: Each TK attack counts as one melee attack/action of the pilot.

Payload: Effectively unlimited.

Bonus: +1 to strike and parry giant-sized opponents, +1 to block/hit a volley of incoming missiles or torpedoes with a 01-33% chance of causing them to explode on impact or make them veer off target, but a deflected volley of missiles/torpedoes may hit an ally or cause collateral damage.

3. Spined Fins: As part of its role in combat, the Scuttler tank often encounters large sea serpents and monsters up close. To shake off melee attackers and dissuade huge sea monsters from trying to eat the sub, it is equipped with a pair of internal spined fin ridges. When activated, they project out of the tank's armor and make wide, circular cuts almost like a buzz saw. Attackers climbing or holding onto the tank must attempt to dodge or take 1D6 M.D. Sea serpents, squid and giants holding the tank in their jaws, hands or tentacles suffer 3D6 M.D. and are quick to let go or jump off.

4. **Scuttler Symbiote and Repairs:** Any damage sustained by the vessel can be "healed" by the symbiote inside the vessel via its limited knowledge of Stone Magic. To do so, the symbiote must *stop* the vessel (hover or float stationary, on land or the sea floor), extend one of its tendrils and remold the damaged stone shell. It can repair 2D6 M.D.C. per melee round. The symbiote itself heals 3D6 M.D.C. per 24 hours, though magical healing can also be used.
5. **Sensor System Note:** Same as the Sea Dart Interceptor, which relies on psychic powers for sensory input, and has the following abilities: Empathy (4), Presence Sense (4), See the Invisible (4), Sense Dimensional Anomaly (4), Sense Time (2), Sixth Sense (2) and Telepathy (4), plus TK Defense (see above, at no additional I.S.P. cost).

Base I.S.P.: 1D6x10+33

Range: 1,000 feet (305 m); double along ley lines.

Wind Seer

Probe, Sentry and Assassin Drone

The Wind Seer is essentially an unmanned version of the Lemurian Symbiote Conduit in a spherical shape. The Wind Seer is not heavily armed as it is meant for support, tracking, tailing and observing enemy targets or guarding strategic locations and campsites, relaying data to a pilot of one of the larger vehicles. With no requirement for a pilot, Wind Seers are designed to be unobtrusive, silent and have incredible depth tolerance. They are often used for the dangerous mission of exploring and scouting deep ocean trenches, where water pressure, lack of light and the minions of the Lord of the Deep are all serious threats.

Model Type: "Wind Seer."

Class: Unmanned Sensor Probe and Assassin Drone.

Crew: None; unmanned.

M.D.C. by Location:

* Symbiote – 6D6+12

Force Field – 50

** Main Body – 90

* The symbiote is a hard target to hit; both the force field and the main body of its shell must be destroyed before harm can be done to it. Destroying the symbiote will render the sub inoperative; a new symbiote must be implanted to make it work again.

** Depleting the M.D.C. of the main body will shut the vehicle down completely, making it useless.

Speed:

Land: Not possible.

Flying: Mach 1 (770 mph/1,232 km). TK Projectors allow the air-sub to hover and take off or land vertically.

Water Surface: The Wind Seer can fly within 3 feet (0.9 m) of the ground or water surface at up to 500 mph (800 km).

Underwater: 100 mph (160 km) maximum.

Speed Note: When on patrol or observing, the orb's speed is likely to be less than 50 mph (80 km).

Maximum Depth Tolerance: 8 miles (12.8 km).

Statistical Data:

Size: 3.5 feet (1 m) in diameter.

Weight: 550 lbs (248 kg).

Cargo: None.

Power System: Wind Seer Symbiote Conduit: 100 year life span. Must spend at least two hours charging on a ley line (or one hour on a nexus or stone pyramid) every seven days or the ship will be unable to use its weapons and be limited to a speed of 100 mph (160 km) in the air and 30 mph (48 km) underwater.

Cost: 2 million credits to raise the symbiote and prepare the lodestone.

Weapon Systems:

1. Ionic Charge Imbalancer: Just like its bigger brothers, the Wind Seer drone can use its propulsion drive's energy as a weapon to fire electric bolts 360 degrees in any direction.

Primary Purpose: Assault.

Secondary Purpose: Anti-Aircraft.

Range: 500 feet (152 m) in all environments; double the range when on or within one mile of a ley line or nexus point.

Mega-Damage: 2D6 M.D. per blast.

Rate of Fire: Each blast counts as one melee attack/action.

Payload: Effectively unlimited as long as the vessel is charged.

2. Wind Seer Symbiote and Repairs: Any damage sustained by the observation drone can be "healed" by the symbiote inside it via its limited knowledge of Stone Magic. To do so, the symbiote must *stop* (hover stationary or land), extend one of its tendrils and remold the damaged stone shell. It can repair 2D6 M.D.C. per melee round. The symbiote itself heals 2D6 M.D.C. per 24 hours, though magical healing can also be used.

3. Sensor System Note: The Wind Seer relies on a wide range of psychic powers for sensory input: Empathy (4), Mind Block (4), Presence Sense (4), Read Dimensional Portal (6), See the Invisible (4), Sense Dimensional Anomaly (4), Sense Evil (2), Sense Magic (3), Sense Time (2), Sixth Sense (2) and Telepathy (4).

Base I.S.P.: 2D4x10+36

Range: 1,000 feet (305 m); double along ley lines.

Enemies of Lemuria

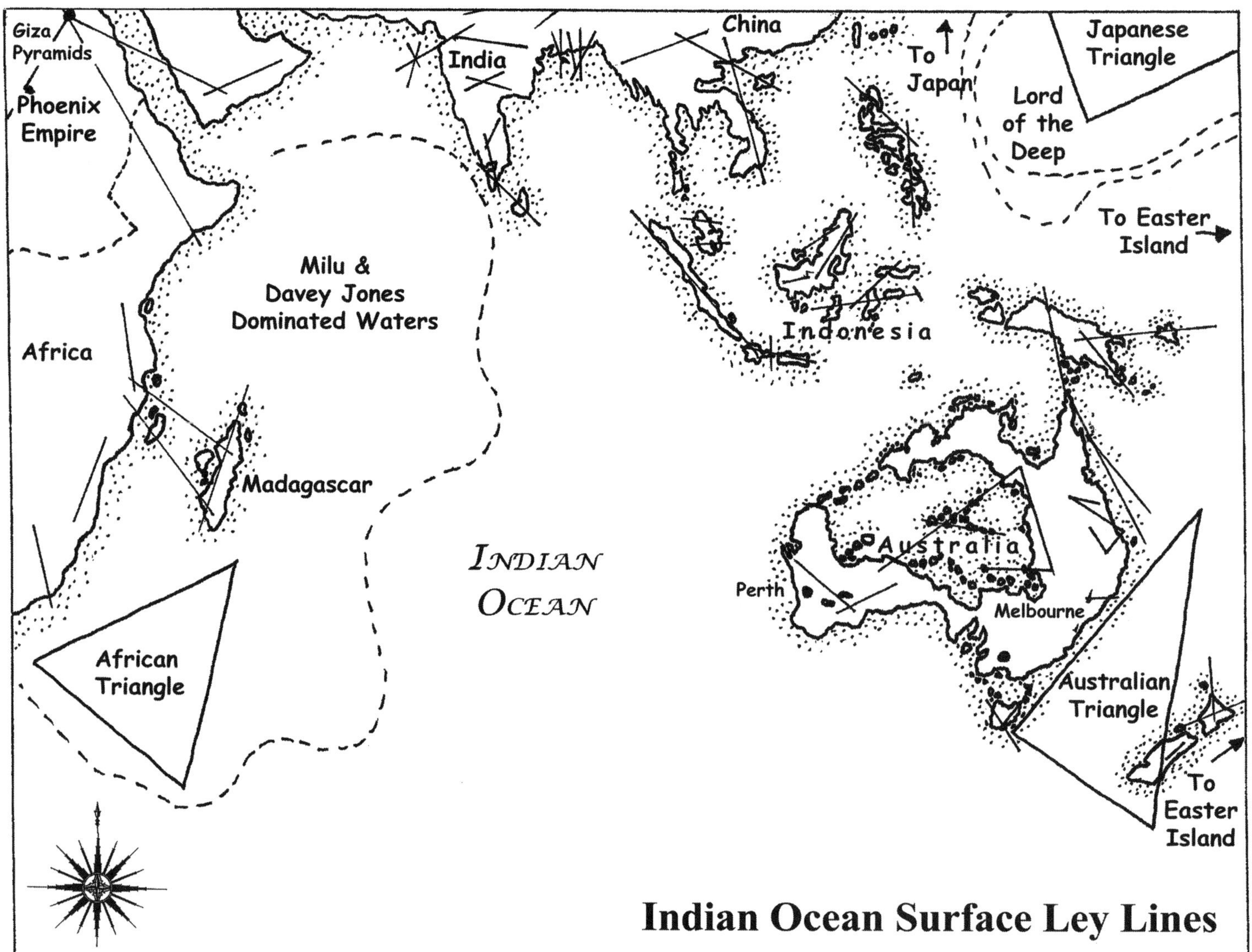

Indian Ocean Surface Ley Lines

Milu

The Milu are a crab-like humanoid race with one large crab claw arm, a humanlike arm and four crab-like legs all encased in a bony exoskeleton. Eons ago, the Milu rose to prominence on an alien ocean world known as Ka-pa'a-he'o. Their ascension to power came from the development of an alien form of Necromancy and the worship of an alien Vampire Intelligence known as **The Dark Warmth of Cold Death**. The Milu had evolved from bottom-feeding scavengers who fed upon carrion, so Necromancy was an easy fit for them. When The Dark Warmth of Cold Death offered even greater Necromantic power and immortality, the Milu embraced him, worshiped him and let the icy tendrils of Cold Death into their world. The other people of their world had never known of vampires – aquatic or otherwise – and succumbed to death. As their numbers and bone kingdoms grew, the Milu went from passive scavengers to an aggressive and warlike people that conquered and enslaved their enemies. Their greatest weapon, the very enemies that fell to them, restored to undead life as vampires or undead Zombie Servants. Other fallen enemies were drained of their blood, eaten by the living Milu, or used as components for the Necromantic arts and their bones as building materials.

After the Milu and the Mahiki Milu (their vampires) overran their world, The Dark Warmth of Cold Death bid them to seek out worlds to conquer, and happily provided portals to new frontiers. The Dark Warmth was alerted to Rifts Earth during the Great Cataclysm, when the deaths of billions of humans and the surge of incredible magic energy reached out to them even in their alien dimension. An army of conquering Milu arrived through dimensional Rifts in the ocean where they clashed with another invader, the Naut'Yll, and then the Minions of Splugorth, and other monsters. These armies, as well as the forces of chaos ravaging the planet, decimated the Milu forces and slammed shut the dimensional door the Milu had used to arrive on Earth. Despite brutal battles, deadly rivalry, and incredible losses, the Milu, Naut'Yll and Splugorth all managed to survive and carve out their own kingdoms on Earth. The Milu, despite many setbacks and constant battle with Lemurians, continue to rebuild and regrow their numbers, conquer and kill in a bid to eventually claim dominion over the oceans of Rifts Earth. They are far from defeated, and as immortals (vampires), waiting a few hundred years to gain a permanent foothold is hardly any time at all.

The Milu people are divided into two main types, the living and the living dead – vampires known as the *Mahiki Milu.*

The living Milu are the exalted chosen ones who spend most of their time as dutiful worshipers and death cultists of their god, *The Dark Warmth of Cold Death*. As such, living Milu do whatever their dark god or the Mahiki Milu tell them to do. The ordinary Milu are *not* vampires, but even as living, flesh and blood, mortals, the Milu are walking tanks with natural M.D.C. armor and Supernatural Strength. All living Milu are either death worshipers (70%) or Necromancers. When Mahiki Milu are reduced in number, living Milu are selected to become new vampires via the Slow Kill Bite of Mahiki Milu. It is a great honor to be chosen to join the Mahiki, and no Milu has ever been known to turn it down.

Roughly one third (33%) of the Milu population are the Mahiki Milu – aquatic vampires (described below). The *Mahiki Milu vampires* are the aristocracy, rulers, and warrior elite. The Mahiki Milu seldom "feed" upon their fellow Milu, but rather they prey upon the people they conquer and enslave, or defeat in battle. Of course, they are careful not to turn such inferior beings (i.e. non-Milu) into vampires unless they desire to do so. When a non-Milu vampire (human, Lemurian, Meran, D-Bee) is created, he is always a subservient soldier in the Milu army and barely more than a slave and known as "They Who Walk the Path of the Mahiki." Such inferior "Path Walkers" instinctively know they are undead soldiers who must remain obedient to all Milu, or be destroyed. The Path Walkers have many of the powers of their Mahiki Milu makers, but cannot create other vampires. Instead, they create Zombie Servants, an even more inferior type of undead that is dull of mind and completely obedient to them, the Mahiki Milu and Milu.

Zombie Servant is the fate of the conquered people taken captive by the Milu and not drained of blood or kept as livestock. Zombie Servants are used as the labor force, guards and cannon fodder. Thousands upon thousands may be sent to besiege an enemy or sent into the (undersea) world to capture or slaughter the enemy. Zombie Servants have no rights in Milu society and are little more than undead killing machines and labor force that exists to serve the Milu. As such, they have no memories, emotions, hopes or desires, except to serve and kill.

Slaves. At the bottom of Milu society, even below the Zombie Servant, are the living slaves. Slaves are always the conquered people defeated and captured by the Milu and their undead legions. This means slaves are always beings other than a Milu. As the chosen people, a Milu is never enslaved no matter his crime, and would sooner be exiled or executed than placed into slavery. Slaves have no rights and are treated worse than animals, used for labor, sport, torture, feeding and for making into Zombie Servants.

Animated dead. Mahiki Milu, Path Walkers and Necromancers can also animate the dead and command them to perform physical labor or attack and kill the enemy. These are true, mindless automatons made from the corpses and skeletons of the dead and controlled by the Necromancer or undead that raised them. They, like the Zombie Servants, are often used to lay siege and soften up the enemy, using their own fallen comrades, murdered slaves and fallen enemy soldiers against the living. It gives the Milu an unfair advantage as they turn the dead against the very people they once fought to protect.

Mortal henchmen and minions. Milu find all humanoid life forms repulsive and disgusting, but are not beneath tricking, bribing, hiring or otherwise using them to infiltrate their enemies and engage in specialized work, including sabotage and assassination.

Living and undead Milu are creatures of the deep, and their domain is the ocean depths. They can come on dry land, but must do so at night, because the sun blinds living Milu and destroys Mahiki Milu, Path Walkers and Zombie Servants. Even entering sunlit water hurts their eyes and does 5D6 M.D. per melee round to Milu undead.

"Living" Milu – NPC Villain

Alignment: Diabolic (45%), Miscreant (32%), Aberrant (10%), and Anarchist (10%). Only living outcasts and renegades (not undead Mahiki Milu) can be Unprincipled or Scrupulous.

Attributes: I.Q. 1D6+9, M.E. 1D6+11, M.A. 1D6+7, P.S. 2D6+13 (Supernatural), P.P. 2D6+5, P.E. 2D6+7, P.B. 2D6, Spd 2D6+9 running and swimming.

Height: 7-8 feet (2.1 to 2.4 m), 9-12 feet (2.7 to 3.6 m) wide when legs are fully extended.

Weight: 600-1,200 lbs (270 to 540 kg).

M.D.C.: 4D6x10 + P.E. attribute number and +1D6 per level of experience. (On S.D.C. worlds the Milu have a bony exoskeleton that provides Hit Points equal to P.E. attribute x2 +1D6 per level of experience, 1D6x10+60 S.D.C., and a Natural A.R. 17. Something about their unusual crustacean physiology makes them M.D.C. creatures and imbues the mortal Milu with Supernatural Strength on Rifts Earth.)

Horror Factor: 11

P.P.E.: 6D6

Age: 90-130 years for the living Milu, but one third of them are the immortal, undead *Mahiki Milu.*

Gender: Male and female Milu are almost indistinguishable except females are typically 20% larger. During the mating season the females lay egg sack clusters in a communal birthing chamber and the males come and fertilize them. The eggs hatch and the Milu are born ready to work. At about 10% of adult size they are sent out to scavenge and collect items, bringing them to city builders, Necromancers or those who have requested specific things. They also quickly learn from others (through observation or direct instruction) and assist until someone takes them on as an apprentice. The lucky ones become Necromancers, learn the Path of the Mahiki and never die. The others become minions or mindless abominations to be summoned and controlled like the rest of the corpses collected by the Milu at the Dead Pools.

Disposition: Most Milu are aggressive, cold-blooded and uncaring cutthroats who have no regard for other people. They see all non-Milu as nothing but food and opportunity – slaves waiting to be conquered and a resource to turn into undead or zombies. Once they establish a foothold on a new world, their thoughts quickly turn to global domination and the genocide of the indigenous people.

Among their own kind they work together, but like most vampires and death cultists, have a fatalistic and nihilistic view of life, and care about their own prosperity above all others. When their individual survival or position is jeopardized, many Milu have sacrificed friends, allies and even loved ones to preserve their power base.

Natural Abilities: Nightvision 3,000 feet (914 m) and underwater vision, depth tolerance of 12 miles (19.2 km), resistant to cold (half damage), and even the mortal Milu are tough, strong and possess Supernatural Strength and Endurance.

Heightened Senses: The Milu have exceptional Nightvision and roughly human level hearing, but the majority of their sensory input comes from a pair of antennae on the top of their heads. These antennae are highly sensitive to chemicals and tastes in the water, allowing them to "smell" dead flesh, blood and decomposition up to three miles (4.8 km) away; double for Milu vampires. **Base Skill:** 60% +3% per level of experience to identify and track such smells to their source.

They can also sense electrical currents and magnetic field of the Earth via their feelers, allowing the Milu to find the magnetic North and navigate underwater. They are so sensitive that they also pick up electrical signals from organic creatures which lets the Milu "see" the silhouette of the creature at a range of 50 feet (15 m) even in complete darkness, murky water or through vegetation, even if that creature is using magic invisibility. They are also sensitive to vibrations and can pick up motion up to 200 feet (61 m) away underwater; one third that out of water.

Milu communicate by reaching out with their antennae and touching each other's antennae. They also "talk" using a variety of chirps, creaks and bubbling noises for longer distances.

Optional O.C.C.: 30% of the Milu are Necromancers. No other O.C.C. is available. 33% are the undead Mahiki Milu.

R.C.C. of the Living Milu: These are not vampires, but they are death worshipers who possess considerable power and work hand in hand with the Mahiki Milu vampires.

The Milu R.C.C. (70% of the living population) has the following skills: Appraise Goods (+30%), Barter (+10%), Begging (+15%), Climbing (+15%), Dance (+20%), Dowsing (+10%), Fasting (+15%), Gambling (+10%), Hand to Hand: Assassin, Sing (+20%), Imitate Voices & Sounds (+20%), Language (Native; roughly the same as the Ichthylean and Junk Crab tongue) at 95%, Palming (+20%), Pick Locks (+15%), Pick Pockets (+10%), Prowl (+20%), Tailing (+10%), Tracking (people; +20%), Underwater Navigation (+10%), Underwater & Sea Survival (+10%), W.P. Knife or Blunt (pick one), W.P. Energy Pistol, W.P. 1D4 of choice (any).

Vulnerabilities & Penalties: 1. Fair swimmers. Despite being an aquatic race, live Milu are not fast or proficient swimmers.

2. Sensitivity to light. Milu are sensitive to sunlight, dislike it and avoid it. In sunlight, even on an overcast day, the Milu have trouble seeing in its glare. They can only see 500 feet (152 m) in bright light or sunlight, and are -3 on Perception Rolls, -2 on initiative, -1 on all combat rolls, lose one melee attack, and are -15% on skill performance when exposed to it. Dim to moderate artificial light hurts their eyes, but doesn't inflict penalties.

3. Breathing on land. Mortal Milu cannot breathe air and need to extract oxygen from the water like fish. They can, however, store enough water/oxygen in their system to remain out of water for 1D4+6 hours at a time, usually at night. **Note:** Mahiki (Milu vampires) can survive on the surface or underwater indefinitely, provided they stay out of sunlight.

Attacks per Melee: As per Hand to Hand: Assassin.

Bonuses: +2 on Perception Rolls, +2 on initiative, +1 to strike, +2 to save vs psionics, possession and mind control, +6 vs Horror Factor, +4 to save vs toxins, drugs and disease, +10% to save vs coma/death.

Mega-Damage: Living Milu have Supernatural Strength and inflict damage as per their Supernatural P.S. The giant crab-claw does an additional 1D6 M.D. from a stab or punch. The claw does 5D6 M.D. from a pincer/scissor-cut attack, or the Milu may use a weapon in the other hand.

Magic: Only via the Necromancer O.C.C. (See **Rifts® Africa**, page 99, or **Rifts® Mystic Russia**, page 83).

Psionics: None.

Habitat: Individuals on the prowl, pairs and small groups of 1D4+2 Milu or Mahiki Milu can be encountered anywhere, as can any number of their or Davey Jones's "zombies" (5D6 is typical). However, the Milu community/stronghold is found at Davey Jones's Locker and the City of Bones located in the depths of the Indian Ocean, along the African coast and in and around Madagascar, as well as the many *Dead Pools* in that ocean. If left unchecked, however, their forces could flourish at a deadly rate!

Allies: Only their own kind. Any alliance with other evil beings will be short-lived, lasting only as long as it serves the Milu's purpose. *Davey Jones* is, in effect, a Master Vampire of the Dark Warmth, a Milu demigod and their General of the Army on Earth.

Enemies: Lemurians are Enemy Number One as they are one of the Milu's biggest obstacles in their conquest of Earth. Followed by the Lemurians' allies, the Minions of Splugorth and vampire hunters. However, Milu and Mahiki Milu consider all sentient life forms to be food, playthings and enemies. The Naut'Yll, Lord of the Deep, the Vampire Kingdoms, Splugorth and other supernatural forces are enemies of the Milu because they are conquering rivals. The New Navy and Tritonia have also battled or joined battles against the Milu, but fighting the undead is a bit out of their league.

Mahiki Milu – Milu Vampires

The Mahiki Milu is a Milu crab person that has been turned into a vampire by another Mahiki, usually under the direction of their god, The Dark Warmth of Cold Death. They possess all the same basic stats of the Milu, but are transformed into the equivalent of a Secondary Vampire with the following changes and vampire powers.

Alignment: Diabolic (45%), Miscreant (35%), Aberrant (13%), and Anarchist (7%).

Attributes: I.Q. 1D6+13, M.E. 1D6+13, M.A. 1D6+13, P.S. 3D6+30 (Supernatural), P.P. 2D6+7, P.E. 2D6+13, P.B. 2D6, Spd 2D6+13 running and swimming.

M.D.C.: 4D6x10 +66 and +2D6 M.D.C. per level of experience and as vampires, are impervious to most mortal weapons. (On S.D.C. worlds the Mahiki Milu have Hit Points equal to P.E. attribute x3 +2D6 per level of experience, 1D6x10+60 S.D.C., and are impervious to all but weapons made of wood, silver, and sunlight. Magic does half damage.)

Special Abilities of the Milu Undead/Vampires:

- Gift of (Undead) Immortality: **The Mahiki Milu** can drink the blood of any sentient being, from humans to Merans, to D-Bees and fellow Milu. However, they seldom turn any but the Milu race into vampires – the others are seen as too inferior, repulsive and unworthy – and when they are turned into a vampire, the non-Milu vampires (i.e. humans and D-Bees) are something less than a Secondary Vampire but more than a Wild Vampire.

  Path Walkers – Non-Milu Undead/Vampires. Mortals such as humans, Lemurians and D-Bees, made into vampires by the *Mahiki Milu* are known to the Milu as *"They Who Walk the Path of the Mahiki,"* or *"Path Walkers"* for short. These mortal humanoids are, in effect, made into a Milu version of an aquatic vampire. They possess the same degree of intelligence as the classic Secondary Vampire, but are always subservient to the *Mahiki Milu* and *Milu Necromancers*, and never threaten or harm a living Milu. In fact, a Path Walker will fight to protect the living Milu as well as their maker and other Mahiki Milu. These humanoid vampires of the Milu have all the basic powers of the Mahiki Milu (described below) and suffer all the same weaknesses. However, though they have a Slow Kill Bite, Path Walkers can NOT create other vampires, they can only create *Zombie Servants*.

Create Zombie Servant (also known as Undead Servant): While the Mahiki Milu (and Davey Jones) can make other aquatic vampires, the Path Walker vampires who are not themselves Milu (i.e., humans, Merans, Amphibs, D-Bees, etc.) CANNOT create other vampires. Instead, the *Slow Kill Bite* of a Path Walker gives unlife to a different type of undead: a *Zombie Servant*.

The undead Zombie Servant is a shadow of the person it was in life. Most memories and emotions are gone, I.Q., M.E., M.A., P.B. and Spd are all *reduced by half*, and P.P. is reduced by one third. P.S. and P.E., however, get a +2D6 bonus and become Supernatural. Meanwhile, the zombie's flesh turns white or light gray and becomes hard as a Milu's shell, Hit Points and S.D.C. are combined and become M.D.C., and the undead Zombie Servant is impervious to most weapons just like a vampire. The Zombie Servant retains 1D6+3 O.C.C. or R.C.C. skills, but they do not improve with experience, and all other skills are forgotten in the same fog that consumes the identity they had when alive. These dull-witted zombies are fiercely obedient to the one who made them and all Milu, living and undead. They follow orders to the letter, know no fear, and fight to the death without mercy, sorrow or hesitation. In that regard, they are like sharks – aggressive and murderous – but killing machines that have no desires or dreams of their own; undead automatons who live to serve the Milu.

Vulnerabilities of the Zombie Servants: Same as the *Mahiki Milu's* vulnerabilities to silver, wood, sunlight, magic, and Bio-Energy (see below for details). The same applies to the humanoid vampires who Walk the Path of the Mahiki. **Note:** Thankfully, the Path Walker (non-Milu Secondary Vampire) can only create one Zombie Servant a week, and must use the Slow Kill process to do so. Path Walkers cannot perform metamorphosis nor summon animals, but can animate 1D4 dead and have all the other vampire powers and vulnerabilities of the Mahiki Milu.

The Mahiki Milu vampire. Think of the Mahiki as Secondary Vampires. These aquatic undead possess the M.D.C. and R.C.C. skills of the Milu and the usual powers of Secondary Vampires with the following exceptions and differences.

- Vampire Metamorphosis. Can NOT turn into mist or into any type of surface animal. Metamorphosis of the Mahiki Milu is limited to that of a black or dark gray manta ray or shark (any large type) with red eyes. The inferior Path Walkers cannot perform any type of metamorphosis.
- Summon Vermin. Mahiki Milu cannot summon land vermin like mice or insects, but can summon crabs of different varieties. (No giant crabs.)
- Summon Wolves of the Sea. Mahiki Milu cannot summon and control wolves or dogs, but can summon sharks or barracudas.
- Animate and Control Dead: Mahiki Milu, Milu Necromancers, and their non-Milu humanoid vampires also make extensive use of the recently deceased, animating them like marionettes to build their cities and to attack the living in great swarms of animated corpses. Each Milu Necromancer can raise and command animated dead as per the Animate and Control Dead spell; a Mahiki Milu can animate 1D4x10 undead, and their non-Milu humanoid vampires can raise 1D4 animated dead.
- Soil of the Homeland: Not applicable.
- Undead Mahiki Milu Vulnerabilities. Same as usual for vampires (silver, wood, sunlight, holy symbols, etc.), except not running water. Running water does no damage. Holy Water does half damage. Most magic spells and weapons inflict half damage. They are also vulnerable to life-radiant Bio-Energy (double damage), making Lemurians and Biomancers their most hated of enemies.

  Wood, even ordinary S.D.C. wood, penetrates the M.D.C. armored hide of the Mahiki Milu and inflicts Mega-Damage point for point. Thus, if a wood weapon does 1D6 S.D.C. to normal beings, it does 1D6 M.D. to the Mahiki Milu and their Undead Minions. This includes their humanoid vampires and Zombie Servants.
- Sunlight hurts, blinds and kills Mahiki Milu and their Undead Minions. The Milu are creatures of the deep. Even the living Milu dislike sunlight and have trouble seeing in its glare. Sunlight and sunlight-based attacks against *Mahiki Milu* and their undead minions (*Path Walkers* and *Zombie Servants*) are devastating. Sunlight does double the usual damage to them as M.D. plus Mahiki Milu, Path Walkers and Zombie Servants are blinded by sunlight (-10 to all combat rolls). The Globe of Daylight does 4D6 M.D. per melee round to them and they cannot bear to enter even dimly sunlit waters (suffer 4D6 M.D. per melee round in dimly sunlit water, and 1D6x10 M.D. per melee round in sunlight). Futhermore, they cannot Bio-Regenerate in the light of day.
- Hunger for Blood. Same as it is for all vampires.
- Blood Scent. Double the scent capabilities of the Milu (same for Path Walkers).
- Vampire Mind Control and Enslavement. Same as it is for all vampires.
- Psionics: Standard as per vampires.
- Prowl: Underwater: 50% +2% per level of experience; -20% on dry land and impossible in sunlight.
- Immortality. Same as it is for all vampires.
- Undead. Does not need to breathe or eat, is impervious to disease, does not radiate heat, and has all the other basic, common features of vampires.

Note: The Vampire Intelligence of the Milu known as The Dark Warmth of Cold Death is not on Rifts Earth. He resides in another dimension of black water. That's why killing Davey Jones will break the monster's connection to Earth and lead to the Milu's eventual decimation. See Davey Jones for details.

Davey Jones

Master Vampire & General of the Milu

Davey Jones began life as a human during the age of pirates. He did a little privateering and pirating on the open seas before collecting enough loot to retire back home in London, England. There he purchased and opened up a pub with his ill-gotten gains. As Davey spent his money and grew greedier, the cutthroat waylayed unsuspecting drunks and patrons at his tavern by adding a sedative to the brew he served them. He'd then lock his victims

away in his wine cellar/locker and sell them to discreet pirates and smugglers going out to sea as slave crew and labor. A number of his unfortunate victims made it back to Britain several years later and exacted their revenge upon Davey. They drugged him, took him aboard their ship, and after he gained consciousness, they tortured and tormented him for weeks. Davey was finally made to walk the plank with an iron ball chained to his leg to send him to the ocean's deep.

To save himself, Davey Jones offered to serve whatever dark god would have him. As the waves engulfed him, Davey thought he heard a voice in the darkness calling to him. When the pirate reawakened, he was transformed into something no longer human. The dark warm voice spoke to him again, this time from the cold, black, ocean depth. It explained that his plea had been heard, that he, Davey Jones, had been chosen and reshaped into a lesser god. A god of vengeance and death destined to lead an army against the forces of goodness and light. Davey would do so by destroying all that was good, raising the dead and helping the dark deity's chosen people – monstrous beings the voice named the Milu – conquer the world. With Davey Jones to lead them as their General, they would make the oceans of Earth their new domain. Davey's reward, besides immortality, the title of Supreme General, and the power of a god, was all the treasure and loot he could take. To be granted the power to make this happen, all Davey Jones had to do was to forsake humanity and embrace his new, dark god and live as a god among men and Milu. Davey Jones had forsaken humanity long ago, so the choice was an easy one.

Somehow, Davey Jones didn't care that his transformation had taken centuries or that the world around him had changed as drastically as he had. Instead, he embraced the chaos, weird aliens and new challenges. In fact, he is often said to laugh and boast how he was made for this new world and dreams of the day when all within it will bow down before him.

Davey's savior and master is a rare and ancient type of Vampire Intelligence that creates undead monsters that live in the sea. This particular Alien Intelligence calls itself **The Dark Warmth of Cold Death**. In addition to making Davey Jones its Master Vampire and link to Rifts Earth, the Dark Warmth is worshiped by a race of crab people known as the **Milu**. It was, the Dark Warmth who brought the Milu the secrets of Necromancy and created the **Mahiki Milu**, a type of aquatic vampire that preys upon the living. The Milu are worshipers of death and the willing minions of The Dark Warmth of Cold Death.

Davey Jones is, himself, a sort of undead monster and the Milu's demigod General on Earth. He has spent centuries building a vast army of vampires and Zombie Servants, making quite a legend for himself as the demonic General of the Milu army on Earth. He is feared by all aquatic people and seafaring folk of Rifts Earth, and is seen as the harbinger of slavery and undeath to the seven seas. Though many have fought him and the Milu's undead legions, including the Minions of Splugorth, the Naut'Yll, and the New Navy, the Lemurians and their allies have been the scourge of the Milu, Davey Jones and The Dark Warmth of Cold Death. Lemurian Biomancy and life energy are the very antithesis of death and undeath, and the two species have become mortal enemies in a continuing battle between good and evil.

Constantly harassed and attacked by Lemuria, it took Davey Jones seven attempts and nearly 200 years before he was able to build his "Locker" stronghold to serve as his permanent base of operations, treasure trove, and prison. It is located on the bottom of the Indian Ocean where it has become the cornerstone for the Milu invasion force. Prisoners taken by Davey Jones are able to survive transportation and captivity in his Locker even if they cannot normally survive such depths. Of course, such captivity is said to be a fate worse than death. According to rumor, the prisoners are tortured for the amusement of Davey Jones and used like cattle, drained of their blood just shy of killing them, over and over again by the Mahiki Milu – the vampire Milu. It also said that the Locker is where Davey makes new vampires and prisoners are eventually made into Zombie Servants.

The Milu leadership on Earth decided to build their **City of Bones** around the Locker, and with their General's blessings, have created a city of the damned that seems indestructible. The Lemurians have experienced great success destroying every Milu stronghold and colony they discover, but when they do, the survivors limp back to the City of Bones. Though they have tried many times, successfully laying siege to the City of Bones and destroying it has eluded Lemuria. One problem is the depth. Another is the highly defendable trench in which it lies, and that at each ley line nexus in the area amasses a huge Dead Pool, which the Milu use to build their weapons of war and create new undead minions. It is only a matter of time before the Milu and their armies attempt to again push out from the City of Bones into the Indian Ocean and beyond. The Lemurians will do all they can to track down and destroy them, but as long as Davey Jones, his

Locker and the City of Bones survive, the Milu and their undead legions will keep trying to conquer more.

Davey Jones – NPC Villain

Davey Jones is, in effect, the *Master Vampire* of *The Dark Warmth of Cold Death.* Destroy Davey Jones, and the Milu not only lose their cunning and evil General, but they lose their link to The Dark Warmth of Cold Death. When that happens, the Milu and Mahiki Milu on Earth become trapped there and more vulnerable to attack, for without this direct link through Davey to the evil god, new essence fragments of the Intelligence cannot enter our dimension, and the Milu cannot create new undead. Such is the strange nature of The Dark Warmth of Cold Death. That means the numbers of Milu vampires can no longer be replenished, and with each of their deaths, the Milu and their undead come one step closer to being completely wiped from the depths of the Earth's oceans. This also means the Milu and Mahiki Milu do everything in their power to protect Davey Jones from harm and rescue him when in danger. Not one will hesitate to sacrifice themselves or do whatever is necessary to keep Davey Jones alive. A fact the mad general relies upon.

Davey Jones always takes the appearance of a human clad in a sea captain's uniform from the bygone pirate era of 18th Century England, including a large hat, long coat, boots, belt, gloves and cutlass. He finds the appearance adds drama and strikes fear into his mortal enemies. If stripped of his uniform, Davey's body is gaunt, his pale gray skin shriveled around his bones. His face is equally gaunt and skeletal, though it is hard to tell from beneath the brim of his hat and his thick, black beard. His mouth is wide and his smile sinister, though his vampire fangs only display when Davey is angry or ready to feed upon the living. The only part of his body that doesn't look dead are his icy blue eyes, but they radiate with cruelty, hate and madness.

Aliases: Davey, David Jones, Duffy Jones, Duffy Jonah and David Jonah.

Alignment: Diabolic.

Attributes: I.Q. 14, M.E. 11, M.A. 24, P.S. 23 (Supernatural), P.P. 17, P.E. 14, P.B. 11, Spd 13 running (52 underwater/36 mph/57.6 km or 31 knots). P.S. and P.E. are Supernatural.

M.D.C.: 240, but as a vampire is impervious to most mortal weapons, including Mega-Damage weapons. Vulnerabilities are the same as the Mahiki Milu vampires.

Size: Six feet tall (1.8 m), 170 lbs (76.5 kg) and looks 40 years of age.

Horror Factor: 14 when his opponents realize who and what he is.

P.P.E.: 30

Disposition: It is impossible to tell whether Davey was this malicious in life or if it was taking the Path of the Mahiki that further hardened his demeanor. Legends of his life before becoming a Master Vampire made him out to be a ruthless pirate and cruel slaver.

A monster on Rifts Earth, Davey Jones is even crueler, but just as in life, he possesses a beguiling charm made all the more powerful thanks to his vampire powers. Charm and abilities he uses to trick heroes and to seduce and entice evil henchmen and "partners" to join his schemes and do his bidding. Davey doesn't mind that he is the servant of a dark god because he believes he is himself a god, and enjoys his "work" and the power he wields. Despite this, to Davey, power means wealth, and this mad god is a miser consumed by greed, so his treasure trove is never enough, and the need to acquire more treasure drives him to take foolish risks.

Natural Abilities: Has all the same powers and abilities of the *Mahiki Milu* vampires; see their description for details. Plus, Nightvision 2,000 feet (610 m; can see in complete darkness), impervious to disease, toxins and poisons, does not need air to breathe, impervious to ocean pressures, physical punches and attacks do no damage, nor do Mega-Damage weapons or M.D. energy attacks (excluding fire), magic and magic weapons do half damage, and Davey Jones Bio-Regenerates 2D6 M.D.C. per melee round.

Skills of Note: Language: English (Native), French, Portuguese, Dutch, Spanish, and Ichthylean/Milu, Pilot: Sail Boats and Sailing Ships, Barter, Boxing, Brewing, Climbing, Dance, Disguise, Navigation, Impersonation, Palming, Pick Locks, Pick Pockets, Prowl, Public Speaking, Radio: Basic, Rope Works, Swimming, Underwater Navigation, Undersea Survival, and Undersea Salvage, all at 98%. W.P. Knife, W.P. Sword, W.P. Handguns, W.P. Energy Pistols and W.P. Paired Weapons, all at 10th level proficiency.

Experience Level: 13th level Pirate, now a 300-year-old Master Vampire.

Attacks per Melee: Seven hand to hand attacks.

Bonuses (including all bonuses): +3 on Perception Rolls, +5 on initiative, +5 to strike, +7 to parry and disarm, +6 to pull punch, +5 to disarm, +2 roll with impact, +7 to save vs Horror Factor, 80% to evoke trust or intimidate, and impervious to all forms of mind control, possession, and magic sleep, paralysis and domination.

Mega-Damage: Restrained punch 4D6 S.D.C., punch or kick 2D6 M.D., Power Punch does 4D6 M.D. (counts as two attacks), bite can do as little as 1D4 S.D.C., but in combat, as much as 2D6 M.D., or by weapon. Davey prefers to use his Slayer Flintlock and his Dirge Cutlass.

Vulnerabilities: Same as the Mahiki Milu, including S.D.C. weapons made of wood or silver, Bio-Energy, sunlight, and so on.

Magic: Magic Lore and tales of magical items, which he covets as part of his treasure. Davey owns and knows how to use several magic items in his vast treasure horde but has no actual skill or abilities in the use of magic.

Psionics: As per all vampires, nothing extra.

Allies: He commands the Milu, Mahiki Milu and Zombie Servants on Rifts Earth, but he also enjoys manipulating, charming, and hiring mortal dupes, stooges, and henchmen to do his bidding.

Enemies: The living in general, and Lemurians most of all.

Guardians & Servants: Wherever Davey Jones goes, he is always accompanied by no fewer than four Mahiki Milu (Milu vampires), 1D4+1 Milu (the +1 being a level 1D6+4 Necromancer), and 2D6 Zombie Servants. Back at the Locker or the City of Bones, or out on a "pleasure cruise," Davey Jones likes to surround himself with 2D6+6 mortal servants and slaves (often captives in chains) to serve him and suffer his terrible desires. Like all vampires, he enjoys using the living as his playthings.

Weapons of Note: Davey retains a love for firearms, particularly pistols, revolvers and old-style flintlocks.

The Slayer Flintlock: The flintlock pistol is a TW weapon, or something similar, possibly designed for a Vampire Hunter. Range: 120 feet (36.6 m). Damage: Can fire any type of bullet of any size up to an 18 mm ball. Rate of Fire: Each shot counts as one attack. Payload: Despite looking like an old flintlock, it can hold six rounds. For the cost of 20 P.P.E. the weapon generates six silver bullets.

The Dirge Cutlass: A silver magic sword that does 2D6 S.D.C. to mortal foes, 2D6 M.D. to most Mega-Damage beings, and 5D6 M.D. to undead, demons, other evil supernatural beings as well as creatures vulnerable to sonic attacks. This unusual blade "sings" in combat, unleashing an eerie stream of humming that sounds like a synthesized guitar.

Armor: Davey seldom wears armor, but will consider it when he knows he's entering a major battle. He can wear any armor suitable for humans.

Vehicles: Whenever he needs or wants one, Davey is fond of raiding and commandeering ocean vessels. He'll force half the crew to follow his orders or die, replace the other half with Milu and Zombie Servants, and lock the rest up until he's ready to take them to his Locker or let his Mahiki Milu (or himself) feed on them.

The City of Bones: Davey Jones's Locker and the City of Bones are the creations of Necromancy, Milu engineering and the power of The Dark Warmth of Cold Death. His "Locker" is part underground bunker, part macabre palace, part treasure vault and half prison. The City of Bones and the Locker are made of stone and bones using Necromancy magic, slaves and Zombie Servants to construct them. Using the vast resources of the dead and undead, they built their general a nearly impregnable fortress and their City of Bones around it. Both are a disturbing monument to their undead conquest, eerie and frightful in every way imaginable. Forced back by the Lemurians, the Milu and their minions continue to gather and collect the dead from the Dead Pools to build a bigger and more powerful army. Much like the Coalition's mega-cities and the 'Burbs, a central impenetrable fortress made from the remains of the dead is surrounded by a crude shanty town of homes and businesses pieced together from the remains of the dead, and inhabited by the lesser members of Milu society, slaves, and Zombie Servants.

Other Enemies

Despite the Lemurians' quest to find peace and harmony in life and nature, they have found themselves cast in the unlikely role of Earth's defenders. Though they try to avoid war and unnecessary violence whenever possible, their technology (i.e. Biomancy, Earth Magic/Stone Magic and Bio-Energy) has made them a force to notice and fear, especially by supernatural evil. This has earned Lemurians the deep and lasting enmity of the invading *Naut'Yll,* the undead worshipping *Milu,* the aggressive *Lord of the Deep,* the Splugorth of Atlantis, and all their legions of minions, henchmen and monsters. This has forced the peace-loving Lemurians to learn to fight or be destroyed. Furthermore, as Lemurians learned more about their demonic enemies and life on Rifts Earth, they have become the self-appointed defenders of the innocent and all people of Earth. To the noble and empathetic Lemurians it was the right thing to do.

Though they have, so far, restricted most of their efforts to the depths of the oceans and seas, they have been helping fellow underwater people, seafarers and coastal people – often in secret or without credit – since the Great Cataclysm returned them to Earth.

Horune Pirates. Not only do Horune Pirates hire themselves out to the Splugorth as slavers and henchmen, but they are also independent pirates who raid and plunder humans, D-Bees, Lemurians and anyone who has valuables or things they want. Horune Pirates are the scourge of the seven seas and may associate with evildoers of mortal or supernatural origins, and should never be trusted. They hate Lemurians just on the principle that they are too nice and too good-looking. Lemurian weapons, armor and magic always fetch a high price, making them targets for attacks, kidnaping and ransom.

The Lord of the Deep: This wicked supernatural being is certainly the Lemurians' most relentless enemy. The mad god is obsessed with revenge upon the Lemurians by seeing them utterly destroyed. The monster has a vendetta against them because they unwittingly stole his way off planet Earth in the aftermath of the Atlantis Catastrophe and trapped him on Earth. Without sufficient magic energy to draw upon, the severely weakened Lord of the Deep was forced to hibernate most of the millennia that followed, awakening only for brief periods to sink a ship or small fleet, before having to vanish back into his trench. This is no way for a god to live even for a short 15,000 years, and even in his dreams the Lord of Deep festered with hatred for the ones who brought him to such an ignoble fate. The Great Cataclysm woke the wicked god and the Earth's ley lines seething with magic energy gave him more power than he had known in many an eon. The Lord of the Deep reveled in the chaos and added to the carnage. He liked this new world.

The Coming of the Rifts also brought the Lemurians back to Earth as well, and when the Lord of the Deep realized it was they who had made him suffer, he vowed to make them pay. So it has been that a vengeful and hate-filled dark god hunts Lemurians and plots their slow and painful destruction. However, the Lemurians in the magic rich environment of Rifts Earth are also more powerful than ever, and have managed to not only survive, but thrive. After the first century of constant attacks, hiding and unable to reason with the evil god, they quickly adapted to war. The stronger the Lemurians became, the better they were able to avoid, counter and fend off the Lord of the Deep's minions and attacks. Two centuries later, the ongoing war with the insane god has turned Lemurians into courageous warriors and heroes who have embraced the job of being protectors of Earth, or at least its oceans. The ongoing war with the Lord of the Deep is an accepted part of Lemurian life and has inspired many of their designs for weapons, armor, riding animals and developments in magic. Not only that, but it was the Lord of the Deep's campaign against them that made them realize *someone* had to step up to protect the oceans and all the innocent creatures living in them from horrors such as him.

It is ironic, but the Lord of the Deep has, in effect, created a force for good that now seeks his destruction and works to thwart his every evil deed. Lemurians are now the Lord of the Deep's greatest nemesis, hunting down and destroying his minions and battling other dark forces like the Milu and Naut'Yll.

The Mauian Order has been covered in detail earlier, but bears mentioning again, for they are truly the evil within, and may consider working with any of Lemuria's enemies to bring down their brothers or rise to power.

The Naut'Yll. When the Lemurians first encountered the Naut'Yll, they approached them with open arms and the dream of making a new friend and ally. The invading Naut'Yll, bent on conquering Earth's oceans and mistakenly believing the Lemurians to be weak and few in number, unleashed a merciless onslaught upon them. Though most surface dwellers don't have a clue or care about the people or battles under the sea, the Naut'Yll are alien invaders come to Earth with the express purpose of conquering the entire planet. As fate would have it, the Lemurians were the first to encounter the hostile Naut'Yll and the two have been at odds ever since. The Naut'Yll regard Lemurians as rivals to be conquered and enslaved, or destroyed. Lemurians see the Naut'Yll for what they really are, evil, alien invaders intent on conquering the world. This has resulted in frequent skirmishes over the last 300 years in an ongoing war that has frustrated the Naut'Yll's relentless efforts to build an army and conquer the people of the oceans and seas. Naut'Yll attack Lemurians whenever they think they have the upper hand, and also engage in acts of sabotage, kidnaping and vindictive assaults designed to hurt and cripple their hated enemy. For the Lemurians' part, they have come to terms with the fact that the Naut'Yll refuse reason and peace and are yet another monster to be annihilated to protect the people and planet of Earth. They are assisted in this effort by cetaceans, Merans, Ichthyleans, and by Tritonians, the New Navy, and Milu, all of whom also recognize the danger represented by the Naut'Yll and engage them in their own campaigns to wipe out or send the invaders packing. These combined efforts have contained and diminished the Naut'Yll forces, causing the monsters to lose ground in their scheme of conquest. Unless something dramatic changes soon for the Naut'Yll, their days on Earth are numbered.

The Splugorth of Atlantis and their Minions. All nations of Rifts Earth know about the Splugorth, their Slavers, Minions and the island continent of Altantis. A place regarded as a dangerous nation of monsters and villainy. But what few people realize is that the Splugorth and their Minions are, themselves, amphibious beings equally at home under the sea. They do not realize that they dominate the waters around Atlantis, the Demon Sea (Bermuda Triangle), and the Mid-Atlantic, nor that the Splugorth cities sprawl for miles around Atlantis in the ocean depths. It is a realization that shocks surface dwellers and makes them wonder how they could have been so blind. The large, black "fish eyes" and teeth of *Splugorth High Lords* hint at their evolution from deep ocean life forms; the *Conservators* with their six limbs and crab-like exoskeletons are clearly aquatic; the iconic Slavers with their tentacles are further evidence of aquatic origins, but most people don't realize that detached from their magic barge, the monsters have a long fish tail. The Metztla are perhaps the most

C·WALTON

primordial and obviously aquatic of the Splugorth's Minions, living inside a shell and covered in tentacles. Surface people are the least familiar with the Metztla because they are rarely encountered, but under the waves, there are vast fleets of these giant monsters inhabiting the waters around Atlantis, and keeping her safe from rivals and enemies.

For political reasons involving rival Splugorth, dark gods, and other considerations, the Splugorth have refrained from conquering Rifts Earth, but their kingdom underwater is expansive and their influence greater than surface dwellers imagine. This means the Minions of Splugorth dominate the Atlantic Ocean, where Metztla and Splugorth Slavers prey upon aquatic people with daring impunity. In fact, it is rival supernatural forces like the *Lord of the Deep* and *the Milu*, as well as human forces like the *New Navy* and *the Lemurians*, that help to keep them in check under the waves. Though not outright "enemies" of Lemuria, Metztla prey upon aquatic wildlife and intelligent life forms, and raiding parties of Splugorth Slavers and Metztla are found in all the oceans and seas of the world, hunting Lemurians, Merans and other aquatic people and animals for the gladiatorial arena, zoos and slave markets on Atlantis and across the Megaverse. Meanwhile, High Lords and Conservators perform inhumane Bio-Wizard experiments (the dark magic cousin to Biomancy) upon Lemurians and other aquatic people, as well as covet many of the secrets of Lemurian magic. Thus, conflicts between the Minions of Splugorth and Lemurians fall way short of war, but their relationship is one of adversarial rivals under the sea.

Undead of the Ocean: The Threat of the Milu. Undead under the sea falls into a few categories, including creations spawned in *Dead Pools* and by the *Lord of the Deep* (both described in **Rifts® Underseas**). However, the Milu are the boldest hostile invader to command undead and, perhaps, the gravest threat.

Milu and Lemurians are polar opposites. The Milu represent death and destruction. The Lemurians, life and peaceful harmony. The two even wield opposing magicks, with the Milu commanding power over Necromancy and the undead and the Lemurians commanding Biomancy and Bio-Energy.

The Milu undead fight on two fronts, with *Davey Jones*, the Milu's Master Vampire General on Earth creating and overseeing legions of undead and Zombie Servants sent against Lemurians and their allies, and the Milu themselves doing likewise, while building secret strongholds, hiding places and their City of Bones on the ocean floor. Lemurians have tried to target and destroy Davey Jones many times, but he always seems to pull an ace out of his sleeve to escape a lasting death time and time again. If they could destroy him, it would leave only the Milu and their legions to deal with in battle.

Lemurians might not have survived the combined assaults of three powerful enemies, the Lord of the Deep, the Naut'Yll and the Milu, except that they have been joined by other heroic forces to battle them. Tritonia and the New Navy have been relentless against the Naut'Yll. Merans, Ichthyleans, cetaceans, and a host of practitioners of magic and other people oppose the Lord of the Deep. And *everyone* battles the Milu undead legions. Everyone, including the Minions of Splugorth who see them as the invading minions of another Alien Intelligence, the Naut'Yll who also see them as demonic rivals for the conquest of Earth, Merans, Ichthyleans, Amphibs, pirates, heroes and any mortal who learns of their existence stand to destroy the Milu and their undead. For to do otherwise is to accept slavery and death.

Few captured Lemurians get turned into Milu Undead or zombies. In most cases, they fight to the death or are rescued by their comrades before it is too late. Due to the threat that the Milu, Davey Jones, and the Lord of the Deep represent, many Lemurians have dedicated their lives to fighting the evil that grows in the ocean depths.

Vampires. Lemurians loath undead of every variety and have begun to play a more active role in the exploration and liberation of Mexico. Their plan is to help the human survivors as much as they can to help eradicate the undead that dominate that part of the world. So far, this has included joining and helping vampire hunters in the region to fight the undead, defending villages and helping slaves escape their clutches. Lemurians are trying to get better reconnaissance and intelligence on the full level of power and number of vampires before taking more extreme action. Lemurians stand against the undead and anyone who contaminates or destroys the environment or exhibits a disdain for life.

Lemurian Relations with Other Peoples

Lemurians have few true allies with any real weight or power at this time. The Merans, Ichthyleans, and several dozen bands of adventurers and some coastal communities around the world are chief among their closest friends and allies.

Amphibs (Friends). These mutants of Tritonia are amphibious like Lemurians and Merans. Perhaps it's because Lemurians and Amphibs encounter each other so often that the two species get along well, despite the politics of their leaders. Lemurians accept Amphibs without fear or apprehension and treat them with respect and courtesy. Likewise, Amphibs appreciate the Lemurians' harmonious existence with nature and see them as fellow "creatures of the sea." The two often stop to exchange data, warn each other of danger in the area and come to each other's aid when in trouble. Amphibs are even welcomed in Lemurian cities, and individuals often strike up lasting friendships. Fun fact: Amphibs were among the first to discover the existence of Lemurians and their floating cities.

Atlanteans (Friends and Associates). Though Atlanteans and Lemurians were once great friends and allies, that was thousands of years ago. Other than a shared history and the positive nature of their past relationship, there is no direct contact or political relationship between these two civilizations. However, both Atlanteans and Lemurians have many enemies in common and are quick to give the other the benefit of the doubt in a given situation. Individual Atlanteans and Lemurians often strike up quick friendships, though the Atlanteans have a darker and more aggressive view of life, and look upon Lemurians as being well-intentioned but innocent and naive to the ways of evil in the Megaverse.

Pneuma-Biform Cetaceans and Whalesingers (Friends and Allies). As noble creatures of the sea, many have banded together with the Lemurians to fight against the Lord of the Deep and other invaders of the oceans. Both keep each other safe from the clutches of the Lord of the Deep, Milu and Minions of Splugorth, and a special relationship has formed between the two groups. The Pneuma-Biforms are welcomed guests at all Lemurian cities, outposts and gardens, and both exchange information, aid and share knowledge.

Lemurians get along well with the intelligent dolphins and whales of Rifts Earth, and both Lemurians and cetaceans regard each other as good friends and allies. However, while they may visit and help each other, they tend to live separate lives, joining forces only when the situation calls for it.

Merans and Ichthyleans (Friends and Allies). These two simple, tribal people of the ocean are two of Lemuria's staunchest allies. Lemurians help, watch out for and protect them, and they do the same for Lemurians. Ironically, Merans and Ichthyleans are not fond of each other, and it is their friendship with Lemurians that keeps these two rivals from a more adversarial relationship. Thus, these two allies of Lemuria often consider each other friendly rivals and even friendly enemies, especially between certain tribes. Due to the influence of Lemuria, the animosity between these two has softened considerably over the last few generations, and some Merans and Ichthyleans have become true friends of one another. However, the majority of Merans and Ichthyleans (60%) still treat each other like competitive siblings, always trying to outdo the other, or prove they are superior to the other. Lemurians, Merans and Ichthyleans work together to fight their common enemies and build a better life for all.

As close friends and allies of both of these aquatic people, Merans and Ichthyleans can be found living and working in and around Lemurian Gardens, cities and outposts. Likewise, it is not unusual to see Lemurians living in and visiting Meran and Ichthylean communities. Both people are treated as complete equals by Lemurians and will come to their aid whenever they are in need. Both also trade with the Lemurians and share information on an open basis.

New Navy (Friends and Associates). Lemurians and the New Navy might be thought of as friendly, good neighbors under the sea. As neighbors, they smile and wave to each other, or stop to chat whenever they bump into one another. They have both come to like and respect each other, and when one is seen to be in trouble, the other is quick to come to their aid and assist in whatever way they can. In fact, the humans of the New Navy and Lemurians have fought side by side against the Naut'Yll, the Lord of the Deep and many other invaders and monsters of the sea many times, but shortly after the danger has passed, both departed and go their separate ways. However, there are no official ties nor any lines of direct communication, trade or military alliance. As a result, one cannot call the other in times of need, and they have no idea of how to contact each other. That having been said, they encounter each other on a rather frequent basis and often stop to exchange information and intelligence about an area or enemy activity, as well as break bread and trade goods and services. It seems only a matter of time before these two make their friendship public and form an official alliance. Then again, this might cause trouble for the New Navy and its friendship with Tritonia, and may be the reason ties with Lemurians have not yet been formalized.

Ocean Wizards and Other Practitioners of Magic (Friends and Associates). Ocean Wizards, Sea Druids, Sea Inquisitors and many other mages and people with ties to the sea know about Lemurians (rumors if nothing else), what they stand for, and may, from time to time, join forces with them against common enemies, share information and trade goods and services.

Surface Dwellers of Polynesia (Friends and Allies). Lemurians have made contact, helped and traded with many of the people of Polynesia for years. They have a good relationship with most of these people and protect them from monsters and invaders.

Surface Dwellers of Tech-Based Nations (Distrusted Rivals). So far, Lemurians have steered clear of most advanced civilizations. They see most of these governments as unstable, isolated, extreme, and dangerous. Virtually all are regarded as savage, brutal and narrow-minded, with little concern for the welfare of nonhumans or the environment. Lemurians understand why the people and nations of Rifts Earth are so polarized and militant, but see most of them as a danger to themselves and others, and have avoided them like the plague. In recent years, however, the Lemurians have started to make forays into the surface world to observe, gather intelligence, and make better assessments about the many fragmented kingdoms there and whether they should make contact with them or not. Such reconnaissance operations are being undertaken in secret and by Lemurian adventurers and explorers curious about the surface world. For now, however, surface-dwellers are regarded with fear, suspicion and distrust.

Tritonia (Rival and Friendly Enemy). Lemurians understand what Tritonia is, and have come to the aid of the human community or groups of Tritonian seafarers on several occassions. However, the two don't see eye-to-eye and rub each other the wrong way. This has led to a number of disagreements and clashes. Both see each other as arrogant elitists unwilling to accept any ideology other than their own. This is not entirely true of either side, but that's the perception. As a result, the two forces don't like or trust one another, have no formal relationship, no trade, minimal contact and avoid official interaction. If the New Navy is Lemuria's friendly neighbor, then Tritonia is the grouchy neighbor best to be avoided.

Part of the problem between these two is their technologies and ways of life. Tritonia is a typical human civilization that is a polluter, has little regard for the environment, and is set in its ways and unwilling to change. Lemuria may be the opposite, but they are equally unwilling to change or accept Tritonia as it is, so they resent each other and clash. Tritonians also have concerns about Lemurian magic and why they are so secretive and elusive, changing the locations of their cities and always being on the move. This leaves the Triotonians wondering if Lemurians can really be trusted, or whether they have something to hide. Lemurians, on the other hand, do not trust the supposed "renegade" and "outcast" Naut'Yll embraced by Tritonia and suspect they are spies and saboteurs out to destroy Tritonia and their allies from within.

It is ironic then, that individual Tritonians and Lemurians often get along well, and are happy to exchange information, trade goods and services and help each other out. It is primarily the leadership, military and politics of the two nations that keep them apart. Also see Amphibs, above.

Exotic Creatures of the Sea

Blue Otter
Death Hunter Fish
Giant Sea Slug
Ichthyosaur
Jonah's Fish
Kilmoran's Eel
Line Ray
Mega-Ray
Narcassai Swordfish
Saber-Toothed Sea Lion
Sea Dragon Turtle
Storm Crab
Terror Eel
Twisted Treasure Sea Horse

Blue Otter

This peculiar mustelid is highly intelligent, inquisitive and agile. The Blue Otter's nature and personality is reminiscent of the river and sea otter: They are playful, love the company of people and make a great companion or Familiar. They are fascinated by humanoids and seem especially attracted to humans, Lemurians, the mutant Amphibs and other similar D-Bees. Their curiosity is infamous and Blue Otters, like dolphins, have been known to play with swimmers, help mariners in distress and sometimes even try to warn and protect the innocent from danger. Their affable personality and attraction to humans makes young Blue Otters easy to domesticate. They are actually smarter than dogs and become fiercely loyal to their owners.

The most unique thing about "Blue" Otters is their mystical capabilities. Like the Mystic, the animal possesses several innate magic abilities and psionics. This has led some people to wonder if they might be some kind of Faerie. Their ability to tap into ambient P.P.E. and cast spells makes them a highly sought after commodity as Familiars and companions to Lemurians, Ocean Wizards, Sea Druids and even mainland practitioners of magic in China, Japan, Canada and the Americas.

Some people believe that the Lemurians developed Blue Otters as pets, however, they are animals from an alien world that were drawn through a dimensional Rift and adapted well to Rifts Earth.

Blue Otter Stats

Also Known As: Mystic Otters and Blues.

Alignment: Most are considered to be Unprincipled (80%) though Scrupulous (10%) and Anarchist (10%) alignments are not unheard of.

Attributes: I.Q. 1D6+8 (high animal intelligence), M.E. 2D6+8, M.A. 2D6+9, P.S. 1D4+6, P.P. 2D6+10, P.E. 2D6+7, P.B. 2D6+7, Spd 2D6+7, double in water.

Size: 4-6 feet (1.2 to 1.8 m) long and weighs 80-120 lbs (36 to 54 kg).

Hit Points: P.E. attribute number +1D6 per level of experience.

S.D.C.: 2D6. **Note:** Hit Points and S.D.C. become M.D.C. when traveling along ley lines and within a ley line triad like the Bermuda Triangle.

Horror Factor: Not applicable.

P.P.E.: P.E. attribute number x4, +1D6 per level of experience or every four years of age (whichever the G.M. wants to use).

Average Life Span: 3D6+12 years.

Experience Level: Typically 1D4 or as the Game Master desires up to level 9, never more.

Equivalent Skills: Swimming 98%, Climbing 50%, Prowl 60%, Detect Concealment 30%, Detect Ambush 40%, and Escape Artist 35%. All go up 3% per level of experience.

Natural Abilities: Hold breath for up to 3D4+10 minutes, nightvision 120 feet (36.6 m), impervious to cold (even magic cold and magic ice weapons do half damage), swim and tolerates depths up to 600 feet (183 m).

Heightened Sense of Smell (special): Enables the animal to track by smell 40% +2% per level of experience and identify foods 60% +3% per level of experience.

Heightened Sense of Touch (special): Otters also have long, bristly whiskers on the face that detect motion and vibrations in the water and air, alerting them to predators and helping them locate prey. This and other heightened senses reduces penalties from fighting blind or an invisible opponent to -5 to strike, parry and dodge.

Ley Line M.D.C. (special): Hit Points and S.D.C. become M.D.C. when the creature is traveling along ley lines or within a ley line triangle like the Bermuda Triangle. No P.P.E. cost to become M.D.C., it just happens automatically. Bites still do S.D.C. damage.

Ley Line Speed Doubler: The same as dolphins, the Blue Otter has the innate ability to swim at twice its normal speed without fatigue whenever swimming along a ley line. Does not work on dry land nor flying in the air; must be in water.

Sense Ley Line (special): Same as the Ley Line Walker O.C.C. ability.

Also see Magic for spell casting abilities and Psionics.

Vulnerabilities: None, per se, except their curiosity and tendency to like and trust humans can get them into trouble, captured or killed.

Attacks per Melee: Three.

Damage: Bite does 1D6 S.D.C.; claws do 1D4 S.D.C.

Bonuses (in addition to possible attribute bonuses): +3 to Perception Rolls, +3 to initiative, +2 to strike, +4 to automatic dodge (the act of dodging does not use up a melee attack) and +4 to pull punch. Note: Reduce all combat bonuses by half on dry land; round down.

Magic: Born with an intuitive understanding of magic, Blue Otters are able to cast the following spells at level one: Armor of Ithan (10), Cleanse (6), Float in Air (5), Sense Evil (2), and Sense Direction Underwater (4). Base P.P.E.: P.E. attribute number x4, +1D6 per level of experience. For each additional level of experience, ONE new spell becomes known to the Blue Otter. Spells may be selected from Ocean Magic and/or from Spell Invocations levels 1-3. **Note:** Blue Otters tend to develop defensive and helpful magic spells, and seldom combat or harmful spells.

Psionics: Blue Otters have Bio-Regeneration (self; 6), Empathy (4), See the Invisible (4), Sense Magic (3), Sense Time (2), Sixth Sense (2) and Stop Bleeding (4). Base I.S.P.: M.E. attribute number x2, +1D4 per level of experience. Select one additional psionic ability from the Sensitive category per each new level of experience (seldom more than level 4).

Habitat: Rocky sea coast. Cool climates are preferred, but they can survive in all temperature ranges.

Allies: Lemurians, humans, and humanoid D-Bees, but prefer the company of easy-going, playful practitioners of magic, Mystics, and Amphibs most of all.

Enemies: Those who hunt them, including sea monsters, sharks and Horune Pirates, cruel and wicked people and supernatural evil (including the Lord of the Deep and his undead legions and the Minions of Splugorth).

Value: As a pet or zoo animal they can fetch a price of 15,000 credits. Their magical aptitude is rarely usable by their owners and is pure instinct. Their fur fetches up to 10,000 credits per pelt, however they are highly prized as Familiars and can easily sell for over 40,000 credits to the right buyer.

Death Hunter Fish

The Death Hunter Fish vaguely resemble barracudas. They are long and slender with a savage looking maw of sharp teeth. They are strong enough to bite through the toughest of bone or armored hide, and are unafraid of the ocean's other monsters. Their vicious jaws open wide like many species of snakes, unhinging to gorge on large chunks of dead flesh, other carrion and the *undead.* While they can survive on carrion, they seem to prefer the taste and challenge of hunting the undead above all else. They have a keen sense of smell and can track the scent of blood, death and decay with pinpoint accuracy, as well as a supernatural sense that allows them to home in on the necromantic energy of the undead and Necromancers.

Their hunger for dead and decaying things makes these fearsome predators threats to the Milu and other undead that lurk at the bottom of the sea. Thankfully, Death Hunters leave the living alone, biting only when they feel threatened or cornered. The one exception is those with the "stink of death" – i.e. the presence of necromantic energy, like Necromancers, Witches allied to gods of death, and those rare few who practice Soulmancy and Demon Magic on Rifts Earth. Death Hunter Fish are, themselves, supernatural and can become Mega-Damage creatures. One marine Biologist from Tritonia noted, while performing an autopsy on a specimen, that it contained an elevated level of silver in its system, which is the bane of the undead and may be one of the primary factors explaining their anti-undead abilities. They glisten with what some have described as a "silvery tint" and their telltale flash when moving to strike has become a thing to fear amongst the undead of the sea.

Death Hunter Fish Stats

Also Known As: Keoni I'a – The Righteous (Hunter) Fish.

Alignment: Considered to be Anarchist.

Attributes: I.Q. 1D4+2 (animal intelligence), M.E. 1D4+2, M.A. 1D4+2, P.S. 1D6+6, P.P. 2D6+2, P.E. 2D6, P.B. 1D4, swimming Spd 3D6+10.

Size: 2 to 5.5 feet (0.6 to 1.7 m) long and up to 1 foot (0.3 m) wide.

Weight: 36 to 103 lbs (16 to 46 kg).

Hit Points: 3D6+8. **S.D.C.:** 1D6x10. **Natural A.R.:** 9, but can temporarily transform into a Mega-Damage creature, see Bio-Energy Field below.

Horror Factor: 10 for most, but 12 for the undead.

Average Life Span: 2D6+6 years.

P.P.E.: 2D6+10

Equivalent Skills: Swimming 98%, Prowl 80% and Underwater Navigation 90%.

Natural Abilities: Good underwater vision, nightvision 2,000 feet (610 m) and tolerate depths up to 7 miles (11 km). Attack in groups of 1D6+4, but swim in schools of 3D4x10 fish.

Bio-Energy Field M.D.C. Transformation (special): The Death Hunter Fish can focus all of its energy (P.P.E.) to transform itself into a minor M.D.C. creature and cause its natural bite to inflict double normal damage against the undead. This power is used at the start of any attack leveled against the undead, turning *Hit Points* (not S.D.C.) into M.D.C., point for point. With each undead a school of Death Hunter Fish slay, those within a 90 foot (27.4 m) radius of the kill get supercharged by the monster's P.P.E. at the time of its death, increasing the M.D.C. (or restoring M.D.C. lost in combat) of each fish by 1D4+6 points per fish. The M.D.C. transformation remains in place for as long as there is even one undead within a mile (1.6 km) of the fish.

Chemoreceptors (special): A highly advanced sense of taste and smell lets the Death Hunter Fish detect salinity and toxicity of the water, which enables it to taste and track the scent of blood, decaying flesh and the distinct smell of *the undead.* **Base Skill**: 86% to track and locate undead and dead/decaying flesh; 68% to track and locate source of blood, identify chemicals, toxins or specific creatures by scent trails. **Range of Detection:** Five mile (8 km) radius.

Sense Undead (special): In addition to their keen sense of smell, the Death Hunter has a magical sense like a Dog Boy or Psi-Stalker that enables it to detect and zero in on the location of undead creatures by their necromantic energy. **Base Skill:** 95% to track and locate undead. **Range of Detection:** Two miles (3 km).

Eat Undead (special): In addition to its hardy stomach and digestive system that can handle dead and decaying flesh, the Death Hunter Fish can actually harm the undead. Whether this is some kind of innate magical ability or an excessive amount of silver in their system is hard to say. The end result is they can slay and devour the undead. Their digestive enzymes retard the undead flesh's ability to regenerate and quickly break down and transform the flesh (and necrotic energy) into usable calories. An undead eaten by the Death Hunter Fish is slain and forever destroyed!

Any undead foolish enough to bite into the flesh of a Death Hunter, or try to drain the blood from it, is in for a nasty surprise: A mouthful of meat or blood that burns like acid, inflicting 4D6 Hit Points/M.D. per bite. Undead that pass through the seeping blood of a wounded or dead Death Hunter Fish also takes 4D6 damage per melee that it is exposed to the blood. **Note:** On the surface, coating one's blade or weapon in Death Hunter Fish blood does an extra 1D6+3 points of damage to vampires and other undead. However, the blood loses its potency against the undead 10 minutes after it dries. Splashing or spraying Death Hunter Fish blood on a vampire/undead is the same as Holy Water.

Vulnerabilities: None per se.

Attacks per Melee: Two.

Damage: A bite does 3D6 S.D.C. damage to normal, mortal creatures, a tail slap or butt does 1D4 S.D.C.

To the undead, however, its bite inflicts 5D6 damage to their Hit Points/M.D.C. to armor worn by undead. Against evil supernatural creatures, the damage of their bite is 1D6 M.D., but demons and other "living" supernatural beings are seldom targeted.

Tend to attack as lone individuals, pairs, trios and in small groups of 5-10 fish, but may gather and hunt in schools as large as 120.

Bonuses (in addition to possible attribute bonuses): +2 to Perception Rolls, +4 on initiative against the undead, +4 to strike and +3 to dodge.

Magic: None.

Psionics: None.

Enemies: Undead of all kinds, especially the undead of the Milu as their prey of choice, as well as humanoids and monsters allied to and empowered by gods of death/the dead/undead, Bonelings, Naga Deevils, Death Demons, Ghouls, Nasu, Soul Catcher demons, Necromancers and Witches, mages and monsters who wield Necromancy, Soulmancy and Demon Magic.

Allies: They leave the living alone and most other predatory fish and sea monsters don't bother Death Hunters. Lemurians love these fish and use their abilities to commune with animals to send them against the undead and to guard permanent underwater Lemurian outposts. Lemurians, Merans and Ichthyleans consider seeing one or two small schools of Death Hunters as good luck. However, seeing several or large schools (3D4x10 fish) means the presence of the undead or a place of death nearby.

Habitat: Death Hunters congregate in schools and hunt in and around Dead Pools, recently sunken ships, underwater battlefields and, of course, Milu strongholds and any area dominat-

ed by the undead. They may show up out of the blue to pick or scavenge from carcasses.

Value: Lemurians and some aquatic D-Bees and Undead Hunters use small packs or even a solo Death Hunter Fish to hunt and track the undead. A trained fish can sell for as much as 1D6x10,000 credits, a school of four as much as 4D6x10,000 credits. Their flesh is not harmful to mortals, but their consumption of undead flesh makes their own meat taste fatty and foul.

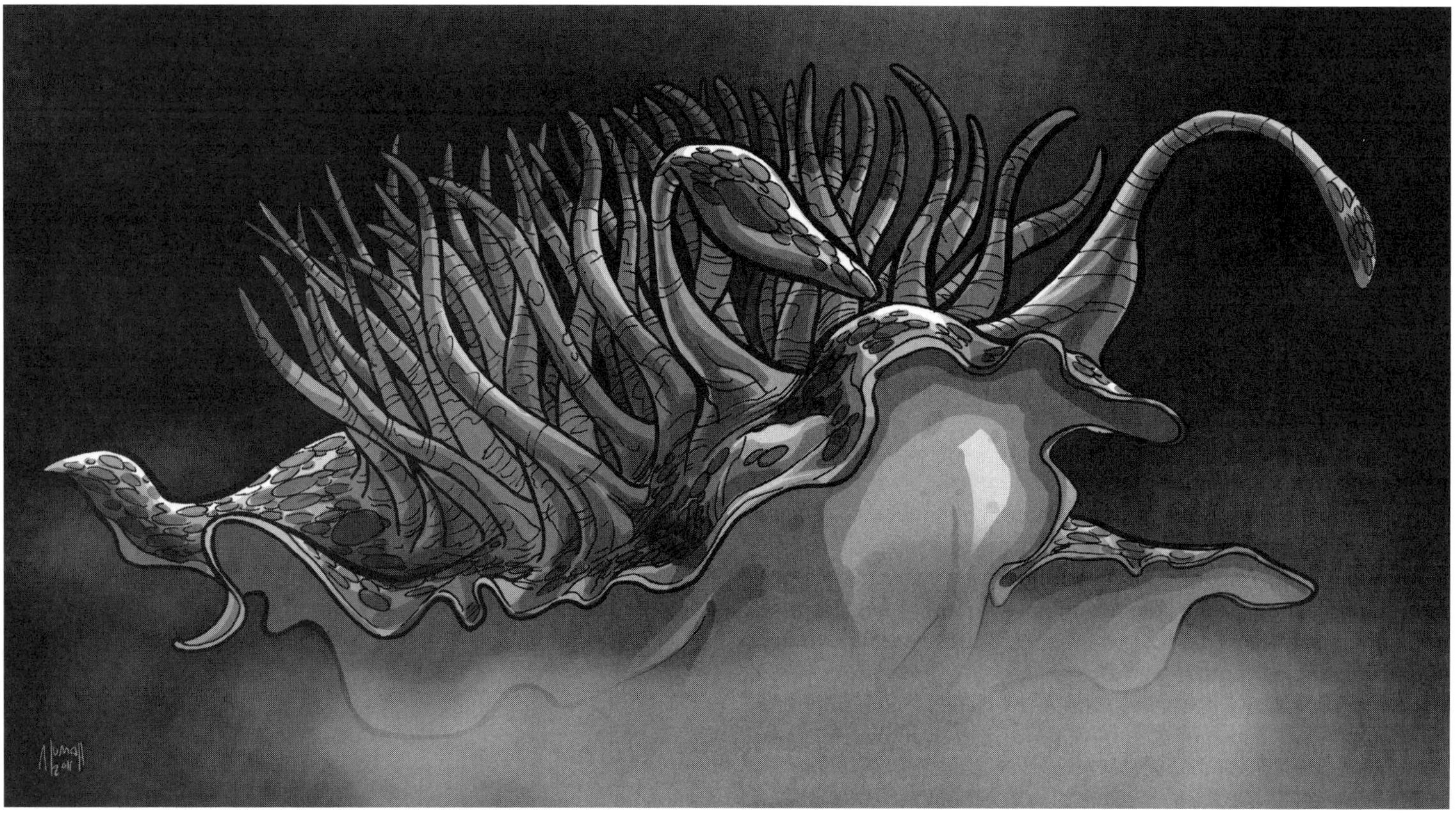

Giant Sea Slug

This unusual creature appears to be a cross between a sea anemone and a normal sea slug. It was originally designed by the Lemurians to feed on garbage and decaying material in an effort to help clean up the ocean. The exotic digestive system of these Giant Sea Slugs enables them to tackle all kinds of noxious substances, even drums of toxic waste, oil and fuel dumped over the centuries by surface dwellers. Whether it was the Lemurians' original intent or a side effect of feeding on carcinogenic and mutagenic toxins, the slugs grow to enormous sizes. When no garbage, waste or toxic chemicals are available, the Giant Sea Slugs devour whatever they can find, including vast sections of coral reefs, crops of plants, wood, carrion, and even attack sick and injured fish, animals and people!

Many of these sea slugs have found a safe refuge at Dead Pools, feeding on the dead and discarded equipment and artifacts. Supernatural predators, sea serpents and the undead have taken to feeding on the Giant Sea Slugs, keeping their numbers in check. They start small, about the size of a robin's egg, but can grow to the size of a house by eating rotting matter, garbage and toxic chemicals. The slug's hide is a rainbow of color like the toxins they feed upon. They also possess hundreds of thick hairs or tentacles on their backs which are their gills. Some species of fish, like the clown fish, live in and amongst these tentacles just as if they were sea anemones.

It has been found that young Giant Sea Slugs can be kept at their small size, making them acceptable as pets and Familiars if they are not allowed to voraciously consume food. If they are fed a steady, conservative diet the slugs remain somewhere between the size of a grapefruit and a watermelon and can rest or cling to their master's shoulder, hide in a bag or float along the currents.

Giant Sea Slug Stats

Also Known As: Living Garbage Disposals, the Devourer and Rainbow Slugs.

Alignment: Considered to be Anarchist or Miscreant.

Attributes: Low animal intelligence (basically an eating machine); I.Q. of 1D4, M.E. 1D4, M.A. 1D4, P.S. 40+2D6 (Robotic), P.P. 1D6+5, P.E. 1D6+28, P.B. 2D6 (often brightly colored), Spd. 1D6+2 swimming and 2D4+4 crawling.

M.D.C.: 1D6x100 M.D.C. (On an S.D.C. World: 3D6x10 Hit Points and 4D6x10 S.D.C., with a Natural A.R. of 9. Small ones, like those used as Familiars, have one-third the Hit Points and S.D.C. of mature wild slugs.)

Horror Factor: 10

Size: "Giants" range in size from that of an automobile to a semi-truck and trailer. Most are 16-24 feet (4.8 to 7.3 m) long, but the largest reach a length of 60 feet (18.3 m) long and 20 feet (6.1 m) tall and wide.

Weight: 3-5 tons on average, 15-20 tons for the largest.

Average Life Span: 2D6+40 years. When they do die, a bizarre chemical reaction takes places during decomposition which neutralizes and purifies any toxins in their body, transforming their dead biomass into fertile and usable remains (no longer toxic or harmful to the environment).

P.P.E.: 2D6. For such a large creature it has very little P.P.E.

Equivalent Skills: Swimming 50%. The slug wiggles its body in an up and down motion to propel itself. It is not fast or graceful, nor agile while swimming, preferring to crawl along the ocean bottom.

Natural Abilities: Impervious to toxins, oil, fossil fuel, chemical toxins, rotten food, and cold (magic cold does one third damage), resistant to heat (half damage) and tolerates depths up to 6 miles (9.6 km).

Chemoreceptors (special): The Giant Sea Slug can taste toxins, toxic chemicals and waste material up to ten miles (16 km) away. Track by Scent: 80%. Recognize other chemicals, toxins, blood and water salinity at 60%.

Heightened Sense of Hearing (special): The slug can locate moving objects in water 90% and hear and understand the dangers of various sounds as well as use them to help it find its food. It is drawn to mechanical sounds, as they are often a source of pollution. It can also hear into the ultrasonic range, mostly for mechanical sounds.

Vulnerabilities: These strange creatures are rarely bothered by natural predators other than the largest sea monsters and undead, but they do have three notable weaknesses:

Blind: Giant Sea Slugs have no eyes or other forms of optical sensors, they rely totally on other senses to find food or fight back.

Breathing Tentacles: The Giant Sea Slug breathes through the tentacles on its back, which serve as a form of external gill. Removing all the tentacles causes the Giant Sea Slug to suffocate and die! Most have 2D6x10 tendrils, and each tendril has 1D6+1 M.D.C.

Slow and Ponderous: Not very maneuverable, the behemoths rely on their size, rubbery M.D.C. hides and distasteful flesh to keep most predators away.

Attacks per Melee: Two.

Damage: Big Tentacle Strike: The two large tentacles at the front of the creature can hit like a pile driver, doing damage as per Robot P.S. (typically 1D6 M.D. on a restrained punch and 3D6 on a full strength attack), or bite attack. Its bite does 1D4x10 M.D. and its massive maw filled with rows of sharp teeth can shred and devour just about anything it sinks its teeth into. It is a slow eater, and it is easy to escape from, but objects (especially stationary ones) that are in its path may fall victim to its vicious maw.

Bonuses (in addition to possible attribute bonuses): +1 to strike with a bite, can sense invisible foes and attack using its sense of hearing alone (no additional penalties for being blind).

Magic: None.

Psionics: None.

Enemies: Almost none, but large animals, sea monsters and other monsters sometimes feed on the slug. The undead of the Milu in and around the Dead Pools of the Indian Ocean also feed upon the slugs as they are slow and provide a wonderful source of nourishment (live flesh).

Allies: None, other than their own kind. Small ones are sometimes used by Lemurians as pets or Familiars.

Habitat: Dead Pools, toxic waste dumps, the sites of toxic spills and the occasional coral, animal or person.

Value: None.

Ichthyosaur

Skimming the surface like dolphins, these massive predators were first thought to be another one of the Lord of the Deep's sea monsters that melded a crocodile and a dolphin together. However, ancient archives and fossil records show the monster is an *Ichthyosaur* dinosaur that existed long before the Great Cataclysm. Some believe it has come to Rifts Earth through a dimensional anomaly from the past or is a similar species from another world, though there are also those who believe it has been recreated by Gene Splicers or rogue Lemurian Biomancer Gene-Mages.

In the wild, Ichthyosaurs hunt in small packs of 2D4+1 creatures, pursuing large fish like tuna and marlin. They are not above taking down a sea monster or supernatural monster if the pack is capable of doing so, and they happily feed upon humanoids and other mammals. While not as intelligent as dolphins or other cetaceans, Ichthyosaurs are quite cunning, using tactics and traps to outmaneuver and kill their prey.

The Ichthyosaur breathes air, like dolphins and whales, but is covered in thick, smooth scales which give it maximum protection and good maneuverability in the water. Its "reptilian brain" makes the creature a calculating hunter, but animals raised by Lemurians make reliable, loyal and friendly pets, work animals or riding animals. They are prized companions to many Lemurians, Merans and Ichthyleans who use the creatures as riding animals, watchdogs and attack animals. In fact, those raised by humanoids from a young age are very tame and enjoy the company of aquatic humanoids. In the wild, they often travel with and defend dolphins and whales.

Ichthyosaur Stats

Also Known As: Mo'o I'a (Lizard Fish), Dolphin Lizard, and Ichthy (pronounced ick thee).

Alignment: Considered to be Unprincipled or Anarchist.

Attributes: I.Q. 1D6+6, M.E. 1D6+6, M.A. 2D6+3, P.S. 4D6+6 (Robotic), P.P. 2D6+10, P.E. 2D6+11, P.B. 1D6+6, swimming Spd 3D6+45 (on average 32-38 mph/51.2 to 60.8 km).

M.D.C.: 1D6x10+15 M.D.C. for juveniles. Add 1D4x10+20 M.D.C. for every 100 years of age. (On an S.D.C. World: 5D6+10 Hit Points, 1D6x10 S.D.C. and a Natural A.R. of 12; +5D6 Hit Points and 1D6x10 S.D.C. per each 100 years of life.)

Horror Factor: 10 for juveniles, 12 for adults (looks like a cross between a dolphin and a crocodile).

Size: Juveniles: 9-15 feet (2.7 to 4.6 m) long.

Adults (more than 100 years old): 20-30 feet (6.1 to 9.1 m).

Ancient (more than 400 years old): 35-40 feet (10.6 to 12.2 m).

Weight: Juveniles: 600-2,000 lbs (270 to 900 kg). Adults: 5-10 tons.

Average Life Span: 600 years (roll 1D6 for random determination). The first 1-100 years is the "juvenile" stage of the monster's life. They start to grow even larger and become much tougher as they pass the 100 year mark.

P.P.E.: 4D6 to start, +1D6 per 100 years.

Equivalent Skills: Swimming 98%, Prowl 60%, Underwater Navigation 98%, Track and Hunt Sea Animals 90%.

Natural Abilities: Tough, scaly hide, nightvision 200 feet (61 m), tolerate depths up to 2 miles (3.2 km), resistant to cold (half damage), can locate moving objects in water 90% by keen hearing (can hear prey up to 3,000 feet/914 m away). Sensitive to electromagnetic energy; can follow electrical impulses, machines, electrical cables/conduits and muscle movement (no penalties for being blind, even in absolute darkness against living creatures); 3,000 foot (914 m) range.

Sense Magnetic North: Same as a dolphin; can always tell where magnetic north is precisely located. This is an immense help in navigating the oceans. A powerful blow to the head may temporarily (3D4 minutes) knockout this ability.

Magnetic Resonance Imaging (M.R.I.) Probe: Same as the dolphin's Ultrasonic Probe, only it uses electromagnetic energy. This probe is so precise that it can detect the thickness of walls, locate weak spots (thin or damaged areas), locate heat sources, sonar and communication arrays, engine rooms, and pinpoint crew location (-40% skill and range when probing large ships or thick armored vessels).

When used on living beings, it can detect whether or not an animal or humanoid is pregnant, has a cancer or tumor, locate the tumor or cancer, as well as locate bullets, foreign objects, blood clots, and scar tissue; detect and locate bionics or brain/M.O.M. implants, cybernetic appendages and even recognize Bio-Systems and artificial skin. This also enables the creature to make positive identification of a species by determining the physiology of the subject being scanned, identify creatures of magic and supernatural beings, and identify shape-changers in disguise (not applicable to magic metamorphosis). **Base Skill:** 65%. **Range:** 100 feet (30.5 m) or closer for maximum accuracy. Up to 200 feet (61 m) but at a skill penalty of -20%.

Dolphin Combat & Maneuvers: The Ichthyosaur can perform many aquatic acrobatics similar to dolphins, such as the following.

Dive: A high speed dive straight down, or at a slight angle, at double normal speed. Maximum depth is 500 feet (152 m) +100 feet (30.5 m) per level of experience. Roll to strike if the creature is trying to dive and hit or grab something.

Mid-Air Leap: Seven feet (2.1 m) for juveniles, 14 feet (4.2 m) for adults. Performed to show off, do tricks and to play.

Mid-Air Precision Leaping: Seven feet (2.1 m) for juveniles, 14 feet (4.2 m) for adults. Performed to grab a fish or object flying close to the surface of the water or to grab or knock an item out of a humanoid's hand. The player must announce this leap before the dice are rolled and must announce whether his Ichthyosaur is trying to grab or knock the item away. Then roll a 20 sided die to *strike* as normal (+2 to strike in addition to other bonuses). The character holding the item can use a parry roll to try to pull the item away. The Ichthy can also try to *slap* an item away or strike a person with its tail while in mid-leap, but gets no bonuses to do so. This move can also be used to leap through hoops, windows, onto boats, etc. Counts as three melee actions.

Quick Turns & Stops: Roll as if this maneuver was an automatic dodge or parry. A roll of 14 or higher means success. A failed roll means the creature couldn't turn or stop in time and either shoots by or slams into something/somebody.

Speed Burst: Can swim at double its normal speed for one minute. This maneuver can be performed six times per hour before tuckering the creature out too much to try it again. This move is performed for a quick dodge (+2 in addition to other bonuses) or getaway, a quick strike (+2 in addition to other bonuses) or to move toward or away from somebody or some place quickly.

Swim Breaching/Skimming: The Ichthy swims in an up and down motion, breaking the water in short, full body leaps, plunging back into the water and leaping out again in a fast forward motion. This is usually considered fun and playful. Ichthyosaurs can pace ships in this fashion and have been known to play escort with strangers for as a long as two hours. Reduce maximum speed by 20% and *speed bursts* are not possible when skimming the surface.

Tight Circle/Turn: The monster can make reasonably tight circles and turns in an area as small as 12 feet (3.6 m) in diameter.

Vulnerabilities: Ichthyosaurs need air to breathe, but can hold their breath for up to 1D4x10+20 minutes before needing to surface. They can only survive out of the water for 1D4+1 hours before their skin dries out and they die from dehydration.

Attacks per Melee: Three.

Damage: Restrained bite or nip inflicts 3D6 S.D.C., bite does 3D6 M.D., ram with nose 3D6 M.D., restrained tail slap does 4D6 S.D.C. and full strength tail slap does 1D6 M.D.; double damage for ancient Ichthyosaurs 500-600 years old.

Bonuses (in addition to possible attribute bonuses): +3 on Perception Rolls, +2 to initiative, +3 to strike, +2 to dodge, +2 to pull punch and +2 to roll with punch, fall or impact; double bonuses for ancient Ichthyosaurs 500-600 years old.

Magic: None.

Psionics: None.

Enemies: Large marine predators, sea serpents and sea monsters.

Allies: Fellow Ichthyosaurs, dolphins and whales. Many aquatic people, including Lemurians, Ichthyleans, Merans and Naut'yll use the creatures as pets, watchdogs, and riding and attack animals.

Habitat: Oceans around the world wherever dolphins and whales are found.

Value: The Ichthyosaur is a great pet, underwater companion and riding animal. Tamed and trained animals sell for 20,000-40,000 credits and exotic animal shows and arenas. Ichthy M.D.C. hides can be made into light body armor (32 M.D.C., weighs 10 lbs/4.5 kg, no movement penalties).

Jonah's Fish

Moving silently through the deep like an aquatic Trojan horse, the Jonah's Fish looks like a massive fish the size of a large house or small office building. Little does the unwitting observer know that Lemurians use the creature as a secret transport vehicle to carry them – a hidden cargo of Lemurian warriors – behind enemy lines from within the giant fish. Lemurians hidden inside the great fish travel in silence and without any mechanical sound, sonar or heat signatures to give themselves away. It is a subterfuge that has won them many a battle. In the event that they are discovered (or suspected of being inside), and the fish is attacked, its tough body scales protect the cargo of Lemurian warriors as they make a speedy retreat into deep water.

The Jonah's Fish stays afloat through the use of two large air bladders on either side of the body which offset the extreme weight of its own thick hide and natural armor. These air bladders have a secondary use, allowing the fish to secretly carry Lemurians into battle. Inside the fish's mouth are two muscle flaps leading to the air bladders which the Lemurians can climb into. They then use their ability to commune with animals to have the Jonah's Fish transport them to their desired location. The Lemurians have used such fishes to sneak up on enemies or to access the shores of the surface world without detection, using the fish to hide their presence as they are delivered behind enemy lines or onto distant shores. Lemurians also use the fish as floating tanks, ramming into ships and "swallowing" up prisoners and valuables that fall into the water. Those who find hiding inside the belly of a fish distasteful usually construct lashes to ride on the exterior of the fish.

Jonah's Fish Stats

Also Known As: Carrier Fish, Transport Fish, Armored Fish.

Alignment: Considered to be Unprincipled (70%) or Anarchist (30%).

Attributes: Low animal intelligence (basically a giant fish); I.Q. 1D4+2, M.E. 1D6+6, M.A. 1D6+4, P.S. 2D4+40 (Supernatural), P.P. 1D6+6, P.E. 2D6+10, P.B. 1D6, Spd 1D4x10+40 swimming (35-55 mph/56 to 88 km).

M.D.C.: +1D4x100+600 M.D.C. (On an S.D.C. World: 2D6x100 Hit Points and 4D6x100 S.D.C. and an A.R. of 16.)

Horror Factor: 9; looks like a giant, fat, ugly fish.

Size: Full grown adults reach a length of 100 to 120 feet (30.5 to 36.6 m), a width of 30-40 feet (9.1 to 12.2 m), a height of 25-30 feet (7.6 to 9.1 m), and weigh 60-70 tons.

Average Life Span: 2D6+50 years.

P.P.E.: 5D6

Equivalent Skills: Swimming 98% and Prowl 70%.

Natural Abilities: Fast swimmer, Supernatural P.S. and P.E., tough outer scales, low thermal reading (like most fish; the Lemurians inside are concealed and undetectable by most sensors until they exit through the mouth of the giant fish), nightvision 1,000 feet (305 m), resistant to cold (half damage, even magic cold does half damage), tolerate depths up to 8 miles (12.8 km) though it's Lemurian cargo cannot exceed their usual depth tolerance.

Air Bladders (special): The air bladders used for buoyancy can also hold 1D6+4 human-sized passengers per bladder and still function. Passengers can remain inside for three days before things become too uncomfortable. Carbon dioxide is removed from the bladder and expelled out of the fish's gills, while new oxygen is drawn in and stored in the bladders. The Jonah's Fish surface every three days to clear out its bladders of garbage and debris, including any Lemurian passengers whether they want to exit or not. The fish's mouth and a dual-flapped muscle structure act as an airlock, allowing passengers to disembark out of the fish's mouth while submerged and still maintain the air pressure and buoyancy on the inside. Lemurians direct the Jonah's Fish via psionic Empathy and Telepathy. Since the giant is docile and is seldom used to attack, it is very compliant and willing to travel where directed.

Cloaking: The Jonah's Fish's own biological signature masks anything hiding inside it, even if it is a powerful source of magical energy, making them/it invisible to the outside world. Like most fish, it also swims quietly (natural prowl of 70%), radiates no heat and is often assumed to be an ordinary, dumb animal when it is detected.

Vulnerabilities: Not very smart or maneuverable, it relies on its armor for protection.

Attacks per Melee: Two, but the Jonah's Fish is not very aggressive, eating small fish by swallowing schools of them at a time in its giant maw. It only attacks people and ships when threatened by them or commanded by a Lemurian.

Damage: Bite 3D6 M.D., tail slap 4D6 M.D., ram 1D6x10 M.D. and counts as two attacks.

Bonuses (in addition to possible attribute bonuses): +1 to dodge underwater.

Magic: None.

Psionics: None.

Enemies: Sea monsters, sea serpents, Splugorth Metztla, and similar giant monsters eat Jonah's Fish. Some seafaring and aquatic people, including Horune Pirates, hunt the Jonah's Fish like whales for its meat, oils and thick skin, using its armored hide, bones and teeth to make M.D.C. armor, shelters, boats, tools and weapons. **Note:** Despite its giant mouth and rows of dagger- to short sword-sized teeth, the Jonah's Fish feeds on small fish, shrimp, and even plankton and krill, swallowing them whole.

Allies: Its own kind and Lemurians. Only Lemurians use the Jonah's Fish to hide inside its air bladders and use it like a living transport vehicle. They also use it to pull heavy cargo. This use of the animal compels them to feed and protect it. Some aquatic D-Bees and humans ride on its back, holding onto its fins or gills, or attaching rope and lashes to the great beast. **Note:** Unlike most fish, Jonah's Fish don't often school together in large numbers. They are most often encountered as lone individuals, pairs and quartets. A large school of Jonah's Fish is 8-12 of them.

Primitive people (not Lemurians) fashion their thick, scaly hides into heavy body armor, tough M.D.C. boats (100-200 M.D.C. for a small boat or raft), huts and shelters (50-200 M.D.C.), and use the bones and teeth to make light M.D. weapons (they inflict 1D4, 1D6 and 2D4 M.D. as spearheads, knives, short swords, and war clubs) and tools. Jonah's Fish Armor has 140 M.D.C. (-15% movement penalty and reduces running and swimming speed by 10%).

Habitat: The oceans of the world from deep sea to shallow waters and coral reefs.

Value: To Lemurians, who use the creature as a submarine or living transport vehicle as well as a giant work animal hauling cargo, a tamed behemoth has a value of 50,000 to 75,000 credits.

Kilmoran's Eel

Like a ghostly apparition, heard, but seen only out of the corner of the eye, the giant Kilmoran's Eel is a frightening adversary in the confines of a labyrinth, sunken ship or rocky canyon. While these giant eels are fast and deadly in the open sea, they thrive in close quarters where there are ample places to hide. They are highly agile and dart back and forth through crevasses, tunnels and passageways like a snake in its underground burrow. Their namesake comes from an animal handler, Eric Kilmoran, who provided a number of these creatures to several undersea gladiatorial arenas in the South Pacific. Kilmoran marketed them as vicious pit and maze monsters, setting up a glass screen on top so spectators could watch the eels pick apart groups of gladiators sent to hunt them inside the underwater maze. While many have tried to follow in his footsteps, he is still heralded as the man who brought the deadly monster eels to the public.

Known as *Moana Makani Puhi* to Polynesians, they move as gracefully and silently as the wind. Renowned Serpent Hunters consider these monster eels as one of their favorite non-sea serpent riding animals to try and master. Their agility combined with their own battle prowess has made them a valued mount in confined areas, tunnels, narrow ravines, and underwater cities, something some species of sea serpents have trouble with.

As fish, they do not survive for very long out of water. However, their snake-like bodies give them an advantage over normal fish, allowing them to slither on dry land with surprising speed, and they can rear up on their tail, carrying a Lemurian warrior into battle on the land for short engagements.

Kilmoran's Eel Stats

Also Known As: Moana Makani Puhi (The Wind Sea Eel), Giant Eel and Giant Cave Eel.

Alignment: Considered to be Anarchist (tamed) or Miscreant (wild).

Attributes: I.Q. 1D4+5 (high animal intelligence), M.E. 2D6+3, M.A. 2D4, P.S. 2D4+29 (Supernatural), P.P. 2D6+12, P.E. 2D6+8, P.B. 1D6+4, swimming Spd 2D6+60 (42-48 mph/67 to 77 km/36 to 41 knots), and when crawling on land, Spd is 28 mph (45 km).

M.D.C.: 3D6x10+20 M.D.C. (On an S.D.C. World: 1D6x10+20 Hit Points, 2D4x10+20 S.D.C. and a Natural A.R. of 12.)

Horror Factor: 13

Size: 30-50 feet (9.1 to 15.2 m) long, with a diameter of 3-5 feet (0.9 to 1.5 m).

Weight: 1,000-3,000 pounds (450 to 1,350 kg).

Average Life Span: 300-500 years.

P.P.E.: 6D6

Equivalent Skills: Climbing 30%, Detect Ambush 80%, Detect Concealment 40%, Escape Artist 45%, Prowl 80%, Swimming 98%, Track and Trap Undersea Animals 80% and Underwater Navigation 98%.

Natural Abilities: Supernatural P.S. and P.E., tough outer skin, natural swimmer 98%, nightvision 2,000 feet (610 m), resistant to cold (half damage), tolerate depths up to 6 miles (9.6 km), and can locate moving objects in water 90% by their keen hearing which can detect prey up to a distance of 3,000 feet (914 m).

Amphibious Nature (special): Kilmoran's Eels can breathe and travel on dry land for up to 1D4+1 hours before becoming distressed, 1D6+28 hours in swampy, damp environments, and two hours in deserts and frozen wastelands. After that period, the giant eel begins to suffer, dehydrates and dies within 1D4 hours. During this period, reduce the eel's M.D.C., attacks per melee and combat bonuses by half for every hour until death. If placed back in the ocean before it expires, the Kilmoran's Eel completely recovers in 4D6+24 hours.

Automatic Dodge: These agile creatures can swerve and move their entire bodies to effortlessly dodge incoming attacks and projectiles. An automatic dodge is the ability to dodge so quickly and easily that it does not count as a melee attack.

Photographic Memory and Land Navigation (special): Not only is the Kilmoran's Eel good at memorizing the places it has traveled (Undersea Navigation 98%), it has an innate ability to understand three-dimensional structures, allowing it to predict where a tunnel might lead, or even how thick a wall is. Coincidentally, the eels never forget a face and will always remember an ally or enemy if encountered again. Land Navigation (surface and underwater): 95%.

Quick Turns & Stops: Roll as if the maneuver was an automatic dodge or parry. A roll of 12 or higher means success. A failed roll means the giant eel couldn't turn or stop in time and either shoots by or slams into something or somebody.

Speed Burst: Can swim at double normal speed for one minute. This maneuver can be performed six times per hour before tiring the monster eel out. This move is performed for a quick dodge (+1 in addition to other bonuses) or get away, or a quick strike (+2 in addition to other bonuses) or to move towards or away from something or someplace quickly.

Tight Circle/Turn: Can make a reasonably tight circle and turns in an area as small as 15 feet (4.6 m) in diameter.

Vulnerabilities: Dehydration on dry land, and sometimes too aggressive in the wild; will sometimes fight to the death. Fire and heat attacks inflict 50% greater damage – Kilmoran's Eels hate fire and it has a Horror Factor of 11 for them.

Attacks per Melee: Four.

Damage: Restrained bite or nip does 5D6 S.D.C., a full strength bite does 4D6 M.D. Ram with nose or body does 1D6x10 M.D. but counts as two attacks. Restrained tail slap does 1D4 M.D. and a full strength tail slap does 4D6 M.D.

Bonuses (in addition to possible attribute bonuses): +3 on Perception Rolls, +3 on initiative, +6 M.D. to bite damage, +2 to strike, +5 to automatic dodge, +4 to pull punch/bite and +2 to roll with impact.

Magic: None.

Psionics: None.

Habitat: Prefer tropical and warm oceans, underwater mountains, and coastal waters, but can be encountered anywhere but the arctic, and found wherever there are Lemurians who use them as guardian and riding animals.

Allies: Tolerate their own kind, but tend to hunt and travel alone or in pairs, never in schools. Dislike most humanoids, but thanks to the Lemurians' connection with nature, they have managed to foster a bond with them. The occasional aquatic race has also managed to tame and ride these giants.

Enemies: Large marine predators, sea monsters, sea serpents and Metztla. In the wild, humanoids are considered easy prey and Kilmoran Eels are happy to gobble them up. An aggressive predator, they have even been known to capsize or sink canoes and small boats to get to the people inside. Preys upon fish of all sizes, otters, dolphins, seals, walrus and similar animals up to 10 feet (3 m) in length.

Value: As a trained riding mount or guardian, they can easily fetch 10,000-20,000 credits among Lemurians, but two or three times more among most other people. Wild, untamed Kilmoran's Eels sell to zoos and gladiatorial arenas as monsters for 1D4x10,000 credits.

Line Rays

These magnificent creatures are believed to be the work of Lemurian Biomancers who wanted to create a powerful underwater riding animal that possessed intelligence, grace and agility. Line Rays are three to four times the size of a normal Manta Ray, and are an aqua-green color with a creamy white underbelly. They have twin tails to assist in swimming and maneuvering, and which Lemurian swimmers wanting to catch a free ride often grab onto.

Like a few other animals that have adapted to the high levels of magic energy on Rifts Earth, Line Rays possess innate and instinctive psionic and magic abilities reminiscent of human Mystics, as well as the ability to use ley lines. For Lemurians and Ocean Wizards, their talent for magic and the channeling of magical energy enhances their value many times over. In addition, Line Rays are even-tempered, calm under duress and exhibit extreme loyalty to their riders and owners. As if that were not enough, Line Rays are able to "swim through the air" above the waves or on dry land when traveling along ley lines. This gives them limited water-to-air capabilities that can come in handy in many situations, particularly rescue operations, scouting and swooping in undetected on unsuspecting pirate camps, defilers of nature or undead strongholds.

Line Ray Stats

Also Known As: Makani Hahalua (Wind Manta Ray), Keheu Hahalua ("Winged" Manta Ray), Ley Line Rays or Flying Rays.

Alignment: Considered to be Unprincipled (65%) or Scrupulous (35%).

Attributes: I.Q. 1D6+7 (high animal intelligence), M.E. 2D4+10, M.A. 2D6+9, P.S. 2D6+13 (Supernatural), P.P. 2D4+15, P.E. 2D6+15, P.B. 2D6+10, Spd 3D6+21 (15-23 mph/24 to 36.8 km or 13-20 knots) swimming underwater (double along ley lines) or in the air.

M.D.C.: P.E. attribute number x10. (On S.D.C. worlds: 2D4x10 +P.E. attribute number for Hit Points and 4D6x10 S.D.C. with an A.R. of 8.)

Horror Factor/Awe Factor: 11 on their own, but H.F. 13 against the enemies of Lemuria.

Size: 18-25 feet (5.4 to 7.6 m) long from the front of the face to the rump. The two tails add another 8-10 feet (2.4 to 3 m) and the "wingspan" is 30-40 feet (9.1 to 12.2 m).

Weight: 3-5 tons.

Average Life Span: 120-200 years in the wild, double in the care of Lemurians. It is suspected they gather to mate at ley line locations.

P.P.E.: 3D4x10+ P.E. attribute number.

Equivalent Skills: Swimming 98%, Prowl 65%, Underwater Navigation 95% and Land Navigation 80%.

Natural Abilities: Supernatural P.S. and P.E., Nightvision 1,000 feet (305 m), can locate moving objects in water 90% via keen hearing (can hear prey up to 3,000 feet/914 m), sensitive to vibration and can sense movement in the water around them within 60 feet (18.3 m), 10 mile (16 km) depth tolerance and heals twice as fast as humans.

Limited Amphibious Nature (special): Line Rays can fly in the air along ley lines and breathe air out of water for one minute per P.E. attribute point. Line Rays cannot crawl or walk on land (they flop around like a fish out of water), but can survive out of water for minutes equal to their P.E. attribute number x2 (x5 when along a ley line). After that period, the Line Ray begins to suffer, dehydrates and dies within 1D4 hours. During this period, reduce the creature's M.D.C., P.P.E., I.S.P., attacks per melee and combat bonuses by half for every hour until death. If placed back in the ocean before it expires, the Line Ray completely recovers in 3D6+12 hours.

Impervious to Ley Line Storms (special): Line Rays can ride a Ley Line Storm at triple their normal flying speed and NEVER get struck by the bolts of energy unleashed during these storms.

Ley Line Energy Blast (special): Like the dolphin, the Line Ray can mentally create and fire mystic energy bolts.

Preparation Time: Counts as one melee action/attack.

Duration: Instant.

Limitations: The Ray can only create energy bolts as long as it is on a ley line.

Range: 1,000 feet (305 m) +400 feet (122 m) per level of experience.

Damage: The Line Ray can create S.D.C. or M.D.C. bolts as desired. It can also regulate the amount of damage in increments of 1D6. Damage is up to 2D6 points (S.D.C. or M.D.C.); does not advance with age or experience.

P.P.E. Cost: One for S.D.C. bolts or five for M.D.C., regardless of the total amount of damage inflicted.

Ley Line Flight (special): This power is very similar to the Ley Line Walker's power of *Ley Line Drifting*, except that the Line Ray can swim through the water at double its usual speed or "swim through the air" (fly) at its normal swimming speed. Maximum altitude is 1,000 feet (305 m) above the water or ground. The moment the animal leaves the ley line, the power of flight vanishes.

Ley Line Healing (special): Recovers at a rate of 2D6 M.D. per hour along a ley line and can completely regenerate lost tails in 1D6 days, lost portions of "wings" in 1D6+6 days and an entire wing within 3D6+12 days.

Ley Line Hopping (special): Again, like dolphins, Line Rays swimming at top speed can mentally create a small dimensional Rift that pops them from one ley line to a *neighboring* one. In this way, the creature and as many as two passengers/riders can hop from one ley line to the next, sometimes spanning miles in a matter of seconds. The Line Ray can also "Rift" from one location to another on the same ley line.

Preparation Time: It takes 1D4 melee rounds (15 to 60 seconds) to mentally focus and create the mini-Rift.

Limitations: The neighboring ley line cannot be more than three miles (4.8 km) away for young rays, six miles (9.6 km) for adults and ten miles (16 km) for truly ancient rays over 100 years in age.

P.P.E. Cost: 10

Vulnerabilities: Their dependence on ley lines for the bulk of their special power is a limitation, as is their size and association with Lemurians.

Attacks per Melee: Three.

Damage: A flap from a "wing" does 2D6 M.D., a tail swipe does 2D4 M.D. and a full speed ram does 3D6 M.D.

Bonuses (in addition to possible attribute bonuses): +2 to initiative, +2 on Perception Rolls (+4 if it pertains to a ley line, such as an oncoming Ley Line Storm), +2 to dodge, +1 on all saving throws.

Magic: A sort of animal version of a Mystic, the Line Ray has limited magical and spell casting abilities.

Ley Line Walker Equivalent Abilities: *Sense Ley Lines and Magical Energy, Read Ley Lines,* and *Ley Line Phasing* (including any passengers they might be carrying).

Spell Casting: The Line Ray can work the following magic spells: Chameleon (6), Cleanse (6), Globe of Daylight (2), Ley Line Fade (20), Invisibility: Simple (6), Negate Poison/Toxin (5), See Aura (6), See the Invisible (5), and Sense Evil (2). Does not gain new spells over time.

Psionics: Has the abilities of Resist Fatigue (4), Resist Hunger (2), Sense Dimensional Anomaly (4) and Sense Time (2). I.S.P. Base: M.E. attribute number +2D6; I.S.P. and abilities do not increase over time.

Habitat: Oceans around the globe, but prefer tropical and temperate areas. May be encountered as lone animals, in pairs, trios and small schools of 2D6+4. Often travel with Mega-Rays, dolphins and whales.

Enemies: Like their Lemurian allies, they despise supernatural evil, fear and hate the undead, and consider demons, the Milu, the Lord of the Deep and the Splugorth and their minions as natural enemies.

Allies: Fellow Line Rays, Mega-Rays, dolphins and whales, Lemurians, Merans, Ichthyeans, and Sea Druids (especially those of the Manta Ray totem), and will associate with and allow themselves to be tamed by other peaceful, nature loving people (mainly aquatic races). They are the preferred riding animal of some Serpent Hunters and many Oceanic Guardsmen, Wilderness Scouts, Biomancer Gene-Mages and other aquatic practitioners of magic.

Value: They love to associate with and help Lemurians, and are happy to serve as riding animals. However, it is one thing to willingly help others, it is another to be enslaved and forced into being work or riding animals. When this happens, Line Rays often (01-75% chance) stop eating and die within 2D4 weeks of captivity or enslavement. That is, unless the clever and resourceful creature can manage to escape.

Mega-Rays

Mega-Rays are enormous manta rays that have been sculpted using the powers of Biomancy. Their bodies are now natural Mega-Damage structures, and they have been given two, long tails to make the distinction between Mega-Rays and Line Rays more difficult to outsiders. Mega-Rays come in a variety of green colors with a dark underbelly. They have been tamed and incorporated into the Lemurian way of life where they are used as work and riding animals by the general public and often equipped with specialized saddles that add weapons and assist normal riders.

Mega-Rays can feed on fish and normal prey, but their mouths can also be used as filters, and most often the huge animals are found swimming in giant, lazy circles pursuing krill and plankton. When brought into battle, however, they are almost invisible on sonar, silent and unafraid to rend enemy sea monsters and submarines with their Mega-Damage teeth. They have limited psionic powers as well, and can use them for defense, stealth and extra-sensory perception.

Mega-Rays are bred and kept in Lemurian habitations where they are allowed to roam free in vast feeding circuits. They can be called to service via psionics, but some have bonded with their riders and remain near them most of the time. Others have migrated out into the open oceans where they live like any other wild animal. Only on occasion is their value as a riding animal and ally understood, but Sea Druids and Ocean Wizards can perceive their power and the Mega-Rays swim with Line Rays, normal rays, dolphins and whales. **Note:** Two Mega-Rays are depicted in the background on the cover of this book.

Mega-Ray Stats

Also Known As: Giant Rays, Sea Kites and Lemurian Manta Rays.

Alignment: Considered Unscrupulous or Anarchist. The majority of Mega-Rays are tamed and domesticated creatures used by the Lemurians and other aquatic people.

Attributes: I.Q. 1D6+3 (high animal intelligence), M.A. 2D6, M.E. 2D6+2, P.S. 2D4+24 (equal to Robot Strength), P.P. 1D6+11, P.E. 1D6+16, P.B. 1D6+11, Spd 2D6+33 swimming (on average 30 mph/48 km or 26 knots).

Size: 25-40 feet (7.6 to 12.2 m) long from the front of the face to the rump. The twin tails add another 10-12 feet (3 to 3.6 m) and the "wingspan" is 40-70 feet (12.2 to 21.3 m) wide.

Weight: 5-8 tons.

M.D.C.: 2D4x10+57. (On S.D.C. worlds: 1D4x10 +P.E. attribute number for Hit Points and 2D6x10 S.D.C. with an A.R. of 8.)

Horror Factor: 12 if it should appear suddenly or make an aggressive attack. When seen from afar they seem slow, graceful and unthreatening.

P.P.E.: 1D4x10+8

Average Life Span: 25-30 years in the wild, 50% greater when cared for by Lemurians.

Equivalent Skills: Swim 98%, Fishing 88%, Prowl 55%, and Land Navigation 70%.

Natural Abilities: Nightvision 1,000 feet (305 m), can locate moving objects in water 80% via keen hearing (can hear prey up to 3,000 feet/914 m), impervious to normal cold (magic cold does half damage), and has a depth tolerance of 5 miles (8 km).

Sonar Stealth (special): Mega-Rays' small cross-sections make them poor reflectors of sound waves. Any attempt to detect a Mega-Ray using sonar is at -30%. They also move without motors or engines, and propel themselves using graceful, silent wing strokes. Anyone trying to detect a Mega-Ray with superior hearing senses or listening devices is -35% on skills/abilities and -2 on Perception Rolls to detect a Mega-Ray passing by or coming in.

Attacks per Melee: Two.

Damage: Bite inflicts 1D6+1 M.D., a wing slap does 2D4 M.D., and a full speed ram does 2D6 M.D. but counts as two melee attacks.

Bonuses (in addition to possible attribute bonuses): +2 on Perception Rolls, +2 to dodge and +3 to save vs possession/mind control.

Magic: None.

Psionics: Bio-Regenerate (self; 6), Empathy (4), Increased Healing (10), Presence Sense (4), and See the Invisible (4). Base I.S.P.: M.E. attribute number x3.

Habitat: As large animals, Mega-Rays prefer open water where they can move unrestrained. As filter feeders, they follow schools of krill and plankton and can often be found cruising over coral reefs or around seamounts. Mega-Rays are most concentrated around Lemurian cities and outposts, but small numbers of them can be found in oceans throughout the world, though they tend to avoid the colder polar seas.

Behavior: Living in the wild, Mega-Rays are peaceful filter feeders that fight to defend themselves. After mating, the female carries the eggs internally for up to a year before giving birth to live young. The average litter size is only two, meaning Mega-Rays are slow animals to breed and are prized by Scouts, Lemurian Biomancers and Serpent Hunters for their stealth capabilities.

Allies: Lemurians, Merans and Icthyeans. Mega-Rays can read people with Empathy, however, and wild rays may trust anyone who does not seek to harm them, passing close by, eating out of their hand and tolerating divers who ride on their backs for short periods.

Enemies: The Milu, the Lord of the Deep and the Splugorth, who enslave the rays and use them in underwater arenas, use them in labor or incorporate them into horrible Bio-Wizard experiments.

Value: Between 75,000 and 150,000 credits as a trained riding animal to outsiders, a quarter of that amount in Lemuria where Mega-Rays are common.

Narcassai Swordfish

The Narcassai Swordfish is a large, fast moving and deadly underwater predator that resembles an Earth swordfish, with a few important and deadly distinctions. One, Narcassai are larger than Earth swordfish; two, they have purple and red scales on their body, with a light blue underbelly; and three, they prey upon humanoids as well as small to medium fish, birds and mammals. They also possess a strange ability to phase their sword bill. All of this puts them in the category of sea monster.

Though many believed the Narcassai Swordfish – also known as Blood Swordfish – to be a creation of the Lemurians, the fish comes from an alien world via the Rifts. Nobody knows where the fish got its name, but it is presumed "Narcassai" is the name of the world (or some version of the name) from which the creature originated. The Narcassai behaves in a similar way as Earth swordfish in that they are solitary hunters, swim at great speeds, and use their sword bill to kill. The Blood Swordfish kills its prey by either thrashing about with its head and sword to batter, slice and chop at prey, stunning or killing its target, or by impaling prey with the sword bill. The aggressive predator has even been known to stab through the bottom and sides of boats, picking off human prey as they drown on the sinking vessel or flounder in the water after jumping ship. When man-sized prey is impaled, the Narcassai typically shakes its head side to side or up and down until it severs a limb or cuts its victim in half.

It is when the sword bill gets stuck or something gets stuck on it, that the fish is able to momentarily (six seconds) make it intangible, enabling the fish to simply turn and swim away unstuck or unencumbered. The Narcassai Swordfish can swim and dive at high speeds and strikes with its sword like a torpedo. When it finds itself impaled and the sword bill stuck, in prey, objects, a ship or the ocean floor, it can escape in a heartbeat to resume its attack or to swim away.

Narcassai Swordfish Stats

Also Known As: Pepehi Kohe-ta áma I'a (Hammering Sheathed Sword of the Burning Light Fish), Blood Swordfish and Phase Swordfish.

Alignment: Considered to be Miscreant and deadly, like a shark.

Attributes: I.Q. 1D6+3 (animal intelligence), M.E. 1D6+1, M.A. 1D6, P.S. 2D4+24 (Robot equivalent strength), P.P. 1D6+12, P.E. 1D6+10, P.B. 1D6+9, Swimming Spd 4D6+76 (on average 60 mph/96 km or 52 knots).

M.D.C.: P.E. attribute number x10. (On S.D.C. worlds it has 6D6+12 Hit Points, 2D4x10 S.D.C., and a Natural A.R. of 9.)

Horror Factor: 12

Size: 12-18 feet (3.6 to 5.4 m) long.

Weight: 1,200 pounds (540 kg) to one ton.

Average Life Span: 1D6+10 years.

P.P.E.: 1D6x10

Equivalent Skills: Swimming 98% and Underwater Navigation 90%.

Natural Abilities: Incredibly fast swimmer, can dive up to 1,000 feet (305 m), leap out of water (breaching) up to 15 feet (4.6 m) high, has excellent underwater vision, Nightvision 600 feet (183 m), can smell blood up to one mile (1.6 km) away, and can tolerate depths up to 8 miles (12.8 km).

Phase Shift Sword (special): The Narcassai Swordfish can phase its sword bill out to become intangible, allowing it, for a couple of seconds, to pass through solid matter to remove it after an impaling attack. This requires the expenditure of 5 P.P.E. and is only used to make a quick exit or release of the sword.

Vulnerabilities: The aggressive animal sometimes takes on tougher opponents than it can handle, but being so fast, the swordfish can flee if necessary.

Attacks per Melee: Three.

Damage: Striking/hitting with its rock hard, but blunt part of the sword bill inflicts 1D6 M.D., the sharp, pointed end of the sword slashes and cuts to inflict 2D6 M.D., and a tail slap does 1D6 M.D. However, a diving or torpedo-like charge, using all three attacks that melee round does 1D6x10 M.D.

Bonuses (in addition to possible attribute bonuses): +1 to Perception Rolls, +3 on initiative, +4 to strike, and +5 to automatic dodge (the act of dodging does not use up a melee attack).

Magic: None.

Psionics: None.

Habitat: All Earth's oceans and seas, but favors Pacific waters.

Enemies: None per se. The fish considers most creatures smaller than it as potential prey.

Allies: None. These lone hunters don't even like to associate with their own species except to mate. Lemurians have tried to tame the beasts, but the Narcassai Swordfish has proven too aggressive, murderous and single-minded (they want to hunt and feed) to be used as a reliable riding animal or companion. Still, some Serpent Hunters use the Blood Swordfish as a fast riding animal. However, the fish doesn't follow orders well and would require considerable Biomancy genetic manipulation to be turned into a reliable mount or domesticated animal. Merans, Ichthyeans and even Naut'Yll hate and fear the monster.

Value: The meat of the Narcassai Swordfish is delicious, but few hunt the beast lest they fall victim to its deadly blade. For reasons even Lemurians don't fully understand, the sword bill of the creature does Hit Point equivalent damage to vampires and other undead.

Saber-Toothed Sea Lions

Not to be mistaken for a giant walrus, these enormous, sea lion-like creatures have a large, muscular, lower jaw with a set of huge saber-teeth protruding upwards from the mouth. They are tough skinned, muscular and violently territorial. Groups of these marine predators can be found roaming coastal waters, hunting fish and smaller marine mammals such as seals or heading into deeper water in packs to take on larger prey. The Saber-Toothed Sea Lion's pack mentality makes them amenable to submitting to a strong leader and being riding animals or pets of aquatic and amphibious D-Bees, especially when the animal is raised from a pup. These big lugs can be as loyal as a puppy and as ferocious as a pit bull – a half ton pit bull. Some Serpent Hunters and Oceanic Guardsmen like to ride the Saber-Toothed Sea Lion standing on the creature's back or in a crouched position like a jockey riding a racehorse.

Saber-Toothed Sea Lion Stats

Also Known As: Niho-Peata Sila (Shark Toothed Seal), Saber-Tooth Walrus and Saber Seal.

Alignment: Considered to be Anarchist, though pets and riding animals exhibit a strong sense of pack loyalty and will sacrifice themselves to protect their owner/rider.

Attributes: I.Q. 1D6+2 (animal intelligence), M.E. 2D6, M.A. 2D6, P.S. 2D6+16 (Supernatural), P.P. 2D6+7, P.E. 1D6+18, P.B. 1D6+8, Spd Swimming 2D6+34 (30 mph/48 km or 26 knots), 1D6+2 crawling on land.

M.D.C.: P.E. attribute x6. (On S.D.C. worlds it has P.E. attribute number x2 for Hit Points, 2D4x10+18 S.D.C. and an A.R. of 10.)

Horror Factor: 12 for one or 15 when facing a pack.

Size: 6-8 feet (1.8 to 2.4 m) for adolescents (typically "attack dogs") but 10-18 feet (3 to 5.5 m) for adults (the preferred sized for riding animals).

Weight: 500-1,000 lbs (225 to 450 kg) for adolescents, 2 tons for adults.

Average Life Span: 50-60 years in the wild, but 100 to 120 years in the care of Lemurians.

P.P.E.: 3D6+5

Equivalent Skills: Detect Ambush 40%, Prowl 45%, Swimming 97%, Track and Hunt Sea Animals 75%, Underwater Navigation 98%, and Wrestling.

Natural Abilities: Hold breath for up to 40 minutes at a time, good vision, keen sense of smell (track by scent 55%), resistant to cold (half damage), tolerate depths up to 2 miles (3.2 km) and Bio-Regenerate 1D6 M.D.C. per hour.

Sense Magnetic North: Same as Dolphins and Whales.

Heightened Sense of Hearing: The Saber-Toothed Sea Lion has an extraordinary sense of hearing and can hear into the ultra-high frequency range of sound.

Sonic Echolocation: Same as a Dolphin.

Ultrasonic Probe: Same as a Dolphin.

Ultrasonic Communication: Saber-Toothed Sea Lions communicate with each other through a series of ultrasonic whistles, clicks, hums and reverberations, but also respond to human words and commands like a dog.

Vulnerabilities: The Saber-Toothed Sea Lion is a creature of the sea, meaning that while it can survive out of water for hours at a time, its flippers, forearms and tail make it clumsy, slow, awkward and vulnerable to attack on land. Sonic based attacks and explosions do double damage.

Attacks per Melee: Five.

Damage: A full strength bite or gore attack with its large, saber-like teeth inflicts 6D6 M.D., a partial strength bite does 3D6 M.D., a swim-by slashing with the teeth does 2D6+2 M.D., a flipper slap, head butt or chest thump does 2D6 M.D., while a tail strike does 3D6 M.D. and the tail can be used to unleash a power punch that does 6D6 M.D., but counts as two melee attacks. A speeding underwater body block/ram also does 6D6 M.D. but counts as three melee actions.

Entangle/Pin (special): Another tactic of the Saber Seal is to pin opponents, especially humanoid opponents on dry land, by knocking them down with the sweep of its tail or fin (does 5D6 S.D.C. damage or one M.D.), and then hold the victim down with its tail, under one fin leaning with the weight of half its body, or by sitting on the victim. A successful entangle or pin maneuver holds the victim down and unable to use his arms and weapons on the creature; counts as two melee attacks/actions, one to knock the person down (the target gets to dodge) and one to pin (the target gets to dodge again).

Bonuses (in addition to possible attribute bonuses): +1 on Perception Rolls (+3 if based on sound), +2 on initiative, +3 to strike, +4 to strike with a knockdown attack/tail sweep, +2 to dodge underwater only, +1 to disarm, +4 to entangle/pin, +3 to pull punch and +3 to roll with impact.

Magic: None.

Psionics: None.

Habitat: Coastal waters in cold regions are their preferred hunting grounds, but they can be found throughout the oceans hunting big and small prey. Small packs can also be found run by lone Lemurians all over Lemurian territory and sometimes beyond.

Enemies: Large predators and humanoids, including Horune Pirates and the minions of the Lord of the Deep.

Allies: Only other pack members, however Lemurians, Merans, Ichthyeans and a few other aquatic D-Bees have all "tamed" or taken control of a pack, making the rest of the pack fiercely loyal to them.

Value: Saber Seals make excellent companions and riding animals, and are favored by Lemurian scouts, explorers and Oceanic Guardsmen. Merans, Amphibs and Naut'Yll sometimes use them as riding animals but more often as pet companions and watch/attack dogs. As a trained riding animal or guard animal, it can sell for 6,000-12,000 credits in Lemuria, but can get three times that amount among surface dwellers and pirates.

Sea Dragon Turtles

These majestic and noble creatures resemble a giant sea turtle with a long head crowned by a pair of large, goat-like horns and a wispy beard under its chin. The shell is lined with fins and covered in algae. When lazying about and floating on the surface of the water, they may look like a small island. Though Sea Dragon Turtles are not true dragons, their regal appearance and great size certainly create a similar impression.

By day they bask in the warmth of the sun on the surface of the water or up on shore, using their stiff flippers to climb onto the best places for sunbathing in order to supercharge their unique solar collecting bodies. When done charging up, they slide back into the water and plummet down into the darkness of the abyss. Intelligent and empathic animals from another dimension, Sea Dragon Turtles are Creatures of Light who possess a natural and instinctive hatred of the undead, demons and most supernatural creatures of darkness. Supernatural horrors that retreat from the sun of the surface world are sought out, destroyed and eaten by Sea Dragon Turtles. In the depths below, the mighty turtle brings sunlight to discharge from its stores of solar energy. They also sense the good in people and help and protect them, including Lemurians, Merans, Ichthyleans, Junk Crabs, Amphibs, D-Bees and humans of good alignment as well as dolpins and whales. Of course, this makes Dragon Turtles the natural enemies of Naut'Yll, Horune Pirates, the Minions of Splugorth, the Lord of the Deep and Davey Jones and his undead horde; all of whom try to capture and enslave or kill the noble creatures. A Sea Dragon Turtle will happily allow itself to serve as a riding animal or raft to help or rescue humanoids of good alignment, and will protect them from monsters, sharks and evildoers. They have been friends to Lemurians since they reappeared on Rifts Earth and allow themselves to be riding animals, protectors, war steeds and even as heavy combat platforms and royal escorts. Sea Dragon Turtles are the symbol of light, peace and hope to Lemurians who consider them friends and allies rather than as dumb animals or lesser beings. In fact, Lemurians insist the great turtles are nearly as intelligent as humans, but live a simpler existence and have a different perspective of the world.

Sea Dragon Turtle Stats

Also Known As: La Mo'o Kea (Sun Lizard Tortoise), Giant Solar Turtles or Sun Turtles.

Alignment: Principled (40%), Scrupulous (50%), and Unprincipled (10%).

Attributes: I.Q. 2D4+8 (generally considered to be high animal intelligence), M.E. 2D4+14, M.A. 2D4+10, P.S. 4D4+24 (Supernatural), P.P. 2D4+3, P.E. 2D4+20, P.B. 3D4+8, Spd 1D4x10+40 (triple along ley lines), 1D4+4 on land.

M.D.C.: 3D4x100 M.D.C. (On an S.D.C. world the Sea Dragon Turtle would have 1D4x100 Hit Points, 1D6x100 S.D.C. and A.R. 18.)

Horror/Awe Factor: 14

Size: 40-50 feet (12 to 15 m) long from nose to end of the shell. The tail adds an additional 12-15 feet (3.6 to 4.6 m), and the neck can stretch 15 feet (4.6 m). The Sea Dragon Turtle can tuck its legs close to the body, but they cannot retract fully inside the shell like freshwater turtles; neither can the head. Height is 15-20 feet (4.6 to 6.1 m). Width of the shell is 25-35 feet (7.6 to 10.6 m) and the "wingspan" of the legs when fully extended to swim is 50-65 feet (15.2 to 19.8 m) depending on the overall size of the turtle.

Weight: 12-30 tons.

Average Life Span: P.E. attribute number 30.

P.P.E.: 2D4x10 +P.E. attribute number.

Experience Level: 1D4 +1 per 100 years of existence. Not recommended as a player character.

Equivalent Skills: Swimming 98%, Astronomy and Navigation 84%, Dowsing 64%, Identify Plants & Fruit 78%, Land Navigation 70%, Mathematics: Basic 84%, Tailing (underwater only) 70%, Underwater Navigation 88%, and Wilderness Survival 88%. **Note:** All skills except Swimming advance at a pace of 1% per level of experience.

Natural Abilities: Supernatural Strength and Endurance, nightvision 600 feet (183 m), can see in all spectrums of light, including ultraviolet and infrared, has polarized vision (impervious to bright light and glare, and cannot be blinded), extraordinary sense of hearing, resistant to fire, heat and cold (all do half damage even if magical), can tolerate depths up to 8 miles (12.8 km) and Bio-Regenerates 1D4 M.D.C. per melee round.

Absorb Sunlight (special): The primary source of food and energy of the Sea Dragon Turtles is sunlight and they must sunbathe at least 14 hours a week, whether it is all at once or two hours a day. Most soak up the energy they need for the week in a day or two.

Amphibious (special): Can survive on dry land or in the water indefinitely, but must come up for air to breathe from time to time; can hold breath two hours per P.E. attribute point.

Chemoreceptors (special): A highly advanced sense of taste/smell that lets the Sea Dragon Turtle detect salty contents and toxicity of the water and taste and track its food source. Base skill to track: 60% +5% per level of experience. Identify chemicals, toxins or specific creatures by taste trails: 40% +5% per level of experience.

Create Sunstone (special): This rough, yellow, stone-like sphere might be thought of as a crude Sea Turtle Dragon pearl, except it is the size of a basketball. As often as once a month, the turtle can cough up and let a Sunstone roll out of its mouth. The stone radiates magic and glows like the sun (same effect as Globe of Daylight; 30 foot/9.1 m radius). The creation requires the Sea Dragon Turtle to expend 40 P.P.E., but the basketball-sized stone radiates sunlight up for 12 hours and can light up a 50 foot (15 m) radius bright enough to read a book at the bottom of the ocean. On top of that, the sphere can be recharged by leaving it in bright sunlight for two hours. If used to strike an evil supernatural or undead creature, the Sunstone explodes in a brilliant flash of sunlight that inflicts 1D4x100 Hit Points/M.D. to the undead and blinds those who were not expecting the flash of light and failed to look away or cover their eyes for 1D4 melee rounds. Mortals and supernatural creatures of a good alignment are unaffected by the blast. Selfish supernatural creatures feel uncomfortable, but are otherwise unharmed. A Sunstone has 1D4+4 M.D.C.

Devour the Undead (special): Sun Turtles can kill and feed on the remains of the undead. Any undead slain and eaten by this creature are permanently destroyed.

Sense Magnetic Fields (special): Extreme sensitivity to the Earth's magnetic field (Sense Magnetic North and Undersea Navigation 98%) as well as those given off by electrical cabling, iron ships and rail guns.

Sun Aura (special): The Sea Dragon Turtle can radiate light like a nimbus cloud with the sun behind it. To most it is a warm, soothing light that is bright, but not blinding. For the undead and evil supernatural creatures harmed by sunlight, the effects are the same as the *Globe of Daylight* spell and will keep them 100 feet (30.5 m) away from the Sea Dragon Turtle and anyone swimming along side of it.

Solar Eye Beams (special): The Sea Dragon Turtle can unleash a powerful laser-like beam of sunlight from its eyes once per melee round. The beam does 4D6 M.D. to most foes, but those harmed by sunlight take 1D6x10 M.D. (or Hit Point) damage per blast. Range of the beam is 3,000 feet (910 m) in an atmosphere, half underwater.

Also see Psionics.

Vulnerabilities: The Sea Dragon Turtle is at its best in water, but it can crawl around on land using its flippers to pull itself along.

Darkness: Powered by solar energy; when the Sea Dragon Turtle is prevented from recharging with 14 hours of sunlight a week, reduce all physical attributes, the number of attacks, eye beam damage, bonuses and P.P.E. by half, and skills are -10%. Furthermore when underpowered, the turtles cannot create Sunstones and become lethargic and sad. When deprived of light for more than two weeks, the Sea Dragon Turtle is unable to generate its eye beams, reduce skills by 30%, its ability to Bio-Regenerate stops and it starts to die of starvation without light at a rate of 1D4x10 M.D.C. a week. Seven hours of sunbathing stops the loss of M.D.C., but 28 hours of light over a week's time is required to restore its abilities to full.

Attacks per Melee: Four.

Damage: As per Supernatural P.S. for all attacks, including bite. A full speed ram with the horns does 1D4x10 M.D., but uses up three melee attacks.

Bonuses (in addition to possible attribute bonuses): +3 on Perception Rolls, +1 to initiative when fighting undead, +2 to strike, +4 to strike with Solar Beam Eyes, +4 to disarm and pull punch, +2 to dodge when underwater only, +6 to save vs possession and mind control.

Magic: None.

Psionics: Empathy (4), Meditation (0), Psychic Diagnosis (4), See Aura (6), See the Invisible (4), Sense Evil (2), Sense Time (2), and Suppress Fear (8). I.S.P. is M.E. attribute number x3 +1D4 per level of experience.

Habitat: Oceans and seas around the world, but as many as 2D4x10 can be found around Lemurian outposts, gardens and cities. May travel as a lone individual, but more often in groups of 2 (often a mated pair) or 2D4 turtles.

Enemies: Supernatural evil and the undead, including zombies and animated dead, but especially the Milu, and the minions and undead servants of the Lord of the Deep, Davey Jones, and the Splugorth.

Allies: Lemurians, Merans, Ichthyleans and all humanoids of good alignment; leery of Unprincipled and distrustful of Anarchist and evil alignments.

Value: Most seafaring people regard Sun Turtles as a sign of good luck. Since they are known to rescue people from drowning and even tow or carry boats and small ships in distress to safe waters, most seafarers of good alignment rarely hunt them. However, Anarchist and evil people, including the Horune Pirates and slavers, may hunt the turtles for their M.D.C. shells, horns, tasty meat and oils. A suit of heavy body armor made from Sun Turtle shell has 3D4+90 M.D.C., weighs 60 pounds (27 kg) and has a -15% movement penalty to Physical skills like Climbing and Prowl, but not Swimming as the buoyant nature of the armor actually makes it easier to swim (+5% to Swimming skill). Suits of non-environmental turtle armor sell for 35,000-45,000 credits.

Storm Crabs

Rising up out of the sea in a torrent of mist, lightning and crashing waves, these behemoths can often be seen charging up onto the beach like a tropical hurricane on legs. They are enormous, tank-like monsters that were designed and raised to be the front-line "battle tanks," troop carriers and artillery units for the Lemurian *Oceanic Guardsmen*. These amphibious monsters have marched into the underwater strongholds of the Naut'Yll, have decimated the ranks of Davey Jones' undead and stormed beaches held by alien invaders and destructive surface dwellers.

Storm Crabs are slow moving, but can dish-out as well as take incredible punishment. Rumor suggests they are nearly unstoppable, which is not true, but they do make a terrifying opponent on the field of battle. Their heavy M.D.C. shells and massive pincer claws make them extremely tough, and combined with the crabs' Supernatural Strength should make any opponent think twice about confronting one of these things. Underwater, they are scary enough, but as the Storm Crab climbs onto shore it generates a crackling array of lightning bolts that creates a mist that quickly turns into a rolling, mini-thunderstorm. This electrical build-up is used to launch devastating lightning strikes, taking out enemy positions and frying enemy troops. This is why they are known as Storm Crabs. Submerged underwater, the lightning blasts and electrical fog making are rendered useless, but on beaches and dry land, watch out.

Storm Crab Stats

Also Known As: Ino Papa'I (Storm Crab) or Hekili 'ino Papa'I (Thunderstorm Crab).

Alignment: Considered an Anarchist animal used as a riding animal and living war machine.

Attributes: I.Q. 1D4+3 (animal intelligence), M.E. 2D6+4, M.A. 2D6, P.S. 3D6+38 (Supernatural), P.P. 1D6+15, P.E. 1D6+15, P.B. 1D6+1, Spd 2D6+20 on dry land (18 mph on average, 29 km), half scuttling across the ocean floor or swimming (9 mph/14.4 km or 7.8 knots).

M.D.C. by Location:

* Eye Stalks (two, small) – 45 each

Legs (6) – 300 each

Pincer Arms (2) – 500 each
Main Body (top) – 1D6x100+760
Main Body (underbelly) – 1D6x100+150

* Eye stalks are small and difficult targets to hit with a ranged weapon and the attacker is -6 to strike. Destroying both only inflicts a blindness penalty of only -3 as the creature relies more on its other senses than its poor eyesight in the first place. Lost eyes grow back in days.

(On an S.D.C. world the Storm Crab would have 1D4x100+64 Hit Points, 2D6x100 S.D.C. and A.R. 17.)

Horror Factor: 14 underwater, 16 on the surface with the electrical discharges and rolling fog.

Size (adult): The body is 50-70 (15.2 to 21.3 m) in diameter, but when the legs are extended for walking/running, Storm Crabs are 100-120 feet (30.5 to 36.6 m) wide. The monster stands 30-40 feet (9.1 to 12.2 m) tall and the claws have a reach of 25 feet (7.6 m).

Weight: 120-200 tons.

Average Life Span: 700-1,000 years.

P.P.E.: 1D4x100; recovers at a rate of 1D4x10 P.P.E. per hour.

Equivalent Skills: Climbing 65%, Detect Ambush 45%, Excavation 55%, Hunting Prowl 40% (underwater only), Swimming 60% (Storm Crabs are neither strong nor fast swimmers), Tailing 60% (underwater only), Track (by sight and smell) 60%.

Natural Abilities: P.S. and P.E. are Supernatural, can walk and run forward, backward and sideways, leap 40 feet (12.2 m) high and across (counts as two melee attacks/action), breathe water and air, impervious to electricity (including magical and M.D. lightning) and Ley Line Storms, takes half damage from sonic attacks, is resistant to cold (half damage) and can tolerate depths up to 6 miles (9.6 km).

Amphibious (special): Can survive on dry land or in the water indefinitely.

Bio-Regeneration (special): 1D4x10 M.D.C. per minute, regenerates lost eyes and eye stalks in 1D6 days, lost legs in 2D4 weeks, a lost pincer in 3D4 weeks; half that time when staying at a ley line until healed, something Storm Crabs do instinctively.

Chemoreceptors: A highly advanced sense of taste/smell that lets the Storm Crab detect salinity and toxicity of the water and taste and track its food source in the water 60%. It can also identify chemicals, toxins or specific creatures by taste trails 40% and can "smell" ozone and oncoming storms in the air when it surfaces 60% (+15% to sense Ley Line Storms).

Create Static Fog: The Storm Crab can create a fog-like mist from the sea, using its potent electrical powers to churn the water and shroud itself (and its Lemurian allies riders). This can only be done when the crab is on the surface of the water and along the shoreline. The fog cloud created by one Storm Crab covers a 200 foot (61 m) radius and up to 60 foot (18.3 m) high area. A platoon of Storm Crabs can easily shroud an amphibious army or conceal an outpost or city. The mist stays with the Storm Crab for as long as it deliberately works to create it and for 5D6+6 minutes after it stops. However, a strong wind (25 mph/40 km or stronger) easily blows it away.

Electrical Discharge/Lightning: The Storm Crab can channel electricity along its massive claws to fire devastating lightning bolts (point and shoot) or to strike with electrified claw strikes.

Range: 1,200 feet (366 m), hand to hand or proximity attack.

Mega-Damage: 4D6+10 M.D. per lightning bolt. An electrified claw strike as per Supernatural P.S. +10 M.D. It can also unleash a crackling stream of energy along its underbelly for a full melee round. This attack inflicts 2D6 M.D. to everything/one underneath the behemoth for every 5 seconds exposed. The crab must wait two melee rounds (30 seconds) before it can do the proximity attack again.

Rate of Fire: Each blast or claw strike counts as one melee attack. The electrified underbelly is a bonus attack.

Bonus: +3 to strike with each lightning blast.

Payload: Each lightning bolt costs 10 P.P.E. to fire. The electrified claw strike and underbelly strike have no P.P.E. cost.

Electromagnetic Sense: The Storm Crab can sense electromagnetic fields, the flow of electricity and even the bio-electric impulses of living creatures, giving it a direct and precise "feel" for everything around it like radar. It can also sense the direction of magnetic north as well as incoming barrages from rail guns.

Attacks per Melee: Four.

Mega-Damage: As per Supernatural P.S. or electrical attack. A stomp or kick does +10 M.D., a leaping pounce or ram/body block does +30 M.D. (counts as two attacks) and a pincer cut does P.S. damage +12 M.D.

Bonuses (in addition to possible attribute bonuses): +2 on initiative, +2 to strike, +4 to parry, +6 to pull punch, +2 to roll with impact, impervious to electricity, resistant to cold, +1 on all saving throws.

Vulnerabilities: Comparatively slow moving, has poor vision (relies on other keen senses), and it is a big, scary target that is likely to draw fire.

Magic: None, other than the natural and instinctive use of P.P.E. to create electricity and fire lightning bolts.

Psionics: None.

Habitat: Though from another world, Storm Crabs have adapted well to Rifts Earth. May be found anywhere in the wild where they are likely to be considered monsters, but most prefer Pacific waters. Each Lemurian city and secret Garden has at least a dozen to 2D4 dozen of the giants used as living tanks and as heavy construction vehicles for digging, excavation and similar work.

Enemies: Sea monsters and surface dwellers. Both prey upon the giant crabs, especially before they reach full size, and vice versa afterwards. Humanoids sometimes hunt the crabs for their armor, delicious meat and organs, or for use as monsters in the arena. Most creatures under 50 feet (15.2 m) in size are seen as potential prey to these giant animals, especially humans and D-Bees who are comparatively tiny. As omnivores, Storm Crabs eat just about anything that can't eat them, from plants to fish to people.

Allies: Respectful of certain humanoids, primarily Lemurians and Merans, who raise and tame Storm Crabs for use as work, riding and battle animals. Few other beings have the patience or ability to control these giants.

Value: As a monstrous pet or mount, they can easily sell for 10 million credits, otherwise their M.D.C. plating can be turned into M.D.C. body armor or building materials, provided it is done just right. Letting the crab's armor just dry out makes it brittle with one-tenth the M.D.C. it should have. Horune Pirates, Metztla, Lemurians and a handful of other people know the secret to preserving it. A suit of heavy body armor made from Storm Crab shell has 6D6+120 M.D.C., weighs 50 pounds (22.5 kg) and has a -15% movement penalty to Physical skills like Climbing and Prowl, but only -10% to Swimming. Full suits of non-environmental armor sell for 45,000-50,000 credits. The meat sells for 20 credits a pound.

Terror Eels

Terror or Screaming Eels are living banshees who subdue their prey by attacking in small schools and unleashing a shrieking sound to stun and disorient their prey before attacking. A variety of other clicks, whistles and noises are used to lure unsuspecting prey, like dolphins, into their clutches, as well as to taunt, warn and scare other sea animals. Terror Eels swim and hunt in small schools of 1D4+4 and use tag team tactics, taking turns to bite and kill their prey. They are also excellent at team tactics to distract, separate and corral one man-sized or dolphin-sized target from the others in its group, while other eels dart in to take bites and work to slay the prey. Their screams and other scary noises create a Horror Factor of 15. Humans and D-Bees have proven to be easy prey for these hunters and have become a favored meal. As a result, Terror Eels sometimes patrol beaches and areas where they know humanoids are located and even follow boats and ships to hunt humanoids by drawing would-be victims with their sounds, including a call that sounds like a woman or child crying. As pack hunters, Terror Eels work extremely well together. Their dark black scales and blood-red eyes only add to their fearsome visage. Elder Terror Eels often develop silver or white streaks in their scale patterns and on their spine fins. This usually accentuates them from other members of the pack, but in the darkness, of the water, gives them an elusive, ethereal appearance.

Terror Eel Stats

Also Known As: Scream Eels.

Alignment: Considered Miscreant or Diabolic, as the monsters like to torment and play with their food before killing it.

Attributes: I.Q. 1D4+3 (animal intelligence, but cunning hunters), M.E. 1D6+8, M.A. 1D6, P.S. 1D6+11, P.P. 1D6+19, P.E. 1D6+13, P.B. 2D6, Spd 2D6+20 swimming (18 mph/29 km or 15.6 knots).

Hit Points: 4D6+6

S.D.C.: 1D6x10 and has a Natural A.R. of 8.

Horror Factor: 10 on their own, but 15 as a pack, making all kinds of scary noises.

Size: 7-10 feet (2.1 to 3 m) long.

Weight: 90-130 lbs (40.5 to 58.5 kg).

Average Life Span: 15-30 years.

P.P.E.: 1D6

Equivalent Skills: Imitate Voices (30%) and Sounds 80%, Prowl 80%, Swimming 98% and Tailing 85%.

Natural Abilities: Nightvision 2,000 feet (610 m), resistant to cold (half damage, magic cold does full damage), tolerate depths up to 7 miles (11 km), can locate moving objects in water 90% through their keen sense of hearing (can hear prey up to 3,000 feet/914 m). They themselves are quite fearless and are +6 to save vs Horror Factor. Each Terror Eel knows how to work as a team with others of their kind.

Terror Shriek (special): Warning Shriek has a Horror Factor of 10, Attack Shriek H.F. 13, Terror Shriek H.F. 15 and hurts the ears of most animals. The Terror Shriek can stun small fish and disorient dolphins, orca and most humans and D-Bess (reduce the number of attacks and combat bonuses of the victims by half, they lose initiative, and skill performance is -30%). Furthermore, the Terror Shriek is so painful, that even those using listening equipment must turn it off or suffer the same penalties. Communications equipment is fouled, broken up with bursts of static and ear-piercing squeals, all of which makes communications fragmented at best and incomprehensible at worse, as well as interfering with sonar systems (-50% to get an accurate reading, -4 to strike using a sonar or sound based targeting system). **Vulnerabilities:** The Terror Eels can get cocky and may underestimate more powerful prey, relying on their ability to create fear. However, such tactics don't always work, especially on some of the creations of the Lord of the Deep, sea dragons and other powerful, underwater supernatural creatures.

Attacks per Melee: Three per eel and the members of the group take turns attacking while maintaining the terror shriek to keep their prey disoriented.

Damage: Bite does 3D6 S.D.C., nose jab, head butt or tail slap does 2D4 S.D.C.

Bonuses (in addition to possible attribute bonuses): +2 to initiative, +3 on Perception Rolls, +2 to strike, +1 to dodge.

Magic: None.

Psionics: Empathy; always on at no I.S.P. cost. They can actively feel the emotions of those around them and become excited in the presence of fear.

Habitat: Can be found anywhere in the Pacific Ocean and other tropical oceans and seas. Though they can survive at considerable depths, they prefer costal waters and reefs, but are found where prey is plentiful, which includes coastal areas populated by people.

Enemies: None, per se, they hunt just about anything they think they can kill.

Allies: Fellow Terror Eels only. The average pack consists of 1D6+4 members, sometimes as large as 2D6+6.

Value: None, per se, though some tribal people eat them.

Twisted Treasure Seahorse

This large seahorse has a turquoise or blue skin covered in gold lines or veins, and is a favorite Familiar amongst Ocean Wizards and Ocean Druids. The small animals, seldom larger than 12 inches (0.3 m), can be seen hanging from the cloak, necklace, hair, belt or strap of many a mage or floating at his side or trailing closely behind their master ready to assist; or, perhaps, quietly swimming forward to scout ahead or spy on someone. They get their name from the fact that while they look like an ordinary seahorse, they are M.D.C. beings that possess strange powers. Twisted Treasure Seahorses are very aware of their surroundings, very alert and perceptive, and Familiars are tied into their master's emotions on a more sensitive level than any other animal that may be chosen as a Familiar. Many Ocean Wizards, Aquatic Biomancers and even Sea Druids have learned to use the creature's unique perspective and avoid the pitfalls related to it.

Twisted Treasure Seahorse Stats

Also Known As: Kopeka Kura Moana Lio (Twisted Treasure Seahorse) or Whina Moana Lio (Helper Seahorse) or just Treasure Seahorse.

Alignment: In the wild, they are considered to be Anarchist. As a Familiar, and even a pet, the creature's alignment mirrors its master's.

Attributes: I.Q. 1D6+8 (high animal intelligence), M.E. 1D6+9, M.A. 1D6+9, P.S. 1D6 (Supernatural), P.P. 1D6+7, P.E. 1D6+9 (Supernatural), P.B. 2D6+11, Spd 1D6+16 swimming or flying (12 mph/19.2 km or 10 knots).

M.D.C.: 1D6+6. (On an S.D.C. world it has P.E. attribute number for Hit Points, 4D6 S.D.C. and an A.R. 8.)

Size: 8-12 inches (20 to 30 cm) tall, with a tail that uncurls for an additional 12 to 20 inches (30 to 51 cm).

Weight: 2-5 lbs (0.9 to 2.3 kg).

Average Life Span: 200-600 years.

P.P.E.: 6D6+10

Equivalent Skills: Detect Ambush 80%, Detect Concealment 75%, Detect Traps and Mines 70%, Dousing 90%, Find Contraband 60%, Gardening 65%, Identify Plants & Fruit 80%, Land Navigation 75%, Lore: Demons & Monsters 60%, Prowl 70% (+10% underwater), Swimming 98%, Tailing 88%, Track and Hunt Sea Animals 60%, Tracking (Humanoids) 65%, and Underwater Navigation 88%.

Natural Abilities: Supernatural P.S. and P.E., the ability to swim and fly through the air, can breathe both air and water, resistant to fire, heat and cold (half damage), tolerates depths up to 4 miles (6.4 km) and Bio-Regeneration (one M.D.C. point per melee).

Fly in Air (special): Treasure Seahorses can hover, float, glide on the wind and fly under their own power in the air. Maximum altitude is 2,000 feet (610 m). Speed is a slow 12 mph (19.2 km), but flying (and swimming) speed is doubled along ley lines.

Innate Understanding of People and their Emotions (special): This is due, in part, to the Treasure Seahorse's keen awareness of its surroundings and others, and its psionic nature. The gentle creature can sense the emotions of others and is attracted

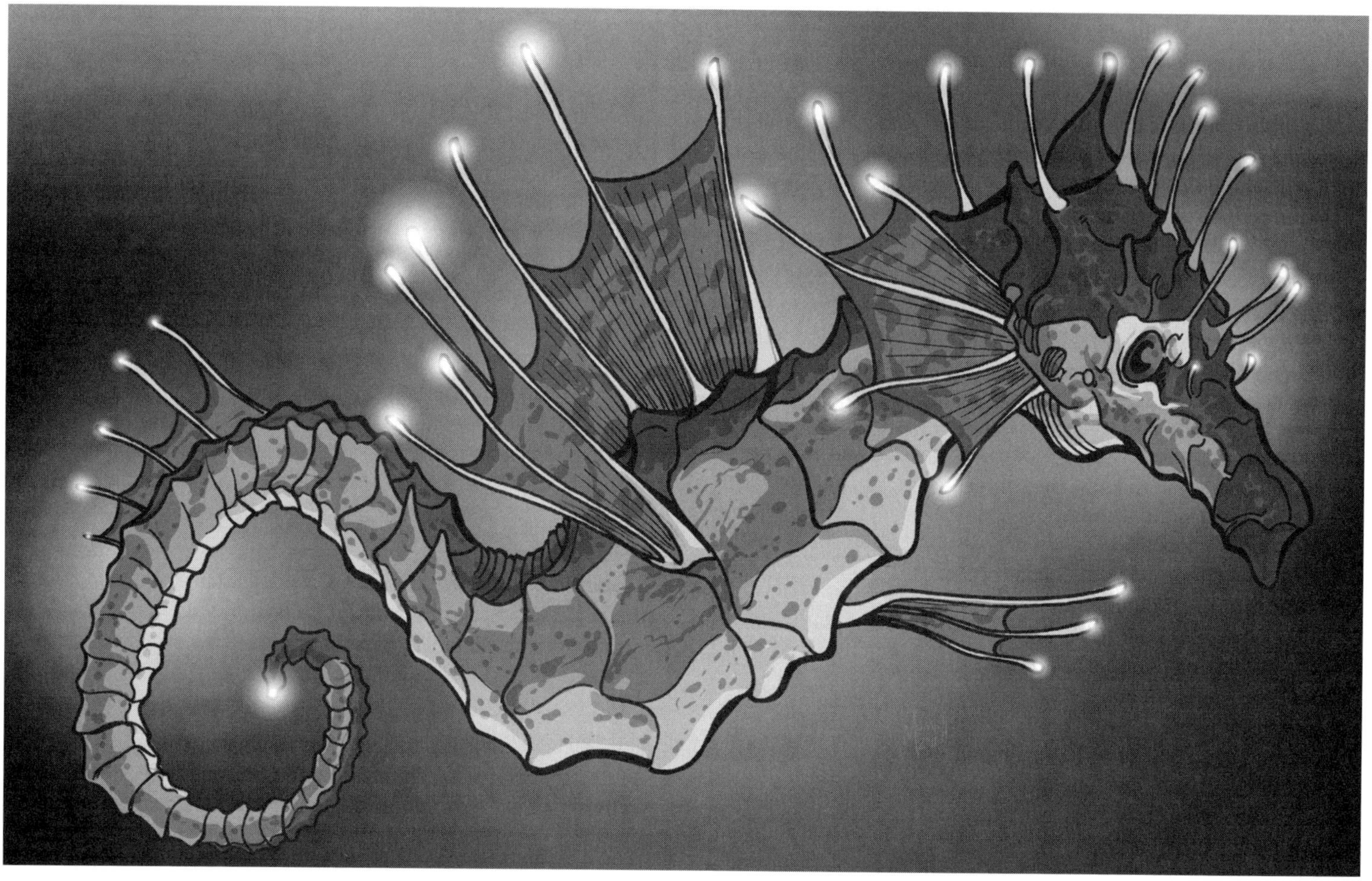

to goodness, joy, laughter and other positive emotions. This sensitivity to others is strongest when linked to a mage as a Familiar. As a Familiar, the seahorse is loyal, attentive and aware of its master's every need, sometimes before he knows it himself.

Light-Up Fin Tips (special): The tips of the fins and frills can be made to glow at will. This light show is enough to create a dim light (roughly equal to a 40 watt lightbulb) for a 4 foot (1.2 m) radius around the seahorse to see in dark waters, or to signal others. Along a ley line they glow automatically and at twice the intensity and three times the range.

Limited Amphibious Nature (special): Treasure Seahorses can hover and fly in the air out of water for two hours per P.E. attribute point. They cannot crawl or walk on land (they flop around like a fish out of water), but can climb bushes and trees and swing from branches and vines. After the Twisted Treasure Seahorse has reached the limit it can endure out of water, it must return to the sea or it begins to suffer, dehydrates and dies within 1D6+1 hours. During this period, reduce the seahorse's M.D.C., P.P.E., I.S.P., attacks per melee and bonuses by half for every hour until death. If placed back in the ocean before it expires, the seahorse completely recovers in 1D6 hours.

Vision, Full Spectrum: The Twisted Treasure Seahorse can see in the entire spectrum of light including infrared and ultraviolet as well as see electro-magnetic energy and magic energy.

Prehensile Tail: The Twisted Treasure Seahorse has two small "flippers" on its upper body which it uses to swim and fly, but must rely on its long and extremely agile tail to grab and hold onto things. The tail is as agile as that of a monkey but is much stronger and can push buttons, pull levers, turn doorknobs, and carry very small objects as well as large packages, bags, suitcases and parcels that have handles, rope or something for the seahorse to hold onto; can carry up to 100 pounds (45 kg) due to its Supernatural P.S.

Also see Psionics.

Attacks per Melee: Two.

Damage: A tail slap or a crush/squeeze attack with its long, prehensile tail does 3D6 S.D.C. damage with a full strength strike, one M.D. with a power punch (counts as two attacks). A body ram does the same range of damage.

Bonuses (in addition to possible attribute bonuses): +6 on Perception Rolls, +1 on initiative, +3 to dodge, +4 to save vs Horror Factor, and +7 to save vs illusions.

Magic: None, but when the animal is a Familiar for a mage, the sorcerer can share draw upon up to two thirds of the animal's P.P.E. reserve.

Psionics: Empathy (4), See Aura (6), See the Invisible (4), Sense Magic (3), Sense Evil (2) and Telepathy (4). Has a base I.S.P. of M.E. attribute x3.

Habitat: Can be encountered in the oceans and seas worldwide, but Treasure Seahorses much prefer tropical coral reefs as they are generally the most vibrant, alive and beautiful of places. They are also found living in Lemurian undersea gardens and in Lemurian cities.

Enemies: Sea monsters and evil supernatural beings. It dislikes the supernatural and regards the Splugorth, Lord of the Deep, the Milu, demons and undead as natural enemies.

Allies: Lemurians, Merans, Ichthyeans, and other people who exude good intentions, good alignments and a sense of compassion. Since the Treasure Seahorse prefers to spend most of its time underwater, it has limited contact with surface people, but the same conditions apply. Is attracted to goodness and beauty, and likes humans, Lemurians and Merans.

Value: They make ideal companions and familiars, easily selling for 100,000 to 500,000 or even a million credits. Of course, Lemurians never buy or sell Twisted Treasure Seahorses, but invite them to become an ally or "partner" (i.e. Familiar).

Sea Monsters & War Steeds

By Kevin Siembieda and Greg Diaczyk

Sea Serpents, Sea Monsters & War Steeds

Panther Shark
Sea Lance
Sea Saber
Sea Whip
Seal Serpent
Serpent Seahorse
Shadow Serpent
Thrall Sea Serpent
Tiger Serpent

Sea Dragons

Leviathan
Ghost Dragon
Hydros Dragon
Octo Dragon
Sand Dragon

In the case of War Steeds created via genetic manipulation by Lemurian Biomancer Gene-Mage Masters, the animals were created for the specific purpose of serving as riding animals, work animals and war horses for Lemuria. This means they did not exist in the wild of Rifts Earth, but were created. However, even the diligent and careful Lemurians could not possibly keep track of every single War Steed, and some, over the years, that lost their rider and failed to find their way back home, have survived in the wild. This means there are some lone War Steeds, mated pairs and small packs/schools/groups encountered from time to time in the wild. These often fall prey to monsters, slavers, pirates and other people who may try to capture them for their own use, place them in gladiatorial contests or kill them out of fear.

Lemurians take great care in keeping War Steeds safe and well cared for, and as noted elsewhere, consider them to be more like partners and companions than pets or slaves. While they do share War Steeds with some of their aquatic allies, they do so only with the most respected and trusted of individuals. Likewise, Lemurians may, sometimes, give a War Steed to an outsider/surface dweller who has proven himself to be a kind, caring and trustworthy hero who will take care of such noble animals, but such a grand gesture is a rarity. The Master Biomancy Gene-Mages NEVER share the secrets of their creations with outsiders, and even most Lemurian Gene-Mages do not know the secrets. As a result, when Lemurian War Steeds come on to the open market (captured in the wild or taken from a slain warrior), such amazing and trained animals fetch hundreds of thousands of credits. In fact, they can often command 50% to 200% more than the prices listed in the descriptions.

Panther Shark

There can be little doubt that the Panther Shark is a Lemurian Biomancer Gene-Mage creation. The massive creature is surprisingly fast on both land and sea, and possesses obvious, lethal combat capabilities, from a massive maw filled with shark teeth, to claws and excellent agility. On dry land, Panther Sharks can run at great speed, leap, climb and pounce. Their massive front claws can parry and tear opponents apart, the mouth capable of taking off a limb with a single bite, and the underbelly is lined with blade-like spikes to slash and cut. The unusual belly-blades can fold to retract inside a flap of belly skin or extend to slash opponents as the creature leaps over them or to do additional damage from a pounce or grappling attack.

Panther Sharks range in color for light to dark gray with a white underbelly. They are a favorite of Oceanic Guardsmen, Scouts and Serpent Hunters. Unlike some War Steeds, Panther Sharks are very aggressive and love to be on the prowl, stalking enemies or prey, hunting or fighting. Their "killer's instinct," fearlessness, agility and loyalty to their rider, makes them high performance War Steeds ideal for land operations.

Panther Shark Lemurian War Steed

Also Known As: Devil Shark and Running Shark.

Alignment: Any, but most are considered to be Scrupulous (40%), Unprincipled (30%) or Anarchist (20%).

Attributes: I.Q. 1D4+5 (high animal intelligence), M.E. 1D6+10, M.A. 1D6+3, P.S. 1D6+20 (Supernatural), P.P. 1D6+18, P.E. 2D6+12, P.B. 1D6+6, Spd 2D4+60 running (40 mph/64 km), 30 mph (48 km or 26 knots) in water; increase running speed 50% and swimming speed by 30% along a ley line. Can run at full speed for 30 minutes (swim for one hour) per P.E. attribute point before feeling fatigued and necessary to reduce speed to one third for a period half as long, before the steed needs to rest for a minimum of five hours. Can swim or run at a leisurely pace for one hour per P.E. point.

Size: 14-18 feet (4.3 to 5.5 m) long from snout to rump, plus another 6-8 feet (1.8 to 2.4 m) of tail, and 5-6 feet (1.5 to 1.8

m) wide at the shoulders, and 7-9 feet (2.1 to 2.7 m) tall at the shoulders (shark fin adds another 4 feet/1.2 m).

Weight: 2-3 tons; females tend to be 25% larger than males.

M.D.C. 3D6x10+70 M.D.C. +P.E. attribute number. (On S.D.C. worlds, Panther Sharks have 2D6x10+40 Hit Points, 2D4x10 S.D.C. and a Natural A.R. of 14.)

Horror Factor: 14

P.P.E.: 5D6+5

Disposition: Aggressive, cunning, natural predator that lives to hunt and battle, but makes a loyal and reliable steed.

Average Life Span: 1D6x10+60 years.

Equivalent Skill Abilities: Climbing 88%/55%, Land Navigation 90%, Tailing 85% (on land and underwater), Tracking (people or animals on land) 65% (+15% to follow blood scent), Underwater Navigation 90%, and learns/understands spoken languages quickly (65%); understands Lemurian and Oceanic at 90%.

Natural Abilities: Supernatural P.S. and P.E., swim 98%, can breathe air or water with equal ease for an indefinite period, depth tolerance of five miles (8 km), Nightvision 1,000 feet (305 m), excellent day and underwater vision, keen underwater sense of smell (track by scent alone, 75% +20% to follow blood scent underwater), resistance to cold (half damage). Can leap 40 feet (12.2 m) high or across from a standing still position, increase by 50% with a running start. Bio-Regenerates at a rate of 2D6 per hour (typically about 120-180 points per 24 hours).

Attacks per Melee: Four.

Mega-Damage: A nip does 4D6 S.D.C., full strength bite and claw attacks do 4D6 M.D. (cannot do a power bite), power claw strike does 1D4x10+4 (counts as two melee attacks), a belly slash does 3D6 M.D. Tail slap does 2D6 M.D. This War Steed will not do head butts, stomps or ramming attacks.

Pounce Attack (special): A pounce attack with belly blades extended does 6D6 M.D. and the victim must make or roll with impact to avoid getting "pinned" by the Panther Shark. A failed roll with impact means he is knocked down, loses initiative, loses one melee attack and there is a 01-60% chance that he is pinned down by the War Steed. If pinned, the victim loses half his attacks, is -5 to strike, parry and dodge and the Panther Shark can continue to attack with bites or from its rider.

Bonuses (in addition to possible attribute bonuses): +2 on Perception Rolls involving blood, hunting and combat, +3 to initiative, +3 to strike, +4 to parry, +4 to automatic dodge on land and water, and +6 to save vs Horror Factor.

Habitat: Feels equally at home hunting and fighting on land or sea, but the ocean is its home.

Enemies: Large marine predators, sea serpents, sea monsters, humanoids, and the enemies of Lemuria.

Allies: Lemurians, the people who created this War Steed, but they may also be used by humans and aquatic D-Bees. The animal gets along with other sharks, but most mammals and aquatic life forms consider it to be a dangerous predator.

Value: As a trained War Steed it is worth 500,000 credits. The hide of the Panther Shark cannot be made into body armor or clothing, but the teeth can be made into arrowheads, knives and war clubs, and the belly blades into knives, short swords and spearheads. Its meat is tasty and sells for (whole animal) 300-500 credits.

Sea Lance

The Sea Lance is another Lemurian Biomancer Gene-Mage creation that is all smooth lines, grace and swimming ability. It is the smallest of the Lemurian War Steeds, and the least threatening. There is something peaceful and majestic about this steed. In water, it swims with the same motion as dolphins but given greater speed by its "wings." Like dolphins and flying fish, the Sea Lance can breach the waves and leap into the air in a forward motion. Here the wings add height and distance to the out of water leap, enough to enable them to land on the decks of boats and ships, as well as docks and beaches. They always land on their feet, ready to run or engage in combat. Along ley lines, the Sea Lance can run 50% faster and, if it so chooses, leap into the air and fly. Along underwater ley lines, swimming speed is doubled.

Though gentle and graceful, Sea Lances are steady and unshakeable in combat. The War Steed will never abandon its rider and have been known to fight to the death to protect him or innocent people, especially children. Sea Lances are a favorite of Lemurian Scouts, explorers, Biomancers and other practitioners of magic. It has the least natural armor (M.D.C.), so Bio-Barding is often a must.

Sea Lance War Steed

Also Known As: Winged Dolphin and Ocean Unicorn.

Alignment: Any, but most are considered to be Principled (30%), Scrupulous (30%), Unprincipled (20%) or Anarchist (10%).

Attributes: I.Q. 1D4+7 (high animal intelligence, though not as intelligent as sentient cetaceans), M.E. 1D6+14, M.A. 1D6+18, P.S. 1D6+15 (Supernatural), P.P. 1D6+14, P.E. 1D6+14, P.B. 1D6+14, Spd 2D4+50 running (36 mph/57.6 km), double Spd in water (72 mph/115 km or 62 knots); double Spd when running or swimming along a ley line, but not flying Spd (see below). Double running and swimming speed along a ley line. Can swim or run at full speed for one hour per P.E. attribute point before feeling fatigued and necessary to reduce speed by half. The reduced pace can be maintained for half as long before the steed must stop and rest for at least five hours. Can swim, run and fly at a leisurely pace indefinitely.

Flying/Gliding: The Sea Lance can leap out of the water and glide 10-20 feet (3-6.1 m) above the waves for a distance of up to 200 feet (61 m). Or the creature can leap upward to land on a ship deck or other surface above water up to 40 feet (12.2 m) high.

Ley Line Flying: This leap and glide only becomes actual flying through the air along ley lines, equal to the animal's running speed, 36 mph (57.6 km). Maximum flying altitude is 600 feet (183 m).

Size: 14-18 feet (4.3 to 5.5 m) long from snout to tail tip, 3-4 feet (0.9 to 1.2 m) wide at the shoulders. Wingspan when fully extended is 18 feet (5.5 m).

Weight: 800-1,200 pounds (360 to 540 kg); males tend to be 20% larger than females.

M.D.C. by Location:

Horn (1) – 2D6+6
Head – 5D6+40
Large Wing Fins (2) – 1D6x10+45 each
Small Wing Fins (2, on front legs) – 3D6+22 each
Legs (4) – 1D4x10+50 each
Tail – 1D4x10+50
Main Body – 1D6x10+55

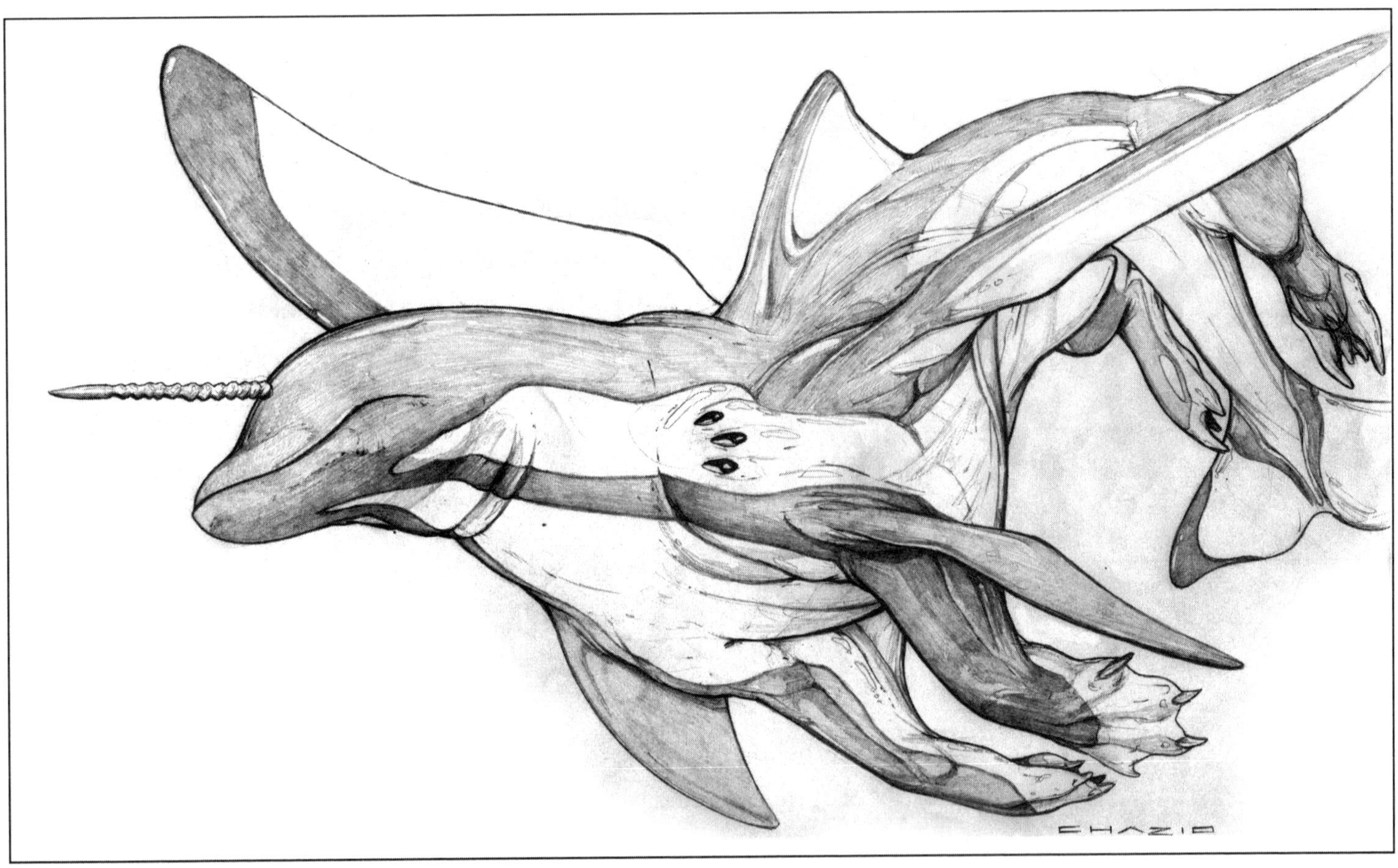

Horror/Awe Factor: 11

P.P.E.: 6D6+20

Disposition: Gentle, easygoing, helpful, cooperative, and caring. Steadfast and calm under duress and combat, fiercely loyal to friends, innocent people, and fellow Sea Lances. When not in combat situations, Sea Lances are playful and loving, and will try to help people in need.

Average Life Span: 1D6x10+30 years.

Equivalent Skill Abilities: Land Navigation 80%, Tailing 75% (on land and underwater), Prowl 50%, Underwater Navigation 90%, and learns/understands spoken languages quickly (75%); understands Lemurian and Oceanic at 90%.

Natural Abilities: Supernatural P.S. and P.E., swim 98%, hold breath for up to 30 minutes +2 minutes per P.E. point, depth tolerance of four miles (6.4 km), Nightvision 1,000 feet (305 m), excellent day and underwater vision, resistance to cold (half damage). Bio-Regenerates at a rate of 1D6 per hour (typically about 80 points per 24 hours).

Attacks per Melee: Four.

Mega-Damage: A nip does 1D6 S.D.C., a restrained bite 4D6 S.D.C., a full strength bite does 1D6 M.D., stomp or front leg kick does 1D6 M.D., Head butt (blunt) or nose strike 1D6+1 M.D. wing strike does 1D6+1 M.D., horn strike or rear leg kick does 2D6+3. Cannot do a power bite or kick. Tail slap does 2D6 M.D. and an underwater ram attack with horn or body does 3D6+3 M.D. but counts as two melee attacks.

Bonuses (in addition to possible attribute bonuses): +3 on Perception Rolls, +2 on initiative, +3 to strike, +1 to parry, +4 to automatic dodge in air, water and on land, +3 to pull punch, +3 to roll with impact, +4 to save vs Horror Factor, +1 to save vs illusions and mind control.

Habitat: Found wherever Lemurians are found, especially among their cities, gardens and outposts. Home is in the ocean with Lemurians, but the Sea Lance does well on dry land, especially when there is water to take a nice, refreshing dip.

Enemies: Sharks and large marine predators, sea serpents, sea monsters, humanoids, and the enemies of Lemuria.

Allies: Namely Lemurians, the people who created this War Steed, but they may also be used by humans and aquatic D-Bees. Gets along with other cetaceans and loves Sea Whips, Serpent Seals and other fun-loving animals and kind people, but most small fish and crustaceans consider it to be a dangerous predator.

Value: As a trained War Steed it is worth 150,000-200,000 credits. The hide of the Sea Lance cannot be made into body armor or clothing, only the horn can be used as a stabbing weapon or spearhead (does 1D6 M.D.). Its meat is not very tasty and there is no market for it.

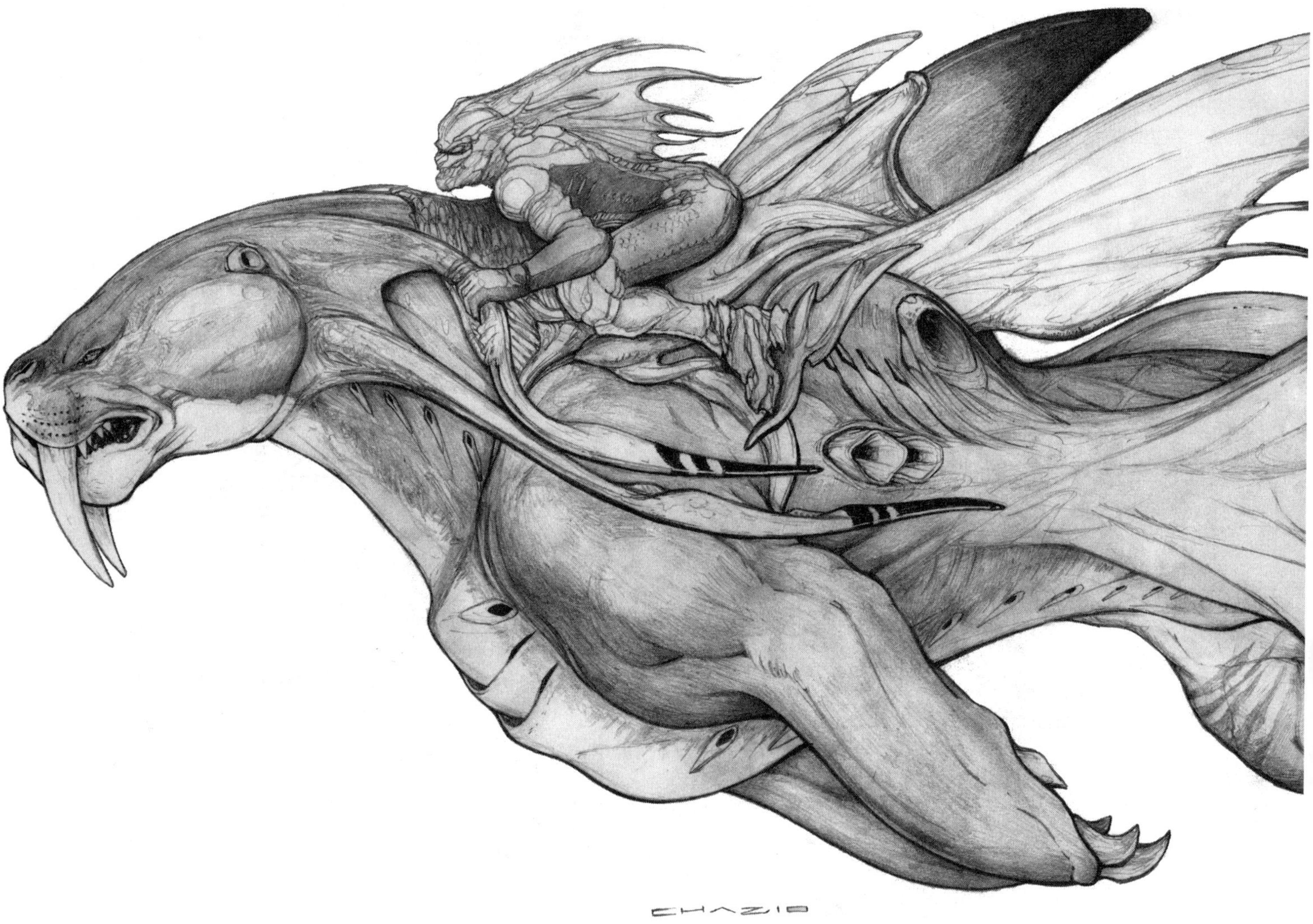

Sea Saber

The Sea Saber is a Lemurian Biomancer Gene-Mage creation built for speed in all terrains – land, water and air. When stretched out with its legs tucked in for "flight" underwater or in the air, it looks like a long ribbon with teeth undulating in the current and coming up a surprising pace.

The Sea Saber is part feline, part manta ray and part fish wrapped in fury. Underwater, its large, manta-like wings and tail catch and ride the currents, requiring little effort to swim. When greater speed is desired, the large, clawed front and hind legs push through water in a loping, running motion, while the iridescent fish-fin wings provide additional thrust and lift. When desired, the Sea Saber can rise to the surface and breach the water with one coordinated thrust of its legs and wings. Like a dolphin or flying fish, the Sea Saber hurls out of the water, but unlike the flying fish, its top wings provide greater lift and the kite-like tail catches air currents, enabling the beast to rise as high as 100 feet (30.5 m) above the water's surface or, if preferred, to skim just a few feet (a meter) above it. When needed, the War Steed can kick it into high speed via a Biomancer Gene-Mage biological air intake system and thrusters in its back behind the shoulders and off to the side of the wings. Underwater the same bio-thrusters propel the War Steed up to 80 mph (128 km or 69.5 knots). On dry land, the thickly muscled, legs take over the job of locomotion, running, leaping great distances and even taking wing to leap over opponents, walls and vehicles with the speed of a Cheetah.

In combat, the saber-toothed War Steed is armed with a pair of tusk-like fangs the length of short swords and massive, wicked claws to rip enemies to shreds. Its flight capabilities enables the Sea Saber to make quick stops, sharp turns and gliding leaps that can cover half the length of a football field, and even hover in mid-air for a few minutes where it can claw at giant robots, engage flying power armor troops, land on rooftops or low flying aircraft, or to get an elevated perspective of the battlefield. The ability to glide comes in handy for leaping over debris fields, fences, walls and areas that may be mined or booby-trapped. The cat nature of the Sea Saber and its retractable claws, gives the War Steed climbing abilities good enough to scale the corners of buildings and sheer cliffs without risk of falling for the first 15 stories (150 feet/45.7 m). Nor do they have a problem leaping from rooftop to rooftop in urban environments. Most riders sit in a crouched position, hugging the animal's body like a racehorse jockey, and use two of the animal's tentacle-like feelers as reins. This War Steed is a favorite of *Oceanic Guardsmen* and, when they use one, *Sea Sentinels*.

Sea Sabers have a thick, rubbery hide like dolphins that is a mountain lion colored brown or tan, with a cream or light gray colored underbelly. Claws are a darker brown color, the saber teeth an off-white and their eyes a vibrant green. The fish-wings

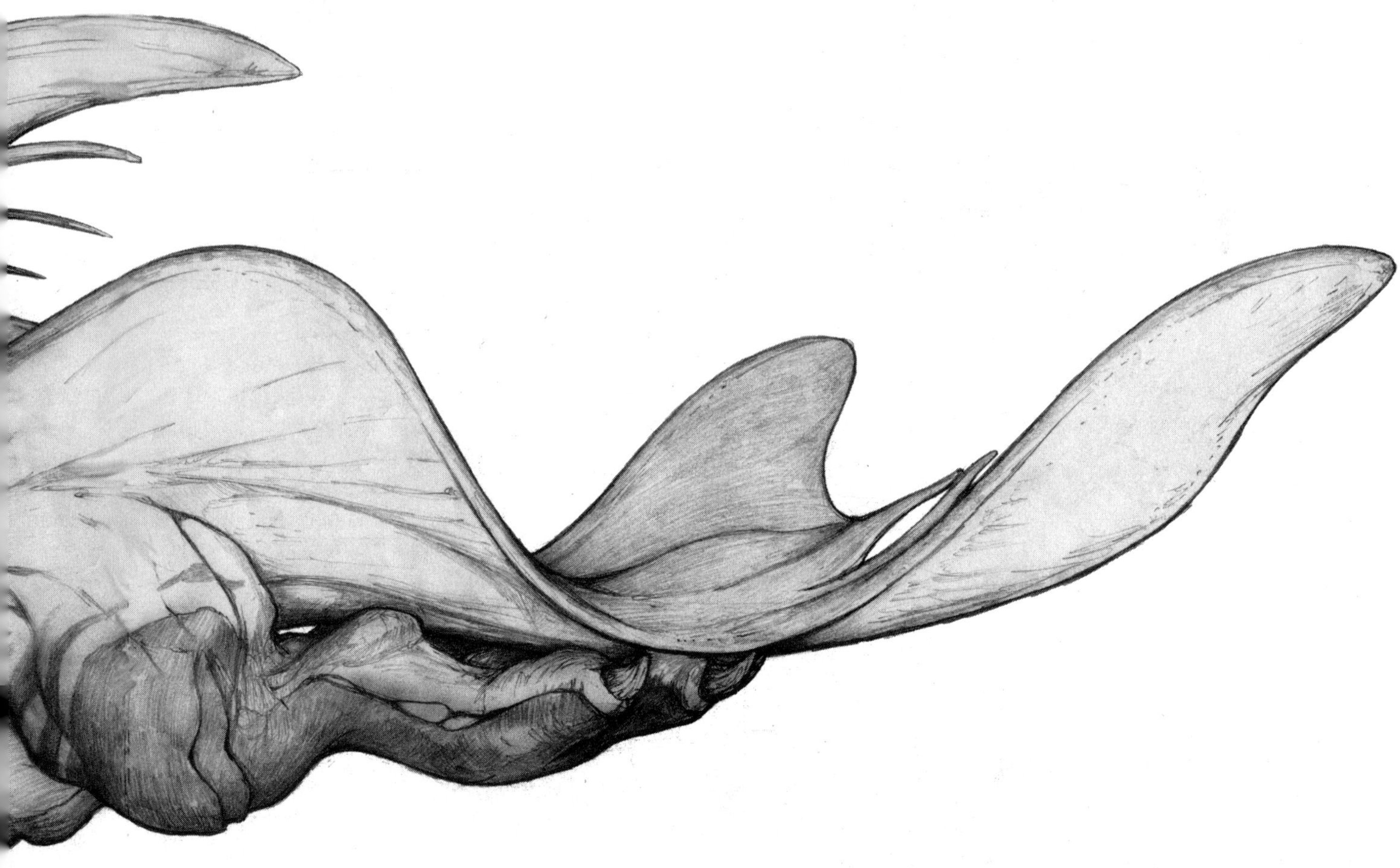

on the back are an iridescent pearl white with a hint of pink and sparkling flecks of white, blue, green and purple.

Sea Saber War Steed

Also Known As: Sea Cat and Wind Cat.

Alignment: Any, but most are considered to be Principled (20%), Scrupulous (30%), Unprincipled (20%) or Anarchist (20%).

Attributes: I.Q. 1D4+6 (high animal intelligence, though not as intelligent as sentient cetaceans), M.E. 1D6+12, M.A. 1D6+15, P.S. 1D6+24 (Supernatural), P.P. 1D6+14, P.E. 1D6+14, P.B. 1D6+14, Spd 2D4+72 running (58 mph/93 km). Can swim or run at full speed for one hour per P.E. attribute point, before feeling fatigued and require a minimum of six hours rest. Can swim or run at a leisurely pace for twice as long. See below for other types of locomotion and speeds.

Climbing: The Sea Saber can climb a sharp vertical incline or sheer wall at half its running speed for the first 15 stories, reduce to one third the rest of the way.

Leaping: 60 feet (18.3 m) high and across from a standing position, double with a running start.

Gliding Leap: Up to 200 feet (61 m); double when leaping into a strong wind blowing in the direction of the leap or on a ley line, and can glide up to 100 feet (30.5 m) high as the result of a leap, though most leaps are a third or half that height.

Flying: A Sea Saber can ride wind and ocean currents to 20 mph (32 km) faster than the wind/current speed. With no wind or light wind, 20 mph (32 km) is the maximum speed possible. Altitude is limited to 1,000 feet (305 m). However, when the wind is stronger than 20 mph (32 km) or the jet bio-thrusters are engaged, the Sea Saber can triple its present air speed and attain an altitude as high as one mile (1.6 km). Needs to leap into the air to take flight, but can stop and hover for 1D4+1 minutes. Jet thruster speed can be maintained in the air for five minutes per P.E. attribute point. **Note:** Increase speed and duration by 50% when along a ley line.

In Water: The Sea Saber can glide on water currents with minimal effort at whatever the speed of the current (typically under 10 mph/16 km). Swimming under its own power has a maximum speed of 50 mph (80 km or 43 knots). However, when the bio-thrusters are engaged, the Sea Saber can rocket through water at 80 mph (128 km or 69.5 knots). Jet thruster speed can be maintained underwater or on the water's surface for 10 minutes per P.E. attribute point. **Note:** Increase speed and duration by 50% when along a ley line.

Also see Natural Abilities.

Size: 14-17 feet (4.3 to 5.2 m) long from snout to rump, plus an additional 11-13 feet (3.3 to 3.96 m) for the manta-wing tail. When running, the manta-wings and tail fold up and lay flat against the animals' body. 4-5 feet (1.2 to 1.5 m) wide at the shoulders, and the manta-wingspan is 12-15 feet (3.6 to 4.6 m) when fully extended.

Weight: 1-2 tons; males tend to be 20% larger than females.

M.D.C. by Location:

Head – 6D6+60
Manta Tail Section & Wings (2) – 2D4x10+45 each
Fish-Wings (2, back) – 1D6x10+40 each
Back Fin (1) – 1D6x10+70
Legs, Front (2) – 1D6x10+60 each
Legs, Rear (2) – 2D6x10+50 each
Main Body – 2D6x10+70

Horror Factor: 13

P.P.E.: 1D6x10+35

Disposition: Alert, quick to take action and aggressive in combat, but otherwise, gentle, easygoing and loyal. Steadfast and calm under duress and combat, fiercely loyal to its rider/partner and fellow Sea Sabers. When not in combat situations, Sea Sabers like to sun themselves on the surface, explore, hunt and play.

Average Life Span: 1D6x10+30 years.

Equivalent Skill Abilities: Climbing 95%/70%, Land Navigation 90%, Tailing 85% (on land and underwater), Prowl 75% (on land and underwater), Track Animals (on land; 75%), Underwater Navigation 90%, and learns/understands spoken languages quickly (65%); understands Lemurian and Oceanic at 90%.

Natural Abilities: Supernatural P.S. and P.E., swim 98%, can breathe water and air indefinitely, Nightvision 1,000 feet (305 m), excellent day and underwater vision, resistance to cold (half damage). Bio-Regenerates at a rate of 1D6 per hour (typically about 80 points per 24 hours). **Note:** Depth tolerance is four miles (6.4 km), however, Sea Sabers much prefer being in much shallower waters illuminated by the sun, as well as skimming the surface like dolphins and flying fish. They also enjoy spending time on dry land more than any other Lemurian War Steed, with the possible exception of the Serpent Seahorse.

Attacks per Melee: Five.

Mega-Damage: A nip does 2D6 S.D.C., a restrained bite 1D6 M.D., a full strength bite does 5D6 M.D., a claw strike does 4D6 M.D., kick from the rear legs 6D6 M.D., a pawing blunt attack (claws retracted), 2D6 M.D., a wing strike does 1D6 M.D., and a tail slap does 3D6 M.D. Cannot do a power bite or claw strike.

Bonuses (in addition to possible attribute bonuses): +3 on Perception Rolls, +3 on initiative, +4 to strike, +3 to parry, +3 to automatic dodge in air, water and on land, +3 to pull punch, +4 to roll with impact and if successful, lands on its feet, and +5 to save vs Horror Factor.

Habitat: Found wherever Lemurians are found, especially among their cities, gardens and outposts. Home is in the ocean with Lemurians, but the Sea Saber does very well on dry land and likes to explore and hunt on islands and coastal forests.

Enemies: Sharks and large marine predators, sea serpents, sea monsters, humanoids, and the enemies of Lemuria.

Allies: Namely Lemurians, the people who created this War Steed, but they may also be used by humans and aquatic D-Bees. Gets along with other cetaceans, Sea Whips, Serpent Seals, Serpent Seahorses and other fun-loving animals. Wary of people it does not know and sees most fish and mammals, including people, as potential prey.

Value: As a trained War Steed it is worth 350,000-600,000 credits. The hide cannot be made into body armor or clothing. Only the two saber teeth can be used as a stabbing weapon, pick or spearheads (does 1D6 M.D. each). Its meat is inedible.

Sea Whip

The Sea Whip is one of the Master Lemurian Biomancer Gene-Mages' most creative concepts for a War Steed. A sleek War Steed inspired by the orca and redesigned for torpedo speed underwater and excellent combat capabilities and speed on dry land. The animal's skin is smooth and rubbery like an orca, and skin coloring is gray with a white throat, underbelly and highlights and additional black trim and accents. The barrel-chested beast has powerful forward limbs and hindquarters made for running and leaping. Grown into its back and hindquarters is the Master Gene-Mages most advanced living propulsion system to date. It is capable of rocketing the Sea Whip through water at impressive speeds. At the end of the Sea Whip's thick, long, prehensile tail is a wide, flat paddle bigger than a surfboard. It is used as both a rudder and a weapon. As a weapon, the big, flat, rock hard plate is used to slap, hammer and pound opponents. The tail is so long and agile, it can be used to strike opponents from behind, above, below, on the sides and even in front of the War Steed's face. It can even parry attacks and try to bat away incoming missiles. On dry land, the powerful hind legs are capable of big forward leaps, and straight up leaps in which the tail can swing down to whack opponents as the creature soars by overhead. To enemies seeing a four-legged, roaring orca bearing down on them, batting away troops and light vehicles as it charges, the Sea Whip is a living nightmare.

Despite its frightening visage and tooth-filled mouth, Sea Whips are graceful, playful and can be amazingly gentle. Sea Whips are steady and unshakeable in combat, never abandon their riders and have been known to fight to the death to protect their Lemurian partners or innocent people, especially children. It is a favorite War Steed of Oceanic Guardsmen, first responders and Lemurian Scouts.

Sea Whip War Steed

Also Known As: Whip Dolphin and Monster Dolphin.

Alignment: Any, but most are considered to be Principled (30%), Scrupulous (30%), Unprincipled (20%) or Anarchist (10%).

Attributes: I.Q. 1D4+6 (high animal intelligence, though not as intelligent as sentient cetaceans), M.E. 1D6+15, M.A. 1D6+15, P.S. 1D6+25 (Supernatural), P.P. 1D6+13, P.E. 1D6+14, P.B. 1D6+10, Spd 2D4+50 running (36 mph/57.6 km), double Spd in water (72 mph/115 km or 62 knots); increase running speed 50% and double swimming along a ley line. Can swim or run at full speed for one hour per P.E. attribute point before feeling fatigued and require a minimum of five hours rest. Can swim or run at a leisurely pace for two hours per P.E. point. See below for other types of locomotion.

Leaping: 30 feet (9.1 m) high and across from a standing position, double with a running start.

Torpedo Speed: The Sea Whip can engage an organic rocket system, and when the bio-thrusters are engaged, the Sea Whip can rocket through water at 130 mph (208 km or 112 knots). Jet thruster speed can be maintained underwater or on the water's surface for 20 minutes per P.E. attribute point. **Note:** Increase speed and duration by 50% when along a ley line.

Size: 13-16 feet (3.9 to 4.9 m) long from snout to rump. The prehensile tail is an additional 18-22 feet (5.5 to 6.7 m) long. The combat paddle/rudder is 8-11 feet (2.4 to 3.3 m) of the tail's overall length and is 4-5 feet (1.2 to 1.5 m) at its widest point. The barrel chest and broad shoulders are 8-10 feet (2.4 to 3 m) wide, but the animal tapers to 3 feet (0.9 m) wide at the waist where the rider sits.

Weight: 3-5 tons; females tend to be 10% larger than males.

M.D.C. by Location:

Head – 1D6x10+80
Fins (2, top) – 5D6+20 each
Thruster Jets (6, back) – 4D6+35 each
Legs, Front (2) – 1D6x10+70 each
Legs, Rear (2) – 1D6x10+80 each
Tail – 4D6x10+350
Main Body – 2D6x10+120

Horror/Awe Factor: 14

P.P.E.: 6D6+20

Disposition: Confident and aggressive in combat, but gentle, easygoing, and caring toward its rider, people in general and cetaceans. Steadfast and calm under duress and combat, fiercely loyal to friends, innocent people and fellow Sea Whips and Sea Lances. When not in combat situations, Sea Whips are playful and loving, and much like dolphins, will try to help people in need.

Average Life Span: 1D6x10+50 years.

Equivalent Skill Abilities: Land Navigation 80%, Tailing 75% (on land and underwater), Prowl 50%, Underwater Navigation 90%, and learns/understands spoken languages quickly (75%); understands Lemurian and Oceanic at 90%.

Natural Abilities: Supernatural P.S. and P.E., swim 98%, can breathe water and air indefinitely, Nightvision 1,000 feet (305 m), excellent day and underwater vision, resistance to cold (half damage). Bio-Regenerates at a rate of 2D6 per hour (typically about 140 points per 24 hours). **Note:** Depth tolerance is four miles (6.4 km), however, Sea Whips much prefer sunlit waters, reefs, and skimming the surface like dolphins and flying fish. They also enjoy spending time on dry land more than any other Lemurian War Steed.

Attacks per Melee: Five.

Mega-Damage: A nip does 3D6 S.D.C., a restrained bite 3D6 M.D., a full strength bite does 5D6 M.D., a claw strike does 3D6 M.D., kick from the rear legs 4D6 M.D., head butt 3D6 M.D. Tail Strikes: Restrained tail "tap" does 1D6x10 S.D.C., restrained tail strike does 3D6 M.D., full strength hit does 5D6 M.D. and a power strike does 1D6x10 M.D. but counts as two melee attacks. Cannot do a power bite or claw strike.

Bonuses (in addition to possible attribute bonuses): +2 on Perception Rolls, +3 on initiative, +3 to strike with most combat attacks (+5 to strike with tail), +3 to parry (+4 to parry with tail), +2 to automatic dodge in water and land, +5 to pull punch, +2 to roll with impact, +5 to save vs Horror Factor and +1 to save vs illusions and mind control.

Habitat: Found wherever Lemurians are found, especially among their cities, gardens and outposts. Home is in the ocean with Lemurians, but the Sea Whip does well on dry land, provided it has regular access to places it can swim and bathe.

Enemies: Sharks and large marine predators, sea serpents, sea monsters, humanoids, and the enemies of Lemuria.

Allies: Namely Lemurians, the people who created this War Steed, but they may also be used by humans and aquatic D-Bees. Gets along with other cetaceans, Serpent Seals and other

fun-loving animals and kind people, but most small fish and crustaceans consider it to be a dangerous predator. They love being around other animals and people.

Value: As a trained War Steed it is worth 350,000-500,000 credits. The hide cannot be made into body armor or clothing, only the tail plate can be used as an M.D.C. material for building. Its meat is not very tasty and there is no market for it.

Seal Serpent

These sleek, Lemurian War Steeds are reminiscent of seals with the exceptions of being gigantic, and having a long neck, long body and a long, serpent-like tail. They are a medium to dark green or grayish brown in color with a warm gray or cream colored underbelly. Despite their frightening appearance, Seal Serpents are curious, playful and love chasing and roughhousing with each other and whales. Like dolphin, Serpent Seals have been known to come to the rescue of people at sea, keeping small boats from sinking and sometimes towing them to shallow waters and land, or letting humanoids ride on their back to land or until rescue arrives. They enjoy playing with Lemurians, who are quickly adopting them as one of their favorite War Steeds, as well as playing with other sea serpents, marine mammals such as seals, otters, walruses, dolphins and whales, but also have an affinity for humans and human-like D-Bees. Lemurians and other aquatic people have been using them as riding animals, work animals, guardians and pets for centuries. Since even wild Seal Serpents are so friendly and playful, swimmers can grab hold of

the tail or a foot/flipper and even hop on the back to hitch a ride. Serpent Hunters and some Lemurian Scouts are so skilled with their Seal Serpent steed that they can ride bareback, hunched in a crouched position like a racehorse jockey, and when on the water's surface or on dry land, ride standing up.

Seal Serpents are much slower on land than in the water, but are loyal to their rider and good in a fight. The animal's bite can inflict good damage, but it is the Seal Serpents clubbing tail that is most dangerous. The tip of its tail is a rock-hard bone appendage that can be used to club opponents and sea monsters. On land, the Seal Serpent fights in the same manner as the Stegosaurus dinosaur, with its rear end facing its opponent, tail poised for downward or sideways strikes, while the long neck of the Seal Serpent is cranked to look back at its primary enemy. However, 120 degree peripheral vision enables the Seal Serpent to notice any attackers coming at it from the front where it can bite with its mouth or slash with its feet.

Seal Serpent Lemurian War Steed

Also Known As: Giant Seal and Monster Seal.

Alignment: Any, but most are considered to be Scrupulous (55%), Unprincipled (30%) or Anarchist (10%).

Attributes: I.Q. 1D6+7 (high animal intelligence), M.E. 1D6+10, M.A. 1D6+16, P.S. 1D6+19 (Supernatural), P.P. 1D6+16, P.E. 2D6+9, P.B. 1D6+12, Spd 1D6+12 running (waddles), Spd x4 swimming in water (roughly 40 mph/64 km or 34.7 knots), and can swim at full speed for hours equal to P.E. attribute divided by half. Swim or run at a leisurely speed for one hour per P.E. point.

Size: 30-35 feet (9.1 to 10.6 m) long from snout to rump, plus another 14-16 feet (3.26 to 4.8 m) of tail; 7-8 feet (2.1 to 2.4 m) wide at the shoulder. The neck is 10-12 feet (3-3.6 m) long all by itself.

Weight: 4-6 tons; males tend to be 25% larger than females.

M.D.C. 4D6x10 M.D.C. +P.E. attribute number. (On S.D.C. worlds, Seal Serpents have 2D6x10 Hit Points, 1D6x10 S.D.C. and a Natural A.R. of 13.)

Horror/Awe Factor: 10

P.P.E.: 5D6+20

Disposition: Inquisitive, gentle and playful.

CHAZIO

Average Life Span: 1D4x10+70 years.

Equivalent Skill Abilities: Land Navigation 65%, Tailing 65% (in or under water only), Underwater Navigation 90%, and learns/understands spoken languages quickly (80%); understands and speaks Cetacean 90%, understands Lemurian and Oceanic 90%.

Natural Abilities: Supernatural P.S. and P.E., swim 98%, hold breath for up to 30 minutes +1 minute per P.E. point, depth tolerance of two miles (3.2 km), Nightvision 1,000 feet (305 m), excellent day and underwater vision, keen sense of smell (track by scent 45%), resistance to cold (half damage). Bio-Regenerates at a rate of 1D6 per hour (typically about 80 points per 24 hours).

Attacks per Melee: Four.

Mega-Damage: Nip does 4D6 S.D.C., full strength bite and claws does 2D6 M.D. (cannot do a power bite or power claw strike), head butt and stomp attack does 1D4 M.D., tail strike (a clubbing or slashing attack) does 3D6 M.D., and a power tail strike does 6D6 M.D. but counts as two melee attacks.

Bonuses (in addition to possible attribute bonuses): +2 on Perception Rolls, +1 on initiative, +1 to strike with bite attacks, +3 to strike with tail attacks, +4 to automatic dodge in water (only attribute dodge bonus on dry land), and +4 to save vs Horror Factor.

Habitat: Found wherever Lemurians are found, especially among their cities, gardens and outposts. In the wild, the creatures prefer coastal areas in most climates. They love being around other animals and people.

Enemies: Large marine predators, sea serpents, sea monsters, Milu and their undead, and humanoid hunters from the surface.

Allies: It gets along with most aquatic D-Bees, humans, Lemurians and marine mammals.

Value: The hide of the Seal Serpent can be made into waterproof light body armor (1D4x10+7 M.D.C., -5% Prowl and movement penalty, the armor typically sells for 20,000 credits), the teeth can be made into knives, short swords and spearheads, and the bone tail can be made into an M.D.C. surfboard (5D6+8 M.D.C.). Meat (whole animal) sells for 200-600 credits and does not taste awful, but is a heavy, greasy and fatty meat.

Serpent Seahorse

The Serpent Seahorse is the newest creation of the Lemurian Master Biomancer Gene-Mage engineers and has only been available for the last four years. It is a fierce yet majestic looking creature that radiates confidence and strength. They are a golden brown color with white and black markings and accents, and gold flecks in their hard, armored hide. The head is that of a giant seahorse with many frilled and spiky fins. The body is also horse-like, but more like what if a horse was combined with a bulldog, with a barrel chest and muscular physique. However, the thick, armored legs go beyond any thing that resembles a dog, and the tail is that of an elegant serpent. The biggest innovation, beside the armored hide, are placements for Stonecaster cannons and ion blasters above them that mount right into the armor of the War Steed's shoulders. Moreover, they draw on the Serpent Seahorse's P.P.E. to charge/reload.

There are a few downsides to the innovations, at least on this War Steed. The rider sits up on the neck of the Serpent Seahorse and must lean to one side or the other to see around the head. This makes a large area on the opposite side is a massive blind spot. To get a good view of the battlefield, the rider must frequently lean from side to side. The heavy armor hampers speed and mobility, and the Serpent Seahorse seems to be a bit less reliable than other War Steeds. It obeys its rider and has moments where it shows concern or affection, but most of the time it is aloof and unfriendly, as if it does what it is asked but is uninterested in much else. In many regards, the Serpent Seahorse is more like a slow moving, living armored tank than the other fast War Steeds that behave and move like animals. On one hand, the sense of connection is less. On the other, the animal makes both an excellent heavy infantry unit and armored troop support. The *Serpent Hunters* and *Oceanic Guardsmen* who have ridden the Serpent Seahorse into combat have all given it positive marks for strength, power and increased combat capabilities, especially against technological enemies. It also makes an excellent work animal able to pull heavy loads.

Serpent Seahorse War Steed

Also Known As: Armored Seahorse and Gun Horse.

Alignment: Any, but most are considered to be Scrupulous (15%), Unprincipled (25%) or Anarchist (50%).

Attributes: I.Q. 1D4+5 (high animal intelligence, though not as intelligent as sentient cetaceans), M.E. 1D6+15, M.A. 1D6+5, P.S. 1D6+30 (Supernatural), P.P. 1D6+12, P.E. 1D6+19, P.B. 1D6+17, Spd 2D4+50 running (36 mph/57.6 km), increase swimming Spd in water by 50% (54 mph/86.4 km or 46.9 knots); double Spd when running or swimming along a ley line. Can swim or run at full speed for one hour per P.E. attribute point before feeling fatigued and requires a minimum of three hours rest. Can swim or run at a leisurely pace for twice as long.

Size: 15-20 feet (4.6 to 6.1 m) tall from the top of its head to its toes, and 17-22 feet (5.2 to 6.7 m) long from snout to rump. The thick, frilly serpent's is tail 30-33 feet (9.1 to 10 m) long, and the barrel chested steed is 7-10 feet (2.1 to 3 m) wide at the shoulders.

Weight: 1-2 tons; males tend to be 20% larger than females.

M.D.C. by Location:

Head – 1D6x10+130
Shoulder Fin Shields (2) – 1D6x10+100 each
Shoulder Stonecasters (2) – 90 each
Shoulder Ion Guns (2) – 35 each
Back Fin (1) – 1D6x10+70
Legs, Front (2) – 1D6x10+160 each
Legs, Rear (2) – 2D6x10+180 each
Serpent Tail – 3D6x10+115
Main Body – 6D6x10+280 (470 on average)

Horror/Awe Factor: 13

P.P.E.: 1D6x10 + P.E. attribute number.

Disposition: Stoic and calm even under heavy fire, this War Steed often keeps its emotions to itself, and is stingy with its displays of affection or what it might be thinking. Compared to the shy normal seahorse, the Serpent Seahorse is very aggressive, bold and almost defiant, as if unafraid of dying and seems to enjoy combat. Steady as a rock under duress and combat, and appears to be loyal to its rider/partner and others

of its species, but indifferent to all others. When not in combat situations, Serpent Seahorse tend to keep to themselves and like to swim around, explore and hunt (they eat small fish).

Average Life Span: 1D6x10+40 years.

Equivalent Skill Abilities: Land Navigation 65%, Tailing 60% on land (+5% underwater), Underwater Navigation 85%, and learns/understands spoken languages quickly (65%); understands Lemurian and Oceanic at 80%.

Natural Abilities: Supernatural P.S. and P.E., swim 90%, can breathe water and air indefinitely, Nightvision 1,000 feet (305 m), excellent day and underwater vision, resistance to cold (half damage). Bio-Regenerates at a rate of 3D6 per hour (typically about 180 points per 24 hours). **Note:** Depth tolerance is four miles (6.4 km), but prefers reefs and gardens, where the Serpent Seahorse always seem to become more friendly, happy and playful. They also enjoy spending time on dry land for a few hours at a time, but feel most at home underwater.

Also see weapon systems under Mega-Damage.

Attacks per Melee: Four.

Mega-Damage: Melee Combat: A nip does 2D6 S.D.C., a restrained bite 1D4 M.D., a full strength bite does 2D6 M.D., front leg kick or tail strike does 4D6 M.D., a kick from the rear legs 5D6 M.D., a stomp or head butt does 3D6 M.D. Cannot do a power bite, kick or tail swipe.

Stonecaster Shoulder Guns (2): One is built into each shoulder. They can only shoot forward but have a 45 degree up and down arc of fire. The weapons are usually fired by the rider via Telepathic command or a physical signal like three taps on the neck. However, if the rider is incapacitated, slain or dismounted, the War Steed can fire the guns itself.

Range: 4,000 feet (1,219 m), half underwater.

Mega-Damage: Sedimentary Rock: 3D6 M.D. to a 15 foot (4.6 m) area. Igneous Molten Rock: 4D6 M.D. on impact and 2D6 M.D. additional for the next two melee rounds. Metamorphic Stone (armor piercing): 6D6 M.D. **Note:** Double damage when the guns in each shoulder are fired simultaneously at the same target.

Rate of Fire: Each single or simultaneous dual shot counts as one melee attack of the rider, unless the War Steed is in control.

Payload: 60 blasts regardless of type. The weapon can be recharged/reloaded on a ley line, nexus or stone pyramid (regenerates one blast a minute), or any mage can pump 60 P.P.E. into the cannon for an instant reload. Otherwise, it regenerates projectiles at a rate of one per hour when no source of magic energy is available.

Ion Blasters: Mounted above each of the Stonecasters is a short-range ion blaster. They shoot forward but have a 45 degree up and down arc of fire. The weapons are controlled by the rider via Telepathic command or a physical signal like three taps on the neck. However, if the rider is incapacitated, slain or dismounted, the War Steed can fire the guns itself.

Range: 1,000 feet (305 m) in air and underwater.

Mega-Damage:

4D6 M.D. per single blast, 1D4x10 when the guns in each shoulder are fired simultaneously at the same target.

Rate of Fire: Each single or simultaneous dual shot counts as one melee attack for the rider, unless the War Steed is in control.

Payload: 30 blasts. The weapon can be recharged/reloaded on a ley line, nexus or stone pyramid (regenerates one blast a minute), or any mage can pump 30 P.P.E. into the blaster for an instant reload. Otherwise, it regenerates at a rate of one blast every three hours when no source of magic energy is available.

Bonuses (in addition to possible attribute bonuses): +2 on Perception Rolls, +3 on initiative, +4 to strike, +1 to parry, +3 to automatic dodge in water and on land, +2 to pull punch, +3 to roll with impact, and +6 to save vs Horror Factor.

Habitat: Found wherever Lemurians are found, especially among their cities, gardens and outposts. Home is in the ocean with Lemurians, but the Serpent Seahorse does very well on dry land and likes to explore and hunt on islands and coastal forests.

Enemies: Sharks and large marine predators, sea serpents, sea monsters, humanoids, and the enemies of Lemuria.

Allies: Namely Lemurians, the people who created this War Steed, and Ichthyleans, but they may also be used by humans and aquatic D-Bees. Gets along with other serpents and tolerates most others War Steeds. Wary of people and most other creatures except Lemurians and Ichthyleans (whom they like for some unknown reason). They see most large fish and mammals, including people, as potential threats and enemies.

Value: As a trained War Steed it is worth 500,000-650,000 credits. The Serpent Seahorse's hide cannot be made into body armor or clothing. Only its spines can be used as spikes, stabbing weapons, picks or spearheads (inflict 1D6 M.D. each). Its meat is inedible.

Shadow Serpent

Some people are of the opinion that these mysterious serpents are creatures from the dark abyss or from the same home dimension as Shadow Beasts. Others claim they are mutants or aliens who have adapted to the darkness of the abyss and magical energies of Rifts Earth. When exposed to light (which is almost never deep underwater), these jet black sea serpents are seen to be covered in large, black, blue-black, or charcoal gray scales, their eerie yellow eyes glowing much like a cat's. Their hands and feet are webbed and tipped with wicked, black claws, and their tail is covered with spikes like a stegosaurus.

Whether hunting the shallows in the dead of night or stalking in the open darkness of the abyss, these sea serpents feast on a wide assortment of fish and squid. However, sharks, whales, dolphins, humans and D-Bees are their favorite prey. They have a high animal intelligence and enjoy cat-and-mouse style games with their prey, and use hit and run tactics, surprise attacks and ambushes from the shadows. The serpents Shadow Melding powers enables them to completely merge with the darkness to the point where it prevents others locating Shadow Serpents via echolocation and sonar systems. Being exposed to any kind of light, even something as small as a flashlight, illuminates and reveals the Shadow Serpent. However, while cloaked in shadow or darkness, only thermal/infrared systems can detect the serpent, and even then the devices are -30% to accurately pinpoint and register the monster.

Though many people mistake Shadow Serpents for *dragons*, the creature is a "sea serpent" – a comparatively dull-witted and weaker cousin to dragons. As such, they are smart, possess the ability to cast a limited number of magic spells and are considered creatures of magic, but they live and behave more like wild animals or savage barbarians than people or dragons. Wild Shadow Serpents are often evil and prey upon other intelligent life forms as well as animals. Lemurians have learned, however, that with the right training and influence, especially when raised from a young age, Shadow Serpents can be become loyal and valiant War Steeds and partners in the defense of Lemuria. In that capacity, they behave like children or smart animals that can talk. Even tamed and well-intentioned Shadow Serpents remain creatures of passion who need their Lemurian rider/partner to provide their moral compass and rein them in. It is in the serpents' nature to be cunning, deceitful, treacherous, and brutal. In combat, they like to lay in wait, attack from behind, and lay traps.

Shadow Serpent

Available As: NPC Sea Serpent Villain or Lemurian War Steed.

Alignment: In the wild, most are Diabolic (20%), Miscreant (30%) or Anarchist (30%). Those influenced by good Lemurians and used as War Steeds are Scrupulous (20%), Unprincipled (35%) or Anarchist (40%).

Attributes: I.Q. 1D4+8 (human-like intelligence, but driven by animal instincts and behavior), M.E. 1D6+6, M.A. 1D6+6, P.S. 1D6+24, P.P. 1D6+11, P.E. 2D6+10, P.B. 2D6+10, Spd 1D6+18 (15 mph/24 km) on land, Spd in water 2D6+46 (50 mph/80 km or 43 knots). Can swim or run at full speed for 30 minutes per P.E. attribute point before needing to rest for at least five hours. Swimming or walking at a leisurely pace can be maintained for one hour per P.E. point.

Size: 20-30 feet (6.1 to 9.1 m) long from snout to rump, the tail is an additional 25 to 30 feet (7.6 to 9.1 m).

Weight: 8 to 12 tons.

M.D.C. by Location:

Head – 1D6x10+120

Legs, Front (2) – 1D6x10+60 each

Legs, Rear (2) – 2D4x10+80 each

Serpent Tail – 3D6x10+120

Tail Blade (1; tip) – 1D6x10+180

Main Body 4D6x10+100

Shadow M.D.C. (Special): While in darkness the Shadow Serpent receives a bonus of +120 M.D.C. Only daylight or being illuminated in bright light dispels the bonus M.D.C. A flashlight or a small Globe of Daylight is not sufficient; however, three or more Globe of Daylight spells or multiple headlights that completely cover the Shadow Serpent will work and eliminate its bonus M.D.C. (On an S.D.C. world, the Shadow Serpent has 1D6x10+40 Hit Points, 4D6x10 S.D.C. +100 in darkness, and a Natural A.R. of 16.)

Horror Factor: 12

Average Life Span: 1D6x100+800 years.

Average Level of Experience: 1D8 for Non-Player Characters or as desired by the G.M. War Steeds of player characters should be first or second level. Use the Dragon Experience Table.

Disposition: Sneaky, tricky, clever and cunning; driven by predatory instincts and a natural inclination to be deceitful and self-serving.

R.C.C. Equivalent Skills: Camouflage 55%, Detect Ambush 65%, Detect Concealment 60%, Escape Artist 60%, Land Navigation 80%, Lore: Demons and Monsters 50%, Lore: Sea Creatures 70%, Prowl 50% (+25% when Shadow Melding), Tailing 60% (+20% in darkness or from shadows), Track Animals 65%, Track and Hunt Sea Creatures 80%, Underwater Navigation 90%; all skills improve at a rate of +1% per level of experience.

Natural Abilities: Supernatural P.S. and P.E., natural swimmer 90%, resistant to cold (half damage), Nightvision 4,000 feet (1219 m; can see in complete and unnatural darkness), poor day/light vision 400 feet (122 m; double in low light), keen sense of hearing, good sense of smell, can breathe both air and water, and Bio-Regenerates 2D6 M.D.C. per melee round, 4D6 M.D.C. in total darkness. Shadow Serpents magically understands and speaks all languages

Blade Tail (special): The last 4-6 feet (1.2 to 1.8 m) of the serpent's prehensile tail is a bone blade made for stabbing and cutting. On the top side of the blade portion are stegosaurus-like spikes that can be used to hit with blunt force or impale with the spikes. The Tail Blade does 4D6+2 M.D. per attack. Blunt tail strike or blunt side of the blade or spikes does 3D6 M.D. Spike strike/impaling Attack: 4D6 M.D.

Depth Tolerance: 7 miles (11.2 km).

Shadow Meld: As per the spell, the Shadow Serpent can completely meld with shadows or darkness. In the depths of the sea this makes them nearly invisible. The Shadow Serpent's ability is even more powerful than the common spell, allowing them to partially shift into the shadow dimension. This makes them difficult to detect with echolocation (passes right through or reflects a very weak response) and sonar. Only bright light can dispel this completely, partial light (like from a flashlight) will weaken the shift to the shadow dimension enough that they are still hard to see, but can be detected by sonar and echolocation systems. Anyone trying to use echolocation or sonar to detect does so at half the usual skill level and any bonuses are halved (such as the Lemurian's crude echolocation sense, which normally reduces penalties for being blind or fighting an unseen target to -1 to strike, parry and dodge, now becomes a -4 to strike parry and dodge against Shadow Serpents).

Size Metamorphosis (special): Unlike dragons, Shadow Serpents cannot shape change to look like other beings, but can reduce their natural size by as much as 60%.

Also see Magic.

Attacks per Melee: Four.

Mega-Damage: Restrained Bite: 1D4x10 S.D.C. Bite attack: 3D6 M.D., Claw Strike: 4D6+3 M.D. Also see Blade Tail, above.

Bonuses (all): +3 on Perception Rolls in darkness only, +1 on initiative, +6 to strike, +4 to parry, +5 to automatic dodge in darkness or shadow, +5 to pull punch, +2 to roll with impact, +1 to save vs psionics and illusions, +3 to save vs magic and poison, +5 to save vs Horror Factor.

Vulnerabilities/Penalties: Light: The Shadow Serpent really does not like the light; bright light dispels their shadow powers and weakens them (less M.D.C.). Bright lights blind the Shadow Dragon (e.g. the Blinding Flash spell, camera flashes, bright sunlight, etc.) with double the duration for penalties. They can operate out in daylight, but squint and shade their sensitive eyes; loses one attack and is -2 to strike, parry and dodge as they block out the sun with one of their hands or tail.

Magic: Starts with Cleanse (6), Cloak of Darkness (6), Fear (5), and Shadow Meld (10). Instinctively knows one new spell selected from levels 1-3 of Spell Invocations for each new level of experience. **P.P.E.:** 1D6x10 + P.E. attribute number, plus 2D6 per level of experience.

Psionics: None.

Habitat: They prefer the darkness of night or depths of the abyss. However, in their search for prey they often rise to the surface at night and hunt fish, animals, and humanoids in and out of the water; cattle are easy prey as are unsuspecting villagers or sailors. Sometimes they attack coastal communities or ships.

Allies: None, per se in the wild where they tend to hunt as lone predators or gather in small groups of 1D4+1. Some may ally themselves to evil practitioners of magic and dark forces. Those used by Lemurians as War Steeds are friends and allies of Lemurians, Ichthyleans, Merans, and friends of Lemura. As a rule, Shadow Serpent War Steeds do not hunt humanoids or sentient beings, and stick to fish and animals. Shadow Serpent War Steeds have proven they can be made to care about their riders and other people and show strong loyalty for their human "partner."

Enemies: Generally view most people and animals as prey. Wild serpents hate creatures of light and those who radiate with light or possess light abilities. (Lemurian War Steeds dislike and distrust them). The creature views other sea serpents, monster and dragons as rivals and potential enemies. Rumor has it that a band of pirates also raise Shadow Serpents as riding animals, pets and assassins; of course these serpents are Anarchist or evil.

Value: 300,000-400,000 credits for one tamed as a War Steed, half that as an attack animal/guardian. The hide of cannot be made into body armor or clothing, but the teeth can be made into arrowheads, knifes and warclubs, and the tail blade can be turned into a giant-size sword, propeller blade, rudder or the blade of a ram prow. Its meat is disgusting and unedible.

Thrall Sea Serpent

One might think of the Thrall Sea Serpent as an aquatic Tyrannosaurus Rex. The creature has a large head and massive, tooth-filled maw that can bite a Great White Shark in half. Its forearms are short, as are its hind legs, but both end in large claws. The body is long, round and snake-like, and ends with a long, tapered tail that can be used like a whip. The Thrall Sea Serpent was the very first Biomancer Gene-Mage creation, and it remains a favorite of Oceanic Guardsmen, Serpent Hunters and Lemurian Scouts. The monster is especially adept in the ocean, where it has excellent speed and agility. On land, its short legs and long, serpentine body makes it a comparatively large, slow target. Or so it would seem. One of the unique capabilities of the Thrall Sea Serpent is it can rear up on its hind legs, reminiscent of a cobra. In this combat position, it can bob and weave out of the way of incoming attacks, as well as parry and attack with its claws, and make lightning fast (counts as one melee attack) and devastating bites. Thralls can also jab and butt with their nose and perform sideways head slaps/butts without harm to their thick-boned skulls. The roar of a Thrall Sea Serpent rearing up like a 30 foot (9.1 m) tall King Cobra is enough to give the most experienced of warriors second thoughts about pressing an attack. Lemurian Serpent Hunters love this snake attack capability because it allows them to leap off the back of the monster to engage the enemy while their mighty War Steed fights at their side or behind them, taking out other enemies, flying enemies, and those coming from the side, and is very much a fighting companion, that also happens to be a War Steed.

Perhaps the most surprising trait about the Thrall Sea Serpent is they are like giant, loving puppy dogs. Thralls are among the most affectionate and loyal to their rider of all the Lemurian War Steeds. In combat, they are fury unleashed and will stand at their rider's side till death if necessary. If their warrior falls, the Thrall goes into a killing fury to destroy, and often devour, the enemy responsible. Once the perpetrator has been destroyed/eaten, the Thrall will usually pick up its fallen Lemurian companion in its mouth and try to carry him to a Lemurian base for medical attention or a proper burial. If their combat partner dies, there is a 01-40% chance the serpent stops eating and starves itself to death in grief. Truth be told, the owners of Thralls usually feel the same about their War Steeds, and the loss of one is equal to losing a best friend. When not in combat, Thrall Sea Serpents love to play, chase, fetch, wrestle, perform aquatic acrobatics, have its belly rubbed (they also love having their neck under their jaw rubbed), and sun themselves between romps.

A hatchling Thrall Sea Serpent is often assigned to a young Lemurian Serpent Hunter (sometimes an Oceanic Guardsman, Biomancer Gene-Mage, or member of the Royal Family) who trains, teaches and cares for his new ally for the rest of his days. Retired Lemurian Serpent Hunters always keep their Thralls as a pet and companions, and many go on to collect and raise Thralls and other sea serpents on small underwater ranches, giving them up at a young age to Lemurian warriors and members of the royal family.

Thrall Sea Serpents have crimson, orange or reddish brown bodies with dark patches on the nose, head and paws, a light, creamy tan or greenish white underbelly, white teeth and black

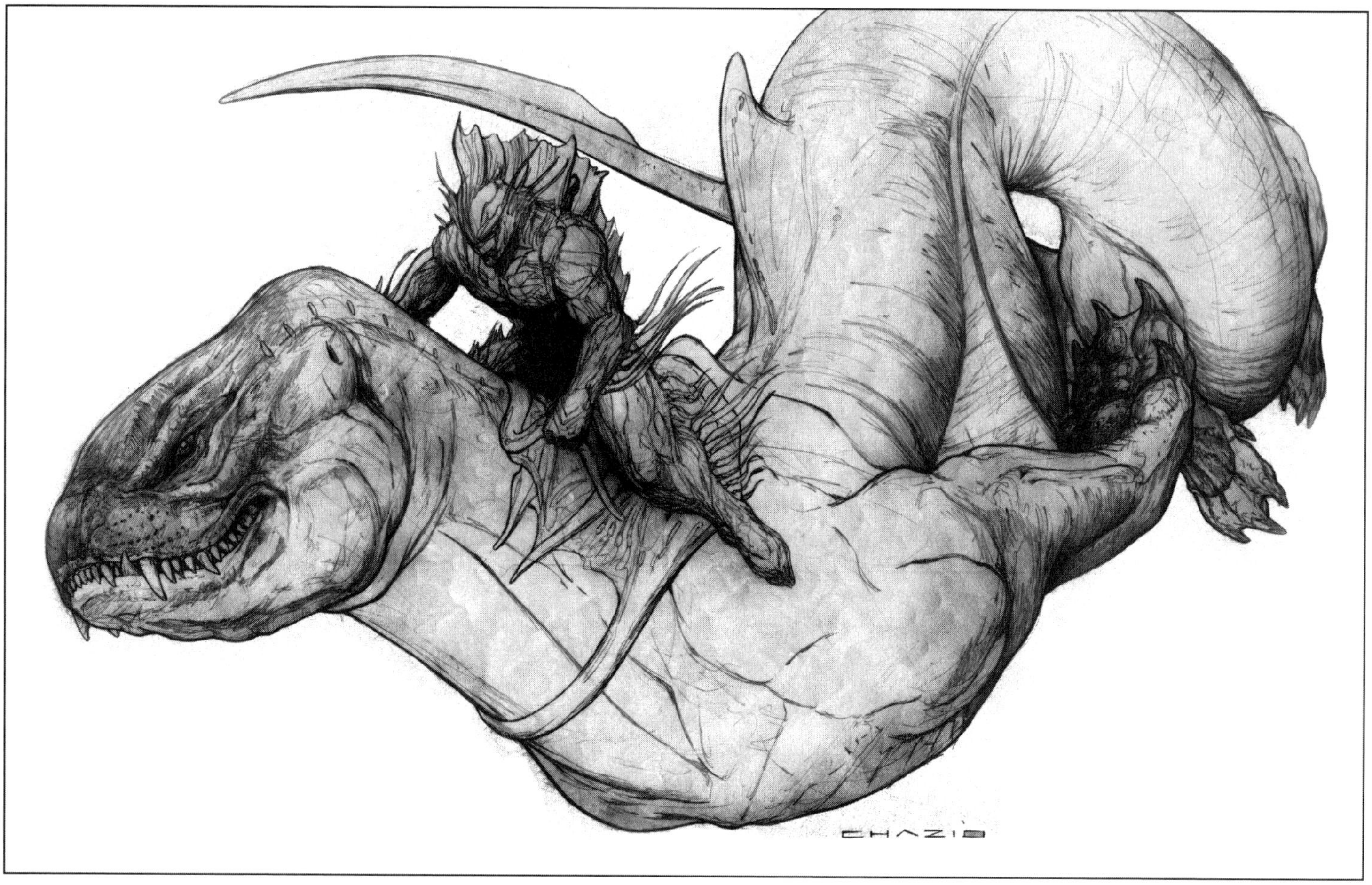

claws. The texture of their skin is like a thick, rough, wrinkled leather, but their underside is smooth.

Thrall Sea Serpent

Also Known As: The Hunter Serpent and Royal Serpent.

Alignment: Principled (45%), Scrupulous (35%), or Unprincipled (15%). Few have a darker nature.

Attributes: I.Q. 1D4+7 (high animal intelligence, though not as intelligent as sentient cetaceans), M.E. 1D6+15, M.A. 1D6+17, P.S. 1D4+30 (Supernatural), P.P. 1D6+15, P.E. 1D6+15, P.B. 1D6+8, Spd 2D4+48 running (36 mph/57.6 km or 31 knots), double swimming Spd in water (72 mph/115 km or 62 knots); increase running and swimming speed 50% along a ley line. Can swim or run at full speed for one hour per P.E. attribute point before feeling fatigued and requires a minimum of three hours rest. Can swim or run at a leisurely pace indefinitely.

Size: 35-40 feet (10.6 to 12.2 m) long from snout to rump. The tail is an additional 22-28 feet (6.7 to 8.5 m) long. Stands 12-15 feet (3.6 to 4.6 m) from toes to the top of the head, but can stand on its hind legs in a cobra-like stance, towering 30+ feet (9.1 m). The body is roughly 5-6 feet (1.5 to 1.8 m) in diameter, and 10-12 feet (3 to 3.6 m) in width at the shoulders and hips; the rider sits above the front legs and up on the neck. The head is 4-5 feet (1.2 to 1.5 m) long and 4 feet (1.2 m) wide.

Weight: 5-8 tons; males tend to be 15% larger than females.

M.D.C. by Location:

Head – 2D6x10+220
Fins (2, top) – 5D6+20 each
Legs, Front (2) – 1D6x10+90 each
Legs, Rear (2) – 1D6x10+100 each
Tail – 3D6x10+150
Main Body – 3D6x10+120

Horror/Awe Factor: 15

P.P.E.: 6D6+15

Disposition: A terror on the battlefield, the Thrall Sea Serpent likes to roar and bellow to frighten opponents, but becomes silent, other than growls and hisses when locked in actual combat. The serpent enjoys combat, is ferocious and fearless, and never leaves its rider's side. Away from battle, the monster is a playful puppy, at least with its humanoid partner, but can go from fun-loving to fighting mode in a split second. Gentle and attentive toward its rider, and highly protective of him.

Average Life Span: 1D6x10+75 years.

R.C.C. Equivalent Skills: Land Navigation 75%, Tailing 75% (underwater only), Prowl 45% (underwater only), Track and Hunt Sea Creatures 80%, Underwater Navigation 90%, and learns/understands spoken languages quickly (75%); understands Lemurian and Oceanic at 90%.

Natural Abilities: Supernatural P.S. and P.E., swim 98%, can breathe water and air indefinitely, Nightvision 1,000 feet (305 m), excellent day and underwater vision, resistance to cold (half damage). Bio-Regenerates at a rate of 3D6 per hour (typically about 200 points per 24 hours).

Chemoreceptors (special): A highly advanced sense of taste/smell that lets the Thrall Sea Serpent track its prey underwater, detect salinity and toxicity of the water and taste blood in the water like a shark. Can identify chemicals, toxins or specific creatures by taste and smell. Identify chemicals and scents by taste: 50%. Track by taste/scent: 70% (+10% to track its rider or blood scent). Range: One mile (1.6 km).

Crude Echolocation System (special): The Thrall Sea Serpent can also hear and discern the reflection or echoes of sounds they make to sense large objects around them. While nowhere near as precise as a whale, dolphin or bat's echolocation sense, it helps them navigate underwater and in the dark, and detect unseen objects and creatures; reduces penalties for being blind or fighting invisible foes by half.

Depth Tolerance: 8 miles (12.8 km).

Ultrasonic Communication (special): Besides being able to hear into the ultrasonic sound range, Thrall Sea Serpents can also create high frequency noises just like the cybernetic Inaudible Frequency Transmission implant. They use this ability to communicate underwater, with whales/dolphins, Lemurians and other Thrall Sea Serpents.

Attacks per Melee: Four while running, swimming, or standing and fighting on all fours, but six when the Thrall Sea Serpent takes its "cobra" stance on land.

Mega-Damage: A nip does 5D6 S.D.C., a restrained bite 3D6 M.D., a full strength bite does 5D6+4 M.D., Power Bite does 1D6x10+5 M.D. (but counts as two melee attacks), a claw strike does 5D6 M.D., head butt 3D6 M.D. Tail Strikes: Restrained tail "tap" does 1D4x10 S.D.C., restrained tail strike does 2D6 M.D., full strength hit does 4D6 M.D. Cannot do a power tail or claw strike.

Bonuses (in addition to possible attribute bonuses): +2 on Perception Rolls, +3 on initiative, +3 to strike with most combat attacks (+5 to strike with tail), +3 to parry (+4 to parry with tail), +2 to automatic dodge in water and land, +5 to pull punch, +2 to roll with impact, +6 to save vs Horror Factor, +2 to save vs illusions and mind control, and +5 to save vs poison and disease.

Vulnerabilities: Sometimes too fearless and loyal, which may causes it to take on overwhelming odds, take foolish chances and fight to the death at the side of its rider.

Habitat: Thrall Sea Serpents coexist with Lemurians and fight alongside them. They are wherever Lemurians are found, especially among their cities, gardens and outposts. Home is in the ocean, and they can be found in any of Earth's oceans and occasionally, on land along coastal regions and deep lakes. A number have gone wild and inhabit remote parts of the Pacific Rim and Indian Ocean.

Allies: Lemurians and their allies. Wild ones can be found alone, in pairs, in small family groups of 3-8, and with pods of cetaceans and other sea serpents. They love being around other animals and people.

Enemies: The Milu, Lord of the Deep, large marine predators, sea serpents, sea monsters, humanoids, and the enemies of Lemuria.

Value: Lemurians treasure them and the Lemurian Serpent Hunters value them as a brother and comrade in arms. As a trained War Steed it commands 350,000-600,000 credits. The hide cannot be made into body armor or clothing, only the teeth can be used to make daggers, spikes, spearheads and jewelry. Its meat is tough and not very tasty and there is no market for it. Besides, the Lemurians typically collect their dead, including slain War Steeds, and especially their beloved Thralls.

Tiger Serpent

These magnificent sea serpents are presumed to be creatures from another dimension, though there are some ancient Indian and Chinese myths that suggest they could originate on Earth. Tiger Serpents have a long snake-like body covered with large, orange or golden scales and black tiger-stripe markings on their face, fins and body. The face is very much feline, the eyes a dark green, and its webbed front feet end in tiger-like retractable claws. Tiger Serpents are solitary hunters who prefer to travel and stalk prey alone or in pairs, and seem to prefer ocean reefs, seaweed forests and comparatively shallow, sunlit waters, though it is believed they retreat to lairs in the ocean depths. Tiger Serpents are masters of stealth and like hunting in jungles and forests on land as much as in the ocean. A favorite tactic is to lurk amongst seaweed beds or tall grass, waiting for the right moment to strike, darting out with lightning speed to snag its prey. Like crocodiles, the serpent also likes laying in wait underwater, but near the surface. When prey or an enemy target comes within range along the water's edge, the serpent lunges up, grabs hold with its claws and pulls its unsuspecting victim into the water where it, presumably, has the advantage. The animal loves to lay in wait, tail opponents, set ambushes and attack with the element of surprise.

As a Lemurian War Steed, Tiger Serpents are surprisingly loyal and obedient to the warrior they bond with. The rider can sit anywhere along the length of its body, but the usual place is just behind the shoulders. A Tiger Serpent can rear up on its snake-like body, but only for a few melee rounds and remains low to the ground where it can claw, bite and pin its victims. Tiger Serpents also like to coil around prey to hold it underwater until it drowns or to hold it in place while it attacks with tooth and claw. **Note:** Tiger Serpents cannot perform a cobra stance.

Tiger Serpent

Also Known As: Tiger Python and Striped Death.

Alignment: Any, but in the wild, they are considered Anarchist or evil, animalistic predators. Lemurian trained Tiger Serpents are usually Scrupulous (15%), Unprincipled (20%) or Anarchist (40%).

Attributes: I.Q. 1D4+6 (high animal intelligence, though not as intelligent as sentient cetaceans), M.E. 1D6+16, M.A. 1D6+11, P.S. 1D4+25 (Supernatural), P.P. 1D6+16, P.E. 1D6+14, P.B. 1D6+16, Spd 2D4+25 running/slithering like a snake (20 mph/32 km), double swimming Spd in water (40 mph/64 km or 34 knots); increase running and swimming speed 50% along a ley line. Can swim or run at full speed for one hour per P.E. attribute point before feeling fatigued and must reduce speed by half, but can continue for another 2D4 hours before it is necessary to rest for five hours. Can swim or run at a leisurely pace indefinitely.

Size: 40-60 feet (12.2 to 18.3 m) long from snout to the tip of the tail. The creature's body is 2-3 feet (0.6 to 0.9 m) in diameter, but tapers to a point along the tail. 5-6 feet (1.5 to 1.8 m) wide at the shoulders and stands 6-8 feet (1.8 to 2.4 m) tall supported by its front legs, its serpentine body trailing off behind it. Rears up to be 10-14 feet (3 to 4.3 m) tall.

Weight: 3-6 tons; females are 20% larger than males.

M.D.C. by Location:

Head – 2D4x10+120

CHAZIO

Fins (many) – 4D6 each

Legs, Front (2) – 1D6x10+80 each

Legs, Rear (none, see Main Body and Tail)

Main Body & Tail – 3D6x10+220

(On S.D.C. worlds, the Tiger Serpent has 2D6x10 Hit Points, 2D6x10 S.D.C. and a Natural A.R. of 15.)

Horror Factor: 14

P.P.E.: 2D4x10 + P.E. attribute number.

Disposition: Behaves very much like a cat, showing affection when it wants to and indifference or disdain when it desires to be left alone. Sneaky, observant and quick to respond. Loves to chase, hunt and play cat and mouse games.

Average Life Span: 2D4x10+100 years.

Equivalent Skill Abilities: Climbing 85%/60% (performed at half the serpent's running Spd), Prowl 60% (+15 underwater), Land Navigation 80%, Tailing 90% (underwater and on land), Tracking (people; 65% on land only), Track and Hunt Sea Creatures 85%, Underwater Navigation 90%, and learns/understands spoken languages quickly (75%); magically understands all languages at 70%, but cannot speak.

Natural Abilities: Supernatural P.S. and P.E., Nightvision 1,000 feet (305 m), excellent daylight vision and sense of hearing, natural swimmer 95%, can breathe both air and water indefinitely, resistant to cold (half damage), and depth tolerance of 6 miles (9.6 km). Bio-Regenerates at a rate of 3D6 per hour (typically about 200 points per 24 hours).

Camouflage: Tiger stripes/plant patterned scales provide +5% to Prowl or hide among fallen trees or seaweed in shallow to medium depth water.

Lightning Quick Strike or Dart Attack: The Tiger Serpent can lunge up to 15 feet (4.6 m) from a hiding place or from where it seems to be standing to attack with bites and claw strikes or to grab its prey and pull it into the water, much like a crocodile. +2 to strike and the attack is considered a surprise or sneak attack.

Venomous Bite: The Tiger Sea Serpent has infectious bacteria living in its mouth (similar to Komodo dragons). The bacteria helps the Tiger Serpent break down its food and prepare it for digestion, and does not harm or further infect the Tiger Serpent. However, those unlucky enough to be bitten and survive an attack must roll to save vs poison (14 or higher), or quickly develop debilitating symptoms as the bacteria engulfs and disables the them. A failed roll means within 12 hours the victim begins to suffers with cramps and soreness of joints, reducing running and swimming speed by 20%, -1 attack per melee round and -2 to strike, parry and all other combat moves. Furthermore, all physical skills are performed with a -20% penalty. The effects last for 2D6 hours as the body fights off the infection, at which point the victim must roll to save again, but with a +2 bonus to save. Another failed roll means the bacteria continues to ravage the body doing 1D4 damage direct to Hit Points (2D4 if an M.D.C. creature) and the cramps, soreness and penalties continue for 3D6 hours. This continues until the victim finally makes a save vs disease or the poison is negated via magic, psionics or medication/antibiotics (the latter takes effect and stops penalties within 1D4 hours; magical and psionic cures have an instant effect).

Attacks per Melee: Four.

Mega-Damage: A nip does 3D6 S.D.C., a restrained bite 2D6 M.D., a full strength bite does 4D6 M.D., a claw strike does 4D6+4 M.D., a power claw strike does 1D4x10+4, and a tail strike does 3D6 M.D. Cannot do a power bite or tail strike.

Bonuses (in addition to possible attribute bonuses): +3 to Perception Rolls, +5 on initiative, +3 to strike, +4 to parry, +2 to dodge, +4 to roll with impact, +2 to disarm, +3 to pull punch, +8 vs Horror Factor, +1 vs psionics and mind control and +6 to save vs disease.

Magic: None.

Psionics: None.

Vulnerabilities: Sometimes too fearless and loyal, which may cause it to take on overwhelming odds, take foolish chances and fight to the death at the side of its rider.

Habitat: Tiger Serpents are found in the wild and living with Lemurians as War Steeds and hunting animals. They are wherever Lemurians are found, especially among their cities, gardens and outposts. Home is in the ocean, and they can be found in any of Earth's oceans and seas as well as on land along coastal regions, swamps, jungle and rain forests.

Allies: Lemurians and their allies. Wild ones are solitary creatures that can be found alone or in mated pairs.

Enemies: The Milu, Lord of the Deep, large marine predators, sea serpents, sea monsters, humanoids, and the enemies of Lemuria.

Value: Lemurian War Steeds command 250,000-400,000 credits. Their tough hide can be used to make a decent suit of medium armor. Many pirates and aquatic bandits like the armor for its durability and comparative light weight. A suit of medium Tiger Serpent Armor has 3D6+55 M.D.C. and a mobility penalty of -7% to Prowl, climb and other physical activities; sells for 50,000-65,000 credits.

Sea Dragons

Most dragons enjoy the water, and are unafraid to explore and live in its depths. However, *Sea Dragons* feel most at home in water and spend the majority of their time in the oceans and seas of Rifts Earth.

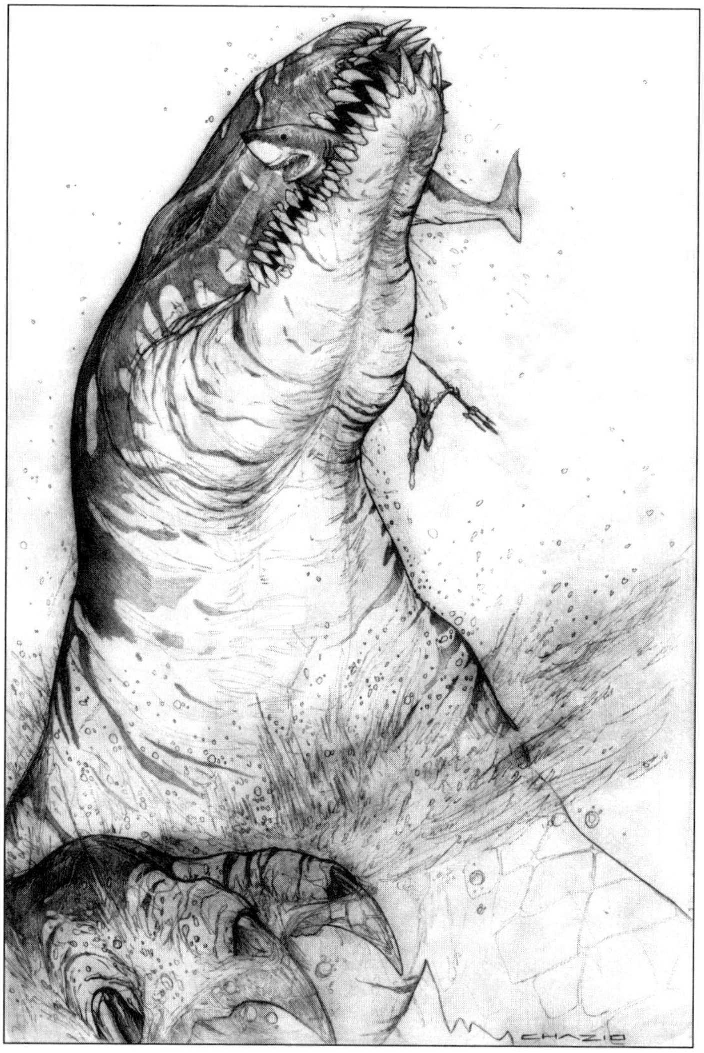

The Leviathan

"If you lay a hand on him, you will remember the struggle and never forget it again! Any hope of subduing him is false; the mere sight of him is overpowering. No one is fierce enough to rouse him. Who then is able to stand against me? Who has a claim against me that I must pay? Everything under the heavens belongs to me. "I will not fail to speak of his limbs, his strength and his graceful form. Who can strip off his outer coat? Who would approach him with a bridle? Who dares open the doors of his mouth, ringed about with his fearsome teeth? . . .

"When he rises up, the mighty are terrified; they retreat before his thrashing. The sword that reaches him has no effect nor does the spear or the dart or the javelin. Iron he treats like straw and bronze like rotten wood. Arrows do not make him flee; sling stones are like chaff to him. A club seems to him but a piece of straw; he laughs at the rattling of the lance. His undersides are jagged potshards, leaving a trail in the mud like a threshing sledge. He makes the depths churn like a boiling caldron and stirs up the sea like a pot of ointment. Behind him he leaves a glistening wake; one would think the deep had white hair. Nothing on earth is his equal – a creature without fear. He looks down on all that are haughty; he is king over all that are proud."

– Chapter 41, the Book of Job, The Bible

Leviathans are a feared and ancient race of sea monster that appear to be some sort of primordial dragon. It is believed that they are native to Earth and predate the appearance of humans. Some have theorized that they are highly evolved aquatic dinosaurs or a reptilian equivalent to whales or dolphins. Their very presence strikes terror in the hearts of the brave and courageous and their brutality and strength are legendary. The Lemurians, instead of trying to conquer or destroy them, as many have tried and failed, have appealed to the monsters sense of self-importance and have managed to forge a tentative alliance. This is perhaps possible because Lemurians show the Leviathans respect and have exhibited considerable courage by daring to even approach them. Moreover, the Lemurian Serpent Hunters show bravery and trust by willingly stepping into the maw of the beast and letting it close in order to receive their fabled Leviathan Bio-Armor. As a result, most Leviathans do not hunt Lemurians and these Kings of the Deep assist them by attacking and destroying Milu, Milu undead, Naut'Yll, demons and other evil supernatural forces. Moreover, both Lemurian and monster are able to call upon the other for assistance in these matters, but for the most part, it has only been the Lemurians who have done so – playing up and coddling to the Leviathans' needs to feel superior and "in charge."

New talks have been opened up between the Leviathans and the Lemurian Serpent Hunters, who seem to have a natural understanding and connection to the cranky monsters. The discussion is to have the monster take a more proactive stance about "unnatural" threats represented by the Lord of the Deep, Davey Jones, the Milu and other evil supernatural forces. The Leviathans' response has been mixed. There is no Leviathan society or one leader, so each of the great beasts must be approached on an individual basis. A few have agreed, while others don't see why any of this is "their" problem. Who cares what "little things" such as Milu and humans do to each other? As long as there are plenty of sea creatures to prey upon, and the "dark forces" and "undead" stay away from Leviathans, there is no issue between them. Other Leviathans complain that Milu and the Lord of the Deep's minions taste bad and undead cannot be digested. That being said, there are a couple dozen of the estimated one hundred or so Leviathans in existence who have agreed, and an equal number who will consider "helping" on a situation by situation basis.

Meanwhile, most Leviathan do as they please, feeding on sea serpents, sea monsters (including many of the creatures Lemurian use as War Steeds), whales, dolphins, large fish, and surface dwellers. Anarchist and evil Leviathans may also chase, threaten, attack and prey upon people for amusement or food, including Naut'Yll, Ichthyleans, Merans, Junk Crabs, Amphibs, Tritonians, humans and other people at sea. Some even dare attack Lemurians when the mood strikes them. People who anger or annoy the monsters are devoured without hesitation. Sometimes a Leviathan will attack a ship or small fleet of ocean vessels, sinking ships and devouring the crew just for fun or to illustrate their power. The only beings to ever be allowed to ride on the shoulder of a Leviathan is the *Lemurian Serpent Hunter*, but only if the Hunter asks permission first and the creature *allows* it. Likewise, people marvel that any Leviathan would allow Biomancer Gene-Mages to create Leviathan Bio-Armor from them, with the compliance of the Leviathans. However, make no mistake, Lemurians hold no thrall nor dominance over the great beasts and are sometimes preyed upon by the monsters themselves.

Leviathans do not learn nor wield magic and are not as intelligent as true dragons, but they remain a force to be reckoned with. A reality they are happy to demonstrate to any dragon who cares to try to take a stand against them. Most dragon hatchlings would be wise to avoid Leviathans and should never reveal that they are young dragons. The Leviathans' fragile ego and need to prove themselves superior, compels them to hunt and devour young dragons that come into their ocean environment.

Leviathan Non-Player Character Monster

Alignment: Any, but most are Unprincipled (3%), Anarchist (30%), Aberrant (30%), Miscreant (20%) or Diabolic (15%).

Attributes: I.Q. 1D4+6 (average human level intelligence, but cunning, devious and perceptive, M.E. 1D6+16, M.A. 1D6+13, P.S. 3D6+40, P.P. 1D6+13, P.E. 2D6+13, P.B. 1D6+4, Spd 2D6+38 swimming (on average 32 mph/51 km or 27.8 knots), 1D6+9 crawling on dry land (around 8 mph/13 km).

Size: 100-130 feet (30.5 to 39.6 m) long from snout to rump, plus another 60-90 feet (18.3 to 27.4 m) for the tail! The forward flippers/arms (which end in a pair of claws) are 50-60 feet (15.2 to 18.3 m) long, each, for a combined wingspan of 150 feet (45.7 m) fully extended. The smaller, middle flippers toward the rear are about half the size of the front pair, and the rear pair are half again (about 12 feet/3.6 m); the four rear flippers do not have claws. Width of the Leviathan with flippers flush to the side of its body is 50-60 feet (15.2 to 18.3 m), and the head is 28-33 feet (8.5 to 10 m) wide and 10-15 feet (3 to 4.6 m) tall from the bottom to top above the eyes.

Weight: 60 to 90 tons.

M.D.C. by Location*:

Head – 4D6x100 +50 per century of life

Front Flippers (2) – 2D4x100 each

Rear Mid-Flippers (2, smaller) – 1D4x100 each

Rear Flippers (2, smallest) – 2D6x10 each

Tail (1; long) – 3D6x100 +30 per century of life

Main Body – 1D6x1,000 +100 per century of life.

(* All numbers are reduced by half, and rounded down, for Leviathan young.)

Horror Factor: 18

P.P.E.: 1D4x100

Disposition: Arrogant and aggressive. They see themselves as the kings and queens of the oceans, and bow down to no one.

Average Life Span: 2D6x100+800 years. Leviathans are very long-lived creatures that reach full size and maturity at 100 years of age. When there is not enough food (or magic energy) available, the creature can spend decades hibernating. Females can give birth to one live young once every 100 years for the first 1,000 years.

Average Level of Experience: One level per every hundred years of life; 2D4 on average for NPC monsters, or as desired by the G.M. Use the Dragon Experience Table.

R.C.C. Skills Note (Non-Player Character Monster): Astronomy and Navigation 90%, Languages: Cetacean, Dragonese, Lemurian, Milu and Oceanic, all at 87%, and two Earth languages of choice at 70%, Lore: Demons and Monsters 60%, Lore: Sea Creatures 80%, Prowl 50% (+10% in dark waters, not applicable on land), Tailing 70%, Track and Hunt Sea Animals 87%, and Underwater Navigation 90%. Skills improve at a rate of +2% per level of experience.

Natural Abilities: Supernatural P.S. and P.E., natural swimmer 92%, Nightvision 2,000 feet (610 m), keen sense of hearing, can breathe both air and water, impervious to fire and heat, electricity and cold do half damage, magically understands and speaks all languages at 85%, and Bio-Regeneration 4D6 M.D.C. per melee round.

Breathes Fire (special): Much like a dragon, the Leviathan breathes fire. The fiery blast is so hot that it can boil through water to scald and burn creatures even underseas. Rate of Fire: Twice per melee round. Range: 60 feet (18.3 m) as a cone (90° spread) or 150 feet (45.7 m) as a stream (hits a single target); half range underwater. Damage: 5D6 M.D. to all inside the fiery cone, 1D4x10 M.D. as a fire stream at a single target. **Note:** The Leviathan can also shoot out a stream of superheated steam same as above, but it does 4D6 S.D.C. and 1D4x10 S.D.C., respectively. Steam is used to express annoyance and frustration, and as a warning to leave it alone.

Chemoreceptors (special): A highly advanced sense of taste/smell that enables the Leviathan to track its prey. They can also determine the salt content or toxicity of the water, especially useful in locating volcanic vents where they like to sleep, as well as to taste blood in the water like a shark. Base Skill: 70% +2% per level of experience to track. 50% +5% per

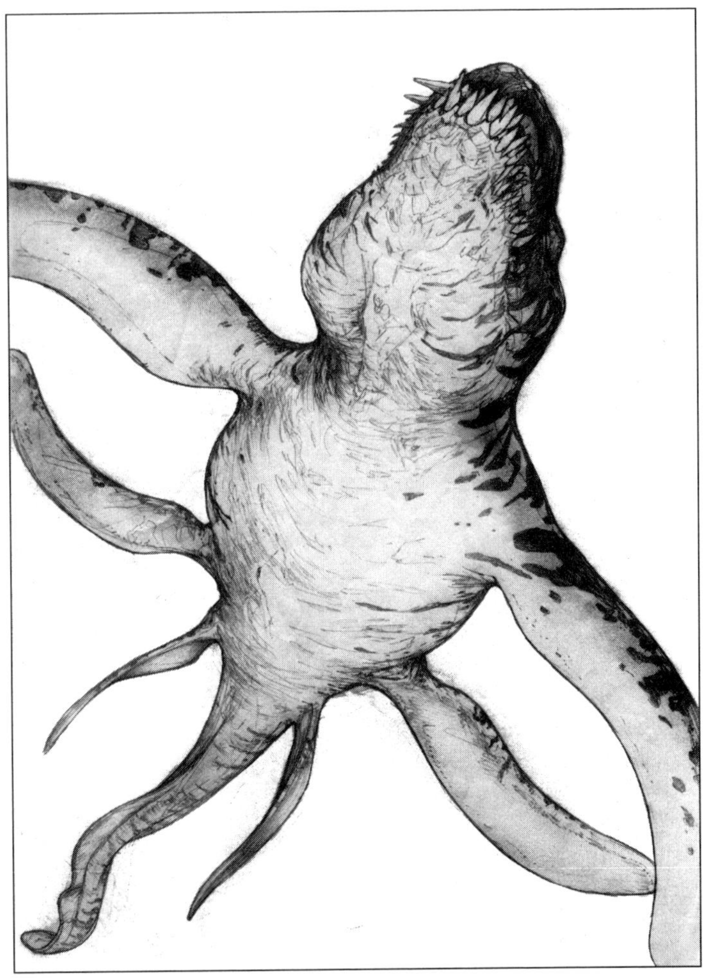

level of experience to identify chemicals, toxins or specific creatures by "sampling" scent trails.

Sense and See Electromagnetic Energy (Special): Leviathans are highly sensitive to electromagnetic energy and can sense and see it. When available, they can see in all spectrums of light (including the visible range, ultraviolet and infrared) and sense the heat given off by most creatures, underwater volcanoes and the slight variation of water temperature called thermoclines (most fish and aquatic life don't give off heat and blend in with their surroundings, but this is useful for hunting aquatic mammals, including humans). They can see the electromagnetic energy of the planet that directs compasses and is what helps them navigate underwater. Leviathans can also see electro-chemical energy emitted by living creatures through their nervous systems and as they contract their muscles (much like the shark's electromagnetic sensitivity). This ability lets them see most invisible creatures and hunt in pitch-black conditions at the bottom of the ocean. Range: 2,000 feet (610 m).

Sense and See Magic Energy (special): Leviathans can see and sense magic energy (P.P.E.) just like a Ley Line Walker. This ability lets them sense and hunt the energy-rich supernatural beings and creatures of magic that now inhabit the oceans.

Attacks per Melee: Five physical attacks per melee, or 2 physical and three fire breath attacks (or any combination thereof).

Bonuses (all): +3 on Perception Rolls, +3 on initiative, +6 to strike, +4 to parry and dodge underwater (half on dry land), +5 to pull punch and bite, +5 to roll with impact, +8 to save vs possession and mind control, +5 to save vs magic, +10 to save vs poison, and is impervious to Horror Factor.

Mega-Damage: As per Supernatural P.S. (on average 42-50). Biting nip or restrained bite does 1D6x10 S.D.C. or 1D6 M.D. depending on the monster's intent. Full strength bite attack does 1D6x10 M.D., a power bite 2D6x10 M.D. (but counts as two attacks), claw swipe 6D6+10 M.D., blunt flipper or tail slash 6D6 M.D., full speed ram attack 3D6x10 M.D., but counts as two attacks.

Vulnerabilities: The monster's arrogance, fearlessness, aggressiveness and size sometimes works against it.

Magic: None, though they find it interesting and respect its power.

Psionics: Meditation (0), Mind Block (4), Sense Magic (3), Sense Time (2), and Telepathy (4). I.S.P.: M.E. attribute x2 +2D6 per level of experience/100 years of age. Considered a Minor Psychic.

Habitat: The ocean depths where they enjoy their solitude, but they do swim to higher levels, the surface and even venture onto dry land to hunt and feed – prey upon fish, animals, humans and D-Bees alike. Many make their lairs at or near underwater volcanoes, and enjoy the ambient heat.

Allies: The Leviathans are feared by almost every creature in the sea, especially people and cetaceans; the Lord of the Deep and Splugorth being two exceptions. Even Davey Jones and the Milu tread carefully around these powerful beasts. The Lemurians are the only ones who routinely communicate with them and have established a tentative, if shaky and uncertain, friendly relationship with them.

Enemies: Leviathans see most smaller and weaker creatures as their inferiors and prey, including sea monsters, sea serpents, Lemurian War Steeds and all people. The Lemurians are an exception, though it's not entirely clear why this is. It may have to do with the fact that Lemurians have gone above and beyond to reach out to the mighty behemoth, ask for their help, and have never hunted them. Still, there are Leviathans who have no tolerance for Lemurians, and are happy to devour them and their War Steeds.

Leviathans have an ongoing feud with the Minions of Splugorth who sometimes hunt and slay them, and Leviathans despise the Metzla. Dragons of all kinds are regarded as arrogant and untrustworthy rivals and showoffs, regardless of their alignment, and are sometimes hunted, slain and eaten by Leviathans, especially hatchlings. Nor do Leviathans hold any love for the Milu or the Lord of the Deep and his minions and monstrous creations, but they tend to leave the Lord of the Deep alone (whom they see as a force of nature like themselves), attacking only the creatures that serve him. Thanks to the Lemurians bringing them to their attention, there is a growing animosity toward the Milu and their undead legions.

Value: Their skin/hide is lightweight, but extremely tough, able to shrug off blows even from rail guns and torpedoes. Its light, resilient nature makes it sought out for body armor. However, capturing (let alone killing) a Leviathan is nearly impossible. Such skins can make a suit of non-environmental/homespun body armor with 1D6x10+90 M.D.C. (-10% Prowl and movement penalty and would sell for 80,000 to 120,000 credits just because of its legendary origin). The teeth can be made into knives, swords, spearheads, staves and other weapons, as well as sculptures, works of art and jewelry. The meat is inedible.

Ghost Dragon

In its natural form, the Ghost Dragon appears as a pale white dragon with a light gray, light blue or light green underbelly and hair. Its head is surrounded by a crown of horns and spikes, with more wicked looking, shark-tooth shaped spikes running down its spine. On its head is a beard, two long, tentacle-like feelers that pass for a mustache, and a shaggy mane of hair that runs down its back. Its eyes are solid white and minus pupils. The Ghost Dragon is more akin to eastern dragons, having a long serpentine body and short limbs. It has a long tail that resembles that of a fish, but ends with a fan-like cluster of fur.

The Ghost Dragon earns its name not just from its white color, but also from the fact that four times a day it can become ethereal. In this "ghost" form, the dragon retains its appearance, but is translucent. In mist, fog and water, the Ghost Dragon seems to vanish completely, becoming partial visible, as if made of water or glass, when it is within 10 feet (3 m) of another person. However, when you can see the Ghost Dragon in its ethereal form, you're probably about to be attacked. To attack, using magic, psionics or physical attacks, the Ghost Dragon must become tangible again, at least for one full melee round (15 seconds). This is when the dragon is most vulnerable, but also at its most deadly.

The Ghost Dragon is relatively new to Rifts Earth, and is a carrion feeder, thriving on the remains of the dead and decaying, as well as feeding upon the entities that are fostered in such an environment. This means Ghost Dragons are attracted to Dead Pools and many are happy to strike up an alliance with Necromancers, the Milu, Davey Jones, the Lord of the Deep, and other supernatural beings and people who control or deal with the dead, undead, and animated dead or are involved in war or murder. As a result, sunken ships, ship graveyards, Dead Pools, battlefields, ocean ley line triangles, and similar places are appealing to Ghost Dragons as locations to hunt, lurk and establish lairs. They also like looking for sunken treasure. Gold, gems, magic items and ancient artifacts are all coveted by the dragon. Likewise, they use places reputed to harbor treasure troves as locations to lure unsuspecting adventurers and seafarers to their doom. Though Ghost Dragons prefer to feed upon the remains of the dead, they don't have a problem with slaughtering the living and letting the bodies rot for a few days before chowing down on their remains. Find a cave or shipwreck full of bloated dead bodies, and you've probably found the lair or meat locker of a Ghost Dragon. Beware, or you may be added to the meal.

Ghost Dragons seldom allow themselves to serve humans, but may ally themselves to humans and other beings if it serves their purpose. Though the monsters can be any alignment, they are seldom good, and more often ally themselves with the enemies of Lemuria and mortals, than the good guys. These are one of the dragons hunted and slain by Serpent Hunters. Any Ghost Dragon that allies itself with heroes, especially Serpent Hunters, are either renegades or the union serves them in some way. Heroes need to be careful, because the Ghost Dragon may be manipulating them for its own insidious agenda or setting them up for a fall.

Ghost Dragon

Also Known As: Spectral Dragon and Sea Mist Dragon.

Alignment: Any, though most are Anarchist (35%), Diabolic (15%), Miscreant (30%) or Aberrant (10%). However, Hatchlings can start off at any alignment.

Attributes (Adult Dragon): I.Q. 2D6+12, M.E. 2D6+14, M.A. 2D6+12, P.S. 3D6+20, P.P. 2D6+10, P.E. 2D6+10, P.B. 2D6+12, Spd 4D6+10 running but most take flight (same ability they use to swim) and can travel at a speed of 1D6x10+100. P.S. is considered Supernatural.

Attributes (Hatchling): I.Q. 2D6+9, M.E. 2D6+5, M.A. 2D6+5, P.S. 2D6+9, P.P. 2D6+5, P.E. 2D6+9, P.B. 2D6+9, Spd 2D6+7 running, double swimming speed, or via "Ghost Flight" (see Natural Abilities).

Size: 20-24 feet (6.1 to 7.3 m) long from snout to the rump, and an additional 10-15 feet (3-4.6 m) for the tail. The Ghost Dragon stands 7-9 feet (2.1 to 2.7 m) tall from toe to the top of its head, and is 4-6 feet (1.2 to 1.8 m) wide at the shoulders.

Weight: 3-5 tons.

M.D.C.: Adult: 4D6x100 +1,300; +1D4x1,000 for ancient Ghost Dragons. (On S.D.C. worlds, the adult has 3D6x10+40 Hit Points, 2D6x100+100 S.D.C. and a Natural A.R. of 12.)

Hatchling: 2D6x10+100. (On S.D.C. worlds, hatchlings have 5D6+7 Hit Points, 2D6x10+25 S.D.C. and a Natural A.R. 8.)

Horror Factor: Adult: 14; Hatchling: 10.

P.P.E.: Adult: 1D4x100. Hatchling: 1D6x10 +10 points per level of experience.

Disposition: Deceitful schemers, and manipulative backstabbers. Like most dragons, they consider themselves far superior to mere mortals, be they humans, Lemurians or Atlanteans, and love to manipulate and use them to their own ends. Ghost Dragons also enjoy causing mischief, calamity, war and death, and enjoy urging mortals into bloody conflicts so they may feast on those who die.

Average Life Span: 1D6x1,000+2,000 years, but some have been known to reach 10,000.

Level of Experience: 2D4 for adult NPCs (Non-Player Characters), 1D4 for hatchlings, or as desired by the Game Master. Hatchling player characters start at level one.

R.C.C. Skills (Hatchling): Advanced Math (+20%), Basic Math (+25%) Barter (+15%), Computer Operation (+10%), Land Navigation (+10%), Literate in Dragonese/Elven (+20%), Lore: Demons and Monsters (+30%), Lore: Faerie & Creatures of Magic (+20%), Prowl (+20%), Seduction (+20%), and Underwater Navigation (+20%) as well as a total of four skill selections from the following skill categories only: Communication, Rogue, Technical, Wilderness and Weapon Proficiencies. See page 156 of **Rifts® Ultimate Edition** for more information about playing dragon characters.

Natural Abilities: Supernatural P.S. and P.E., Nightvision 800 feet (244 m), excellent color vision, see invisible (including Astral Travelers, Entities and essences of Alien Intelligences), magically understands and speaks all languages at 90%, turn invisible at will, Bio-Regeneration 1D4x10 M.D.C. per minute, impervious to cold (does no damage, not even magic M.D. cold), depth tolerance is unlimited (in either form), Teleport Self 80% (+15% if the location is well known), and Dimensional Teleport 32% +4% per level of experience.

Breathing: Breathes without air and can survive the pressures of the ocean or the emptiness of space without any difficulties.

Breath Weapon: P.P.E. Leech Attack (special): This particular breath weapon is a little like a Chinese dragon's animus. The Ghost Dragon breathes out a *white mist* that surrounds and attacks those caught in its embrace. The mist covers a 5 foot (1.5 m) radius and can be directed at a specific target or group up to 50 feet (15.2 m) away. All those exposed lose 2D6 P.P.E. Mages and creatures of magic who are in control of their P.P.E. may make a save vs magic (14 or higher). Success means no P.P.E. is lost, however, failure means they lose 2D6 P.P.E. Moreover, the P.P.E. is not so much "lost" as "stolen" and absorbed by the Ghost Dragon. All stolen P.P.E. can be stored for up to one minute per level of experience and used by the dragon to cast its own magic spells. This power can only be used once per melee round.

Depth Tolerance (special): Unlimited.

Ghost Flight (special): When in Ghost Form, the dragon can swim and fly at double its usual speed. Flight is limited to an altitude of two miles (3.2 km).

Ghost Form (special): While most dragons can shapeshift into a variety of forms, the Ghost Dragon can only change into three: **1.** A physical, pale human or human-looking being (Lemurians, Elves, etc.) with white, blue or green hair but nothing smaller than a cat and nothing larger than its natural form. **2.** A small, physical version of itself, up to half its normal size. **3.** A ghost version of itself. Duration: Six hours per level of experience of any altered state.

As a "ghost," the dragon is intangible, allowing it to pass through walls and solid objects, but it is clearly visible as a ghostly, transparent version of itself; it cannot turn invisible in Ghost Form. However, its transparent ghost form cannot be seen in mist, fog and water until it comes within 10 feet (3 m) of a person. Moreover, the dragon can run and swim at double its usual speed when a ghost and can fly in the air. Magic and psionic energy fields are one of the few things it cannot pass through. However, while most weapons and attacks cannot hurt the dragon in Ghost Form, it cannot attack or hurt other people, not even with psionics. **Note:** The Ghost Dragon must turn into its physical form to harm people in the physical world. Once transformed into a ghost, or from ghost to physical form, the Ghost Dragon must maintain that form for at least one full melee round (15 seconds), before it can change back. Can turn from ghost to physical and back as many times in a day as it desires without spending P.P.E.; natural ability.

Slay Ghosts and Entities: When in its Ghost Form, the dragon can attack other "spirits," including Astral Travelers, Entities and essences of Alien Intelligences with its claws, teeth, and psionic powers. If slain by the Ghost Dragon, the Entity's P.P.E. is eaten by the dragon which restores 1D4x10 M.D.C. and makes the dragon feel powerful. The "eaten" P.P.E. cannot be used to cast magic. The Ghost Dragon cannot harm people in the physical world by any means while in Ghost Form.

Vulnerabilities & Weaknesses: When the Ghost Dragon turns ethereal, it cannot be harmed by most physical attacks, but is vulnerable to weapons that can harm ghosts and Entities, and dragon slaying magic weapons can still hurt them in Ghost Form, but at half the weapons normal dragon damage. Only psionic attacks do full damage to the ethereal Ghost Dragon. Other types of magic weapons and spells inflict half damage and last one third the duration when leveled against an ethereal Ghost Dragon. Magic that summons or protects against spirits, ghosts and Entities will hold ethereal Ghost Dragons at bay, but only while it is ethereal. Otherwise, all attacks (except cold), will do damage to the dragon when it is in physical form.

Attacks per Melee: Adult: Eight physical attacks per melee or two by magic, or up to four breath weapon attacks.

Hatchling: Four physical or two by breath weapon attacks.

Mega-Damage: Varies with Supernatural P.S. The prehensile tail can be used to strike at its enemies like a whip but does half the P.S. damage of a punch and a power tail strike and bite are not possible. A bite attack does punch damage +3 M.D., a claw attack does punch damage +2D6 M.D., or the dragon may use its magic, psionics or a weapon.

Bonuses (in addition to attribute bonuses): Adult: +3 to Perception Rolls, +2 to initiative, +4 to strike, +3 to parry and dodge, +5 to pull punch, +3 to roll with impact, +7 to save vs Horror Factor and +2 on all other saving throws.

Hatchling: +1 to initiative, +2 to strike, +1 to parry and dodge, +2 to pull punch, +2 to roll with impact, +3 to save vs Horror Factor and +1 on all other saving throws.

Magic Knowledge of an Adult: Most Ghost Dragons learn *Ocean Magic* (30%), Wizard/Spell Invocations the same as a *Ley Line Walker* (30%), or *Necromancy* (40%). The dragons do not like linking themselves to other beings and stay away from the Warlock and Shifter O.C.C.s. An adult is likely to know 3D6+10 magic spells from its chosen area of knowledge.

Hatchling: All Dragon Hatchlings are born with a full understanding of magic, but they know no spells at level one. They can, however, learn magic and use Techno-Wizard, Biomancy and other magical weapons and devices. See the **Rifts® Ultimate Edition**, starting on page 156, for rules and guidelines for playing a Dragon Hatchling.

Psionics: Adult: I.S.P. 3D4x10 + M.E. attribute number and 5 I.S.P. for each level of experience. Considered to be a Master Psychic. Psionic Powers: All Sensitive psionic abilities as well as Empathic Transmission (6) and Radiate Horror Factor (8).

Hatchling: I.S.P. 1D4x10 + M.E. attribute number, +2D4 per level of experience. Considered to be a Master Psychic. Psionic Powers: Commune with Spirits (6), Machine Ghost (12), Mind Block (4), Sense Magic, Sense Time (2), and three psychic powers from the Sensitive psionic category. Select one additional at levels 4, 8, 12 and 16, and gets Empathic Transmission (6) at level 8.

Habitat: Ghost Dragons enjoy the depths of the ocean, especially in and around sunken ships, graveyards and Dead Pools, but can be encountered anywhere. Some have even been known to actively hunt the living to add their corpses and vessels to their personal graveyards and lairs.

Allies: Evil and Anarchist Ghost Dragons are likely to find the Milu, Lord of the Deep, Minions of Splugorth, the undead, demons, pirates, slavers, Necromancers, and others of selfish and evil alignments to make suitable henchmen, lackeys and associates. As with most dragons, they avoid their own kind.

Enemies: They see other dragons, even their own species, as dangerous rivals and enemies. Evil and selfish Ghost Dragons, of course, see heroes and people of good alignment as fools, suckers and likely enemies to be manipulated, tricked, cheated and eaten. Entities are the natural enemy and prey of Ghost Dragons.

Hydros Dragon

These beautiful dragons are a metallic-looking silver-blue with a silver underbelly and highlights. They are sometimes mistaken for a sea serpent because the creature has no hind legs in dragon form, but a snake-like tail that narrows to a point. Their front legs/arms are powerful and their webbed hands end with deadly silver claws – literally "silver," making them deadly weapons to supernatural beings vulnerable to the metal. The dragon has "whiskers" or tentacle-like appendages around its mouth that it uses to sense things in darkness and at the bottom of the ocean, though it also has good Nightvision. Most people assume the Hydros Dragons prefers the water over dry land, but except for desert environments, they are equally comfortable on land or in water. Their favorite places are beautiful landscapes, such as jungles and forests, coral reefs, lagoons, waterfalls, etc., but they tend to find the beauty in all environments, from the tropics to the arctic.

Hydros Dragons are highly intelligent and sensitive to beauty and joy, and hate ugliness, cruelty and the suffering of others. Thus, it is no surprise that they often join forces with the Lemurians and other heroes to combat evil, especially the undead and supernatural evil. This makes them the natural enemy of vampires, the Milu, the Lord of the Deep and wicked dragons. Hydros also get along well with Merans and sentient cetaceans (dolphins and whales), and love to swim and play with both. Thus, it can be a startling transition to see these noble, gentle and kind dragons transform into bellowing monsters when engaged in combat. When the peace-loving Hydros enter battle, they fight with a primordial fury and intensity that can chill the soul, crushing evil without hesitation. Though they are no man's "war steed" or "pet," Hydros Dragons have been known to let human and D-Bee heroes ride on them, usually behind the shoulders or on the neck behind the base of the head.

Hydros Dragon

Also Known As: Water Dragons or Aqua Dragons.

Alignment: Any, but tend to be Principled (35%), Scrupulous (30%), Unprincipled (10%), or Anarchist (10%).

Attributes (adult): I.Q. 2D6+12, M.E. 2D6+15, M.A. 2D6+12, P.S. 2D6+28, P.P. 2D6+10, P.E. 3D6+10, P.B. 4D6+6, Spd 1D6+18 on land where it moves like a snake (roughly 15 mph/24 km), swimming Spd is 1D6x10+90 (75-80 mph/120 to 128 km or 65 to 69 knots) and can swim indefinitely without tiring.

Attributes (hatchling): I.Q. 2D6+6, M.E. 2D6+4, M.A. 1D6+12, P.S. 2D6+18, P.P. 2D6+6, P.E. 2D6+12, P.B. 2D6+3, Spd 2D6+10 crawling like a snake on land or 6D6+30 swimming in or underwater; P.S. is considered Supernatural.

Size: 36-50 feet (10.9 to 15.2 m) long.

Weight: 12-20 tons.

M.D.C.: Adult: 1D6x1,000 +800; +1D6x1,000 for ancient Hydros Dragons. (On S.D.C. worlds, the adult has 4D6x10+100 Hit Points, 3D6x100+200 S.D.C. and a Natural A.R. of 14.)

Hatchling: 1D6x100.(On S.D.C. worlds, hatchlings have 180 Hit Points, 2D6x10+25 S.D.C. and a Natural A.R. 10.)

Horror Factor: Adult: 14; Hatchling: 10.

P.P.E.: Adult: 1D6x100+180. Hatchling: 2D6x10 +2D6 points per level of experience.

Disposition: Peace-loving, compassionate, merciful and passionate about life. This dragon appreciates music and the arts, beauty in all forms, and believes in the goodness of sentient beings. Hates ugliness, evil and the demonic and wickedness. Usually kind and caring to those mortals with whom they become attached.

Average Life Span: 1D6x1,000 +2,000 years, but some have been known to reach 9,000.

Level of Experience: 2D4 for adult NPCs (Non-Player Characters), 1D4 for hatchlings, or as desired by the Game Master. Hatchling player characters start at level one.

R.C.C. Skills (Hatchling): Art (+30%), Computer Operation (+15%), Dowsing (+30%), Firefighting (+20%), Gemology (+20%), Land Navigation (+12%), Literate in Dragonese/Elven (+20%), Lore: Demon and Monster (+30%), Mathematics: Basic (+25%), Philosophy (+20%), Pilot: Sail Boats (+20%), Pilot: Water Scooters (+10%), Pilot: Water Skiing and Surfing (+40%), Prowl (+10% in water only), and Underwater Navigation (+20%), as well as a total of four skill selections from the following skill categories only: Aquatic, Communication, Domestic, Science, Technical and Wilderness. See page 156 of **Rifts® Ultimate Edition** for more information about playing dragon characters.

Natural Abilities: Supernatural P.S. and P.E., Nightvision 800 feet (244 m), excellent color vision, see invisible (including Astral Travelers, Entities and essences of Alien Intelligences), magically understands and speaks all languages at 90%, turn invisible at will, Bio-Regenerates 1D4x10 M.D.C. per minute, impervious to cold (does no damage, not even magic M.D. cold), Teleport Self 50% +3% per level of experience (+20% if the location is well known), and Dimensional Teleport 24% +4% per level of experience.

Breathing: Breathes without air and can survive the pressures of the ocean or the emptiness of space without any difficulties.

Breath Weapon: Cold (special): The Hydros Dragon can unleash a blast of icy mist that inflicts 3D6 M.D. from cold (5D6 M.D. from adults). Each blast counts as one melee attack. Range is 120 feet (36.6 m).

Depth Tolerance (special): Unlimited.

Metamorphosis (special): This is a natural ability common to most dragons. The Hydros can transform into any type of animal or humanoid (with legs to walk on) that is no smaller than a rabbit, and the maximum size cannot exceed its own. The transformation lasts for three hours per level of experience.

Metamorphosis: Water (special): The Hydros Dragon can transform into a creature of living water. On the surface, this transformation is performed to turn into a puddle to flow under doors or pour itself through small openings, vents, grates, down a drain and through water pipes to travel or gain access to an area without having to break down a door or alert people to its presence. Speed of travel as water is half its running speed, and NO attacks are possible in this form.

Underwater, the Hydros Dragon that becomes water is completely invisible to all conventional means of detection including sonar, nightvision, sound, heat/thermal detection, and even see the invisible (because the dragon is not invisible, it's "water" which just cannot be seen while in other water!). While in water form, the dragon is impervious to physical attacks but cannot attack by any means itself; it must become physical to attack even with psionics.

Quick Turns & Stops (special): Stops on a dime and can completely turn around in tight spaces or areas underwater.

Sense Magnetic North (special): Same as a dolphin

Chemoreceptors (special): A highly advanced sense of taste/smell that enables the Hydro Dragon to track its prey. They can also determine the salt content or toxicity of the water, as well as to taste blood in the water like a shark. Base Skill: 76% +2% per level of experience to track. 60% +2% per level of experience to identify chemicals, toxins or specific creatures by "sampling" scent trails.

Vulnerabilities & Weaknesses: Does not like fire, heat and fire attacks; M.D. plasma and magic fires inflict double damage.

Attacks per Melee: Adult: Seven physical or psionic attacks per melee or four by magic. Hatchling: Four physical or psionic attacks, or two by magic. Or any combination thereof.

Mega-Damage: Varies with Supernatural P.S. The prehensile tail can be used to strike at its enemies like a whip at does the same damage as a punch; a power tail strike does double damage but counts as two melee actions. A claw strike does punch damage +2D6 M.D., goring with mouth tusks does punch damage +3D6 M.D., a bite does 5D6 M.D. (+2D6 M.D. from adults). A full strength ram (swimming at close to full speed) does 2D4x10 M.D. (The tusks and bone in the chin add to the damage) but counts as three melee actions.) In the alternative, the dragon may use magic, psionics or a weapon.

Bonuses (in addition to attribute bonuses): Adult: +2 on Perception Rolls (but +5 to anything involving water), +2 to initiative, +3 to strike and parry, +1 to dodge (+4 to automatic dodge underwater), +5 to pull punch, +4 to roll with impact, +6 to save vs Horror Factor and +2 on all other saving throws.

Hatchling: +1 on Perception Rolls (+2 to anything involving water), +1 to initiative, +2 to strike, +1 to parry and dodge, +2 to pull punch, +2 to roll with impact, +3 to save vs Horror Factor and +1 on all other saving throws.

Magic Knowledge of an Adult: Most Hydros Dragons learn *Ocean Magic* (40%), or Wizard/Spell Invocations the same as a *Ley Line Walker* (30%), or *Whale Songs* (30%); pick one area of magic. The dragon does not like linking itself to other beings and stays away from the Warlock and Shifter O.C.C.s as well as dark magic like Necromancy. An adult is likely to know 3D6+16 magic spells from its chosen area of knowledge.

Hatchling: All Dragon Hatchlings are born with a full understanding of magic, but they know no spells at Level One. They can, however, learn magic and use Techno-Wizard, Biomancy and other magical weapons and devices. See the **Rifts® Ultimate Edition**, starting on page 156, for rules and guidelines for playing a Dragon Hatchling.

Psionics: Adult: I.S.P. 3D6x10 +M.E. attribute number and 10 I.S.P. for each level of experience. Considered to be a Master Psychic. Psionic Powers: All Hydro-Psionic Abilities, plus the Super-Psionic abilities of Group Mind Block (22), Hydrokinesis (varies), Mind Bolt (varies), and P.P.E. Shield (30).

Hatchling: I.S.P. 1D6x10 +M.E. attribute number, +10 per level of experience. Considered to be a Master Psychic. Psionic Powers: Empathy (4), Meditation (0), Mind Block (4), and five Hydro-Psionic abilities of choice (see the *Spouter O.C.C.* for these powers), +1 new Hydro-Psionic ability for each new level of experience and the Hydrokinesis Super-Psionic Power at level 4 and P.P.E. Shield at level 8.

Habitat: Hydros Dragons enjoy the depths of the ocean, especially around coral reefs and other places full of life and beauty, but can be encountered anywhere. They also enjoy beautiful environments on dry land, including the arctic, and many make remote, frozen places the location of their secret lair and treasure trove.

Allies: In general, heroes and beings of good alignment. Several Hydros Dragons have friendly relationships with Lemuria.

Enemies: The Milu, Lord of the Deep, Minions of Splugorth, Ghost Dragons, the undead, demons, pirates, slavers, Necromancers, and other wicked and cruel people and beings who enjoy enslaving hurting and killing innocent people. The dragon has a strong fear of fire, so it dislikes and distrusts most fire-based creatures and dragons (fire breathers), and those who practice fire types of magic or have natural powers over fire, like Bursters.

Octo Dragon

This bizarre creature is believed to be a monstrosity from another dimension or an experimental creation/minion of the Lord of the Deep that has gone rogue. Other dragons that have encountered an Octo Dragon insist that it is a true dragon as they can sense its presence.

The Octo Dragon has a long serpentine body and large head that is more reminiscent of a giant, monstrous eel than a dragon or sea serpent. Its massive jaw is lined with two sets of sharp teeth the size of short swords and a tail that ends in a wicked blade used for slashing and stabbing. A row of spines run down the monster's back from the base of the head to about two-thirds of its body. The hide is covered in tiny, fine scales. Instead of legs or wings, the beast has eight long, octopus-like tentacles, each of which, and the tail, are prehensile, agile and strong. Octo Dragons swim using their tail and eight limbs, but speed is slow compared to most other Sea Dragons and sea serpents. Of course, the octopus arms are also used to crawl, climb, carry heavy objects and to grab, hold and manipulate objects. Most Octo Dragons can adjust the color of their skin, including blotchy patterns and markings, to camouflage themselves, just like true octopus and squid, so colors can range from white to black to every color in the rainbow. However, it is believed that their natural coloring is a light brownish gray with a pink underbelly and pink coloration on the underside of the tentacles.

Octo Dragons are renowned for their short tempers, aggressiveness, their savagery and brutality in combat. They seem to be intolerant of all weaker life forms and regard them as prey or playthings. This dark nature has caused many Octo Dragons to serve the Lord of the Deep who treats them as generals put in charge of lesser minions. Others associate with the Splugorth of Atlantis, with several making Atlantis or the waters around Atlantis their home. Others have established small kingdoms of their own above and below the waves, where the dragon rules over terrified aquatic people or coastal and island people as a tyrant king or self-appointed god. The only advantage such dragon-ruled "kingdoms" (actually city-states with 4D6x100 people) enjoy is that the possessive "King" protects them from monsters, invaders and outsiders. However, that is likely to result in isolation, and any visitors to the island, other than sanctioned pirates and traders, are likely to be added to the enslaved

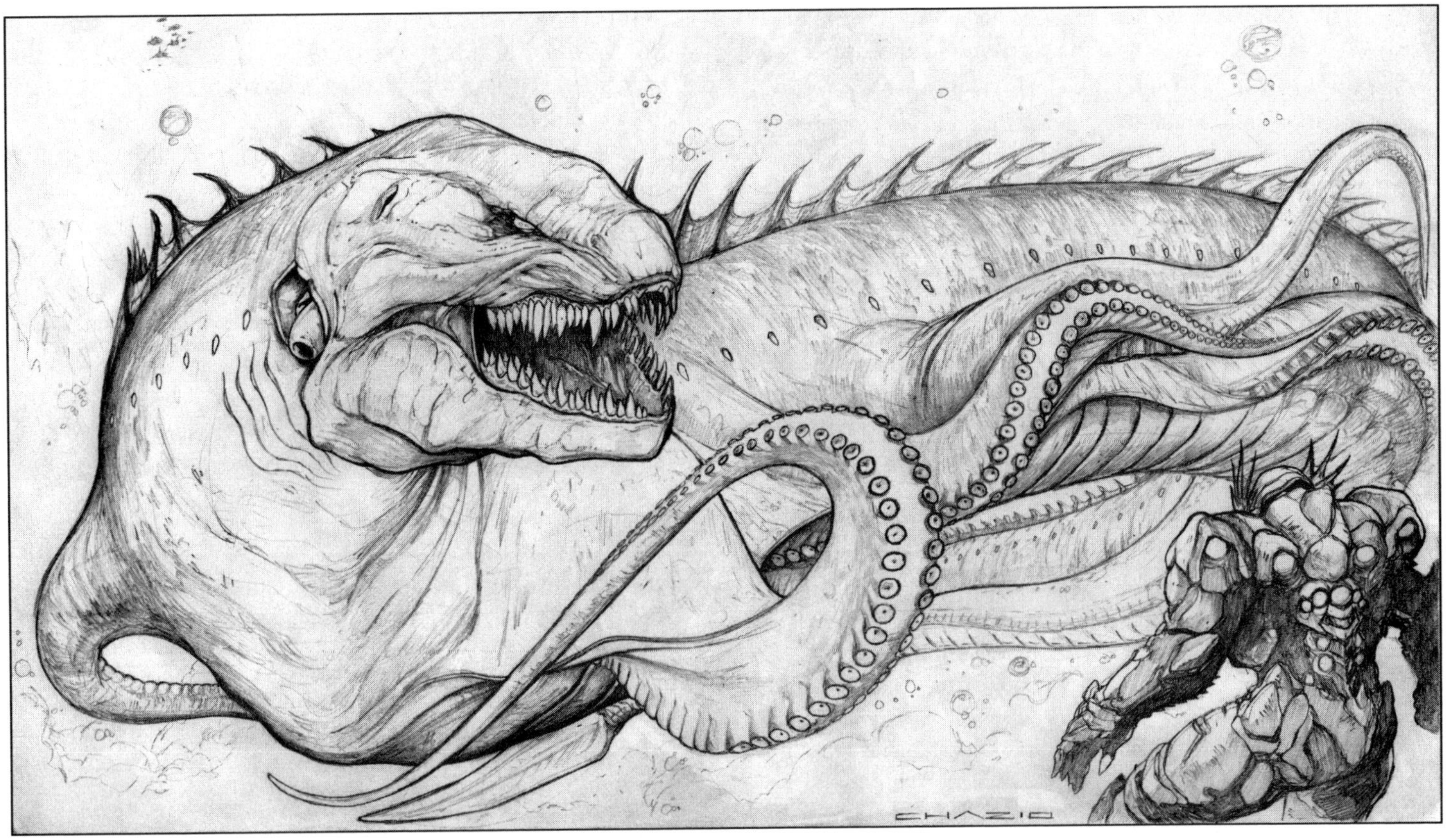

population. Those who try to escape or stand against the monster are beaten into submission or slain and eaten, probably after torture. Most Octo Dragons will have 3D4 evil henchmen who function as managers, spies and enforcers, as well as an association with pirates and other evildoers.

While most Octo Dragons are evil and do not interact with other races in a peaceful manner, not all are evil. There are some that are simply selfish and those that are good, but even they tend to be short-tempered and quick to violence to resolve a problem.

Octo Dragon

Also Known As: Tentacle Dragon and Tyrant Dragon.

Alignment: Any, though most are Diabolic (25%), Miscreant (40%), Aberrant (10%), or Anarchist (15%).

Attributes (Adult): I.Q. 2D6+16, M.E. 2D6+16, M.A. 2D6+8, P.S. 2D6+32, P.P. 2D6+16, P.E. 2D6+16, P.B. 1D6+6, Spd 3D6+10 slithering like a snake on its belly or using its tentacles to crawl (15 mph/24 km), swimming Spd is 2D6+20 for an average swim speed of 2D6+36 (around 30 mph/48 km or 26 knots); the act of swimming does not tire the dragon out.

Attributes (Hatchling): I.Q. 2D6+8, M.E. 2D6+8, M.A. 2D6+4, P.S. 2D6+20, P.P. 3D6+8, P.E. 3D6+3, P.B. 2D6+3, Spd 3D6 slithering like a snake or using tentacles to crawl. Swimming Spd is 1D6+18 (20 mph/32 km or 17 knots); the act of swimming does not tire the dragon out.

Size: 30-40 feet (9.1 to 12.2 m) long from snout to the section of its back where the tentacle end, plus 90-100 feet (27.4 to 30.5 m) of tail. The head is 8-10 feet (2.4 to 3 m) in diameter and each tentacle is 30-40 feet (9.1 to 12.2 m) long.

Weight: 30-50 tons.

M.D.C.: Adult: 2D4x1,000 +1,600; +1D4x1,000 for ancient Octo Dragons. (On S.D.C. worlds, the adult has 5D6x10+160 Hit Points, 3D6x100 S.D.C. and a Natural A.R. of 12.)

Hatchling: 2D4x100.(On S.D.C. worlds, hatchlings have 240 Hit Points, 2D6x10+80 S.D.C. and a Natural A.R. 9.)

Horror Factor: Adult: 15; Hatchling: 11.

P.P.E.: Adult: 2D4x100+160. Hatchling: 2D4x10 +2D6 points per level of experience.

Disposition: Highly aggressive and prone to violence, many of these natural predators are wicked and cruel. They are merciless in combat, and engage in acts of brutality and cruelty for pleasure.

Average Life Span: 1D6x1,000 +1,600 years, but some have been known to reach 9,000.

Level of Experience: 2D4 for adult NPCs (Non-Player Characters), 1D4 for hatchlings, or as desired by the Game Master. Hatchling player characters start at level one.

R.C.C. Skills (Hatchling): Camouflage (+25%), Climbing (+30%), Escape Artist (+30%), Gemology (+20%), Intelligence (+10%), Interrogation (+20%), Land Navigation (+14%), Literate in Dragonese/Elven (+10%), Lore: Demons and Monsters (+20%), Mathematics: Basic (+15%), Pilot: Sail Boats (+20%), Prowl (+20%), Tailing (+20%), and Underwater Navigation (+20%), as well as a total of five skill selections from the following skill categories only: Aquatic, Communication, Rogue, Technical, Wilderness and W.P. See page 156 of **Rifts® Ultimate Edition** for more information about playing dragon characters.

Natural Abilities: Supernatural P.S. and P.E., Nightvision 500 feet (152 m), excellent color vision, see the invisible, can see clearly in murky water, magically understands and speaks all languages at 85%, turn invisible at will, Bio-Regenerates 1D4x10 M.D.C. per minute, impervious to cold (does no damage, not even magic M.D. cold), Teleport Self 48% +2% per level of experience (+10% if the location is well known), and Dimensional Teleport 16% +4% per level of experience.

Breathing: Breathes without air and can survive the pressures of the ocean or the emptiness of space without any difficulties.

Breath Weapon: Ink Cloud (special): The Octo Dragon spews out a dark liquid, much like the ink cloud of an octopus. On the surface the ink turns into a dense, black cloud that shrouds an area of 30x30x30 feet (9x9x9 m) and lasts for 1D4 melee rounds. Everyone caught inside the magical darkness fights as blind until they can exit the cloud (-10 to strike, parry, dodge and all other combat moves). The cloud is a weird ink, not smoke, so infrared and passive nightvision goggles do not work, nor does Nightvision! Underwater, the ink cloud covers an area twice as large; same duration and effects.

Camouflage Quick Change (special): Like a real octopus, the dragon can change its skin color and patterns to imitate and blend into its surroundings. It takes only one melee action/attack to complete the change and can be performed as frequently as desired. Adds +10% to Prowl and Tailing skills when it is used.

Chemoreceptors: In its mouth are advanced sense of taste sensors that enable the Octo Dragon to detect minute changes in the salinity and chemical components of the water. Identify chemicals by taste: 72% +1% per level of experience. Track by taste: 72% +2% per level of experience; range: One mile (1.6 km).

Depth Tolerance (special): Unlimited.

Metamorphosis (special): This is a natural ability common to most dragons. The Octo Dragon can transform into any type of animal or humanoid (with two legs and arms, unless the creature it is copying has more limbs, up to eight total) that is no smaller than a wolf, and the maximum size cannot exceed its own. The transformation lasts for two hours per level of experience.

Vulnerabilities & Weaknesses: Does not like fire. Normal fire does half damage as M.D. (e.g. a fire that does 4D6 S.D.C. does 2D6 M.D. to the Hydros Dragon), while M.D. plasma, fire and magical fire does double damage. Also hates captivity and becomes incredibly angry and violent, thrashing around and bellowing until it is exhausted.

Attacks per Melee: Adult: *Nine* physical or psionic attacks per melee round or four by magic.

Hatchling: Four physical attacks per melee round or two by magic.

Mega-Damage: As per Supernatural P.S. The prehensile tail can be used to strike at its enemies like a tentacle that ends with a giant blade that does 6D6+12 M.D. A blunt tail strike does the same damage as a punch, a power tail strike does double damage but counts as two melee actions. Bite damage is 1D6x10 M.D. Tentacles can also grab and hold opponents or squeeze and crush, doing up to 3D6 M.D. per squeeze. Each squeeze counts as one melee attack.

Bonuses (in addition to attribute bonuses): Adult: +1 on Perception Rolls, +4 to initiative (+6 in water), +8 to strike and parry, +8 to disarm and entangle, +3 to dodge, +6 to pull punch, +2 to roll with impact, +8 to save vs Horror Factor and +2 on all other saving throws.

Hatchling: +1 to initiative (+2 in water), +2 to strike, +4 to parry and disarm, +4 to entangle, +1 to dodge, +2 to pull punch, +2 to roll with impact, +3 to save vs Horror Factor and +1 on all other saving throws.

Magic Knowledge of an Adult: Adult: Octo Dragons are very direct and simple creatures, so the main magic they learn is Wizard/Spell Invocations the same as a *Ley Line Walker* (90%). Only a few study *Ocean Magic* (6%) or Necromancy or other dark magic (4%). The dragon does not like accepting anyone as its better, so it avoids magicks that require linking itself to other beings and stays away from the Warlock and Shifter O.C.C.s. An adult is likely to know 3D6+16 magic spells from its chosen area of knowledge.

Hatchling: All Dragon Hatchlings are born with a full understanding of magic, but they know no spells at Level One. They can, however, learn magic and use Techno-Wizard, Biomancy and other magical weapons and devices. See the **Rifts® Ultimate Edition**, starting on page 156, for rules and guidelines for playing a Dragon Hatchling.

Psionics: Adult: I.S.P. 2D6x10+16 +M.E. attribute number and 10 I.S.P. for each level of experience. Considered to be a Master Psychic. Psionic Powers: All Physical psionic abilities, plus the Super-Psionic ability of Radiate Horror Factor (8).

Hatchling: I.S.P. 1D6x10 +M.E. attribute number, +2D4 per level of experience. Considered to be a Master Psychic. Psionic Powers: Death Trance (1), Meditation (0), Mind Block (4), and five Physical psionic powers, +1 new Physical ability for each new level of experience, plus Radiate Horror Factor (8) at level 12.

Habitat: Octo Dragons enjoy the depths of the ocean and can be found anywhere, but because they like to enslave and dominate lesser beings, many have established their own little despot kingdom above and/or below the waves, or like to raid and terrorize coastal communities.

Allies: Evil and Anarchist Octo Dragons find Davey Jones, the Milu, the Lord of the Deep, and the Splugorth and their minions to be worth "associates" and "allies." At least a half a dozen to a dozen Octo Dragons appear to serve the *Lord of the Deep* as the generals of his monstrous legions and/or as elite assassins and henchmen. Similarly, Octo Dragons often find that the undead, demons, pirates, slavers, evil mages and other beings of selfish and evil alignments make suitable henchmen, servants, slaves and worshipers. Only beings who are powerful yet subservient may be treated like an actual trusted associate. As with most dragons, they avoid their own kind and see them as rivals and potential enemies.

Enemies: Evil Octo Dragons despise Hydros Dragons, Sand Dragons, Lemurians (especially Serpent Hunters), creatures of light and heroes. They see other dragons, especially their own species, and Ghost Dragons, as dangerous rivals and enemies. Octo Dragons enjoy terrorizing mortals and see them as potential slaves, worshipers, playthings and food.

Sand Dragon

These magnificent, though slightly odd, dragons range in color from bone white or cream to gold with a green or red frilled fin skirting the neck and a matching color trail of fins that runs down their spine. Sand Dragons love to play in the sand of beaches, deserts and the sea floor, and have an affinity for building things out of sand. They also love the environment of sandy beaches and love to sunbathe, sleep and relax on them. The dragon's affinity for sand often starts out with building small sand castles and sculptures, but eventually moves onto grander and grander things. There are rumors that huge underwater sand castles have been put together with ordinary sand, silt and material from the sea floor bottom. These elaborate and beautiful creations can be found on dry land or underwater, and are held together by magic, or would otherwise dissolve with the ebb and flow of the tides and wind. The wind and waves eventually tear down most of their creations, but half the fun for the dragon is rebuilding them again and again.

Sand Dragons enjoy the depths of the oceans just as much as they do an open desert or sandy beach, and can be found in either locale. They are among the most calm and peaceful of known dragons, and try to avoid taking sides and fighting, in favor of building, albeit, temporary works of art, deep thinking, long conversations with people of all kinds, exploration and enjoying art and nature. Sand Dragons are seasoned dimensional travelers, so their presence on Rifts Earth is a new experience for them and the people of Earth. This means Sand Dragons have no allegiances to anyone and are rather confounded by the level of rivalry and violence seemingly exhibited by everything on the planet. They find Lemurians especially interesting and something of kindred spirits, but even they have a violent side to them and are locked in an ongoing war the Sand Dragon has trouble understanding.

Sand Dragon

Also Known As: Sand Masters, Earth Dragons and Castle Builders.

Alignment: Any, but tends to be Scrupulous (20%), Unprincipled (25%), and Anarchist (30%).

Attributes (Adult): I.Q. 2D6+12, M.E. 2D6+15, M.A. 2D6+12, P.S. 2D6+26, P.P. 2D6+10, P.E. 3D6+10, P.B. 3D6+7, Spd 3D6+38 running (around 35 mph/56 km), swimming Spd is 4D6+60 (averaging 50 mph/80 km or 43 knots); the act of swimming does not tire the dragon out.

Attributes (Hatchling): I.Q. 2D6+8, M.E. 2D6+6, M.A. 3D6+6, P.S. 3D6+10, P.P. 2D6+5, P.E. 2D6+9, P.B. 2D6+4, Spd 3D6+6 running, swimming Spd is 3D6+30 (averaging 30 mph/48 km or 26 knots).

Size: 20-30 feet (6.1 to 9.1 m) long from snout to rump, plus 30-40 feet (9.1 to 12.2 m) of tail.

Weight: 18-30 tons.

M.D.C.: Adult: 1D6x1,000 +1,200; +1D4x1,000 for Ancient Sand Dragons. (On S.D.C. worlds, the adult has 5D6x10+120 Hit Points, 2D6x100 S.D.C. and a Natural A.R. of 15.)

Hatchling: 1D6x100.(On S.D.C. worlds, hatchlings have 220 Hit Points, 2D6x10+30 S.D.C. and a Natural A.R. of 11.)

Horror Factor: Adult: 13; Hatchling: 10.

P.P.E.: Adult: 1D6x100+400. Hatchling: 1D6x10+50 +2D6 points per level of experience.

Disposition: Tend to be easygoing, imaginative, creative and artistic. Most welcome strangers and find them and their devices extremely interesting. Natural builders – not of machines, though they find them curious – but of statues, art and buildings, Sand Dragons spend a lot of time making sand constructs for enjoyment. The dragons prefer to avoid physical combat as much as possible, but are not afraid to fight and make deadly combatants when drawn to battle.

Sand Dragons do not handle criticism about their sand castles, sculptures and creations well, and are easily offended even by well-intentioned constructive suggestions.

Average Life Span: 1D6x1,000 +2,000 years, but some have been known to reach 10,000.

Level of Experience: 2D4 for adult NPCs (Non-Player Characters), 1D4 for hatchlings, or as desired by the Game Master. Hatchling player characters start at level one.

R.C.C. Skills (Hatchling): Art (+20%), Calligraphy (+10%), Computer Operation (+20%), Dowsing (+30%), Excavation (+10%), Gemology (+20%), General Repair and Maintenance (+10%), Land Navigation (+16%), Literate in Dragonese/Elven (+30%), Mathematics: Basic (+25%), Military Fortifications (+15%), Philosophy (+15%), Pilot: Sail Boats (+20%), Pilot: Water Skiing and Surfing (+12%), Prowl (+10% in sand and water only), Underwater Navigation (+20%), and Whittling and Sculpting (+25%), as well as a total of four skill selections from any the following skill categories only: Aquatic, Communication, Domestic, Science, Technical and Wilderness. See page 156 of **Rifts® Ultimate Edition** for more information about playing dragon characters.

Natural Abilities: Supernatural P.S. and P.E., Nightvision 500 feet (152 m), excellent color vision, see the invisible, magically understands and speaks all languages at 90%, turn invisible at will, Bio-Regeneration 1D4x10 M.D.C. per minute, impervious to fire (does no damage, not even magic M.D. fire, and it likes to play in hot lava), Teleport Self 60% +3% per level of experience (+15% if the location is well known), and Dimensional Teleport 28% +3% per level of experience.

Breathing: Breathes without air and can survive the pressures of the ocean or the emptiness of space without any difficulties.

Breath Weapon: Sand (special): The Sand Dragon can unleash a blast of sand that inflicts 3D6 M.D. and opponents whose eyes are not protected by goggles, a helmet with face plate, armor or magic get grit in their eyes and are blinded until they can rinse them clean with water. (-10 to strike, parry, dodge and other combat moves while blind.) Range is 120 feet (36.6 m).

Depth Tolerance (special): Unlimited.

Metamorphosis (special): This is a natural ability common to most dragons. The Sand Dragon can transform into any type of animal or humanoid that is no smaller than a fox, and the maximum size cannot exceed its own. The transformation lasts for three hours per level of experience.

Build with and Fortify Sand (special): The Sand Dragon first enchants an area of sand to build his monument or castle upon. He then goes to work molding the sand into the desired shape (sand castle, sculpture, etc.). When the building or sculpting and the magic ritual is completed, the sand solidifies with channeled P.P.E., becoming as hard as M.D.C. concrete. The whole structure glows dimly with mystical energy and can be sensed by fellow practitioners of magic within 1,000 feet (305 m). Each 12 foot (3.6 m) area/section has 10 M.D.C. and the sand structure will last for one week per level of the dragon's experience. If the sand structure is built upon a ley line it will last for one month per level of experience, or one year per level of experience at a nexus or stone pyramid. Each 12 foot (3.6 m) section requires the expenditure of 25 P.P.E. by the Sand Dragon.

Vulnerabilities & Weaknesses: Cold attacks do double damage. Sand Dragons hate dark, ugly places, and being trapped in such an environment makes the dragon depressed (-1 attack per melee, no Perception Roll and initiative bonuses, -20% on the performance of skills, -1 on all combat moves, and reduce Spd by 20%).

Attacks per Melee: Adult: Six physical attacks per melee or three by magic. Hatchling: Four physical or two by magic.

Mega-Damage: Varies with Supernatural P.S. The prehensile tail can be used to strike at its enemies like a whip. The tail does the same damage as a punch, a claw strike does the same damage as a punch +1D6 M.D., and a bite does 4D6 M.D. Cannot do a power strike with claws or tail.

Bonuses (in addition to attribute bonuses): Adult: +4 on Perception Rolls, +2 to initiative, +3 to strike and parry, +2 dodge (+4 to automatic dodge underwater), +6 to pull punch, +3 to roll with impact, +4 to save vs Horror Factor and +2 on all other saving throws.

Hatchling: +1 on Perception Rolls (+2 to anything involving building), +1 to initiative, +1 to strike, +1 parry and dodge, +2 to pull punch, +1 to roll with impact, +2 to save vs Horror Factor and +1 on all other saving throws.

Magic Knowledge of an Adult: Most Sand Dragons learn *Ocean Magic* (25%), or Wizard/Spell Invocations the same as a *Ley Line Walker* (25%), or Earth Warlock Magic (30%), or *Temporal Magic* (20%); pick one. The dragon avoids dark magic like Necromancy. An adult is likely to know 2D6+14 magic spells from its chosen area of knowledge.

Hatchling: All Dragon Hatchlings are born with a full understanding of magic, but they know no spells at Level One. They can, however, learn magic and use Techno-Wizard, Biomancy and other magical weapons and devices. See the **Rifts® Ultimate Edition**, starting on page 156, for rules and guidelines for playing a Dragon Hatchling.

Psionics: Adult: I.S.P. 3D6x10 +M.E. attribute number and 10 I.S.P. for each level of experience. Considered to be a Master Psychic. Psionic Powers: All Psionic Sensitive or Healing abilities, plus the Super-Psionic abilities of Hydrokinesis (varies), Telemechanics (10), and Telemechanics Mental Operation (12).

Hatchling: I.S.P. 1D6x10 +M.E. attribute number, +1D6+2 per level of experience. Considered to be a Master Psychic. Psionic Powers: Empathy (4), Object Read (6), and five of choice selected either from Healing or Sensitive categories (pick one). Select one new psionic power from that specific category for each new level of experience and gets Telemechanics at level 6.

Habitat: Sand Dragons enjoy the oceans and seas, and love beaches, deserts and sand to play and build in. However, they are curious by nature and new to Rifts Earth, so they can be found wandering, building and exploring just about anywhere.

Allies: None per se. Sand Dragons tend to be loners and are content as can be off by themselves building giant sand castles or exploring by themselves. When they do associate with other people, they generally like heroes and beings of good alignment. Several Sand Dragons have friendly relationships with Lemuria.

Enemies: None per se, though the enemies of Lemuria generally assume a friend of Lemuria is an enemy of their's. The Milu, Lord of the Deep, Shadow Serpents, Ghost Dragons, Octo Dragons, the undead, demons, pirates, slavers, Necromancers, and other wicked and cruel beings usually hate Sand Dragons the instant they meet one. The Splugorth of Atlantis and their Minions are accepting of all dragons. The Sand Dragons have a strong dislike of cold and darkness, so it dislikes and distrusts most creatures and dragons of darkness.

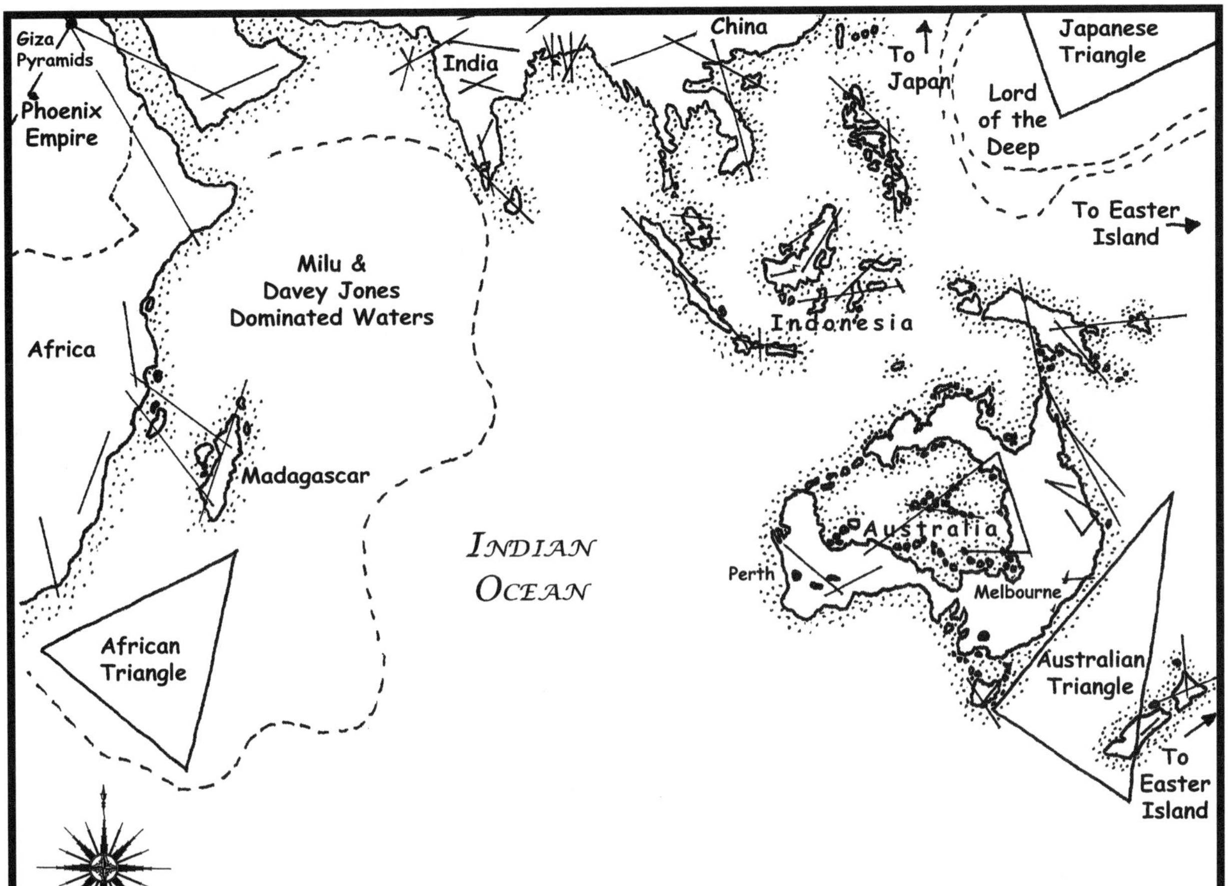

Indian Ocean Surface Ley Lines

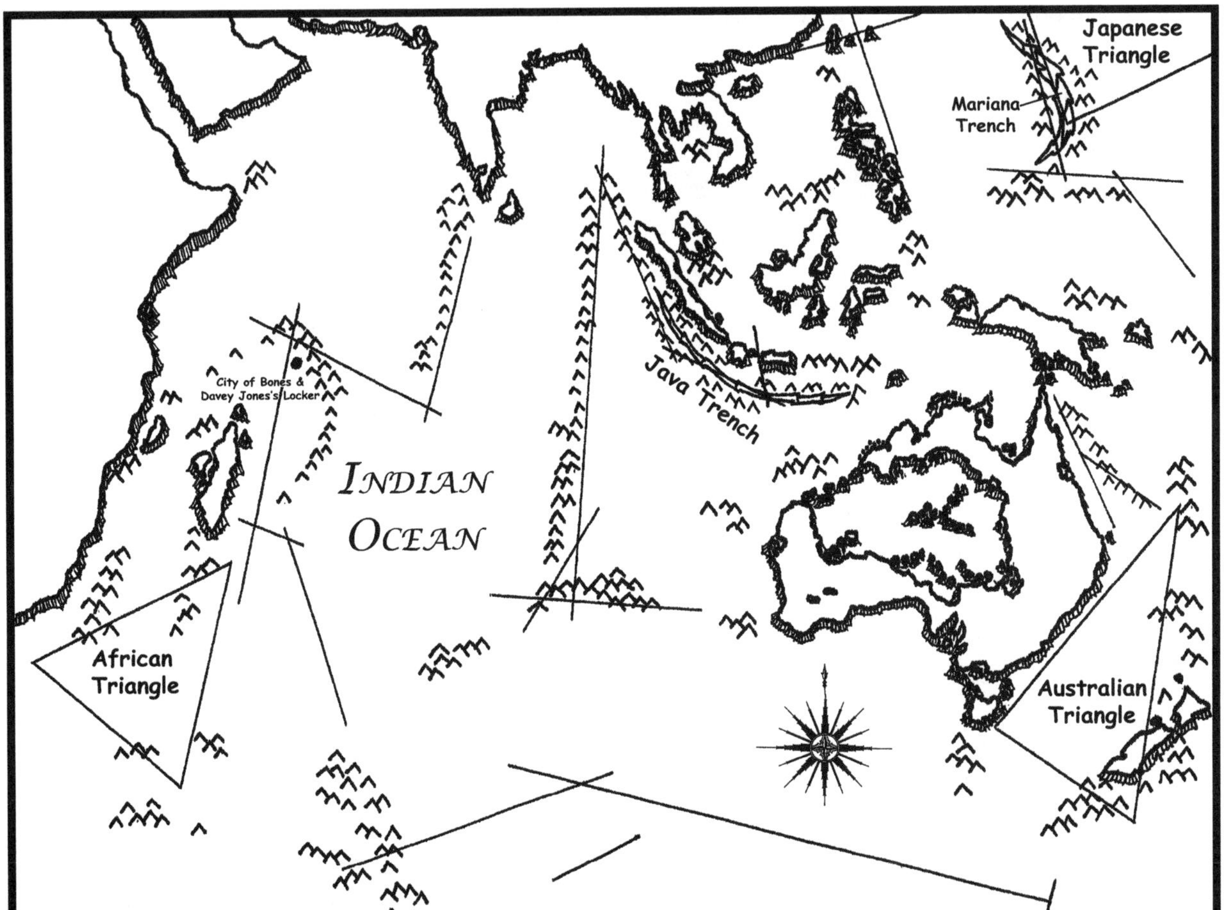

Indian Ocean Underwater Ley Lines

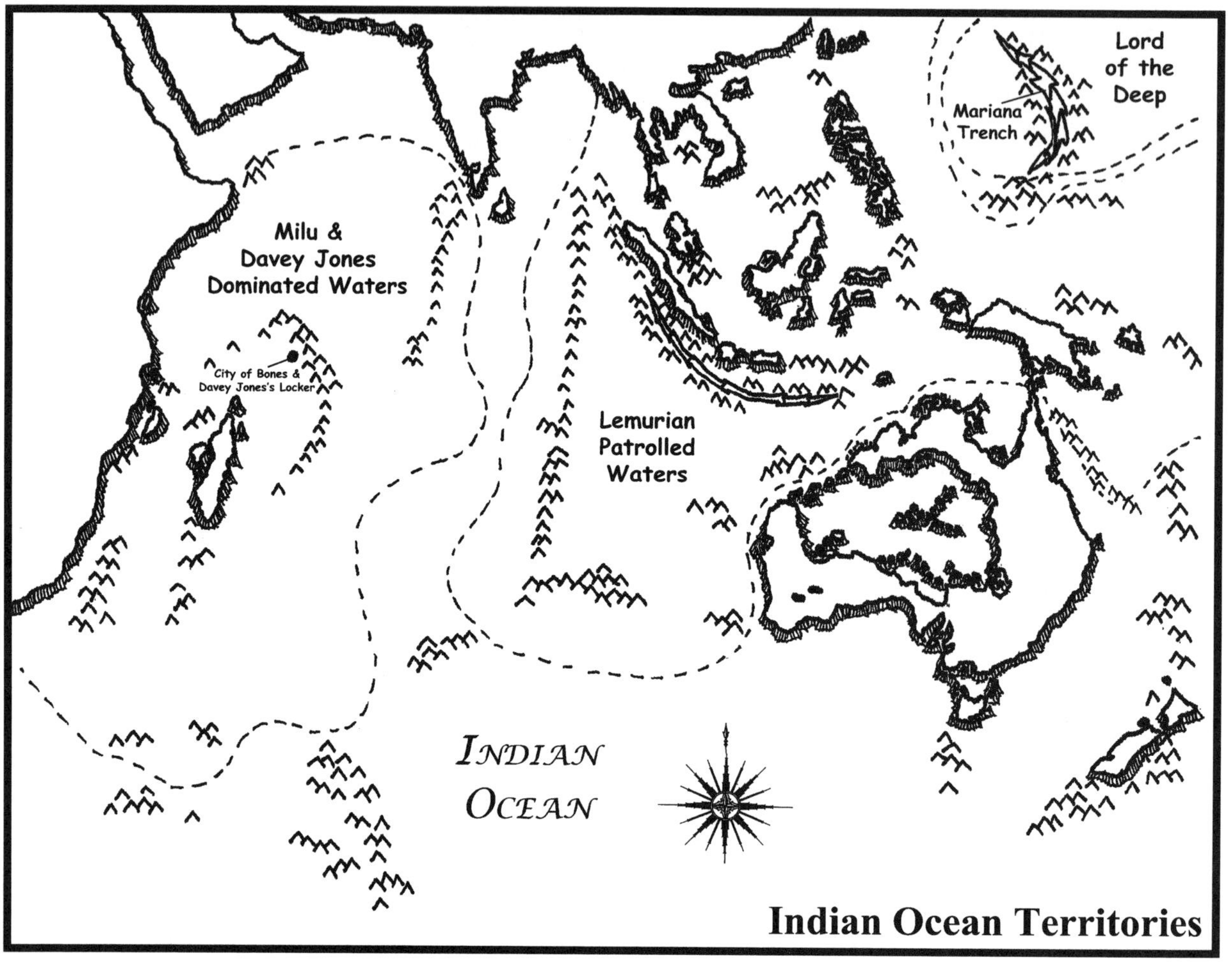
Lord of the Deep
Mariana Trench
Milu & Davey Jones Dominated Waters
City of Bones & Davey Jones's Locker
Lemurian Patrolled Waters
INDIAN OCEAN
Indian Ocean Territories

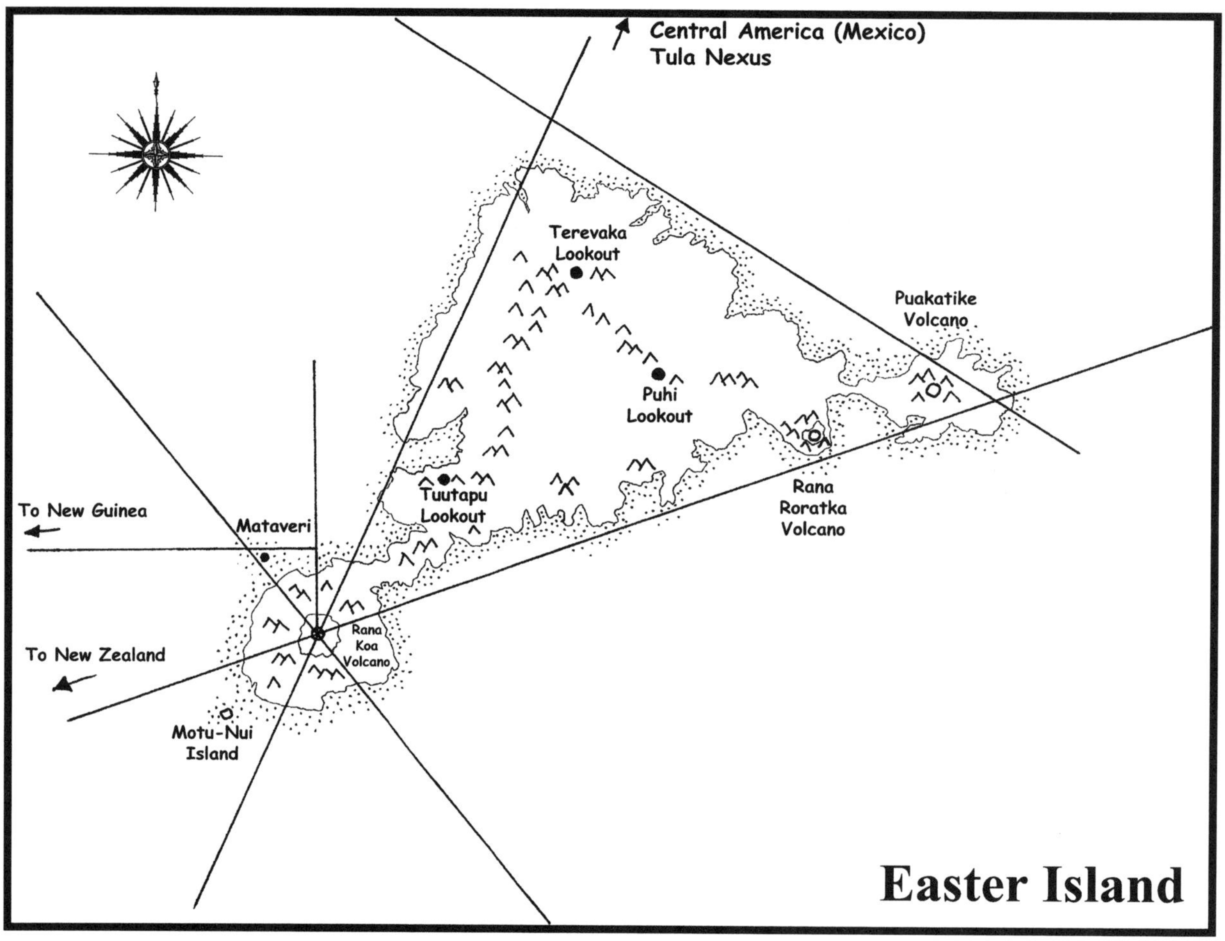
Central America (Mexico) Tula Nexus
Terevaka Lookout
Puakatike Volcano
Puhi Lookout
Tuutapu Lookout
Rana Roratka Volcano
To New Guinea
Mataveri
Rana Koa Volcano
To New Zealand
Motu-Nui Island
Easter Island

Recent & Upcoming Releases from Palladium Books®

Rifts® Path of the Storm™

– One writer's vision for the Rifts® movie

Everyone wants to know what's going on with the **Rifts® movie**. Well, this book presents an insight and behind the scenes info on that front by Kevin Siembieda, plus an entire screenplay written on speculation by *Matthew Clements* as well as game stats and artwork for major characters in the script. Kevin was so impressed with the writer's screenplay that he had Matthew make changes and improvements and sent the second draft to *Jerry Bruckheimer Films* for their consideration..

We thought it would be fun to let Rifts® gamers and Palladium fans see the type of **Rifts® movie** we at Palladium Books would like to see made. So we are presenting Matthew's screenplay as a **proposed Rifts® movie script** and **Rifts® sourcebook**. The screenplay is a fast, fun adventure story that is sure to please Rifts fans. To make it more fun, the author has statted out the key characters in the script and gamers can use the heroes, villains and story ideas in their own campaign should they choose to do so.

- **A complete movie screenplay, with dialog.**
- **A story that captures the look, feel and attitude of Rifts®.**
- **Character stats for inclusion in your own games.**
- **Use the story and ideas in your own Rifts® campaign.**
- **Some concept art and character illustrations.**
- **A fun read and insight to behind the scenes at Palladium.**
- **Cover and interior artwork by Charles Walton.**
- **Written by Matthew Clements. Notes by Kevin Siembieda.**
- **96 pages – $12.95 retail – Cat. No. 305.**

Rifts® Vampires Sourcebook™

Unknown to most humans, deep within Mexico the vampires have established entire kingdoms. There they live like tyrants and gods, dominating an underclass of cattle people used as slaves and food stock. Learn more about the vampires, their rivals, allies and the humans who willingly serve their supernatural masters for a chance to join the undead. A must-have guide for those who wish to travel deeper into the *Vampire Kingdoms* or play as vampire hunters.

- **More anti-vampire gear including Techno-Wizard weapons.**
- **Magic-based Vampire Hunters and human strongholds.**
- **Profiles for Doc Reid and key Reid's Rangers.**
- **Fort Reid, an entire city devoted to hunting the undead.**
- **Secret vampire groups that exterminate Vampire Hunters.**
- **The Yucatan Peninsula, overrun by demons and monsters.**
- **The werebeasts of Mexico and Central America.**
- **New O.C.C.s, the return of ancient gods and much more.**
- **$16.95 – 128 pages. Cat. No. 884.**

Rifts® Black Market™

– A Rifts® Sourcebook

On Rifts® Earth, the Black Market is the most prevalent trader in weapons, contraband and magic items outlawed by the Coalition. Explore the day to day business of the market along with its smuggling routes, practices, policies and nefarious products. Encounter the five major Black Market factions in North America and foreign groups like the Yakuza, Green Scarf Sect and the Underground Railroads of Atlantis and the Vampire Kingdoms.

- **New O.C.C.s like the Con Man, Coyote and Venture Criminal.**
- **Black Market services, products, practices and customers.**
- **Criminal jobs like the Enforcer, Hit Man and Defense Attorney.**
- **Major smuggling corridors and routes through Coalition territory.**
- **Smuggling methods, both magical and conventional.**
- **The Five Factions of North America and other Black Market groups.**
- **More equipment from Bandito Arms and specialized smuggling gear.**
- **Tables for creating Traveling Merchants, Caravans, Market Outlets, Market Towns, Clubs and Bars, Body-Chop-Shops and more!**
- **Information on the Coalition prison system and border security.**
- **Written by Matthew Clements and Taylor White with additional material by Kevin Siembieda and Alex Marciniszyn.**
- **160 pages – $20.95 retail – Cat. No. 886.**

Rifts® World Book:

Northern Gun™ One

The largest independent manufacturer of weapons, robots and adventure gear in North America is *Northern Gun*™. Located in Michigan's Upper Peninsula, they have been the premier outfitter of mercenaries and adventurers for decades, and are a major hub for hiring military contractors. With a whole new product line to offer their customers, the future looks bright for Northern Gun™.

- **The arms giant Northern Gun profiled for the first time!**
- **The Kingdom of Ishpeming, a puppet-state propped up by NG.**
- **Full 109 P.A. catalog of Northern Gun products!**
- **New weapons, power armor, vehicles, robots and adventure gear.**
- **The Ishpeming military, essentially a framework for hiring mercenaries and privateers.**
- **The NG Bounty Board, the largest collection of bounties and mercenary contracts anywhere on Rifts® Earth.**
- **Hover trains, supply ships and sales outlets.**
- **Northern Gun's relationship with the Coalition States, Triax Industries, the Black Market and others.**
- **Written by Matthew Clements.**
- **Interior Artwork by Nick Bradshaw, Chuck Walton and others.**
- **160 pages – $20.95 retail – Cat. No. 887.**

Rifts® Megaverse® in Flames™

The Minion War spills across Rifts Earth, where demons and infernals hope to recruit allies and use the Rifts as gateways of destruction.

- **Soulmancer and Blood Magic.**
- **Seven Deadly Plagues and Demon Plagues across the globe.**
- **Battleground: Earth – demons & infernals amass their legions.**
- **Rifts Calgary – also known as Hell's Pit – described.**
- **Ciudad de Diablo and other notable Hell holes on Earth.**
- **Lord Doom, Pain and other demonic leaders.**
- **Horune treachery, Dimension Stormers and other villains.**
- **Global chaos, notable characters and many adventure ideas.**
- **192 pages – $24.95 retail – Cat. No. 876.**

Go to **www.palladiumbooks.com** for weekly updates, news, online store, message boards and more.